Personality Disorder Reviewed

Edited by
PETER TYRER
GEORGE STEIN

Personality Disorder Reviewed

GASKELL

©The Royal College of Psychiatrists 1993

Gaskell is an imprint of the Royal College of Psychiatrists,
17 Belgrave Square, London SW1

British Library Cataloguing-in-Publication Data
Personality Disorder Reviewed
  I. Tyrer, Peter   II. Stein, George
✳ 616.85
ISBN 0-902241-52-4

Distributed in North America
by American Psychiatric Press, Inc.
ISBN 0-880486-18-X

The views presented in this book do not necessarily
reflect those of the Royal College of Psychiatrists,
and the publishers are not responsible for any error
of omission or fact.

Cover illustration ©The Oskar Schlemmer Theatre Estate,
Badenweiler, Germany. Photograph: Photo Archive C.
Raman Schlemmer, Oggebbio, Italy.

Phototypeset by Dobbie Typesetting Limited, Tavistock, Devon
Printed in Great Britain by Bell & Bain Limited, Glasgow

Dedicated to
Jonathan, Clare, Freya
and Ann
and
Benjamin, Joseph
and
Suzanna
and
our parents

Contents

Contributors

Hagop S. Akiskal, Professor of Psychiatry, University of California at San Diego, La Jolla, California, USA (presently on leave at the National Institute of Mental Health, Rockville, Maryland, USA)

Mark Berelowitz, Consultant Psychiatrist, Department of Child and Adolescent Psychiatry, The Maudsley Hospital, Denmark Hill, London SE5 8AZ, UK

German E. Berrios, Consultant and University Lecturer in Psychiatry, University of Cambridge, Addenbrooke's Hospital, Hills Road, Cambridge CB2 2QQ, UK

Patricia Casey, Professor of Psychiatry, Mater Misericordiae Hospital, Eccles Street, Dublin, Republic of Ireland

Jeremy Coid, Senior Lecturer in Forensic Psychiatry, Department of Psychological Medicine, St Bartholomew's Hospital, West Smithfield, London EC1A 7BE, UK

Brian Ferguson, Consultant Psychiatrist, Mapperley Hospital, Nottingham, UK

Peter Fonagy, Freud Memorial Professor, Psychoanalysis Unit, University College, London, UK

Anna Higgitt, Consultant Psychiatrist and Honorary Senior Lecturer, St Charles' Hospital, Exmoor Street, London W10 6DZ, UK

Peter McGuffin, Professor of Psychological Medicine, Department of Psychological Medicine, University of Wales College of Medicine, Heath Park, Cardiff, UK

Herschel Prins, Professor, Midlands Centre for Criminology and Criminal Justice, University of Loughborough, UK, and Visiting Professor in Clinical Criminology, Nottingham Trent University, UK

George Stein, Senior Lecturer, King's College Hospital, and Consultant Psychiatrist, Farnborough Hospital, Farnborough Common, Orpington, Kent BR6 8ND, UK

Michael H. Stone, Professor of Clinical Psychiatry, Columbia College of Physicians and Surgeons, Columbia, USA

Digby Tantam, Professor of Psychotherapy, Department of Psychology and School of Postgraduate Medical Education, University of Warwick, Coventry CV4 7AL, UK

Alex Tarnopolsky, Consultant Psychotherapist, The Maudsley Hospital, Denmark Hill, London SE5 8AZ, UK

Anita Thapar, MRC Training Fellow, Department of Psychological Medicine, University of Wales College of Medicine, Heath Park, Cardiff, UK

Peter Tyrer, Professor of Community Psychiatry, Academic Department of Psychiatry (St Mary's Hospital Medical School), St Charles' Hospital, London W10 6DZ, UK

Jane Whittaker, Registrar in Psychiatry, Withington Hospital, Manchester M20 8LR, UK

Stephen Wilson, Consultant Psychotherapist, Oxford Mental Health Unit, and Clinical Lecturer, University of Oxford, UK

Sula Wolff, Honorary Fellow, University of Edinburgh, Department of Psychiatry, Royal Edinburgh Hospital, Morningside Park, Edinburgh EH10 5HF, UK

Introduction

PETER TYRER and GEORGE STEIN

Sometimes in lecturing about the difficult subject of the personality disorders, we realise just how vast is our lack of knowledge in this area and are tempted to consider the subject as being 'on the other side of the moon'. The side of the moon that we can see with ease, that is, the insanities and the more florid disturbances of mental state, has been exposed to both public and professional gaze for many centuries, as well as being the focus of a considerable degree of scientific scrutiny. Regrettably, the equally important component of personality abnormality, because it has been barely visible, has been neglected and remains obscure. Perhaps we should not carry the moon analogy too far, because now that modern space technology has given us a glimpse of the other side of the moon, we realise that it looks very similar to the side we can see. By contrast, the more we learn about the personality disorders, the more we realise just how different they are from the more familiar disorders of mental state. Nevertheless, because an individual with a personality disorder may suffer seriously or inflict much suffering on others we sometimes make the mistake of thinking that these conditions are fundamentally the same as the mental state disorders and this leads us into error.

Indeed, one of the important early pioneers in the study of antisocial personality disorder, Hervey Cleckley, believed that people with these disorders were truly insane, afflicted by an illness almost as severe as a psychosis, and so chose the title *The Mask of Sanity* for his classic book on the subject (Cleckley, 1941). At the other end of the range are those who believe that personality disorder is a redundant term, describing either a moral judgement or an untreatable condition, or that such a label is a technique used by psychiatrists to dispose of patients they do not wish to treat.

We hope that this review of personality disorders will advance the debate a stage further. Whatever the outcome, patients with personality disorders are important consumers of health services, particularly in the emergency and forensic settings. They also present rather more difficult problems in management than most other mental state disorders, yet this should hardly be a reason for abandoning them.

Despite this, there have been important advances in our understanding of the personality disorders during the past 20 years, mostly in the area of more accurate clinical description, diagnosis, and classification. These advances have helped place much of the previous literature into a more comprehensible perspective and have also allowed treatment and management to be studied rather more scientifically than was the case a generation ago.

Psychiatry has, until recently, been rather poor at defining its own terms and the personality disorders have been one of the main casualties of psychiatric vagueness. Looking at earlier literature it is now easy to see that previous diagnoses such as pseudoneurotic schizophrenia, chronic resistant neurosis, and borderline personality disorder are really one and the same condition. However, because for a long time they were held to be different conditions, understanding and study was greatly delayed.

In *Personality Disorder Reviewed* we try to prevent this confusion by defining exactly what we mean before moving on to other aspects of personality disorder. The reviews are written by leading authorities in different areas of research into personality disorders. Some of these articles have already appeared in the *British Journal of Psychiatry*, usually in shorter form, but others are published here for the first time. The aim has not been to cover the field of personality disorders in its entirety but to concentrate on those areas where there have been recent advances and developments.

The book is roughly divided into three sections. In the first few chapters the nature of personality disorder, its definition and separation from mental state disorders, and the history of the concept are considered. In the first chapter we set up the market stall for personality disorders, showing exactly what is on offer, how it is described, and how it differs from other disorders. Dr Berrios follows this with an erudite examination of the development of the concept, which explains the origins of many of the current controversies concerning personality disorder. He illustrates well that some of the earliest writings on the subject describe patients who would not nowadays be considered as having a primary disturbance of personality.

The emotive question of whether personality disorders are created as much through our genes as through our environment is examined by Professor McGuffin and Dr Thapar and holds the hope that some of the major advances in genetics of the past two to three years could be used with advantage to examine the personality disorders in much greater detail. Dr Sula Wolff examines one of the more important, but often neglected, areas of psychiatry, the development of disorder in childhood into adult disorder, a subject on which she has made major contributions to the literature in her studies of schizoid and withdrawn personalities. She highlights the curious fact that, despite some continuity of disorder which fits in with developmental theories, it is surprising how many children from quite appalling environmental backgrounds manage to achieve stability in adult life against all the odds.

The second section is devoted to the personality disorders that arouse the greatest controversy, the borderline personality disorder and those associated with antisocial behaviour, which for many is the most important constituent of abnormal personality. Throughout this subject the confusing adjective 'borderline' permeates; although many have criticised the concept of borderline personality disorder, it has dominated research into the subject in the US.

Drs Berelowitz and Tarnopolsky have set the scene by bringing us up to date with current thinking on borderline personality disorder. They illustrate that the concept is alive and well and continuing to stimulate research into diagnosis, treatment and outcome despite reservations in some quarters about the exclusivity of the concept. The overlap with the general notion of psychopathy is illustrated by Dr Coid, a forensic psychiatrist, in the following chapter. The late Sir Aubrey Lewis considered psychopathy to be "a most elusive category"; Dr Coid pins it down and examines its roots, its current definition and likely future. Like the term borderline, psychopathy continues to hold attractions for many people because it neatly encapsulates many characteristics that are consistently found in a group of patients now categorised as antisocial personality disorder (DSM–III–R; American Psychiatric Association, 1987), and dissocial personality disorder in the recent ICD-10 scheme (World Health Organization, 1992).

The concept of borderline still hovers in the background in later chapters by Dr Stephen Wilson on multiple personality disorder and in a chapter on self-mutilation by Professor Digby Tantam and Dr Jane Whittaker. It could be argued that multiple personality disorder should not be in this book at all because all the more recent classifications consider it to be a type of dissociative phenomenon, or one of the hysterical disorders. However, both this condition and the phenomenon of self-mutilation are ways in which some personality disordered people respond to stress and present to the helping professions. These chapters illustrate both the fascination and the horror that is aroused by such behaviour; fascination because of the kaleidoscopic disguises that mask the true problem, and horror that they lead to such punitive action and disturbing behaviour.

Also in this section Professor Akiskal, one of the world's foremost authorities on depressive disorders, critically considers the arguments in favour of the depressive personality. This condition is not a formal personality disorder and has been given various titles, including the one of sub-affective temperament by Akiskal. Whatever the more formal classifications decree, there is no doubt that Professor Akiskal is writing about a gloomy group of people whose depressive characteristics are so much part of their personality structure that it is difficult to regard them as having a separate mental state disorder.

The last four chapters illustrate the failures and successes of treatment of this group of conditions that has for so long been regarded as quite untreatable. In a penetrating review, Dr Higgitt and Professor Fonagy illustrate the usefulness of the borderline concept for those treating personality disorders. The seminal value of Kernberg's structural model and Kohut's deprivation model of borderline personality disorder are well described and their influence on psychotherapeutic technique is discussed. This chapter also illustrates well the peculiar combination of toughness and tolerance that is required of the therapists who treat the borderline subject. If the term countertransference did not exist it would have to be invented for this group of disorders, for the therapist often acts out just as much as the patient after prolonged psychotherapeutic contact.

Borderline personality disorder also features heavily in the drug treatment of abnormal personalities, which is reviewed in careful detail by Dr Stein. This chapter examines the early history of drug trials in these conditions and illustrates how too many conclusions have been drawn from too little evidence. However, well designed recent studies incorporating placebo controls have confirmed that some drugs, particularly low dosage neuroleptics and lithium carbonate, do appear to have some value in the treatment of some borderline individuals. This chapter also highlights how other drugs such as the benzodiazepines and the tricyclics may have paradoxical effects and can actually worsen those with borderline personality disorders.

In the final chapter Professor Michael Stone has perhaps the most taxing task of all. In examining the outcome of personality disorders over many years he has to allow for the fact that diagnostic habits will have changed dramatically over this time. However, in his own study in New York, he manages to trace over 95% of his group of borderline patients some 15 years after their initial assessment, a remarkable achievement that sets a benchmark for future researchers. We are encouraged by his findings that many subjects with borderline personality disorders may do well. This is despite the frustration and despair they invoke in their therapists during the acute treatment phase. However, those who have been abused during childhood or have additional antisocial personality characteristics still do badly.

We hope the pages that follow will help the reader to navigate through the hills and valleys that lie on the other side of the psychiatric moon. Although large areas remain unexplored, others are now quite well trodden and are even beginning to seem like familiar territory. The scenery is sometimes threatening and challenging but never boring, although so far we see little evidence of a Sea of Tranquility, where all is settled and calm.

July 1992

References

AMERICAN PSYCHIATRIC ASSOCIATION (1987) *Diagnostic and Statistical Manual of Mental Disorders* (3rd edn, revised) (DSM–III–R). Washington, DC. APA.

CLECKLEY, H. (1941) *The Mask of Sanity*. London: Henry Kimpton.

WORLD HEALTH ORGANIZATION (1992) *The ICD–10 Classification of Mental and Behavioural Disorders*. Geneva: WHO.

1 Personality disorder in perspective

PETER TYRER, PATRICIA CASEY and BRIAN FERGUSON

'Personality disorder' remains a term that to many still lacks respectability. For many years it has been imbued with the negative qualities of degeneracy (Koch, 1891), untreatability (Maudsley, 1868) and conflict (Henderson, 1939). Most psychiatric labels can be interpreted as pejorative, but whereas 'schizophrenia' and 'depression' at least have the compensatory status of being recognised illnesses, 'personality disorder' is a term that takes away little or no personal responsibility from the victim. It also tends to be a diagnosis of despair. When a difficult patient has been assessed and treated fully without a favourable response, the problem is often reformulated as a diagnosis of primary personality disorder. The trouble with this change of diagnosis is that it can have all the properties of a primary delusion: it offers a deceptively simple explanation of events and behaviour that may be quite independent of the truth. This can be doubly unfortunate if the diagnosis leads to abandonment of care on the grounds that patients with personality disorder have no 'formal' mental illness and are therefore not the province of a normal psychiatric service. Gunn (1988) points out the curious ambivalence attached to the term 'personality disorder' among many professionals in the psychiatric service. Care, sympathy and tolerance are given in abundance if the patient is regarded as having an 'illness', but when the disorder is considered to be one of personality, the behaviour is construed as deliberately difficult, malicious or manipulative, and value judgements are made accordingly.

In this first chapter we shall briefly touch on all the issues that make the study of personality disorder so important and yet which, for reasons that will become clear, have been relatively neglected until recently. Although personality disorder has long been part of the language of psychiatry its words have often been obscure and misappropriated by others outside the profession. As a consequence its validity has been undermined and it is not surprising that a minority, albeit a shrinking one, regard personality disorder as a non-diagnosis that is prejudicial to good clinical practice. We hope that this book will win over these doubters and persuade them that the term 'personality disorder' is an essential component of psychiatric practice.

As an introduction we shall cover briefly the development of personality disorder as a clinical concept, its value in practice, and the advantages of a bi-axial system of classification of mental disorders that allows every individual to be classified by both mental and personality status. This emphasises that debates about patients having *either* a personality disorder *or* a mental illness are sterile; of much greater importance is the accurate delineation of each in the evaluation of a clinical problem. Although personality is clearly in a different domain of function than mental state this unnatural dichotomy in clinical practice has been reinforced by almost all major psychiatric textbooks; personality disorders are given their own separate chapters (or occasionally lumped inappropriately with neurotic disorders) and not considered in conjunction with other conditions. This state of affairs clearly has important historical roots and needs to be considered in the context of other parallel developments in society as a whole.

The development of the concept

Disorders of personality have been recognised in many cultures since early times. Many centuries BC, the peripatetic philosopher Theophrastus described his 'characters' in a way which parallels our modern classification systems (Adlington, 1925). Nevertheless, in his account there is no suggestion of illness in the distinct personality types he describes, only that they are different from normal. Similar distinctions were made in Asian, Arabic and Celtic cultures, and nearly all are noted for their insistence that the personality characteristics which separate such people from normal are disagreeable ones. Hence an element of social judgement invariably enters into the basic concept. The secondary assumption is made that the possessors of such characteristics are responsible for them and must bear the consequences of the associated behaviour.

It is no accident that the first clinical separation of personality disorder from mental illness, by Pinel, occurred shortly after the onset of the French Revolution, with its implications for social organisation and change. Man was no longer born to a pre-determined status in life but had equal liberties and rights together with their ensuing responsibilities. Clearly, some people were afflicted by illnesses that were questionably under their control and were therefore unable to exercise those responsibilities. A need arose to separate illness behaviour from the rest. Pinel's celebrated nobleman who pushed a woman down a well in a fit of rage was clearly not ill, and possessed a clear, intact reasoning ability, and showed no evidence of delusional beliefs (Pinel, 1801). In other respects his conduct and behaviour were characteristic of the mentally disturbed at the time. This central notion of bizarre behaviour in the presence of otherwise normal reasoning processes has remained one of the cornerstones of diagnosis of abnormal personality to this day. The nobleman in Pinel's account was therefore distinguished from the mentally ill as a case of '*manie sans délire*', but none the less was sentenced to a life in custody in the Bicêtre.

During the course of the 19th century this distinction was refined, although the process was not always an easy one. By focusing on the 'moral faculty' Prichard in Bristol and Benjamin Rush in the United States were influential in this regard, but many of their cases would now be reclassified as forms of mental illness. In 1868 Henry Maudsley set the stage for the present British concept of personality disorder by again emphasising the finding of a normal mental state and the acceptance of personal responsibility. The categorisation of personality disorder did not receive any firm support until the time of Schneider. His classification, based on clinical observations (Schneider, 1923), together with similar work by Kahn, Kraepelin and Kretschmer, formed the foundation of the present international classifications.

A significant move away from some of these principles was elaborated by Hervey Cleckley, who initially argued that the level of maladjustment in psychopathic patients was such that he believed them to be psychotic. Developments in genetic and organic research seemed to give weight to the idea that personality disorder was indeed a 'mask of sanity' covering a more significant pathological process (Cleckley, 1941). These ideas need to be considered in the light of similar moves to regard alcoholism as a disease, which again beg the question whether sufferers from such disorders can reasonably be held responsible for their asocial actions. Mental health legislation in the UK still retains the idea that such patients may not be legally competent to judge their own affairs, but commital to mental hospital can only occur when the condition is considered 'treatable'.

In the last 30 years, the standard bearers of research into personality disorders have portrayed the Stars and Stripes more than any other banner, and much of the credit for this falls on a persistent few, notably Gunderson, Jacobson and Kernberg for their work on the dynamics of borderline and narcissistic personalities, and another group involved in defining personality disorders in the American Psychiatric Association's *Diagnostic and Statistical Manual* (DSM), in which Frances, Millon, Spitzer and Widiger have played major roles.

The interests of these groups at first seem opposed: one is deeply rooted in the psychodynamic tradition, with concern for the structure and development of personality and intrapsychic phenomena; and the other is preoccupied with accurate and reliable descriptions of behaviour that can be fashioned into the operational criteria of a DSM diagnosis. It says a great deal for the flexibility of personality disorder as a concept that these approaches have been married successfully, whereas for other subjects, particularly the neuroses, there has been a public and bad-tempered divorce

(Bayer & Spitzer, 1985). 'Borderline' is the common key to this success. Although it is accused of being an elusive adjective only (Akiskal *et al*, 1986) and unless "used to signify a class that borders on something, has no clinical or descriptive meaning at all" (Millon, 1981, p. 332), it permeates the literature on personality disorder in all its contexts. Indeed, to many 'personality disorder' is interpreted as 'borderline', illustrating the adaptability of a word that, after Lewis Carroll's *Through the Looking Glass*, could be described as a 'Humpty Dumptyism' ("when I choose a word", Humpty Dumpty said in a rather scornful tone, "it means just what I choose it to mean, – neither more nor less"). However, whatever one's individual views about the usefulness of the term, borderline personality disorder is a major focus of research, theory and clinical practice and this is acknowledged by the chapters devoted specifically to the subject in this book.

Definition and classification

Although the concept of personality is well established, it is very difficult to define. Vernon (1964) gives six definitions of personality, involving habitual behaviour, attitudes and roles, organised traits, transactions between dispositions and situations, subjective and external appraisal, and relationships with others. None of these is satisfactory on its own and it is difficult to synthesise them into a single description without oversimplifying.

Defining personality disorder presents equal difficulties (Table 1.1) and all short definitions lose important elements. Whereas abnormalities of mental state can be defined by observations or symptoms that stand alone (e.g. symptoms of depression and the rituals of obsessional disorders), disorders of personality intertwine persistent behaviour, attitudes, subjective distress, and impact on relationships. The last is considered by many to be the most important but is difficult to interpret: the one who suffers is not necessarily the one who is disordered. Since the time of Schneider it has been stressed that personality disorder must always be judged by its effects on others, be they friends, relations or others in close contact with the patient, or society as a whole. Society thereby imposes its own yardstick on the definition of personality disorder. This is often unsatisfactory, particularly when the society from which normative behaviour and relationships are derived is itself abnormal. Using Schneider's definition literally, Heinrich Himmler and Hermann Goering had normal personalities between 1933 and 1943, and Andre Sakharov and Nelson Mandela are personality disordered, since they have caused suffering to themselves and others through trying to reform the widest manifestation of society, the state. The study of the personality status of major historical figures, a discipline that could be christened 'personography', reveals that many had personality disorders but were none the less successful at important times in their lives possibly because the

TABLE 1.1
Some definitions of personality disorder (only global definitions are included)

Source	Definition
Schneider (1923)	Abnormal personalities who suffer through their abnormalities and through whose abnormalities society suffers
Rado (1953)	Disturbances of psychodynamic integration that significantly affect the organism's adaptive life performance, and its attainment of utility and pleasure
World Health Organization (1978)	Deeply ingrained maladaptive patterns of behaviour generally recognisable by the time of adolescence or earlier and continuing throughout most of adult life, although often becoming less obvious in middle and old age. The personality is abnormal either in the balance of its components, their quality and expression, or in its total aspect
American Psychiatric Association (1987)	Behaviour or traits that are characteristic of the individual's recent (past year) and long-term functioning (generally since adolescence or early adulthood). The constellation of types of behaviour or traits causes either significant impairment in social or occupational functioning, or subjective distress
Davis (1987)	An enduring way of perceiving, relating to, and thinking about the environment that causes distress in social and occupational functioning
Rutter (1987)	A persistent, pervasive abnormality in social relationships and social functioning generally
Tyrer & Ferguson (1988)	A persistent abnormality of personal and social functioning that is independent of mental integration

prevailing social milieu was itself abnormal (Henry, 1975, 1979; Henry *et al*, 1993).

The other important aspect of personality function is that it needs to be considered independently of mental state. This is acknowledged formally in the American classifications (DSM) and implicitly in the World Health Organization's *International Classification of Diseases* (ICD). Nevertheless, personality disorder can lead to mental state disorders and vice versa, and the new diagnosis of 'enduring personality change' proposed in the latest draft of ICD–10 (World Health Organization, 1992) recognises this.

Categorisation

The current classification of personality disorder is illustrated in Table 1.2. There is good agreement between DSM–III–R and the draft version of ICD–10, with most of the differences between the two systems being minor ones of terminology. The combination of these disorders under a common heading is perhaps surprising because their origins are so disparate. The criteria for antisocial ('dissocial') personality disorder derive from careful

TABLE 1.2

Comparison of current classifications of personality disorder

Description	Code
ICD–10[1]	
Paranoid – excessive sensitivity, suspiciousness, preoccupation with conspiratorial explanation of events, with a persistent tendency to self-reference	F60.0
Schizoid – emotional coldness, detachment, lack of interest in other people, eccentricity and introspective fantasy	F60.1
Schizotypal – no equivalent category in ICD–10	
Anankastic – indecisiveness, doubt, excessive caution, pedantry, rigidity and need to plan in immaculate detail	F60.5
Histrionic – self dramatisation, shallow mood, egocentricity and craving for excitement with persistent manipulative behaviour	F60.4
Dependent – failure to take responsibility for actions, with subordination of personal needs to those of others, excessive dependence with need for constant reassurance and feelings of helplessness when a close relationship ends	F60.7
Dissocial – callous unconcern for others, with irresponsibility, irritability and aggression, and incapacity to maintain enduring relationships	F60.2
Narcissistic – no equivalent category in ICD–10	
Anxious – persistent tension, self-consciousness, exaggeration of risks and dangers, hypersensitivity to rejection, and restricted lifestyle because of insecurity	F60.6
Impulsive – inability to control anger, to plan ahead, or to think before acts, with unpredictable mood and quarrelsome behaviour	F60.30[3]
Borderline – unclear self-image, involvement in intense and unstable relationships	F60.31[3]
DSM–III–R[2]	
Paranoid – interpretation of people's actions as deliberately demeaning or threatening	301.00
Schizoid – indifference to relationships and restricted range of emotional experience and expression	301.20
Schizotypal – deficit in interpersonal relatedness with peculiarities of ideation, appearance and behaviour	302.22
Obsessive–compulsive – pervasive perfectionism and inflexibility	301.40
Histrionic – excessive emotion and attention-seeking	301.50
Dependent – persistent dependent and submissive behaviour	301.60
Antisocial – evidence of repeated conduct disorder before the age of 15 years	301.70
Narcissistic – pervasive grandiosity, lack of empathy, and hypersensitivity to the evaluation of others	301.81
Avoidant – pervasive social discomfort, fear of negative evaluation and timidity	301.82
Borderline – pervasive instability of mood and self-image	301.83
Passive–aggressive – pervasive passive resistance to demands for adequate social and occupational performance	301.84

1. World Health Organization (1992).
2. American Psychiatric Association (1987).
3. Included under heading of emotionally labile personality disorder.

follow-up studies, notably of children into adult life (e.g. Robins, 1966), while those for borderline and narcissistic personality disorders come from dynamic theory and psychotherapy in practice (Hoch & Polatin, 1949; Kohut, 1971; Gunderson & Singer, 1975; Kernberg, 1975), and schizoid and anankastic personality disorders derive from European phenomenology. One diagnosis, 'avoidant personality disorder', comes from academic psychology (Millon, 1969), and another 'schizotypal personality disorder', has a joint origin from genetics and dynamic theory, being popularised by the results of the Danish adoption studies of schizophrenia (Rosenthal *et al*, 1971), although they were formulated much earlier in dynamic terms (Rado, 1953).

This catholicism of source has created a certain stability in consensus, in that all those interested in diagnosing abnormal personality feel that their discipline has made some contribution to classification. There are many who abhor classification in psychiatry but none the less accept some of these divisions within the field of personality disorder. Nevertheless, the classification has its critics because there is considerable overlap between many of the categories, which argues for a simpler and smaller grouping (Rutter, 1987).

Livesley, who has carried out a series of valuable studies into the consistency of criteria for assessing personality disorders, has demonstrated that some of the operational criteria for the DSM–III and DSM–III–R personality disorders (American Psychiatric Association, 1980, 1987, respectively) are common to two or more different categories, or even if the conditions were fundamentally distinct, patients could qualify for more than one category (Livesley, 1987; Livesley & Jacobson, 1988).

Apart from this descriptive overlap, there is a more independent overlap between several disorders, commonly described as 'comorbidity' in the American literature. It is not always possible to separate these two types of overlap, but there is no doubt that it is too great to be satisfactory, with co-occurrence of borderline and histrionic personalities as high as 46% and multiple diagnosis of personality disorder of 15% or above in borderline, schizotypal, antisocial, histrionic, avoidant, dependent and passive–aggressive disorders (Dahl, 1986; Pfohl *et al*, 1986; Zanarini *et al*, 1987; Morey, 1988; Widiger & Rogers, 1989). The danger is that once a diagnosis becomes established it can survive all evidence that it is merely a heterogeneous mix by claiming comorbidity as an explanation. For example, in 180 in-patients, Fyer *et al* (1988) found that pure borderline personality disorder was only present in 8% of patients, while 46% had one additional diagnosis and 46% two or more additional diagnoses; 64% had at least one additional diagnosis in the affective group. Diagnosis ceases to become an economical exercise with such profligacy of pathology.

The DSM–III personality disorders are conventionally divided into three major clusters: the flamboyant and dramatic (borderline, antisocial, narcissistic, histrionic), the odd or eccentric (schizoid, schizotypal, paranoid), and the fearful (avoidant, obsessive–compulsive, passive–aggressive, dependent). Many studies have economically confined themselves to these groupings (e.g. Reich & Thompson, 1987).

The standard approach to the newer classifications of both mental illness and personality disorders has been the introduction of operational criteria in DSM–III and DSM–III–R. These criteria have the merit of clear definition; a requisite number needs to be present before a diagnosis can be made. This achieves greater reliability in diagnosis but may give a spurious impression of accuracy. Once a great deal is known about a subject it is reasonable to introduce criteria that are universally acceptable in order to improve reliability. In the case of personality disorders there is little that is agreed by all, and there is a danger in introducing operational criteria at this early stage that reliability will replace validity. This danger is illustrated by the multiplicity of instruments in the US that measure DSM–III and DSM–III–R diagnoses (Ferguson & Tyrer, 1989); these instruments only have to satisfy the demands of the operational criteria for each of the diagnoses. A more fundamental question as to whether the operational criteria are indeed true measures of the disorders concerned has sometimes been forgotten (Tyrer, 1988).

Because every personality is, in the strictest sense, unique, it is always possible to argue for the introduction of a new group. This is tending to happen in the US, where sadistic and self-defeating personality disorders are close to being included in the next classification, DSM–IV. Unless there are clear dividing lines between the categories, the extent of the overlap between them squanders good diagnosis. At present there is no accepted system of ordering personality disorders when several co-exist. In practice this means that many can be present in the same person at one time (Pfohl *et al*, 1986; Loranger *et al*, 1987; Coid, 1989). Mere reiteration of these in sequence is not good diagnostic practice.

There are ways of assigning priority so that only a single diagnosis is made, but care must be taken to avoid the mistake of ignoring those conditions that are pathological but lower in the hierarchy. Attempts at achieving an adequate priority of personality disorder classification include the introduction of a dimensional system (Widiger *et al*, 1987) so that each disorder can exist in several grades of severity. This allows several diagnoses to be recorded but can order them in importance. One instrument, the Personality Assessment Schedule (PAS), takes this to the extreme of only recording one personality disorder in diagnosis, the one that has the greatest impact on social functioning (Tyrer & Alexander, 1979; Tyrer *et al*, 1988). Although this has its merits and can be justified on both theoretical and practical grounds, doctors must prefer working with categorical diagnoses and so these are likely to persist.

Epidemiology

Recent interest in diagnosing personality disorder independently of mental state has shown that these conditions are more prevalent than was originally thought, both in psychiatric practice and in other populations. The older literature on personality disorder in the general population is sparse and confusing, not least because personality disorder has often been equated with only one of its elements, sociopathy. There has also been uncertainty about the threshold of diagnosis. Thus early epidemiological studies of personality disorder give prevalence figures varying from 6% to 11% (Srole *et al*, 1962; Leighton *et al*, 1963), while more recent studies, with more restrictive criteria, give lower figures of 2% to 4% (Weissman *et al*, 1978; Myers *et al*, 1984). Epidemiological studies from the UK are few, but one investigation (Casey & Tyrer, 1986), using a structured interview, identified disorders of personality in 13% of an adult urban population. Explosive and anankastic types were the most common. Findings that are common to all these studies are: an excess of personality disorders among men, decreasing rate with increasing age, and a significantly higher prevalence in urban communities (Dohrenwend & Dohrenwend, 1969; Myers *et al*, 1984; Casey & Tyrer, 1986).

Prevalence figures of personality disorder in primary care are between 4% and 8% for primary personality disorder diagnosed by both clinical and research criteria (Kessel, 1960; Cooper, 1965; Shepherd *et al*, 1966; Hoeper *et al*, 1979). However, a more recent study (Casey *et al*, 1984) which made both axis I and II diagnoses using structured interviews to assess those with conspicuous morbidity found that 34% had personality disorder. The most common associations of personality disorder were with axis I diagnoses of anxiety states and of alcohol abuse. Comparisons were made with a rural general practice (Casey, 1985) where personality disorder was significantly less common (20%) but the anankastic type was found in greater proportion.

The prominence of personality disorder in parasuicide has been described in a number of studies. Recurrent suicidal gestures and acts are one of the criteria for the diagnosis of borderline personality disorder in DSM–III–R. High prevalences (48–65%) for personality disorder among those attempting suicide have been described by several workers (Philips, 1970; Ovenstone, 1973) and this finding has been upheld even when a structured, relatively bias-free schedule was used (Casey, 1989). Abnormalities of personality are especially common in those making suicidal gestures and minor attempts (Pallis & Birtchnell, 1977). An association between obsessional personality and serious attempts has been postulated (Murthy, 1969) although this has not been replicated in more recent work (Pierce, 1977; Casey, 1989).

Another group subject to bias in assessment is the forensic one, where the risk of assuming that abnormal behaviour among prisoners is inevitably caused by personality disorder can inflate apparent prevalence. Studies have found that between 20% and 70% of prisoners have abnormal personalities (Bluglass, 1977; Gunn *et al*, 1978) and predictably the antisocial (sociopathic) type predominates.

The advent of case registers and medical audit should facilitate studies of personality disorder in hospital populations. This will be of value only if diagnostic practice is improved by psychiatrists avoiding both the temptation to classify mental state and personality disorders on a single axis and the arbitrary use of value-laden, unreliable terminology (e.g. 'hysterical', 'immature') to describe personality disorders (Thompson & Goldberg, 1987). In England and Wales, 7.6% of all admissions have a diagnosis of personality disorder (Department of Health and Social Security, 1985) and a similar proportion are so diagnosed in Ireland (O'Hare & Walsh, 1986), but both these figures are almost certainly underestimates because mental state disorders take precedence (Frances, 1980). Recent inquiries into the prevalence and type of personality disorders in psychiatric in-patients has shown that nearly half qualify for the diagnosis of a personality disorder as well as one of mental state (Cutting *et al*, 1986; Dahl, 1986; Loranger *et al*, 1987; Widiger *et al*, 1987). Studies of out-patient samples have shown lower figures, but even in this group between 20% and 40% have an identifiable personality disorder (Tyrer *et al*, 1983*a*; Kass *et al*, 1985; Morey, 1988). Similarly, in emergency clinics dealing with emotional problems between 7.4% and 31% of clients have personality disorders (Muller *et al*, 1967; Bowman & Sturgeon, 1977), the disparity being explained by variations in method.

Thus, unless we explain these results as artefacts of mental illness, or an error in method that sets the criteria for diagnosis at too low a level, we must conclude that personality disorder is a ubiquitous companion to psychiatric practice and not just a subject for the specialist in fields such as drug dependence or forensic psychiatry.

Treatment

There has long been an opinion, often amounting to conviction, that personality disorders are impervious to treatment. This may have been true in the 18th and 19th centuries (Prichard, 1837; Maudsley, 1868), but is open to question today. In the following chapters in this book, the efficacy of both pharmacological and psychological treatments in different personality disorders, in which the category of 'borderline' is most prominent, will be described.

The treatment of personality disorders is long, arduous and difficult to complete. Anticipation of the obstacles to success is one of the main facets of treatment (Horowitz, 1977; Waldinger, 1987). It is important to take a long-term perspective because short-term treatment followed by resolution is unrealistic. One of the important consequences of better classification and awareness of personality problems is the recognition that people with personality disorders suffer considerably and merit help, even if it cannot always be given in reliable and effective form. In the past, many therapeutic disciplines have tended to regard personality disorders as not really part of psychiatry's province, and believed that they should therefore be separated from 'real' mental illness. This view is often implicit and rarely finds its way into print but is unfortunately common in practice. Views of treatment are now changing. Psychotherapy in particular, which has always maintained that personality disorders are part of its territory, has persevered in attempts to understand and modify the harmful attitudes that dominate the personal lives and relationships of people with personality disorders, and has helped to transfer this awareness to others.

Taken together, there are grounds for believing that some forms of long-term psychotherapy (Waldinger & Gunderson, 1987), group therapy (Parloff & Dies, 1977), behaviour therapy (Dahl & Merskey, 1981), and drug therapies, particularly low-dose antipsychotic drugs (Soloff *et al*, 1986), are effective in the treatment of some personality disorders. This is a wide range of potential treatments and it is sad that only drug treatments have been tested in satisfactory clinical trials. Although the ethical, financial and organisational challenges of mounting the necessary long-term studies of treatment in personality disorders must not be underestimated they are not insuperable, and these studies are essential before satisfactory recommendations for the treatment of personality disorder can be made.

Development and course

It would be wrong to pretend that personality disorder is easy to treat, and any success in preventing its development would be a major advance. The causes of personality disorder remain extremely difficult to determine, and while the environment (particularly the emotional one) is undoubtedly important, the role of inherited characteristics is likely to be equally so. To understand the development of personality disorder, careful longitudinal studies are needed with initial assessment at an early age, and these should involve close collaboration between child and adult psychiatry. Detailed follow-up studies (e.g. Wolff & Chick, 1980) are of great value here.

Although definitions of personality disorder refer to their enduring characteristics, the adjective 'enduring' should not be taken as 'permanent'. Examination of the prevalence and outcome of personality disorders suggests that some categories, particularly borderline personality disorder, improve significantly over as little as five years (Pope *et al*, 1983; McGlashan, 1984). When personality disorders are studied with regard to age, two groups can be identified: immature personality disorders that improve over time, and mature personality disorders that tend to persist into late middle or old age (Tyrer & Seivewright, 1988) (Table 1.3).

The influence of personality disorder on the course of mental state diagnoses is important and needs greater emphasis in clinical practice, particularly when assessing prognosis. When the outcome of mental state

TABLE 1.3
Separation of mature and immature personality disorders

Mature (little variation with increasing age)	Immature (tends to improve over time)
Anankastic (obsessive–compulsive)	Antisocial (dissocial)
Paranoid	Borderline (impulsive)
Schizoid (and schizotypal)	Histrionic
Anxious	Dependent
	Narcissistic

Adapted from Tyrer & Seivewright (1988).

disorders, of whatever type, is examined in groups with and without concurrent personality disorder, there is invariably a worse outcome in those with personality disorders (Greer & Cawley, 1966; Zimmerman *et al*, 1988). This is true across the range of personality disorder, and individual categorisation has little impact.

Closer examination of the data suggests that there are two components to this poor outcome: greater mental state pathology and greater vulnerability to relapse. Thus although short-term improvement may be similar in those with and without concurrent personality disorder (Zimmerman *et al*, 1988; Tyrer *et al*, 1990), this is not maintained and relapse is accompanied by much greater demands on the psychiatric services at all levels (Tyrer & Seivewright, 1988).

Beyond the horizon

The concept of personality disorder is not likely to disappear from psychiatry, despite its critics (Blackburn, 1988; Lewis & Appleby, 1988), and once it is accepted universally there will be no need to give a nervous laugh or act as though the subject is a parenthetical appendage whenever it is mentioned. It is indispensable to psychiatric practice and there is now greater awareness of its importance in affecting many aspects of aetiology and management.

There are many possibilities for new developments. Life-events research, which has examined the social factors responsible for the onset of mental illness (Brown & Harris, 1978, 1989) and its recovery (Brown *et al*, 1992) in great detail, could also with profit examine the relationship between personality status and life events. Preliminary findings suggest that certain personality features, particularly those of the flamboyant personality disorders, create, or are at least associated with, greater rates of life events, and that anankastic (obsessional) personalities have fewer events than those with no personality disorder (Seivewright, 1987, 1988).

The relationship between personality disorder and suicide attempts may also offer scope for selective preventive strategies, and the similar association between personality status and potential for drug dependence (Tyrer *et al*,

1983*b*) may also be useful in preventing dependence. If those, for example, who are at great risk of developing dependence on benzodiazepines (Tyrer, 1991) are not prescribed these drugs for longer than a few weeks then much iatrogenic disorder might be prevented.

The evidence that patients with personality disorder receive longer periods of hospital treatment (Stone *et al*, 1987) and more contact from psychiatric services (Seivewright & Tyrer, 1988) also has important implications for those involved with service planning. Currently the demand for medical services is dominated by the degree of social deprivation in the community concerned (Jarman, 1983) but the likely proportion of those with personality disorder might be a better predictor.

It is likely that many more apparently 'stable' elements of knowledge of mental state disorders will be shown to be dependent on personality factors that are currently undetected because they have never been investigated. The subject seems destined to increase in importance but we need better unbiased measurements; these are likely to be biosocial ones that need cross-disciplinary collaboration. Our perspective for personality disorders needs to be a combination of broad vision and fine-grained detail; all parts of the subject deserve to be better focused.

References

ADLINGTON, R. (ed. & trans.) (1925) *A Book of Characters* (by Theophrastus). London: George Routledge.

AKISKAL, H. S., CHEN, S. E., DAVIS, G. C., *et al* (1986) Borderline: an adjective in search of a noun. In *Essential Papers on Borderline Disorders: One Hundred Years at the Border* (ed. M. S. Stone), pp. 549–568. New York: New York University Press.

AMERICAN PSYCHIATRIC ASSOCIATION (1980) *Diagnostic and Statistical Manual of Mental Disorders* (3rd edn) (DSM–III). Washington, DC: APA.

—— (1989) *Diagnostic and Statistical Manual of Mental Disorders* (3rd edn, revised) (DSM–III–R). Washington, DC: APA.

BAYER, R. & SPITZER, R. L. (1985) Neurosis, psychodynamics and DSM–III: a history of the controversy. *Archives of General Psychiatry*, **42**, 187–196.

BLACKBURN, R. (1988) On moral judgements and personality disorders. The myth of psychopathic personality revisited. *British Journal of Psychiatry*, **153**, 505–512.

BLUGLASS, R. S. (1977) *A Psychiatric Study of Scottish Prisoners*. MD thesis, St Andrew's University.

BOWMAN, M. J. & STURGEON, D. A. (1977) A clinic within a general hospital for the assessment of urgent psychiatric problems. *Lancet*, *ii*, 1067–1068.

BROWN, G. & HARRIS, T. (1978) *The Social Origins of Depression*. London: Tavistock Publications.

—— & —— (1989) *Life Events and Illness*. London: Unwin and Hyman.

——, LEMYRE, L. & BIFULCO, A. (1992) Social factors and recovery from anxiety and depressive disorders. *British Journal of Psychiatry*, **161**, 44–54.

CASEY, P. R. (1985) *Psychiatric Morbidity in General Practice: A Diagnostic Approach*. MD thesis, National University of Ireland.

—— (1989) Suicide intent and personality disorder. *Acta Psychiatrica Scandinavica*, **79**, 290–295.

——, TYRER, P. J. & DILLON, S. (1984) The diagnostic status of patients with conspicuous psychiatric morbidity in primary care. *Psychological Medicine*, **14**, 673–681.

—— & TYRER, P. J. (1986) Personality, functioning and symptomatology. *Journal of Psychiatric Research*, **20**, 363–374.

CLECKLEY, H. (1941) *The Mask of Sanity*. London: Henry Kimpton.

COID, J. W. (1989) Psychopathic disorders. *Current Opinion in Psychiatry*, **2**, 750–756.

COOPER, B. (1965) A study of one hundred chronic psychiatric patients identified in general practice. *British Journal of Psychiatry*, **111**, 595–605.

CUTTING, J., COWEN, P. J., MANN, A. H., *et al* (1986) Personality and psychosis: use of the Standardized Assessment of Personality. *Acta Psychiatrica Scandinavica*, **73**, 87–92.

DAHL, A. (1986) Some aspects of the DSM–III personality disorders illustrated by a consecutive series of hospitalized patients. *Acta Psychiatrica Scandinavica*, **73**, 61–66.

DAVIS, D. R. (1967) How useful a diagnosis is borderline personality? *British Medical Journal*, **294**, 265–266.

DEPARTMENT OF HEALTH AND SOCIAL SECURITY (1985) *Mental Illness in Hospitals and Units in England. Results from the Mental Health Inquiry Statistical Bulletin, Government Statistical Services*, London: HMSO.

DOHRENWEND, B. P. & DOHRENWEND, B. S. (1969) *Social Status and Psychological Disorder. A Causal Inquiry*. New York: Wiley Interscience.

FERGUSON, B. & TYRER, P. (1989) Personality disorders. In *The Instruments of Psychiatric Research* (ed. C. Thompson), pp. 239–251. Chichester: Wiley.

FRANCES, A. (1980) The DSM–III personality disorders section: a commentary. *American Journal of Psychiatry*, **137**, 1050–1054.

FYER, M. R., FRANCES, A. J., SULLIVAN, T., *et al* (1988) Co-morbidity of borderline personality disorder. *Archives of General Psychiatry*, **45**, 348–352.

GREER, H. S. & CAWLEY, R. H. (1966) *Some Observations on the Natural History of Neurotic Illness*. Australian Medical Assocation, Mervyn Archdall Medical Monograph No. 3. Glebe, Australia: Australasian Medical Publishing Company.

GUNDERSON, J. G. & SINGER, M. T. (1975) Defining borderline patients: an overview. *American Journal of Psychiatry*, **132**, 1–10.

GUNN, J. (1988) Personality disorder: a clinical suggestion. In *Personality Disorders: Diagnosis Management and Course* (ed. P. Tyrer), pp. 33–42. London: Wright.

——, ROBERTSON, G., DELL, S., *et al* (1978) *Psychiatric Aspects of Imprisonment*. London: Academic Press.

HENDERSON, D. K. (1939) *Psychopathic States*. New York: Norson.

HENRY, D. (1975) The personality of Oliver Cromwell. *Practitioner*, **215**, 102–110.

—— (1979) Stonewall Jackson: a soldier eccentric. *Practitioner*, **223**, 580–587.

——, GEARY, D. & TYRER, P. (1993) Adolf Hitler: a reassessment of his personality status. *Irish Journal of Psychological Medicine* (in press).

HOCH, P. & POLATIN, P. (1949) Pseudo-neurotic forms of schizophrenia. *Psychiatric Quarterly*, **23**, 248–276.

HOEPER, E. W., NYEZ, G. R., CLEARY, P. D., *et al* (1979) Estimated prevalence of RDC mental disorder in primary medical care. *International Journal of Mental Health*, **8**, 6–15.

HOROWITZ, M. J. (1977) *Hysterical Personality*. New York: Jason Aronson.

JARMAN, B. (1983) Identification of underprivileged areas. *British Medical Journal*, **286**, 1705–1709.

KASS, F., SKODOL, A., CHARLES, E., *et al* (1985) Scaled ratings of DSM–III personality disorders. *American Journal of Psychiatry*, **142**, 627–630.

KERNBERG, O. F. (1975) *Borderline Conditions and Pathological Narcissism*. New York: Jason Aronson.

KESSEL, N. (1960) Psychiatric morbidity in a London general practice. *British Journal of Preventive and Social Medicine*, **14**, 16–22.

KOCH, J. L. A. (1891) *Die psychopathischen Minderwertigkeiten*. Dorn: Ravensburg.

KOHUT, H. (1971) *The Analysis of the Self*. New York: Inernational Universities Press.

LEIGHTON, D. C., HARDING, J. S., MACKLIN, D. B., *et al* (1963) Psychiatric findings of the Stirling County study. *American Journal of Psychiatry*, **119**, 1021–1026.

LEWIS, G. & APPLEBY, L. (1988) Personality disorder: the patients psychiatrists dislike. *British Journal of Psychiatry*, **153**, 44–49.

LIVESLEY, W. J. (1987) A systematic approach to the delineation of personality disorders. *American Journal of Psychiatry*, **144**, 772–777.

—— & JACKSON, D. (1988) The internal consistency and factorial structures of behaviors judged to be associated with DSM–III personality disorders. *American Journal of Psychiatry*, **139**, 1360–1361.

LORANGER, A. W., SUSMAN, V. L., OLDHAM, M. M., *et al* (1987) The Personality Disorder Examination: a preliminary report. *Journal of Personality Disorders*, **1**, 1–13.

MAUDSLEY, H. (1868) *A Physiology and Pathology of Mind* (2nd edn), p. 516. London: Macmillan.

MCGLASHAN, T. H. (1984) The Chestnut Lodge follow-up study. i. Follow-up methodology and study sample. *Archives of General Psychiatry*, **40**, 573–585.

MILLON, T. (1969) *Modern Psychopathology: A Biosocial Approach to Maladaptive Learning and Functioning*. Philadelphia: Saunders.

—— (1981) *Disorders of Personality, DSM–III: Axis II*. New York: Wiley.

MOREY, L. (1988) Personality disorders in DSM–III and DSM–III–R: convergence, coverage, and internal consistency. *American Journal of Psychiatry*, **145**, 573–577.

MULLER, J. J., CHAFETZ, M. E. & BLARE, H. T. (1967) Acute psychiatric services in the general hospital: III, statistical survey. *American Journal of Psychiatry*, **124**, 56.

MURTHY, V. N. (1969) Personality and the nature of suicide attempts. *British Journal of Psychiatry*, **115**, 791–795.

MYERS, J. K., WEISSMAN, M. M., TISCHLER, G. L., *et al* (1984) Six month prevalence of psychiatric disorders in three communities, 1980–1982. *Archives of General Psychiatry*, **41**, 959–967.

O'HARE, A. & WALSH, D. (1986) *Activities of Psychiatric Hospitals and Units 1983*. Dublin: The Medico-Social Research Board.

OVENSTONE, I. K. (1973) Spectrum of suicidal behaviours in Edinburgh. *British Journal of Preventive and Social Medicine*, **27**, 27–35.

PALLIS, D. J. & BIRTCHNELL, J. (1977) Seriousness of suicide attempts in relation to personality. *British Journal of Psychiatry*, **130**, 253–259.

PARLOFF, M. B. & DIES, R. R. (1977) Group psychotherapy outcome research, 1966–1975. *International Journal of Group Psychotherapy*, **27**, 281–319.

PFOHL, B., CORYELL, W., ZIMMERMAN, M., *et al* (1986) DSM–III personality disorders: diagnostic overlap and internal consistency of individual DSM–III criteria. *Comprehensive Psychiatry*, **27**, 21–34.

PHILIPS, A. E. (1970) Traits, attitudes and symptoms in a group of attempted suicides. *British Journal of Psychiatry*, **116**, 475–482.

PIERCE, D. W. (1977) Suicide intent and self-injury. *British Journal of Psychiatry*, **130**, 377–385.

PINEL, P. (1801) *A Treatise on Insanity* (trans. D. D. Davis, 1962). New York: Hafner.

POPE, H. G., JONAS, J. M., HUDSON, J. I., *et al* (1983) The validity of DSM–III borderline personality disorder: phenomenologic, family history, treatment response and long-term follow-up study. *Archives of General Psychiatry*, **40**, 23–30.

PRICHARD, J. C. (1837) *A Treatise on Insanity and Other Diseases Affecting the Mind*. Philadelphia: Harwell, Barrington & Harwell.

RADO, S. (1953) Dynamics and classification of disordered behaviour. *American Journal of Psychiatry*, **110**, 406–416.

REICH, J. & THOMPSON, W. D. (1987) DSM–III personality disorder clusters in three generations. *British Journal of Psychiatry*, **150**, 471–475.

ROBINS, L. N. (1966) *Deviant Children Grown Up*. Baltimore: Williams & Wilkins.

ROSENTHAL, D., WENDER, P. H., KETY, S. S., *et al* (1971) The adopted-away offspring of schizophrenics. *American Journal of Psychiatry*, **128**, 307–311.

RUTTER, M. L. (1987) Temperament, personality and personality disorder. *British Journal of Psychiatry*, **150**, 443–458.

SCHNEIDER, K. (1923) *Die Psychopathischen Personlichkeiten*. Berlin: Springer.

SEIVEWRIGHT, N. (1987) Relationship between life events and personality in psychiatric disorder. *Stress Medicine*, **3**, 163–168.

—— (1988) Personality disorder, life events and the onset of mental illness. In *Personality Disorders: Diagnosis, Management and Course* (ed. P. Tyrer), pp. 82–92. London: Wright.

SHEPHERD, M., COOPER, B., BROWN, A. C., *et al* (1966) *Psychiatric Illness in General Practice.* Oxford: Oxford University Press.

SOLOFF, P. H., GEORGE, A., NATHAN, R. S., *et al* (1986) Progress in pharmacotherapy of borderline disorders: a double blind study of amitriptyline, haloperidol and placebo. *Archives of General Psychiatry*, **43**, 691–697.

SROLE, L., LANEER, T., MICHAEL, S., *et al* (1962) *Mental Health in the Metropolis.* New York: McGraw Hill.

STONE, M., HURT, S. & STONE, D. (1987) The PI 500: long-term follow-up of borderline inpatients meeting DSM III criteria. *Journal of Personality Disorders*, **1**, 291–298.

THOMPSON, D. J. & GOLDBERG, D. (1987) Hysterical personality disorder: the process of diagnosis in clinical and experimental settings. *British Journal of Psychiatry*, **150**, 241–245.

TYRER, P. (1988) What's wrong with DSM–III personality disorders? *Journal of Personality Disorders*, **2**, 281–291.

——— (1991) Qui devient dependant des benzodiazepines? In *Les Nouvelles Addictions* (ed. J. L. Venisse), pp. 142–147. Paris: Masson.

——— & ALEXANDER, J. (1979) Classification of personality disorder. *British Journal of Psychiatry*, **135**, 163–167.

———, CASEY, P. & GALL, J. (1983*a*) The relationship between neurosis and personality disorder. *British Journal of Psychiatry*, **142**, 404–408.

———, OWEN, R. & DAWLING, S. (1983*b*) Gradual withdrawal of diazepam after long-term therapy. *Lancet*, *i*, 1402–1406.

——— & FERGUSON, B. (1988) Development of the concept of abnormal personality. In *Personality Disorders: Diagnosis, Management and Course* (ed. P. Tyrer), pp. 1–11. London: Wright.

——— & SEIVEWRIGHT, H. (1988) Studies of outcome. In *Personality Disorders: Diagnosis, Treatment and Course* (ed. P. Tyrer), pp. 119–136. London: Wright.

———, ALEXANDER, J. & FERGUSON, B. (1988) Personality assessment schedule. In *Personality Disorders: Diagnosis, Management and Course* (ed. P. Tyrer), pp. 140–167. London: Wright.

———, SEIVEWRIGHT, N., FERGUSON, B., *et al* (1990) The Nottingham study of neurotic disorder: relationship between personality status and symptoms. *Psychological Medicine*, **20**, 423–431.

VERNON, P. E. (1964) *Personality Assessment: A Critical Survey*, pp. 240–241. London: Methuen.

WALDINGER, R. O. (1987) Intensive psychodynamic therapy with borderline patients: an overview. *American Journal of Psychiatry*, **144**, 267–274.

——— & GUNDERSON, J. (1987) *Effective Psychotherapy with Borderline Patients.* New York: Macmillan.

WEISSMAN, M. M., MYERS, J. K. & HARDING, P. S. (1978) Psychiatric disorder in a US urban community. *American Journal of Psychiatry*, **135**, 459–462.

WIDIGER, T., TRULL, T., HURT, S., *et al* (1987) A multidimensional scaling of the DSM–III personality disorders. *Archives of General Psychiatry*, **44**, 557–563.

——— & ROGERS, J. H. (1989) Prevalence and comorbidity of personality disorders. *Psychiatric Annals*, **19**, 132–136.

WOLFF, S. & CHICK, J. (1980) Schizoid personality in childhood: a controlled follow-up study. *Psychological Medicine*, **9**, 85–100.

WORLD HEALTH ORGANIZATION (1978) *Mental Disorders: Glossary and Guide to their Classification in Accordance with the Ninth Revision of the International Classification of Diseases* (ICD-9). Geneva: WHO.

——— (1989) *International Classification of Diseases*, draft of 10th revision (ICD-10). Geneva: WHO.

ZANARINI, M., FRANKENBURG, F., CHAUNCEY, D., *et al* (1987) The Diagnostic Interview for Personality Disorders: interrater and test–retest reliability. *Comprehensive Psychiatry*, **28**, 467–480.

ZIMMERMAN, M., CORYELL, W., PFOHL, B., *et al* (1988) ECT response in depressed patients with and without a DSM–III personality disorder. *American Journal of Psychiatry*, **143**, 1030–1032.

2 Personality disorders: a conceptual history

GERMAN E. BERRIOS

'Personality disorders' are defined by DSM–III–R as clusters of "personality traits [which] are inflexible and maladaptive and cause either significant functional impairment or subject distress" (p. 335) (American Psychiatric Association, 1987). 'Personality traits' thus remain the conceptual unit of analysis, and are defined as "enduring patterns of perceiving, relating, and thinking about the environment and oneself exhibited in a wide range of important social and personal contexts" (p. 335). Clinicians are "directed to find a *single specific personality disorder* that adequately describes the person's disturbed personality functioning. Frequently this can be done only with difficulty, since many people exhibit traits that are not limited to a single personality disorder" (my italics) (p. 336). ICD–10 (World Health Organization, 1992), in turn, suggests explanatory mechanisms: "conditions and patterns of behaviour [that] emerge early in the course of individual development, as a resultant of both constitutional factors and social experience, while others are acquired later in life" (p. 150).

Both the DSM–III–R and ICD–10 accounts of personality disorder can best be described as palimpsests whose earlier European text has been hidden by recent layers of 'empirical' varnish; to read the original meanings the clinician must scratch the surface away and remind him- or herself of the rich French and German conceptual traditions of thinking on character types from which recent scripts have emerged. During the last 150 years, terms such as personality, personality disorder, character, temperament, constitution, self, type, trait, and psychopathic inferiority, have changed and exchanged meanings. Although it is known that such combinations and permutations have been presided over by scientific, ideological, and social factors (Jeanmaire, 1882; Ribot, 1912; Anonymous, 1921; Allport, 1937; Werlinder, 1978; Tyrer & Ferguson, 1990), it remains unclear to the clinician which of the obscurities besetting the concept of personality disorder are man-made and which *in re*. This paper examines the history of these issues between the beginning of the 19th century and World War II.

17

Historiographical issues

Untold confusion has been caused by mixing up the history of 'personality disorder' as a term, a behavioural form, and a concept. Words have their own linguistic space, and are the concern of historical semantics. Patterns of behaviour similar to those currently called personality types or disorders, albeit named differently, have been known for millennia. For example, Theophrastus (1967 translation) marvelled that: "albeit the whole of Greece lies in the same clime and all Greeks have a like upbringing, we have not the same constitution of character" and proceeded to describe 29 traits including arrogance, backbiting, boorishness, buffoonery, cowardice, and distrustfulness. Concepts (models and theories) have been created throughout time to 'explain' such behavioural patterns (e.g. Freud, 1925; Theophrastus, 1967; Cloninger, 1987). The historian must locate the moment at which name, behaviour and concept converged: in the case of the 'personality disorders', such convergence seems to have taken place during the 1920s. Along the historical path thus outlined, answers will be found for questions such as the following. What is the pedigree of the concept of 'personality trait'? Is it structurally different from 'symptom'? Should 'type' or 'trait' be the unit of clinical analysis for personality disorder? What is the relationship between 'trait' and 'dimension'? Has the old notion of 'moral insanity' anything to do with the more recent one of 'psychopathic behaviour'? Is the latter best conceived as a disorder of personality or as a form of insanity? Should the 'neuroses' be considered as periodic forms of personality disorder? What is the relationship between psychoses and disorder of personality? When did the concept of psychopathic personality become contaminated by 'moral' nuances? Are the terms currently favoured any better than older ones, such as moral insanity, impulsion, impulsive insanity, lucid insanity, volitional insanity, psychopathy, monomania, non-delusional insanity, or reasoning insanity? (See Maughs, 1941; Saussure, 1946; Gurvitz, 1951; Ey, 1952; Craft, 1965; Whitlock, 1967, 1982; Lewis, 1974; Fullinwider, 1975; Blair, 1975; Werlinder, 1978; Pichot, 1978; Smith, 1979; Lanteri-Laura, 1979*a,b*; Kageyama, 1984; Schmiedebach, 1985; Huertas, 1987; Ellard, 1988; Motte-Moitreux, 1990).

The 19th-century intellectual background

There were two predominant psychological theories during the 19th century. Faculty psychology, the oldest, conceived the mind as a set of functions: intellectual (cognitive), emotional (orectic), and volitional (or conative) (Berrios, 1988*a*); versions of this theory have existed since classical times (Blakey, 1850). Associationism, the second theory, started in the work of

Locke and other British philosophers (Warren, 1921) who conceived the mind as an empty slate: knowledge originated from ideas obtained from the external world, or from their combination by means of rules of association (Hoeldtke, 1967). By the late 18th century, Thomas Reid and other Scottish philosophers (Brooks, 1976) as well as Kant (Hilgard, 1980) had expressed a preference for faculty psychology, their main argument being that experience alone could not explain all knowledge – 'innate' structures were necessary.

At the beginning of the 19th century these psychological theories vied for supremacy. Faculty psychology (Albrecht, 1970) inspired phrenology, a scientific theory which led to new ideas on personality profiling and brain localisation (Spoerl, 1936; Hecaen & Lanteri-Laura, 1978); associationism, in turn, was instrumental in the development of psychophysics and quantification in psychology (Claparède, 1903). Both theories contributed to the creation of the new descriptive psychopathology, psychiatric taxonomy, and the concepts of trait, type, and character.

Maine de Biran and *habitude*

During the early 19th century, the view that human 'character' was innate was challenged by the belief that behaviour was also shaped by environmental factors. Maine de Biran (1929) made popular the notion of *habitude* (habit) to explain the origin of behaviour which, on account of its persistence, seemed innate and/or inherited (Moore, 1970). The term 'habitude' has a complex semantic past (Lalande, 1976) which includes old references to the 'form of being' of objects, regardless of their origin (in the sense, for example, of 'leptosomic habitus'). Maine de Biran (Delacroix, 1924), and later Ravaisson (1984), emphasised the 'learning' aspect of habitude, thereby providing an important explanatory mechanism for the formation of character. By the second half of the century, the term habitude was incorporated into medical parlance (Dechambre, 1886a). Terms derived from the same Latin stem were later used by Kretschmer (1936) and Sheldon (1942) to refer to specific types of human physique.

Types, traits and their measurement

Faculty psychology and associationism also made possible the view that the mind and behaviour could be divided into recognisable parts or 'traits'; for the first time monolithic descriptions of human character were broken up into their ingredients, thereby transforming 'molar' descriptions into 'molecular' ones. Traits became the unit of analysis of human behaviour, measurement scales developed, and as cerebral localisation theories gained acceptance, correlation between traits and brain sites were sought.

B

The concept of 'type' also has an interesting history (Abbagnano, 1961). The word 'typus', originally meaning 'mark' or 'impression', was used by Plato to refer to model, form, scheme, or cluster of features. Galen imported 'typus' into medicine to refer to the 'form' of disease, and Juan Huarte and La Bruyère (Ferrater Mora, 1958) used the term in Theophrastus' sense to refer to recognisable forms of human behaviour. By the beginning of the 19th century, psychological 'typologies' were, therefore, well known, and constituted the theoretical framework within which the new concept of character was to be analysed.

Psychological measurement was highly developed by the end of the 19th century. In addition to sensory events, reaction times, and memory performance, efforts were also made to quantify personality traits (Boring, 1961; Zupan, 1976). The latter was helped by the work of Francis Galton (a cousin of Charles Darwin), and the expansion of statistics and probability theory which, in the event, was to permeate all Western science (Porter, 1986; Gigerenzer *et al*, 1989; Hacking, 1990).

The notion of 'correlation' (Galton, 1883) provided a new form of 'scientific' evidence for the view that some personality traits went together; Galton believed that "the fundamental and intrinsic differences of character that exist in individuals are well illustrated by those that distinguish the two sexes, and which begin to assert themselves even in the nursery . . . the subject of character deserves more *statistical investigation* than it has yet received" (my italics) (pp.39–42). He also believed that intellectual differences had a 'hereditary' origin (Buss, 1976), and with regard to his own book *Hereditary Genius* (1879), Galton wrote: "during the fourteen years that have elapsed since this book was published, numerous fresh instances have arisen of distinction being attained by members of the gifted families whom I quoted as instances of heredity, thus strengthening my argument" (p. 57). Some 20th century measurements of personality and physique were modelled on the anthropometric indices developed by Galton.

Relevant 19th-century terms

The words 'constitution', 'temperament', 'self', 'character', and 'personality' were imported into the 19th century from earlier 'epistemes' (forms of discourse now lost), so they had to be shelled and refurbished with new meanings (Berrios, 1984).

'Constitution', 'temperament' and 'self'

The word 'constitution' has, since Greek times, played an important descriptive and explanatory role in Western medicine (Pinillos *et al*, 1966).

Equivalent to 'diathesis', 'conformation of the body', or 'habit' (in the sense of 'pyknic' habit), constitution was used until the end of the 19th century to refer to "the harmonious development and maintenance of the issues and organs of which the body is made up" (p. 381) (Quain, 1894). This body-centred view differed from Hippocratic usage which emphasised environmental variables, for example, "the climactic conditions of such a marked type as to give a distinguishing character to a period of time" or "to denote a fixed type prevalent at any particular time" (p. 141) (Jones, 1923). It is beyond the scope of this paper to explain this major change in meaning (for this see Brochin, 1876; Pinillos *et al*, 1966): suffice it to say that at the end of the 19th century the concept of personality was remodelled on that of constitution to mean 'harmonious' organisation of psychological parts.

The word 'temperament' was equally influential; in Greek medicine it was used to provide a 'biological' explanation for the individuality of the self and its traits (Haupt, 1858; Dechambre, 1886*b*; Staehelin, 1941; Roccatagliata, 1981). The Hippocratic fourfold humoral view of the temperaments lasted well into the 18th century, when Richerand attempted to re-explain temperaments in terms of the size and predominance of certain bodily organs; this view was challenged by Royer-Collard (1843), who found no physiological reasons or post-mortem evidence to support the claim that the size of the heart, brain, or liver were related to behaviour. The last European effort to return to the classical notion of temperament was Stewart's (1887). The theory of temperaments provided the modern notion of disorder of personality with the crucial principle that psychological 'types' are determined by an organic substratum (Bloor, 1928; Burt, 1938; Dublineau, 1943; Eysenck, 1951).

During the 19th century, the philosophical analysis of character, personality, consciousness, and introspection revolved around the concept of 'self'. Although ideas equivalent to self can be found in pre-Cartesian writings, there is agreement that it achieved clarity only in the work of Descartes (Frondizi, 1952; Viney, 1969), and later in the philosophical systems of Locke, Leibniz, and Kant (Burns, 1979). Thus, by the beginning of the 19th century, three views were recognised: the old Cartesian conception of the self as consciousness or self-awareness, the self as a core (unity or structure), and the self as a bundle of relationships (Abbagnano, 1961). All three views have been important to the development of the notions of character and personality.

Descartes conceived the self as the enduring substance that provided man with 'ontological continuity'. This view doubled as a solution to the 'personal identity' problem (Penelhum, 1967) but was challenged by Hume (Pears, 1975), who questioned the existence of a substance and redefined the self as a series of perceptual moments, linked by memory. During the 19th century, this emphasis on subjectivity led to the 'psychologisation' of the self. Human scepticism, however, had undermined the ontological view of personal identity so much (Hamilton, 1859) that the latter issue continued besetting even the psychological version of the self. This is one of the reasons why, during the last century, refurbished concepts such as character, constitution and, in the event, personality, were made to act as conceptual props for the personal identity problem. Towards the end of the century, writers such as Royce and Baldwin offered a redefinition of the self in terms of human relationships (Baldwin & Stout, 1901), that is, feedback from others on the continuity of one's character was important to the development of the sense of identity; this view was to become the conceptual core from which 'interactionist' theories of personality grew during the 20th century (Ekehammar, 1974).

'Character' and 'personality'

The 19th-century usage of the term 'character' emphasised, more than that of personality, the 'unchangeable' core of the individual's behaviour, that which made him/her different from others (Roback, 1927). Of classical provenance, the term was revived by Kant to name the empirical and logical character of objects (Ferrater Mora, 1958). Noticing its psychological potential, J. S. Mill suggested that a new book on human 'characters' needed writing and Alexander Bain – produced his *On the Study of Character, Including an Estimate of Phrenology* in 1861. Character soon achieved popularity as the preferred name for 'psychological type' (Azam, 1885). It is important to remark that during this period, and indeed until the turn of the century, the word 'personality' was used to refer to the 'conscious aspects of behaviour' (Jeanmaire, 1882). 'Characterology' became the science of character, and found a niche within psychology. By the early 20th century, the word 'character' was replaced by 'personality', which by then had acquired a wider meaning.

'Personality' started life as a philosophical word, for example Aquinas meant by it the "condition or mode of appearance of a person" ('person' being the Greek term for mask). The term was 'psychologised' in the work of Hume and Kant, and the process completed by Maine de Biran and J. S. Mill (Jeanmaire, 1882). During most of the 19th century, however, 'personality' remained related to the subjective aspects of the self. This is the reason why Janet as late as 1896 pleaded that "the study of personality, still conceived as a metaphysical problem, should become a topic for experimental psychology" (p. 97). Influenced by Comte, the French writer identified three periods in the history of personality: a metaphysical one, lasting up to the beginning of the 19th century, during which writers attempted (not always successfully) to distinguish personality from a deeper substance or principle; then an associationist period, in which a search was made for the mental elements underlying the feeling of unity of the self or personality; and Janet suggested that a third or scientific period was about to start, in which personality would be defined in objective terms and on the basis of material obtained from new sources such as the study of the mentally ill.

Analysis of Continental work on personality during this period, however, shows that all three approaches coexisted (Paulhan, 1880; Caillard, 1894; Galton, 1895; Martí y Juliá, 1899; Renouvier, 1990), and that most writers equated personality with self-awareness. Noticing this, Jeanmaire (1882) – the greatest historian of personality during the 19th century – complained that the concept was caught between the scepticism of the British empiricists and the rationalism of the French spiritualists, and cautioned that the only way out was to emphasise its 'psychological' aspects (as Maine de Biran had indeed attempted to do). After examining the use of the term 'personality' in 12 popular French books published between 1874 and 1882, Beaussire (1883) concluded that scientific psychology had not yet resolved the problem that while "personality manifests itself by means of consciousness, the latter is *not sufficient to constitute the personality*" (my italics) (p. 317).

Perusal of contemporary books on either the 'disorders' (Ribot, 1912), 'variations' (Paulhan, 1882) or 'alterations' (Binet, 1892) of the personality shows that none of these works dealt with personality types or disorders in the current sense; instead they analysed the mechanisms of awareness of the self, and phenomena concerning the disintegration of consciousness such as somnambulism, hysterical anaesthesia, automatic writing, hallucinations, multiple personalities, and memory disorders. This suggests that clinical and experimentalist writers shared the view that personality was tantamount to the 'internal self'. During the early 20th century, attempts were made to escape from this narrow approach by suggesting that pathological changes in awareness (as those listed above) reflected alterations in the 'perception' of the personality (Anonymous, 1921; Dwelshauvers, 1934). These earlier beliefs also explain why the DSM–III–R category "personality disorders" has been translated in France not as *troubles de la personnalité* but as *personnalités pathologiques* (Garrabé, 1989).

Disorders of 'character' as forms of insanity

In 19th-century psychiatry, diagnostic categories were created for a number of reasons, but mostly to deal with the insanities. Some described disorders sharing a number of clinical features (active naming), others referred to clinical states not fitting into any classification (passive naming or naming by exclusion); yet others grouped clinical states having only one feature in common. *Manie sans délire*, moral insanity, and *folie lucide* illustrate these modes.

'Manie sans délire'

It is not easy to decide whether Pinel (1809) intended 'mania without delusions' to be a new clinical category. His classification, based on faculty psychology, empirical observation, and his determination to preserve the notion of 'total insanity', included four categories: *manie* (*délire général*), *mélancolie* (*délire exclusif*), *démence* (*abolition de la pensée*), and *idiotisme* (*obliteration des facultés intellectuelles et affectives*). These definitions cut across the universe of mental disorders in ways opaque to the current clinician; indeed, it would be difficult to find patients to fit into any of them. Pinel proceeded to subdivide *manie* into *la manie avec délire* and *la manie sans délire*. The view of the historian is obscured here by the meanings of the French word *délire* and *manie*. During this period the former referred to disorders of intellect, emotions, or conation, and hence cannot be fully translated as 'delusion' (which, since the 17th century, had had an intellectualistic meaning); *manie* referred to states of persistent furor and florid psychosis and had little to do with the current notion of mania (Berrios, 1988*b*). This is why Pinel asked whether mania could exist without a lesion of the intellect (p. 155); he believed it could, and criticised John Locke for "considering mania as inseparable from délire: when I started working at Bicêtre, I used to think like this author, and I was not a little surprised to see many patients who at no time showed any lesion of the intellect, and who were dominated by a sort of furor, as if their affective faculties were disordered" (pp. 155–156).

As examples, Pinel reported the case of a self-indulgent young man suffering from temper tantrums during which he would even kill his own pet animals; after attacking a woman he was forcefully admitted to hospital. Another man, with "a more advanced state of the same form of insanity" (p. 157), had periodic attacks of furor started by intense thirst, pain in his bowels, constipation, and a feeling of heat which spread to his chest, neck and face "making them red" and his "arterial pulses fast and visible" (were these porphyria attacks?); he would then attack the first person he met. Insight into this behaviour would afterwards make him contrite and suicidal. The third case was a chronic patient, who after claiming improvement and looking normal, was released only to become agitated and aggressive after joining a political demonstration. Pinel suggested that all three patients shared a disease characterised by disordered affect (*facultés affectives lésées*). But recall that Pinel did not mean depression, euphoria or anxiety, but simply 'furor' or aggression.

Debate on what Pinel meant by *manie sans délire* raged during most of the 19th century. Some German writers accepted the new disease with reservation (e.g. Hoffbauer, Reil, Heinroth), while others (like Henke) rejected it, based on the principle of unity of the human mind, and on the belief that mental functions could not become diseased independently

(Société Médico-Psychologique, 1866, p. 385; Motte-Moitroux, 1990). In France, Esquirol and his followers, although accepting the faculty psychology principle that mental functions could become ill independently, were uneasy about the notion of *manie sans délire*; alienists from other groups (e.g. the Falrets) opposed it from the start. As late as 1866, in a famous debate at the Société Médico-Psychologique, the crucial argument was rehearsed by Falret junior (1866) that the only reason for entertaining a category such as *manie sans délire* was to use it as a defence in court. Analysis of Pinel's work, however, suggests that he was indeed trying to construct a new form of *insanity*, whose definition was no longer based on the presence of delusions but which still preserved its forensic value (Motte-Moitroux, 1990). Be that as it may, Pinel's clinical intentions had little to do with the 'personality disorders'.

'Monomanie'

Esquirol was unhappy with *manie sans délire*; he rarely if ever used the term, and instead propounded another – monomania (and to deal with depressive illness, lypemania). On the former he wrote

"Pinel, more than other alienists, has drawn the attention of observers to this condition that is called reasoning mania (*folie raisonnante*) but which our illustrious master called *manie sans délire*. Fodéré has also accepted its existence and called it *fureur maniaque* . . . but does this variety of mania in which the sufferers preserve the sanity of their reason while abandoning themselves to the most condemnable acts really exist? Can there be a pathological state in which men are irresistibly led to perform acts that their conscience rejects. I do not think so. I have seen many patients deploring these impulses, and all intimated that at the time of the act they felt something which they could not explain, that their brain was under pressure, and that they experienced great difficulty in the exercise of their reason . . . thus, all the clinical facts of *manie sans délire*, as reported by other authors, belong into monomania or lypemania, species of insanity characterised by fixed and specific delusions." (Esquirol, 1838, vol. 2, pp. 95–96)

Esquirol had his own reasons for not using *manie sans délire*. The notion of monomania, that he tried so hard to popularise, also had a chequered career (Saussure, 1946; Alvarez-Uría, 1983), and was killed at a meeting of the Société Médico-Psychologique in 1854 when it was made clear that because it assumed the independent functioning of the mental faculties it offered no advantage over Pinel's old notion (Brierre de Boismont, 1853; Société Médico-Psychologique, 1854; Falret, 1864). Furthermore, it was felt that it was a tautological notion, as the behaviour it tried to explain was often the only evidence for the fixed or specific *délire* (as in the case of 'suicidal' monomania) (Berrios & Mohanna, 1990).

Moral insanity

The earlier claim that this term, coined by J. C. Prichard, was a forerunner of 'psychopathic disorder', has been effectively discredited (Smith, 1981; Whitlock, 1967, 1982; Ey, 1978). One of these writers said it clearly: "There [is] not the remotest resemblance between their examples [Pinel's and Prichard's] and what today would be classed as psychopathic personality" (p. 57) (Whitlock, 1982). But, then, what was Prichard attempting to describe? Like Pinel, Esquirol and Georget (his sources), Prichard (1835) was influenced by the Scottish version of faculty psychology and called into question Locke's delusional definition of insanity. The latter had become an embarrassment to alienists appearing in court, for unless delusions were clearly elicited, judges would not countenance the insanity plea (in England, this reached its highest point after the creation of the McNaughton rules) (West & Walk, 1977). Definitions of insanity based on delusions also went against views, fashionable during Prichard's time, that affective and volitional insanities were a clinical possibility, for mental functions could become diseased independently. There is little doubt that the category 'moral insanity' was created by Prichard (1835) to include the latter two (Müller, 1899).

In general, insanity was for the English writer "a disorder of the system by which the sound and healthy exercise of the mental faculties is impeded or disturbed" (Prichard, 1835 p. 2). Because this definition required that states such as organic delirium, stupor, and apoplexy had to be ruled out on each occasion, Prichard offered a 'positive' list which included melancholia, mania, partial insanity, and incoherence (dementia) (all these still considered in their pre-19th-century meaning). Prichard added to them an extra category, 'moral insanity', to refer to behavioural disorders whose only common feature was absence of delusions. He criticised Pinel's poor choice of examples to illustrate his category *manie sans délire*, and even reported a personal conversation with Esquirol during which the latter admitted feeling uneasy about Pinel's view.

Historical analysis, however, shows that Pinel, Esquirol and Prichard had different reasons for suggesting the existence of a form of insanity without delusions. In the case of Prichard, his main worry seems to have been finding a niche for cases of manic–depressive illness with no psychotic features. Thus, he describes as typical 'moral insanities' (pp. 17–21) cases where:

"tendency to gloom and sorrow is the predominant feature . . . the individual, though surrounded with all the comforts of existence . . . becomes sorrowful and desponding. All things present and future are to his view involved in dreary and hopeless gloom . . . a state of gloom and melancholy depression occasionally gives way after an uncertain period to an opposite condition of preternatural excitement: in other cases this is the primary character of the disease . . . in this form of moral derangement the disordered condition of the mind displays itself in a want of self-government, in continual excitement, an unusual expression of strong feelings . . . a female modest and circumspect becomes violent and abrupt in her manners, loquacious, impetuous, talks loudly and abusively.'' (pp. 18–19)

Prichard's cases often got better (p. 26), or would become ill for the first time in old age (p. 25), and eccentricity of behaviour alone or bad propensities were *not* sufficient for the diagnosis (p. 23). It should be clear that Prichard was not talking about psychopathic personalities.

Prichard did for British psychiatry what Pinel had done for his own: break away from the intellectualistic definition and widen the boundaries of insanity to the point that symptoms affecting other mental function might be sufficient to make a diagnosis. By successfully creating the 'moral insanity' category he incorporated manic–depressive states with no delusions or hallucinations into the main stream of the insanities (psychoses). Apart from being forensically convenient, this also encouraged the development of a descriptive psychopathology for the affective disorders.

Folie lucide

Ulysse Trélat (1861), a French alienist and revolutionary of the first half of the 19th century, coined the term '*folie lucide*' to name an array of behavioural disorders: "the patients I am to describe have not been studied before. Lucid madmen, in spite of their disturbed reason, respond all questions to the point, and to the superficial observer look normal''; they included 77 patients with a variety of disorders: idiocy, satyrism and nymphomania, monomania, erotomania, jealousy, dipsomania, adventurism and dissolution, haughtiness, cruelty, kleptomania, suicidality, inertia, and lucid mania. Trélat claimed that up to 56% of these cases had a family history of insanity, and that the law had not, until then, been firm enough when dealing with them. The book had excellent reviews (e.g. Lunier, 1861) in spite of the fact that it was written in a format and style already obsolete, offered no clinical criteria for the classification of patients, and ignored the advances achieved by the various debates held at the Société Médico-Psychologique. It gives the impression that Trélat, because of his busy political life, had been, as far as psychiatry was concerned, in a time warp. It is, therefore, all the more strange that Tuke (1892) thought that *folie lucide* was but a synonym of moral insanity.

'Impulsive insanity'

During the late 19th century, aggressive acts committed by the insane were characterised as 'unreflexive or involuntary' and dealt with under the notion of *impulsion* (Bourdin, 1896). Some explained these acts as unmotivated *motor* explosions occurring without warning; others as disorders of the will, i.e. as irresistible feelings difficult to control (Ribot, 1904). The category impulsive insanity (Dagonet, 1870) was created to include behavioural states, such as homicidal and suicidal monomania (Grasset, 1908; Grivois, 1990). In his *Frontiers of Insanity*, Hesnard (1924) classified the *déséquilibrés* into *passionnés* and *impulsifs*. Impulsive insanity remained associated until the end of the 19th century with *manie sans délire*, *folie avec conscience*, and other categories into which impulsive acts, unaccompanied by other symptoms, had been originally included. By the time of Magnan, impulsive insanity also became linked to degeneration theory, in whose association it remained until the 20th century. Impulsion and impulsive insanity thus provided one of the kernels around which the notion of psychopathic personality was to be organised (Caroli & Olie, 1979). By the 1930s, impulsions were considered to be stereotyped actions of affective, motor, or obsessive origin (Ey, 1950). The volitional explanation, once popular, had by then disappeared as the philosophical and psychological aspects of the concept of 'will' came under scrutiny (Horwicz, 1876; Aveling, 1925; Keller, 1954; Kimble & Perlmuter, 1970; Daston, 1982). By the early 20th century, impulsions began to be explained in organic and psychodynamic terms, but during the 1920s observation of the major behavioural sequelae of lethargic encephalitis tilted the balance in favour of an organic explanation (Thiele, 1953). Cruchet (1943), for example, reported that encephalitis in childhood gave rise to severely antisocial behaviour (the so-called 'apache' or 'perverse' children). In French psychiatry, interest in the study of *impulsion* lasted well into the second half of this century. For example, Porot & Bardenat (1975) classified this symptom along two dimensions – spontaneous or reflex, and constitutional or acquired – suggesting three assessment criteria: affective loading, degree of awareness, and inhibitory capacity.

'Psychopathic disorders' as a degeneration of the character

The terms psychopathic personality and disorder have disappeared from current classifications: in ICD–10 they have been incorporated into 'dissocial personality disorder' (F60.2), and in DSM–III–R into cluster B (antisocial personality disorder; 301.70). The types of behaviour to which these terms referred, however, remain diagnostically relevant, hence their turbulent history needs exploration (Maughs, 1941; Craft, 1965; Pichot, 1978).

'Degeneration theory' is the general term for a view developed by B. Morel (1857), a French psychiatrist of Austrian origin, according to which noxae such as alcoholism (Bynum, 1984) or masturbation caused alterations in the human seed which in later generations expressed themselves as mental illness (successively, melancholia, mania, and dementia) and physical stigmata (Dallemagne, 1895; Ribot, 1906; Mairet & Ardin-Delteil, 1907). Morel was a Roman Catholic and his theory was permeated by the theological metaphor of the Fall; he also assumed a sort of Lamarckian mechanism for the inheritance of acquired traits. Valentin Magnan, and later followers, played down the religious overtones of the theory and emphasised its neurobiological aspects (Saury, 1886).

Without the framework of degeneration theory (Genil-Perrin, 1913), the concept of psychopathic inferiority (Koch, 1891; Gross, 1909) would have made little sense. But this concept also was influenced by a host of other factors such as the pre-Darwinian phrenological studies on the criminal mind (Gall, 1825), the atavistic criminology of Lombroso (Peset, 1983; Pick, 1989), Darwinism (Hilts, 1982), the model of the hierarchical nervous system propounded by Herbert Spencer and Hughlings Jackson (Berrios, 1985), and the view that some human beings are born with a higher propensity to eccentric and antisocial behaviour than others (Saury, 1886). Degeneration theory, in turn, was relevant to the survival of endangered clinical categories such as *folie raisonnante* (Saury, 1886; Sérieux & Capgras, 1909), and to the development of later typologies such as those of Kretschmer (1936), Schneider (1950), Kahn (1931), and Henderson (1939). Degenerational views can still be detected in France as late as the 1930s, in the new doctrine of constitutions (Charpentier, 1932; Delmas, 1943).

During the late 19th century, the adjective 'psychopathic' meant 'psychopathological' and applied to any form of mental disorder (Werlinder, 1978; Schmiedebach, 1985). A narrower meaning appeared in the work of Koch (1891) who under 'psychopathic inferiority' grouped abnormal behavioural states resulting from "weakness of the brain" which were not to be considered as 'diseases' in Kahlbaum's sense, and which might be chronic or acute, congenital or acquired. Inferiorities ranged from mild to severe; the latter, always the result of degeneration, included antisocial behaviour. Years later, Schneider (1950) remarked that Koch's main classificatory criterion had been 'moral' rather than scientific, and that, in this regard, the 'psychopathies' were "essentially, a German problem".

Another important landmark is the work of Otto Gross, the Austrian alienist, already well known for his hypothesis of the cerebral 'secondary function' (Gross, 1904). According to this view, differences in the time nervous cells took to regain electrical steady state after the primary discharge caused differences in character. In his book on the *Psychopathic Inferiorities*, Gross (1909) differentiated between subjects with short secondary functions, who responded rapidly but were distractible, and those with longer secondary functions (whom he called inferiorities) who showed 'narrow' consciousness. Gross's ideas influenced the work of Jung (1964), who called Gross's types extroverts and introverts, respectively.

Schneider

Kurt Schneider (1950) published the first edition of *Psychopathic Personalities* in 1923 as part of Aschaffenburg's *Handbuch der Psychiatrie*. By opting for the term 'personality', he contributed to making the words 'temperament' and 'character' obsolete; the ninth edition of this book, which includes a long preface and ripostes to critics, finds its strength in the simplicity of its operational criteria and empirical approach. Schneider (1950) conceived the psyche as a harmonious combination of intelligence, personality, and feelings and instincts, and defined 'personality' as the stable "composite of feelings, values, tendencies and volitions" (p. 25); thus excluding cognitive functions and corporal sensations. Abnormal personality, in turn, he defined as a state of divergence from the mean, acknowledging that 'ideal' definitions of normality were also important. Psychopathic personalities were a *subclass* of the abnormal personalities, and referred to those "who themselves suffer, or make society suffer, on account of their abnormality" (p. 27). Abnormal and psychopathic personalities were not pathological in a 'medical sense', and hence fell outside the 'disease' model; none the less, they were assumed to have distinctive somatic bases. Schneider had little to say about abnormal personalities *per se*, and concentrated on ten psychopathic groupings: hyperthymic, depressive, insecure, fanatical, lacking in self-esteem, labile in affect, explosive, wicked, aboulic, and asthenic; he conceived these categories as 'forms of being' and not as 'diagnostic' entities (p. 70), and readily accepted that none was new. Furthermore, they were not even permanent for, as Kahn (1931) suggested, they could be "reactive and episodic" (p. 74). Schneider did not see any relationship between his types and the neuroses or psychoses, but suggested that personality, whether normal or abnormal, might modulate the form of the psychoses.

As Schneider noticed, his book enjoyed "a wide circle of readers"; none the less, it was subject to criticism. For example, Edmund Mezger (1939, 1944), a professor of criminology at Munich, did not agree with his definition of normality, which he found "unworkable in the courts" (p. 60). He also believed that "in the last instance all psychopathy must be called degeneration" (p. 64), quoting in his support the notorious book by Baur *et al* (1927). Mezger's view illustrates well the way in which the notion of psychopathic personality got trapped into the eugenic atrocities committed in Germany at the time (Müller-Hill, 1988). A more determined attack took place at the 105th meeting of the Swiss Society of Psychiatry when F. Humbert (1947) and A. Repond scorned Schneider's definition of psychopathic as 'tautological' (p. 180) and as a melee of "sociological, characterological and constitutional criteria" (p. 181). Humbert also accused Schneider of having borrowed all his clinical categories from others, and of creating artificial separations (e.g. between depressives and hyperthymics). On the basis of French sources, Humbert denied the existence of a separate clinical category for psychopathic disorders, believing that they were either attenuated forms of psychotic illness (schizothymic, cyclothymic, etc.) or acquired states, "childhood neuroses of character" (p. 194), susceptible to psychodynamic treatment. Schneider (1950) curtly replied that it was "self-deception to believe that there are no psychopaths, and that abnormal personalities are but developmental syndromes" (p. 29).

Kahn

In 1928, Eugen Kahn published his *Psychopathischen Persönlichkeiten* as part of Bumke's *Handbuch der Geisteskrankheiten*. He used the word 'psychopathic' to "designate a large number of characteristics or conditions which lie in the broad zone between mental health and mental illness (psychosis)" (p. 55) and supported Schneider's original definition of 'psychopathic personality' as states which made their bearer or society suffer (pp. 56–57) (Kahn, 1931). He conceived personality as a three-legged concept whose final profile was determined by the relative contribution of impulse, temperament, and character: "not everything in the psychopathic personality was [however] psychopathic" (p. 60). Kahn was influenced by the psychological notions of Stern: "by psychopathic personality we understand those discordant personalities which on the causal side are characterised by quantitative peculiarities in the impulse, temperament, or character strata, and in their unified goal-striving activity are impaired by quantitative deviations in the ego- and foreign evaluation" (p. 69). Kahn classified psychopathic personalities in terms of three components: the first group included impulsive, weak, and sexual psychopaths; the second hyper-, hypo-, and poikilothymic; and the third ego-overvaluers, undervaluers, and ambitendents. The Schneiderian groups he called "complex psychopathic states", and suggested that they could be analysed out in terms of physique, impulse-life, temperament, and character.

Henderson

D. K. Henderson's book on *Psychopathic States* (1939) was an extended version of his Salmon Memorial Lectures. This unsophisticated and badly referenced work revolved around the notion of 'constitution' that Adolf Meyer (1903) had borrowed from Paulhan (1894). Henderson defined constitution as "the whole being, physical and mental, it is all partly inborn, partly environmental, and is in a state of flux varying from day to day and even from hour to hour" (p. 32), and psychopathic state as:

> "the name we apply to those individuals who conform to a certain intellectual standard, sometimes high, sometimes approaching the realm of defect but yet not amounting to it, who throughout their lives, or from a comparatively early age, have exhibited disorders of conduct of an antisocial or asocial nature, usually of a recurrent or episodic nature, which, in many instances, have proved difficult to influence by methods social, penal, or medical care and treatment, and for whom we have no adequate provision of a preventive or curative nature . . . [it] constitutes a *true illness* for which we have no explanation." (my italics) (pp. 16–17).

Henderson believed that the proportion of "psychopathic states, not only amongst the prison population, but in ordinary social life, is very high indeed, and that in our ordinary work we do not realise half-seriously enough that it is the psychopathic state which constitutes the rock on which our prognosis and treatment in relation to many psychoneurotic and psychotic states becomes shattered" (p. 37). He suggested three clusters: predominantly aggressive, passive, and creative; each including core and accessory types of behaviour: in the first group suicide, murder and assault, alcoholism and drug addiction, epilepsy, and sex variants; in the second, cycloid and schizoid states; and in the third, talent. Werlinder (1978) has suggested that Henderson was influenced in this last grouping by the French concept of '*dégénéré supérieur*'. Craft (1965) rightly commented of it: "although Henderson continued to use this term most authors have found it difficult to use" (p. 13).

Later typologies

Typological classifications continued to develop during the early 20th century; although conceptually similar to those popular during the previous century, these differed in that they sought to correlate personality types with anatomical forms and mental disorders. During the 19th century, personality disorders were mostly conceived as *formes frustres* of insanity. After the latter notion was narrowed down into the new concept of 'psychosis' (Berrios, 1987), however, the concept of *forme frustre* lost meaning, and as a consequence, a large group of disorders lost their clinical abode; some, like the obsessive–compulsive states, were soon incorporated into the redefined class of the 'neuroses' (Berrios, 1989), others formed the core of the newly invented group of the 'character' disorders. Psychodynamic ideas, which were very important in modulating these changes, are dealt with elsewhere in this volume.

Typologies based on the classical notion of constitution had reached their zenith during the second half of the 19th century; for instance, the popular treatise on *Our Temperaments* by Alexander Stewart (1887) can be considered as the last manifestation of the Hippocratic humoral and physiognomonic approaches; this author believed to have identified among the British people examples of sanguine, bilious, lymphatic, and nervous temperament. Others, like Beneke (1881) suggested a bipolar typology: scrofulous-phthisical versus rachito-carcinomatous, based on three-dimensional measurements of internal organs, and believed that most people fitted into one of these body-types; and that organ-size correlated with age and disease. Di Giovanni (1919) was likewise interested in the relationship between the size of internal organs and morbidity as was Galton (1883), who attempted to identify the features and dimensions constituting the typical English face and body shape (pp. 1–17).

But it is C. G. Jung (1964) who can be said to have rescued the concept of 'type' for the 20th century: no longer interested in stereotyped behavioural forms, or humours, he suggested that the human personality was a combination of features or 'dimensions'. Influenced by the neurophysiological speculations of Otto Gross (1904), Jung proposed an introversion/extroversion dimension around which mental functions such as thinking, feeling, sensation and intuition might be organised. Also influenced by Gross was the work of the Dutch psychologists Heymans & Wiersma (1906), who propounded an eightfold typology based on a dimensional view of behavioural traits which included the amorphous, apathetic, nervous, sentimental, sanguine, phlegmatic, choleric, and impassioned characters.

Typologies based on biological speculation also developed during this period. Berman (1922) believed that since "a single gland can dominate the life history of an individual" (p. 202) it was possible to talk about 'endocrine types', and suggested adrenal, pituitary, thyroid, thymocentric, and gonadocentric personalities. In 1921, Kretschmer (1936) propounded a simpler and more influential typology: following Kraepelin's division of the psychoses, he suggested cycloid and schizoid temperaments, which he believed influenced most aspects of human behaviour. There were four types of physique: asthenic or leptosomatic, athletic, pyknic or pyknosomatic, and dysplastic: correlations existed between manic–depressive illness and the pyknic type, and between schizophrenia and the leptosomatic, asthenic and (less frequently) the dysplastic character. During the 1940s, his work was criticised, particularly in Great Britain, on methodological grounds (Rees, 1961). Typological classifications, however, continued in the USA, for example, in the work of Sheldon (1942) who created a scale for measuring temperament whose items (representing a combination of behavioural traits) factorised out into three components: viscerotonia, somatotonia, and cerebrotonia.

During the 1920s, the French developed a more conceptual approach to human personality called the doctrine of the 'constitutions' (Dupré, 1925) which was to be widened into a general theory of mental disorder (Gayat, 1984). According to Dupré, "personality whether normal or pathological, represents the sum or synthesis of all organic and functional activities" and "mental diseases, in effect, are diseases of the personality", "mental diseases result from anomalies of general sensibility, of alterations of organic consciousness, in a word, of vices – whether constitutional or acquired – of the nervous system" (p. 79) (Dupré, 1984). This author recognised eight groups: unstable in their physical sensibility (hypo- and hyperaesthesics, and coenesthopathics); unstable in their motor function; emotive (e.g. erethics); disordered in appetite; disordered in instinct; disordered in mood; paranoid; and those with pathological imagination (e.g. mythomanics). When present in a minor degree, these types of behaviour might just tinge the personality, but when excessive caused mental illness. Dupré's doctrine, the last important manifestation of the degeneration theory in France, was influenced by the ideas of Bouchard, Magnan, and particularly Duprat, who had published in 1899 a great book on *L'instabilité Mentale* which contained the germ of the doctrine of constitutions.

Discussion and conclusions

Current definitions of personality disorder, whether enshrined in DSM–III–R, ICD–10, or British approaches (Ferguson & Tyrer, 1990), are informational composites based on three data sources: reporting of direct (and hopefully unedited) subjective experiences, autobiographical accounts, and narratives by others. Hence, their reliability is dependent on the degree of informational convergence: the higher the convergence the more stable the cluster or profile; in some cases it is stable enough even to warrant the postulation of a neurobiological substratum. Historically, all three sources of information have required justification. Subjective accounts of self were allowed only when introspection became legitimised as a method of analysis (Boring, 1953; Danziger, 1980; Wilson, 1991), autobiographical and biographical accounts only when mental disorder began to be conceived as a longitudinal process (Pistoia, 1971). On the other hand, the idea that stable behavioural profiles may warrant the postulation of a neurobiological substratum is an offshoot of the old anatomoclinical model of disease (Ackerknecht, 1967). More recently, yet another evidential method emerged – statistical corroboration. Anecdotal observation is no longer considered a guarantee for convergence; instead everything seems to revolve around the plausibility of some pattern-recognition techniques such as cluster and principal-component analysis. This switch in scientific paradigm is perhaps the only difference that the historian can find between 19th- and 20th-century approaches to personality disorders. In wider terms, the historical analysis presented in this paper suggests the conclusions outlined below.

(a) The concept of 'personality (or character) disorder' appeared in the psychiatric literature of the 19th century only after a *psychological* definition of character and personality became available, and after the 'self' was considered as a 'mental' function.'

(b) During this period, the word 'personality' had a *different* meaning from the current one; what nowadays is called personality was then called character, temperament, and constitution.

(c) From the start, the psychiatric concept of 'disordered' character included reference to an 'organic' substratum; this was a manifestation of the anatomical/clinical view.

(d) During the 19th century, personality disorder meant alteration of consciousness and included states such as hysterical dissociations.

(e) This explains why, up to World War I (and to a certain extent to the present time), the psychiatric and psychological study of 'personality' (and its disorders) has not been convergent.

(f) During the 19th century, there were three causal models for personality 'disorders': according to faculty psychology they resulted from failures in the mental faculty of the 'will'; associationism postulated a loss of coherence between cognitive, emotional, and volitional information; and the 'automatism' hypothesis suggested that personality disorders resulted from lower forms of behaviour escaping the control of higher ones, i.e. to a horizontal 'splitting' of 'consciousness' (defined in a Jacksonian fashion as a hierarchy of levels).

(g) All three models made use of explanations based on degenerational (genetic) and acquired (learning) mechanisms. Hence, views on personality disorders seemed more unified than in fact they were.

(h) The language of 'types' and 'traits' originated from the phrenological and psychometric traditions, respectively.

(i) Intellectual context and historical fashion, rather than empirical research, determined which of these three views was the predominant one during a particular period. For example, when the notion of 'will' fell out of fashion, volitional models of psychopathy rapidly disappeared; likewise, the 'developmental' dimension was only added to the concept of personality disorder after the inception of Freudian ideas; (current) neurobiological explanations, however, are a manifestation of the early assumption that behaviour, whether normal or pathological, is entirely dependent on specific neurochemical events.

References

ABBAGNANO, N. (1961) *Dizionario di filosofia*. Turin: Unione tipografic-editrice.
ACKERKNECHT, E. H. (1967) *Medicine at the Paris Hospital: 1794–1848*. Baltimore: Johns Hopkins.
ALBRECHT, F. M. (1970) A reappraisal of faculty psychology. *Journal of the History of the Behavioural Sciences*, **6**, 36–40.
ALLPORT, G. W. (1937) *Personality*. New York: Henry Holt.
ALVAREZ-URIA, F. (1983) *Miserables y locos*. Barcelona: Tusquets.
AMERICAN PSYCHIATRIC ASSOCIATION (1987) *Diagnostic and Statistical Manual of Mental Disorders* (3rd edn, revised) (DSM–III–R). Washington, DC: APA.
ANONYMOUS (1921) Personalidad. In *Enciclopedia Universal Illustrada*, Vol 43, pp. 1173–1184 Bilbao: Espasa-Calpe.
AVELING, F. (1925) The psychology of conation and volition. *British Journal of Psychology*, **16**, 339–353.
AZAM, B. (1885) Le caractère dans les maladies. *Annales Médico-Psychologique*, **43**, 386–406.
BALDWIN, J. M. & STOUT, G. F. (1901) Self. In *Dictionary of Philosophy and Psychology*, Vol 2, (ed. J. M. Baldwin), pp. 507–508. London: Macmillan.
BAUR, E., FISCHER, E. & LENZ, F. (1927) *Menschliche Erblichkeitslehre und Rasenhygiene*. Munich: Springer.
BEAUSSIRE, E. (1883) La personnalité humaine d'après les théories récents. *Revue de Deux Mondes*, **55**, 316–361.
BENEKE, F. W. (1881) *Konstitution und Konstitutionelles kranksein des Menschen*. Marbourg: Elwert.
BERMAN, L. (1922) *The Glands Regulating the Personality*. New York: Macmillan.
BERRIOS, G. E. (1984) Descriptive psychopathology: conceptual and historical aspects. *Psychological Medicine*, **14**, 303–313.
––––––– (1985) Positive and negative symptoms and Jackson. *Archives of General Psychiatry*, **42**, 95–97.
––––––– (1987) Historical aspects of the psychoses: 19th century issues. *British Medical Bulletin*, **43**, 484–497.
––––––– (1988*a*) Historical background to abnormal psychology. In *Adult Abnormal Psychology* (eds E. Miller & P. J. Cooper), pp. 26–51. Edinburgh: Churchill Livingstone.
––––––– (1988*b*) Depressive and manic states during the nineteenth century. In *Depression and Mania* (eds A. Georgotas & R. Cancro), pp. 13–25. New York: Elsevier.
––––––– (1989) Obsessive-compulsive disorder: its conceptual history in France during the 19th century. *Comprehensive Psychiatry*, **30**, 283–295.
––––––– & MOHANNA, M. (1990) Durkheim and French views on Suicide during the 19th century. *British Journal of Psychiatry*, **156**, 1–9.
BINET, A. (1892) *Les altérations de la personnalité*. Paris: Alcan.
BLAIR, D. (1975) The medicolegal implications of the terms 'psychopath', 'psychopathic personality' and 'psychopathic disorder'. *Medicine, Science and the Law*, **15**, 51–61, 110–123.
BLAKEY, R. (1850) *History of the Philosophy of Mind*. London: Longman, Brown, Green & Longmans.
BLOOR, C. (1928) *Temperament. A Survey of Psychological Theories*. London: Methuen.
BORING, E. G. (1953) A history of introspection. *Psychological Bulletin*, **50**, 169–189.
––––––– (1961) The beginning and growth of measurement in psychology. *Isis*, **52**, 238–257.
BOURDIN, J. (1896) De l'impulsion: sa définition, ses formes et sa valeur psychologique. *Annales Médico-Psychologique*, **3**, 217–239.
BRIERRE DE BOISMONT, A. (1853) De l'état des facultés dans les délires partiels ou monomanies. *Annales Médico-Psychologique*, **5**, 567–591.
BROCHIN, M. (1876) Constitutions Médicales. Constitutions épidémiques. In *Dictionnaire Encyclopédique des Sciences Médicales*. Vol 19 (eds A. Dechambre & L. Lereboullet), pp. 751–806. Paris: Masson.
BROOKS, G. P. (1976) The faculty psychology of Thomas Reid. *Journal of the History of the Behavioural Sciences*, **12**, 65–77.

BURNS, R. B. (1979) *The Self. Theory, Measurement, Development and Behaviour.* London: Longman.

BUSS, A. R. (1976) Galton and the birth of differential psychology and eugenics: social, political, and economic forces. *Journal of the History of the Behavioural Sciences*, **12**, 47–58.

BURT, C. (1938) The analysis of temperament. *British Journal of Medical Psychology*, **17**, 158–180.

BYNUM, W. F. (1984) Alcoholism and degeneration in 19th century European medicine and psychiatry. *British Journal of Addiction*, **79**, 59–70.

CAILLARD, E. M. (1894) Personality as the outcome of evolution. *Contemporary Review*, **65**, 713–721.

CAROLI, F. & OLIE, J. P. (1979) *Nouvelles formes de déséquilibre mental.* Paris: Masson.

CHARPENTIER, R. (1932) De l'idée de dégénérescence à la doctrine des constitutions. *Journal of Neurology and Psychiatry*, **32**, 137–169.

CLAPARÈDE, E. (1903) *L'Association des Idées.* Paris: Doin.

CLONINGER, C. R. (1987) A systematic method for clinical description and classification of personality variants. *Archives of General Psychiatry*, **44**, 573–588.

CRAFT, M. (1965) *Ten Studies into Psychopathic Personality.* Bristol: Wright.

CRUCHET, R. (1943) *Nuevos Conceptos de Patologia Nerviosa.* Buenos Aires: Editorial Médico-Quirúrgica.

DAGONET, H. (1870) Des impulsions dans la folie et de la folie impulsive. *Annales Médico-Psychologique*, **4**, 5–32, 215–259.

DALLEMAGNE, J. (1895) *Dégénérés et Déséquilibrés.* Paris: Alcan.

DANZIGER, K. (1980) The history of introspection reconsidered. *Journal of the History of the Behavioural Sciences*, **16**, 241–262.

DASTON, L. J. (1982) The theories of will versus the sciences of mind. In *The Problematic Science. Psychology in the 19th century* (eds W. R. Woodward & M. G. Ash), pp. 88–115. New York: Praeger.

DECHAMBRE, A. (1886a) Habitude. In *Dictionnaire Encyclopédique des Sciences Médicales*, Vol. 48 (eds A. Dechambre & L. Lereboullet), pp. 8–15. Paris: Masson.

——— (1886b) Tempérament. In *Dictionnaire Encyclopédique des Sciences Médicales*, Vol. 95 (eds A. Dechambre & L. Lereboullet), pp. 312–325. Paris: Masson.

DELACROIX, M. H. (1924) Maine de Biran et L'Ecole Médico-Psychologique. *Bulletin de la Societé Francqise de Philosophie*, **24**, 51–63.

DELMAS, F. A. (1943) Les constitutions psychopatiques. Le rôle et la signification des constitutions en psychiatrie. *Annales Médico-Psychologique*, **101**, 119–232.

DUBLINEAU, J. (1943) La psychiatrie et le problème des tempéraments. *Annales Médico-Psychologique*, **101**, 200–218.

DUPRAT, G. L. (1899) *L'Instabilité Mentale.* Paris: Alcan.

DUPRÉ, E. (1925) *Pathologie de l'Imagination et de l'Émotivité.* Paris: Payot.

——— (1984) Les déséquilibres constitutionnels du systeme nerveux. *Revue Internationale d'Histoire de la Psychiatrie*, **2**, 77–91.

DWELSHAUVERS, G. (1934) *Traité de Psychologie.* Paris: Payot.

EKEHAMMAR, B. (1974) Interactionism in personality from a historical perspective. *Psychological Bulletin*, **81**, 1026–1948.

ELLARD, J. (1988) The history and present status of moral insanity. *Australian and New Zealand Journal of Psychiatry*, **22**, 383–389.

ESQUIROL, E. (1838) *Des Maladies Mentales.* 2 Vols. Paris: Baillière.

EY, H. (1950) *Études Psychiatriques.* Vol. 2, pp. 83–102, 163–212. Paris: Desclée de Brouwer.

——— (1978) La notion de "maladie morale" et de "traitement moral" dans la psychiatrie française et allemande du debut du XIXème siècle. *Perspectives Psychiatriques*, **1**, 12–35.

EYSENCK, H. J. (1951) Cyclothymia and schizothymia as dimensions of personality. I. Historical review. *Journal of Personality*, **19**, 123–152.

FALRET, J. P. (1864) De la non-existence de la monomanie. In *Des Maladies Mentales*, pp. 425–455. Paris: Baillière.

——— (1866) Discussion sur la folie raisonnante. *Annales Médico-Psychologique*, **24**, 382–426.

FERGUSON, B. & TYRER, P. (1990) Classifying personality disorder. In *Personality Disorders* (ed. P. Tyrer), pp. 12–32. London: Wright.

FERRATER MORA, J. (1958) *Diccionario de Filosofía*, 4th Edition. Buenos Aires: Editorial Sudamericana.

FREUD, S. (1925) *Collected Papers*, Vol. 4. London: The Hogarth Press.

FRONDIZI, R. (1952) *Substancia y función en el problema del yo*. Buenos Aires: Editorial Losada.

FULLINWIDER, S. P. (1975) Insanity as the loss of self: the moral insanity controversy revisited. *Bulletin of the History of Medicine*, **49**, 87–101.

GALL, F. J. (1825) *Fonction du Cerveau*. Paris: Baillière.

GALTON, F. (1883) *Inquiries into Human Faculty*. London: Macmillan.

────── (1895) Personality. *Nature*, **62**, 517–518.

────── (1979) *Hereditary Genius* (First edition 1869). London: Friedmann.

GARRABÉ, J. (1989*a*) *Dictionnaire Taxonomique de Psychiatrie*. Paris: Masson.

────── (1989*b*) Dissociation et refoulement. *Annales Médico-Psychologique*, **147**, 1011–1016.

GAYAT, G. (1984) Introduction a la lecture de la leçon inaugurale d'Ernest Dupré. *Revue Internationale d'Histoire de la Psychiatrie*, **2**, 67–76.

GENIL-PERRIN, G. (1913) *Histoire des Origins et de l'Évolution de l'Idée de Dégénérescence*. Paris: Leclerc.

GIGERENZER, G., SWIJTINK, Z., PORTER, T., *et al* (1989) *The Empire of Chance*. Cambridge: Cambridge University Press.

GIOVANNI, A. DI (1919) *Clinical Commentaries Deduced from the Morphology of the Human Body*. London: Eyre.

GOLDSTEIN, J. (1987) *Console and Classify. The French Psychiatric Profession in the Nineteenth Century*. Cambridge: Cambridge University Press.

GRASSET, J. (1908) *Semi-locos y semi-responsables* (transl. G. Gonzales). Madrid: Sáenz de Jubera.

GRIVOIS, H. (ed) (1990) *Les Monomanies Instinctives*. Paris: Masson.

GROSS, O. (1904) *Zerebrale Sekundärfunktion*. Leipzig: Vogel.

────── (1909) *Über psychopathische Minderwertigkeiten*. Wien und Leipzig: Wilhelm Braumüller.

GURVITZ, M. (1951) Developments in the concept of psychopathic personality (1900–1950). *British Journal of Delinquency*, **2**, 88–102.

HACKLING, I. (1990) *The Taming of Chance*. Cambridge: Cambridge University Press.

HAMILTON, W. (1859) *Lectures on Metaphysics*, Vol. 2. Edinburgh: Blackwood.

HAUPT, T. VON (1858) *Die Temperamente des Menschen im gesunden und kranken Zustande*. Würzburg: Stahel.

HÉCAEN, H. & LANTERI-LAURA, G. (1978) *Evolution des Connaissances et des Doctrines sur les Localisations Cérébrales*. Paris: Desclée de Brouwer.

HENDERSON, D. K. (1939) *Psychopathic States*. New York: Norton.

HESNARD, A. (1924) *Les Psychoses et les Frontières de la Folie*. Paris: Flammarion.

HEYMANS, G. & WIERSMA, E. (1906) Beiträge zur speziellen Psychologie auf grund einer Massenunterschung. *Zeitschrift fur Psychologie*, **42**, 81–127, 253–301.

HILGARD, E. R. (1980) The trilogy of mind: cognition, affection, and conation. *Journal of the History of the Behavioural Sciences*, **16**, 107–117.

HILTS, V. (1982) Obeying the laws of hereditary descent: phrenological views on inheritance and eugenics. *Journal of the History of the Behavioural Sciences*, **18**, 62–77.

HOELDTKE, R. (1967) The history of associationism and British medical psychology. *Medical History*, **11**, 46–64.

HORWICZ, A. (1876) Histoire du développement de la volonté. *Revue Philosophique*, **1**, 488–502.

HUERTAS, R. (1987) *Locura y degeneración*. Madrid: Clavileño.

HUMBERT, F. (1947) Les états dits psychopathiques constitutionnels; terms, notions et limites. *Schweizer Archiv fur Neurologie und Psychiatrie*, **59**, 179–195.

JANET, P. (1896) Résumé historique des études sur le sentiment de la personnalité. *Revue Scientifique*, **5**, 98–103.

JEANMAIRE, CH. (1882) *L'Idée de la Personnalité dans la Psychologie Moderne*. Toulouse: Douladoure-Privat.

JONES, W. H. S. (1923) Notes. In *Hippocrates*, Vol. 1. London: Heinemann.

JUNG, C. G. (1964) *Tipos Psicológicos* (transl. Ramón de la Serna). Buenos Aires: Editorial Sudamericana.

KAGEYAMA, J. (1984) Sur l'histoire de la monomanie. *L'Evolution Psychiatrique*, **49**, 155–162.

KAHN, E. (1931) *Psychopathic Personalities*. New Haven: Yale University Press.

KELLER, W. (1954) *Psychologie und Philosophie des Wollens*. Basel: Reinhardt.

KIMBLE, G. A. & PERLMUTER, L. C. (1970) The problem of volition. *Psychological Review*, **77**, 361–384.

KOCH, J. A. (1891) *Die psychopathischen Minderwertigkeiten*. Ravensburg: Maier.

KRETSCHMER, E. (1936) *Physique and Character* (transl. W. J. H. Sprott). London: Kegan Paul, Trench, Trubner & Co.

LALANDE, A. (1976) *Vocabulaire Technique et Critique de la Philosophie*, 11th Edition. Paris: Presses Universitaires de France.

LANTERI-LAURA, G. (1979*a*) *Lecture des Perversions. Histoire de leur Appropriation Médicale*. Paris: Masson.

—— (1979*b*) Conditions théoriques et conditions institutionelles de la connaissance des perversions au XIXe siècle. *L'Evolution Psychiatrique*, **44**, 633–662.

LEWIS, A. (1974) Psychopathic personality: a most elusive category. *Psychological Medicine*, **4**, 133–140.

LUNIER, L. J. J. (1861) Review of Trélat's Folie Lucide. *Annales Médico-Psychologique*, **7**, 658–664.

MAINE DE BIRAN (1929) *The Influence of Habit on the Faculty of Thinking* (transl. M. D. Boehm). London: Baillière.

MAIRET, A. & ARDIN-DELTEIL, P. (1907) *Hérédité et et Prédisposition*. Montpellier: Coulet.

MARTÍ Y JULIÁ, D. (1899) Concepto de la personalidad. *Revista de Ciencias Médicas de Barcelona*, **25**, 281–292.

MAUGHS, S. (1941) The concept of psychopathy and psychopathic personality: its evolution and historical development. *Journal of Criminal Psychopathology*, **2**, 329–356.

MEYER, A. (1903) An attempt at analysis of the neurotic constitution. *American Journal of Psychology*, **14**, 90–94.

MEZGER, E. (1939) Zum Begriff der Psychopathen. *Monatschrift für Kriminologie*, **30**, 190–213.

—— (1944) *Kriminalpolitik auf Kriminologischer Auflage* (3rd edn). Munich: Enke.

MOORE, F. C. T. (1970) *The Psychology of Maine de Biran*. Oxford: Clarendon Press.

MOREL, B. A. (1857) *Traité des Dégénérescences Physiques, Intellectuelles et Morales de l'Espèce Humaine*. Paris: Baillière.

MOTTE-MOITREUX, J. F. (1990) Philippe Pinel et la manie sans délire. *Information Psychiatrique*, **66**, 1016–1021.

MÜLLER, E. (1899) Über "moral insanity". *Archiv für Psychiatrie und Nervenkrankheiten*, **31**, 325–377.

MÜLLER-HILL, B. (1988) *Murderous Science. Elimination by Scientific Selection of Jews, Gypsies and others in Germany 1933–1945*. Oxford: Oxford University Press.

PAULHAN, F. (1880) La personnalité. *Revue Philosophique*, **5**, 49–67.

—— (1882) Les variations de la personnalité a l'état normal. *Revue Philosophique*, **13**, 639–653.

—— (1894) *Les caractères*. Paris: Alcan.

PEARS, D. (1975) Hume's account of personal identity. In *Questions in the Philosophy of Mind* (ed. D. Pears), pp. 208–223. London: Duckworth.

PENELHUM, T. (1967) Personal identity. In *The Encyclopedia of Philosophy*, Vol. 6 (ed. P. Edwards), pp. 95–107. New York: Macmillan.

PESET, J. L. (1983) *Ciencia y marginación*. Barcelona: Grijalbo.

PICHOT, P. (1978) Psychopathic behaviour. A historical overview. In *Psychopathic Behaviour: Approaches to Research* (eds R. D. Hare & D. Schalling), pp. 55–70. New York: Wiley.

PICK, D. (1989) *Faces of Degeneration*. Cambridge: Cambridge University Press.

PINEL, PH. (1809) *Traité Médico-Philosophique sur L'Aliénation Mentale*, 2nd Edition. Paris: Brosson.

PINILLOS, J. L., LÓPEZ PIÑERO, J. M. & BALLESTER, L. G. (1966) *Constitución y personalidad. Historia y teoría de un problema.* Valencia: Guerris.

PISTOIA, DEL L. (1971) Le problème de la temporalité dans la psychiatrie française classique. *L'Evolution Psychiatrique,* **36**, 445–474.

POROT, A. & BARDENAT, CH. (1975) Impulsions, impulsivité. In *Manuel Alphabétique de Psychiatrie* (ed. A. Porot), pp. 339–341. Paris: Presses Universitaires de France.

PORTER, T. M. (1986) *The Rise of Statistical Thinking: 1820–1900.* Princeton: Princeton University Press.

PRICHARD, J. C. (1835) *A Treatise of Insanity.* London: Sherwood, Gilbert, and Piper.

QUAIN, R. (1894) *A Dictionary of Medicine,* 2 vols. London: Longmans, Green.

RAVAISSON, J. G. F. (1984) *De L'Habitude* (First edition 1838). Paris: Fayard.

REES, L. (1961) Constitutional factors and abnormal behaviour. In *Handbook of Abnormal Psychology* (ed. H. Eysenck), pp. 344–392. London: Pitman.

RENOUVIER, CH. (1900) La personnalité. *L'Année Philosophique,* **10**, 1–38.

RIBOT, TH. (1904) *Les Maladies de la Volonté.* Paris: Alcan.

––––––– (1906) *L'Hérédité Psychologique.* Paris: Alcan.

––––––– (1912) *Las enfermedades de la personalidad (translation of R. Rubio).* Madrid: Jorro.

ROBACK, A. A. (1927) *The Psychology of Character. With a Survey of Temperament.* London: Kegan Paul, Trench, Trubner & Co.

ROCCATAGLIATA, G. (1981) *Storia della psichiatria biologica.* Firenze: Guaraldi.

ROYER-COLLARD, H. (1843) Des tempéramens, considérés dans leurs rapports avec la santé. *Mémoires de la Academie Royale de Médecine,* **10**, 134–169.

SAURY, H. (1886) *Etude Clinique sur la Folie Héréditaire.* Paris: Delahaye.

SAUSSURE, R. DE (1946) The influence of the concept of monomania on French medico-legal psychiatry (from 1825–1840). *Journal of the History of Medicine,* **1**, 365–397.

SCHMIEDEBACH, H. P. (1985) Zum Verständniswandel der "psychopathischen" Störungen am Anfang der naturwissenschaftlichen Psychiatrie in Deutschland. *Nervenarzt,* **56**, 140–145.

SCHNEIDER, K. (1950) *Die psychopatischen Personlichkeiten.* Vienna: Deuticke.

SERIEUX, P. & CAPGRAS, J. (1909) *Les Folies Raisonnantes.* Paris: Alcan.

SHELDON, W. H. (1942) *The Varieties of Temperament.* New York. Harper.

SMITH, R. (1979) Mental disorder, criminal responsibility and the social history of theories of volition. *Psychological Medicine,* **9**, 13–19.

––––––– (1981) *Trial by Medicine.* Edinburgh: Edinburgh University Press.

SOCIÉTÉ MÉDICO-PSYCHOLOGIQUE (1854) Debate on monomania. *Annales Médico-Psychologique,* **6**, 99–118, 273–298, 461–474, 629–644.

––––––– (1866) Debate on reasoning insanity. *Annales Médico-Psychologique,* **24**, 382–431.

––––––– (1989) *L'Automatism Psychologique de Pierre Janet 100 ans après.* Paris: Masson.

SPOERL, H. D. (1936) Faculties versus traits: Gall's solution. *Character and Personality,* **4**, 216–231.

STAEHELIN, J. T. (1941) Zur Geschichte der Lehre von den Temperamenten. *Schweizerische Medizinische Wochenschrift,* **22**, 1401–1402.

STEWART, A. (1887) *Our Temperaments: Their Study and Their Teaching.* London: Crosby Lockwood.

THEOPHRASTUS (1967) *Characters* (transl. J. E. Edmonds & A. D. Knox), Loeb Classical Edition. London: Heineman.

THIELE, R. (1953) Zum Begriff und zur Pathologie der Dragerscheinungen. *Psychiatrie, Neurologie und Medizinische Psychologie,* **5**, 51–59.

TRÉLAT, U. (1861) *La Folie Lucide.* Paris: Delahaye.

TUKE, D. H. (ed) (1892) *A Dictionary of Psychological Medicine,* 2 vols. London: Churchill.

TYRER, P. & FERGUSON, B. (1990) Development of the concept of abnormal personality. In *Personality Disorders* (ed. P. Tyrer), pp. 1–11. London: Wright.

VINEY, L. (1969) Self: the history of a concept. *Journal of the History of the Behavioural Sciences,* **5**, 349–359.

WARREN, H. C. (1921) *History of Association Psychology.* New York: Scribner's sons.

WERLINDER, H. (1978) *Psychopathy: a History of the Concepts.* Motala: Borgströms.

WEST, D. J. & WALK, A. (1977) *Daniel McNaughton. His Trial and Aftermath.* London: Gaskell.
WHITLOCK, F. A. (1967) Prichard and the concept of moral insanity. *Australian and New Zealand Journal of Psychiatry*, **1**, 72–79.
—— (1982) A note on moral insanity and psychopathic disorders. *Bulletin of the Royal College of Psychiatrists*, **6**, 57–59.
WILSON, F. (1991) Mill and Comte on the method of introspection. *Journal of the History of the Behavioural Sciences*, **27**, 107–129.
WORLD HEALTH ORGANIZATION (1992) *The ICD-10 Classification of Mental and Behavioural Disorders.* Geneva: WHO.
ZUPAN, M. L. (1976) The conceptual development of quantification in experimental psychology. *Journal of the History of the Behavioural Sciences*, **12**, 145–158.

3 The genetics of personality disorder

PETER McGUFFIN and ANITA THAPAR

Psychopathy, a term usually reserved in the English-speaking world for the most deviant types of personality, is an elusive concept (Lewis, 1974) and it follows that lesser degrees of abnormal personality tend to be even more difficult to define and to measure reliably. This does not present a promising state of affairs for genetic research, since of all the biological sciences, genetics is perhaps the one which depends most heavily on dealing with characters, or phenotypes, which are unequivocally recognisable and which tend to be stable and enduring in a variety of circumstances (Penrose, 1971). Nevertheless, a considerable amount of energy has been expended in attempts to explore the genetic basis of certain personality disorders, particularly those where antisocial behaviour is a prominent feature. Indeed, genetic research has in recent years gone far beyond concern just with antisocial personality and at least one widely accepted category, schizotypal personality disorder, exists almost entirely as a result of genetically orientated research.

Traditionally, psychiatric thinking on personality disorder has been concerned with various (presumed) diagnostic entities and this is still clearly reflected in current classifications such as DSM–III–R (American Psychiatric Association, 1987) and ICD–9 (World Health Organization, 1978). However, much of the dissatisfaction with the concept of psychopathy and other personality deviations stems from the recognition that few patients judged clinically to have abnormal personalities fit neatly into any of the conventional categories but rather have a repertoire of repeated behaviours which differ in some quantitative sense from the clinician's view of the average or "normal".

Furthermore, many individuals are encountered who do not warrant a diagnosis of personality disorder but who do have certain exaggerated traits which may or may not be maladaptive. Against this background it is necessary for the genetic researcher to consider a quantitative approach to the assessment of personality and to consider what contribution genes may make to personality variation within the normal range. We will therefore begin by briefly reviewing research into the genetic basis of personality before going on to discuss what is currently known about hereditary influences on personality disorder.

The genetics of personality

The evidence that there is a genetic contribution to individual differences in personality comes from three main sources. The first two are indirect, comprising animal studies of temperamental attributes which might be akin to human personality traits, and studies of individual differences in psychophysiological measures which could possibly reflect the 'biological substrate' of personality. The third approach depends on attempts to measure personality directly with questionnaires usually of the 'paper and pencil' type, and to assess the resemblance in relatives reared together, relatives who have been separated, and in pairs of monozygotic (MZ) and dizygotic (DZ) twins.

Animal studies

Long before anything was known of the science of genetics, animal breeders carried out artificial selection for desirable attributes and although it was probably never explored in a systematic way, temperamental qualities were among those thought to be inherited. This makes sense to anyone familiar with the obvious variations in aggressiveness or sociability among various breeds of dogs. However, the problem about the systematic study of animal behaviour is that it can only be measured by observer ratings and in most respects the behaviour is simpler and the repertoire more limited than the sorts of measures we usually consider in relation to human personality.

One of the best known models is provided by the Maudsley reactive (MR) and non-reactive (MNR) strains of rats which were selected first to provide a means of studying 'emotionality' (Wimer & Wimer, 1985). Selection was based on the open-field test in which rats were placed in a brightly lit enclosure and where frequency of defaecation was taken as a measure of emotionality. Although there has been debate about the validity of this simple measure and whether it really provides a useful comparison with more complex human manifestations of emotion, it does have the virtue of being simple and easily quantified. The underlying principle of studying inbred strains is that after many generations (at least 20) of brother–sister matings, heterozygosity is eliminated and strains of animals are produced which are virtually genetically identical. Inbreeding experiments are more costly and time-consuming in larger mammals but intriguing observations have been made with certain strains of dog, most notably so-called 'nervous' pointers

(Reese, 1979). These show normal activity in the presence of other dogs but become timid and fearful when approached by man, showing immobility and freezing. Nervous pointers are poor at operant conditioning and show low heart rates. Various other physiological and pharmacological response characteristics have been studied and are summarised by Wimer & Wimer (1985). A very useful recent summary of animal models of fearfulness has also been provided by Marks (1986).

Psychophysiological studies

It has long been suggested that psychophysiological characteristics might reflect the central and autonomic nervous system substrata upon which personality is based. There is much evidence that psychophysiological characteristics are partly genetically determined. One classic study was quite striking in demonstrating the importance of genetic factors in resting encephalographic (EEG) patterns so that blind raters of EEG tracings were able to distinguish zygosity in twin pairs with a high degree of accuracy (Lennox *et al*, 1945). Furthermore, EEG similarities persist in MZ twins who have been reared apart (Juel-Neilsen & Harvald, 1958). By contrast, auditory or visual evoked responses appear to have only a modest heritability (Lewis *et al*, 1972) and correlations in alpha blocking have not been found to be significantly greater in MZ than in DZ pairs (Young *et al*, 1971). Regarding peripheral measures, twin studies suggest that habituation of the galvanic skin response (GSR) and spontaneous fluctuations in GSR and pulse rate (Lader & Wing, 1966; Hume, 1973) and finger tremor (Tyrer & Kasriel, 1975) are to a large extent genetically determined.

More recent studies of psychophysiological trait measures have focused on their possible relevance to abnormal personalities and to psychopathology. In particular, it has been suggested that abnormalities of smooth pursuit eye movements characterise patients with schizophrenia and a proportion of their relatives. It has therefore been proposed that a dysfunction in 'eye tracking' might be a genetically influenced marker of schizotypy or vulnerability to schizophrenia (Iacono & Koenig, 1983). Certainly there is evidence from twin research of a genetic influence on variations in eye tracking (Iacono, 1982), but a recent claim that a single dominant gene can account for both eye-tracking dysfunctions and the inheritance of schizophrenia (Holzman *et al*, 1988) seems to be an oversimplification of a complex problem (McGue & Gottesman, 1990).

Personality questionnaire studies

Virtually all studies which have been based on questionnaire measures of personality agree in finding evidence of a genetic effect (Loehlin *et al*, 1988; Eaves *et al*, 1989; Plomin & Rende, 1991). However, one area of some dispute is whether there is a modest but significant genetic contribution for all traits (Loehlin & Nichols, 1976), or whether there is a differential heritability of various aspects of personality. Among some of the earlier studies on twins there was fairly good agreement using the Minnesota Multiphasic Personality Inventory (MMPI) that the scales measuring social introversion, depression, psychopathic deviance and schizophrenic-like traits were heritable but there was poor agreement across studies relating to other traits (Gottesman, 1963, 1965; Reznikoff & Honeyman, 1967). Some inconsistencies may have stemmed from sampling errors and sampling bias. There is little doubt that large-scale twin studies depending on volunteers usually attract an excess of pairs who are monozygotic and female. A reanalysis of earlier twin studies using the California Psychological Inventory showed that MZ correlations were consistent across studies despite the fact that DZ correlations and MZ/DZ differences were less easy to replicate (Carey *et al*, 1978).

Recent studies of personality in twins have sought to reduce error by obtaining samples which are large, and as representative as possible of the population. In analysing their data, most researchers now adopt biometric model-fitting approaches. The details of these differ, but the common theme is that there is an attempt to estimate the heritability, or proportion of variance contributed by genes (or more strictly by additive gene effects), the proportion of variance contributed by shared family environment, and the proportion of variance which can be attributed to non-familial environmental effects. The importance of each of these contributors can be tested by fitting reduced models, e.g. a model where there is no heritability or where there is no common environmental effect, and seeing whether these can explain the data just as well (Fulker, 1981). A consistent finding across all domains of personality testing, which has now emerged in such studies, is of heritability of around 35–50% for traits measured by questionnaires, for example, extroversion or neuroticism (Martin & Jardine, 1986; Tellegen *et al*, 1988; Eaves *et al*, 1989). A more curious, but again highly consistent, finding is that shared family environment produces a negligible contribution to the variance and can nearly always be dropped from the model without adversely affecting the fit; i.e. although at least 50% of the variance in most personality traits is environmental it is comprised entirely of non-shared, non-familial factors. The only scales in which family environment does play a detectable part relate to conservatism, and even here the size of the effect appears to be modest at around 20% (Martin & Jardine, 1986).

Interestingly, these recent findings seem to be in keeping with the much earlier results obtained on MZ twins reared apart (MZA). For example, Shields (1962) found that MZA pairs were actually more alike on some personality measures than MZ pairs reared together and suggested that the common environment of reared-together twins had little effect on personality. If anything, Shields suggested, reared-together twins 'react' against one another, presumably in some attempt to assert individual identities. A more recent study of MZA twins confirmed that virtually all of the environmental variance for self-reported measures of personality was of the non-shared type (Pedersen *et al*, 1988). However, there was a hint that common environment might affect some traits so that twins who were reunited shortly after separation were more alike for neuroticism and impulsivity than were twins who never met again after separation. Another important aspect of this study was that it avoided the selection biases present in some earlier MZA studies which recruited twin pairs by advertisement since it was based on a systematic sampling method via the Swedish Twin Registry. This may in part account for the fact that estimates of heritability were slightly lower than those from previous studies. This latter finding is actually in keeping with recent adoption study results (reviewed by Loehlin *et al*, 1988) which showed quite modest biologically based correlations for various personality traits.

Personality disorder

Despite the difficulties in definition and measurement, the results of animal studies, psychophysiological investigations and studies using questionnaires, suggest that personality probably has a partly genetic basis. We would therefore seem to be on reasonably safe ground to go and explore the genetic basis of personalities which deviate from normality. In doing so we will somewhat arbitrarily divide personality disorders into three main groups which have some similarities to the main clusterings contained in DSM–III (American Psychiatric Association, 1980) and we will call these antisocial personality, anxious or 'avoidant' personalities and schizoid–schizotypal personalities. In doing so, we are not attempting any new method of classification nor are we suggesting that these groupings have any inherent biological validity but we are simply using them as a means of facilitating description and of reviewing a literature where a lot of empirical data have been generated by many different investigators using different terminologies and theoretical frameworks.

Antisocial personality

Although few researchers will accept a simplistic argument that criminality and antisocial personality are one and the same, a history of convictions for criminal offences, particularly repeated convictions, is at least a reliable marker. An early and influential study was by Lange (1931) who, in a provocatively entitled book *Crime as Destiny*, reported concordance for criminality in 10 of 13 MZ pairs compared with only two of 17 DZ pairs.

Like many early twin studies, this one suffered from methodological problems. In particular there was non-blind diagnosis and non-systematic ascertainment of twins, which usually results in an overinclusion of the most conspicuous sort of pairs (i.e. MZ twins who are concordant). Ascertainment biases are best overcome using twin registers, and the study of Christiansen (1974; Cloninger & Gottesman (1987) update the results), based on a survey of several thousand pairs, showed concordance for criminality of 51% in MZ twins compared with 30% in DZ twins. Another Scandinavian study based upon a smaller but again systematically ascertained sample, produced even more modest MZ/DZ differences with a concordance of 41% in 31 MZ pairs compared with 26% concordance in 54 DZ pairs (Dalgaard & Kringlen, 1976).

The results of combining data in twin studies of criminality need to be viewed with caution because of differing methods, definitions and base rates across different centres. Nevertheless, McGuffin & Gottesman (1984) considered that there was enough comparability to pool the results of seven studies of adult criminality and five studies of juvenile delinquency where twin concordance was reported as actual numbers and where ascertainment could be presumed to be systematic. The weighted-mean concordance for adult criminality in MZ twins was 51% and in DZ twins was 22% suggesting a definite genetic contribution. By contrast, for juvenile delinquency there was little difference in the MZ and DZ concordance rates at 87% and 72% respectively, suggesting that juvenile delinquency is almost certainly familial but probably does not have a genetic component.

Criminality in most cultures is much less common in women than in men and this was evident in the Danish study of Christiansen (1974). These data were reanalysed by Cloninger *et al* (1978) who applied a two-threshold model. Here it is assumed that liability to become criminal is contributed by an additive combination of genetic and environmental factors, and those whose liability at some stage exceeds a certain threshold, manifest criminal behaviour. Under this model, the threshold for women is more extreme than that for men and, hence, female criminals will have more of a genetic loading than male criminals. This hypothesis appears to fit very well with the Danish twin data.

Adoption studies have been more consistent than twin studies in suggesting a genetic contribution to antisocial personality. In a study of adoptees with 'psychopathy', Schulzinger (1972) found that a significantly greater proportion of biological relatives compared with adoptive relatives and controls could be given the same diagnosis. Similarly, Cadoret (1978), Cadoret & Cain (1980) and Cadoret *et al* (1985), in a series of adoptee family studies, reported a genetic influence on antisocial behaviour and the diagnosis of antisocial personality. In studies of the offspring of female offenders, adopted offspring had significantly more convictions, repeated arrests and incarceration for an offence than controls and also had higher rates of antisocial personality (Crowe, 1972, 1974). The study of Bohman (1978) at first appeared to go against this general trend in failing to show a genetic influence on criminality. However, the findings may have been partly confounded by problems of alcohol abuse and subsequently this author reported that non-alcoholic criminal adoptees had an excess of petty crime without alcohol abuse in their biological compared with their adopting parents (Bohman *et al*, 1982). Whereas petty property offences appeared to be genetically influenced, violent and highly repetitive crime appeared to be more closely related to alcoholism. Similarly, Mednick *et al* (1984) found a significant relationship between biological relatedness for criminality concerning property offences but not violent crimes.

In a cross-fostering study using the Danish register, Hutchings & Mednick (1975) found that when neither biological nor adoptive parents had a criminal record, 11% of adoptees were 'known to the police'. This did not differ significantly from the rate of 12% of having a police record in those adoptees where the adoptive father also had a police record. However, where only the biological father was known to the police, 21% of adoptees had a criminal record, and this rose to 36% where both biological and adoptive fathers were known to the police. The advantage of a cross-fostering design of this type is that genetic factors and factors to do with the environment of rearing can be examined at the same time. Thus there is a suggestion here that family background does play a part, but only when there is already a genetic pre-disposition towards criminality. More recent studies extending the Swedish adoption investigations of Bohman have also suggested that most of the explained variability concerning criminality is due to differences in genetic predisposition (Cloninger *et al*, 1982; Sigvardsson *et al*, 1982). However, environmental contributions were also identified. In particular, the risk of criminality was increased in those with prolonged institutional care; it was also higher in men who had had multiple temporary placements and where the socioeconomic status of the adoptive home was low.

A controversial area is whether criminal behaviour and antisocial personality has a familial or genetic association with other types of abnormal personality. In particular, it has been suggested that somatisation disorder or Briquet syndrome is a sort of female equivalent to antisocial personality, and that there is a high prevalence of antisocial personality disorder among the relatives of women diagnosed as having Briquet syndrome (Guze *et al*, 1967; Cloninger & Guze, 1973; Cloninger *et al*, 1975). Again, a multiple-threshold model has been evoked whereby Briquet syndrome and antisocial personality in women occupy differing positions on a continuum of liability. Those women whose liability exceeds the less extreme threshold present as Briquet syndrome, and those beyond a more extreme threshold present with criminal or antisocial behaviour. At least one set of family data has been held to fit with this hypothesis (Cloninger *et al*, 1975). Similarly, the results of at least one adoption study support an association between antisocial personality and 'hysteria' of the Briquet type (Cadoret, 1978). We return to the topic of Briquet syndrome in discussing the genetics of hysterical personality.

Even more controversial is the suggestion of a genetic association between antisocial personality and schizophrenia. One recent study (Silverton, 1988) found a familial association between criminal or antisocial behaviour and schizophrenia. Similarly, Heston's (1966) classic adoption study found that eight of 42 offspring of schizophrenic mothers had criminal records, compared with only one out of 50 control adoptees. High rates of criminality have not been a consistent feature of other adoption studies of schizophrenia, however, and we cannot exclude the possibility that there was a high rate of criminality among the fathers of the adoptees in Heston's study (Gottesman & Shields, 1982).

In summary, most twin and adoption studies suggest that antisocial personality, albeit often crudely defined in terms of criminal convictions or repeated convictions, has a partly genetic aetiology. There is a strong suggestion that the heritable form of criminality has to do with petty recidivism and property offences rather than violent crimes against the person. It remains to be seen whether the results so far obtained are relevant when modern operational definitions of antisocial personality are applied.

Anxious or avoidant personalities

In genetic studies, as in clinical real life, one of the major problems is in differentiating between neurotic *traits* and anxious *states*. There certainly appears to be evidence from twin studies that anxiety disorder is partly genetic, showing consistently higher concordances in MZ than in DZ twins (Slater & Shields, 1969; Torgersen, 1983). There is also good evidence that the more extreme forms of anxiety, manifesting as panic disorder, are highly familial (Crowe *et al*, 1981). Similarly, we have already discussed how neuroticism, e.g. as measured by the Eysenck Personality Questionnaire (Eysenck & Eysenck, 1975), has shown a consistent modest level of heritability in twin studies. What is less clear is whether there are certain individuals who have lifelong high levels of anxiety and whether this too is heritable.

One approach to this problem has been to focus on 'normal' phobias in non-patient samples of twins. Torgersen (1979) interviewed 99 twin pairs ascertained via the Norwegian National Register. All subjects responded to a phobia questionnaire and the results were submitted to an analysis which yielded five factors. MZ twins were found to be more alike with respect to fears of animals, social fears, mutilation fears (medical procedures, blood etc.), 'nature fears' (heights, enclosed spaces, etc.) and separation fears which include agoraphobic-like items. Only separation fears showed a non-significant MZ/DZ difference. Similarly, Rose *et al* (1981) administered a fear questionnaire to 91 MZ and 60 DZ college-age twin pairs and a proportion of their parents. There was a substantial heritability for many common fears and, for example, animal phobia appeared to be 72% heritable. As with the questionnaire measures of normal personality described earlier there was little evidence of a common environmental effect. Rose *et al* (1981) remarked that the question of a genetic basis for trait anxiety had been considered more than a century earlier by Charles Darwin, who pointed to the selective advantage of fearfulness in certain circumstances. It is of particular interest in this context that the range of common phobic cues in modern man is quite limited (Marks, 1986). Snakes and spiders often produce phobic results whereas guns and knives rarely do so, suggesting that as Darwin put it, the phobic cues represent "the inherited effects of real dangers . . . during ancient savage times".

Obsessional personality

Obsessive–compulsive disorder and obsessional personality disorder are often difficult to disentangle, both in research studies and in clinical practice. Slater (1943) noted, in his classic study of 'neurotic constitution' in soldiers, that obsessional neurosis seemed to be more closely associated with pre-existent personality traits than are most other neurotic disorders. Most studies which have focused on obsessional disorders have shown an increased risk of obsessional traits among family members but the estimated rates vary widely from 5% (Carey *et al*, 1978) to 37% (Lewis, 1935) which must surely reflect varying breadths of diagnostic inclusiveness. There have been various case reports of concordance for obsessive–compulsive disorder and obsessional traits in MZ twins (McGuffin & Mawson, 1980; Marks, 1986). However, to date only one systematic twin study of overt obsessive–compulsive disorder has been published (Carey & Gottesman, 1981) which showed a proband-wise concordance rate of 13 out of 15 in MZ twins compared with seven out of 15 DZ twins when concordance was defined broadly according to obsessional features in the co-twin. A study of obsessional traits and 'normal symptoms' in a large sample of volunteer twins used the Leyton Obsessional Inventory Test (Clifford *et al*, 1984). MZ twins were more highly correlated than DZ twins and the estimated heritabilities were 0.4 for obsessional traits and 0.47 for obsessional symptoms. These authors also found a highly significant correlation between obsessional symptom scores and N scores measured by the Eysenck Personality Questionnaire (Eysenck & Eysenck, 1975). It was therefore suggested that genetic factors contribute to obsessional neurosis by influencing both obsessional personality traits and a more general neurotic tendency such that these two in combination may manifest as obsessional symptoms.

Somewhat surprising in view of this, Torgersen (1980) found that an obsessional dimension derived from factor analysis was not heritable and Young *et al* (1971) found that obsessional symptoms in the Middlesex Hospital Questionnaire (MHQ) were not influenced genetically. Again differences of definition must be playing a part in these disparate findings. However, it has to be said that the study of Clifford *et al* (1984) which did find evidence of a modest but significant genetic component in obsessionality used better established measures and a more sophisticated approach to genetic analysis than the earlier negative investigations.

Hysterical personality

Hysterical personality disorder provides particular difficulties for reviewers of genetic studies because researchers have used the term 'hysteria' in so many different ways. When considered as a personality trait measured by the MMPI, Gottesman's (1963) twin study of normal adolescents showed negligible genetic influences. By contrast, Torgersen (1980) found that a hysterical dimension derived by factor analysis showed higher correlations in MZ than in DZ twins, especially in women. Yet another twin study, this time using the MHQ, suggested that there was a modest genetic influence on hysterical personality traits (Young *et al*, 1971). Here, however, the authors expressed doubts as to whether it was extraversion rather than hysterical personality traits as such which were being measured by the questionnaire. In a small twin study of classical conversion or dissociative symptoms, Slater (1961) found zero concordance in both 12 MZ and 12 DZ pairs. However, a rather different clinical concept of hysteria is prevalent in some parts of the United States influenced in particular by the Washington University, St Louis School. Arkonac & Guze (1963) proposed that hysteria could be defined as a syndrome occurring in early adult life, mainly affecting women and presenting as recurrent and often dramatic symptoms affecting many organ systems. The syndrome is said to be similar to that originally described by the 19th-century French clinician, Briquet, and hence the eponymous term 'Briquet syndrome'. A somewhat modified concept has been incorporated in DSM–III (American Psychiatric Association, 1980), and is called somatisation disorder. Although it is strictly a DSM–III axis-I diagnosis and hence is not classified as a personality disorder, the early onset of the condition, its enduring nature and its supposed familial relationship to antisocial personality (mentioned earlier) make somatisation disorder a concept which is more closely allied to a personality defect than an illness.

Schizoid–schizotypal disorders

Here again the definition of terms and the derivation of concepts need to be carefully considered. Family and genetic studies have played a particularly influential role and there has long been a view among researchers that the relatives of schizophrenics show an excess of individuals with abnormal personalities and schizophrenic-like features in the absence of overt schizophrenia.

Meehl (1962) coined the terms 'schizotaxia' to cover the psychological abnormalities inherent in the predisposition to schizophrenia and 'schizotypy' to describe characteristic symptoms in those predisposed but still non-schizophrenic individuals. A much broader concept of 'schizoid disease' was put forward by Heston (1970) in his formulation of a monogenic hypothesis of transmission of schizophrenia. Schizoid disease included not just classical schizoid and paranoid features but also creative and intellectual abilities. Subsequently, the publication of Danish adoption studies demonstrated that there appeared to be a broad range of abnormalities, so-called 'schizophrenia spectrum disorders', which were commoner in the biological relatives of schizophrenics than in adoptive relatives or controls (Kety *et al*, 1971). While the veracity of the adoption study findings was widely accepted, the concept of spectrum disorders seemed unacceptably broad for some researchers. Therefore, based on the Danish adoption study records, Spitzer *et al* (1979) devised stricter, more explicit operational criteria for schizotypal personality disorder. This was later incorporated in a somewhat modified form in DSM–III (American Psychiatric Association, 1980).

Deriving from a quite different conceptual background of psychoanalytic clinical practice is the notion of borderline states. The term is particularly confusing since schizophrenia spectrum disorders have sometimes been referred to as 'borderline schizophrenia' (Kety *et al*, 1971). However, borderline states, as described by Gunderson & Singer (1975) show more depressive-like features (Stone, 1981), and provided the basis for Spitzer *et al*'s (1979) description of 'unstable personality' which was later modified and incorporated in DSM–III as borderline personality disorder. Most recent authors concur that borderline personality disorder does not show a genetic relationship to schizophrenia or schizotypy but rather have emphasised the higher rate of affective disorder in individuals with borderline personalities, and in their first-degree relatives (Loranger *et al*, 1982; Baron *et al*, 1985). Family studies have also suggested that the rate of borderline personality is increased among the relatives of borderline probands but that the category of borderline personality disorder is very mixed so that there is an increased risk also of histrionic and antisocial personality disorder among relatives (Pope *et al*, 1983). The one available twin study was based on a very small sample and suggested that although borderline personality disorder may be familial, there is no evidence to support genetic transmission (Torgersen, 1984).

Genetic studies of schizotypal personality disorder suffer from two shortcomings. First, most studies have been based upon schizophrenic probands and have attempted to identify schizophrenia and schizotypal personality disorder among relatives. Few studies have taken schizotypal probands as their starting point. Second, several of the key published papers have consisted of 'recycling' exercises where new criteria have been applied to old data. Moreover, the most frequently used dataset in diagnostic reanalysis has been the Danish adoption study from which the forerunners of DSM–III criteria for schizotypal personality disorder were derived. Despite the inherent circularity of the exercise, the reanalysis of the Danish adoption data has been informative. For example, the original non-operational clinical diagnosis applied in the adoptees family study of Kety *et al* (1971) produced rates of schizophrenia and related disorders of 20% in the biological relatives of schizophrenics compared with 6% in the adoptive relatives and controls. However, when the diagnostic criteria were restricted to DSM–III schizophrenia and schizotypal personality disorder, the rates became 22% in the biological relatives of schizophrenics versus 2% of adoptive relatives and controls (Kendler *et al*, 1981). The increase in magnitude of the difference between those genetically related and those not genetically related to a schizophrenic suggests that the DSM–III concept of schizotypal personality disorder is not only a more restricted concept but, from a genetic point of view, has a greater validity than the less explicit concept of spectrum disorder. Some support for the genetic relationship between schizophrenia and schizotypal personality disorder comes also from a reanalysis of a classic twin study of schizophrenia (Gottesman & Shields, 1972). On applying DSM–III criteria, a definition of illness in co-twins, which included schizotypal personality disorder as well as schizophrenia, produced a higher MZ to DZ concordance ratio than when the diagnosis was restricted to schizophrenia alone (Farmer *et al*, 1987). Although MZ:DZ ratio provides a fairly crude measure of how genetic is a condition, the findings support the idea that adding schizotypy to schizophrenia enhances the definition of the phenotype and is not simply adding 'noise'. Almost all studies of the families of schizophrenic probands have found an excess of both schizophrenia and schizotypal personality disorder among relatives (Kendler *et al*, 1984; Baron *et al*, 1983). Only one study so far has failed to find a relationship between schizotypal personality disorder and either schizophrenia or other psychoses (Coryell & Zimmerman, 1989).

As we have pointed out, there have been few studies of families ascertained via schizotypal probands. There has been one report that schizotypal personality disorder aggregates in families, particularly in the families of probands with pure schizotypal disorder rather than a mixed schizotypal/borderline personality type (Baron *et al*, 1985). However, this and most other published studies did not show an increased risk of schizophrenia among the relatives of probands with schizotypal personality disorder (Soloff & Millward, 1983; Schulz *et al*, 1986). How then do we reconcile these two groups of findings, evidence of a genetic relationship between schizotypy and schizophrenia in studies based on schizophrenic probands but not in studies based on schizotypal probands? One explanation is to invoke a severity-liability model as we have done elsewhere in this article. Here schizophrenia and schizotypy could be regarded as lying on the same continuum of liability with schizotypy being a milder, commoner disorder where only a moderately high liability is required to cross the threshold of being affected, whereas schizophrenia is considered as a more severe and less common disorder occupying a more extreme position on the liability continuum. We would then predict that the relatives of schizophrenics would have higher rates of both schizotypy and schizophrenia than the relatives of schizotypal personality disorder probands. In general, this would then mean that larger sample sizes would be required to detect an excess of schizophrenia among the relatives of schizotypal probands than among the relatives of schizophrenics, and hence any failure to detect such an excess in a family study might reflect a lack of power rather than a true absence of familial relationship between schizophrenia and schizophrenia personality disorder. However, results of a more recent Italian family study differ from previous findings (Battaglia *et al*, 1991). Relatives of 21 schizotypal probands (unlike other studies, most were not mixed schizotypal/borderline) showed a significantly higher morbidity risk for chronic schizophrenia than those of controls. Thus the co-occurrence of another personality disorder may influence genetic findings.

A different approach to the problem is, as with other types of personality disorder, to regard schizotypy as something measurable on a continuous scale rather than a disorder which is qualitatively distinct from normality. Various scales attempting to measure schizotypy have been devised (Claridge, 1988; Venables *et al*, 1990) and there is some evidence from a twin study of a heritable component in schizotypy scores (Claridge & Hewitt, 1987). However, measurements of schizotypy in general tend to be correlated with neuroticism scores and so it is hard to decide whether they are measuring true schizotypy or some more general propensity to psychopathology. Schizotypy scores derived from MMPI items have been shown to have positive correlations within families and moreover to have a pattern of distribution which would be compatible with major factor inheritance (Moldin, 1990). The search for continuous measures of schizotypy is important. If reliable and valid continuous measures of schizotypy can be devised they have considerable potential in genetic studies of schizophrenia as an indicator of which unaffected relatives of a schizophrenic have a schizophrenia-prone genotype. This applies both in statistical studies which attempt to resolve mode of transmission and in studies using DNA polymorphisms as genetic linkage markers.

Molecular genetics and the biological basis of personality disorder

Although the data are fragmentary and the definitions of the phenotypes untidy, the traditional methods of psychiatric genetics, family, twin and adoption studies, suggest a genetic contribution to personality disorders. However, it becomes apparent that in studying personality disorders we are not dealing with 'all-or-none' traits, but rather with phenotypes which are best regarded as continuous or semi-continuous. That is, we can either regard personality disorders as one extreme of a continuum which blends imperceptibly with normality or we can impose a dichotomy where the population is divided into those with or without personality disorders. If we take this second course, the personality disorder group itself varies from those who have a set of comparatively mild abnormal behaviours to those who are severely disordered. It follows that the patterns of inheritance must be complex and we are not dealing with traits where simple monogenic explanations of transmission will suffice. In fact, personality disorders do not show simple mendelian patterns of transmission, and concordances in MZ twins of well below 100%, or correlations well below unity, mean that there must be a substantial environmental component. For personality measures within the normal range, we have seen that this environmental component is nearly always non-familial but this is not necessarily true of deviant personalities and it seems likely that at least part of the reasons for the familial aggregation of criminality lie in shared family environment.

Given this complicated series of affairs, can we go any further with the genetics of personality disorder and progress from stating that *something* is transmitted to specify more precisely *what* is transmitted? Cytogenetic studies initially appeared to offer an improved insight into the physical basis of personality disorder. In particular, the finding that men with an extra Y chromosome having the so-called 47XYY karyotype accounted for about 3% of the inmates of Carstairs, a hospital for mentally abnormal offenders in Scotland, provoked considerable interest (Jacobs *et al*, 1968). Subsequent studies have found a consistent slight excess of men with the 47XYY constitution in similar institutions. Such men have a mean IQ below that of the rest of the population but are thought to have no characteristic physical abnormalities other than greater than average height. The incidence of the abnormality among new-born boys is in the region of 1 to 2 per 2000 (0.05 to 0.1%) and the syndrome has not been shown to shorten life. It therefore seems that the majority of infants reach adulthood and hence only a very small minority of XYY males are so conspicuously abnormal as to be placed in special institutions. A survey of over 4000 ostensibly normal men of greater than 1.84 metres in height uncovered 12 individuals (0.3%) with the 47-XYY karyotype (Witkin *et al*, 1976). Five of these (42%) turned out to have had criminal records compared with only 9% of normal XY males. The offences committed by the XYY subjects were not predominantly acts of aggression and included relatively minor crimes. This study therefore suggests that there is an increased risk of social deviance among non-institutionalised XYY men but seriously sociopathic or criminal individuals account for only a tiny proportion of those with this syndrome. It may be, therefore, that the initial impression of an association between the XYY constitution and serious crime requiring treatment in a special hospital reflects socio-legal factors, rather than purely genetic influences. A court faced with sentencing a convicted offender who is tall and dull may be more inclined to recommend disposal in a special hospital than if the offender is of average height and intelligence.

Biochemical genetics have so far shed little light on the causes of personality disorder and we have very few clues about biochemical markers which might possibly indicate personality deviations. The suggestion that lowered activity of platelet monoamine oxidase characterises subjects with schizophrenia and some of their relatives or co-twins has proved controversial (Reveley *et al*, 1986). However, the finding has led to researchers studying other aspects of personality than those which may obviously be related to schizophrenia. In particular, a relationship has been reported between scores on sensation-seeking scales and platelet monoamine oxidase levels (Buchsbaum *et al*, 1976). Unfortunately, it is still not clear how firm a finding this is or indeed what is the mechanism by which monoamine oxidase activity and sensation seeking are associated.

In summary then, the explanatory power of cytogenetic techniques is limited, and biochemical markers or the sorts of psychophysiological measures which we discussed earlier can at best provide us with 'endopheno-types' which lie a step closer to the abnormal genotypes than do clinical descriptions, but still represent vague and indistinct signposts on the complicated pathway between abnormal genes and abnormal behaviour. A more attractive proposition might be to utilise the techniques of recombinant DNA research and go straight for the genotypes themselves. Recent rapid advances in the discovery of DNA polymorphisms has allowed the construction of a nearly complete human genetic linkage map covering the 22 pairs of autosomes and the sex chromosomes (Donis-Keller *et al*, 1989). This means that it is feasible to undertake linkage studies with any inherited trait where there is a real prospect of major gene effects. For example, there have now been several studies focusing on manic–depressive illness (McGuffin & Katz, 1989), and schizophrenia (Owen & Mullan, 1989; Owen & McGuffin, 1991). The aim here is to study the co-segregation within families of the disease and DNA polymorphisms with the aim of detecting co-inheritance of a marker and the disease. This assumes that the inheritance of the disorder is, at least in some families, explicable in terms of a gene of major effect and not just multiple genes of small effect at many loci. Therefore, the important question is whether the approach can be extended further to cover even more loosely defined entities than the major psychoses, including personality disorders. We think that this probably would not be wise. The main reasons are those outlined earlier which persuade us that personality traits within the normal range and personality deviations are most likely to have polygenic modes of transmission. That is, there are likely to be many genes of small effect at different loci acting in a predominantly additive fashion and each on its own accounting for only a small proportion of the variance. This unfortunately means that linkage strategies are unlikely to prove successful.

If this is so, can genes of minor effect be detected or usefully studied at all using molecular genetic techniques? The best evidence that they can be studied comes from recent experiments in plant and laboratory animal breeding. For example, by studying crosses and then back-crosses between domestic tomato and wild South American tomato, Paterson *et al* (1988) made use of a complete genetic linkage map consisting of DNA restriction fragment length polymorphisms (RFLP) distributed throughout the tomato genome. The aim was to define so-called quantitative trait loci (QTL), that is, loci responsible for certain forms of continuous variation. These workers were able to map six QTL controlling fruit mass, five influencing fruit pH and four influencing liquid soluble concentrations in tomato fruit. They have thus provided a convincing demonstration that comparatively simple continuous traits in plants are polygenically inherited and that the polygenes can be localised. As Plomin (1990) has put it, it seems unlikely that human behaviour will turn out to be "less complicated than salad"! Indeed, experiments described by Plomin using recombinant inbred strains of rat strongly suggest that behaviour which can be quantified in the laboratory is most unlikely to be monogenically transmitted. Hence animal behaviour which might be viewed as a prototype for human personality is more likely to be elucidated by a search for QTL than by classical linkage strategies. More recently, loci affecting continuous traits, for example blood pressure in rats (Hilbert *et al*, 1991), have been identified.

Searching for QTL which may influence human personality is much more problematic. Just as Mendel's insights into patterns of transmission came from breeding experiments with plants, so also has the discovery of QTLs, discrete mendelian factors encoding for quantitative traits, come from plant genetics. The application of mendelian genetics in studies of human disease took some time because breeding experiments are not possible, and the investigator has to rely on 'natural experiments' such as observing recurrence risks of 'inborn errors' in siblings (Garrod, 1908).

In searching for markers of small genetic effects it may be necessary to focus not on the segregation of disorders in families but on their distribution in populations. It has long been known that consistent population associations between genetic markers and diseases can be demonstrated even when association accounts for only a tiny proportion of variance. For example, the association between blood group O and duodenal ulcer explains just over 1% of the variance in liability to the disorder (Edwards, 1965). Associations with particular marker alleles occur for a variety of reasons but the most important are either that the marker allele has some pleiotropic influence on the trait of interest or there is very tight linkage between the trait locus and the marker resulting in *linkage disequilibrium*. This means that the two loci are so physically close that a particular marker allele continues to be co-inherited with the trait over many generations. Probably the maximum physical distances between loci which would still be compatible with linkage disequilibrium is about 10^6 base pairs. Since the human genome is about 3×10^9 base pairs long, a minimum of 1500 evenly spaced DNA markers would be required therefore in order to be fairly confident of detecting QTL in association studies. This would obviously be an enormous undertaking in studies of human personality but one way of reducing the work entailed in the initial search might be to focus on loci of bio-behavioural interest, for example, genes encoding for neuroreceptors or other proteins involved in neurotransmission (Plomin, 1990).

This 'candidate gene' approach depends for its success upon variability detected by molecular biological methods actually having some effect on function. This is not guaranteed since most variability in DNA resulting in RLFP is probably due to random base changes in introns (or non-coding intervening sequences of DNA). Nevertheless, mapping of the human genome is progressing so rapidly that it seems inevitable that all functional human genes including QTL will eventually be detected and localised. How long we mean by 'eventually' is impossible to say. The vast majority of genes discovered so far are not of relevance to complex traits which are polygenic and partially environmental; however, the total number is about 2000 and already accounts for 2–4% of all human genes. This represents a more than ten-fold increase over the past decade suggesting that the end, if not in sight, is definitely foreseeable.

Summary

Most measurable aspects of normal personality appear to be at least moderately heritable, with direct evidence coming from family, twin and adoption studies and indirect support deriving from psychophysiological research and breeding experiments on animals. Interestingly, genetic studies also shed light on the environmental sources of variation in personality and suggest that shared family environment rarely, if ever, has any positive effect on similarity between relatives. Despite problems of classification, and variations in the use of terms, a survey of the literature provides reasonably consistent evidence of a genetic contribution to several categories of abnormal personality, which we here divide into three groups, antisocial, anxious/ avoidant, and schizoid–schizotypal personalities. However, personality disorders are complex traits that do not show simple Mendelian patterns of inheritance and so far molecular genetics has been of no help in understanding their aetiology. Fortunately, techniques are now becoming available that enable the detection and potential localisation of genes of small effect and which may help elucidate the molecular basis even of (probably) polygenic traits such as abnormal personality.

References

AMERICAN PSYCHIATRIC ASSOCIATION (1980) *Diagnostic and Statistical Manual of Mental Disorders* (3rd edn) (DSM–III). Washington, DC: APA.
—— (1987) *Diagnostic and Statistical Manual of Mental Disorders* (3rd edn, revised) (DSM–III–R). Washington, DC: APA.
ARKONAC, O. & GUZE, S. B. (1963) A family study of hysteria. *New England Journal of Medicine*, **268**, 239–242.
BARON, M., GRUEN, R., ASNIS, L., *et al* (1983) Familial relatedness of schizophrenic and schizotypal states. *American Journal of Psychiatry*, **140**, 1437–1442.
——, ——, RAINER, J. D., *et al* (1985) A family study of schizophrenic and normal control probands: implications for the spectrum concept of schizophrenia. *American Journal of Psychiatry*, **142**, 447–455.
BATTAGLIA, M., GASPERINI, M., SCIUTO, G., *et al* (1991) Psychiatric disorders in the families of schizotypal subjects. *Schizophrenia Bulletin*, **17**, 659–665.
BOHMAN, M. (1978) Some genetic aspects of alcoholism and criminality. A population of adoptees. *Archives of General Psychiatry*, **35**, 267–276.
——, CLONINGER, R., SIGVARDSSON, S., *et al* (1982) Predisposition to petty criminality in Swedish adoptees. Genetic and environmental heterogeneity. *Archives of General Psychiatry*, **39**, 1233–1241.
BUCHSBAUM, M. S., COWSEY, R. D. & MURPHY, D. L. (1976) The biochemical high risk paradigm. Behavioural and family correlates of low platelet monoamine oxidase activity. *Science*, **194**, 339–341.
CADORET, R. J. (1978) Psychopathology in adopted-away offspring of biologic parents with antisocial behaviour. *Archives of General Psychiatry*, **35**, 176–184.
—— & CAIN, C. (1980) Sex differences in predictors of antisocial behaviour adoptees. *Archives of General Psychiatry*, **37**, 1171–1175.
——, O'GORMAN, T. W., TROUGHTON, E., *et al* (1985) Alcoholism and antisocial personality – interrelationships, genetics and environmental factors. *Archives of General Psychiatry*, **42**, 161–167.
CAREY, G., GOLDSMITH, H. H., TELLEGEN, A., *et al* (1978) Genetics and personality inventories. The limits of replication with twin data. *Behavior Genetics*, **8**, 299–313.
—— & GOTTESMAN, I. I. (1981) Twin and family studies of anxiety, phobic and obsessive disorders. In *Anxiety: New Research and Changing Concepts* (eds D. F. Klein & J. Rabkin), pp. 117–135. New York: Raven Press.
CHRISTIANSEN, K. O. (1974) The genesis of aggressive criminality. Implications of a study of crime in a Danish twin study. In *Determinants and Origins of Aggressive Behaviour* (eds J. De Wit & W. W. Hartup). The Hague: Mouton.
CLARIDGE, G. (1988) Schizotypy and schizophrenia. In *Schizophrenia: The Major Issues* (eds P. Bebbington & P. McGuffin), pp. 187–200. Oxford: Heinemann Medical.
—— & HEWITT, J. K. (1987) A biometrical study of schizotypy in a normal population. *Personality and Individual Differences*, **8**, 303–312.
CLIFFORD, C. A., MURRAY, R. M. & FULKER, D. W. (1984) Genetic and environmental influences on obsessional traits and symptoms. *Psychological Medicine*, **14**, 791–800.
CLONINGER, C. R. & GUZE, S. B. (1973) Psychiatric illness in the families of female criminals. A study of 288 first-degree relatives. *British Journal of Psychiatry*, **122**, 697–703.
——, REICH, J. & GUZE, J. B. (1975) The multifactorial model of disease transmission II. Sex differences in the familial transmission of sociopathy. *British Journal of Psychiatry*, **127**, 11–22.
——, CHRISTIANSEN, K. O., REICH, T., *et al* (1978) Implications of sex differences in the prevalences of antisocial personality, alcoholism and criminality for familial transmission. *Archives of General Psychiatry*, **35**, 941–945.

60 McGuffin and Thapar

——, SIGVARDSSON, S., BOHMAN, M., et al (1982) Predisposition to petty criminality in Swedish adoptees II. Cross-fostering analysis of gene-environment interaction. Archives of General Psychiatry, **39**, 1242–1253.

—— & GOTTESMAN, I. I. (1987) Genetic and environmental factors in antisocial behaviour disorders. In Causes of Crime: New Biological Approaches (eds S. A. Mednick, T. E. Moffitt & S. A. Stack). Cambridge: Cambridge University Press.

CORYELL, W. H. & ZIMMERMAN, M. (1989) Personality disorder in the families of depressed, schizophrenic and never ill probands. American Journal of Psychology, **146**, 496–502.

CROWE, R. R. (1972) The adopted offspring of women criminal offenders—a study of their arrest records. Archives of General Psychiatry, **27**, 600–603.

—— (1974) An adoption study of antisocial personality. Archives of General Psychiatry, **31**, 785–791.

——, PAULS, D. L., KERBER, R. E., et al (1981) Panic disorder and mitral valve prolapse. In Anxiety: New Research and Changing Concepts (eds C. D. F. Klein & J. Rabkin). New York: Raven Press.

DALGAARD, O. S. & KRINGLEN, E. (1976) A Norwegian study of criminality. British Journal of Criminology, **16**, 213–232.

DONIS-KELLER, H., HELMS, C. & GREEN, P. (1989) A human genetic linkage map with more than 500 RFLP loci and average marker spacing of 6 centimorgans. Cytogenetics and Cell Genetics, **51**, 991.

EAVES, L. J., EYSENCK, H. J. & MARTIN, N. (1989) Genes, Culture and Personality. New York: Academic Press.

EDWARDS, J. H. (1965) Association between blood groups and disease. Annals of Human Genetics, **29**, 77–83.

EYSENCK, H. J. & EYSENCK, S. B. G. (1975) Manual of the Eysenck Personality Questionnaire. London: Hodder and Stoughton.

FARMER, A. E., McGUFFIN, P. & GOTTESMAN, I. I. (1987) Twin concordance for DSM–III schizophrenia. Scrutinising the validity of the definition. Archives of General Psychiatry, **44**, 634–641.

FULKER, D. W. (1981) Biometrical genetics and individual differences. British Medical Bulletin, **37**, 115–120.

GARROD, A. E. (1908) Croonian lecture on inborn errors of metabolism. Lancet, **ii**, 1–7.

GOTTESMAN, I. I. (1963) Heritability of personality: a demonstration. Psychological Monograph, **77**, 1–21.

—— (1965) Personality and natural selection. In Methods and Goals in Human Behaviour Genetics (ed. S. G. Vanderberg). New York: Academic Press Inc.

—— & SHIELDS, J. (1972) Schizophrenia and Genetics: A Twin Vantage Point. New York and London: Academic Press.

—— & —— (1982) Schizophrenia: The Epigenetic Puzzle. New York: Cambridge University Press.

GUNDERSON, J. G. & SINGER, M. T. (1975) Defining borderline patients: an overview. American Journal of Psychiatry, **132**, 1–10.

GUZE, S. B., WOLFGRAN, E. D., MCKINNERY, J. K., et al (1967) Psychiatric illness in the families of convicted criminals. A study of 519 first-degree relatives. Diseases of the Nervous System, **28**, 651–659.

HESTON, L. L. (1966) Psychiatric disorders in foster home-related children of schizophrenic mothers. British Journal of Psychiatry, **112**, 819–825.

—— (1970) The genetics of schizophrenia and schizoid disease. Science, **167**, 249–256.

HILBERT, P., LINDPAINTNER, K., BECKMANN, J. S., et al (1991) Chromosomal mapping of two genetic loci associated with blood-pressure regulation in hereditary hypertensive rats. Nature, **353**, 521–529.

HOLZMAN, P. S., KRINGLEN, E., MATTHYSSE, S., et al (1988) A single dominant gene can account for eye-tracking dysfunction and schizophrenia in offspring of discordant twins. Archives of General Psychiatry, **45**, 641–647.

HUME, W. I. (1973) Physiological measures in twins. In Personality Differences and Biological Variations: A Study of Twins (eds G. Claridge, S. Canter & W. I. Hume). Oxford: Pergamon Press.

HUTCHINGS, B. & MEDNICK, S. A. (1975) Registered criminality in the adopted and biological parents of registered male adoptees. In *Genetics, Environment and Psychopathology* (eds S. A. Mednick, F. Schulzinger, J. Higgins, *et al*). Amsterdam: Elsevier.

IACONO, W. G. (1982) Eye tracking in normal twins. *Behaviour Genetics*, **12**, 517–526.

—— & KOENIG, W. G. R. (1983) Features that distinguish the smooth pursuit eye-tracking performance of schizophrenic, affective disorder and normal individuals. *Journal of Abnormal Psychology*, **92**, 29–41.

JACOBS, P. A., PRICE, W. H., COWER-BROWN, W. M., *et al* (1968) Chromosome studies on men in maximum security hospitals. *Annals of Human Genetics*, **31**, 339–358.

JUEL-NIELSEN, N. & HARVARD, B. (1958) The electroencephalogram in uniovular twins brought up apart. *Acta Genetica*, **8**, 57–64.

KENDLER, K. S., GRUENBERG, A. M. & STRAUSS, J. S. (1981) An independent analysis of the Copenhagen sample of the Danish adoption study of schizophrenia. II. The Relationship between schizotypal personality disorders and schizophrenia. *Archives of General Psychiatry*, **38**, 982–984.

——, MASTERSON, C. C., UNGARO, R., *et al* (1984) A family history study of schizophrenic related personality disorders. *American Journal of Psychiatry*, **141**, 424–427.

KETY, S. S., ROSENTHAL, D., WENDER, P. H., *et al* (1971) Mental illness in the biological and adoptive families of adopted schizophrenics. *American Journal of Psychiatry*, **128**, 302–306.

LADER, M. & WING, L. (1966) *Physiological Measures, Sedative Drugs and Morbid Anxiety*. Oxford: Oxford University Press.

LANGE, J. (1931) *Crime as Destiny*. London: Allen & Unwin.

LENNOX, W. G., GIBBS, E. L. & GIBBS, F. A. (1945) The brain wave pattern: an hereditary trait. Evidence from 74 'normal' pairs of twins. *Journal of Heredity*, **36**, 233–243.

LEWIS, A. (1935) Problems of obsessional illness. *Proceedings of the Royal Society of Medicine*, **29**, 325–336.

—— (1974) Psychopathic personality: a most elusive category. *Psychological Medicine*, **4**, 133–140.

LEWIS, E. G., DUSTMAN, R. E. & BECK, C. (1972) Evoked response similarity in monozygotic, dizygotic and unrelated individuals: a comparative study. *Electroencephalography and Clinical Neurophysiology*, **32**, 309–316.

LOEHLIN, J. C. & NICHOLS, R. C. (1976) *Heredity, Environment and Personality. A Study of 850 sets of Twins*. Texas: University of Texas Press.

——, WILLERMAN, L. & HORN, J. M. (1988) Human behaviour genetics. *Annual Review of Psychology*, **39**, 101–133.

LORANGER, A. W., OLDHAM, J. M. & TULIS, E. H. (1982) Familial transmission of DSM–III borderline personality disorders. *Archives of General Psychiatry*, **39**, 795–799.

McGUE, M. & GOTTESMAN, I. I. (1989) Genetic linkage in schizophrenia: perspective from genetic epidemiology. In *Genetic Approaches in the Prevention of Mental Illness* (eds V. Bulyzhenkov, Y. Christen & L. Prilipko), pp. 24–38. Berlin: Springer-Verlag.

McGUFFIN, P. & MAWSON, D. (1980) Obsessive compulsive neurosis: two identical twin pairs. *British Journal of Psychiatry*, **137**, 285–287.

—— & GOTTESMAN, I. I. (1984) Genetic influences on normal and abnormal development. In *Child Psychiatry: Modern Approaches* (2nd edn) (eds M. Rutter & L. Hersov). London: Blackwell.

—— & KATZ, R. (1989) The genetics of depression and manic depressive illness. *British Journal of Psychiatry*, **155**, 294–304.

MARKS, I. (1986) Genetics of fear and anxiety disorders: a review. *British Journal of Psychiatry*, **149**, 406–418.

MARTIN, N. & JARDINE, R. (1986) Eysenck's contributions to behaviour genetics. In *Hans Eysenck: Consensus and Controversy* (eds S. Modgil, C. Modgil), pp. 13–47. Philadelphia: Falmer.

MEDNICK, S. A., GABRIELLI, W. F. & HUTCHINGS, B. (1984) Genetic influences in criminal convictions: evidence from an adoption cohort. *Science*, **224**, 891–894.

MEEHL, P. E. (1962) Schizotaxia, schizotypy schizophrenia. *American Psychologist*, **17**, 827–831.

MOLDIN, S. O. (1990) Transmission of a psychomatic indicator for linkage to schizophrenia in normal families. *Genetic Epidemiology*, **7**, 163–176.

OWEN, M. J. & MULLAN, M. J. (1989) Molecular genetic studies of manic depression and schizophrenia. *Trends in Neuroscience*, **13**, 29–31.

—— & MCGUFFIN, P. (1991) DNA and classical markers in schizophrenia. *European Archives of Psychiatry and Clinical Neuroscience*, **240**, 197–208.

PATERSON, A. H., LANDER, E. S., HEWITT, J. D., *et al* (1988) Resolution of quantitative traits into mendelian factors by using a complete linkage map of restriction fragment length polymorphisms. *Nature*, **335**, 721–726.

PEDERSEN, N. L., PLOMIN, R., MCLEARN, G. E., *et al* (1988) Neuroticism, extraversion, and related traits in adult twins reared apart and reared together. *Journal of Personality and Social Psychology*, **55**, 950–957.

PENROSE, L. S. (1971) Psychiatric genetics (editorial). *Psychological Medicine*, **1**, 265–266.

PLOMIN, R. (1990) The role of inheritance in behavior. *Science*, **248**, 183–188.

—— & RENDE, R. (1991) Human behavioral genetics. *Annual Review of Psychology*, **42**, 161–190.

POPE, H. G., JONAS, J. M., HUDSON, J. I., *et al* (1983) The validity of DSM–III borderline personality disorder: a phenomenologic, family history, treatment response, and long term follow-up study. *Archives of General Psychiatry*, **40**, 23–30.

REESE, W. G. (1979) A dog model for human psychopathology. *American Journal of Psychiatry*, **136**, 1168–1172.

REVELEY, M. A., REVELEY, A. M., CLIFFORD, C., *et al* (1986) Genetics of platelet MAO activity in discordant schizophrenic and normal twins. In *Contemporary Issues in Schizophrenia* (eds A. Kerr & P. Snaith), pp. 310–317. London: Gaskell, Royal College of Psychiatrists.

REZNIKOFF, M. & HONEYMAN, M. S. (1967) MMPI profiles of monozygotic and dizygotic twin pairs (Abstract). *Journal of Consulting Psychology*, **31**, 100.

ROSE, R. J., MILLER, J. Z., POGUE-GEILE, M. F., *et al* (1981) Twin-family studies of common fears and phobias. In *Twin Research 3: Intelligence, Personality and Development*, pp. 169–174. New York: Alan R. Liss.

SCHULZINGER, F. (1972) Psychopathy, heredity and environment. *International Journal of Mental Health*, **1**, 190–206.

SCHULZ, P. M., SCHULZ, S. C., GOLDBERG, S. C., *et al* (1986) Diagnoses of the relatives of schizotypal outpatients. *Journal of Nervous and Mental Diseases*, **174**, 457–463.

SHIELDS, J. (1962) *Monozygotic Twins Brought Up Apart and Brought Up Together*. Oxford: Oxford University Press.

SIGVARDSSON, S., CLONINGER, C. R., BOHMAN, M., *et al* (1982) Predisposition to petty criminality in Swedish adoptees. III. Sex differences and validation of the male typology. *Archives of General Psychiatry*, **39**, 1248–1253.

SILVERTON, L. (1988) Crime and the schizophrenia spectrum – a diathesis-stress model. *Acta Psychiatrica Scandinavica*, **78**, 72–81.

SLATER, E. (1943) The neurotic constitution: a statistical study of two thousand soldiers. *Journal of Neurological Psychiatry*, **6**, 1–16.

—— (1961) The Thirty-fifth Maudsley lecture: 'Hysteria 311'. *Journal of Mental Science*, **107**, 359–381.

—— & SHIELDS, J. (1969) Genetic aspects of anxiety. In *Studies of Anxiety* (ed. M. H. Lader). British Journal of Psychiatry Special Publication No. 3. Ashford: Headley Brothers.

SOLOFF, P. H. & MILLWARD, J. W. (1983) Psychiatric disorders in the families of borderline patients. *Archives of General Psychiatry*, **40**, 37–44.

SPITZER, R. L., ENDICOTT, J. & GIBBON, M. (1979) Crossing the border into borderline personality and borderline schizophrenia. *Archives of General Psychiatry*, **365**, 17–24.

STONE, M. H. (1981) Psychiatrically ill relatives of borderline patients: a family study. *Psychiatric Quarterly*, **58**, 71–83.

TELLEGEN, A., LYKKEN, D. T., BOUCHARD, T. J., *et al* (1988) Personality similarity in twins reared apart and together. *Journal of Personality and Social Psychology*, **54**, 1031–1039.

TORGERSEN, S. (1979) The nature and origin of common phobic fears. *British Journal of Psychiatry*, **134**, 343–351.

—— (1980) The old, obsessive and hysterical personality syndrome. A study of heredity and environmental factors by means of the twin method. *Archives of General Psychiatry*, **37**, 1272–1277.

—— (1983) Genetic factors in anxiety disorders. *Archives of General Psychiatry*, **40**, 1085–1089.

—— (1984) Genetic and nosological aspects of schizotypal and borderline personality disorders. A twin study. *Archives of General Psychiatry*, **41**, 546–554.

TYRER, P. & KASRIEL, J. (1975) Genetical components of physiological tremor. *Journal of Medical Genetics*, **12**, 160–164.

VENABLES, P. H., WILKINS, S., MITCHELL, D. A., *et al* (1990) A Scale for the Measurement of Schizotypy. *Personality and Individual Differences*, **11**, 481–495.

WIMER, R. E. & WIMER, C. C. (1985) Animal behavior genetics: A search for the biological foundations of behavior. *Annual Review of Psychology*, **36**, 171–218.

WITKIN, H. A., MEDNICK, S. A. & SCHULSINGER, F. (1976) Criminality in XYY and XXY men. *Science*, **193**, 547–555.

WORLD HEALTH ORGANIZATION (1978) *Mental Disorders. Glossary and Guide to their Classification in Accordance with the Ninth Revision of the International Classification of Disease* (9th revision) (ICD-9). Geneva: WHO.

YOUNG, J. P. R. & FENTON, G. W. (1971) An investigation of the genetic aspects of the alpha attenuation response. *Psychological Medicine*, **1**, 365–371.

——, —— & LADER, M. H. (1971) The inheritance of neurotic traits: a twin study of the Middlesex Hospital Questionnaire. *British Journal of Psychiatry*, **119**, 393–398.

4 Personality disorder in childhood

SULA WOLFF

Personality disorder is rarely diagnosed in childhood. There are two good reasons for this. First, although ICD-10 (World Health Organization, 1992) defines some personality disorders as emerging early in the course of individual development, and DSM-III-R (American Psychiatric Association, 1987) defines personality disorders, except those associated with organic brain damage, as beginning in childhood or adolescence, many children with symptoms retrospectively associated with the personality disorders may never develop these. This is known to be so in the case of dissocial (ICD-10) or antisocial (DSM-III-R) personality disorder. Of adult sociopaths, 60% have been seriously, and a further 30% moderately, antisocial in childhood, while over 50% of highly antisocial children do not develop later sociopathy (Robins, 1978). The association between childhood symptoms and adult personality for this disorder at least, is strong looking backwards but not looking forwards (Rutter, 1989a).

Second, the personality disorders are by definition enduring, so a diagnosis of personality disorder spells a gloomy prognosis. This could act as a self-fulfilling prophecy in clinical practice, reinforcing the often counter-productive negative evaluations, especially of antisocial children, on the part of parents, teachers and the wider society (Wolff, 1984). Hope as an ingredient of treatment must be preserved when, in the majority of cases, the outcome for an individual child cannot be accurately predicted.

The discontinuity in diagnostic usage between childhood and adult life also has its disadvantages. Spurious differences may, as we shall see, be suggested, for example, between some of the developmental disorders of childhood and those personality disorders grouped together in DSM-III-R as 'Cluster A', namely the paranoid, schizoid, and schizotypal personality disorders of adult life. The practice recommended in DSM-III-R seems on the face of it sensible: personality disorder categories should be applied to children and adolescents in those 'unusual circumstances' in which the maladaptive traits appear to be stable. One exception to this rule, however, is

64

antisocial personality disorder. Here a diagnosis of conduct disorder should be made under the age of 18 and the personality disorder label confined to older people (American Psychiatric Association, 1987). Yet Birley (1990) has argued that such a recommendation, to call the same condition by different names, is an unhelpful sleight of hand. He suggests rather that the task is to discover those variables which determine whether or not a child will 'grow out of' the antisocial proclivity.

A further disadvantage of differing diagnostic conventions in childhood and adult life is to bolster the differences in clinical attitudes and practices between child and adolescent psychiatrists, and general psychiatrists. Child psychiatrists do not usually exclude children from attention because they are 'not psychiatrically ill': very few child psychiatric patients in fact warrant an 'illness' diagnosis. Nor are children who are unlikely to respond to treatment excluded from psychiatric care. In adulthood, in contrast, the most deviant and, to the lay mind, often the most inexplicable forms of behaviour, because not easily remedied, may be excluded from psychiatric concern (Wolff, 1987).

This chapter will review in turn: (a) disorders in which constitutional factors loom so large that some aspects of childhood behaviour are very likely to be permanent (e.g. constitutional hypersensitivity or shyness with similarities to avoidant (DSM–III–R) or anxious (avoidant) (ICD–10) personality disorder in later life), and constitutional hyperactivity often leading to impulsive type of emotionally unstable personality disorder or contributing to dissocial personality disorder (ICD–10) later; (b) those constitutional disorders which, as evidence suggests, are so fixed that a personality disorder diagnosis is appropriate even in childhood: schizoid/schizotypal disorders (Asperger's syndrome); (c) the childhood antecedents, constitutional and environmental, of dissocial (antisocial) personality disorder; and (d) other personality disorders as yet only tentatively identified in childhood.

The chapter will thus focus on the rare conditions which merit a personality disorder diagnosis even in childhood, and on those childhood antecedents which are known to contribute causally to adult personality disorder. An appreciation of childhood causal factors is essential if one is to make sense of repetitive maladaptive behaviour in adult life not due to psychiatric illness. The evidence may now be purely historical and must be sought for in the memories of patients and their relatives and in medical, social service and educational records. One of the aims of this chapter is to highlight the importance of the childhood origins of adult personality disorders, especially antisocial personality.

Two preliminary issues must be raised. First on what basis do we decide that a childhood disorder is equivalent to its counterpart in adult life? Second, what determines the continuity of personality characteristics during childhood?

The basis for diagnostic continuities

Despite the modifying effects of developmental immaturity on some clinical conditions, disorders of childhood can be taken to be equivalent to their adult counterparts only if their essential symptoms and signs correspond. This is clearly so for anorexia nervosa, for depressive disorders, for obsessive–compulsive disorders and for schizophrenia of early onset. It should be the basis too of a childhood diagnosis of personality disorder. Zeitlin (1986) in a study of referred children who also became psychiatric patients as adults, demonstrated the continuity of symptoms rather than diagnoses over time and discussed the confusions that arise when 'masked' diagnoses are inferred in childhood in the absence of those symptoms necessary for the diagnosis in adulthood.

The basis for stability of personality characteristics in childhood

Children are often thought to be endlessly open to change. That this is not so has been demonstrated by studies of the stability of intelligence over time and also, as we shall see, by studies of childhood temperament. Both intelligence and temperament reflect constitutional determinants of behavioural continuities, largely but by no means solely based on genetic factors. But there are other causes of behavioural stability over time: environmental continuities of culture, sub-culture, family circumstances and schooling, which often exert their effects throughout childhood; mutually reinforcing interactions (or transactions) between the child and his/her caregivers, teachers and peers, about which much more will be said later; and inner, experiential continuities based on remembered life events and circumstances and their emotional and cognitive impact. This impact reflects a child's developmental level as well as his/her past experiences and determines in turn the individual child's expectations of others and the interpretations of and responses to subsequent occurrences.

Childhood temperament and personality disorder

Temperament is generally defined as personality traits with at least some continuity over time, which appear in early childhood and have a constitutional, largely genetic, basis (see also Buss & Plomin, 1984; Plomin *et al*, 1988). Temperament is thought of as style rather than content or motivation, the 'how' rather than the 'what' of behaviour and experience. The New York Longitudinal Study (Chess & Thomas, 1984) explored temperament with detailed interview and observational methods from infancy to adult life.

All nine dimensions of temperament defined in this study: activity level, approach/withdrawal to novelty, positive or negative mood, threshold of sensitivity to stimuli, intensity of response, rhythmicity of biological functions, adaptability to novel situations or people, distractibility, and persistence, increase in stability after early childhood. Approach/withdrawal (later subsumed by others in a shyness dimension) accounts for more variance between children than any other trait, and increases in stability during the pre-school years. Activity level, intensity of response, and threshold are all relatively stable over time, and adaptability is the most stable trait of all (Thomas & Chess, 1986; Plomin *et al*, 1988).

A genetic basis for such normal differences in temperament beginning in childhood has been more firmly established than that for schizoid/ schizotypal disorders of childhood, as a result of twin and adoption studies (Goldsmith, 1983). Plomin's early work, although based only on factor analyses of short questionnaires (derived from the nine dimensions of the New York Longitudinal Study (NYLS) (Thomas & Chess, 1986)) completed by parents about their children (Buss & Plomin, 1975), suggested that four aspects of normal temperament are in large measure genetically determined: activity level; emotionality (with loadings on approach/withdrawal, mood, intensity, and threshold); affiliativeness or sociability (with two components: sociability and warmth, and with loadings on approach/withdrawal, adaptability, and threshold); and impulsivity. Impulsivity was excluded in later studies, in part because it is identified only after the second year of life.

In a more recent longitudinal twin study, using detailed interview data from mothers, Torgersen (1989) found that of the nine aspects of temperament defined in the NYLS, activity level and approach/withdrawal to novel stimuli, including people, were among the most genetically influenced variables both at separate ages and developmentally. Mood (predominantly positive or negative) did not have such a genetic basis. Her study provided evidence for both genetic and environmental determinants of temperamental qualities.

Plomin & Daniels (1987) have argued that, among environmental variables, it is those unique to the individual rather than those shared by children within the same family that are important. They reviewed the evidence for the conclusion that most environmental variation affecting psychological development lies in the non-shared (or 'specific') environment of children within the same family. This includes adverse events, birth order and gender, differential interactions with parents and siblings, extrafamilial experiences, but also differential perceptions of life events and circumstances. (Perceptions too may well in part be genetically determined and thus more similar in monozygotic (MZ) than dizygotic (DZ) twins. But they will also be influenced by a person's previous experiences, which will differ for each partner of both MZ and DZ pairs.) Yet, as Henderson (1982) has cogently argued, while it is now clear that temperament and cognition are much less open to cultural influences than was once thought, the idea that common environmental influences are negligible goes against much evidence suggesting that culture can powerfully affect personality and its development. We are now clearer about the sources of individual differences of childhood personality, including intelligence and temperament. We know also that a particular constellation of early childhood temperament, the 'difficult child syndrome': irregularity of biological functions, withdrawal from novel stimuli, poor adaptability, intensity of responses, and negative mood, contribute both to childhood psychiatric disorder and to adult maladjustment (Chess & Thomas, 1984). But the relationship between temperamental deviance in childhood and later personality disorder is not, as yet, well documented. There is evidence that some aspects of temperament contribute, or even form a part of, both child and adult psychiatric disorders: excessive withdrawal and shyness, and overactivity, for example. Both may have other than genetic causes, such as prenatal or perinatal damage in the case of overactivity. But there is no one-to-one relationship between extremes of childhood temperament and personality disorder except possibly in the case of constitutional shyness (probably equivalent to low scores on the approach/withdrawal dimension with an admixture of low adaptability).

Constitutional shyness and avoidant personality disorder

Children's initial responsiveness to novel events, especially to unfamiliar people, is one of the qualities of behaviour whose stability over time has been well documented. Of 2- and 3-year old children, 10–15% regularly become quiet, vigilant and subdued in such a context; and this is independent of social class and IQ (Kagan *et al*, 1988). Kagan and his colleagues followed up cohorts of children who in their second year were observed to be either consistently shy or consistently sociable in the presence of unfamiliar people, objects, and rooms. At the age of seven, most of the children who had earlier been shy and inhibited were still quiet and socially avoidant with unfamiliar children and adults, while those who had been spontaneous were now talkative and interactive. Unusual fears and greater autonomic reactivity characterised the shy children. Yet environmental factors also contributed to such a development: two-thirds of the sociable children had been first born, without interfering siblings in their earliest years; while two-thirds of the shy children had been later born. In a subsequent study by the same investigators (Kagan *et al*, 1989) only children at the extremes of either restraint and inhibition, or spontaneity and disinhibition, maintained these temperamental characteristics over time. Moreover, the preservation of uninhibited behaviour was stronger than that of inhibition, and stronger for boys than for girls. Only at the extreme of inhibition was there significantly higher cardiac acceleration in response to cognitive stress. The authors emphasise the importance of studying extremes of behavioural variations in addition to the correlates of continuous dimensions.

In a classic adoption design study, Daniels & Plomin (1985) correlated infant shyness with parents' ratings on an adult social temperament scale. In non-adoptive families infant shyness correlated with mothers' self-reports of shyness, introversion, and low sociability. In adoptive families the correlations were less, and the correlations between the self-assessments of biological mothers and their adopted-away children, while still significant, were even fewer than those between these children and their adoptive parents. The authors speculate that shy and socially anxious mothers may expose both themselves and their offspring less often to novel situations and that this would then reinforce the constitutional tendency of their children to social shyness.

One of the difficulties in this area is the variety of terms and definitions used for temperamental traits, so that one can never be sure how comparable the results of different investigations really are.

Despite this, a long-term study of the adult outcome of shy children is of great interest. Archival behavioural data accumulated in the Berkeley longitudinal study of children's problem behaviour, initiated now over 60 years ago, was the starting point (Capsi & Elder, 1988). Boys rated shy and reserved at 8 to 10 years were found at 40 years to have married, become fathers, and established careers later and to have less good occupational achievements, with more work and marital instability than subjects not so rated in early life. It is not possible now to be sure that among these 'shy' boys there were not also some with schizoid traits, which might have confounded the outcome picture. Shy girls in this study, in contrast, more often followed a conventional pattern of marriage and home making. Fewer of them, than of girls not rated shy, were working, but the occupational status of their partners was higher. Shyness in early childhood based on mothers' reports, had correlated with teachers' assessments at 10 and 12 years, and with an index of adult shyness at 30.

The authors discuss what they call the 'cumulative continuity' of personality traits, whereby an individual's disposition causes him/her to select or construct environments which will in turn reinforce and sustain such dispositions. They describe individual development as a sequence of reciprocal dynamic transactions between the person and the environment, through both behavioural and cognitive mechanisms. They contrast their findings for shy children grown-up with those for children who had been rated earlier as ill tempered and explosive. (This earlier study will be summarised when we discuss the antecedents of dissocial disorders.)

Both ICD–10 and DSM–III–R define the childhood psychiatric disorders based on extreme shyness and withdrawal from novelty rather differently from the adult personality disorders that might be an expected later outcome. In ICD–10, social sensitivity disorder of childhood is defined as persistent, unusual and socially impairing fear or avoidance of strangers (adults or peers) beginning before the age of six, not part of a more generalised emotional disorder, and occurring in children with normal attachments to parents and other familiar people. Anxious (avoidant) personality disorder in this classification is defined rather differently, in terms of tension, anxiety and insecurity (not specifically in novel settings or with strangers) and a need for social acceptance. In DSM–III–R, avoidant disorder of childhood or adolescence is also defined in terms of incapacitating anxiety evoked by, and social avoidance of, strangers, as well as a wish for acceptance by, and for close relationships with, familiar people, all beginning after 2½ years of age. Avoidant personality disorder is defined rather similarly to ICD–10 in terms of oversensitivity to possible rejection, social withdrawal, low self-esteem, and a wish for affection and acceptance. In DSM–III–R this diagnosis can be applied to children if their avoidant disorder is pervasive and persistent.

Clinicians certainly, although rarely, see children with extreme constitutional shyness and social withdrawal, often associated with oversensitivity and poor adaptability to novel situations and people, whose social life outside the family is grossly impaired by these traits of temperament. Such children are basically sociable and, in contrast to schizoid children, long to be able to mix better with other children. Similar traits are often reported for other members of the family. How many of such children will later come to resemble their shy and socially withdrawn relatives, how many may have other psychiatric disorders in adult life, and whether girls and boys are affected similarly, is not known. Nor do we know the childhood antecedents, in terms of temperament and life experiences, of those adults who merit a diagnosis of avoidant personality disorder. The differential diagnosis of constitutional shyness in childhood, especially from depressive illness and autistic conditions, has recently been discussed by Hall & Hill (1991).

Constitutional overactivity, the hyperkinetic disorders and associated antisocial conduct

Much more familiar to the clinician than avoidant disorders are the hyperkinetic disorders of childhood. Activity level is, as we have seen, one of the more stable qualities of temperament. This constitutional proclivity certainly contributes to, but is not the only factor in, the genesis of the clinical syndromes of childhood hyperkinesis.

Taylor *et al* (1991), in an epidemiological study of 7–8 year old boys, found 1.7% with severe, pervasive overactivity and attention deficit, often associated with conduct disorders. These workers compared pure hyperkinetic, mixed hyperkinetic/conduct-disordered, pure conduct-disordered, and normal boys, and found that both types of symptoms were more severe in the mixed group. This group of children was also more impaired in concentration and delayed in reading, and the onset of conduct disorders was earlier than in the purely conduct-disordered group. Neurodevelopmental disorders were more commonly (but not invariably) present in the hyperactive children, with lower IQ, clumsiness, language delay (in almost one half) and a history of perinatal risk factors (neonatal delay in establishing respiration, seizures and 'jitteriness'). This was so especially in the mixed hyperkinetic/conduct-disordered group.

Adverse family relationships, with parental hostility expressed towards the child, poor parental skills in coping with the child's problem behaviour, inconsistency between parents, and maternal depressive symptoms, were greater in all three disturbed groups, but again especially in the children with mixed hyperkinetic/conduct disorders. Marital discord, in contrast, was if anything greater in the families of purely conduct-disordered children and so was a family history of delinquency. Because this was essentially a cross-sectional study, little can be said about the direction of causal influences. It seems most likely that the more seriously affected hyperkinetic children are also those with neurodevelopmental impairments and specific delays of eductional functioning; and that their parents' adverse child rearing behaviour is, at least in part, secondary to the children's difficulties. The adverse home environment then in turn has the effect of reinforcing the children's disruptive behaviour and educational failure, as well as engendering and reinforcing antisocial conduct, with the result that what might have been a transient disturbance persists. A review of the children's developmental records showed hyperactivity to precede conduct disorders in the mixed group. Richman *et al* (1982) also found that a complaint of overactivity at three years strongly predicts antisocial behaviour at eight. Conduct disorders are in many cases likely to be secondary to the effects, educational and familial, of the hyperkinetic disorder.

A recent twin study (Goodman & Stevenson, 1989*a*, *b*) showed pervasive hyperactivity to be more common in boys, and confirmed the association with inattention, lower IQ, specific learning difficulties, and antisocial conduct. About half the variance of activity and inattentiveness in a broader group of pervasively hyperactive children was accounted for by genetic factors. This is consonant with the view that deviance on the temperamental dimensions of activity, and perhaps distractability and persistence too, is likely to contribute also to the clinically more important syndrome of pervasive hyperkinesis. Taylor *et al* (1991) did not examine impulsivity, because of difficulties of definition. Hyperkinetic children were, however, found to be quicker and less accurate on problem-solving tasks.

There is evidence for a continuity between childhood hyperkinesis and adult sociopathy, but only with associated conduct disorder as a mediating factor. Moreover, children with both hyperkinesis and conduct disorder have a worse outcome than conduct-disordered children without hyperkinesis.

The evidence is as yet not totally conclusive because of differences in the definitions of childhood hyperkinesis used and the attrition of subjects, likely to be the most disturbed, at follow-up in some studies. Weiss *et al* (1979) found that a quarter of hyperkinetic children, especially boys, and especially if also aggressive and exposed to socio-economic disadvantage or family strife, were delinquent at adolescence, often with continuing impulsivity, disorganised behaviour and educational failure. In these children, hyperactivity decreased with age, but aggressiveness did not. In early adult life (Weiss *et al*, 1985), many had developed an antisocial personality disorder.

Mannuzza *et al* (1989) using the DSM–III concept of attention deficit disorder with hyperkinesis (ADDH), less severe and more common than ICD–10 hyperkinetic disorders of childhood, compared the outcome at 16–23 years of 103 boys diagnosed as having ADDH at 6–12 years with that of 100 normal controls. Criminality in adult life was much commoner in the clinic group with 39% compared with 20% having been arrested and 9% compared with 1% incarcerated. The presence of a clinical diagnosis of antisocial personality disorder completely accounted for the differences, while continuing attention and hyperactivity problems were not themselves associated with arrest. In this study, almost half the children with ADDH had developed conduct disorders by 18 years, and of these over half had substance abuse disorders.

In summary, the clinical syndrome of severe and pervasive childhood hyperkinesis, to which temperamental overactivity may well contribute, is largely brought about by brain dysfunction (Taylor *et al*, 1991). Low intelligence and developmental learning difficulties are often associated. Conduct disorder is a very common development in early or middle childhood, especially when, either in response to the child's difficulties or for other reasons, there is an adverse family environment. When conduct disorder, especially aggressive behaviour, supervenes, the risk of a dissocial personality development is high.

Schizoid/schizotypal personality disorders of childhood (Asperger's syndrome)

In 1944 the paediatrician, Hans Asperger, not then aware of Kanner's (1943) first description of early infantile autism, reported clinical details of four patients and summarised 200 other cases of what he called autistic psychopathy of childhood which he thought was an enduring personality disorder. Affected children had life-long personality features among which the most salient were: solitariness; abnormalities of gaze, expression, and gesture limiting emotional contact with others; insensitivity to social cues; lack of feeling for other people, sometimes amounting to callousness; oversensitivity as well as insensitivity; 'autistic intelligence', inventive rather than imitative; with specific interests in restricted fields such as chemistry, poisons, mathematics or art which could lead to creative achievements. Educational delays of all kinds were common and pressure to conform could lead to outbursts of rage or tears. Social adaptation often improved with age and the work adjustment of gifted autistic psychopaths was good, but their basic personality features persisted and intimate relationships remained impaired. Sexual interests were often limited even in adult life, and sometimes deviant. The full syndrome in childhood was confined to boys. Girls with a partial syndrome frequently had evidence of brain damage. Yet among adult biological relatives of affected children, the full syndrome was seen in women too.

Asperger considered but dismissed the possibility that the condition was pre-schizophrenic. Apparently, only two of 400 such children he saw later developed this illness (Weber, 1985). In every case, however, one or more biological relatives were affected with the full or partial syndrome. In later years Asperger distinguished between autistic psychopathy of childhood and Kanner's early infantile autism and described the children, who differed from any he had seen before, as "highly intelligent . . . with interesting peculiarities, yet . . . with behaviour so difficult that they were almost impossible to keep in family or school . . . . They achieve the highest university professorships or become artists – yet their quirks and peculiarities . . . remain with them for life" (Asperger, 1979).

Two developments in diagnostic practice have occurred since then. Lorna Wing (1981) reported on 34 seriously impaired children and adults with the features Asperger had described, and Digby Tantam (1986, 1988*a*, *b*) studied 60 adult psychiatric patients with "life-long social isolation and conspicuous eccentricity". Of these only two had ever married and only one had been in continuous employment since leaving school. Many of these patients had had the symptoms of early infantile autism beginning in later childhood. Wing described the characteristics of her subjects as a failure in two-way social interaction; difficulty in verbal and non-verbal communication; and impaired imagination, and she coined the diagnostic label 'Asperger's syndrome'. This she held to be equivalent to high-level autism (i.e. with normal IQ and no gross early language delays). The concept of an 'autistic spectrum' (Gillberg, 1989; Gillberg & Gillberg, 1989) derives from this work. Wing's criteria were later used by Gillberg (1990) to clarify the similarities and differences between Asperger's syndrome and infantile autism.

The second development arose from the identification of a group of children referred to a psychiatric clinic who described themselves or were described by others as 'loners'. They had the features of schizoid personality disorder as recorded in the older psychiatric literature (perhaps not so familiar to Asperger, the paediatrician). While much less impaired than Wing's and Tantam's cases, they too resembled the children Asperger had described. They were predominantly boys (sex ratio 4:1) and made up about 4% of new clinic referrals. They were of slightly above average IQ, and came from an upwardly skewed social class background. Referral took place during the school years and the main difficulty was often an apparently inexplicable failure to conform to the ordinary demands of school life. Aggressive outbursts and pathological lying sometimes occurred. With few exceptions these children were regarded as 'awkward' rather than handicapped. Their clinical features were (a) solitariness, especially in the boys; (b) impaired empathy and emotional detachment; (c) rigidity of mental set including the single-minded pursuit of special interests; (d) increased sensitivity at times with paranoid ideation; and (e) unusual or odd styles of communication including overcommunicativeness, especially in the girls. Over half the children were outgoing but a few were withdrawn and uncommunicative, and very occasionally they presented with elective mutism.

A predictive validation study (Chick *et al*, 1979; Wolff & Chick, 1980) showed the syndrome in boys to be very stable over time. Of 'schizoid' children grown up, 90% could be distinguished from a matched group of other referred children in adult life by an interviewer blind to the original diagnoses, and the five postulated core features also differentiated significantly between the two groups. At a mean age of 22 years, two of 22 schizoid subjects had developed a schizophrenic illness. Schizoidness was not related to Eysenck's neuroticism or introversion (Chick *et al*, 1979).

A more recent study showed that, when adult, three quarters of 'schizoid' boys fulfilled DSM–III diagnostic criteria for schizotypal personality disorder (American Psychiatric Association, 1980) on a well validated schedule to measure these (Wolff *et al*, 1991). At a mean age of 27 years, many 'schizoid' subjects had good work achievements and many had married, but their overall work adjustment, their heterosexual adjustment, and their psychiatric status were worse than those of other referred children grown up.

A retrospective case note analysis of 32 'schizoid' children and 32 other referred children showed that three of the 'schizoids' had had some symptoms of autism although they were never given this diagnosis; three had had elective mutism; but most of them had presented with the features of 'schizoid' personality described above, associated with educational difficulties or with the kind of conduct or mixed conduct and emotional disorders usually regarded as secondary to adverse life experiences. Multiple or serious specific developmental delays, usually involving language-related skills, occurred in 15 of the 32 'schizoid' boys, but in only 4 of 32 controls (Wolff, 1991a). Szatmari *et al* (1990) had also found early developmental delays in children given a diagnosis of Asperger's syndrome.

The 'schizoid' children were very like the children described as schizotypal by Nagy & Szatmari (1986). They also shared some of the clinical features reported for the 'high risk' offspring of schizophrenic mothers and for children subsequently known to have developed schizophrenia (Wolff, 1991a).

Yet they certainly resembled Asperger's cases and overlapped with Wing's, Tantam's and Gillberg's patients. Although all descriptions of these disorders report a strong familial incidence, definitive genetic studies are now needed. These should also help to clarify whether such a schizoid/schizotypal/Asperger picture represents a unitary syndrome or several related syndromes, and whether it is part of an autistic or a schizophrenic spectrum or both. Tentative evidence to support the former comes from a comparative study of parents of well functioning autistic children and of children with other handicaps. More parents of the autistic group had 'schizoid' features and they were also more 'intellectual' (Wolff *et al*, 1988; Narayan *et al*, 1990). Social handicaps in addition to cognitive deficits have been found in the biological relatives of autistic children (Bolton & Rutter, 1990) and in children with severe specific developmental language delays (see Bishop, 1989).

Autism and schizophrenia do not overlap in families, and very few autistic children later develop schizophrenia. Yet the possibility remains that, at least in some cases of each condition, a genetic predisposition to schizoid/schizotypal disorder may be a necessary cause, in addition to other genetic and/or non-genetic necessary factors different for the two conditions.

Further work on the diagnosis of these disorders is not only of theoretical interest but of clinical importance. Children with severe forms of Asperger's syndrome will need the same services as well functioning autistic children. The more intelligent and less obviously handicapped schizoid/schizotypal children, however, require above all to be identified as constitutionally impaired. Their special make-up must be understood. They may also need special arrangements made, particularly at school, in the knowledge that many of them in later life, when pressures for conformity are less than during the school years, will be able to find their social niche, and a few may be able to develop their rather exceptional gifts.

The diagnostic status of these conditions: whether pervasive developmental disorders of childhood or personality disorders beginning in childhood, is not of primary clinical importance. Moreover, the concept of pervasive developmental disorders remains ambiguous (World Health Organization, 1992) because, unlike the specific developmental disorders which may be associated, pervasive developmental disorders do not tend to improve with age relative to developmental expectations. What is important is not to call the same conditions by different names because they are identified in childhood rather than in adult life. Meanwhile, my own preference is to use personality disorder labels for those affected children whose social functioning, while deviant, does not amount to a gross handicap; and to group both schizotypal and schizoid disorders with the personality disorders, as in DSM–III–R, rather than to group the former with the schizophrenias, as in ICD–10. Schizotypal personality disorder is common; schizophrenia is rare; and their association in families and individuals, while significantly higher than expected, is only moderate (Torgersen, 1984).

The conditions described so far are thought to be primarily genetic, with little evidence that life events and circumstances significantly affect their outcome.

The antecedents of dissocial (antisocial) personality disorder

The conduct disorders of childhood are very common (Rutter *et al*, 1975), affecting between 4% and 10% of the population in middle childhood. They are also, like the antisocial personality disorders of adult life, among the most worrying psychiatric disabilities. They bring misery to affected individuals, their families and other people; they inevitably evoke negative responses; their prognosis is not good (Robins, 1966, 1978); and effective intervention is difficult.

Severe and pervasive hyperkinesis in boys, although relatively rare, is often followed by childhood conduct problems and later dissocial personality disorder. Here, other factors associated with the persistence of childhood conduct disorder over time, and likely to contribute to the development of later personality disorder, specifically dissocial personality, will be discussed.

Robins (1991) has recently clarified developments in the classification of conduct disorders and antisocial personality in ICD-10, DSM-III and DSM-III-R. Both systems have moved away from the view that disorders brought about by constitutional factors together with deficiencies of parenting, can be distinguished from those reflecting subcultural norms. In fact, the latter are no longer recognised, because it is thought that, if conduct problems reflect subcultural norms and violate only the standards of a wider culture, they should not be considered as psychiatric disorders. Both systems now acknowledge the fact that hyperkinesis (and/or attention deficit) and conduct disorder are frequently associated, and both recognise that conduct disorder in childhood often, but by no means invariably, progresses to dissocial (antisocial) personality disorder. Robins views childhood conduct disorder as a middle phase of chronic psychiatric disorder, typically beginning in early life and continuing into adulthood, but one which can abort at any time.

The manifestations tend to be temper tantrums, arguments and stubbornness in the preschool years, oppositional behaviour somewhat later, stealing and firesetting at 8–10 years, and truancy, vandalism and substance abuse in the early teens. Aggressive, uncontrolled behaviour, perhaps because it tends to start very early in life and is, as we shall see, for a variety of reasons, a rather stable form of behaviour, predicts antisocial conduct at adolescence much more strongly than any other personal or environmental variables. Children, most often girls, whose antisocial conduct begins for the first time at adolescence, did not have the low IQ, school problems and attention deficit so common among other delinquents, and their prognosis was better. We shall see later that early physical maturity may be a factor in evoking antisocial conduct at this age.

In Robins' epidemiological studies of adults (1991), antisocial personality was assessed, and a detailed enquiry about childhood symptoms of DSM–III antisocial personality, almost equivalent to ICD–10 criteria for conduct disorders, was made. In this retrospective study, the total number of conduct disorder symptoms was the best predictor of adult antisocial personality disorder, with age of onset the second best. A quarter of children with five to seven symptoms under the age of six had an antisocial personality development, compared with only 10% if the onset was after 12. With eight or more symptoms beginning under six (a rare occurrence), over 70% developed antisocial personality disorder, and almost 50% if the onset of such multiple symptoms was after six years of age. Yet only a quarter of children with three or fewer conduct disorder symptoms before the age of 15 develop antisocial personality disorder later.

Childhood aggression is stable and predicts later antisocial conduct

In his 20-year follow-up study of Swedish children aged 10, 13 and 15 years, Magnusson (1988) traces the interactive antecedents of adult criminality, investigating specifically hyperactive and aggressive childhood behaviours and low adrenalin excretion at 13. All three are significantly related to adult criminality in boys. Almost half the boys rated as extremely aggressive at 13 had recorded crimes (half of these serious) at 18–26 years. But, when hyperactivity at 13 was present also, the proportion of adult criminals was even higher. Overactivity without aggression predicted criminality more strongly than aggression without overactivity. Both types of behaviour at 13 were correlated with low adrenalin excretion, but the small group of overactive children was responsible for the association between aggressive conduct disorder and low adrenalin excretion. Magnusson suggests that low adrenalin excretion is reflected by low arousal and the need for 'monotony avoidance', and that affected children are fearless, with low reactivity to external stimuli and inefficient appraisal of their environment. (This is in complete contrast to the features of constitutionally shy children outlined above.)

Aggression is one of the most stable personality characteristics, resembling IQ in its predictability over time, especially in boys (Olweus, 1979, 1980; Cummings *et al*, 1989). Olweus identified the following variables as promoting aggressivity: high temperamental scores on activity level and intensity; mothers' early expectations of their sons' behaviour; mothers' tolerance of aggression; and the use by parents of 'power-assertive' methods of child rearing.

Huesmann *et al* (1984) followed-up over 600 children from 8 to 30 years of age. Those high on aggressiveness at 8 (on a peer-nomination index) remained aggressive at 30. In addition, early aggressiveness predicted serious antisocial behaviour (including criminality), spouse abuse and self-reported physical aggression in adult life. The stability of aggressiveness at comparable ages across generations in the same family (measured in terms of parental punitiveness, and aggressiveness of the subjects and their children) was even more stable than within the individual. Stability over time increased with age and was greater for men than women. Aggression at 30 varied with birth factors, socio-economic status, IQ, and punitiveness of upbringing, but was most highly associated with aggressiveness at the age of eight.

These findings are supported by another longitudinal study of aggressive behaviour, based on the early Berkeley study (Capsi *et al*, 1987). Boys rated at 8–10 years as having serious temper tantrums and lower educational achievements, and those with poor educational attainments tended to have a downward and unstable occupational path, especially if they had come from middle class families. More men with an early history of temper tantrums had divorced and, if they also had a poor work history, they tended to be more bad tempered as fathers. Women with severe temper tantrums in childhood married men of lower occupational status, and were more likely to divorce and to become ill-tempered mothers than other women.

Aggression is thus not only stable from childhood to adult life and across the generations, but is also highly predictive of subsequent antisocial and delinquent conduct. Yet, as Capsi & Elder (1988) make clear, there are, of course, always exceptions: "... some people refuse to be ensnared in social traps", and particular turning points occur in their experience which disconfirm previous relational styles and open up new life paths.

Some constitutional determinants of childhood aggression

Sex

Males are more aggressive than females in many species from infancy onwards. Manning *et al* (1977), for example, found three-year old boys to display more rough-and-tumble play aggression than girls. While cultural expectations of differential behaviour, and child-rearing methods and circumstances certainly play a large part, from early infancy onwards, in transmitting the sex role behaviours of a culture to its children, constitutional factors also contribute to this process (see also Wolff, 1989). Boys are more muscular, more active, more vigorous and more impulsive; girls are more sensitive. Hormonal factors may in part be responsible. It is known that female animals can be made more aggressive by injecting their mothers with male hormones in pregnancy; and pre-birth male sex hormone levels have been found to correlate with gender-role behaviour in children, that is, with the styles of play and imitative behaviour which distinguish between boys and girls (Meyer-Bahlburg *et al*, 1986).

Pre-school boys in an unstructured playgroup setting learn to become even more aggressive through social interactions with other boys (Patterson *et al*, 1967). Only boys low on sociability and activity escape such a development, and we shall see that shyness and low sociability can also protect boys against those environmental influences known to promote a delinquent way of life (Farrington *et al*, 1988).

Boys are more vulnerable than girls to the environmental hazards associated with the development of antisocial conduct, such as marital discord and parental hostility, often associated with parental psychiatric illness or family disruption (Cardoret & Cain, 1980; Quinton & Rutter, 1988). The stability of aggression over time is also, as we have seen, greater for boys than for girls (Huesmann *et al*, 1984); and the adult sequelae of childhood aggression are different and less severe for girls (Capsi *et al*, 1987).

The same antecedents can lead to different outcomes in girls and boys. Guze (1976), in an early series of follow-up and family studies of offenders, found hysteria (Briquet's syndrome) and sociopathy to cluster in the same families, and women with hysteria to have shown the same antisocial childhood behaviour patterns and the same adverse family circumstances as antisocial men. He suggests that the same causal factors may give rise to different clinical pictures in men and women: antisocial personality in the former; 'hysteria' in the latter, and that both constitutional, family and cultural factors contribute to these different manifestations in the two sexes. Robins (1966) too, in her long-term follow-up of child guidance clinic attenders, found that, in contrast to antisocial boys, 26% of antisocial girls had a diagnosis of hysteria in adult life; and in a later study (Robins, 1986) she found conduct disorders in girls to lead to a variety of adult social and emotional disorders rather than predominantly to delinquency as in boys. And Zeitlin (1983), in his study of subjects attending both child and adult psychiatric clinics, found conduct-disordered and delinquent girls more often than boys to have been diagnosed as depressed and less often as personality disordered in adult life.

Temperament

It will be clear from what has been said that high levels of activity, sociability, and impulsiveness contribute to the development of aggressive behaviour and to some forms of delinquent conduct. Shyness and withdrawal as well as low activity levels can be protective. It has been suggested that the absence of temperamental sex differences in the NYLS was because appropriate composite measures were not used (Berger, 1985). Another temperamental quality associated with aggressive and later antisocial behaviour may be the need for thrills and risk taking with fearlessness and inefficient appraisal of the environment, associated with low arousal (Magnusson, 1988).

Possible constitutional obstacles to the development of an effective conscience

The effects of conscience on the inhibition of aggressive and other antisocial impulses has as yet been quite inadequately explored. Kagan (1981) demonstrated the development of a sense of right and wrong as well as self-awareness of competence in the second year of life, and Hoffman (1987) has stressed the importance of a capacity for empathy for the distress of others, as a basis for prosocial behaviour. Accurate empathy also begins to develop in the second year. Children with schizoid/Asperger disorders lack empathic qualities, and some later develop aggressive antisocial behaviour (Wolff & Cull, 1986). The emergence of dissocial personality disorder in such children, rare as they are, may well have a rather different basis from that in the more common conduct-disordered children, and their later functioning too is likely to be different (Wolff, 1991*b*).

Experiential antecedents of chronic aggressive and antisocial conduct

Disruption and distortion of early attachments

Early parent loss and institutional care feature prominently in the past histories of antisocial people, and the short term sequelae of distorted early mother–child interactions, often associated with maternal depression, have been well documented (see Wolff, 1989). Disruption of parent–child relationships certainly fosters aggression in children, particularly in the setting of parental discord; and after divorce, boys especially are at increased risk of conduct disorders, usually short lived. But the later effects both of disrupted and distorted early ties are so confounded by other associated or consequential adversities, such as institutional care and continuing exposure to family disharmony, that any specific contributions of abnormal early bonding or abnormal early socialisation to the persistence of later antisocial conduct are not readily traced.

Coercive child rearing

What is clear is that to be brought up in a family in which there is chronic discord between the parents for whatever reason and hostility between parents and the child, fosters conduct disorder and delinquency especially in boys (Wolkind & Rutter, 1985). Olweus (1979, 1980), as we saw, identified child-rearing methods as well as aspects of temperament as associated with the persistence over time of aggressive behaviours.

A major contribution both to the understanding of the family processes involved in the genesis of childhood aggression and delinquency, and of possible treatment interventions has come from the work of Patterson (1982, 1986). He starts with the premises that children do not tend to outgrow aggressive behaviour, that antisocial conduct is correlated with many other problems such as academic failure, peer rejection and low self-esteem, and that conduct-disordered children have parents who lack family management skills. These consist of a failure to monitor their children's behaviour adequately and, even more important, of a coercive approach to child training. This evokes counter-aggression from the child so that a mutually reinforcing coercive process is set up between parents and children with ever increasing levels of violence: relatively trivial non-compliance on the part of the child evokes excessive punitiveness from the parents; this puts a temporary stop to the child's irritating behaviour, rewarding the parents for their inappropriate intervention; inevitably the child misbehaves again, once more provoking parental punishment. A second possible sequence is for the parents to intrude aggressively on the child's activities, evoking counter-aggression from the child, followed by parental withdrawal which then reinforces the child's aggression. A regular sequence is seen in children from such families: from non-compliance to physical violence. Parental behaviour is characterised by threats not carried through, by nagging, scolding, and periodic physical attacks on the child.

Children with a 'difficult temperament' are most at risk of evoking such coercive responses. Parents most at risk of responding coercively are the socio-economically deprived, especially when depressed, under external stress, or under the influence of alcohol or drugs. Faulty parenting techniques tend to be transmitted from one generation to the next (Patterson & Dishion (1988) argue for a mediation rather than a genetic model to account for this), and they interfere with enjoyable parent–child interactions and with the expression of affection which is in fact often felt. The aggressive children from such families arrive at school with inadequate social skills and are rejected by other children. They tend to fail academically and their self-esteem is poor. Patterson believes that non-aggressive children who steal manifest a different form of non-compliance to their parents. They often have parents who are themselves delinquent and, while less openly hostile than the parents of aggressive children, they are insufficiently attached to their offspring.

Farrington *et al* (1988) also showed that among the non-behavioural predictors of persisting delinquency are: poor intellectual abilities, having criminal parents, and coming from a large and economically deprived family, with parents who have poor child-rearing skills.

Educational failure

Educational retardation is highly associated with childhood conduct disorder, and both are much more common in boys. On the Isle of Wight, both disorders and reading retardation occurred in about 4% of children, but one-third of conduct-disordered boys were retarded in reading and fully one-third of reading-retarded boys were conduct disordered (Rutter *et al*, 1970). We saw also that educational retardation and other developmental delays are common in hyperkinetic children and that these too are frequently also conduct disordered.

There is evidence, however, that educational failure *per se* does not lead to later dissocial behaviour, only when associated with childhood conduct disorder (Maughan, personal communication).

Poor peer relationships and stigma

Rutter (1989*b*) suggests that poor peer relationships in childhood, as yet not widely studied, contribute to the persistence of antisocial conduct. There is also evidence that labelling of antisocial behaviour by others, especially at adolescence, can stigmatise affected children, alter their self-image in conformity with the label, and cause what might have been a transient disorder to persist. West & Farrington (1973) found adolescent delinquents with convictions to be significantly more likely to re-offend than youngsters with equal numbers of self-reported offences who had not been convicted.

The aggressive child's frame of mind

Although it is increasingly accepted that "cognitive, introspective psychology . . . can no longer be ignored experimentally, or written off as 'a science of epiphenomena' " (Sperry, 1982), little work has been done on how aggressive children view the world. An exception is a study by Dodge (1980) taking social attribution theory as a starting point. Boys aged 6 to 10 years, rated aggressive both by peers and teachers, were compared with non-aggressive boys in their responses to an experimental experience of being frustrated by an unseen peer. All children correctly interpreted and responded to frustrating peers if they were obviously heard to be hostile or benign in intent. But if the intent conveyed was ambiguous, aggressive boys attributed hostile (and non-aggressive boys benign) intent to the frustrating peer, and their behaviour and comments in the test situation reflected this. When subsequently questioned about how they and other children were likely to think and act under similar circumstances, aggressive children attributed hostile intentions to peers 50% more often than non-aggressive children, predicted that the target of frustration would react aggressively, and said they would not trust the frustrating child in future, and would themselves retaliate aggressively. The authors conclude that aggressive boys, when frustrated, tend to infer hostile intent and react with defensive aggression which then increases their own reputation of being aggressive. They are "caught up in a spiralling cycle of reputation and behaviour".

Early puberty in girls

Magnusson (1988) found that girls who reached puberty early often, although not invariably, associated with older friends. When this happened, but not otherwise, such girls had higher rates of norm-breaking behaviour at adolescence, such as smoking, alcohol use, early dating, and staying out late, than later maturers. They tended to leave school earlier and had fewer educational qualifications than other girls. At 26 years, they had had more children, and slightly more recorded crime, but the stability of their heterosexual relationships was not impaired. While early puberty was clearly not a major hazard it did, when it led to mixing with older friends, have some disadvantageous long-term effects.

Early substance abuse

Robins (1988, unpublished lecture) has shown that one of the factors making for persistence of antisocial conduct in young adolescents is alcohol abuse. Her recommendation is "not now, but later".

Factors protecting against an antisocial development

Farrington examined a series of boys from highly criminogenic backgrounds, who did *not* later become delinquent (Farrington *et al*, 1988). Such boys tended to have non-delinquent parents, well adjusted siblings, and mothers who thought well of them. They spent less leisure time with their fathers than unsuccessful boys from similarly criminogenic backgrounds. Their personal characteristics were that between eight and ten years they were rated as more 'neurotic', better behaved, less daring, and with no or fewer friends than boys later judged to be unsuccessful. Shyness was thought to act as a protective factor against delinquency for non-aggressive boys but as an aggravating factor if the boys had been aggressive. Yet even those shy boys who did not become chronically delinquent often had other difficulties. They tended to be anxious, nervous, timid, inhibited, and apathetic.

Werner & Smith (1982) stressed the protective effects of a harmonious family environment for vulnerable children. Birth hazards which might otherwise result in poor later educational achievements and maladjustment, had far fewer ill effects when the family was stable and the mother had positive regard for the baby. The work on hyperkinetic children also showed those with an adverse family environment to be more at risk of associated conduct disorder.

D

The skills of teachers and specific aspects of the school environment can both foster educational achievements and, probably as a consequence of an improved self-image, protect children against later delinquency, at the pre-school stage in the case of disadvantaged children, and in the later school years (for a summary see Wolff, 1989).

Another factor now known to protect children from the adversity of family discord, although less specifically against delinquency, is having a good relationship with an adult outside the immediate family circle (Jenkins & Smith, 1990).

Sociopathy is not all of a kind

Adult dissocial personality disorders are often discussed as if they were a single syndrome. Despite the graphic case descriptions of 'sociopaths' in Cleckley's *The Mask of Sanity* (1976), his clinical case histories do not enable one to tease out the likely interacting constitutional and environmental causes. He stresses the absence of regularly identifiable adverse parenting and the superficial charm and normality of his subjects, suggesting one must look behind the 'mask' to discern these people's real difficulties in leading a socially acceptable life. Yet what these difficulties are is not made clear. Some of the cases reported may well have had schizoid personality traits and there is evidence that some sociopathic people have features of schizoid personality/Asperger's syndrome (see Wolff & Cull, 1986). Hare and Schalling both discuss 'psychopathy' as if it were either unitary or could be subdivided on the basis of adult behavioural characteristics alone (Schalling, 1978; Hare & Cox, 1978). Hopefully, increasing knowledge about the childhood influences which can result in persistent dissocial conduct can lead to a more rational classification of the dissocial personality disorders in adult life, and to a recognition of the overlap there undoubtedly is between dissocial and impulsive, and dissocial and schizoid personality disorders.

Which personality disorders should be diagnosed in children?

ICD-10 makes no provisions for the diagnosis of personality disorders in childhood, schizoid disorders of childhood being grouped with the pervasive developmental disorders. In DSM-III-R only two personality disorders are specifically applicable to children, if their disturbance is pervasive, persistent and unlikely to be limited to a developmental stage: avoidant personality disorder (corresponding to childhood avoidant disorder), already discussed, and borderline personality disorder (corresponding to childhood identity disorder), for which there is no counterpart in ICD-10. Despite a vast literature on borderline personality in adult life, the validity of this diagnostic category must remain in doubt (Pope *et al*, 1983; Tarnopolsky & Berelowitz, 1987). Attempts to differentiate borderline from schizoid/schizotypal disorders in childhood are also not persuasive (Petti & Vela, 1990). The dissociative condition of multiple personality disorder, which certainly, although rarely, occurs in children, is not, despite its name, part of the personality disorder category (either in DSM–III–R or ICD–10). Nor are the abnormalities of gender identity, sexual preference, or the impulse disorders of pathological stealing and firesetting, which also begin in childhood. Much less is known about their course from childhood to adult life than about the dissocial disorders, and their origins as well as their often extraordinary fixity remain largely unexplained.

Conclusions

Only two types of personality disorder are clearly identifiable in childhood: schizoid/schizotypal disorders and sensitivity (avoidant) disorders. However, the conduct disorders of childhood frequently, although by no means always, lead to a later dissocial personality development. The multiple, interacting hazards, among them temperamental deviance, early aggressivity, neurodevelopmental abnormalities, hyperkinesis, educational failure, and family adversities, including aggressive/coercive child rearing, have been discussed. It will be clear also, that the persistence of dissocial conduct depends in part on mutually reinforcing transactional processes between the affected children and their parents, teachers, and peers. In the appraisal of sociopathic adults, the childhood origins of their disorder are likely to shed much light on the nature of their difficulties and may yet point the way to helpful interventions.

References

AMERICAN PSYCHIATRIC ASSOCIATION (1980) *Diagnostic and Statistical Manual of Mental Disorders* (3rd edn) (DSM–III). Washington, DC: APA.
—— (1987) *Diagnostic and Statistical Manual of Mental Disorders* (3rd edn, revised) (DSM–III). Washington, DC: APA.
ASPERGER, H. (1944) Die autistischen Psychopathen im Kindesalter. *Archiv für Psychiatrie und Nervenkrankheiten*, **177**, 76–137.
—— (1979) Problems of infantile autism. *Communication*, **13**, 45–52.
BERGER, M. (1985) Temperament and individual differences. In *Child and Adolescent Psychiatry: Modern Approaches* (eds M. Rutter & L. Hersov), pp. 3–16. Oxford: Blackwell.
BIRLEY, J. L. T. (1990) DSM–III: from left to right or from right to left? *British Journal of Psychiatry*, **157**, 116–118.
BISHOP, D. V. M. (1989) Autism, Asperger's syndrome and semantic-pragmatic disorder. *British Journal of Communication*, **24**, 107–121.

BOLTON, P. & RUTTER, M. (1990) Genetic influences in autism. *International Review of Psychiatry*, **2**, 67–80.

BUSS, A. H. & PLOMIN, R. (1975) *A Temperamental Theory of Personality*. New York: Wiley.

—— & —— (1984) *Temperament: Early Developing Personality Traits*, pp. 84–85. Hillsdale, New Jersey: Lawrence Erlbaum.

CAPSI, A., ELDER, G. H. & BERN, D. J. (1987) Moving against the world: life course patterns of explosive children. *Developmental Psychology*, **23**, 306–313.

—— & —— (1988) Emergent family patterns: the intergenerational construction of problem behaviour and relationships. In *Relationships within Families: Mutual Influences* (eds R. H. Hinde & J. Stevenson-Hinde), pp. 218–240. Oxford: Clarendon Press.

——, —— & BERN, D. J. (1988) Moving away from the world: life course patterns of shy children. *Developmental Psychology*, **24**, 824–831.

CARDORET, R. J. & CAIN, C. (1980) Sex differences in predictors of antisocial behavior in adoptees. *Archives of General Psychiatry*, **37**, 1171–1175.

CHESS, S. & THOMAS, A. (1984) *Origins and Evolution of Behavior Disorders*. New York: Raven Press.

CHICK, J., WATERHOUSE, L. & WOLFF, S. (1979) Psychological construing in schizoid children grown up. *British Journal of Psychiatry*, **135**, 425–430.

CLECKLEY, H. (1976) *The Mask of Sanity* (5th edn). St Louis: The C.V. Mosby Co.

CUMMINGS, E. M., IANNOFFI, R. J. & ZAHN-WAXLER, C. (1989) Aggression between peers in early childhood: individual continuity and developmental change. *Child Development*, **60**, 887–895.

DANIELS, D. & PLOMIN, R. (1985) Origins of individual differences in infant shyness. *Developmental Psychology*, **21**, 118–121.

DODGE, K. A. (1980) Social cognition and children's aggressive behavior. *Child Development*, **51**, 162–170.

FARRINGTON, D. P., GALLAGHER, B., MORLEY, L., *et al* (1988) Are there any successful men from criminogenic backgrounds? *Psychiatry*, **51**, 116–130.

GILLBERG, C. (1989) Asperger Syndrome in 23 Swedish children. *Developmental Medicine and Child Neurology*, **31**, 520–531.

—— (1990) Autism and pervasive developmental disorders. *Journal for Child Psychology and Psychiatry*, **31**, 99–119.

GILLBERG, I. C. & GILLBERG, C. (1989) Asperger syndrome – some epidemiological considerations: a research note. *Journal of Child Psychology and Psychiatry*, **30**, 631–638.

GOLDSMITH, H. H. (1983) Genetic influences on personality. *Child Development*, **54**, 331–355.

GOODMAN, R. & STEVENSON, J. (1989*a*) A twin study of hyperactivity-I. An examination of hyperactivity scores and categories derived from Rutter teacher and parent questionnaires. *Journal of Child Psychology and Psychiatry*, **30**, 671–689.

—— & —— (1989*b*) A twin study of hyperactivity-II. The aetiological role of genes, family relationships and perinatal adversity. *Journal of Child Psychology and Psychiatry*, **30**, 691–709.

GUZE, S. B. (1976) *Criminality and Psychiatric Disorders*. London: Oxford University Press.

HALL, D. M. B. & HILL, P. (1991) Shy, withdrawn or autistic? *British Medical Journal*, **302**, 125–126.

HARE, R. D. & COX, D. N. (1978) Clinical and empirical conceptions of psychopathy and the selection of subjects for research. In *Psychopathic Behaviour: Approaches to Research* (eds R. D. Hare & D. Schalling). Chichester: Wiley.

HENDERSON, N. D. (1982) Human behavior genetics. *Annual Review of Psychology*, **33**, 403–440.

HOFFMAN, M. L. (1987) The contribution of empathy to justice and moral judgement. In *Empathy and its Development* (eds N. Eisenberg & J. Strayer). New York: Cambridge University Press.

HUESMANN, L. R., ERON, L. D., LEFKOWITZ, M. M., *et al* (1984) Stability of aggression over time and generations. *Developmental Psychology*, **20**, 1120–1134.

JENKINS, J. M. & SMITH, M. A. (1990) Factors protecting children living in disharmonious homes: maternal reports. *Journal of the American Academy of Child and Adolescent Psychiatry*, **29**, 60–69.

KAGAN, J. (1981) *The Second Year: The Emergence of Self-awareness.* Cambridge, Mass.: Harvard University Press.

——, REZNICK, J. S. & SNIDMAN, N. (1988) Biological bases of childhood shyness. *Science,* **240**, 167–171.

——, —— & GIBBONS, J. (1989) Inhibited and uninhibited types of children. *Child Development,* **60**, 838–845.

KANNER, L. (1943) Autistic disturbances of affective contact. *The Nervous Child,* **2**, 217–250.

MAGNUSSON, D. (1988) *Individual Development from an Interactional Perspective: A Longitudinal Study.* Hillsdale, New Jersey: Lawrence Erlbaum.

MANNING, M., HERON, J. & MARSHALL, C. (1977) Styles of hostility and social interactions at nursery, at school and at home: an extended study of children. In *Aggression and Anti-Social Behaviour in Childhood and Adolescence* (eds L. A. Hersov & M. Berger). Oxford: Pergamon.

MANNUZZA, S., GITTELMAN KLEIN, R., HOROWITZ KONIG, P., et al (1989) Hyperactive boys almost grown up: IV. Criminality and its relationship to psychiatric status. *Archives of General Psychiatry,* **46**, 1073–1079.

MEYER-BAHLBURG, H. F. F., EHRHARDT, A. & FELDMAN, J. F. (1986) Long-term implications of the prenatal endocrine milieu for sex-dimorphic behavior. In *Life-Span Research on the Prediction of Psychopathology* (eds L. Erlenmeyer-Kimling & N. E. Miller), pp. 17–30. Hillsdale, New Jersey: Lawrence Erlbaum.

NAGY, J. & SZATMARI, P. (1986) A chart review of schizotypal personality disorders in children. *Journal of Autism and Developmental Disorders,* **16**, 351–367.

NARAYAN, S., MOYES, B. & WOLFF, S. (1990) Family characteristics of autistic children: a further report. *Journal of Autism and Developmental Disorders,* **20**, 523–535.

OLWEUS, D. (1979) Stability of aggressive reaction patterns in males: a review. *Psychological Bulletin,* **86**, 852–875.

—— (1980) Familial and temperamental determinants of aggressive behaviour in adolescent boys: a causal analysis. *Developmental Psychology,* **16**, 644–660.

PATTERSON, G. R. (1982) *Coercive Family Process.* Eugene, Oregon: Castalia.

—— (1986) Performance models for antisocial boys. *American Psychologist,* **41**, 432–444.

—— & DISHION, T. J. (1988) Multilevel family process models: traits, interactions and relationships. In *Relationships within Families: Mutual Influences* (eds R. A. Hinde & J. Stevenson-Hinde), pp. 283–310. Oxford: Clarendon Press.

——, LITTMAN, R. A. & BRICKER, W. (1967) Assertive behavior in children: a step toward a theory of aggression. *Monographs of the Society for Research in Child Development,* **32**, no. 5.

PETTI, T. A. & VELA, R. M. (1990) Borderline disorders of childhood: an overview. *Journal of the American Academy of Child and Adolescent Psychiatry,* **29**, 327–337.

PLOMIN, R. & DANIELS, D. (1987) Why are children in the same family so different from one another? *Behavioral and Brain Sciences,* **10**, 1–60.

——, DE FRIES, J. C. & FULKER, D. W. (1988) *Nature and Nurture During Infancy and Early Childhood.* Cambridge: Cambridge University Press.

POPE, H. G., JONAS, J. M., HUDSON, J. I., et al (1983) The validity of DSM–III criteria for borderline personality disorder. *Archives of General Psychiatry,* **40**, 23–30.

QUINTON, D. & RUTTER, M. (1988) *Parenting Breakdown: the Making and Breaking of Intergenerational Links.* Aldershot: Avebury.

RICHMAN, N., STEVENSON, J. & GRAHAM, P. J. (1982) *Pre-school to School: A Behavioural Study,* London: Academic Press.

ROBINS, L. N. (1966) *Deviant Children Grown Up.* Baltimore: Williams and Wilkins. (Reprinted, 1973, Huntington, New York: Krieger).

—— (1978) Sturdy childhood predictors of adult antisocial behaviour: Replications from longitudinal studies. *Psychological Medicine,* **8**, 611–622.

—— (1986) The consequence of conduct disorder in girls. In *Development of Antisocial and Prosocial Behavior: Research Theories and Issues* (ed. D. Olweus), pp. 385–414. New York: Academic Press.

—— (1991) Conduct disorder. *Journal of Child Psychology and Psychiatry: Annual Research Review,* **32**, 193–212.

88   *Wolff*

RUTTER, M. (1989*a*) Pathways from childhood to adult life. *Journal of Child Psychology and Psychiatry*, **30**, 23–51.

—— (1989*b*) Annotation: child psychiatric disorders in ICD-10. *Journal of Child Psychology and Psychiatry*, **30**, 499–511.

——, COX, A., TUPLING, C., *et al* (1975) Attainment and adjustment in two geographical areas. I: the prevalence of psychiatric disorder. *British Journal of Psychiatry*, **126**, 493–509.

RUTTER, M., TIZARD, J. & WHITMORE, K. (1970) *Education, Health and Behaviour*, London: Longman.

SCHALLING, D. (1978) Psychopathy-related personality variables and the psychophysiology of socialization. In *Psychopathic Behaviour: Approaches to Research* (eds R. D. Hare & D. Schalling). Chichester: Wiley.

SPERRY, R. W. (1982) Some effects of disconnecting the cerebral hemispheres. *Science*, **217**, 1223–1226.

SZATMARI, P., TUFT, L., FINLAYSON, M. A. J., *et al* (1990) Asperger's syndrome and autism. *Journal of the American Academy for Child and Adolescent Psychiatry*, **29**, 130–136.

TANTAM, D. (1986) *Eccentricity and Autism*. PhD Thesis, University of London.

—— (1988*a*) Lifelong eccentricity and social isolation I: psychiatric, social and forensic aspects. *British Journal of Psychiatry*, **153**, 777–782.

—— (1988*b*) Lifelong eccentricity and social isolation II: Asperger's syndrome or schizoid personality disorder? *British Journal of Psychiatry*, **153**, 783–791.

TARNOPOLSKY, A. & BERELOWITZ, M. (1987) Borderline personality: a review of recent research. *British Journal of Psychiatry*, **151**, 724–734.

TAYLOR, E., SANDBERG, S., THORLEY, G., *et al* (1991) *The Epidemiology of Childhood Hyperactivity*. Maudsley Monograph No. 33. Oxford: Oxford University Press.

THOMAS, A. & CHESS, S. (1986) The New York Longitudinal Study: from infancy to early adult life. In *The Study of Temperament: Changes, Continuities and Challenges* (eds R. Plomin & J. F. Dunn), pp. 39–52. Hillsdale, New Jersey: Lawrence Erlbaum.

TORGERSEN, A. M. (1989) Genetic and environmental influences on temperamental development: longitudinal study of twins from infancy to adolescence. In *Early Influences Shaping the Individual* (ed. S. Doxiadis). London: Plenum.

TORGERSEN, S. (1984) Genetic and nosological aspects of schizotypal and borderline personality disorders: a twin study. *Archives of General Psychiatry*, **41**, 546–554.

WEBER, D. (1985) Autistische Syndrome. In *Kinder- und Jugendpsychiatrie in Klinik und Praxis, vol. II* (eds H. Remschmidt & M. H. Schmidt), pp. 269–298. Stuttgart: Georg Thieme.

WEISS, G., HECTMAN, L., PERLMAN, T., *et al* (1979) Hyperactives as young adults. A controlled prospective 10-year follow-up of 75 children. *Archives of General Psychiatry*, **36**, 675–681.

——, HECHTMAN, L., MILROY, T., *et al* (1985) Psychiatric status of hyperactives as adults: a controlled prospective 15-year follow-up of 63 hyperactive children. *Journal of the American Academy of Child and Adolescent Psychiatry*, **24**, 211–220.

WERNER, E. E. & SMITH, R. S. (1982) *Vulnerable but Invincible: A Longitudinal Study of Resilient Children and Youth*. New York: McGraw Hill.

WEST, D. J. & FARRINGTON, D. P. (1973) *Who Becomes Delinquent?* London: Heinemann.

WING, L. (1981) Asperger's syndrome: a clinical account. *Psychological Medicine*, **11**, 115–129.

WOLFF, S. (1984) Annotation: The concept of personality disorder in childhood. *Journal of Child Psychology and Psychiatry*, **25**, 5–13.

—— (1987) Antisocial conduct: whose concern? *Journal of Adolescence*, **10**, 105–118.

—— (1989) *Childhood and Human Nature: The Development of Personality*, London: Routledge.

—— (1991*a*) 'Schizoid' personality in childhood and adult life. III: the childhood picture. *British Journal of Psychiatry*, **159**, 629–635.

—— (1991*b*) Moral development. In *Child and Adolescent Psychiatry: A Comprehensive Textbook* (ed. M. Lewis), pp. 257–266. Baltimore: Williams and Wilkins.

—— & CHICK, J. (1980) Schizoid personality in childhood: a controlled follow-up study. *Psychological Medicine*, **10**, 85–100.

—— & CULL, A. (1986) 'Schizoid' personality and antisocial conduct: a retrospective case note study. *Psychological Medicine*, **16**, 677–687.

——, NARAYAN, S. & MOYES, B. (1988) Personality characteristics of parents of autistic children: a controlled study. *Journal of Child Psychology and Psychiatry*, **29**, 143–153.

——, TOWNSHEND, R., MCGUIRE, R. J., *et al* (1991) 'Schizoid' personality in childhood and adult life II: Adult adjustment and the continuity with schizotypal personality disorder. *British Journal of Psychiatry*, **159**, 620–628.

WOLKIND, S. & RUTTER, M. (1985) Separation, loss and family relationships. In *Child and Adolescent Psychiatry: Modern Approaches* (eds M. Rutter & L. Hersov). Oxford: Blackwell.

WORLD HEALTH ORGANIZATION (1992) *The ICD-10 Classification of Mental and Behavioural Disorders*. Geneva: WHO.

ZEITLIN, H. (1986) *The Natural History of Psychiatric Disorder in Children*. Maudsley Monographs No. 29. Oxford: Oxford University Press.

5 The validity of borderline personality disorder: an updated review of recent research

MARK BERELOWITZ and ALEX TARNOPOLSKY

In 1987 we reviewed the data on the validity of the diagnosis of borderline personality (Tarnopolsky & Berelowitz, 1987), using the research that had become available since the statement by Liebowitz (1979) that:

> "When the St Louis approach to diagnostic validity is used as a guideline, the conclusion reached is that available data do not weight for or against borderline's status as an independent entity."

We concluded in our review that the scale had tipped in favour of the validity of the diagnosis, but that much research was still needed.

The key developments between 1979 and 1987 that made this change possible were the introduction of reliable clinical diagnostic criteria in the DSM–III (American Psychiatric Association, 1980), and reliable research instruments such as the Diagnostic Interview for Borderlines (DIB; Gunderson *et al*, 1981). It became possible, using these instruments, to test the validity of the diagnosis against the criteria of Robins & Guze (1970):

(a) identification of a characteristic phenomenology
(b) phenomenological independence from other psychiatric disorders
(c) follow-up data
(d) family studies
(e) laboratory investigations and psychological tests
(f) treatment response.

We also concluded in 1987 that data were lacking in several areas. It seems appropriate therefore to reassess the situation in the light of recent developments. These include:

(a) general developments in the field of personality disorders
(b) new empirical studies using diagnostic instruments that examine a wider range of DSM–III Axis 2 diagnoses
(c) new data and new concepts on aetiology and long-term outcome

(d) treatment studies
(e) childhood antecedents.

For the convenience of the reader we will follow the basic structure of our 1987 review, updating each section systematically, and adding new sections as appropriate.

As in 1987, the literature remains predominantly from the US, although there is a burgeoning Canadian literature on the subject, as well as a few papers from the UK.

Conceptual models and diagnostic systems

The term 'borderline' has been used in a number of specific ways in psychiatry and psychoanalysis (Jackson & Tarnopolsky, 1990). Firstly, there is a long history of the notion of a condition which was borderline to schizophrenia, in terms of symptoms, course and prognosis. Many of these patients would fit into the category of schizotypal personality disorder in DSM–III–R (American Psychiatric Association, 1987).

Secondly, following Stern (1938), psychoanalysts use the word 'borderline' to describe a group of patients, apparently with neurotic disorders, who are prone to brief psychotic episodes under stress, including the stress of psychoanalysis. These patients were not defined precisely in phenomenological terms, and possibly covered a wide group of diagnostic labels. The clearest contemporary account of such patients has been given by Kernberg (1967), including a diagnostic system (Kernberg, 1981) and a modification of the psychotherapeutic method (Kernberg *et al*, 1989).

Thirdly, a number of psychotherapeutically sophisticated American psychiatrists (Grinker *et al*, 1968; Gunderson & Kolb, 1978; Spitzer *et al*, 1979) combined the psychoanalytic ideas, empirical research, and their own clinical experience to construct phenomenological profiles for borderline personality disorder (BPD). The specific consequences of their work include a semistructured research instrument, the Diagnostic Interview for Borderlines (DIB) (Gunderson *et al*, 1981; Zanarini *et al*, 1989), and the DSM–III diagnostic set for Borderline Personality Disorder (Spitzer *et al*, 1979). These instruments identify a group of patients with a specific personality disorder characterised by a particular instability in areas of behaviour, relationships, identity, and emotional experience, as well as a vulnerability to psychotic-like episodes. Although a term like unstable or labile personality disorder may well have been more appropriate for this group, the word 'borderline' has persisted, for better or for worse. It is the validity of borderline personality as defined by Spitzer and Gunderson that will be the focus of this paper.

We will begin by reviewing the reliability of the diagnostic instruments; we will then assess the validity of the diagnosis, using the criteria of

Robins & Guze (1970); lastly we will examine some of the data on childhood antecedents.

Reliability

Reliability refers to the agreement between different assessors about the presence of a disorder, and to the consistency of the assessment over time. Reliable diagnostic instruments are a precondition for empirical research. The coefficient kappa (x) is a good measure of reliability with $x = 0$ indicating chance agreement and $x = 1$ showing full agreement). In general x values above 0.7 are considered acceptable.
  Two instruments will be considered here.

(a) Diagnostic Interview for Borderlines (DIB; DIB–R) (Gunderson *et al*, 1981; Zanarini *et al*, 1989). This is a semistructured interview which identifies characteristic affects, impulse–action patterns, interpersonal relationships, and cognitions, including psychotic-like phenomena. The new version (DIB–R) contains 186 questions, divided into several sections, which are weighted to provide a numerical score.
    Acceptable agreement, with x values in some cases above 0.8, has been demonstrated for live interviews (Kroll *et al*, 1981a; Frances *et al*, 1984; Hurt *et al*, 1984) and case notes (McGlashan, 1983a; Armelius *et al*, 1985); and for two interviews of the same patient by different clinicians at least one week apart (Cornell *et al*, 1983). Inter-rater reliability for the subscales of the DIB was also high, with the exception of the section on affects (Frances *et al*, 1984).

(b) DSM–III Borderline Personality Disorder. Spitzer *et al* (1979) partitioned a muddled field into two distinct personality disorders: schizotypal personality, related to schizophrenia, and borderline personality, discussed here. This work formed part of the development of the DSM–III, and the form and content of the diagnostic method are very much within the spirit of the DSM–III – there is an eight-item checklist, five of which must be present for the diagnosis. The checklist identifies chronically unstable, vulnerable individuals, with difficult relationships, poor self-control, and identity problems. The definitions of three items were improved for DSM–III–R. The DSM–III criteria have latterly been incorporated into research instruments (e.g. Spitzer *et al*, 1987). Good reliability with x values above 0.7 was obtained with clinical interviews (Frances *et al*, 1984), case notes (McGlashan, 1983a), and with new research interviews ($x = 0.85$, Stangl *et al*, 1985; x between 0.52 and 1.0, Zanarini *et al*, 1987; see also Kavoussi *et al*, 1990).

Validity: an application of the criteria of Robins and Guze

The paucity of objective indicators of psychiatric disorder means that validity is best assessed by marshalling data from a number of different areas. The criteria of Robins & Guze (1970) remain useful for this purpose, despite criticism (Livesley, 1991).

A unitary clinical description

"In general, the first step is to describe the clinical picture of the disorder" (Robins & Guze, 1970). Does the research identify a homogeneous group of patients?

During the 1980s many studies have applied both the DIB and the DSM–III criteria to case notes (McGlashan, 1983*a*; Pope *et al*, 1983) and interviews (Frances *et al*, 1984; Akiskal *et al*, 1985*a*). Kroll's group (Kroll *et al*, 1981*b*, 1982; Barrash *et al*, 1983) thoroughly examined a series of 252 admissions in the US and the UK, applying both sets of criteria in interviews. The DIB identified a larger number of patients than the DSM–III. There were some false positives and false negatives, mostly cases which met the DIB criteria and not the DSM–III. The commonest diagnosis for these discordant cases was 'non-borderline' personality disorder. Cluster analysis further improved the agreement and yielded a high sensitivity (0.83) and specificity (0.89) for the DIB against the DSM–III. However, there is a problem in assessing these data: the DIB is a research tool, whereas the DSM–III criteria are in the form of an unstructured clinical interview.

Zanarini *et al* (1991) tested the DSM–III and DSM–III–R criteria against so-called LEAD diagnoses (i.e. clinical diagnoses made by experienced clinicians – Longitudinal Expert All Data, see also Spitzer, 1983). There were a number of misclassified cases, indicating that the DSM criteria did not accurately reflect what senior clinicians had in mind when diagnosing BPD. Overall the DSM criteria identified a wider range of personality pathology than did the clinical diagnoses.

By means of this and other research (Gunderson, 1977; Sheehy *et al*, 1980; Soloff & Ulrich, 1981) a characteristic phenomenological set of core features has been identified: unstable interpersonal relationships, idealisation and denigration of others, intense unpredictable feelings, and impulsive and self-destructive behaviour. Similarly, Maudsley psychiatrists thought that the most frequent items among the borderline patients were a pattern of unstable, intense interpersonal relationships, and impulsiveness and unpredictability in potentially self-damaging areas (both DSM–III items); the most discriminating item, however, was brief, stress-related, psychotic episodes or regressions (a Gunderson item) (Tarnopolsky & Berelowitz, 1984). With regard to psychotic features, Links *et al* (1989) found that loosely defined 'psychotic' symptoms such as depersonalisation/derealisation and drug-free paranoid experiences predict a diagnosis of BPD, while borderline patients with highly specific symptoms like delusions and hallucinations often merited additional diagnoses of major affective disorder or drug/alcohol abuse. Bateman (1989) reported the only diagnostic study of UK patients undertaken by a local author. He compared in-patient DIB-diagnosed borderline patients with PSE-diagnosed neurotic and psychotic controls. A particularly high level of anxiety and irritability, externalised as violent destructive behaviour, anger, and hostility at interview, distinguished borderline patients from neurotic patients. In addition, they presented with depressive and non-specific psychotic features.

Kroll *et al* (1982) highlighted certain differences between British and American patients: "The British borderlines (DIB and DSM–III criteria) reported minimal drug abuse and no drug-related psychosis . . . [they] evidenced no interest in caretaker roles; and although the majority reported derealisation and depersonalisation, so did the majority of British non-borderline patients".

Although there is some persistent discordance between the diagnostic instruments, they do nevertheless appear to be tapping the same core of pathology. The agreement between the DIB and the DSM–III is relatively high, particularly considering the uncertainty about psychiatric diagnosis generally.

Phenomenological discrimination from other disorders

The question here is whether patients with an operationally diagnosed borderline personality can be distinguished from patients with other psychiatric conditions, especially schizophrenia, affective disorders, and other personality disorders.

Schizophrenia

Several studies in different centres and using different methods have now placed the phenomenological distinction between borderline personalities and schizophrenic in-patients beyond reasonable doubt (Gunderson *et al*, 1975; Kolb & Gunderson, 1980; Soloff & Ulrich, 1981; Kroll *et al*, 1981*b*, 1982; Pope *et al*, 1983). For example, Gunderson *et al* (1975), using patients drawn from the International Pilot Study of Schizophrenia (Carpenter *et al*, 1973), found that the borderline in-patients had significantly fewer psychotic symptoms than the schizophrenic group, with no evidence of thought disorder. The borderline group was characterised by derealisation, a frenetic and stormy life-style, unusual and occult experiences, marked interpersonal difficulties, and suicide threats.

Other writers confirmed that the psychotic symptoms of borderline patients are not typically schizophrenic (Pope *et al*, 1983; Chopra & Beatson, 1986;

Links *et al*, 1989). Kroll *et al* (1981*b*) found only one DSM–III schizophrenic among 21 DIB positive in-patients, and Pope *et al* (1983) found no DSM–III schizophrenics among 33 in-patients diagnosed as borderline according to Gunderson criteria.

However, the distinction between out-patients from these two groups is less clear and less well studied. Sheehy *et al* (1980), comparing borderlines (diagnosed according to their own criteria) and schizophrenics diagnosed by Carpenter criteria (Carpenter *et al*, 1973), found that deficient management of impulses, intolerably unpleasant feelings, and idealisation/denigration of others were significantly more prevalent among the borderline patients. Pronounced failure of reality testing was more prevalent among the schizophrenic patients, and was the best predictor of group differences. But Koenigsberg *et al* (1983) found that borderline out-patients had only non-significantly higher DIB scores than schizophrenic out-patients. These results are conflicting and throw doubt on the accuracy of the distinction between the disorders.

Affective disorders

The coincidence of affective illness with borderline personality is greater than might be expected statistically (Gunderson & Elliot, 1985; Perry, 1985). The relationship between borderline personality and affective illness is potentially more complicated than the postulated link with schizophrenia. The issue remains complex, and the debates are often heated.

Gunderson & Elliot (1985) listed four possible explanations for the high coincidence. The first two possibilities were that one disorder is a consequence of the other: (a) drug-taking or promiscuity are used to relieve feelings of dysphoria or depression, or (b) depression may be secondary to poor impulse control and unsatisfactory relationships. The third (c) is that both disorders coexist independently in the same subjects; and the fourth (d) postulates that affective symptoms or character traits arise from an interaction of symptoms peculiar to each individual. Research data partially support each hypothesis, although Gunderson & Elliot's analyses at the time led them to accept the fourth.

Turning now to the empirical evidence, Gunderson & Kolb (1978) were able to discriminate borderline personality from neurotically depressed in-patients by the presence of drug-related psychotic experiences, anhedonia and dysphoria, interpersonal difficulties, and paranoid experiences. Sheehy *et al* (1980), with less formal methods, obtained similar results in a series of out-patients. Barrash *et al* (1983), summarising the findings of Kroll's group of 252 in-patients, found 48 with DIB positive borderline personality and 77 patients with affective disorders (unspecified); only three patients with affective disorders were DIB positive. Soloff & Ulrich (1981) found that total scores, scaled section scores, and 19 individual DIB items all effectively differentiated borderline personality from Research Diagnostic Criteria (RDC; Spitzer *et al*, 1975) (major) unipolar depressives. It was also repeatedly noted that the items characteristic of each disorder are different (e.g. impulsivity v. affective state), and that the attendant emotions are different, the depression of the borderline patient having the more schizoid qualities of boredom and emptiness. Borderline personalities also feel easily disappointed and let down, want to hurt themselves, and may be well aware of their rage. These symptomatic differences were confirmed by McGlashan (1987*b*), who also found that borderline patients broke down at an earlier age, and had fewer premorbid instrumental skills than unipolars.

By contrast, other studies of in-patients (Pope *et al*, 1983) and out-patients (Akiskal *et al*, 1985*a*) have found proportions as high as 50% of major and minor affective illnesses among DIB positive patients. Akiskal argued that the symptom set for BPD could easily be rearranged to look like an affective disorder. It is of local interest that the British sample (*n* = 47) studied by Kroll *et al* (1982) showed seven DIB-positive cases, three with a secondary diagnosis of depressive neurosis and one with a primary diagnosis of major affective illness (DSM–III). Also, Bateman's (1989) study in London found that among 11 borderline in-patients (DIB), ten met the PSE criteria for minor, and one for major, depressive disorders, although they differed in other ways (see above). James & Berelowitz (in preparation) found similar results in adolescents.

Soloff *et al* (1987) studied patients who were both borderline and depressed to see if a particular depressive syndrome emerged (i.e. one that could replace BPD as a diagnostic category) – it did not.

Fyer *et al* (1988) used an epidemiological approach to examine comorbidity, and found no increase of affective disorder in BPD patients compared with other patients. Certainly depression was common in other personality disorders as well. Other studies have shown that many affectively disordered patients have abnormal personalities (Friedman *et al*, 1983; Shea *et al*, 1987), but these are not exclusively or even predominantly borderline (Shea *et al*, 1987; Pilkonis & Frank, 1988).

Gunderson has recently updated his review (Gunderson & Phillips, 1991), and now concludes that their third hypothesis is the most tenable, namely that BPD and affective illnesses commonly occur together, but are unrelated. Overall the findings are conflicting, and the field remains unclear. Certainly, affective symptoms and borderline traits are both common, and often occur together, but depression occurs in other personality disorders as well. It is likely that more conceptual as well as empirical work will be needed to clarify these matters.

Personality disorders

In our first review we reported several studies that failed to distinguish between in-patients with borderline (DIB) and non-borderline personality disorders (Kolb & Gunderson, 1980; Kroll *et al*, 1981*b*, 1982). Pope *et al* (1983) found that borderline personality overlapped with histrionic personality disorder in women, and antisocial personality disorder in men (all diagnoses according to DSM–III criteria). However, borderline cases could be clearly distinguished in at least three out-patient samples (Sheehy *et al*, 1980; Perry & Klerman, 1980; Koenigsberg *et al*, 1983). As mentioned above for the comparison with schizophrenia, it is possible that the symptoms which determine admission may be of particular importance. In one refinement of the in-patient studies quoted above, Barrash *et al* (1983) applied cluster analytic methods to the DIB items in Kroll's series, and were then able to distinguish between borderline and other personality disorders.

Several points should be noted. Firstly, in the early 1980s the diagnosis of non-borderline personalities was not standardised. Secondly, the studies quoted made little allowance for dimensional aspects of personality. Thirdly, the use of the DSM–III has become more refined.

Several newer studies have dealt with these points in different ways. Stangl *et al* (1985), studying out-patients, found good overall agreement ($x > 0.7$) for the presence of any personality disorder, and for three particular DSM–III types, borderline, histrionic, and dependent. The most frequent combination was borderline and histrionic. Zanarini *et al* (1990) applied the DIB as well as their own interview for the assessment of other personality disorders to a large sample of in- and out-patients. They were able to distinguish between frequent, discriminating, and specific borderline traits. The latter included seven features evident in both sexes and both settings: quasi-psychotic thought; self-mutilation; manipulative suicide efforts; concerns about abandonment, engulfment, and annihilation; demandingness and entitlement; treatment regressions; and countertransference difficulties. But when the DSM–III and DSM–III–R were compared with so-called LEAD criteria ('expert criteria') on the same sample, the DSM criteria were found to be 'overinclusive', and the LEAD criteria restrictive. The authors suggest that the DSM criteria may identify a relatively non-specific type of severe character pathology. Nurnberg *et al* (1991), using DSM–III–R, reached a similar conclusion.

Borderline personalities can be distinguished at a descriptive level from schizophrenic and affective patients. However, there continue to be problems in distinguishing them from other personality disorders. It may be that the term is being used in two ways, as a relatively precise and distinctive cluster of symptoms which identify a specific personality disorder (DIB), and as a more general measure of severe character pathology (DSM–III, DSM–III–R). The latter notion would also fit with psychoanalytic views such as those of Kernberg (1967). This problem may reflect a fundamental weakness in the concept of borderline personality; alternatively it may merely reflect the conceptual and theoretical difficulties which bedevil the whole field of personality disorders. In summary, the data suggest that borderline personality disorders, as currently described, may be distinct and also coexist, at different levels of severity. This is illustrated by the overlap and distinctiveness of borderline and schizotypal personalities (Spitzer *et al*, 1979; Barrash *et al*, 1983; Frances *et al*, 1984; McGlashan, 1987*a*). Other writers have identified large sets of traits shared by what had been assumed to be separate personality disorders. For example, Nurnberg *et al* (1991) found two broad groups which straddle the boundaries of the DSM–III clusters. Borderline personality is in one group, schizotypal in the other.

Follow-up

Follow-up studies help to establish whether or not, over time, patients who are thought to have one particular condition can be shown to have some other disorder which can better explain their original symptoms (Robins & Guze, 1970). Early studies of borderline personality were not specifically designed for follow-up, and had small sample sizes and short observation periods (Pope *et al*, 1983; Barasch *et al*, 1985; Akiskal, 1985*a*; Mitton & Links, 1988). Some studies have extended over longer periods (as much as 15 years), but most have problems relating to diagnostic reliability, selectivity of the samples, and treatment effects (McGlashan, 1986; Stone *et al*, 1987; Paris *et al*, 1988; Cardish & Silver, 1991). There issues are discussed at greater length by Stone (Chapter 13), this volume.

A central question initially was whether borderline personalities were manifesting an early form of schizophrenia. In a five-year follow-up of borderline and schizophrenic patients, before the DIB and DSM–III were introduced (Carpenter & Gunderson, 1977), all the schizophrenic patients retained their original diagnoses, but there was persistent diagnostic uncertainty about the borderline group. Despite this uncertainty, however, only one of the 24 borderlines was subsequently rediagnosed as schizophrenic. No schizophrenics were found among DIB or DSM–III borderline samples after 4–7 years (Pope *et al*, 1983, *n* = 27) and after three years (Barasch *et al*, 1985, *n* = 30). McGlashan (1983*b*) found that after 15 years 24% of borderline personalities and 55% of schizotypals developed schizophrenia. No specific borderline trait was predictive of schizophrenia (Fenton & McGlashan, 1989).

The second question concerned the relationship between borderline personality and affective illness. Pope *et al* (1983) found that of the mixed cases (borderline personality plus affective illness), 74% had possible/ probable affective illness at follow-up, while the corresponding figure for the 'pure' borderline group was only 23%. Akiskal (1985*a*) found a similar figure of 20% for melancholic episodes among 'pure' borderlines.

Moreover some workers have found major depression to be equally prevalent among borderline and other personality disorders at three years, which argues against a specific link between borderline and affective disorders (Barasch *et al*, 1985). The vast majority of borderline patients do not become depressives: only 11% changed from borderline personality to affective disorder over time (McGlashan 1983*b*, 1987*b*). McGlashan (1987*b*) also found that one-third of unipolar depressives developed BPD.

The third question concerns the stability of borderline personality over time. The majority retained their original diagnosis (65%: Pope *et al*, 1983; 60–90%: Barasch *et al*, 1985; 44–70%: McGlashan, 1983*b*, 1987*b*), but some, in addition, received other personality disorder diagnoses as well, mainly in the DSM–III dramatic or flamboyant group (Pope *et al*, 1983). In only one or two cases was the diagnosis of schizotypal personality considered possible or definite.

The last question concerns social functioning. The presence of similar social outcome is a weaker argument for validity than the persistence of the diagnosis, since there is no one-to-one relationship between psychopathology and social functioning. Nevertheless, when followed up over several years, borderline patients show better social functioning than schizophrenics. This was evident at five years (Carpenter & Gunderson, 1977), although at two years there had been no discernible difference (Gunderson *et al*, 1975). In later studies, 'pure' borderline personalities presented outcomes intermediate between those for schizophrenic illness (worst) and affective illness (best) at around five years (Pope *et al*, 1983; McGlashan, 1983*b*, 1986), and similar to affective illness at 15 years (McGlashan, 1983*b*). Unlike schizophrenics, they tend to improve over time, and are at their best 10–20 years after discharge (McGlashan, 1986; Cardish & Silver, 1991). By comparison with schizophrenics they were more likely to be autonomous, in employment, to be married and have children, despite needing repeated brief hospital admissions (McGlashan, 1986). There was also less completed suicide (Stone *et al*, 1987). The diagnosis distinction between borderline and schizophrenia was found to be a powerful predictor of the type of discharge, circumstances of discharge, and course following discharge (McGlashan & Heinssen, 1988).

In summary, borderline personalities usually retain their diagnoses over time, but in addition they may present with other personality disorders, frequently within the DSM–III 'dramatic' group. Several studies show that only a minority develop schizophrenia, in contrast with schizotypals. Most borderline personalities do not develop affective illness; a variable number display affective symptoms at follow-up, but possibly no more than for other personality disorders. One-third of unipolars appear to develop BPD. Comorbidity with affective disorders (McGlashan, 1987*b*; Shea *et al*, 1987) and alcoholism (Dulit *et al*, 1990) affects the presentation, interpretation and course of the disorder.

At follow-up, patients with BPD either retain their diagnoses or acquire another Axis II diagnosis. It appears that a distinctive course is becoming clearer, with long-term social functioning similar to that of unipolar depressives, and improvement early in the fifth decade.

Family studies

Robins & Guze (1970) argue that finding an increased prevalence of the disorder in the relatives and in the index patients supports the validity of the diagnosis. In particular, twin studies help to disentangle the relative aetiological importance of environment and heredity.

Because of their respective historical roots, in this section we will consider both borderline (DSM–III and DIB criteria) and schizotypal personalities, and their relationship to schizophrenia. In the Danish Adoption Study, Kety *et al* (1968) found evidence supporting a genetic link between 'B-3 or borderline schizophrenics' and the chronic schizophrenic index cases. A sample of B-3 cases was then used by Spitzer to define the criteria for DSM–III Schizotypal Personality Disorder (Spitzer *et al*, 1979). Kendler *et al* (1981) applied Spitzer's criteria blindly to the Danish records and confirmed that schizotypal personality was more common among the biological relatives of chronic schizophrenic patients than among either relatives of controls or relatives of B-3 index cases. Gunderson *et al* (1983) further showed that among the B-3 relatives of chronic schizophrenics, the most common diagnosis was schizotypal personality, not borderline; the commonest diagnosis in the B-3 *index* cases was borderline personality (9 cases out of 10), and their B-3 relatives had borderline rather than schizotypal features. These two studies therefore allow for two genetic propositions: (a) the mentally ill biological relatives of schizophrenics are schizotypal and not borderline, and (b) the mentally ill relatives of borderline personalities are, in the main, themselves borderline. These findings are supported by other studies (Loranger *et al*, 1982; Baron *et al*, 1985). The latter group found that borderline personality was ten times more common among the treated relatives of borderline patients than in the relatives of schizophrenic patients. Links *et al* (1988*a*) found no schizophrenic patients among the relatives of borderlines. A substantive twin study by Torgersen (1984) showed that monozygotic twins of schizotypal patients have schizotypal (33%) and not borderline (0%) disorders.

With regard to the genetic link with affective disorders, Soloff & Millward (1983) are often quoted as they found that more borderline than depressed probands had relatives with mood swings. This result, however, refers to a mixed group of 19 borderline patients, 9 schizotypal patients, and 20 patients who met both criteria: further analysis revealed that depression was actually more prevalent among the relatives of the schizotypal than the borderline patients! Links *et al* (1988) examined the relatives of a sample of borderline patients. The vast majority of patients also had a depressive condition; among the relatives the most frequent diagnoses were alcoholism and recurrent unipolar depressions.

Pope *et al* (1983) and Andrulonis & Vogel (1984) simply separated pure borderline patients from those who also had an affective illness, and found that the prevalence of affective illness was raised only in the relatives of the latter group. Torgersen (1984) found the same: "all the co-twins with an affective disorder were co-twins of schizotypal and borderline patients with a concurrent affective disorder as well". Zanarini *et al* (1988) supported these conclusions. They examined a sample of patients with borderline, antisocial, and other personality disorders. The latter also had dysthmic disorder. The borderline patients were separated into 'pure' and 'depressed' subgroups. In summary, they found that relatives of borderlines were more frequently borderline and relatives of 'antisocials' were more frequently antisocial and relatives of depressed borderlines more frequently had major depressions. Relatives of dysthymic patients with 'other' personality disorders had an even higher rate of major depressions.

Although a number of objections can be raised against these studies (see Tarnopolsky & Berelowitz, 1987, p. 730) we are nevertheless left with consistent evidence, albeit of variable quality, confirming the separateness of borderline and schizotypal personalities, and of borderline personality and major depressive illness. In 1987 we suggested that diagnostically rigorous multicentre research was needed to further clarify these issues – such a study is currently being carried out (Loranger *et al*, 1991).

Laboratory investigations and psychological tests

Biological data are as sparse and inconclusive in the area of borderline personalities as they were for the whole of psychiatry 20 years ago (Robins & Guze, 1970).

Much of the work with biological markers to assess the relationship with affective disorders is questionable, either because the patient had both syndromes concurrently (Carroll *et al*, 1981), or because good controls were not available. Only Kontaxakis *et al* (1987) found similar proportions of dexamethasone non-suppressors (about 50%) among borderline patients and depressive controls. Korzekwa *et al* (1991) found an abnormal DST in only a quarter of borderline personalities comorbid with depression, and, paradoxically, in only 17% of those with endogenous features. Several reviews (Steiner *et al*, 1988; Tarnopolsky, 1991; Korzekwa, 1991) all agree that the DST findings are inconsistent in studies of BPD.

Other indicators have been studied. The findings by Korzekwa (1991) for thyrotropin-releasing hormone were inconclusive. Akiskal *et al* (1985*b*) described a REM sleep pattern in borderline patients similar to that found in depressive patients; there were differences however, between those borderline patients who had an affective illness at any time in the past and those who had not. Silk *et al* (1988) argued that the sleep EEG may be a more useful predictor of endogenous depression among borderline patients than the DST. Coid *et al* (1984) found a raised level of plasma metencephalin (a neuropeptide that blocks pain perception) among self-mutilators who met DSM–III borderline criteria. Coccaro *et al* (1989) found that low CSF 5-HIAA correlates more with traits of aggression and impulsivity than with BPD per se. Only Kutcher *et al* (1987, 1989) are able to argue for a common biological element to BPD and schizophrenia. Using the EEG under experimental conditions, they obtained auditory evoked responses (P300) that distinguished BPD from other personality disorders and from affective disorder, but were shared by schizotypal and schizophrenic patients.

Some of these findings are intriguing, but we have to conclude that there is as yet no diagnostic biological marker of BPD, and no biological proof of its affiliation with another psychiatric disorder.

Singer (1977) has reviewed the literature on psychological tests. In brief, borderline personalities show ordinary reasoning on highly structured tests, but on projective ones they ''demonstrate flamboyantly deviant reasoning and thought processes''. Test results distinguish between borderline and schizophrenic in-patients, but for out-patients the distinction is less clear. Borderline patients' responses to Wechsler (1958) Adult Intelligence Scale, Rorshach (1942) and other tests have been reported (Kernberg *et al*, 1981; Soloff & Ulrich, 1981). Borderline personalities in both the USA and the UK showed a characteristic Minnesota Multidimensional Personality Inventory (MMPI; Hathaway & McKinley, 1967) profile, namely 8,4,2 (8 = schizophrenia, 4 = psychopathic deviate, and 2 = depression) (Kroll *et al*, 1981*b*, 1982). MMPI scores also differentiate borderline from schizotypal personality (Goldberg, 1985; Stangl *et al*, 1985).

Westen *et al* (1990) compared borderline adolescent girls with other psychiatric cases and with normal controls, using the Thematic Apperception Test (TAT). Borderline patients demonstrated more malevolent representations, lower level capacity for emotional investment in people, relationships, and moral values, and attributions of causality which were less accurate, complex, or logical. However, some of their representations of people were overly complex. These interesting findings need replication.

Treatment response

Although not specifically mentioned by Robins & Guze (1970), treatment response contributes to the delineation of a disorder: therapeutic success may suggest the existence of a specific aetiological or pathogenic factor (e.g. Teitelman *et al*, 1979).

Few controlled studies of treatment of borderline patients exist: this is probably because of the lack, until recently, of reliable diagnostic criteria; because psychoanalytic psychotherapy is often described only in case reports; and because of the lack of optimism among many psychiatrists about the treatment of patients with personality disorders.

Pharmacotherapy

Both antidepressants (Klein, 1977) and low-dose neuroleptics have been used (Brinkley *et al*, 1979; Seran & Siegal, 1984). Recently, two double-blind, placebo-controlled trials reported the efficacy of moderate doses of neuroleptics on chronic severe populations. In one sample of out-patients, thiothixene had an effect on psychotic-like symptoms (Goldberg *et al*, 1986); in an in-patient sample haloperidol had an effect on both psychotic-like and affective symptoms (Soloff *et al*, 1986), but patients on amitryptiline got worse.

Other studies of antidepressants (Cowdry & Gardner, 1988; Cole *et al*, 1984) have not shown substantial benefits for antidepressants; in fact they may be positively harmful in some cases (Soloff *et al*, 1986).

Recently there has been an interest in the possible efficacy of serotonin reuptake inhibitors. A trial by Cornelius *et al* (1990) showed that fluoxetine may be effective in treating the depressive and impulsive symptoms of borderline patients, but not the other symptoms.

In a helpful review article Kutcher & Blackwood (1989) provide guidelines for the rational use of medication with borderline patients and the topic is also reviewed by Stein (Chapter 11, this volume).

Individual psychoanalytic psychotherapy

The classic Meninger Clinic project (Kernberg *et al*, 1972) remains the most comprehensive study in this area. The investigators compared supportive psychotherapy, classical psychoanalysis, and 'expressive psychotherapy' conducted in an in-patient setting; borderline patients responded best to the latter. The sophistication of this study makes replication daunting (the researchers raised one million dollars in 1955!), but it is nevertheless surprising that smaller replications have not been attempted.

Recently there has been a shift towards combining pharmacotherapy and psychotherapy, a protocol that has some face validity. This has been described by Waldinger & Frank (1989), Stone (1990) and Brockman (1990), among others, but we are unaware of clinical trials of this treatment combination.

Family therapy

We are unaware of controlled studies of the efficacy of this treatment. However, given our increasing breadth of knowledge about the family histories of borderline patients, such a treatment makes intuitive sense, especially for adolescent patients. This has been reviewed by Clarkin *et al* (1991).

Conclusion

With regard to treatment, our 1987 conclusions remain unchanged. Good studies of treatment are only just becoming available, and have not yet contributed substantially to the issue of validity. Further work needs to be done on medication, on the relative merits of in-patient and out-patient treatment, on different models of psychotherapy, and on combined treatments. The effects of treatment will have to be analysed carefully, both with regard to target symptoms, and also to non-specific measures such as social and psychological morbidity.

Childhood antecedents

In our previous paper we did not deal with aetiology except with regard to genetics, mainly because of a lack of suitable empirical data. However, over the last five years a number of relevant papers have appeared which test certain aetiological theories.

The theory which went unchallenged for many years, especially in the United States, was that of Mahler's group (Mahler *et al*, 1975). They observed a group of mothers and toddlers in a seminaturalistic setting, and observed a particular type of mother–child interaction, during a specific developmental phase, which they felt wa sthe foundation of future personality disorder. They noticed that toddlers aged 18–24 months repeatedly explore away from mother, and then return to her for comfort and reassurance – this phenomenon is called the rapproachment phase of separation–individuation. They argued that through repetitions of this cycle the infant learns both object constancy and the capacity for ambivalence. It was noted that some mothers responded to their returning infants with either aggression or withdrawal, and the infants then alternated between clinginess and withdrawal. The behaviour of the infant was thought to be similar to that of borderline adults.

This research was welcomed uncritically by those seeking a psychological cause for borderline personality disorder. Mahler's ideas fit with Bowlby's empirical work (Bowlby, 1982), and one can see similarities to the way in which the so-called group C infants responded to maternal separation in the strange situation (Bretherton, 1985).

However, there are a number of problems with Mahler's work. Firstly, we are unaware of any follow-up data on the original children which would confirm or deny the hypothesis. Secondly, there is the important caution expressed by Balint (1968) and Stern (1985) about the links that can be drawn between certain types of apparently similar adult and child behaviour. Thirdly, Mahler's sample was unusual in being a volunteer sample of middle-class intellectual academics or spouses of academics, and we are unaware of similar work on more representative samples.

Perhaps in keeping with the spirit of the times, the focus of the more recent empirical research has been on overt physical and sexual abuse, separation and neglect, in the childhood histories of borderline adults, and there has recently been a flurry of papers dealing with this issue.

Links *et al* (1988*b*) compared in-patients with confirmed BPD and those with borderline traits. The BPD cases experienced more separations, family breakdown, foster placement, and physical and sexual abuse. The reason for the separation also differed – in the former group it was usually due to marital breakdown, in the latter group to bereavement.

Herman *et al* (1988) studied patients with BPD and those with other personality disorders, looking specifically for experiences of childhood trauma. Histories of physical and sexual abuse, and the witnessing of serious domestic violence characterised the borderline patients.

Ogata and colleagues compared borderline and depressed patients. Borderline patients had a much higher rate of sexual abuse. Mental illness, personality disorder, drug abuse and marital discord were more common in their parents (Ogata *et al*, 1990).

Nigg *et al* (1991) used projective measures to study the quality of childhood experiences in sexually abused borderline adults. They found that the early memories of the subjects were particularly malevolent and unpleasant.

Also using projective tests, Paris & Frank (1989) found that borderline patients perceived themselves as having received less care as children than did non-borderline controls.

Brown & Anderson (1991) studied the childhood abuse (physical and sexual) histories of nearly 1000 patients admitted to a military centre. An increase in the proportion of patients with borderline personality disorder was noted with increasing levels of reported abuse; 3% of non-abused patients, 13% with either type of abuse, and 29% of those who had suffered both types of abuse had BPD. Borderline personality disorder accounted for nearly 50% of the personality disorder diagnoses in the abused group.

Byrne *et al* (1990) compared early life histories of a sample of 29 borderline and schizophrenic patients. Both physical and sexual abuse were much more common in the borderline group. The pattern of sexual abuse suggested neglectful and disordered family relationships.

Zanarini *et al* (1989) have made a detailed study of this area, with the aim of investigating whether abuse, neglect, disturbed parenting, or separation are aetiologically important. They compared the childhood histories of 50 out-patients with borderline personality disorder, 29 with antisocial personality disorder, and 26 who were dysthymic as well as having a non-borderline Axis II diagnosis. The borderline patients reported significantly more abuse, with 48% reporting physical abuse, 26% reporting sexual abuse, and 80% reporting verbal abuse. There was also a substantial degree of neglect. Abuse was found to be both common and highly discriminating, and neglect and separation were common but less discriminating. Many patients experienced a combination of all three.

All these papers have the problem that they are based on retrospective recall of childhood events. We are unaware of any prospective studies of sexually and physically abused children which demonstrate the later development of BPD. However, the retrospective nature of the above work does not invalidate it. All of the papers were investigating persistent patterns of maltreatment and neglect, rather than one-off incidents. They therefore lend substantial support to the idea that the breeding ground for borderline personality disorder is a childhood environment which combines neglect and instability, marital discord, physical and sexual abuse, and the absence of a good relationship which will buffer the effects of the adverse environment.

There is less support now for the aetiological significance of multiple separations from the mother, as suggested by earlier writers. It seems that those authors overestimated the effects of the separations alone, and did not pay sufficient attention to the family context which led to the separation – namely discord, neglect, and abuse.

These papers also contribute to the discussion (see below) about whether BPD is really best thought of as synonymous with 'severely disabling personality disorder'.

Conclusions

The validity of borderline personality disorder has been scrutinised more intensely than any other personality disorder category. The diagnosis has a complex history, which has led to understandable confusion. However, the rigorous examination of the concept has been greatly assisted by several developments in the last 15 years. Firstly, Spitzer's group partitioned a muddled field into two discreet disorders, namely borderline and schizotypal personalities, and from there developed the DSM–III clinical diagnostic criteria. Secondly, Gunderson's group has developed and refined the DIB, still the best research interiew for diagnosing BPD. Thirdly, diagnostic instruments of acceptable quality have been devised for the diagnosis of non-borderline personality disorders. In 1987 we concluded that there was support for the validity of the diagnosis. The evidence since 1987 has not led to any major new breakthroughs, but serves to add some modest additional validation. We are unaware of any substantial work that calls the diagnosis into question more strongly than before.

The DSM and the DIB continue to be useful instruments, and identify a characteristic phenomenological core. The patients thus identified can be readily distinguished from schizophrenic in-patients, and, with less success, from schizophrenic out-patients. The accumulated evidence suggests that BPD cannot be subsumed under the category of affective illness. There continue to be problems in distinguishing BPD from certain other personality disorders. Follow-up studies show that patients retain their diagnoses over time, or acquire other Axis II diagnoses. They do not appear to develop affective illness or schizophrenia. The condition becomes less disabling in the fifth decade. The family studies thus far indicate that the disorder is genetically distinct, and not linked to schizophrenia or affective illness. The biological research remains speculative. The data on treatment suggest that there is no specific treatment, either psychological or pharmacological. A combination of treatments may be most sensible.

With regard to aetiology, the period since 1987 saw a substantial interest in the quality of care which borderline adults received in childhood. The evidence for a history of abuse and neglect is strong.

Borderline personality disorder is common, disabling, and difficult to treat. It probably has a multifactorial aetiology, and requires a flexible treatment approach. This raises the question of whether it would be easier to see it as a measure of severe personality dysfunction, rather than as a discrete diagnostic entity. However, this issue is complicated by the fact that most personality disorder diagnoses depend partly on the identification of specific symptoms, and partly on measures of social and interpersonal functioning. Nevertheless it may be that 'severe' cases of antisocial personality, borderline personality, and histrionic personality have more in common with one another than with 'mild' cases within the same specific diagnostic category. Further conceptual work is required to clarify these issues.

References

AKISKAL, H. S., CHEN, E. S., DAVIS, G. C., *et al* (1985*a*) Borderline: an adjective in search of a noun. *Journal of Clinical Psychiatry*, **46**, 41–48.
—— , YERAVANIAN, B. I., DAVIS, G. C., *et al* (1985*b*) The nosological status of borderline personality: clinical and polysomnographic study. *American Journal of Psychiatry*, **142**, 192–198.
AMERICAN PSYCHIATRIC ASSOCIATION (1980) *Diagnostic and Statistical Manual of Mental Disorders* (3rd edn) (DSM–III). Washington, DC: APA.
—— (1987) *Diagnostic and Statistical Manual of Mental Disorders* (3rd edn, revised) (DSM–III–R). Washington, DC: APA.
ANDRULONIS, P. A. & VOGEL, N. G. (1984) Comparison of borderline sub-categories to schizophrenic and affective disorders. *British Journal of Psychiatry*, **144**, 358–363.
ARMELIUS, B., KULGREU, G. & RENBERG, E. (1985) Borderline diagnosis from hospital records. *Journal of Nervous and Mental Disease*, **173**, 32–34.
BALINT, M. (1968) *The Basic Fault*. London: Tavistock Publications.
BARASCH, A., FRANCES, A., HURT, S., *et al* (1985) Stability and distinctness of borderline personality disorder. *American Journal of Psychiatry*, **142**, 1484–1486.

BARON, M., GRUEN, R., ASNIS, L., *et al* (1985) Familial transmission of schizotypal and borderline disorders. *American Journal of Psychiatry*, **142**, 927–934.

BARRASH, J., KROLL, J., CAREY, K., *et al* (1983) Discriminating borderline personality disorder from other personality disorders: cluster analysis of the Diagnostic Interview for Borderlines. *Archives of General Psychiatry*, **40**, 1297–1302.

BATEMAN, A. W. (1989) Borderline personality in Britain: a preliminary study. *Comprehensive Psychiatry*, **30**, 385–390.

BOWLBY, J. (1982) *Attachment and Loss. Vol. 1. Attachment* (2nd edn). New York: Basic Books.

BRETHERTON, I. (1985) Attachment theory: retrospect and prospect. In *Growing Points of Attachment Theory and Research* (eds I. Bretherton & E. Waters). *Monographs of the Society for Research in Child Development*, **50**, 3–35.

BRINKLEY, J. R., BEITEMAN, B. D. & FREIDEL, R. O. (1979) Low-dose neuroleptic regimens in the treatment of borderline patients. *Archives of General Psychiatry*, **36**, 319–326.

BROCKMAN, R. (1990) Medication and transference in psychoanalytically oriented psychotherapy of the borderline patient. *Psychiatric Clinics of North America*, **13**, 287–296.

BROWN, G. R. & ANDERSON, B. (1991) Psychiatric morbidity in adult inpatients with childhood histories of sexual and physical abuse. *American Journal of Psychiatry*, **148**, 55–61.

BYRNE, C. P., VELAMOOR, V. R., CERNOVSKY, Z. Z., *et al* (1990) A comparison of borderline and schizophrenic patients for childhood life events and parent–child relationships. *Canadian Journal of Psychiatry*, **35**, 590–595.

CARDISH, R. J. & SILVER, D. (1991) The long term outcome of borderline personality disorder. *Proceedings of the Conference on Borderline Personality Disorder, Hamilton, Ontario, January 1991.*

CARPENTER, W., STRAUSS, J. & BARTKO, J. (1973) Flexible system for the diagnosis of schizophrenia. *Science*, **182**, 1275–1278.

—— & GUNDERSON, J. G. (1977) Five year follow-up comparison of borderline and schizophrenic patients. *Comprehensive Psychiatry*, **18**, 567–571.

CARROLL, B. J., GREDEN, J. T., FEINBERG, M., *et al* (1981) Neuroendocrine evaluation of depression in borderline patients. *Psychiatric Clinics of North America*, **4**, 89–99.

CHOPRA, H. D. & BEATSON, J. A. (1986) Psychotic symptoms in borderline personality disorder. *American Journal of Psychiatry*, **143**, 1605–1607.

CLARKIN, J. F., MARZIALI, E. & MUNROE-BLUM, H. (1991) Group and family treatments for borderline personality disorder. *Hospital and Community Psychiatry*, **42**, 1038–1043.

COCCARO, E. F., SIEVER, L. J., KLAR, H. M., *et al* (1989) Serotonergic studies in patients with affective and personality disorders. *Archives of General Psychiatry*, **46**, 587–599.

COLE, J. O., SALOMON, M., GUNDERSON, J., *et al* (1984) Drug therapy in borderline patients. *Comprehensive Psychiatry*, **25**, 249–254.

COID, J. C., ALLALIO, B. & REES, L. H. (1984) Raised plasma metenkephalin in patients who habitually harm themselves. *Lancet*, **ii**, 545–546.

CORNELIUS, J. R., SOLOFF, P. H., PEREL, J. M., *et al* (1990) Fluoxetine trial in borderline personality disorder. *Psychopharmacology Bulletin*, **26**, 151–154.

CORNELL, D. G., SILK, K. R., LUDOLPH, P. S., *et al* (1983) Test–retest reliability of the Diagnostic Interview for Borderlines. *Archives of General Psychiatry*, **40**, 130–131.

COWDRY, R. & GARDNER, D. (1988) Pharmacotherapy of borderline personality disorder. *Archives of General Psychiatry*, **45**, 111–119.

DULIT, R. A., FYER, M. R., HAAS, G. L., *et al* (1990) Substance use in borderline personality disorder. *American Journal of Psychiatry*, **147**, 1002–1007.

FENTON, W. S. & McGLASHAN, T. H. (1989) Borderline personality disorder and unipolar affective disorder: long term effects of comorbidity. *Journal of Nervous and Mental Disease*, **167**, 467–473.

FRANCES, A., CLARKIN, J. F., GILMORE, M., *et al* (1984) Reliability of criteria for borderline personality disorder – a comparison of DSM–III and the Diagnostic Interview for Borderline Patients. *American Journal of Psychiatry*, **141**, 1080–1084.

FRIEDMAN, R. C., ARNOFF, M. S., CLARKIN, J. E., *et al* (1983) History of suicidal behaviour in depressed borderline patients. *American Journal of Psychiatry*, **140**, 1023–1026.

FYER, M. R., FRANCES, A., SULLIVAN, T., *et al* (1988) Comorbidity of borderline personality disorder. *Archives of General Psychiatry*, **45**, 348–352.

GOLDBERG, S. (1985) The MMPI as a predictor of borderline and schizotypal personality disorders. *Abstracts, Annual Meeting of the Royal College of Psychiatrists*. London: Royal College of Psychiatrists.
───, SCHULZ, S. C., SCHULZ, P. M., *et al* (1986) Borderline and schizotypal personality disorders treated with low-dose thiothixene versus placebo. *Archives of General Psychiatry*, **43**, 698–700.
GRINKER, R. R., WERBLE, B. & DRYE, R. C. (1968) *The Borderline Syndrome*. New York: Basic Books.
GUNDERSON, J. G. (1977) Characteristics of borderlines. In *Borderline Personality Disorders* (ed. P. Hartocollis), pp. 173–192. New York: International Universities Press.
───, CARPENTER, W. T. & STRAUSS, J. S. (1975) Borderline and schizophrenic patients: a comparative study. *American Journal of Psychiatry*, **132**, 1257–1264.
─── & KOLB, J. E. (1978) Discriminating features of borderline patients. *American Journal of Psychiatry*, **135**, 792–796.
───, ─── & AUSTIN, V. (1981) The diagnostic interview for borderline patients. *American Journal of Psychiatry*, **138**, 896–903.
───, SIEVER, L. J. & SPAULDING, E. (1983) The search for a schizotype: crossing the border again. *Archives of General Psychiatry*, **40**, 15–22.
─── & ELIOT, G. R. (1985) The interface between borderline personality disorder and affective disorder. *American Journal of Psychiatry*, **142**, 277–288.
─── & PHILLIPS, K. A. (1991) A current view of the interface between borderline personality disorder and depression. *American Journal of Psychiatry*, **148**, 967–975.
HATHAWAY, S. R. & MCKINLEY, J. C. (1967) *Minnesota Multiphasic Personality Inventory: Manual for Administration and Scoring*. New York: Psychological Corporation.
HERMAN, J. L., PERRY, J. C. & VAN DER KOLK, B. A. (1988) Childhood trauma in borderline personality disorder. *American Journal of Psychiatry*, **146**, 490–495.
HURT, S. W., HYLER, S. E., FRANCES, A., *et al* (1984) Assessing borderline personality with self-report, clinical interview, or semi-structured interview. *American Journal of Psychiatry*, **141**, 1228–1231.
JACKSON, M. & TARNOPOLSKY, A. (1990) Borderline personality. In *Principles and Practice of Forensic Psychiatry* (eds R. Bluglass & P. Bowden). Edinburgh: Churchill Livingstone.
KAVOUSSI, R. J., COCARRO, E. F., KLAR, H. M., *et al* (1990) Structured interviews for borderline personality disorder. *American Journal of Psychiatry*, **147**, 1522–1525.
KENDLER, K. S., GRUENBERG, A. M. & STRAUSS, J. S. (1981) An independent analysis of the Copenhagen sample of the Danish adoption study of schizophrenia: II. The relationship between schizotypal personality disorder and schizophrenia. *Archives of General Psychiatry*, **38**, 982–984.
KERNBERG, O. F. (1967) Borderline personality organisation. *Journal of the American Psychoanalytic Association*, **15**, 641–685.
─── (1981) Structural interviewing. *Psychiatric Clinics of North America*, **4**, 169–195.
───, BURSTEIN, E. D., COYNE, L., *et al* (1972) Psychotherapy and psychoanalysis: final report of the Menninger Foundation's Psychotherapy Research Project. *Bulletin of the Menninger Clinic*, **36**, 1–277.
───, GOLDSTEIN, E. G., CARR, A. C., *et al* (1981) Diagnosing borderline personality: a pilot study using multiple diagnostic methods. *Journal of Nervous and Mental Disease*, **169**, 225–231.
───, SELZER, M. A., KOENIGSBERG, H. W., *et al* (1989) *Psychodynamic Psychotherapy of Borderline Patients*. New York: Basic Books.
KETY, S. S., ROSENTHAL, D., WENDER, P. H., *et al* (1968) The types and prevalence of mental illness in the biological and adopted families of adopted schizophrenics. In *The Transmission of Schizophrenia* (eds D. Rosenthal & S. S. Kety), pp. 345–362. New York: Pergamon Press.
KLEIN, D. F. (1977) Pharmacological treatment and delineation of borderline disorders. In *Borderline Personality Disorders* (ed. P. Hartocollis). New York: International Universities Press.
KOENIGSBERG, H., KERNNBERG, O. F. & SCHOMER, J. (1983) Diagnosing borderline patients in an outpatient setting. *Archives of General Psychiatry*, **40**, 60–63.
KOLB, J. E. & GUNDERSON, J. G. (1980) Diagnosing borderline patients with a semi-structured interview. *Archives of General Psychiatry*, **37**, 37–41.

KONTAXAKIS, V., MARKIONIS, M., VASLAMTSIS, J., *et al* (1987) Multiple neuroendocrinological responses in borderline personality disorder patients. *Acta Psychiatrica Scandinavica*, **76**, 593–597.

KORZEKWA, M. I. (1991) Biological markers in borderline personality disorders. *Proceedings of the Conference on Borderline Personality Disorder, Hamilton, Ontario, January 1991.*

——, STEINER, M., LINKS, P., *et al* (1991) The dexamethasone suppression test in borderline personality disorders. Is it useful? *Canadian Journal of Psychiatry*, **36**, 26–28.

KROLL, J., PYLE, R., ZANDER, J., *et al* (1981*a*) Borderline personality disorder: inter-rater reliability of the Gunderson Diagnostic Interview for Borderlines (DIB). *Schizophrenia Bulletin*, **7**, 269–272.

——, SINES, L., MARTIN, K., *et al* (1981*b*) Borderline personality disorder: construct validity of the concept. *Archives of General Psychiatry*, **38**, 1021–1026.

——, CAREY, K., SINES, L., *et al* (1982) Are there borderlines in Britain? *Archives of General Psychiatry*, **39**, 60–63.

KUTCHER, S. P., BLACKWOOD, D. H. R., ST CLAIR, D. M., *et al* (1987) Auditory P300 in borderline personality disorder and in schizophrenia. *Archives of General Psychiatry*, **44**, 645–650.

—— & —— (1989) Pharmacotherapy of the borderline patient: a critical review and clinical guidelines. *Canadian Journal of Psychiatry*, **34**, 347–353.

——, ——, ST CLAIR, D. M. *et al* (1989) Auditory P300 does not differentiate borderline personality disorder from schizotypal personality disorder. *Biological Psychiatry*, **26**, 645–650.

LIEBOWITZ, M. R. (1979) Is borderline a distinct entity? *Schizophrenia Bulletin*, **5**, 23–37.

LINKS, P. S., STEINER, M. & HUXLEY, G. (1988*a*) The occurrence of borderline personality disorder in the families of borderline patients. *Journal of Personality Disorders*, **2**, 14–20.

——, ——, OFFORD, D. R., *et al* (1988*b*) Characteristics of borderline personality disorder: a Canadian study. *Canadian Journal of Psychiatry*, **33**, 336–340.

——, —— & MITTON, J. (1989) Characteristics of psychosis in borderline personality disorder. *Psychopathology*, **22**, 188–193.

LIVESLEY, W. J. (1991) Borderline personality disorder: aspects of validity. *Proceedings of the Conference on Borderline Personality Disorder, Hamilton, Ontario, January 1991.*

LORANGER, A. W., OLDHAM, J. M. & TULIS, E. H. (1982) Familial transmission of DSM-III borderline personality disorder. *Archives of General Psychiatry*, **39**, 795–799.

——, HIRSHFIELD, R. M. A., SARTORIUS, N., *et al* (1991) The WHO/ADAMHA International Pilot Study of Personality Disorders: background and purpose. *Journal of Personality Disorders*, **5**, 296–306.

McGLASHAN, T. H. (1983*a*) The borderline syndrome: I. Testing three diagnostic systems. *Archives of General Psychiatry*, **40**, 1311–1318.

—— (1983*b*) The borderline syndrome: II. Is it a variant of schizophrenia or affective disorder? *Archives of General Psychiatry*, **40**, 1319–1323.

—— (1986) Long-term outcome of borderline patients. *Archives of General Psychiatry*, **40**, 20–30.

—— (1987*a*) Testing DSM-III symptoms criteria for schizotypal and borderline personality disorders. *Archives of General Psychiatry*, **44**, 143–148.

—— (1987*b*) Borderline personality disorder and unipolar affective disorder: long term effects of comorbidity. *Journal of Nervous and Mental Disease*, **167**, 467–473.

McGLASHAN, T. H. & HEINSSEN, R. K. (1988) Hospital discharge status and long term outcome for patients with schizophrenia, schizoaffective disorder, borderline personality disorder and unipolar affective disorder. *Archives of General Psychiatry*, **45**, 363–368.

MAHLER, M. S., PINE, F. & BERGMANN, A. (1975) *The Psychological Birth of the Human Infant.* London: Hutchinson.

MITTON, J. E. & LINKS, P. S. (1988) Two year prospective follow up of borderlines. *Proceedings and Summary, 141st Annual Meeting, American Psychiatric Association*, p. 225. Washington, DC: APA.

NIGG, J. T., SILK, K. R., WESTEN, D., *et al* (1991) Object representations in the early memories of sexually abused borderline patients. *American Journal of Psychiatry*, **148**, 864–869.

NURNBERG, H. G., RASKIN, M., LEVINE, P. E., *et al* (1991) The comorbidity of borderline personality disorder and other DSM-III-R Axis II personality disorders. *American Journal of Psychiatry*, **148**, 1371–1377.

OGATA, S. N., SILK, K. R. & GOODRICH, S. (1990) The childhood experience of the borderline patient. In *Family Environment and Borderline Personality Disorder* (ed. P. Links). Washington, DC: American Psychiatric Press.

PARIS, J., KNOWLIS, D. & BROWN, R. (1988) Developmental factors in the outcome of BPD. *Proceedings and Summary, 141st Annual Meeting, American Psychiatric Association*, p. 157. Washington, DC: APA.

—— & FRANK, H. (1989) Perceptions of parental bonding in borderline patients. *American Journal of Psychiatry*, **146**, 1498–1499.

PERRY, J. C. (1985) Depression in borderline personality disorder: lifetime prevalence at interview and longitudinal course of symptoms. *American Journal of Psychiatry*, **142**, 15–21.

—— & KLERMAN, G. L. (1980) Clinical features of the borderline personality disorder. *Archives of General Psychiatry*, **137**, 165–173.

PILKONIS, P. A. & FRANK, E. (1988) Personality pathology in recurrent depression: nature, prevalence and relationship to treatment response. *American Journal of Psychiatry*, **145**, 435–441.

POPE, H. G., JONAS, J. M., HUDSON, J. I., *et al* (1983) The validity of DSM–III borderline personality disorder. *Archives of General Psychiatry*, **40**, 23–30.

ROBINS, E. & GUZE, S. G. (1970) Establishment of diagnostic validity in psychiatric illness: its application to schizophrenia. *American Journal of Psychiatry*, **126**, 983–987.

RORSCHACH, H. (1942) *Psychodiagnostics* (5th edn). Berne: Hans Huber.

SERBAN, G. & SIEGEL, S. (1984) Response of borderline and schizotypal patients to small doses of thiothixene and haloperidol. *American Journal of Psychiatry*, **141**, 1455–1458.

SHEA, M. T., GLASS, D. R., PILKONIS, P. A., *et al* (1987) Frequency and implications of personality disorders in a sample of depressed outpatients. *Journal of Personality Disorders*, **1**, 27–42.

SHEEHY, M., GOLDSMITH, L. & CHARLES, E. (1980) A comparative study of borderline patients in a psychiatric outpatient clinic. *American Journal of Psychiatry*, **137**, 1374–1379.

SILK, K. R., LOHR, E., SHIPLEY, E., *et al* (1988) Sleep EEG and DST in borderlines with depression. *Proceedings and Summary, 141st Annual Meeting, American Psychiatric Association*, p. 206. Washington, DC: APA.

SINGER, M. (1977) The borderline diagnosis and psychological tests: review and research. In *Borderline Personality Disorders* (ed. P. Hartocollis). New York: International Universities Press.

SOLOFF, P. H. & ULRICH, R. F. (1981) The Diagnostic Interview for Borderlines: a replication study. *Archives of General Psychiatry*, **38**, 686–692.

—— & MILLWARD, J. W. (1983) Psychiatric disorders in the families of borderline patients. *Archives of General Psychiatry*, **40**, 37–44.

——, GEORGE, A., NATHAN, S., *et al* (1986) Progress in pharmacotherapy of borderline disorders. *Archives of General Psychiatry*, **38**, 686–692.

——, ——, ——, *et al* (1987) Characterising depression in borderline patients. *Journal of Clinical Psychiatry*, **48**, 155–157.

SPITZER, R. L. (1983) Psychiatric diagnosis: are clinicians still necessary? *Comprehensive Psychiatry*, **24**, 399–411.

——, ENDICOTT, J. & ROBINS, E. (1975) Research Diagnostic Criteria (RDC). *Psychopharmacology Bulletin*, **11**, 22–24.

——, —— & GIBBON, M. (1979) Crossing the border into borderline personality and borderline schizophrenia. *Archives of General Psychiatry*, **36**, 17–24.

——, WILLIAMS, J. B. W. & GIBBON, M. (1987) *Structured Clinical Interview for DSM–III–R Axis II Disorders (SCID–II)*. New York: New York State Psychiatric Institute, Biometrics Research.

STANGL, D., PFOHL, B., ZIMMERMAN, M., *et al* (1985) A structured interview for the DSM–III personality disorders. *Archives of General Psychiatry*, **42**, 591–596.

STEINER, M., LINKS, P. & KORZEKWA, M. I. (1988) Biological markers in borderline personality disorders: an overview. *Canadian Journal of Psychiatry*, **33**, 350–354.

STERN, A. (1938) Psychoanalytic investigation of and therapy in the borderline group of neuroses. *Psychoanalytic Quarterly*, **7**, 467–489.

STERN, D. N. (1985) *The Interpersonal World of the Infant*. New York: Basic Books.

STONE, M. H. (1990) Treatment of borderline patients: a pragmatic approach. *Psychiatric Clinics of North America*, **13**, 265–286.

——, STONE, D. K. & HURT, S. (1987) The natural history of borderline patients treated by intensive hospitalisation. *Psychiatric Clinics of North America*, **10**, 185–206.

TARNOPOLSKY, A. (1991) The validity of the borderline personality disorder. In *Handbook of Borderline Personality Disorder* (eds D. Silver & M. Rosenbluth). New York: IUP.

—— & BERELOWITZ, M. (1984) 'Borderline personality': diagnostic attitudes at the Maudsley Hospital. *British Journal of Psychiatry*, **144**, 364–369.

—— & —— (1987) Borderline personality: a review of recent research. *British Journal of Psychiatry*, **151**, 724–734.

TEITELMAN, E., GLASS, J. B., BLYN, C., *et al* (1979) The treatment of female borderlines. *Schizophrenia Bulletin*, **5**, 111–117.

TORGERSEN, S. (1984) Genetic and nosological aspects of schizotypal and borderline personality disorders. *Archives of General Psychiatry*, **41**, 546–554.

WALDINGER, R. J. & FRANK, A. F. (1989) Clinicans' experiences in combining medication and pharmacotherapy in the treatment of borderline patients. *Hospital and Community Psychiatry*, **40**, 712–718.

WECHSLER, D. (1958) *The Measurement and Appraisal of Adult Intelligence* (4th edn). Baltimore: Williams & Wilkins.

WESTEN, D., LUDOLPH, P., LERNER, H., *et al* (1990) Object relations in borderline adolescents. *Journal of the American Academy of Child and Adolescent Psychiatry*, **29**, 338–348.

ZANARINI, M., GUNDERSON, J. G. & FRANKENBURG, F. R. (1987) The diagnostic interview for personality disorders: test–retest and interrater reliability. *Comprehensive Psychiatry*, **28**, 467–480.

——, ——, MARINO, M. F., *et al* (1988) DSM–III disorders in the families of borderline outpatients. *Journal of Personality Disorders*, **2**, 292–302.

——, ——, ——, *et al* (1989) Childhood experiences of borderline patients. *Comprehensive Psychiatry*, **30**, 18–25.

——, ——, ——, *et al* (1989) The revised diagnostic interview for borderlines. *Journal of Personality Disorders*, **3**, 10–18.

——, ——, ——, *et al* (1990) Discriminating borderline personality disorder from other Axis II disorders. *American Journal of Psychiatry*, **147**, 161–167.

——, ——, ——, *et al* (1991) The face validity of the DSM–III and DSM–III–R criteria sets for borderline personality disorder. *American Journal of Psychiatry*, **148**, 870–874.

6 Current concepts and classifications of psychopathic disorder

JEREMY COID

There is considerable debate over whether to retain the term 'psychopathic disorder'. As interest grows in the study of personality disorder, it is likely that this debate will intensify. It is important therefore to clarify the use of the term and point out that it can have four contemporary meanings. Besides lay use as a term of opprobrium, it has been applied in the past as a single diagnostic label and is retained as a legal category of mental disorder within the English Mental Health Act (MHA) 1983. It can also be used as a broad generic term to encompass a wide range of poorly delineated psychopathology exhibited by individuals with severe personality disorder who may exhibit antisocial or other dysfunctional social behaviours. The question of whether to define it in terms of abnormal behaviour or abnormality of personality is still not resolved, although contemporary taxonomists place increasing emphasis on the latter. Unfortunately, the psychopathology associated with psychopathic disorder (however defined) has never fitted easily into the various classifications of personality disorders. At the same time, the condition does not find a suitable place among the major mental disorders.

As a single diagnostic category, psychopathic disorder had increasingly fallen out of fashion until the appearance of dissocial personality disorder in the ICD-10 (World Health Organization, 1992). It was omitted from the ICD-9 (World Health Organization, 1978) and DSM-III-R (American Psychiatric Association, 1987) classifications, having been replaced by 'antisocial personality disorder', and with the ability to add more diagnostic categories when necessary. However, this chapter will demonstrate that no contemporary diagnostic classification is entirely satisfactory. History has demonstrated that the sheer range of psychopathology exhibited by psychopaths and its unusual complexity have always posed major challenges to classification. For this reason, the chapter will begin with a brief examination of the historical development of the diagnostic and legal concepts of psychopathy and the interrelationship between the two. It is also important to re-examine some of the confusions that have arisen over time and the conflicts between different classificatory systems. Five major classifications currently in use will be critically evaluated and the additional importance of taking a longitudinal perspective of these patients' psychopathology will be briefly reviewed. In this chapter, the terms 'psychopathy', 'psychopath', or 'psychopathic' should be understood as relating to the broad generic use of the term unless otherwise stated.

Historical lessons for current concepts of psychopathy

A comprehensive history of the concept of psychopathic disorder is beyond the scope of this chapter and readers are referred to reviews by Lewis (1974) and Pichot (1978). But it is important to understand that several different concepts can be in vogue, sometimes simultaneously, before becoming unpopular and falling into disrepute. One major lesson that can be drawn from the history of psychopathic disorder for the study of personality disorders is that there can be no automatic assumption that current classifications are necessarily comprehensive, valid, or the fundamental basis of what will be employed in the future.

A second important lesson is that at various times, particularly during the 19th century, doctors have considered the psychopathology of individuals now labelled 'psychopathic' as amounting to a more wide-ranging and severe entity than a mere abnormality of 'personality'. This is reflected in recent research demonstrating multiple DSM–III Axis–II and lifetime Axis–I diagnoses in individuals legally detained as psychopaths in maximum security hospitals or demonstrating serious control problems within English prisons (Coid, 1992). These findings merely echo the observations of 19th century psychiatrists who considered psychopathy along a spectrum of severity ranging from near normality to near mental illness. At the same time, the condition could not be explained by major mental illness. Preservation of intelligence was observed but with an impairment in the normal feelings for others, willpower, and morality. Some early authors observed a predisposition to transient psychotic states, affective reactions, and the *psychopathia sexualis* (sexual deviations). Although the condition was often associated with criminal behaviour it was not to be discounted as merely due to a criminal disposition. Those who made the clinical diagnosis (according to the diagnostic fashions of the time) considered that it warranted psychiatric treatment and care rather than punishment. From the beginning of the 19th century, the disorder was considered to have both a constitutional and environmental aetiology. But at various times the idea of a congenital or idiopathic abnormality of personality development has been necessary to explain the apparent absence of environmental disadvantage from the life histories of a subgroup of psychopaths.

In a review of this complex area, Pichot (1978) traces three main historical themes through the 19th century. Firstly, the idea of abnormal personality as defined by social maladjustment, a concept originating in France, but developed most strongly in England with the diagnostic concept of 'moral insanity' and eventually leading to the contemporary legal definition of psychopathic disorder. Within this tradition, psychopathy is defined by the presence of antisocial behaviour. Secondly, a concept developed in France and influenced by the doctrine of mental degeneracy. This included subjects whose personalities were abnormal and who could be antisocial, but who presented primarily with a 'fragility' of their personality and were therefore predisposed to psychotic states of a special nature. Thirdly, the German trend in defining abnormal psychopathic personality types while excluding behaviour from the definition. Many recent debates over classification have centred around the conflict over whether psychopathic disorder should be defined according to abnormal behaviour or abnormal personality. In the UK the position is further confused by a legal definition which borrows the term 'psychopathic' from the German tradition of defining personality disorders without recourse to the inclusion of behavioural abnormality, but applies it to a definition firmly based in the English tradition of observing social maladjustment and abnormal behaviour. This borrowing of a term which categorises one disorder and later applying it to a quite different, or only partially related, one is frequently observed throughout the history of psychopathic disorder.

A further important example of confusion of terms is in the use of 'primary' and 'secondary' to further subdivide the condition. Originally employed by Karpman (1946, 1947) in the USA, primary, idiopathic, or essential psychopathy (anethopathy) was applied to individuals whose antisocial behaviour was the result of a constitutionally determined failure of personality development. Secondary, or symptomatic, psychopathy referred to those whose superficial behaviour might appear to be typical, or even classically psychopathic, but where the underlying motivating or shaping factors would ultimately be explained by other psychopathology. Karpman was largely influenced by psychodynamic thinking and based the primary–secondary subdivision on the eliciting of psychogenic factors in the secondary type, in contrast to a failure to find significant, deep-seated psychic motivations for behaviour in the primary. The primitive development of emotions, fantasy and dream life, social feeling, conscience, etc. rendered most anethopaths untreatable by psychodynamic techniques. Unfortunately, Blackburn (1975, 1986) has also employed a primary–secondary subdivision and partly confused the concept. But his division is based on whether antisocial subjects fall into different groupings according to statistical analysis of Minnesota Multiphasic Personality Inventory (MMPI) scores (Hathaway & McKinley, 1967) (see below). Blackburn (1988) is critical of Karpman's view, yet careful examination of the work of both authors indicates that they are describing different constructs of abnormal personality derived from very different theoretical frameworks.

Once these and other potential sources of confusion are understood, it becomes increasingly clear that the origins of many contemporary debates over classification are firmly rooted in the past. It also becomes clear that different authors are using similar terms to describe quite different concepts or conditions, demonstrating the need to read the original literature if this area is to be understood. This is essential in understanding the origins of the legal category 'psychopathic disorder' within the English MHA.

Origins of the legal category

It is probable that philosophers and physicians recognised individuals corresponding to those later classified as psychopaths as early as the 17th century (Walker & McCabe, 1973). But clearer descriptions of these conditions do not begin to appear until the beginning of the 19th century in the French and German literature. Pinel (1806) described 'manie sans delire' as a pronounced disorder of the affective (emotional) functions and blind impulse to acts of violence, including the possibility of murderous fury, but without perceptible alterations in the intellectual function, perception, judgement, imagination, and memory. His ideas were subsequently developed in France by his pupils into the concept of the 'monomanias' where patients were considered deranged in isolated faculties of the mind resulting in specific abnormalities of behaviour. Examples were later to include an ever growing list of diagnoses based on abnormal behaviour. These were not explained by more generalised and obvious mental disorder and included conditions such as pyromania, kleptomania, nymphomania, homicidal monomania, etc. in ever increasing numbers until the monomanias concept fell widely into disrepute towards the end of the century. However, the notion of an isolated defect or disease of the mind influenced Prichard in England who was later to popularise the concept of a disorder of the moral faculty. Prichard (1835) defined moral insanity as a

> "morbid perversion of the natural feelings, affections, inclinations, temper, habits, moral dispositions and natural dispositions, without any remarkable disorder or defect of the intellect or knowing or reasoning faculties and particularly without any insane illusion or hallucination".

Prichard is usually attributed as the originator of contemporary concepts of psychopathy in the form of 'moral insanity', but this has been disputed by a series of authors, most notably Walk (1954) and Whitlock (1982), who point to a quite different use of the word 'moral' by Prichard and others in early 19th century England, maintaining that a latterday psychiatric equivalent of the word 'moral' would now be 'affective'. Closer examination of Prichard's clinical cases tends to support their observation (Bowden, 1992).

It was not until later in the century that authors such as Maudsley referred to a concept of moral insanity approaching that which is perhaps wrongly attributed to Prichard, the use of the term 'moral' having apparently changed over time. Maudsley (1879) described moral insanity as a

"perverted state of those mental faculties that are usually called the active and moral powers, or included under the feelings and volition – that is to say the feelings, affections, propensities, temper, habits and conduct".

Maudsley believed that morbid emotions could overcome thinking and reasoning, a notion similar to latterday ideas of cognitive distortion secondary to affective disturbance (see Novaco & Welsh, 1989). The overlap of moral insanity with major mental disorder, particularly affective disorder, can be seen both in Maudsley's definition and his suggested aetiology. Like Prichard, he observed 'moral derangement' often preceding or following severe mental disorder, especially melancholia. He also observed that it could occur in relation to epilepsy before or after fits, or appearing in a 'masked' form instead of the convulsion. However, he also recognised an idiopathic form of moral derangement of "more or less congenital defect or imbecility" (Maudsley, 1897).

The concept of a congenital failure of the development of moral sense, as currently defined, existing in the same way as a congenital deficiency of intelligence, can be traced back before Prichard and Maudsley to Grohmann (1818) in Germany. Maudsley later differentiated the moral imbeciles from typical criminals, pointing out that certain children "long before they can possibly know what vice or crime means, [are] addicted to extreme vice, or committing great crimes, with an instinctive facility, and as if from an inherent proneness to criminal actions". He observed that punishment had no reforming effect on them, but believed that as they had no true moral responsibility the threat of punishment would still have a partially inhibiting effect on their behaviour, recommending that, for some, punishment was the best treatment that could be employed.

It is not always clear when reading Maudsley and other writers from the latter part of the 19th century whether 'moral insanity' or 'moral derangement' refers to those patients whose personality or behavioural abnormality is due to a congenital absence of the moral sense or secondary to an active disease process. During this period the idea of a defect or a disease in the hypothetical moral faculty had become widely accepted as European psychiatry came under the influence of French writers who believed these disorders were the result of hereditary degeneration. It was proposed that a degenerative process, which was a physical disorder, showed increasing severity in successive generations, leading finally to the disappearance of affected individuals and their families. In its severe form, the degeneration led to subnormality of intelligence but in the less severe, to moral defects. Physical and psychological stigmata could be identified in both. In this way, English-speaking psychiatrists still associated moral defectiveness with mental defectiveness by the beginning of the 20th century.

Thus, in 1913, the Mental Deficiency Act (valid in Britain with the exception of Scotland and Ireland) covered four classes of subjects: idiots, imbeciles, feeble minded, and moral imbeciles – the fourth class being defined as including "persons who, from an early age, display some permanent moral defect, coupled with strong vicious or criminal propensities on which punishment has little or no deterrent effect". In 1927, the new Mental Deficiency Act began to approach contemporary legislation with a slight modification in nomenclature, moral imbeciles becoming moral defectives, but defined as "persons in whose case there exists mental defectiveness coupled with strong, vicious, or criminal propensities, and who require care, supervision, and control for the protection of others".

English mental health legislation was later to borrow the term 'psychopathic' from the German diagnostic classifications that had developed at the beginning of the 20th century. In this context, psychopathic originally meant no more than 'psychologically damaged' and at that time German psychiatry did not clearly distinguish between conditions that would later be separated into neuroses and personality disorders. But German psychiatry developed further classifications of abnormal personality, culminating in the highly influential work of Schneider (1950) from which certain contemporary categories within DSM–III–R and ICD–10 are ultimately derived. By this time, the term 'psychopathy' equated with contemporary usage of the term 'personality disorder'. Later successive editions of the World Health Organization's *International Classification of Diseases* (ICD) were to substitute the term personality disorder for psychopathy. While keeping to the tradition of borrowing terms from elsewhere and labelling the personality subtypes differently from Schneider, the definitions still tended to leave many of Schneider's original criteria largely intact up until ICD–10.

Meanwhile, Henderson's (1939) broad subdivision of abnormal personalities into 'aggressive', 'inadequate', and 'creative' psychopaths had been highly influential in the UK during the mid-20th century. This subdivision concentrated diagnostic attention on the abnormal and antisocial behaviours of these individuals and simultaneously narrowed down the diagnostic concept while still including a heterogeneous group of individuals. For example, Henderson's predominately 'aggressive' type could include those who injured themselves or others, alcoholics, drug addicts, 'epileptoids', and 'sex variants'. Henderson's classification was never officially adopted but was influential in associating the term 'psychopathic' with antisocial behaviour and implicated a wide range of conditions within a single diagnostic entity.

The more immediate origins of the legal category 'psychopathic disorder' lie with the Royal Commission on the Law relating to mental illness and mental deficiency before the 1959 Mental Health Act. The Commission proposed for broad administrative purposes that three main groups of patients should be recognised. The mentally ill and severely subnormal would constitute two, while higher grade feeble minded, moral defectives, and 'other psychopathic patients' (constituting those with a personality disorder which did not make them severely subnormal but recognised medically as a form of mental disorder resulting in abnormally aggressive or inadequate social behaviour) would constitute a third. Within this third group were individuals who would require different forms of care once admitted to hospital according to their level of intelligence. The Commission therefore subdivided them for administrative purposes into 'subnormality' and 'psychopathic disorder'. None of the final four legal categories of 'mental illness', 'severe subnormality', 'subnormality' or 'psychopathic disorder' constituted a single diagnostic entity or category, but were intended to be generic terms capable of covering a number of specific diagnoses. In legal terms, psychopathic disorder was now defined as

> "a persistent disorder or disability of mind (whether or not including subnormality of intelligence) which results in abnormally aggressive or seriously irresponsible conduct on the part of the patient, and requires or is susceptible to medical treatment".

A very broad range of patients could be compulsorily detained in hospital under this category if psychiatrists so chose. The same category was retained in the 1983 Act, but for compulsory detention a proviso was added that admission "is likely to alleviate or prevent a deterioration of his condition". This treatability qualification meant there should be no obligation to admit these patients unless it is considered that treatment will be effective (Bluglass, 1990).

More recently, the use of this legal category has come under increasing criticism. Grounds (1987) has argued that there are doubts about the nature of the disorder, what constitutes treatment, which patients are actually treatable, the effectiveness of treatment, and whether evidence of psychological change implies a reduced risk of reoffending. He further argues that indeterminate hospital orders may provide an unrealistic and unjust framework for treating psychopaths detained in maximum security hospitals. Dell & Robertson (1988) were exceptionally critical of this legal framework following a study of patients in Broadmoor Hospital which revealed shortcomings in the medical management of psychopaths. More recently, criticisms have been made of the lack of adequate facilities for their treatment and the risk to professional and institutional reputations when these patients reoffend (Coid & Cordess, 1992). Many UK psychiatrists still believe that certain patients with severe personality disorder should be given a trial of treatment in an attempt to ameliorate their conditions. But shortcomings in the terms of the MHA, 1983, subtle political pressures on psychiatrists to continue to detain dangerous patients after treatment has been unsuccessful, and the implied acceptance of professional responsibility for further reoffending, have all resulted in the compulsory admission of such patients becoming increasingly unpopular in the UK. Thus, although approximately 25% of patients in the special hospitals were still detained under the legal category psychopathic disorder in the 1980s (Hamilton, 1990), the proportion was only 0.24% in ordinary NHS facilities (Government Statistical Service, 1991).

Current diagnostic approaches to psychopathic disorder

No single method of classifying personality disorder is entirely satisfactory when applied to psychopaths. In an important review of personality disorder, Rutter (1987) pointed out that three unifying features of these conditions have been: (a) an onset in childhood or adolescence, (b) longstanding persistence over time without marked remission or relapses, and (c) abnormalities that seem to constitute a basic aspect of the individual's usual functioning. When applied to psychopathic disorders, four additional qualifying features can be applied: (a) that it is a particularly severe condition, whether measured according to the number of personality traits present, the level of functioning according to a psychodynamic framework, or the number of diagnostic labels finally applied, (b) that it is resistant to treatment, either as a function of the severity of the condition or an unwillingness or lack of cooperation in treatment by the individual concerned, (c) that the abnormality of personality leads to dissocial behaviour (including behaviour harmful to the individual concerned), and (d) that the behaviour may be sufficiently socially unacceptable to lead to formal interventions such as criminal proceedings, imprisonment, compulsory hospital admission, and can also lead to other forms of serious social breakdown such as homelessness, vagrancy, etc. These four additional features do not separate psychopathic disorder from personality disorder but place it at the far end of a spectrum of severity.

The following sections will examine the current classification of psychopathic disorder according to five different contemporary frameworks.

ICD-10 dissocial personality disorder

The ICD-10 classification of personality disorders is now considerably closer to DSM-III-R Axis-II than ICD-9 (see Table 6.1). The conditions listed have been agreed by advisers and consultants in different countries as a reasonable basis for defining 'typical' disorders. It is recommended that clinicians should generally record as many diagnoses as necessary to cover the clinical picture, but if recording more than one then the main diagnosis should be specified. ICD-10 personality disorders include a variety of conditions which demonstrate that an individual's characteristic and enduring patterns of inner experience and behaviour deviate markedly from the culturally expected and accepted range (World Health Organization, 1992). For research purposes:

(a) the deviation must be manifest in one or more of:
  (i) cognition
  (ii) affectivity
  (iii) control over impulses and needs gratification
  (iv) relating to others and manner of handling interpersonal situations
(b) the deviation must be pervasive in the sense of manifesting itself as behaviour that is inflexible, maladaptive, or otherwise dysfunctional across a broad range of personal and social situations
(c) there is personal distress, or adverse impact on the social environment, or both, clearly attributable to (b)
(d) there must be evidence that the deviation is stable and of long duration, having its onset in late childhood or adolescence
(e) the deviation cannot be explained as a manifestation or consequence of other adult mental disorders, although other episodic or chronic conditions may coexist or be superimposed upon it
(f) organic brain disease, injury, or gross dysfunction must be excluded as a possible cause.

Dissocial personality disorder ICD-10, F60.2 is intended to include previous diagnostic categories of sociopathic, amoral, asocial, antisocial, and psychopathic personality disorder. ICD-10 defines this condition as usually coming to attention because of a gross disparity between behaviour and the prevailing social norms, and is characterised by:

(a) callous unconcern for the feelings of others and lack of the capacity for empathy
(b) gross and persistent attitude of irresponsibility and disregard for social norms, rules and obligations
(c) incapacity to maintain enduring relationships

TABLE 6.1
DSM-III-R and ICD-10 personality disorder classifications

	DSM-III-R	ICD-10
Cluster A:	paranoid	paranoid
	schizoid	schizoid
	schizotypal	dissocial
Cluster B:	antisocial	emotionally unstable:
	borderline	impulsive type
	histrionic	borderline type
	narcissistic	histrionic
Cluster C:	avoidant	anankastic (obsessive-compulsive)
	dependent	anxious (avoidant)
	obsessive-compulsive	dependent
	passive-aggressive	other
Additional:	self-defeating	unspecified
	sadistic	

(d) very low tolerance of frustration and a low threshold for discharge of aggression including violence
(e) incapacity to experience guilt and to profit from experience, particularly punishment
(f) marked proneness to blame others or to offer plausible rationalisations for the behaviour bringing the subject into conflict with society
(g) persistent irritability

For research purposes three or more of these criteria should be present. The usefulness of this diagnostic category must be determined by future research. The criteria suggest an emphasis on personality characteristics rather than types of behaviour. However, personality features such as unconcern, specific attitudes, low tolerance, incapacity to experience certain feelings etc., may ultimately have to be inferred from a patient's behaviour patterns rather than a true understanding of underlying personality abnormalities. Furthermore, additional categories of personality disorder such as 'paranoid', 'emotionally unstable', and 'histrionic' may well have to be added to encompass the broad range of psychopathology exhibited by psychopaths (see Coid, 1992). Criterion (g), persistent irritability, already demonstrates considerable potential for overlap with two criteria for 'emotionally labile personality disorder' within ICD–10, and does not easily distinguish an implied personality trait from an affective disturbance.

ICD–10 appears to have made an attempt to assemble the core personality traits of the psychopathic personality. But whether this will translate successfully into research and clinical practice remains to be seen.

DSM–III–R antisocial personality disorder

DSM–III–R diagnostic criteria for personality disorders refer to types of behaviour or traits that are characteristic of the person's recent and long-term functioning since early adulthood. The constellation of behaviour or traits cause either significant impairment in social or occupational functioning or subjective distress. The classification includes 11 categories divided into three 'clusters' as shown in Table 6.1. These are diagnosed along a separate Axis (Axis-II) from the major mental disorders. Two additional categories, sadistic and self-defeating personality disorders, were proposed but considered in need of further study before formal adoption. The essential features of antisocial personality disorder (ASPD) are patterns of irresponsible and antisocial behaviour beginning in childhood or early adolescence and continuing into adulthood. For the diagnosis to be given, the person must be at least 18 years of age and have a history of conduct disorder before the age of 15 years. The criteria for the condition are summarised below and represent the only personality disorder category that is derived from empirical research (Robins, 1966, 1978).

(a) current age at least 18
(b) evidence of conduct disorder with onset before age 15, as indicated
by a history of three or more of the following:
- (i) truancy
- (ii) running away
- (iii) fights
- (iv) using weapons
- (v) forcing sexual activities on others
- (vi) physical cruelty to animals
- (vii) physical cruelty to people
- (viii) destruction of others' property
- (ix) fire setting
- (x) lying
- (xi) stealing without confrontation of a victim
- (xii) stealing with confrontation of a victim

(c) a pattern of irresponsible and antisocial behaviour since age 15, as
indicated by at least four of the following:

- (i) unable to sustain consistent work behaviour
- (ii) failure to conform to social norms with respect to lawful behaviour
- (iii) irritable and aggressive
- (iv) failure to honour financial obligations
- (v) failure to plan ahead, or is impulsive
- (vi) lack of regard for the truth
- (vii) recklessness
- (viii) lack of ability to function as a parent
- (ix) has never sustained a monogamous relationship for more than
  one year
- (x) lack of remorse

(d) occurrence of antisocial behaviour is not exclusively during the course
of schizophrenic or manic episodes.

Other categories in Axis-II are ultimately derived from Schneider's
classification, or loosely based on psychodynamic concepts and promoted
at the Committee stage of assembling the DSM Glossary. Field trials have
shown a higher inter-rater reliability for ASPD than other Axis-II categories
(Mellsop *et al*, 1982).

DSM–III–R ASPD omits the personality traits component of the
diagnostic construct of psychopathy and substitutes a framework based on
behaviour instead. It is anticipated that the present diagnostic concept will
change yet again in DSM–IV and align itself more closely to the ICD–10
(Hare *et al*, 1991). Successive editions of the Diagnostic and Statistical
Manual have radically changed the construct of psychopathy in the USA

over the latter half of this century. DSM–I (American Psychiatric Association, 1952) divided personality disorders into three groups: personality pattern disturbances, personality trait disturbances, and sociopathic personality disturbance. The latter category included individuals who are "ill primarily in terms of society and of conformity with the prevailing cultural milieu, and not only in terms of personal discomfort and relations with other individuals". Sociopathy included four subcategories: antisocial reaction, dissocial reaction, sexual deviation, and addiction. 'Psychopathic personality' and 'constitutional psychopathic state' were abandoned as independent labels and subsumed under the category 'antisocial reactions'. In the DSM–I, 'Dissocial reaction' referred to a quite different entity than in ICD–10 (a further example of the borrowing of the term from one glossary and applying it to a new diagnostic entity) and included individuals "manifesting a disregard for the usual social codes . . . as a result of having lived all their lives in an abnormal moral environment". This category emphasised an environmental cause for the dissocial behaviour and an ability for the individual to align himself with a particular, albeit antisocial, code of social behaviour which could include subcultural criminal behaviour.

DSM–II (American Psychiatric Association, 1968) underwent a dramatic change to align itself with the ICD–8 (World Health Organization, 1967). Sexual deviations and addictions were now classified elsewhere, and antisocial and dissocial reaction were replaced by antisocial personality disorder which applied to "individuals who are basically unsocialised and whose behaviour pattern brings them repeatedly into conflict with society". However, this category also included a number of personality characteristics such as selfishness, callousness, irresponsibility, impulsiveness, inability to learn from punishment and experience, low frustration tolerance, and a tendency to blame others and offer plausible rationalisations for behaviour. In the DSM–III, ASPD underwent a further, dramatic transformation into a diagnostic construct based entirely on the presence of a series of types of behaviour that had been derived from empirical longitudinal research on conduct-disordered children (Robins, 1966, 1978). The separation of the personality disorders into a separate axis of DSM–III also led to a dramatic increase in research into these conditions and paved the way for important studies of the epidemiology of ASPD.

Epidemiology

Several major epidemiological studies have employed standardised diagnostic criteria for ASPD, making it the most comprehensibly studied personality disorder category in this area of research from any contemporary glossary. The epidemiological catchment area (ECA) study in three US sites surveyed the largest general population samples and showed one month, six months, and lifetime prevalence rates for ASPD of 0.5%, 1.2%, and 2.6% respectively, the lifetime prevalence rate varying between each site from 2.1 to 3.4 (Robins *et al*, 1984; Robins & Regier, 1991). Lifetime prevalence for males was significantly higher (4.5%) than for females (0.8%), highest in the 25–44 age groups, no higher in blacks than whites, commonest in those who had dropped out of high school, and most commonly found in inner-city populations. A more recent US study from six sites also found a one-month prevalence of 0.5% but confirmed a 2.5% lifetime diagnosis (Regier *et al*, 1988).

The Christchurch, New Zealand, psychiatric epidemiological study employed similar methods and revealed six month and lifetime ASPD prevalence rates of 0.9% and 3.1% respectively (Wells *et al*, 1989). Lifetime rates for males were 4.2% compared with 0.5% for females, but differences were not statistically significant, probably because of the smaller sample size. This study included an examination of the one-year recovery rate which showed a surprisingly high level of 51.6% for ASPD. However, this may have reflected a distortion of state effects from substance abuse on the ASPD diagnosis. A subgroup of drug abusers no longer appeared personality disordered following abstinence.

A lifetime prevalence rate of 3.7% (6.5% males, 0.8% females) was found for ASPD in Edmonton, Canada, and was highest in the 18–34 age group and those who were widowed, separated, and divorced (Bland *et al*, 1988*a*,*b*). Rates were considerably lower in Taiwan, ranging from 0.03% in rural settings to 0.14% in metropolitan Taipei (Hwu *et al*, 1989). But these figures generally correlated with overall lower rates of most DSM–III disorders measured in Taiwan. Reich *et al* (1989) and Zimmerman & Coryell (1990) also showed considerably lower rates, of 0.4% and 0.9% respectively, in two US studies, but used different instruments from the other researchers who had employed the Diagnostic Interview Schedule which had been specifically developed for epidemiological study (Robins *et al*, 1981).

Zimmerman & Coryell (1990) also demonstrated that the rates increased from 0.9% to 3% when interviewers were used, suggesting that self-report instruments may well underestimate ASPD.

Studies in prison settings have shown a high prevalence of ASPD, varying from 39–76% of subjects (Hare, 1983, 1984; Bland *et al*, 1990; Cote & Hodgins, 1990). However, prisons vary in their concentrations of hardened, career criminals who might be expected to have higher rates of ASPD than those found in institutions which contain more petty offenders, such as county jails in the USA or remand prisons in the UK. A study of male prisoners who had posed the most serious disciplinary problems in English prisons demonstrated that 86% had a diagnosis of ASPD, the remaining group tending to have organic or psychotic illnesses which had accounted for their disruptive and dangerous institutional behaviour (Coid, 1991, 1992).

Epidemiological studies have also revealed important characteristics of ASPD individuals. Males and females appear to have differing ages of onset, with males tending to present with conduct disorder at an earlier age than females who present around puberty (Robins, 1986). There are also sex differences in presenting symptoms, with men having more traffic offences and arrests, and exhibiting more promiscuity and illegal occupation, whereas women more often desert or hit their spouses or fail to work steadily. Men appear to have a special vulnerability to ASPD. Childhood environments of ASPD females are more disturbed, suggesting that more predisposing factors are required for the disorder to appear in women (Robins, 1985). Similarly, in a child guidance sample, records showed that women later diagnosed as sociopathic had lower IQs, had more frequently been in correctional institutions, more often had parents on welfare or who were chronically unemployed, and more often had alcoholic or sociopathic fathers than did male sociopaths (Robins, 1966).

ASPD appears to be associated with poverty and other indices of social failure. Koegel *et al* (1988) found five times more ASPD among the homeless in Los Angeles than in the general population. Poor school success and poor work history predispose to low status jobs and unemployment. However, Robins (1966) demonstrated that despite originating from families of low socioeconomic status, adult status of sociopaths still tended to fall below that of their parents during a study period which coincided with general economic and social improvement in the USA.

The important finding of an association between ASPD and inner-city residence corresponds to the criminological tradition of linking urbanisation with increasing rates of crime (Shaw & McKay, 1942; Baldwin & Bottoms, 1976; Herbert, 1979). However, it is not established whether high rates of crime in inner-city areas are contributed to significantly by an excess of ASPD residents. Explanations such as a 'drift' of these individuals to inner-city areas requires further examination, as do the observations that unstable and disadvantaged individuals tend to be placed in high crime and socially deprived areas as a result of housing policy in the UK (Rex & Moore, 1967; Gill, 1967).

Black people are disproportionately over-represented in the prison populations in both the USA and the UK. Although they disproportionately reside in inner-city areas of both countries, US studies still show that the inner city black population has higher arrest and conviction rates than the white population (Shannon, 1978). As the best predictor of adult antisocial personality is childhood conduct disorder (Robins, 1978), an association of conduct problems with race would tend to imply a higher rate of ASPD in black people. For example, Rutter *et al* (1974) noted a higher rate of conduct problems in black children in an inner London area than white children. Similarly, the Epidemiologic Catchment Area study retrospectively examined conduct problems in childhood and showed that black children had higher rates than white children. However, black children were less likely to continue these types of behaviour into adult life, resulting in similar rates of ASPD in adulthood.

Antisocial personality disorder appears to predominate in young adulthood and studies have suggested that the symptoms begin to diminish in a proportion during middle age. However, the disorder also involves a higher risk of death during early adulthood. Unfortunately, at least 20% still meet the criteria when aged 45 and constitute 0.5% of the US population, indicating that those who do not remit still pose a serious problem for clinicians and for society. Robins (1986) has also made the alarming proposal that there may be a rising proportion of individuals with ASPD in successive US generations over time.

Criminal psychopaths

Only one UK study has examined the prevalence of DSM-III Axis-II disorders (including ASPD) in patients detained under the legal category psychopathic disorder. In a study of three samples, including male psychopaths detained in an English special hospital, female psychopaths detained in three English special hospitals, and male prisoners detained in three special units in English prisons, (developed specifically for those who have posed difficult and dangerous behaviours), ASPD was found in 53% of the overall total ($n = 243$), coming second to borderline personality (BPD) which was found in the majority (69%) of subjects. BPD featured in 91% of the female psychopaths but the proportion fell to just over half of male psychopaths and male prisoners. However, 86% of male prisoners showed ASPD, and a high proportion also showed a paranoid personality disorder (67%). An important finding was that subjects required multiple Axis-II categories to describe their psychopathology and only two subjects with ASPD presented this condition as a single Axis-II diagnosis. It appeared that ASPD would frequently associate with paranoid, narcissistic, borderline, and/or passive–aggressive personality disorders. These additional diagnoses were necessary to encompass the broad range of severe pathology demonstrated by these subjects (Coid, 1992).

By applying lifetime diagnostic instruments to the same sample, subjects were also found to have multiple Axis-I major mental disorders, with depressive disorder having a lifetime prevalence of 50%. ASPD tended to associate with a lifetime history of substance abuse, whereas affective disturbances such as depressive disorder, dysthymia, mania, panic disorder, and unspecified psychotic episodes tended to associate with an Axis-II diagnosis of BPD. Indicators of neuropsychological abnormality such as perinatal trauma, developmental delay, a history of seizures, etc., did not associated with ASPD but with schizotypal and schizoid personalities. However, factors indicative of an adverse family environment before the age of 15, including parental discord, poverty, physical and sexual abuse, placement in care, and criminal first-degree relatives did associate with ASPD (Coid, unpublished).

Genetic and familial factors

Studies of twins and adoptees have begun to clarify how genetic and environmental factors interact in the development of antisocial behaviour. Genetic studies have examined juvenile delinquency, conduct disorders, adult criminality, ASPD, and substance abuse. But it must be pointed out that although these are overlapping syndromes, they have a quite uncertain genetic relationship to each other and the results from some studies may not entirely apply to ASPD.

Cloninger & Gottesman (1987) have examined the liability to ASPD in first-degree relatives of antisocial probands and found that familial (genetic plus environmental) factors relevant to the development of ASPD are largely the same in men and women. However, sex differences in prevalence are due to a higher threshold for expression in women than in men (Cloninger *et al*, 1975, 1978). Thus, to develop ASPD, women must on average have a greater liability of both genetic and environmental factors than men. On the other hand, it has also been suggested that the clinical counterpart of milder ASPD in men could be Briquet's syndrome or somatisation disorder in women (Cloninger, 1978). Both conditions aggregate in the same families and there is an excess of ASPD and somatisation disorder in the relatives of probands with either disorder. Similarly, women with ASPD have more relatives with either ASPD or somatisation disorder than women with somatisation disorder alone.

Results from the Stockholm adoption study support the sex differences in the expression of liability to ASPD (Bohman *et al*, 1984; Cloninger *et al*, 1984; Sigvardsson *et al*, 1984). Four family types were identified, with different clinical features in men and women and with different genetic and environmental antecedents. Alcohol abuse was the most prominent clinical characteristic of men in two family types (milieu-limited and male-limited alcoholism). Criminal behaviour was the most prominent feature of men in the other two family types. In one of the latter, the men committed property offences but not crimes against the person. Women in those families with a strong genetic loading, usually both biological parents criminal, also committed property offences. With a milder genetic loading the women had multiple somatic complaints from an early age. In the other family type associated with criminal behaviour the men committed a variety of crimes, including crimes of violence. Women in these families had a high rate of somatic complaints and psychiatric disability.

Cloninger & Gottesman (1987) have reviewed the studies of antisocial behaviour in twins and pointed out that the results have markedly different implications for the role of genetic factors in juvenile delinquency and adult criminality. Twin studies reveal no differences between monozygotic and dizygotic rates for juvenile delinquency, indicating that genetic factors are unimportant in most cases of juvenile delinquency. However, results for adult criminality have consistently demonstrated substantial differences according to zygosity, indicating a genetic component.

Adoption studies provide a more sensitive test of gene–environment interaction than twin studies where it must be accepted that monozygotic twins are likely to have shared more similar environmental experiences (see Carey, 1992). Crowe (1972) studied a small sample of adopted-away children of female felons in Iowa and found an increase in adult criminality and ASPD but not alcoholism or other disorders when compared with non-adopted controls. He also showed that children placed late for adoption tended to become criminal more often than controls, late placement suggesting an environmental influence from living with the mother. In a large Swedish adoption study, criminality alone in the biological parents increased the risk of crime in adopted-away sons but alcoholism did not, when compared with the sons of other parents. Sons of parents with both crime and alcoholism were usually alcohol abusers and not criminal. Adopted women with a history of criminal offences had biological parents who had committed an excess of offences and showed criminality in their parents to a more marked degree than the adopted-away criminal male subjects, again suggesting that a genetic predisposition to criminality must be more severe in order for a woman to become criminal than for a man. However, certain postnatal environmental factors also increased the risk of property crime in both sexes, but with different factors important for each sex. Low occupational status of the adoptive father and multiple temporary placements of the adoptee were predictive of criminality in men but not in women. Rural adoptive homes and prolonged institutional care were predictive of criminality in women but not in men. It was concluded that both females and males were unlikely to become criminals unless they were at high risk as a consequence of both their biological-parent background and their postnatal environment (Bohman *et al*, 1982; Cloninger *et al*, 1982; Sigvardsson *et al*, 1982).

A large Danish adoption study showed similar results, detecting contributions towards criminality from both biological and adoptive parents. There was no evidence that the type of biological parent conviction was related to the type of adoptee conviction, but there was a particularly strong relationship between the presence of chronic criminal behaviour in the adopted-away children and a history of conviction in biological parents. A number of potentially confounding environmental variables were considered in this study but none proved sufficient to explain the genetic relationship. It was therefore concluded that some biological factor must be transmitted genetically to increase the likelihood that the adopted children would be convicted of criminal offences, particularly the chronic offenders (Mednick *et al*, 1987).

Comment

It is thought that ASPD is the personality disorder most likely to undergo change in the DSM–IV, with simplified criteria and the addition of items associated with personality characteristics of the psychopath rather than an emphasis on behavioural disturbance alone (Hare *et al*, 1991). Current DSM–III–R criteria have been criticised as too long and cumbersome, yet ASPD is the only Axis-II category derived from empirical research and its criteria have obtained the highest inter-rater reliability. There have been criticisms that the criteria are too broad, in the sense of including many individuals who are prone to criminal behaviour but do not have the personality traits that would be associated with psychopathy (Millon, 1981); on the other hand they have been criticised as too narrow, leading to the exclusion of many antisocial individuals who do not enter the criminal justice system (Hare, 1983). Perhaps the most important criticisms of the ASPD category come from studies of substance abuse. There is a substantial association between ASPD and these disorders (Docherty *et al*, 1986; Tarter, 1988). But the validity of these findings is partly compromised by the questionable independence of the diagnosis (Gerstley *et al*, 1990; Nathan, 1988).

Certain criteria for ASPD and substance dependence in DSM–III–R are essentially equivalent and it is not always clear whether two disorders are observed in a single individual or one disorder is given two diagnoses (Widiger & Shea, 1991). On the other hand, Brooner *et al* (1992) have argued that the early-onset criteria of ASPD are an important prognostic factor in substance abuse, indicating the importance of further research in resolving these issues (see Alterman & Cacciola, 1991).

The inclusion of a longitudinal component within this diagnostic construct considerably improves its descriptive ability. Furthermore, it could be argued that the addition of other Axis-II diagnostic categories is all that is necessary to complete a more comprehensive diagnostic picture of the psychopath which cannot be provided by other checklists and glossaries. It may therefore be prudent to retain this category until ICD–10 dissocial and the forthcoming DSM–IV replacement have established their validity.

Hare's Psychopathy Checklist

Hare's Psychopathy Checklist (PCL) is not a classificatory system but a unidimensional scale of psychopathy consisting of both personality traits and antisocial behaviours. At the heart of this construct is the notion that psychopathy is a unitary syndrome that can be measured using such a scale. During its development, Hare initially took the list of 16 characteristics considered by Cleckley (1976) to be typical of the psychopath in his seminal work *The Mask of Sanity* and applied them to a series of prisoners (Hare, 1980). After further studies of prison samples, the preliminary PCL was expanded to a 22-item version and ratings of 0–2 applied to each item which could give a maximum possible score of 44. At a cut-off score of 33 or above, a subject would be designated a psychopath for research purposes. For most items in the PCL, data are collected from both interview and from institutional files before scoring 0 = not applicable, 1 = applies partly, or 2 = item applies. Two items were subsequently dropped from the 22-PCL and a further item modified to create a revised version of the checklist (PCL–R) as shown below.

(a) glibness/superficial charm
(b) grandiose sense of self worth
(c) need for stimulation/proneness to boredom
(d) pathological lying
(e) cunning/manipulative
(f) lack of remorse or guilt
(g) shallow affect
(h) callous/lack of empathy
(i) parasitic lifestyle
(j) poor behavioural controls
(k) promiscuous sexual behaviour
(l) early behaviour problems
(m) lack of realistic, long-term goals
(n) impulsivity
(o) irresponsibility
(p) failure to accept responsibility for own actions
(q) many short-term marital relationships
(r) juvenile delinquency
(s) revocation of conditional release
(t) criminal versatility

The corresponding cut-off for the PCL–R is a score of 30 or above (Hare, 1985). Hare and colleagues have now demonstrated high inter-rater and test–retest reliability using both PCL and PCL–R on prisoners and forensic psychiatric hospital in-patients when the checklist is used by properly trained raters.

More recently, Hare and colleagues demonstrated by factor analysis that the PCL and PCL–R contain two correlated factors that have distinct patterns of intercorrelations with other variables. The first factor consists of the personality traits considered to be descriptive of the syndrome, including items (a), (b), (d)–(h), and (p) in the above list, which generally represent the selfish, callous, and remorseless use of others. The second factor reflects socially deviant behaviour, including items (c), (i), (j), (l)–(o), (r) and (s), representing a chronically unstable, antisocial, and socially deviant lifestyle (Harpur *et al*, 1988, 1989). It was suggested that factor 1 core personality traits correspond to DSM–III narcissistic personality disorder and factor 2 features of a chronic, unstable lifestyle to DSM–III antisocial personality disorder.

Reliability

If the PCL–R items are re-examined, they appear generally consistent with several traditional views of the personality traits and types of behaviour defining the construct of psychopathy. A series of earlier authors described psychopaths as selfish, aggressive, feeling no guilt or remorse for their behaviour, lacking in shame, lacking empathy, callous, and having a fundamental incapacity for love or true friendship. They also lack insight, are unable to control impulses or delay gratification, and demonstrate pathological lying, thrill seeking, poor judgement, and disregard for societal conventions, having social and sexual relationships that are superficial but demanding and manipulative. They are able to extricate themselves from difficult situations by producing intricate and at times contradictory lies, together with theatrical and convincing explanations and promises, and present as two-dimensional people able to simulate emotions and affectional attachment when it is advantageous to do so (Karpman, 1961; McCord & McCord, 1964; Craft, 1965; Buss, 1966). Clinical practice measured by surveys of Canadian psychiatrists (Gray & Hutchinson, 1964) and British forensic psychiatrists and prison medical officers (Davies & Feldman, 1981) have also confirmed very similar, or overlapping, features. Similarly, analysis of the research literature on primary features of psychopathy (Fotheringham, 1957) and content analysis of articles on psychopathy (Albert *et al*, 1959) have largely shown the same findings.

Violent criminal behaviour

Early onset of antisocial and criminal behaviour and a wide range of criminal activities (criminal versatility) are important items in Hare's construct. In addition to a high rate of criminal activities in general, psychopaths, as measured on the PCL–R, engage in an inordinate amount of violent and aggressive behaviour compared with other, non-psychopathic criminals (Hare & MacPherson, 1984*a*). Two studies have examined the violent offences of psychopathic prisoners compared with non-psychopathic groups, and found that the latter tended to occur during domestic disputes or during a period of extreme emotional arousal. The victims were usually female and known to them. For psychopaths, victims tended to be male and unknown, the violence tending to have revenge or retribution as the motive and often occurring in a drinking bout. In general, the psychopaths' violence was callous and cold-blooded or part of an aggressive or macho display, but without the affective colouring or understandable motives that accompanied the violence of the non-psychopathic group (Williamson *et al*, 1987; Wright & Wong, 1988).

One longitudinal study has examined the criminal careers of psychopaths based on global ratings of psychopathy (Hare *et al*, 1988). Criminal activities of psychopaths showed a higher level relative to other offenders in the early adult years but tended to peak around the age of 35 or 40 years and then to decrease sharply. However, these age-related changes were more dramatic for the non-violent than the violent crimes. The violent activities of psychopaths remained relatively constant after the sharp drop in their non-violent criminal activities had occurred.

Violent and disruptive behaviour within prisons and in hospital settings also characterised the institutional careers of certain subjects with high PCL and PCL-R scores. It has been observed that the extreme nature of the dangerous and disruptive behaviour of a small group of male psychopaths in the English prison system has now resulted in them being refused admission (or readmission) to maximum security hospitals on the grounds of 'untreatability' according to the criteria of the English MHA (Coid, 1991). As a result, new and alternative initiatives have been taken within UK prisons to effect the humane control and containment of these individuals (Home Office, 1984; Walmsley, 1989; Ditchfield, 1990). Men admitted to the three prison special units show higher PCL scores than psychopaths in the English special hospitals. Similarly, research with samples of Canadian and US prisoners (reviewed by Hare, 1990) has shown a correlation between violent and aggressive behaviour in institutional settings (and the PCL-R) and anti-authoritarian behaviour rated by prison officers in Scottish prisons using the prison behaviour rating scale (Cooke, personal communication).

Predictive value

Hare (1990) points out that psychopaths can deceive and manipulate others in prison as frequently as outside. Although some can be disruptive, others may make heavy use of various constructive programmes which are most likely to impress the parole board. Some appear inordinately successful in obtaining conditional release despite their lengthy criminal records, some of which may include previous violations of conditional release. Four empirical studies reviewed in detail by Hare (1990) have confirmed their poor risk using the PCL or PCL-R scores, providing actuarial demonstration that high scores will correlate with failure measured in terms of the number of subjects whose parole was revoked or who reoffended, and length of time for each before a failure occurred. In two of these studies, PCL factor 1 and factor 2 scores were also examined in relation to failure following conditional release, demonstrating that factor 2 (chronic antisocial lifestyle) correlated most strongly. This would tend to confirm the maxim that previous behaviour is usually the most accurate predictor of future behaviour rather than personality traits.

Laboratory studies

Neuropsychological studies have failed to demonstrate an association between brain damage and dysfunction and high scores on the PCL or PCL-R (Hare,

1984). However, more subtle differences have been found between psychopathic subjects and controls using specific laboratory tests to measure language, attentional processes, and cognitive functioning. It has been suggested from clinical observation that psychopaths have difficulty in experiencing or appreciating the emotional significance of everyday life. Cleckley (1976) suggested that psychopaths suffer from a central and deep-seated semantic disorder in which meaning-related, associative, and elaborative processes are missing. These deficits would be 'masked' by a well functioning expressive and receptive process whereby the psychopath can readily express himself both vividly and eloquently, sometimes charming and conning others, but with a pantomime of feeling rather than a true understanding of the connotative or affective meaning of the words used.

To test this hypothesis, psychopaths have been presented with a procedure to dissociate affective content of word meaning from denotative content (described by Brownell *et al*, 1984) and compared with non-psychopaths. Williamson *et al* (unpublished) found that psychopaths defined by the PCL–R made little use of cognitive content in grouping words in a series of presentations of word triads when they were required to group the two of these words that were closest to each other in meaning. In a further part of this study, subjects were required to match clauses or pictures on the basis of inferred emotional information. Psychopaths tended to confuse emotional polarity (goodness or badness) in linguistic tasks but not pictorial tasks, suggesting that they had difficulty in integrating information in situations in which affective processing in the formation of conceptual relationships was required.

In a more recent study, the same researchers tested the hypothesis that psychopaths failed to use or understand connotative aspects of language with a lexical decision task in which prison inmates pressed a button as quickly as possible whenever a letter-string flashed on a computer monitor (Williamson *et al*, 1991). Normal subjects can make a lexical decision of this sort more quickly when the letter-string is an emotional word than when it is a neutral word. But at the same time some components of their event-related brain potentials are different to emotional words than to neutral ones. The study found that this normal pattern of responding occurred in non-psychopathic inmates but not in psychopathic ones. Psychopaths failed to show normal behavioural (reaction time) and electrocortical differentiation between emotional and neutral words. Both studies are thought to support the hypothesis that some of the affective components of language available to normal people are missing in psychopaths, and that psychopathy could be characterised by poor integration of affective and other components of cognition and behaviour.

Hare (1990) suggested that psychopaths may have difficulty in encoding material that has abstract, affective connotations, citing two studies of language-related hand gestures which proceeded from the hypothesis that hand gestures and speech stem from the same internal processes and that gestures provide an external representation of these processes. Psychopaths did not differ from controls in the use of hand gestures related to semantic content of language but used considerably more 'beats' – another type of gesture unrelated to content of narrative, unintentional, and tending to occur at significant points of discontinuity in the structure of the narrative. The timing of beats observed during discourse demonstrated that psychopathic subjects may use these specific hand gestures (which are thought to usually mark a breakdown in speech process, reflect attempts to reinstate speech flow, and reflect encoding difficulties) more often when they talk about abstract and affectively charged material.

Two additional studies have suggested that psychopathy may be associated with weak or unusual lateralisation of language function. Hare & MacPherson (1984*b*) demonstrated that PCL-defined psychopaths showed a reduced right ear advantage for processing dichotically presented words. In a later study, Hare & Jutai (1988) used a divided visual field procedure to investigate cerebral lateralisation of language processes. There were no differences between psychopaths, non-psychopathic criminals, and non-criminals in the number of errors made when the subjects were required to process words presented tachiscopically to different visual fields. However, when presented with words of an abstract category rather than a specific category, the psychopaths demonstrated a left visual field–right hemisphere advantage in contrast to the non-psychopaths and non-criminals who showed the opposite.

It has also been hypothesised that the disinhibited behaviour of psychopaths is related to a dominant response set for reward. In earlier studies, Hare and colleagues found that psychopaths exhibited an unusual pattern of autonomic activity in anticipation of an unavoidable aversive stimulus, with little or no increase in electrodermal activity but large increases in heart rate (Hare & Craigen, 1974; Hare *et al*, 1978). More recently, Newman and colleagues have carried out a series of studies of passive avoidance learning, disinhibition, and dominant response set in psychopaths to support the hypothesis that their disinhibited behaviour relates to a dominant response set for reward (reviewed by Hare, 1990). Newman has also suggested that the poor passive avoidance behaviour of psychopaths may also result from an inability to switch attentional focus when faced with competing signals for reward and punishment.

Comment

In comparison with an extended 12-category DSM–III–R research interview, the PCL–R measures favourably in terms of brevity. But it omits a considerable amount of psychopathology that has been found relevant for descriptive purposes in a series of individuals considered to be psychopathic in a UK study (Coid, 1992). This research did not entirely support Hare's thesis that psychopathy is a unidimensional entity. However, the emphasis on obtaining information from casefiles, in addition to that obtained at interview, may give it a marked advantage over other research schedules in terms of reliability when applied to subjects who are well versed in presenting themselves in a favourable light at a single interview. More recently, Hare *et al* (1991) have attempted to further shorten and simplify their instrument for clinical use and have produced criteria which partly overlap with ICD–10 dissocial personality disorder.

Blackburn's MMPI profile typology

Dimensional models which describe and classify personality disorder have their roots in academic psychology. The aim of this approach has been to develop a comprehensive conceptual organisation of normally occurring traits in which pathological personality types are seen as extreme variations within the general population (Eysenck, 1952; Leary, 1957; Cattell, 1965). By examining a broad range of personality traits to see how they cluster in normal populations it is possible to distinguish a discrete number of personality types, often separated into symmetrically opposite poles. These dimensional models have the advantages of empirical testability and broad generalisability and have been employed most successfully with psychopaths using the Minnesota Multiphasic Personality Inventory (MMPI). Within this framework the psychopath is described and classified along preset scales which measure factors of personality abnormality according to self-reported traits.

Despite its basis within a dimensional system, Blackburn's typology is in fact an empirical conversion to a categorical scheme. Studies of self-reported personality characteristics using the MMPI in a forensic psychiatric hospital (Blackburn, 1971, 1975, 1986) and prison samples (Holland & Holt, 1973; Widom, 1977; McGurk, 1978; McGurk & McGurk, 1979; Henderson, 1982) have yielded an apparently similar taxonomy when the variables are subjected to cluster analysis. Typically, four profiles have been demonstrated by these authors. Types 1 and 2 are considered to represent two subgroups of psychopaths, whereas types 3 and 4 are considered to be non-psychopathic individuals.

(a) *Type 1 – primary or 4–9 type.*   Blackburn considers this to be close to Cleckley's concept. These individuals are highly extroverted, non-neurotic, guilt-free, have a high level of impulsivity, and are more violent in terms of previous convictions.

(b) *Type 2 – secondary or neurotic.*   These subjects are withdrawn, hypochondriacal, suspicious, prone to depression, tension, and disruptive thoughts, resentful, aggressive, anxious, undersocialised, impulsive, and somewhat introverted. They have a highly abnormal MMPI profile suggestive of paranoid and psychotic disorder, although the samples chosen in various studies did not tend to include psychotic subjects. In samples from maximum security hospitals these individuals tend to be more aggressive and difficult to manage on the wards. Their criminal histories show more sex offences than type 1.

(c) *Type 3 – controlled.* This group tends to show defensive denial about psychological problems; they are sociable, slightly extrovert, highly controlled, and deny experiencing anxiety or other negative affect.

(d) *Type 4 – inhibited.* This group show defensive denial. They are less controlled than type 3 and more suspicious but not notably aggressive. They are characterised by social withdrawal and extreme introversion. They show dysthymic characteristics or a profile of depression and social avoidance. They have difficulty in interpersonal relationships but otherwise there is no typical correspondence with the concept of a psychopath. In the hospital samples, they tended to have committed more sex offences.

Validity

Blackburn (1986) has argued that the first two psychopathic groups are largely differentiated from the second two groups by being undercontrolled according to Megargee's (1966) model of overcontrolled and undercontrolled aggression. Megargee proposed that undercontrolled offenders have weak inhibitions and are likely to respond aggressively to provocation with some regularity. They are also likely to be identified as psychopathic personalities. Overcontrolled offenders, in contrast, have strong inhibitions and will be aggressive only when instigation is sufficiently intense to overcome inhibitions. They are therefore expected to attack others rarely, but with extreme intensity if they do so. Blackburn proposed that the overall description of his four groups represented combinations of two dimensions relating to Megargee's concept of undercontrolled and overcontrolled personality. Factor analysis of scales discriminating between the groups yielded two higher order factors (Blackburn, 1979*a*). The first, which he termed psychopathy or antisocial aggression, is defined by scales of impulsivity, aggression, hostility, and low denial, which distinguished between undercontrolled (primary and secondary psychopaths) and overcontrolled (controlled and inhibited) groups. The second, withdrawal versus sociability, is defined by measures of social anxiety or inhibition and proneness to mood disorders, which have discriminated within the undercontrolled and overcontrolled pairs. Combinations of high and low scores on these two factors produced MMPI and related personality test profiles in further studies which seemed comparable to the four patterns generated by the cluster analysis (Blackburn, 1979*b*; Blackburn & Lee-Evans, 1985).

Laboratory studies

Subjects have been compared on electroencephalogram (EEG) and autonomic indices at rest and during habituation trials to examine differences between the four profiles (Blackburn, 1979*b*). Few differences were found between psychopaths and non-psychopaths but there were clear differences between primary and secondary psychopaths. Secondary psychopaths showed the least level of cortical arousal, fewer spontaneous fluctuations in skin conductance, and the most rapid electrodermal habituation and cortical dearousal, which Blackburn found to correlate with additional trait measures of social withdrawal. Similar contrasts were shown in a study of the imagery characteristics of delinquents by Gillham (1978). Once again, psychopathic and non-psychopathic delinquents were not clearly differentiated, but the secondary psychopaths reported the least vivid imagery, particularly of emotional scenes, whereas primary psychopaths had the strongest imagery. In a review of several other studies, Blackburn (1978) found that the secondary group had higher scores on Cleckley's criteria and lowest scores on Gough's socialisation scale. Primary psychopaths were intermediate between secondary psychopaths and non-psychopaths on these measures. These findings suggested that social insensitivity is a major characteristic of the secondary group who also have the highest degree of self-reported emotionality.

Howard (1984) has given some support to the notion of social withdrawal in psychopaths relating to cortical arousal. In his study of consecutive admissions to Broadmoor Special Hospital (including both mentally ill and psychopathic subjects) those with EEG abnormalities suggestive of cortical underarousal scored higher on Welsh's anxiety measure derived from the MMPI and were more likely to have committed offences against strangers.

Comment

Blackburn's profiles present an alternative, empirically derived classification of psychopathic personality. However, it remains unclear to what extent they correspond to the more widely used ICD-10 and DSM-III-R classification. More recently Blackburn (1990) has carried out a preliminary investigation demonstrating that certain DSM-III Axis-II categories do correspond with his typology. Using the Millon Clinical Multiaxial Inventory (Millon, 1983), Blackburn found that primary psychopaths were more likely to show traits of the DSM-III histrionic, narcissistic and aggressive categories; secondary psychopaths showed mainly schizoid, avoidant, dependent, passive-aggressive, borderline and paranoid categories; controlled patients tended to be mainly dependent; and inhibited patients were schizoid, avoidant, and dependent. Further empirical support might generate a sufficient body of research to promote its wider use among psychiatrists.

But self-report instruments are not ideal for use with psychopathic subjects and MMPI profiles ignore longitudinal factors in the patient's history. Gunderson (1988) has criticised dimensional models as appealing for their heuristic value and comprehensiveness, but sometimes limited because they seem removed from clinical realities.

Psychodynamic classification

The most widely applied psychodynamic classification of psychopathic disorder groups personality types according to their level of severity and dynamic and biogenetic affinities with other diagnostic conditions. This model is derived from Reich's (1949) view, subsequently accepted by many psychoanalysts, that symptomatic disturbances are essentially epiphenomena or secondary extensions of the underlying and more enduring personality disorder. However, psychopathic patients are not commonly engaged successfully in clinical practice so it is unsurprising that there has been a dearth of psychodynamic literature exclusively devoted to this area. More recently, developments in diagnosis have stemmed from the psychodynamic treatment of character-disordered patients described by Kernberg and, to a lesser degree, Kohut.

The psychodynamic concepts of borderline and narcissistic personality organisation are most relevant to psychopathic patients. These are reflected in the patients' primary characteristics, especially; (a) the degree of identity integration, (b) the type of defensive operations habitually employed, and (c) the capacity for reality testing. Kernberg (1975, 1984) proposed three broad structural organisations – neurotic, borderline and psychotic – which stabilise the mental apparatus, mediating between aetiological factors and direct behavioural manifestations of illness. Narcissistic personality disorder is seen as a specific form overlapping with, or in some cases part of, borderline organisation. Psychopaths can be placed at the most severe end of a spectrum of severity of both these forms of personality organisation.

Borderline personality organisation and psychopathy

Kernberg differentiates neurotic–borderline–psychotic personality organisations according to the patient's primary characteristics. Neurotic personality structure presents a defensive organisation centring on repression and other advanced or high-level defences. Borderline and psychotic structures show a predominance of defences centred on splitting. While reality testing is maintained in both the neurotic and borderline organisations, it is severely impaired in the psychotic and may be accompanied by primary process thinking. Borderline personality organisation (BPO) can be further differentiated from neurotic by the presence of certain non-specific manifestations of ego weakness, lack of anxiety tolerance, impulse control, and the capacity for sublimation (see also Vaillant & Drake, 1985).

According to Kernberg, the classical characteristics of BPO include the following.

(a) *Descriptive symptoms.*

  (i) anxiety – chronic, diffuse and free floating
 (ii) polysymptomatic neurosis – two or more of: multiple phobias, obsessive symptoms, multiple elaborate or bizarre conversion symptoms, dissociative reactions, hypochondriasis, paranoid and hypochondriacal trends with any other symptomatic neurosis
(iii) polymorphous perverse sexual trends
 (iv) classical prepsychotic personality structures including (1) paranoid personality (2) schizoid personality (3) hypomanic personality and cyclothymic personality organisation with strong hypomanic trends
  (v) impulse neurosis and addiction – chronic repetitive eruption of impulses which gratify instinctual needs
 (vi) 'Lower level' character disorders – severe character pathology typically represented by the chaotic and impulse-ridden character.

(b) *Lack of integrated identity: identify diffusion.* Represented by a poorly integrated concept of the self and of significant others and reflected in the subjective experience of chronic emptiness, contradictory perceptions, contradictory behaviour that cannot be integrated in an emotionally meaningful way, and shallow, flat, impoverished perception of others.

(c) *Primitive defence mechanisms.* Primitive dissociation or splitting and the associated mechanisms of primitive idealisation, primitive types of projections (particularly projective identification), denial, omnipotence, and devaluation. These defences protect the borderline patient from intrapsychic conflict but at the cost of weakening ego functioning and reducing adaptive effectiveness and flexibility.

(d) *Reality testing.* The capacity to differentiate self from non-self, intrapsychic from external origins of perception and stimuli, and capacity to evaluate realistically one's own affect, behaviour and thought content in terms of ordinary social norms are retained, in contrast to the psychotic.

(e) *Non-specific manifestations of ego weakness.* These include difficulty tolerating increased levels of anxiety without increased symptoms or regressive behaviour, difficulty in experiencing strong urges or emotions without having to act on them, and poor sublimatory effectiveness.

(f) *Lack of superego integration.* The personality organisation is characterised by non-integrated superego precursors, particularly sadistic and idealised object representations.

(g) *Genetic-dynamic characteristics of instinctual conflicts.* A pathological condensation of genital and pregenital instinctual strivings with a predominance of pregenital aggression. This explains the bizarre or inappropriate condensation of sexual, dependent, and aggressive impulses found clinically in these patients.

Gunderson (1984) is not entirely in agreement with the generalised use of Kernberg's BPO, suggesting instead a narrower concept of borderline personality disorder in line with the diagnostic category in DSM–III–R. He suggested a stratification of severity of borderline functioning according to three levels. The third and most severe corresponds to that observed in a proportion of psychopathic patients. This formulation emphasises that the degree to which borderline individuals manifest psychopathology can be understood in terms of relationships to major objects. Major objects refer to any significant current relationship perceived as necessary. Gunderson sees lower levels of psychological functioning emerging regressively and acting to preserve a sense of contact with and control over major object relationships. These are outlined below.

Level I – where a major object is present and supportive. At this level the depressive, bored and lonely features predominate. There is considerable conscious longing for closer attachment but considerable passivity and failure to initiate greater sharing within relationships. There is a capacity to reflect on past failures and to identify conflict and resistances realistically. But considerable concern remains about the objects fragility and concurrent fears of being controlled by becoming dependent.

Level II – angry, devaluative, and manipulative features predominate at the second level where a major object is frustrating or the threat of loss is raised. At this level, anger is only occasionally expressed as open rage and is more often modified, for example, as biting sarcasm or threats of suicide. When there is a danger of anger becoming uncontrolled it may be projected on to the object and paranoid accusations may occur. Gunderson perceives such reactions as efforts to control or coerce the object into staying.

Level III – psychopathic patients frequently function at the lowest level, perceiving an absence or lack of any major object. In reaction to this they can experience brief psychotic episodes, panic states, or impulsive efforts to avoid panic. These can include fights and promiscuity, often assisted by the disinhibiting effects of drugs and alcohol, which reflect desperate efforts to establish contact with, and revive the illusion of, control over some new object. Gunderson sees these phenomena as efforts to ward off the subjective experience of aloneness and badness. An alternative reaction can include prolonged dissociative episodes of depersonalisation and derealisation during which self-mutilation may occur. During such episodes, nihilistic fears may occur which can become beliefs and take on aspects of psychotic depression. Bizarre imagery, simple hallucinatory phenomena, ideas of reference, or transient somatic delusions may also occur. In psychopaths, where major objects are perceived as absent, corresponding to a sense of abandonment and resulting in the severest forms of separation anxiety, these phenomena can be especially severe and the patient will act dangerously and impulsively in desperate efforts to stave off these states.

Narcissistic personality organisation and psychopathy

An understanding of the concept of pathological narcissism is important in making sense of the observation that certain individuals with similar primitive defence mechanisms and highly disturbed superego pathology are still able to superficially retain some normal social functioning in many life situations, sometimes for relatively long periods. These individuals do not manifest the more severe examples of anxiety, polysymptomatic neurosis, and identity diffusion of BPO. Examples are the highly predatory sadistic killer who may otherwise lead a married life and hold a job, or the ruthless criminal who is able to successfully portray himself as the 'family man' to friends and associates. To explain such phenomena, Kernberg (1975) and Kohut (1971, 1977) have postulated that there is another group of patients, also at a level of structural organisation between neurotic and psychotic, but whose personality is not necessarily borderline. Kernberg has argued that in the more severe, or lower-order, examples of narcissistic personality the personality organisation is in fact borderline. But in these cases, the patient is protected from the intense intrapsychic conflicts more typical of borderline pathology by the development of the 'pathological grandiose self'. Whereas the borderline typically presents with highly disturbed identity or identity diffusion (see Bruce-Jones & Coid, 1992), the narcissistic personality usually has an integrated self-concept. However, this self-concept is still pathological and grandiose and its development continues to interfere seriously with superego functioning.

Narcissistic personalities do not usually appear severely regressed but present with an unusual degree of self-reference in their interactions with others. There is a contradiction between their inflated concept of themselves and an inordinate need for positive attention from others. They derive little enjoyment from life except from tributes from others or within their grandiose fantasies. They envy others but idealise those who provide them with narcissistic supplies, deprecating and treating with contempt those from whom they expect nothing. Relationships with others tend to be exploitative and sometimes parasitic. They feel that they have a right to control and possess others and exploit them without guilt. Behind what can be a superficially charming and engaging exterior is coldness and ruthlessness.

Kernberg (1984) describes six levels of superego pathology in these individuals, ranging from those with neurotic character pathology along a continuum of severity to the practically untreatable antisocial personality proper, or psychopath.

(a) At the mildest level are neurotic personalities with an excessively severe and sadistic superego. Freud (1916) referred to these patients as ''criminals from a sense of guilt''. Kernberg believed they suffered from an unconscious dominance of infantile morality, coupled with an oedipal fixation on parental prohibitions and demands. Because of the existence of a superego structure and absence of borderline defences operations, they would not strictly be considered narcissistic personalities and are considered treatable with psychotherapy.

(b) The next level is represented by most BPO patients without antisocial and narcissistic features. They are aware of their strong contradictory impulses which are uncontrollable but show a capacity of concern for themselves and others. While chaotic, dependent and affectively disturbed, they will have capacity for object relations and internalisation of more realistic parental representations. Psychotherapeutic management may be difficult but the prognosis is better than the following, more severe, levels of superego pathology.

(c) Next come narcissistic personalities without antisocial behaviour but who characteristically deny responsibility for their actions. These patients maintain affective discontinuity, an aspect of splitting which protects them from both anxiety and guilt. There is an arrogant 'participant observer' quality to their lives and consequent absence of object relations in depth. Relationships are emotionally vacuous but they still seem emotionally content. Kernberg believed that they have not internalised Jacobson's (1964) third level of superego formation, the realistic parental prohibitions and demands.

(d) These are borderline patients who are dishonest in treatment but show no overt antisocial behaviour. At this level of superego pathology, patients chronically suppress or distort important information regarding their lives or subjective experiences. They tend to lie by omission as well as commission in the treatment situation. The dishonesty appears largely of a 'protective' nature, there is little direct or overt antisocial behaviour, and quality of object relations is better maintained. Consequently, the relative severity of the superego pathology may be overlooked for extended periods during psychodynamic treatment.

(e) Narcissistic personality with antisocial features, and those with malignant forms of pathological narcissism whose aggressive sense of entitlement is expressed in egosyntonic antisocial behaviour, form the next level. Kernberg differentiates this group from the most severe level in having some availability of idealised superego precursors. During treatment they will at least attempt to justify their sadistic and exploitative behaviour to themselves, even if they are not convincing to others. They may also show an aggressive, enraged, vengeful quality, with a paranoid tendency to attribute similar reactions to others. Their internal world of object relations typically includes the image of overpowering parental figures experienced as omnipotent and cruel. Any good, loving, or mutually gratifying relationship with the object is perceived as unavailable, frail, destroyed, or even a direct invitation to attack by the overpowering parent. They typically have a sense that total submission or absorption into the power of the cruel and omnipotent parent was the only condition for survival and therefore all ties to alternative good but weak objects had to be severed. But their identification with a cruel omnipotent object provides an exhilarating sense of power and enjoyment, along with freedom from fear, pain and dread, with a conviction that gratification of aggression is the only significant mode of relating to others. The more severe cases, with examples of overt aggression and sadism, will merge into the most severe samples of superego pathology seen in the final group, the psychopaths.

(f) The final level is the antisocial proper or psychopathic group. These individuals are entirely identified with a grandiose self-structure, the stranger self-object. Their primary mode of relatedness is aggression, usually experienced as sadistic pleasure. They do appear to understand the moral requirements of social reality, to which they may superficially appear to conform, but do not understand that this represents an authentic system of morality that other persons have internalised. They cannot experience authentic investment of love in others or appreciate the difference between such investments others may have for them and ruthless exploitation and manipulation. Meloy (1988) has emphasised the absence of more passive and independent modes of narcissistic repair, the presence of anal-eliminative and phallic-exhibitionistic libidinal themes in the repetitive interpersonal cycles of goal conflict with others, their intent to deceive, the carrying out of the deceptive act, and the final contemptuous delight when victory is perceived.

Kernberg believed that these patients are usually too dangerous to treat in an ordinary psychotherapeutic setting. The enactment of an overt sadistic triumph over the therapist through extreme deprecation, matched with direct financial or other exploitation, may be a frightening experience outside of a secure setting. Among this group, Kernberg saw a continuum between the passive, exploitative, parasitic criminal, and the frankly sadistic criminal. But in the former, confrontation at this level of superego pathology with their antisocial behaviour can still trigger violent paranoid regression in the transference projected on to the therapist. In the most severe cases the grandiose self is infiltrated with aggression and a subsequent egosyntonic search for the gratification of their sadistic urges. It is as if the individual identifies with the primitive, ruthless, totally immoral power that contains satisfaction only through the expression of unmitigated aggression. Unlike the previous subgroup, these individuals do not seek to morally justify their behaviour and demonstrate no adherence to any consistent value other than the exercise of power. Such individuals are particularly at home in social conditions or occupations where they can freely express their primitive aggression and cruelty.

Comment

Psychodynamic formulations of psychopathic disorder provide an important alternative framework to explain many clinical observations of psychopaths' symptoms and their behaviour. Both Kernberg's description of BPD and Gunderson's three levels correlate with empirical research showing multiple DSM–III Axis I and II conditions in these patients. However, these concepts are not widely adhered to by UK psychiatrists, many of whom are not trained in the psychodynamic treatment of character-disordered patients. Furthermore, diagnosis of borderline or narcissistic personality organisation has to be made following a structured clinical interview and much of the psychopathology described above would not become apparent until the patient has spent some time in psychodynamically orientated therapy.

The longitudinal perspective

A longitudinal perspective is vital to the understanding of psychopathy. Several long-term prospective studies of delinquency and behavioural disorder in children have attempted to learn whether behaviour and associated personality traits have long-term stability, and to identify early predictors of adverse outcomes. There are problems with the long-term study of personality traits, however, because these may be expressed differently at different ages. At the same time, continuity of behaviour does not necessarily mean continuity of personality because the meaning of behaviour varies with age. Nevertheless, research has confirmed that a significant proportion of children who demonstrate conduct disorders in childhood, and show poor peer relationships come from disadvantaged, disordered, and disorganised family environments, with parents who suffer from mental illness, display criminality, and practise violent or erratic child rearing. They are more likely to exhibit an adverse outcome in adulthood, including crime, low occupational achievement, substance abuse, and marital instability. In most cases, these original childhood behavioural problems must be present for the adverse outcome, although a subgroup do not display signs until middle or late adolescence.

Markedly different longitudinal courses can be observed. For example, a small subgroup of individuals with a relatively normal childhood can still have an adverse adult outcome. But it appears that overall recovery from behavioural problems presenting before adulthood is common in the majority of children, a subgroup of even the most difficult becoming normal adults. However, a further subgroup remains who not only demonstrate conduct disorder and problems of adult adjustment, but persistence of antisocial behaviour into the fourth decade. This important observation suggests a potential for more accurate classification of psychopathic disorder with inclusion of the essential element of prognosis. It also implies that certain environmental and constitutional factors may be affecting outcome by a process of interaction, possibly at key periods of development, and that strategically-timed treatment programmes could ultimately improve prognosis for at least some psychopathic individuals.

Conduct disorder

It has been estimated that between 4% and 10% of children in Britain and the USA meet the criteria for conduct disorder (CD) (Rutter *et al*, 1975; Kazdin, 1987; Institute of Medicine, 1989). Estimates have also indicated that CD presents in one-third to a half of all child and adolescent clinic referrals (Robins, 1981; Herbert, 1987). This condition is characterised by a persistent pattern of behaviour in which the child violates the basic rights of others and the major age-appropriate social norms. Up to 40% of children so diagnosed can be expected to have serious psychosocial disturbance in adulthood (Robins, 1970; Rutter & Giller, 1983). It has been argued, however, that the diagnosis of CD is too broad, that many subjects may have little in common, and their antisocial behaviour may have different causes and can vary qualitatively and quantitatively, presenting in one setting but not in others (Kazdin, 1987). However, until the concept is refined, clinicians and researchers will require some way to identify young persons whose primary problem is antisocial behaviour. The diagnosis will therefore retain some usefulness if these limitations are recognised (Shamsie & Hluchy, 1991).

Conduct disorder is one of the three subclasses of disruptive behaviour disorder of children along with attention-deficit hyperactivity disorder (ADHD) and oppositional defiant disorder. Clinical evidence suggests that these disorders may transform from one to the other, but usually in a particular order from ADHD to oppositional defiant disorder to conduct disorder and ultimately to ASPD in adulthood. It is unclear whether these conditions should be considered entirely separate or whether CD might be better conceptualised as the middle phase of a very chronic psychiatric disorder beginning in early life and continuing into adulthood, but which can still abort at any point along the way and show improvement (see Loeber *et al*, 1991).

From its appearance in early childhood, aggressiveness is the most stable personality characteristic of CD (Loeber, 1982), although the aggression will be expressed differently at different stages of development. For example, Aschenbach & Edelbrock (1981) found that mothers reported younger problem children to be argumentative, stubborn and prone to tantrums, while older children had oppositional behaviours. At a later date, they present with firesetting and stealing, and finally truancy, vandalism, and substance abuse. Loeber (1982) has determined four factors predictive of chronic delinquency following CD from a review of the literature: (a) frequency of antisocial behaviours, (b) their variety, (c) age of onset, and (d) the presence of antisocial behaviour in more than one setting. These factors not only predispose to adult ASPD (Robins *et al*, 1991), but also to substance abuse (Hesselbrock, 1986), major mental disorder in a subgroup (Robins & Price, 1991), and a higher rate of violent death (Rydelius, 1988).

Attention-deficit hyperactivity disorder

The question of whether children with hyperactivity–impulsivity–attention-deficit problems are at greater risk of presenting with psychopathic disorder in adulthood has been partly resolved with the appearance of research findings based on a prospective series of children reaching early adulthood. However, the disorder has undergone frequent definitional changes from 'the hyperkinetic reaction of childhood' in DSM–II, to 'attention-deficit disorder with or without hyperactivity' in DSM–III, to 'attention-deficit hyperactivity disorder' in DSM–III–R. The latter condition is defined as having three components of developmentally inappropriate degrees of inattention, impulsiveness, and hyperactivity. But the overlap with CD poses specific research problems in disentangling which of the two conditions, CD or attention-deficit hyperactivity disorder (ADHD), relate to certain adverse adult outcomes. Farrington *et al* (1990) have pointed out that many previous studies are confounded by the use of similar measures or definitions for the two conditions. Although they are not entirely separated from each other, there do appear to be separate prognostic implications for an adult outcome. ADHD appears to predict juvenile convictions independently of CD and vice versa. When presenting together, the two conditions have an additive effect predictive of chronic offending in adulthood. ADHD and CD appear to have different background factors, the former relating to criminal parents, low intelligence, and large family size, whereas CD relates more to poor supervision and poor parenting. ADHD requires the presence of these family factors as intervening variables for the appearance of criminal behaviour in later life, but also separates from CD on the basis of various cognitive handicaps (Loney & Milich, 1982; McGee *et al*, 1985; Farrington *et al*, 1990).

Prospective follow-up studies have examined continuity of ADHD, revealing that the majority continue to manifest the condition into mid-adolescence, with approximately a third showing remission by this stage, but with a marked diminution of impairment in late adolescence (Klein & Mannuzza, 1991). Persistence through adolescence is particularly important for the development of ASPD in adulthood, the chances being four times greater than for those who remit during childhood. Approximately half the subjects in different series will have an additional diagnosis of CD, however, and it is still not entirely clear to what extent ADHD alone contributes to ASPD in adulthood. Furthermore, despite the risk of a criminal outcome in adulthood being significantly raised for ADHD children, this increased risk appears to be accounted for by the development of ASPD itself and is unrelated to the retention of ADHD in the absence of ASPD.

F

Hechtman *et al* (1981) have divided adult outcome of ADHD into three broad categories: (a) those who function fairly normally in adulthood, (b) those who continue to have significant concentration, social, emotional and impulse-control problems (the majority can be expected to fall into this group), (c) those who have serious psychiatric and/or antisocial pathology. Some of the latter exhibit co-morbidity with substance abuse in addition to their ASPD and serious criminal behaviour. It has been suggested that the category into which the ADHD individual will ultimately fall depends on the presence of additional risk and protective factors (Hechtman, 1991).

Risk and protective factors

Rutter (1989) emphasised the need to research both risk and protective factors leading to outcome in adulthood. Risk factors are those that influence the probability of a child developing an emotional or behavioural disorder or other form of adverse adult outcome. Protective factors refer to those that protect them from an environment or constitution that places them at high risk of developing such an outcome (Rutter, 1985). Hechtman (1991) has suggested grouping these factors in the following ways.

(a) *Characteristics relating to the child.*   Children with health problems, including problems during pregnancy, perinatally, or during infancy, are more at risk of adult disorder (Werner & Smith, 1982). Children with difficult temperaments are also less adaptive, particularly to new environments or environmental stress, and may be less socially and emotionally responsive to others. They may also have a less reflective cognitive style and be more impulsive, with difficulty controlling their impulses and their aggression. This will interact in turn with their social environment where they are less able to elicit positive responses from their carers and thus find solace and satisfaction (Rutter, 1979; Anthony, 1987; Cohler, 1987). Although intelligence is not traditionally considered important in the development of psychopathy, many studies attest to the superior adult achievement of children with a higher IQ. However, such a constitutional advantage will directly interact with other factors of personality and environment, so that low IQ can show a complex relationship to delinquency (West, 1982). Resilient children also appear to have a greater sense of autonomy and more positive self-esteem, better empathy, social skills and ability to relate to peers. They tend to be more able to ask for help from others and are generally more optimistic about themselves and their futures.

(b) *Family factors.*   Low socioeconomic status clearly relates to the ability of parents to confer various opportunities on their children. But adverse outcome is not related directly to low status without additional mediating factors such as parental competence, living in a delinquent neighbourhood, etc. Authors have frequently stressed the importance of a warm, cohesive, and supportive family environment in influencing outcome (Rutter, 1979;

Werner & Smith, 1982; Garmezy, 1985; Anthony, 1987). Adverse factors include psychiatric disorder in parents (especially personality disorder), marital discord, loss of parents (especially due to divorce), one-parent family situations, large family size (especially with little space between successive children), institutional care of the child, inconsistent discipline, violence between parents, criminality in parents, and lack of structure or chaos in the family environment (Kellam *et al*, 1977; Oliver & Buchanan, 1979; Offord, 1982; West, 1982; Beardslee *et al*, 1983; Rutter & Giller, 1983; Garmezy, 1983; Rutter & Quinton, 1984; Quinton & Rutter, 1984; Oliver, 1988; Lewis *et al*, 1989; Rae-Grant *et al*, 1989).

(c) *Larger social and physical environments.* Members of the extended family, friends, schools, and religious organisations can provide important protective support for children at risk. Change in circumstances over the lifespan, including moving away from a high crime area, where drugs are freely available, or from delinquent associates, and later forming a stable relationship with a wife or girlfriend, can all positively influence outcome (Werner & Smith, 1982; West, 1982; Robins & McEvoy, 1990).

Persistent offending and career criminals

Previous commentators have criticised the inclusion of criminal behaviour in definitions of psychopathy. Indeed, Scott (1963) argued that the construct of psychopathy could not be satisfactorily differentiated from criminal recidivism. Nevertheless, Hare's construct of psychopathy and the DSM–III–R category ASPD are still heavily reliant on criteria involving criminal behaviour. Both constructs emphasise persisting criminal behaviour and overlap with the criminological construct of the career criminal. Until an adequate diagnostic classification is available based exclusively on personality traits, an understanding of the longitudinal course of psychopathic disorder is still heavily reliant on research into criminal behaviour.

Most westernised countries have reported an increase in crime in recent years and a substantial minority of males can expect to receive a conviction at some time in their life. However, convictions are predominately recorded in the early and mid-teenage years. Most offenders desist from crime in late teenage and early adult years. But persistence is observed in a subgroup, which in turn associates with various other indicators of poor adult adjustment. In psychiatric classifications these same associated factors have been adopted as criteria for various diagnostic categories or scales of psychopathy, demonstrating further overlap with criminological constructs.

Research has shown that a large proportion of serious crime is committed by a small segment of the criminal population. For example, Wolfgang *et al* (1972) found that in a series of all males born in Philadelphia in 1945 and still living in the city 10–18 years later, approximately 6 % were responsible for 51 % of offences recorded for the cohort as a whole. When imprisoned or convicted samples have been examined, similar findings emerge (Petersilia *et al*, 1978; Peterson & Braiker, 1980). For example, a study of incarcerated US robbers indicated that their average rate of offending had been five robberies per year. But 5% of the sample had committed 180 to 400 robberies each (Blumstein & Cohen, 1979). Similarly, in a study of the criminal careers of over 24 000 middle-aged US prisoners, 14% had been continuously involved in crime over three age periods of adolescence, young adulthood, and middle age and older. They therefore had the highest overall rates of prior arrests, imprisonments, family members with criminal histories, and a history of drug abuse. They were also the most likely group to have fathered an illegitimate child and exhibited the highest rate of unemployment in the month before commission of the current index offence (Langan & Greenfeld, 1983).

Delinquent careers can develop along several trajectories (Smith *et al*, 1984). However, for career criminals, persistence through four successive stages can be observed: (a) precriminal (10–18 years), (b) early criminal (18–mid/late 20s) (c) advanced (late 20s to early 40s), (d) criminal burnout/maturity stage (early 40s onwards) (Walters, 1990). In the precriminal stage, the majority of arrests are for nuisances and misdemeanours (Petersilia *et al*, 1978). Criminal behaviour is rarely specialised (Hindelang, 1971; Wolfgang *et al*, 1972) but larceny, burglary and car theft are the most common offences (LeBlanc & Frechette, 1989). These offences are frequently committed in the company of other adolescents and thrill-seeking is an important motive. This stage appears to hold the greatest prospect for change, and a significant proportion of juveniles do not carry their criminality on to adulthood. During the second, early criminal stage, the overall number of individuals committing offences progressively declines (Blumstein & Cohen, 1987). However, a subgroup begin to move towards career criminality as they find themselves in contact with new criminal associates, often met during incarceration, learn new criminal techniques, and acquire status in the criminal world (Gibbs & Shelly, 1982). Their overall number of crimes may decrease but their seriousness increases both in the value of property stolen (Langan & Farrington, 1983) and the appearance of violent offences (West & Farrington, 1977; Petersilia *et al*, 1978). Motives also change from thrill-seeking and obtaining peer status to the desire to obtain money for drugs and non-essential material goods.

Voluntary dropping out of crime appears lowest during the advanced criminal stage. Walter (1990) describes these individuals as having now committed themselves to a criminal lifestyle with an associated cognitive style. Their antisocial behaviour appears driven and out of control and they compensate by becoming increasingly concerned with gaining a sense of power and control over others. In the early 40s, a further stage is reached, corresponding with the mid-life transition, when there is a further high rate of termination from a criminal lifestyle (Hirschi & Gottfredson, 1983). At this stage, some individuals begin to exhibit greater maturity associated with a change in their thinking, values, and motivations, accompanying their declining physical and mental energy. However, Walters points out that maturity is not necessarily part of the process of criminal burnout. Many individuals may remain on the fringes of crime, behaving in an irresponsible and self-indulgent manner, but no longer as intrusive in their criminal behaviour.

Factors relating to desistence from crime, and the separate concepts of maturity and burnout, include the stress of continuing a criminal lifestyle, gradual wearing down of criminal drive by accumulation of punishments and incarceration, fear of further (and longer) incarceration, reduced expectations, development of a satisfying relationship, redefining criminal activities as foolish and self-defeating, shifts in aspirations and goals, commitment to legitimate employment, and becoming less self-absorbed, rebellious, and pleasure-seeking (Irwin, 1970; Meisenhelder, 1977; Shover, 1983; Gove, 1985; Cusson & Pinsonneault, 1986; Jolin & Gibbons, 1987). However, a small subgroup will fail to re-evaluate their lives in this way during the mid-life transition and continue to engage in significant criminal behaviour. The relationship of this subgroup of career criminals to the concept of psychopathic personality is an important area for future research, and future classifications may be enhanced by the inclusion of factors relating to persistence of antisocial behaviour and/or the related personality traits.

Co-morbidity

Co-morbidity has received increasing attention as researchers have revealed frequent Axis-I–Axis-II correlations in subjects with personality disorder using the DSM–III–R. The term co-morbidity is generally used to refer to coexisting disorders, that have different aetiologies, in a single patient. Studies using standardised research instruments to evaluate Axis-II have demonstrated that at least 50% of subjects can be expected to have two or more coexisting personality disorders (Pfohl *et al*, 1986; Loranger *et al*, 1987; Oldham *et al*, 1992). Axis-II co-morbidity appears even higher in criminal psychopaths. An English study demonstrated a mean of 3.6 (s.d. 1.8) personality disorders per subject and fewer than 2% of individual Axis-II categories presented as a single diagnosis (Coid, 1992). Preliminary analysis revealed that BPD showed the highest level of co-morbidity, supporting Stone's (1990) hypothesis that the borderline syndrome, however defined, could be a 'final common pathway' which is multifactorial in origin. ASPD is associated with narcissistic, borderline, paranoid, and passive–aggressive personality disorders. This association between narcissistic and ASPD corresponds to Hare's research demonstrating two factors within his unidimensional scale (see above). Passive–aggressive criteria are related to additional traits and types of behaviour associated with the incarceration or compulsory hospital admission of these antisocial individuals and their consequent conflicts with staff. However, the finding that 45% of psychopaths had a paranoid personality disorder contrasts with the low rates found in community samples (Leighton, 1959; Reich *et al*, 1989; Zimmerman & Coryell, 1990), although Langner & Michael (1963) found a rate of 28.4/100 in the Midtown Manhattan study. The addition of paranoid personality disorder to ASPD described the highly suspicious, intolerant, and vengeful attitudes of a subgroup of criminal psychopaths towards others, with a tendency to misinterpret behaviour, and carry out occasional pre-emptive strikes on others to defend themselves from what they perceived as the threat of attack (see Coid, 1991). These additional personality disorders challenge Hare's (1990) claim that psychopathy is a unidimensional construct, unless they are considered secondary diagnoses.

Criminal psychopaths also demonstrated multiple Axis-I mental disorders over their lifetime, with a 50% prevalence of major depression, 35% alcoholism/alcohol abuse disorder, and 27% drug dependence/abuse disorder. At least one in five subjects had lifetime histories of dysthymia, schizophrenia or schizophreniform episodes, phobias, and brief unspecified episodes of florid psychosis lasting less than two weeks. Less than a quarter manifested sexual deviations, but these tended to be multiple. Sexual sadism predominated. An overlapping subgroup had sadistic masturbatory fantasies of rape and homicide (including females), corresponding to the phenomenology described by MacCullough *et al* (1983). A further overlapping group described compulsive homicidal urges they felt unable to resist, which brought them a sense of power, pleasure and (non-sexual) excitement from putting into action (Coid, 1992). This syndrome showed certain similarities to the condition 'homicidal monomania' in diagnostic use up until the end of the 19th century (Tuke, 1892).

Impulse disorders such as pyromania and kleptomania were more common in females and related to a disorder of mood associated with BPD. In two separate studies of female prisoners and psychopaths with BPD, a substantial proportion of their antisocial behaviour related to this mood disturbance (Coid *et al*, 1992; Coid, 1993). Gunderson & Phillips (1991) have previously argued that the affective component of BPD should continue to be considered a personality trait and that the criterion 'affective instability' should be changed to 'affective reactivity' in the future. However, the sheer severity of the mood disturbance in the study of female psychopaths suggested that it might constitute an affective disorder in its own right, demonstrating considerable complexity and specificity in what has previously been considered a criterion for personality disorder (Coid, 1992). A principal-components analysis of reported symptoms revealed four factors of anxiety, irritability, depression, and tension which showed individual patterns of association with additional lifetime diagnoses of

certain Axis-I and Axis-II disorders. These women also presented with multiple, mood-related behaviours which they acted out with a subjective feeling of compulsion and which relieved the original affective symptoms. Furthermore, this affective syndrome demonstrated a specific longitudinal course with appearance around puberty in the majority of subjects and progressive improvement from the third decade onwards. However, a subgroup showed an earlier onset which associated with a poorer prognosis. This study would imply that certain personality disorder categories, such as BPD, could yet undergo substantial re-evaluation and revision after further research into axis co-morbidity. It also supports the views of Akiskal (1992) and Stone (1992) that BPD, or certain components of the condition as currently defined, might be more appropriately placed among the Axis-I clinical syndromes.

Co-morbidity appears inevitable when applying a categorical classificatory system to patients with psychopathic disorder as multiple diagnostic labelling is necessary if the full extent of the psychopathology is to be described. However, Tyrer *et al* (1991) were highly critical of the DSM–III–R framework and co-morbidity resulting from the use of multiple-diagnostic categories. They recommended that research instruments should be used which record the one personality-disorder diagnosis which has the greatest impact upon social functioning. This recommendation has been criticised as an oversimplication when applied to psychopaths (Coid, 1992). Furthermore, Caron & Rutter (1991) have pointed out that the issue of co-morbidity remains unresolved for diagnosticians, is highly complex, and can only be assessed through the use of fully representative epidemiological data. Neglecting co-morbidity may also result in misleading research findings when the correlates of one disorder being investigated are in fact the correlates of another, unspecified, co-morbid condition. Secondly, it is unsafe to assume that the meaning of a given disorder is exactly the same regardless of the presence or absence of other disorders when making diagnoses. Many questions remain unresolved regarding co-morbidity in psychopaths including whether one disorder represents an early manifestation of another, one is in reality a part of another, dimensional diagnostic frameworks are more appropriate than categorical, overlapping diagnostic criteria are being inappropriately applied, and whether syndromes are being artificially subdivided. However, true co-morbidity may still result from shared and overlapping risk factors, the co-morbid pattern constituting a distinct, meaningful syndrome, and one disorder creating an increased risk for another. High levels of co-morbidity in psychopaths may ultimately provide further insight into other current diagnostic concepts. For example, if psychopaths demonstrate a raised lifetime prevalence of schizophrenic psychosis or major depression it has to be questioned whether these conditions are the same or different from those manifesting in individuals without a premorbid antisocial personality.

Conclusion

Recent changes in the classification of personality disorders have shown a trend towards diagnosing psychopathic disorder according to abnormal personality traits rather than abnormal behaviour. In previous DSM classifications an empirically-derived construct of ASPD generated considerable research data, including important epidemiological information. This has now been rejected in favour of the untested construct of dissocial personality disorder in ICD–10. It is anticipated that the forthcoming DSM–IV will be changed to align itself more closely to ICD–10, but whether the dissocial category will prove an adequate description of the core features of the psychopathic personality remains to be seen. This chapter revealed doubts in three areas. Firstly, it is difficult to infer the presence of dissocial personality traits without the presence of certain (primarily antisocial) types of behaviour in the patient's history. Secondly, a longitudinal concept has been omitted from the category, in particular the presence of conduct disorder in childhood. This appears increasingly important in terms of both prognosis and the ability to differentiate antisocial behaviour secondary to other psychiatric conditions occurring in later life. Thirdly, no single diagnostic category or unidimensional scale adequately encompasses the full range of psychopathology that is shown by a subgroup of criminal psychopaths. The literature reviewed in this chapter would therefore suggest that it is premature to shorten and simplify diagnostic instruments for use with psychopaths while their validity remains unproven and while aetiological and prognostic factors remain poorly researched. It is therefore recommended that assessments for research purposes should continue to employ multiple and extended versions of the diagnostic instruments that are currently available.

Treatment programmes for psychopaths are particularly difficult to devise when there is no universal consensus of what it actually is that the clinician is attempting to treat. The literature has demonstrated that three major areas of (a) personality disorder, (b) major mental disorder (clinical syndromes), and (c) behavioural disorder show considerable overlap within contemporary concepts of psychopathy. No diagnostic system has resolved the problem of co-morbidity within or between diagnostic axes, demonstrated the superiority of one trait-based classification or scale over another, successfully separated traits from behaviour, or adequately incorporated a lifespan perspective. It is therefore proposed that a more complex, two-dimensional formulation of psychopathic disorder should be employed which incorporates the three elements of personality disorder, mental disorder, and behaviour disorder, with a lifespan perspective taken of each along the second dimension. This concept is illustrated diagrammatically in Fig. 6.1. which shows the two-way interactions between each of these first three elements, and reflecting the extreme difficulty in separating these

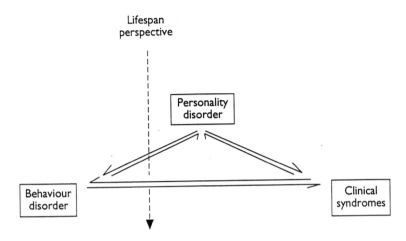

Fig. 6.1. Two dimensional construct of psychopathic disorder

overlapping entities. At the same time, personality disorder, clinical syndromes, and behaviour will change according to the patient's developmental stage. Considerable information is now available on the development of behavioural disorder from infancy to adulthood and some relevant data has already been summarised in this chapter. Similarly, psychiatric research increasingly provides data on the age of presentation and longitudinal course of clinical syndromes, including major mental disorders, substance abuse, etc. But despite the contemporary emphasis on a trait-based classification of personality disorder, little is known of the longitudinal development of personality traits.

In future, a comprehensive clinical assessment of psychopathic disorder should take into account this two-dimensional model with a view to clinical diagnosis. This might include the assessments outlined below.

(a) (i) Personality disorder – an assessment involving one or more of the following constructs: (1) DSM–III–R, Axis-II categorisation, (2) ICD–10, (3) PCL–R score, (4) MMPI Profile, (5) structured clinical interview to provide a psychodynamic formulation.

(ii) Clinical syndromes (Axis-I) – detailed psychiatric history to cover mental disorders, and including paraphilias and substance abuse. Research instruments should include the lifetime perspective rather than the present mental state alone.

(iii) Detailed assessment of the patient's behaviour in relation to culturally-determined social norms, including social adjustment, work record, quality of interpersonal relationships, criminal behaviour, etc. If ASPD is dropped from future glossaries it might be usefully retained within this component of clinical evaluation.

(b) All three components should be considered from a lifespan perspective according to the present level of functioning and previous patterns of development.

By separating these components during the assessment it may ultimately be easier to observe whether potential aetiological factors relate primarily to one component or another. Similarly, treatment programmes can then be evaluated according to which component has been individually targeted. For example, medication might not change certain personality traits but may improve symptoms of major mental disorder or act prophylactically to prevent further episodes, which may in turn have previously interfered with the success of a behavioural modification programme or a patient's ability to cooperate with individual or group psychotherapy.

The sheer complexity and range of psychopathology in psychopathic disorder has previously led to the suggestion that these individuals could be considered to suffer from a series of conditions that would best be subsumed under a broad generic term 'psychopathic disorders' rather than a single entity (Coid, 1989). This would have two immediate advantages. Firstly, it demarcates a poorly defined area that requires further empirical research and where future developments are unlikely to come from a purely trait-based concept of the relevant psychopathology. Secondly, it aligns these syndromes to the legal concept 'psychopathic disorder' within the MHA 1983. Future research in this neglected area may reveal new conditions that have not previously been described and could result in further advances in the classification of other mental disorders.

References

AKISKAL, H. S. (1992) Borderline: an adjective still in search of a noun. In: *The Handbook of Borderline Disorders* (eds D. Silver & M. Rosenbluth), pp. 155–176. Madison, Connecticut: International Universities Press.

ALBERT, R. S., BRIGANTE, T. R. & CHASE M. (1959) The psychopathic personality: a content analysis of the concept. *Journal of Clinical Psychology*, **60**, 17–28.

ALTERMAN, A. I. & CACCIOLA, J. S. (1991) The antisocial personality disorder diagnosis in substance abusers: problems and issues. *Journal of Nervous and Mental Disease*, **179**, 401–409

AMERICAN PSYCHIATRIC ASSOCIATION (1952) *Diagnostic and Statistical Manual of Mental Disorders*. Washington, DC: American Psychiatric Association. Mental Hospital Service.

—————— (1968) *DSM–II Diagnostic and Statistical Manual of Mental Disorders* (2nd edn). Washington, DC:APA.

—————— (1980) *Diagnostic and Statistical Manual of Mental Disorders* (3rd edn) (DSM–III). Washington, DC:APA.

—————— (1987) *Diagnostic and Statistical Manual of Mental Disorders* (3rd edn, revised) (DSM–III–R). Washington, DC:APA.

ANTHONY, J. E. (1987) Children at high risk for psychosis growing up successfully. In *The Invulnerable Child* (eds J. E. Anthony & B. J. Cohler). New York: The Guilford Press.

ASCHENBACH, T. M. & EDELBROCK, C. S. (1981) Behavioural problems and competencies reported by parents of normal and disturbed children aged four through sixteen. *Monographs of the Society for Research in Child Development*, **46**, 1–82.

BALDWIN, J. & BOTTOMS, A. E. (1976) *The Urban Criminal*. Tavistock: London.

BEARDSLEE, W. R., BEMPORN, J., KELLER, M. B., *et al* (1983) Children of parents with major affective disorders: a review. *American Journal of Psychiatry*, **140**, 825–832.

BLACKBURN, R. (1971) Personality types among abnormal homicides. *British Journal of Criminology*, **11**, 14–31.

—— (1975) An empirical classification of psychopathic personality. *British Journal of Psychiatry*, **127**, 456–460.

—— (1978) Personality and the Criminal Psychopath: A logical analysis and some empirical data. Paper presented at the seminar on "The Psychopathic Criminal". International Sociological, Penal and Penitentiary Research and Studies Centre, Messina, Sicily. November 1978.

—— (1979*a*) Psychopathy and personality: the dimensionality of self-report and behaviour rating data in abnormal offenders. *British Journal of Social and Clinical Psychology*, **18**, 111–119.

—— (1979*b*) Cortical and autonomic arousal in primary and secondary psychopaths. *Psychophysiology*, **16**, 143–150.

—— (1986) Patterns of personality deviation among violent offenders: replication and extension of an empirical taxonomy. *British Journal of Criminology*, **26**, 254–269.

—— (1988) On moral judgements and personality disorder. The myth of psychopathic disorder revisited. *British Journal of Psychiatry*, **153**, 505–512.

—— (1990) Treatment of the psychopathic offender. In *Clinical Approaches to Working with Mentally Disordered and Sexual Offenders* (eds K. Howells & C. R. Hollin), pp. 54–66. Issues in Criminological and Legal Psychology. No. 16. Leicester: British Psychological Society.

—— & LEE-EVANS, J. M. (1985) Reactions of primary and secondary psychopaths to anger-evoking situations. *British Journal of Clinical Psychology*, **24**, 93–100.

BLAND, R. C., NEWMAN, S. C. & ORN, H. (1988*a*) Age of onset of psychiatric disorders. *Acta Psychiatrica Scandinavica*, **77** (suppl. 338), 43–49.

——, —— & —— (1988*b*) Lifetime prevalence of psychiatric disorders in Edmonton. *Acta Psychiatrica Scandinavica*, **77** (suppl. 338), 24–32.

——, ——, DYCK, R. J., *et al* (1990) Prevalence of psychiatric disorders and suicide attempts in a prison population. *Canadian Journal of Psychiatry*, **35**, 407–413.

BLUGLASS, R. (1990) The Mental Health Act 1983. In *Principles and Practice of Forensic Psychiatry* (eds R. Bluglass & P. Bowden), pp. 1173–1187. Edinburgh: Churchill Livingstone.

BLUMSTEIN, A. & COHEN, J. (1979) Estimation of individual crime rates from arrest records. *Journal of Criminal Law and Criminology*, **70**, 561–585.

—— & —— (1987) Characterizing criminal careers. *Science*, **237**, 985–991.

BOHMAN, M., CLONINGER, C. R., SIGVARDSSON, S., *et al* (1982) Predisposition to petty criminality in Swedish adoptees: I. Genetic and environmental heterogeneity. *Archives of General Psychiatry*, **39**, 1233–1241.

——, ——, VON KNORRING, A-L., *et al* (1984) An adoption study of somatoform disorders: III. Cross-fostering analysis and genetic relationship to alcoholism and criminality. *Archives of General Psychiatry*, **41**, 872–878.

BOWDEN, P. (1992) Pioneers in forensic psychiatry. James Cowles Prichard: moral insanity and the myth of psychopathic disorder. *Journal of Forensic Psychiatry*, **3**, 113–135.

BROONER, R. K., SCHMIDT, C. W., FELCH, L. J., *et al* (1992) Antisocial behaviour in intravenous drug abusers: implications for diagnosis of antisocial personality disorder. *American Journal of Psychiatry*, **149**, 482–487.

BROWNELL, H. H., POTTER, H. H., MICHELOW, D. (1984) Sensitivity to lexical denotation and connotation in brain damaged patients: a double dissociation? *Brain and Language*, **22**, 253–265.

BRUCE-JONES, W. & COID, J. W. (1992) Identity diffusion presenting as multiple personality disorder in a female psychopath. *British Journal of Psychiatry*, **160**, 541–544.

BUSS, A. H. (1966) *Psychopathology*. New York: Wiley.

CAREY, G. (1992) Twin imitation for antisocial behaviour. Implications for genetic and family environment research. *Journal of Abnormal Psychology*, **101**, 18–25.

CARON, C. & RUTTER, M. (1991) Comorbidity in child psychopathology: concepts, issues and research strategies. *Journal of Child Psychology and Psychiatry*, **32**, 1063–1080.

CATTELL, R. (1965) *The Scientific Analysis of Personality*. Chicago: Aldine.

CLECKLEY, H. (1976) *The Mask of Sanity* (5th edn). St Louis M.O.: Mosby.

CLONINGER, C. R. (1978) The link between hysteria and sociopathy. In *Psychiatric Diagnosis: Exploration of Biological Predictors* (eds H. S. Akiskal & W. L. Webb), pp. 189–218. New York: Spectrum Press.

——, REICH, T. & GUZE, S. B. (1975) The multifactorial model of disease transmission: II Sex differences in the familial transmission of sociopathy (antisocial personality). *British Journal of Psychiatry*, **127**, 11–22.

——, CHRISTIAN, K. O., REICH, T., *et al* (1978) Implications of sex differences in the prevalence of antisocial personality, alcoholism, and criminality for familial transmission. *Archives of General Psychiatry*, **35**, 941–951.

—— & GOTTESMAN, I. I. (1987) Genetic and environmental factors in antisocial behaviour disorders. In *The Causes of Crime: New Biological Approaches* (eds S. A. Mednick, T. F. Moffitt & S. A. Stack), pp. 92–109. Cambridge: Cambridge University Press.

——, SIGVARDSSON, S., BOHMAN, M., *et al* (1982) Predisposition to petty criminality in Swedish adoptees: II. Cross-fostering analysis of gene-environment interaction. *Archives of General Psychiatry*, **39**, 1242–1247.

——, ——, VON KNORRING, A-L., *et al* (1984) An adoption study of somatoform disorders. II. Identification of two discrete somatoform disorders. *Archives of General Psychiatry*, **41**, 863–871.

COHLER, B. J. (1987) Adversity, resilience and the study of lives. In *The Invulnerable Child* (eds J. E. Anthony & B. J. Cohler). New York: The Guilford Press.

COID, J. W. (1989) Psychopathic disorders. *Current Opinion in Psychiatry*, **2**, 750–756.

—— (1991) Psychiatric profiles of difficult/disruptive prisoners. In *Special Units for Difficult Prisoners* (eds K. Bottomley & W. Hay). Hull: Centre for Criminology and Criminal Justice, University of Hull.

—— (1992) DSM-III diagnosis in criminal psychopaths: a way forward. *Criminal Behaviour and Mental Health*, **2**, 78–94.

—— (1993) An affective syndrome in female psychopaths with borderline personality disorder? *British Journal of Psychiatry* (in press).

—— & CORDESS, C. (1992) Compulsory admission of dangerous psychopaths (editorial). *British Medical Journal*, **304**, 1581–1582.

——, WILKINS, J., COID, B., *et al* (1992) Self-mutilation in female remanded prisoners II: a cluster analytic approach towards identification of a behavioural syndrome. *Criminal Behaviour and Mental Health*, **2**, 1–14.

COTE, G. & HODGINS, S. (1990) Co-occurring mental disorders among criminal offenders. *Bulletin of the American Academy of Psychiatry and Law*, **18**, 271–281.

CRAFT, M. J. (1965) *Ten Studies in Psychopathic Personality*. Bristol: John Wright.

CROWE, R. R. (1972) The adopted offspring of women criminal offenders: a study of their arrest records. *Archives of General Psychiatry*, **27**, 600–603.

CUSSON, M. & PINSONNEAULT, P. (1986) The decision to give up crime. In *The Reasoning Criminal: Rational Choice Perspectives on Offending* (eds D. Cornish & R. Clarke). New York: Springer-Verlag.

DAVIES, W. & FELDMAN, P. (1981) The diagnosis of psychopathy by forensic specialists. *British Journal of Psychiatry*, **138**, 329–331.

DELL, S. & ROBERTSON, G. (1988) *Sentenced to Hospital. Offenders in Broadmoor*. Oxford: Oxford University Press.

DITCHFIELD, J. (1990) *Control in Prisons: A Review of the Literature*. London: HMSO.

DOCHERTY, J. P., FIESTER, S. J. & SHEA, T. (1986) Syndrome diagnosis and personality disorder. In *Psychiatry Update*. Vol. 5. 315–355 (eds A. J. Frances & R. E. Hales). Washington, DC: American Psychiatric Press.

EYSENCK, H. J. (1952) *The Scientific Study of Personality*. Chicago: Aldine.

FARRINGTON, D., LOEBER, R. & VAN KAMMEN, W. B. (1990) Long-term criminal outcomes of hyperactivity–impulsivity–attention deficit and conduct problems in childhood. In *Straight and Devious Pathways from Childhood to Adulthood* (eds L. N. Robins & M. Rutter). Cambridge: Cambridge University Press.

FOTHERINGHAM, J. B. (1957) Psychopathic personality: a review. *Canadian Psychiatric Association Journal*, **2**, 52–74.

FREUD, S. (1916) Some character-types met with in psychoanalytic work. *Standard Edition*, **14**, 309–333. London: Hogarth Press.

GARMEZY, N. (1983) Stressors in childhood. In *Stress, Coping and Development in Children* (eds N. Garmezy & M. Rutter). New York: McGraw-Hill.

—— (1985) Broadening research on developmental risk. Implications for studies of vulnerable and stress resistant children. In *Early Identification of Children at Risk* (eds W. F. Frankenburg, R. M. Einde & J. W. Sullivan). New York: Plenum Press.

GERSTLEY, L. J., ALTERMAN, A. I., MCLELLAN, A. T., *et al* (1990) Antisocial personality disorder in patients with substance abuse disorders: a problematic diagnosis. *American Journal of Psychiatry*, **147**, 173–178.

GIBBS, J. J. & SHELLY, P. L. (1982) Life in the fast lane: A retrospective view of commercial thieves. *Journal of Research in Crime and Delinquency*, **19**, 299–330.

GILL, O. (1967) *Luke Street. Housing Policy, Conflicts and the Creation of the Delinquent Area.* London: MacMillan.

GILLHAM, R. A. (1978) *An Investigation of Imagery in Psychopathic Delinquents.* Unpublished BSc. Thesis, University of Aberdeen.

GOVE, W. (1985) The effect of age and gender on deviant behaviour: A biopsychological approach. In *Gender and the Life Course* (ed. A. Ross). Washington, DC: American Sociological Association.

GOVERNMENT STATISTICAL SERVICE (1991) In-patients formally detained in hospitals under the Mental Health Act, 1983, and other legislations, England, 1984–1988/9. *Statistical Bulletin*, **2** (1), 91. Department of Health

GRAY, H. C., HUTCHINSON, H. C. (1964) The psychopathic personality: a survey of Canadian psychiatrists opinions. *Canadian Psychiatric Association Journal*, **9**, 452–461.

GROHMANN (1818) Cited in A. Lewis (1974) Psychopathic personality: a most elusive category. *Psychological Medicine*, **4**, 133–140.

GROUNDS, A. T. (1987) Detention of 'psychopathic disorder' patients in special hospitals: critical issues. *British Journal of Psychiatry*, **151**, 474–478.

GUNDERSON, J. G. (1984) *Borderline Personality Disorder.* Washington, DC: American Psychiatric Press.

—— (1988) Personality disorders. In *The New Harvard Guide to Psychiatry* (ed. A. M. Nicholi). Cambridge, Massachusetts: Harvard University Press.

—— & PHILLIPS, K. A. (1991) A current view of the interface between borderline personality disorder and depression. *American Journal of Psychiatry*, **148**, 967–975.

HAMILTON, J. (1990) Special hospitals and the state hospital. In *Principles and Practice of Forensic Psychiatry* (eds R. Bluglass & P. Bowden), pp. 1363–1374. Edinburgh: Churchill Livingstone.

HARE, R. D. (1980) A research scale for the assessment of psychopathy in criminal populations. *Personality and Individual Differences*, **1**, 111–117.

—— (1983) Diagnosis of antisocial personality disorder in two prison populations. *American Journal of Psychiatry*, **140**, 887–890.

—— (1984) Performance of psychopaths in cognitive tasks related to frontal lobe function. *Journal of Abnormal Psychology*, **93**, 133–140.

—— (1985) *The Psychopathy Checklist.* Unpublished manuscript. University of British Columbia, Vancouver, Canada.

—— (1990) *Manual for the Revised Psychopathy Checklist.* Unpublished manuscript. University of British Columbia, Vancouver, Canada.

—— & CRAIGEN, D. (1974) Psychopathy and physiological activity in a mixed-motive game situation. *Psychophysiology*, **11**, 197–206.

——, FRAZELLE, J. L. & COX, D. N. (1978) Psychopathy and physiological response to threat of an aversive stimulus. *Psychophysiology*, **15**, 165–172.

—— & MCPHERSON, L. M. (1984a) Violent and aggressive behaviour by criminal psychopaths. *International Journal of Law and Psychiatry*, **7**, 35–50.

—— & —— (1984b) Psychopathy and perceptual asymmetry during verbal dichotic listening. *Journal of Abnormal Psychology*, **56**, 710–714.

——, —— & FORTH, A. E. (1988) Male psychopaths and their criminal careers. *Journal of Consulting and Clinical Psychology*, **56**, 710–714.

—— & JUTAI, J. W. (1988) Psychopathy and cerebral asymmetry in semantic processing. *Personality and Individual Differences*, **9**, 329–337.

——, HART, S. D. & HARPUR, T. J. (1991) Psychopathy and the DSM–IV criteria for antisocial personality disorder. *Journal of Abnormal Psychology*, **100**, 391–398.

HARPUR, T. J., HAKSTIAN, A. R. & HARE, R. D. (1988) Factor structure of the Psychopathy Checklist. *Journal of Consulting and Clinical Psychology*, **56**, 741–747.

——, HARE, R. D. & HAKSTIAN, A. R. (1989) Two factor conceptualisation of psychopathy: construct validity and assessment implications. *Psychological Assessment: A Journal of Consulting and Clinical Psychology*, **1**, 6–17.

HATHAWAY, S. R. & McKINLEY, J. C. (1967) *Minnesota Multiphasic Personality Inventory: Manual for Administration and Scoring.* New York: Psychological Corporation.

HECHTMAN, L. (1991) Resilience and vulnerability in long-term outcome of attention deficit hyperactive disorder. *Canadian Journal of Psychiatry*, **36**, 415–421.

HECHTMAN, C., PERLMAN, T., HOPKINS, J., *et al* (1981) Hyperactives as young adults: prospective ten year follow-up. In *Psychosocial Aspects of Drug Treatment for Hyperactivity* (eds K. D. Gadow & J. Loney). Boulder, C.O; Westview Press.

HENDERSON, D. K. (1939) *Psychopathic States.* London: Chapman & Hall.

HENDERSON, M. (1982) An empirical classification of convicted violent offenders. *British Journal of Criminology*, **22**, 1–22.

HERBERT, D. T. (1979) Urban crime: a geographical perspective. In *Social Problems and the City. Geographical Perspectives* (eds D. T. Herbert & D. M. Smith). Oxford: Oxford University Press.

HERBERT, M. (1987) *Conduct Disorders of Childhood and Adolescence: A Social Learning Perspectiove* (2nd edn). Chichester: John Wiley.

HESSELBROCK, M. N. (1986) Childhood behaviour problems and adult antisocial personality disorder in alcoholism. In *Psychopathology and Addictive Disorders* (ed. R. E. Myer). New York: The Guilford Press.

HINDELANG, M. J. (1971) The social versus solitary nature of delinquent involvements. *British Journal of Criminology*, **11**, 167–175.

HIRSCHI, T. & GOTTFREDSON, M. (1983) Age and the explanation of crime. *American Journal of Sociology*, **89**, 552–584.

HOLLAND, T. R. & HOLT, N. (1975) Personality patterns among short-term prisoners undergoing presentance evaluations. *Psychological Reports*, **37**, 827–836.

HOME OFFICE (1984) *Managing the Long-Term Prison System.* Report of the Control Committee. London: HMSO.

HOWARD, R. C. (1984) The clinical EEG and personality in mentally abnormal offenders. *Psychological Medicine*, **14**, 569–580.

HWU, H. F., YEH, E. K. & CHANG, L. Y. (1989) Prevalence of psychiatric disorders in Taiwan defined by the Chinese Diagnostic Interview Schedule. *Acta Psychiatrica Scandinavica*, **79**, 136–147.

INSTITUTE OF MEDICINE (1989) *Research on Children and Adolescents with Mental, Behavioural and Developmental Disorders.* Washington, DC: National Academic Press.

IRWIN, J. (1970) *The Felon.* Englewood Cliffs, NJ: Prentice-Hall.

JACOBSON, E. (1964) *The Self and the Object World.* New York: International Universities Press.

JOLIN, A. & GIBBONS, D. C. (1987) Age patterns in criminal involvement. *International Journal of Offender Therapy and Comparative Criminology*, **31**, 237–260.

KARPMAN, B. (1946) Psychopathy in the scheme of human typology. *Journal of Nervous and Mental Disease*, **103**, 276–288.

—— (1947) Passive parasitic psychopathy: towards the personality structure and pathogenesis of idiopathic psychopathy (anethopathy). *Psychoanalysis Review*, **34**, 102–118, 198–222.

—— (1961) The structure of neurosis: with special differentials between neurosis, psychosis, homosexuality, alcoholism, psychopathy, and criminality. *Archives of Criminal Psychodynamics*, **4**, 599–646.

KELLAM, S. G., ENSMINGER, M. E. & TURNER, R. J. (1977) Family structure and the mental health of children. Concurrent and longitudinal community wide studies. *Archives of General Psychiatry*, **34**, 1012–1022.

KERNBERG, A. (1975) *Borderline Conditions and Pathological Narcissism.* New York: Jason Aronson.

KERNBERG, O. (1984) *Severe Personality Disorders. Psychotherapeutic Strategies.* New Haven: Yale University Press.

KLEIN, R. G. & MANUZZA, S. (1991) Long-term outcome of hyperactive children: a review. *Journal of the American Academy of Child and Adolescent Psychiatry*, **30**, 383–387.

KOEGEL, P., BURMAN, A. & FARR, R. K. (1988) The prevalence of specific psychiatric disorders among homeless individuals in the inner city of Los Angeles. *Archives of General Psychiatry*, **45**, 1085–1092.

KOHUT, H. (1971) *The Analysis of Self.* New York: International Universities Press.

—— (1977) *The Restoration of Self.* New York: International Universities Press.

LANGAN, P. A. & FARRINGTON, D. P. (1983) Two-track or one-track justice? Some evidence from an English longitudinal survey. *Journal of Criminal Law and Criminology,* **74**, 519–546.

—— & GREENFELD, L. A. (1983) *Career Patterns in Crime.* Bureau of Criminal Statistics Special Report NCJ-88672. Washington, DC: Bureau of Justice Statistics.

LANGNER, T. S. & MICHAEL, S. T. (1963) *Life Stress and Mental Health. The Midtown Manhattan Study.* London: Collier, MacMillan.

LEARY, T. (1957) *Interpersonal Diagnosis of Personality: a Functional Theory and Methodology for Personality Evaluation.* New York: Ronald Press.

LEBLANC, M. & FRECHETTE, M. (1989) *Male Criminal Activity from Childhood through Youth. Multilevel and Developmental Perspectives.* New York: Springer-Verlag.

LEIGHTON, A. M. (1959) *My Name is Legion: The Stirling County Study of Psychiatric Disorder and Sociocultural Environment.* New York: Basic Books.

LEWIS, A. (1974) Psychopathic personality: a most elusive category. *Psychological Medicine,* **4**, 133–140.

LEWIS, D. O., LOVELEY, R., YEAGER, C., *et al* (1989) Towards a theory of the genesis of violence: a follow up study of delinquents. *Journal of the American Academy of Child and Adolescent Psychiatry,* **28**, 431–436.

LOEBER, R. (1982) The stability of antisocial and delinquent child behaviour: a review. *Child Development,* **53**, 1431–1446.

——, LAHEY, B. B. & THOMAS, C. (1991) Diagnostic conundrum of oppositional defiant disorder and conduct disorder. *Journal of Abnormal Psychology,* **100**, 379–390.

LONEY, J. & MILICH, R. (1982) Hyperactivity, inattention and aggression in clinical practice. In *Advances in Behavioural Paediatrics.* Vol. 3. (eds M. Wolraich & D. K. Routh). Greenwich C. T.: JAI Press.

LORANGER, A. W., SUSAN, V. C., OLDHAM, J. M., *et al* (1987) The Personality Disorder Examination: a preliminary report. *Journal of Personality Disorder,* **1**, 1–13.

MACCULLOCH, M. J., SNOWDEN, P. R., WOOD, P. J. W., *et al* (1983) Sadistic fantasy, sadistic behaviour and offending. *British Journal of Psychiatry,* **143**, 20–29.

MAUDSLEY, H. (1879) *The Physiology and Pathology of Mind.* 3rd ed. London: Macmillan & Co.

—— (1897) *Responsibility in Mental Disease.* New York: Appleton & Co.

MCCORD, W. & MCCORD, J. (1964) *The Psychopath: An Essay on the Criminal Mind.* Princeton, N. J.: Van Nostrand.

MCGEE, R., WILLIAMS, S. & SILVA, P. A. (1985) Factor structure and correlates of ratings of inattention, hyperactivity, and antisocial behaviour in a large sample of 9-year old children from the general population. *Journal of Consulting and Clinical Psychology,* **53**, 480–490.

MCGURK, B. (1978) Personality types among normal homicides. *British Journal of Criminology,* **18**, 146–161.

—— & MCGURK, R. E. (1979) Personality types among prisoners and prison officers. *British Journal of Criminology,* **19**, 31–49.

MEDNICK, S. A., GABRIELLI, W. F. & HUTCHINGS, B. (1987) Genetic factors in the aetiology of criminal behaviour. In *The Causes of Crime. New Biological Approaches* (eds S. A. Mednick, T. W. Moffitt & S. A. Stack), pp. 74–91. Cambridge: Cambridge University Press.

MEGARGEE, E. I. (1966) Undercontrolled and overcontrolled personality types in extreme antisocial aggression. *Psychological Monographs,* **80**, No. 611.

MEISENHELDER, T. (1979) An exploratory study of exiting from criminal careers. *Criminology,* **15**, 319–334.

MELLSOP, G., VARGHESE, F., JOSHUA, T., *et al* (1982) The reliability of Axis II of DSM-III. *American Journal of Psychiatry,* **139**, 1360–1361.

MELOY, J. R. (1988) *The Psychopathic Mind. Origins, Dynamics and Treatment.* Northvale, NJ: Jason Aronson.

MILLON, T. (1981) *Disorders of Personality: DSM-III, Axis II.* New York: Wiley.

MILLON, R. (1983) *Millon Clinical Multiaxial Inventory.* 3rd ed. Minneapolis: Interpretive Scoring Systems.

NATHAN, P. E. (1988) The addictive personality is the behaviour of the addict. *Journal of Consulting and Clinical Psychology*, **56**, 183–188.

NOVACO, R. W. & WELSH, W. N. (1989) Anger disturbances: cognitive mediation and clinical prescriptions. In *Clinical Approaches to Violence* (eds K. Howells & C. R. Hollin), pp. 39–60. Chichester: John Wiley.

OFFORD, D. R. (1982) Family backgrounds of male and female delinquents. In *Abnormal Offenders; Delinquency, and the Criminal Justice System.* (eds J. Gunn & D. P. Farrington), pp. 129–152. Chichester: John Wiley.

OLDHAM, J. M., SKODOL, A. E., KELLMAN, H. D., *et al* (1992) Diagnosis of DSM–III–R personality disorders by two structured interviews: patterns of comorbidity. *American Journal of Psychiatry*, **149**, 213–220.

OLIVER, J. E. (1988) Successive generations of child maltreatment. The children. *British Journal of Psychiatry*, **153**, 543–553.

—— & BUCHANAN, A. H. (1979) Generations of maltreated children and multiagency care in one kindred. *British Journal of Psychiatry*, **135**, 289–303.

PETERSILIA, J., GREENWOOD, P. W. & LAVIN, M. (1978) *Criminal Careers of Habitual Felons.* Washington, DC: US Government Printing Office.

PETERSON, M. A. & BRAIKER, H. B. (1980) *Doing Crime: A Survey of California Prison Inmates.* Santa Monica, CA: RAND.

PFOHL, B., CORYELL, W., ZIMMERMAN, M., *et al* (1986) DSM–III personality disorders: diagnostic overlap and internal consistency of individual DSM–III criteria. *Comprehensive Psychiatry*, **27**, 21–34.

PICHOT, P. (1978) Psychopathic behaviour: a historical overview. In *Psychopathic Behaviour* (eds R. D. Hare & D. Schalling). Chichester: John Wiley.

PINEL, P. H. (1806) *A Treatise on Insanity.* (Reissued 1962) (transl. D. Davis). New York Academy of Medicine. New York: Hafner Publishing.

PRICHARD, J. C. (1835) *Treatise on Insanity.* London: Gilbert and Piper.

QUINTON, D. & RUTTER, M. (1984) Parenting behaviour of mothers raised 'in care'. In *Longitudinal Studies in Child Psychology and Psychiatry: Practical Lessons from Research Experience.* Chichester: Wiley.

RAE-GRANT, N., THOMAS, B. H., OFFORD, D. R., *et al* (1989) Risk, protective factors and the prevalence of behavioural and emotional disorders in children and adolescents. *Journal of the Academy of Child and Adolescent Psychiatry*, **28**, 262–268.

REGIER, D. A., BOYD, J. H., BURKE, J. D., *et al* (1988) One-month prevalence of mental disorders in the United States. *Archives of General Psychiatry*, **45**, 977–986.

REICH, J., BOERSTLER, H., YATES, W., *et al* (1989) Utilization of medical resources in persons with DSM–III personality disorders in a community sample. *International Journal of Psychiatry in Medicine*, **19**, 1–9.

REICH, W. (1949) *Character Analysis.* New York: Orgone Institute Press.

REX, J. & MOORE, R. (1967) *Race, Community and Conflict: A Study of Sparkbrook.* London: Oxford University Press for the Institute of Race Relations.

ROBINS, L. N. (1966) *Deviant Children Grown Up: A Sociological and Psychiatric Study of Sociopathic Personality.* Baltimore: Williams and Wilkins.

—— (1978) Sturdy childhood predictors of adult antisocial behaviour: replications from longitudinal studies. *Psychological Medicine*, **8**, 611–622.

—— (1981) Epidemiological approaches to natural history research: antisocial disorders in children. *Journal of the American Academy of Child Psychiatry*, **20**, 556–580.

—— (1985) Epidemiology of antisocial personality. In *Psychiatry.* Vol. 3 (ed. J. O. Cavenar), ch. 19, pp. 1–14. Philadelphia: Lippincott & Co.

—— (1986) The consequences of conduct disorders in girls. In *Development of Antisocial and Prosocial Behaviour. Research, Theories and Issues.* (eds D. Olweus, J. Block & M. Radke-Yarrow). Orlando: Academic Press.

——, HELZER, J. E., CROUGHAN, J., *et al* (1981) National Institute of Mental Health Diagnostic Interview Schedule: its history, characteristics and validity. *Archives of General Psychiatry*, **39**, 381–389.

——, ——, WEISSMAN, M. M., *et al* (1984) Lifetime prevalence of specific psychiatric disorders in Three Sites. *Archives of General Psychiatry*, **41**, 949–958.

—— & McEvoy, L. T. (1990) Conduct problems as predictors of substance abuse. In *Straight and Devious Pathways to Adulthood* (eds L. N. Robins & M. R. Rutter). Cambridge: Cambridge University Press.

—— & Price, R. K. (1991) Adult disorders predicted by childhood conduct problems: results from the NIMH Epidemiological Catchment Area Project. *Psychiatry*, **54**, 116–132.

—— & Regier, D. A. (1991) *Psychiatric Disorder in America. The ECA Study*. New York: Free Press.

——, Tipp, P. & Przybeck, T. (1991) Antisocial personality. In *Psychiatric Disorder in America. The ECA Study* (eds L. N. Robins & D. Regier), pp. 258–290. New York: Free Press.

Rutter, M. (1979) Protective factors in childrens responses to stress and disadvantage. In *Primary Prevention of Psychopathology*, Vol. 3. (eds M. W. Kent & J. E. Rolf). Hanover, NH: University Press of New England.

—— (1985) Resilience in the face of adversity: protective factors and resistance to psychiatric disorder. *British Journal of Psychiatry*, **147**, 598–611.

—— (1987) Temperament, personality and personality disorder. *British Journal of Psychiatry*, **150**, 443–458.

—— (1989) Pathways from childhood to adult life. *Journal of Child Psychology and Psychiatry*, **30**, 23–51.

——, Yule, W., Berger, E., *et al* (1974) Children of West Indian immigrants; I. Rates of behavioural deviance and of psychiatric disorder. *Journal of Child Psychology and Psychiatry*, **15**, 241–246.

——, Cox, A., Tupling, C., *et al* (1975) Attainment and adjustment in two geographical areas: I. The prevalence of psychiatric disorder. *British Journal of Psychiatry*, **126**, 493–509.

—— & Giller, H. (1983) *Juvenile Delinquency: Trends and Perspectives*. Harmondsworth: Penguin.

—— & Quinton, D. (1984) Parental psychiatric disorder: effects on children. *Psychological Medicine*, **14**, 853–880.

Rydelius, P. A. (1988) The development of antisocial behaviour and sudden violent death. *Acta Psychiatrica Scandinavica*, **77**, 398–403.

Schneider, K. (1950) *Die Psychopathischen Personalichkeiten* (9th edn.) reissued [1958] as *Psychopathic Personalities* (transl. M. Hamilton). London: Cassell.

Scott, P. (1963) Psychopathy. *Postgraduate Medical Journal*, **39**, 1–7.

Shamsie, J. & Hluchy, C. (1991) Youth with conduct disorder: a challenge to be met. *Canadian Journal of Psychiatry*, **36**, 405–414.

Shannon, L. W. (1978) A longitudinal study of delinquency and crime. In *Quantitative Studies in Criminology* (ed. C. Welford). Beverley Hills, CA: Sage Publications.

Shaw, C. R. & McKay, H. D. (1942) *Juvenile Delinquency and Urban Areas*. Chicago: Chicago University Press.

Shover, N. (1983) The later stages of ordinary property offenders careers. *Social Problems*, **31**, 208–218.

Sigvardsson, S., Cloninger, C. R., Bohman, M., *et al* (1982) Predisposition to petty criminality in Swedish adoptees: III. Sex differences and validation of the male typology. *Archives of General Psychiatry*, **39**, 1248–1253.

——, Von-Knorring, A-L., Bohman, M., *et al* (1984) An adoption study of somatoform disorders: I. The relationship to psychiatric disability. *Archives of General Psychiatry*, **41**, 853–859.

Smith, D. R., Smith, W. R. & Noma, E. (1984) Delinquent career-lines: a conceptual link between theory and juvenile offences. *Sociological Quarterly*, **25**, 155–172.

Stone, M. H. (1990) *The Fate of Borderline Patients*. New York: Guilford Press.

—— (1992) The borderline patient: diagnostic concepts and differential diagnosis. In *Handbook of Borderline Disorders* (eds D. Silver & M. Rosenbluth). Madison, Connecticut: International Universities Press.

Tarter, R. E. (1988) Are there inherited behavioural traits that predispose to substance abuse? *Journal of Consulting and Clinical Psychology*, **56**, 189–196.

Tuke, H. D. (1892) *A Dictionary of Psychological Medicine*. Vol. 1. London: J. and A. Churchill.

Tyrer, P., Casey, P. & Ferguson, B. (1990) Personality disorder in perspective. *British Journal of Psychiatry*, **159**, 463–471.

VAILLANT, G. E. & DRAKE, R. E. (1985) Maturity of ego defences in relation to DSM–III Axis-II personality disorder. *Archives of General Psychiatry*, **42**, 597–601.

WALK, F. (1954) Some aspects of the 'Moral Treatment' of the insane up to 1854. *Journal of Mental Science*, **100**, 807–837.

WALKER, M. & McCABE, S. (1973) *Crime and Insanity in England*. Vol. 2. Edinburgh: Edinburgh University Press.

WALMSLEY, G. R. (1989) *Special Security Units*. Home Office Research Study. no. 109 London: HMSO.

WALTERS, G. D. (1990) *The Criminal Lifestyle. Patterns of Serious Criminal Conduct*. Newbury Park, California: Sage Publications.

WELLS, E. J., BUSHNELL, J. A., HORNBLOW, J., *et al* (1989) Christchurch psychiatric epidemiology study, part I: Methodology and lifetime prevalence for specific psychiatric disorders. *Australian and New Zealand Journal of Psychiatry*, **23**, 315–326.

WERNER, E. E. & SMITH, R. S. (1982) *Vulnerable but Invincible: a Study of Resilient Children*. New York: McGraw-Hill.

WEST, D. J. (1982) *Delinquency. Its Roots, Careers, and Prospects*. London: Heinemann.

—— & FARRINGTON, D. P. (1977) *The Delinquent Way of Life: Third Report of the Cambridge Study in Delinquent Development*. London: Heinemann.

WHITLOCK, F. A. (1982) A note on moral insanity and psychopathic disorders. *Bulletin of the Royal College of Psychiatrists*, **6**, 57–59.

WIDIGER, T. A. & SHEA, T. (1991) Differentiation of Axis-I and Axis-II disorders. *Journal of Abnormal Psychology*, **700**, 399–406.

WIDOM, C. S. (1977) An empirical classification of female offenders. *Criminal Justice and Behaviour*, **5**, 35–52.

WILLIAMSON, S., HARE, R. D. & WONG, S. (1987) Violence: criminal psychopaths and their victims. *Canadian Journal of Behavioural Science*, **19**, 454–462.

——, HARPUR, T. J. & HARE, R. D. (1991) Abnormal processing of affective words by psychopaths. *Psychophysiology*, **28**, 260–273.

WRIGHT, S. & WONG, S. (1988) Criminal psychopaths and their victims cited in R. D. Hare (1990) *Manual for the Revised Psychopathy Checklist*. Dept. of Psychology, University of British Columbia, Vancouver, Canada.

WOLFGANG, M., FIGLIO, R. F. & SELLIN, T. (1972) *Delinquency in a Birth Cohort*. Chicago: University of Chicago Press.

WORLD HEALTH ORGANIZATION (1967) *Manual of the International Statistical Classification of Diseases, Injuries and Causes of Death, 1965 Revision* (8th edn) (ICD–8). Geneva: WHO.

—— (1978) *Mental Disorders: Glossary and Guide to their Classification in Accordance with the Ninth Revision of the International Classification of Diseases (ICD–9)*. Geneva: WHO.

—— (1992) *The ICD–10 Classification of Mental and Behavioural Disorders*. Geneva: WHO.

ZIMMERMANN, M. & CORYELL, W. H. (1990) Diagnosing personality disorders in the community. *Archives of General Psychiatry*, **47**, 527–531.

7 Proposal for a depressive personality (temperament)

HAGOP S. AKISKAL

"A permanent gloomy emotional stress in all the experiences of life . . . usually perceptible already in youth, and may persist without essential change throughout the whole of life . . . [or] there is actually an uninterrupted series of transitions to periodic melancholia . . . in which the course is quite indefinite with irregular fluctuations and remissions . . ." Kraepelin (1921)

The present review evaluates new research efforts to validate the construct of a depressive personality in its various relationships to 'minor' and 'major' affective conditions. Studies supportive and critical of such a construct are both highlighted.

Classical descriptions

The concept of a 'melancholic' temperament, first introduced in the writings of the Hippocratic school, was later formalised by Galen in his humoral theory as one of the basic human types to be considered in understanding disease, as well as adaptation occurring in different seasons, climates, and ages (Klibansky *et al*, 1979). The spleen, by virtue of its position in the human body analogous to that of Saturn in the firmament – and under the influence of this sombre planet – secreted the black humour that caused melancholia.

This ancient theory of the predisposition to depression is actually quite modern, at least conceptually, in drawing attention to an underlying biology – indeed we have yet to formulate any biochemical theory more valid than 'black bile' – as well as in deriving the disease state from pre-existing enduring subclinical traits consisting of lethargy, gloominess, and excessive brooding. Finally, its metaphysics notwithstanding, the saturnine dominance which favours inclination to meditation and introspection provides some justification for Aristotle's claim that this sombre and tormented temperament is over-represented in such professions as poetry, the sciences, philosophy, and public office (which was a serious business in those days) – indeed all professions and crafts requiring dedication to matters for which the ordinary man has no inclination. Mediaeval pictorial representations of the *typus melancholicus* contrast the diligent working habits of the individual prone to melancholy with the impaired functioning – and the 'slothful' hypersomnolence – of the full-blown melancholic state. It is as if in this temperament, preserving sanity necessitates overdedication to work – especially mental overactivity – to compensate for the constant tendency to physical sloth.

Modern formulations

This classical formulation of the predisposition to depression survived to modern times, and such authorities as Kraepelin (1921), Kretschmer (1936) and Schneider (1958) fully endorsed – and expanded – the list of depressive temperamental traits: habitual lassitude, gloominess, brooding, pessimism, low self-confidence, and shouldering the burdens of work and daily existence without their pleasures. Schneider's monograph on *Psychopathic Personalities* includes a chapter on the depressive type, which is generally considered the definitive empirical statement on the subject. Yet it makes intriguing allusions to 'morbid enjoyment' of one's failures and belonging to an 'aristocracy of suffering' as cardinal features of this personality.

The triad of brooding, pessimism, and low self-confidence has found further expression in the negative attributional style of the new cognitive– behavioural approaches to depression (Kovacs & Beck, 1978; Abramson *et al*, 1978; Alloy *et al*, 1988). As for psychoanalytic (Abraham, 1927; Chodoff, 1972) and phenomenological authors (Kraus, 1978; Tellenbach, 1980), they supplanted the classical formulation with greater emphasis on dependency, orderliness, and adherence to conventional social roles that can be linked by the trait of dependability; analogous notions have been developed by Shimoda in Japan (Kasahara, 1991). Sjobring's (1973) dimensional description of the predisposition to depression as a mixture of 'subvalidity' (asthenia) and 'supersolidity' (rigidity) further bridges the classical and psychoanalytic positions.

Descriptively, the construct of a 'masochistic personality' (Asch, 1985; Simons, 1987; Kernberg, 1988) overlaps to some extent with the classical depressive type; however, its pejorative implications for feminine psychology have been criticised by a growing literature (see Widiger, 1987) which has opposed the official adoption of a 'self-defeating personality' type into the main body of DSM–III–R (American Psychiatric Association, 1987). Given space limitations, the present review will focus on systematic clinical studies which have endeavoured to develop operational descriptions of a putative depressive type free of metapsychological assumptions.

Delineating the depressive personality

Terms like 'temperament', 'character' and 'personality' refer to long-term, often lifelong, dispositions that typify a given individual. Although it is widely believed that childhood experiences play the major formative influence on such dispositions, recent evidence (Cloninger *et al*, 1987; Bouchard *et al*, 1990; McGuffin & Thapar, 1992) allocates a significant role to hereditary and/or constitutional factors in their origin. This viewpoint is best subsumed under the ancient term 'temperament', which emphasises dispositions which are closest to the biological underpinnings of drive, affect and cognition (Rutter, 1987). By contrast, characterological attributes are best reserved for the ensemble of defensive operations that the growing child mobilises in its attempts to adapt its endogenous, temperamental dispositions to the vicissitudes of environmental challenge; the ensuing personality compromise is an adaptation that characterises the ego-syntonic coping style of the individual. Psychiatrists are rarely privileged to observe the workings of such adaptive compromise; as physicians they are summoned to witness personality malfunction – i.e. personality (character) disorder in the DSM–III–R sense – when adaptation has already failed, resulting in a major clinical syndrome such as affective illness.

As elaborated elsewhere (Akiskal *et al*, 1983), personality disturbances can precede – although not necessarily predispose to – major affective episodes; they could represent comorbid conditions that bring affectively ill individuals to clinical attention; or they complicate one or more affective episodes. In the latter situation, these disturbances eventually coalesce into 'post-depressive' personality changes (Kraines, 1967; Cassano *et al*, 1983). Although the ambition of researchers investigating the role of personality in mood disorders is the characterisation of premorbid personality styles that predispose to affective episodes, much of the research in this area – for the reasons just outlined – has documented post-morbid personality changes (Hirschfeld *et al*, 1983; Lewinsohn *et al*, 1988). These changes (Shea *et al*, 1987; Pilkonis & Frank, 1988) represent variations on the themes of obsessionality, dependency, and sensitive-avoidance (the so-called 'anxious' cluster of DSM–III–R) and, to a lesser extent, on those of narcissistic, histrionic, and borderline features (or the 'erratic' cluster of DSM–III–R). This ensemble of post-depressive personality disturbances (Akiskal, 1981, 1984) summarised here includes behaviour which often disrupts the therapeutic process (e.g. the first five items) or resists it (e.g. the last five).

(a) Clinging dependence
(b) Hostility
(c) Lability
(d) Demandingness (Entitlement)
(e) Impulsiveness

(f) Manipulativeness
(g) Rigidity
(h) Low self-esteem
(i) Easily hurt
(j) Pessimism
(k) Social withdrawal
(l) Sensitive ideas of reference

The foregoing personality disturbances seem to represent an interaction of premorbid personality traits with depressive illness and its social consequences. The striving for strong partner relationships, orderliness and work- or achievement-orientation can be interpreted as 'defences' against the opposite tendencies during depressive episodes (Tellenbach, 1980). By contrast, characterological attributes from the erratic cluster often reflect the tempestuous interactions of major depressives – especially those suffering from the bipolar II subtype – with others, including their therapists, who assign them such countertransference diagnoses as 'histrionic' and 'borderline' (Akiskal *et al*, 1985*a*). The post-affective nature of these personality disorders is clearly demonstrated in the work of Friedman *et al* (1982) who reported that in a large population of adolescent psychiatric in-patients, borderline diagnoses were largely limited to major affective disorders and that, furthermore, in all instances but one, they followed affective diagnoses. A putative depressive personality therefore should be ultimately distinguished from such state-dependent characterological disturbances which flare up in the aftermath of clinical bouts of depression.

Only four studies (Nystrom & Lindegard, 1975; Angst & Clayton, 1986; Lewinsohn *et al*, 1988; Hirschfeld *et al*, 1989) have succeeded in measuring personality attributes long before the onset of major affective episodes. These studies either failed to reveal personality features that significantly distinguished those who subsequently developed affective episodes from those without such an outcome, or else they could not distinguish minor deviations in personality functioning from minor or subsyndromal mood changes. These findings further underscore the emerging consensus that the premorbid structure in major mood disorders often consists of normal personality traits rather than personality disorder (Angst, 1973; Tellenbach, 1980; Charney *et al*, 1981; Hirschfeld *et al*, 1989; Kasahara, 1991).

The criteria for depressive temperament (Akiskal *et al*, 1980) – as operationalised at the University of Tennessee based on Kurt Schneider's empirical work (1958) – highlight both the virtues and vulnerabilities of individuals prone to pathological mood states. Standage (1978) has demonstrated that such a depressive personality can be reliably diagnosed by clinicians. Klein's recent empirical investigation (1990) has further demonstrated good inter-rater reliability, internal consistency, test–retest stability, as well as convergent and discriminant validity for the seven-item criterion set originally used in our mood clinic.

Our more current 10-item version (revised from Akiskal, 1983, 1989) is modified in light of clinical experience by Kukopoulos *et al* (1990) as well as collaboration with the clinical research team at the University of Pisa (Cassano *et al*, 1989; Perugi *et al*, 1990):

(a) gloomy and brooding
(b) preoccupied with inadequacy, failure, and pessimistic outcomes
(c) sluggish, living a life out of action
(d) scarce social life centred on a small circle of friends
(e) humourless and incapable of fun
(f) few interests which, nevertheless, can be pursued with relative constancy (especially in the realm of work)
(g) non-assertive, self-sacrificing, devoted
(h) self-critical, self-reproaching and guilt-prone
(i) sceptical and hypercritical
(j) habitually long sleeper (>9 hours of sleep).

Although overconscientiousness *per se* is deleted – this being concordant with Klein's (1990) psychometric analyses of the depressive personality – we now consider self-sacrificing devotion to others and overinvestment in work-related activities to the exclusion of leisure as one of the cardinal facets of individuals with intermittent depressive traits (Perugi *et al*, 1988). Their affiliative nature tends to prevent the extreme social avoidance that occurs in more sensitive types. Finally, habitual tendency to oversleep may serve as a discriminatory feature from the anxious personality cluster where intermittent insomnia predominates (Akiskal *et al*, 1984; Akiskal, 1988).

Relationship to dysthymia

The next question to be discussed is the degree of overlap between the putative depressive temperament and low-grade chronic depressive symptoms. Since Kahlbaum coined the term in the latter part of the 19th century, 'dysthymia' (literally 'painful mind' or 'ill-humoured') has been used either as an unofficial rubric for low-grade protracted depressive conditions, or as a personality construct high on the dimensions of 'neuroticism' and 'introversion' (Eysenck, 1952). Its official adoption as a subtype of mood disorder in the American Psychiatric Association's Diagnostic Manual in 1980 (DSM–III; American Psychiatric Association, 1980) – and subsequent retention in DSM–III–R – has generated much research, debate and controversy (Burton & Akiskal, 1990).

In an attempt to delineate a valid dysthymic type, my mood clinic research team in Memphis sought to restrict the nosological territory of the disorder.

Thus, we focused on probands with longstanding low-grade depressive symptoms of early onset. Habitual gloom, self-denigration and self-hatred are so deeply ingrained in these individuals that they appear to be part of the habitual self, hence the broad appeal of the clinical colloquialism of 'characterological depression' in reference to this complex clinical realm.

Such affective disturbances characterise a heterogeneous group of patients who, until recently, were generally considered treatment resistant. We reasoned that the disappointing results with pharmacotherapy were due to the tendency to overlook these patients' social deficits; psychotherapy, on the other hand, was ineffective in reversing the temperamentally based inertia so characteristic of these patients. We therefore coupled vigorous and sequential trials of at least two tricyclic antidepressants (TCAs) and/or lithium with behavioural strategies such as social-skills training (Akiskal *et al*, 1980). One subgroup – who failed to improve significantly on such combined treatment – did not show evidence for external validating criteria for mood disorders. Those who responded to the joint intervention strategy were designated as a 'subaffective dysthymia' in view of an early onset disorder characterised by lethargy, anhedonia, and gloom worse in the morning; although habitually introverted, some were extroverted and driven for brief periods of time, especially upon exposure to TCAs. It is as though in these patients dysthymia consisted of phasic 'minidepressions' coalesced together, but occasionally interrupted by the opposite tendencies. The core features of dysthymia as delineated in Tennessee research are summarised below (adapted from Burton & Akiskal, 1990).

(a) Mood
    (i) gloomy
    (ii) anhedonic
(b) Vegetative
    (i) hypersomnia
    (ii) weight gain
    (iii) diurnality
(c) Cognitive
    (i) low self-esteem
    (ii) guilty ruminations
    (iii) pessimistic outlook
    (iv) thoughts of death
(d) Psychomotor
    (i) lethargy
    (ii) social withdrawal.

Prospective follow-up of dysthymic children has also provided evidence for such subtle hypomanic-like types of behaviour (Kovacs & Gastsonis, 1989). The affective nature of early-onset dysthymia studied by the Memphis team was further reinforced by its frequent complication by major depressive episodes with endogenous features and elevated rates of both unipolar and bipolar illness in their first-degree relatives (Rosenthal *et al*, 1981), now replicated by others (Klein *et al*, 1988*b*). Studies with the reverse strategy have reported an excess of dysthymia in the offspring – even prepubertal children – of both unipolar (Klein *et al*, 1988*a*) and bipolar probands (Akiskal *et al*, 1985*b*). In the latter study with a high-risk prospective design, depressive and related temperaments as well as dysthymia preceded by 3–4 years any superimposed affective episodes.

Even when examined in their 'trait' condition (i.e. when not in a definable depressive episode), subaffective dysthymics display shortened REM latency similar to primary depressive states, yet with a tendency to be long sleepers (Akiskal *et al*, 1984). As expected from these sleep EEG findings in dysthymic–neurotic patients, now replicated by some (Berger *et al*, 1983; Hauri & Sateia, 1984), but not all research groups (Arriaga *et al*, 1990), both the open systematic study at Tennessee (Akiskal *et al*, 1980) and subsequent controlled trials (reviewed in Howland, 1991) have shown efficacy of several classes of thymoleptics in dysthymia. Rihmer's systematic clinical study (1990) reported positive responses – even occasional extroverted behaviour – with sleep deprivation. The therapeutic response to sleep deprivation in dysthymic patients contrasts with the worsening of those with panic (Roy-Byrne *et al*, 1986) and related atypical depressive disorders (Akiskal *et al*, 1984) where protracted initial insomnia is followed by prolonged REM latency, daytime napping and evening fatigue, and worsening of mood, as one would expect in a predominantly anxious group of dysthymics (Akiskal & Lemmi, 1987).

Despite the foregoing research thrust, progress in our understanding of low-grade depression is beset by methodological problems largely due to unresolved boundaries. The DSM–III–R concept of dysthymia, while more restricted than that of its predecessor DSM–III, is still too broad and refers to a heterogeneous group of low-grade depressions. The depressive temperament – proposed here as the core trait of subaffective dysthymia (Akiskal, 1983) – is best correlated with the DSM–III–R rubric of primary early-onset dysthymia. A dysthymic personality type has also emerged in the empirical research of Tyrer (1988) who, like the present author, has been critical of the broader DSM–III rubric; obviously such a broad rubric would overlap with a variety of anxiety and personality disorders (Tyrer *et al*, 1990).

The research by my team has endeavoured to delineate a central thrust within this heterogeneous realm: it is submitted that many habitually anhedonic, gloomy, brooding, guilt-ridden, self-denigrating, lethargic, and hypersomniac individuals are suffering from a lifelong temperamental variant of primary affective illness with attenuated symptoms. Although such a putative subaffective temperament manifests primarily in depressive attributes, subtle hypomanic tendencies are not rare, a conclusion that was anticipated by Kretschmer (1936).

Trait–state relationships in affective illness

Kocsis & Francis (1987) commented on the fluid boundary between dysthymic and major depressive conditions. Recurrent major depression is frequently superimposed on a dysthymic substrate – a situation dubbed 'double depression', in both clinical (Keller *et al*, 1983) and epidemiological samples (Weissman *et al*, 1988). In a community sample of adults and adolescents, Lewinsohn *et al* (1991) have shown that dysthymia more often precedes than follows major depressive episodes and, therefore, it cannot be considered as being merely the residual phase of incompletely remitted episodes.

The foregoing considerations leave unanswered the question of whether the intermittent low-grade depressive condition (Barrett, 1984) – from which major depression develops – is a character style (Bonime, 1966; McCullough, 1991) of developmental origin (Arieti & Bemporad, 1980) or a subthreshold mood disorder with recurrent brief depressions (Angst *et al*, 1990) of constitutional origin (Kretschmer, 1936; Peron-Magnan & Galinowski, 1991). The studies summarised in this review are compatible with a continuum hypothesis whereby the constructs of depressive temperament, intermittent or recurrent brief depression, and subaffective dysthymia represent successive stages in the predisposition to 'major' affective episodes (Fig. 7.1). These episodes, conventionally defined as time-limited syndromal departures from the usual self (i.e. departures from a 'normal' baseline or from that of a depressive personality), appear qualitatively distinct when

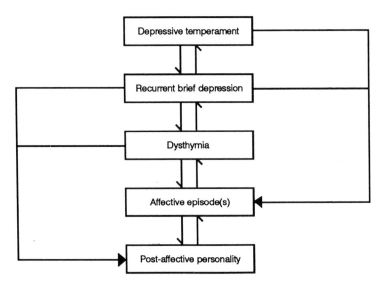

Fig. 7.1.   The hypothesised relationship between the depressive temperament, 'minor' and 'major' affective conditions, and post-affective character disorder

intermediary intermittent brief depressive and more chronically symptomatic dysthymic conditions are eliminated from consideration in the rubric of 'affective disorder'. Recent clinical and epidemiological research focused on subsyndromal affective conditions – variously referred to as 'reactive', 'minor', 'brief', 'intermittent', 'dysthymic', and 'characterologic' – has added weight to the continuum model proposed here. At least one prospective study conducted in the 1970s (Akiskal *et al*, 1978), has shown that 40% of neurotic depressives meeting the foregoing descriptors, when examined over a 3–4 year period, developed more 'classical' episodes with endogenous, psychotic and even bipolar features (Table 7.1). Furthermore, the notion that trait-like attributional biases of the depressive type are restricted to reactive, minor depressive or dysthymic conditions is not supported by current data (Eaves & Rush, 1984; Willner *et al*, 1990); if anything, they appear more pronounced in major depressions with endogenous features.

A continuum of at least some forms of dysthymia and major depression, paradoxically criticised by psychoanalytic authors (Cooper & Michels, 1981), has been subsequently endorsed (Cooper, 1985). Curiously, lingering opposition for such a spectrum concept still exists among neoKraepelinian nosologists (Winokur, 1987; Andrews *et al*, 1990) who continue to regard neurotic depression as being characterologically based and fundamentally different from its 'endogenous' or psychotic counterparts; admittedly, the abnormal personalities in some of these neurotic-type depressions appear more relevant to secondary depressive states in the families of alcoholic and sociopathic individuals (van Valkenburg *et al*, 1987).

Depressive states are obviously heterogeneous, being associated with different personality structures. Nonetheless, up to 40% of primary major depressions seem to develop in the setting of a depressive temperament (Perugi *et al*, 1990; Klein, 1990). Furthermore, the bipolar I form of manic–depressive illness more often seems to evolve from a depressive than a hyperthymic temperament (Cassano *et al*, 1989; Kukopoulos *et al*, 1990).

TABLE 7.1
Three to four year prospective outcome in 100 neurotic depressives[1]

Outcome	Percentage of subjects
Mania	4
Hypomania	14
Psychotic depression	21
Melancholia	36
Suicide	3
'Characterologic depression'	24
Anxiety disorders	12
Other mental disorders	21
No mental disorder	2

1. Summarised from Akiskal *et al* (1978). The total percentage for outcome categories exceeds 100 because more than one outcome occurred in some patients.

These considerations suggest that major affective episodes not infrequently arise from the substrate of the 'opposite' temperament (Akiskal & Akiskal, 1988), a situation that was noted by Kraepelin (1921), but not replicated in more recent German work (von Zerssen & Possl, 1990). A final provocative possibility in need of further study is that such reversal – i.e. manic episodes superimposed on a depressive temperament – might give rise to mixed (dysphoric manic) states (Dell'Osso *et al*, 1991).

It is beyond the scope of the present chapter to discuss other temperaments – cyclothymic and hyperthymic – which also seem to play a predisposing role in major depression (Akiskal & Akiskal, 1992). The same applies to the sensitive–avoidant type (Boyce *et al*, 1990), neuroticism (Fergusson *et al*, 1989) and hysteroid dysphoria (Liebowitz & Klein, 1979), all of which appear generic to a broad spectrum of anxious and related depressive states (Perris *et al*, 1984; Akiskal, 1988; Alnaes & Torgersen, 1990).

The existence of individuals with trait depressive conditions meeting the requirements of a depressive personality type should no longer be in doubt (Akiskal, 1989; Phillips *et al*, 1990). However, discrimination from putative anxious personality types and neuroticism in general is still problematic. Finally, the hypothesised progression from the proposed trait depressive condition to the various affective states should be further tested in a prospective longitudinal research design.

Clinical implications

This chapter has distinguished personality disorders which occur during depression or are comorbid with it (i.e. dependent, avoidant, and borderline) from a depressive type proper which characterises the habitual self of many patients with recurrent mood disorders. This is an important nuance which has been insufficiently emphasised in the otherwise excellent review by Phillips *et al* (1990).

For nearly 2500 years, clinicians have observed individuals with temperamental inclination to melancholy, manifested in the affective sphere (brooding, gloominess, and anhedonia), in biorhythmic disturbances with excessive need for sleep and psychomotor inertia (lethargy, especially prominent in the morning), as well as in cognitive distortions (low self-esteem, pessimism, guilt-prone). These features are optimally manifested in self-sacrifice and devotion in the sphere of work almost to the exclusion of leisure; the downside of this precarious adjustment is represented by recurrent brief depressions which may coalesce into a more or less continuous dysthymic pattern in others. Thus, compared with dysthymia, the depressive temperament or personality emerges as a milder or less symptomatic manifestation in the proposed pathogenetic chain leading to major affective episodes. Descriptively – and to some extent biologically – these overlapping conditions appear to be in continuum with so-called 'major' affective episodes. There is suggestive evidence that 'reversal' from the depressive temperament to 'opposite' affective episodes – hypomania, mania and mixed states – also occurs, providing further support for considering the depressive temperament as a protracted alternative phase of affective illness as originally envisioned by Kraepelin (1921).

Theoretical considerations

The foregoing considerations paint a picture of affective illness sitting on a chronic substrate from which episodes erupt periodically (Akiskal *et al*, 1980; Ceroni *et al*, 1984; Keller *et al*, 1986). This substrate itself is constituted from a melange of personality traits and subaffective symptoms – intermittent or recurrent brief depression – in constant flux. It now appears that this subaffective substrate often generates the life events – even some of the biological stressors – which are known to precipitate major affective episodes (Akiskal, 1990).

The remark by Parker *et al* (1988) that valid subclassification of neurotic depression requires both symptoms and personality constructs is probably relevant to all mood disorders. Even Kraepelin (1921), credited for developing the concept of affective illness as an episodic disorder with 'normal' intermorbid functioning, nonetheless posited that the illness arose from temperamental substrates which he termed *Grundzustande* (fundamental states).

The paradox of why the conventional psychiatric literature considers major depressives with 'endogenous' features to be 'normal' in personality is perhaps best understood in light of the virtues of the melancholic temperament in the areas of devotion, self-sacrifice, and work (von Zerssen & Possl, 1990) – and perhaps even intellectual achievement – noted since Aristotle's time. It is finally befitting to reiterate Kraepelin's suggestion (1921) that future discoveries on the aetiology and pathogenesis of affective illness will come from a better understanding of its temperamental substrates. Such understanding will be difficult without official adoption of an operationally defined concept of depressive personality that clinicians and researchers alike can use. This is a rare occasion where the perspectives of biologically orientated, psychoanalytic and cognitive–behavioural schools meet.

Summary

The ancient concept of a melancholic or depressive temperament played an important role in Kraepelin's and Kretschmer's portrayal of the origin of clinical depression in subdepressive symptoms consisting of gloominess, joylessness, lethargy, and brooding woven into the habitual self. In a related development, Schneider empirically characterised what he termed the 'depressive psychopath'. To bridge the conceptual gap between these classical descriptions and more recent psychodynamic and cognitive–behavioural formulations emphasising such characterological attributes as dependency, orderliness and negative thinking styles, the author has proposed the hypothesis that subaffective (dysthymic) and characterological attributes represent alternative manifestations of primary mood disorders. This position is documented by recent empirical research on dysthymia conceived as a trait depressive condition characterised by high loading of many of the same external validating indices as those with major affective disorders, as well as the clinical overlap between the depressive temperament, recurrent brief depression, dysthymia, and major affective states. These considerations support the merit of reintroducing the construct of a depressive personality in our official nosology, which in turn will facilitate prospective validation of its proposed relationship to major affective states.

Acknowledgements

The author thanks Richard E. Weise, MEd for his assistance in the preparation of this manuscript, and Athanasio Kukopoulos, MD, for his valuable suggestions on the definition of the depressive temperament.

The research summarised in this paper was conducted when the author was at the University of Tennessee, Memphis, before his current position at the National Institute of Mental Health. The opinions expressed in this paper are the author's and do not necessarily reflect those of the Institute.

References

ABRAHAM, K. (1927) Notes on the psycho-analytical investigation and treatment of manic depressive insanity and allied conditions. In *Selected Papers of Karl Abraham*, pp. 418–502. London: Hogarth Press and the Institute of Psychoanalysis.

ABRAMSON, L. Y., SELIGMAN, M. E. & TEASDALE, J. D. (1978) Learned helplessness in humans: critique and reformulation. *Journal of Abnormal Psychology*, **87**, 49–74.

AKISKAL, H. S. (1981) Subaffective disorders: dysthymic, cyclothymic and bipolar II disorders in the 'borderline' realm. *Psychiatric Clinics of North America*, **4**, 25–46.

—— (1983) Dysthymic disorder: psychopathology of proposed chronic depressive subtypes. *American Journal of Psychiatry*, **140**, 11–20.

—— (1984) Characterologic manifestations of affective disorders: toward a new conceptualization. *Integrative Psychiatry*, May–June, 83–96.

—— (1988) Personality in anxiety disorders. *Psychiatrie et Psychobiologie*, **3**, 161s–166s.

—— (1989) Validating affective personality types. In *The Validity of Psychiatric Diagnosis* (ed. L. Robins), pp. 217–227. New York: Raven Press.

—— (1990) An integrative perspective on recurrent mood disorders: The mediating role of personality. In *Psychosocial Aspects of Depression*, (eds J. Becker & A. Kleinman), pp. 215–235. Hillsdale: Lawrence Erlbaum Associates.

——, BITAR, A. H., PUZANTIAN, V. R., et al (1978) The nosological status of neurotic depression: a prospective three- to four-year follow-up examination in light of the primary–secondary and unipolar–bipolar dichotomies. *Archives of General Psychiatry*, **35**, 756–766.

——, ROSENTHAL, T. L., HAYKAL, R. F., *et al* (1980) Characterological depressions. Clinical and sleep EEG findings separating 'subaffective dysthymias' from 'character spectrum disorders'. *Archives of General Psychiatry*, **37**, 777–783.

——, HIRSCHFELD, R. M. & YEREVANIAN, B. I. (1983) The relationship of personality to affective disorders. *Archives of General Psychiatry*, **40**, 801–810.

——, LEMMI, H., DICKSON, H., *et al* (1984) Chronic depressions. Part 2. Sleep EEG differentiation of primary dysthymic disorders from anxious depressions. *Journal of Affective Disorders*, **6**, 287–295.

——, CHEN, S. E., DAVIS, G. C., *et al* (1985*a*) Borderline: an adjective in search of a noun. *Journal of Clinical Psychiatry*, **46**, 41–48.

——, DOWNS, J., JORDAN, P., *et al* (1985*b*) Affective disorders in referred children and younger siblings of manic–depressives. Mode of onset and prospective course. *Archives of General Psychiatry*, **42**, 996–1003.

—— & LEMMI, H. (1987) Sleep EEG findings bearing on the relationship of anxiety and depressive disorders. In *Anxious Depression: Assessment and Treatment* (eds G. Racagani & E. Szmeraldi), pp. 153–159. New York: Raven Press.

—— & AKISKAL, K. (1988) Re-assessing the prevalence of bipolar disorders: clinical significance and artistic creativity. *Psychiatrie et Psychobiologie*, **3**, 29s–36s.

—— & —— (1992) Cyclothymic, hyperthymic and depressive temperaments as subaffective variants of mood disorders. In *American Psychiatric Association Review* (ed. A. Tasman), pp. 43–62. Washington, DC: American Psychiatric Press.

ALLOY, L. B., ABRAMSON, L. Y., METALSKY, G. I., *et al* (1988) The hopelessness theory of depression: attributional aspects. *British Journal of Clinical Psychology*, **27**, 5–21.

ALNAES, R. & TORGERSEN, S. (1990) DSM–III personality disorders among patients with major depression, anxiety disorders, and mixed conditions. *Journal of Nervous and Mental Disease*, **178**, 693–698.

AMERICAN PSYCHIATRIC ASSOCIATION (1980) *Diagnostic and Statistical Manual of Mental Disorders* (3rd edn) (DSM–III). Washington, DC: APA.

—— (1987) *Diagnostic and Statistical Manual of Mental Disorders* (3rd edn, revised) (DSM–III–R). Washington, DC: APA.

ANDREWS, G., NEILSON, M., HUNT, C., *et al* (1990) Diagnosis, personality and the long-term outcome of depression. *British Journal of Psychiatry*, **157**, 13–18.

ANGST, J. (1973) The etiology and nosology of endogenous depressive psychoses. *Foreign Psychiatry*, **2**, 1–108.

—— & CLAYTON, P. (1986) Premorbid personality of depressive, bipolar, and schizophrenic patients with special reference to suicidal issues. *Comprehensive Psychiatry*, **27**, 511–532.

——, MERIKANGAS, K., SCHEIDEGGER, P., *et al* (1990) Recurrent brief depression: a new subtype of affective disorder. *Journal of Affective Disorders*, **19**, 87–98.

ARIETI, S. & BEMPORAD, J. R. (1980) The psychological organization of depression. *American Journal of Psychiatry*, **137**, 1360–1365.

ARRIAGA, F., ROSADO, P. & PAIVA, T. (1990) The sleep of dysthymic patients: a comparison with normal controls. *Biological Psychiatry*, **27**, 649–656.

ASCH, S. (1985) The masochistic personality. In *Psychiatry* (eds R. Michels & J. Cavenar). Philadelphia: J. B. Lippincott.

BARRETT, J. E. (1984) Naturalistic change after 2 years in neurotic depressive disorders (RDC categories). *Comprehensive Psychiatry*, **25**, 404–418.

BERGER, M., LUND, R., BRONISCH, T., *et al* (1983) REM latency in neurotic and endogenous depression and the cholinergic REM induction test. *Psychiatry Research*, **10**, 113–123.

BONIME, W. (1966) The psychodynamics of neurotic depression. In *American Handbook of Psychiatry, Vol. 1*, (ed. S. Arieti), pp. 239–255. New York: Basic Books Inc.

BOUCHARD, T. J., JR., LYKKEN, D. T., McGUE, M., *et al* (1990) Sources of human psychological differences: the Minnesota Study of Twins Reared Apart. *Science*, **250**, 223–228.

BOYCE, P., PARKER, G., HICKIE, I., *et al* (1990) Personality differences between patients with remitted melancholic and nonmelancholic depression. *American Journal of Psychiatry*, **147**, 1476–1483.

BURTON, S. W. & AKISKAL, H. S. (eds) (1990) *Dysthymic Disorder*. London: Gaskell.

CASSANO, G. B., MAGGINI, C. & AKISKAL, H. S. (1983) Short-term, subchronic, and chronic sequelae of affective disorders. *Psychiatric Clinics of North America*, **6**, 55–67.

———, AKISKAL, H. S., MUSETTI, L., *et al* (1989) Psychopathology, temperament, and past course in primary major depressions. 2. Toward a redefinition of bipolarity with a new semistructured interview for depression. *Psychopathology*, **22**, 278–288.

CERONI, G. B., NERI, C. & PEZZOLI, A. (1984) Chronicity in major depression: a naturalistic prospective study. *Journal of Affective Disorders*, **7**, 123–132.

CHARNEY, D. S., NELSON, J. C. & QUINLAN, D. M. (1981) Personality traits and disorder in depression. *American Journal of Psychiatry*, **138**, 1601–1604.

CHODOFF, P. (1972) The depressive personality. A critical review. *Archives of General Psychiatry*, **27**, 666–673.

CLONINGER, C. R. (1987) A systematic method for clinical description and classification of personality variants. A proposal. *Archives of General Psychiatry*, **44**, 573–588.

COOPER, A. M. (1985) Will neurobiology influence psychoanalysis? *American Journal of Psychiatry*, **142**, 1395–1402.

——— & MICHELS, R. (1981) Book review: American Psychiatric Association: Diagnostic and Statistical Manual of Mental Disorders, 3rd Ed. *American Journal of Psychiatry*, **138**, 128–129.

DELL'OSSO, L., PLACIDI, G. F., NASSI, R., *et al* (1991) The manic–depressive mixed state: familial, temperamental and psychopathologic characteristics in 108 female inpatients. *European Archives of Psychiatry and Clinical Neuroscience*, **240**, 234–239.

EAVES, G. & RUSH, A. J. (1984) Cognitive patterns in symptomatic and remitted unipolar major depression. *Journal of Abnormal Psychology*, **93**, 31–40.

EYSENCK, H. J. (1952) *The Scientific Study of Personality*. London: Routledge and Kegan Paul.

FERGUSSON, D. M., HORWOOD, L. J. & LAWTON, J. M. (1989) The relationships between neuroticism and depressive symptoms. *Social Psychiatry and Psychiatric Epidemiology*, **24**, 275–281.

FRIEDMAN, R. C., CLARKIN, J. F., CORN, R., *et al* (1982) DSM–III and affective pathology in hospitalized adolescents. *Journal of Nervous and Mental Disease*, **170**, 511–521.

HAURI, P. & SATEIA, M. J. (1984) REM sleep in dysthymic disorders. *Sleep Research*, **13**, 119.

HIRSCHFELD, R. M., KLERMAN, G. L., CLAYTON, P. J., *et al* (1983) Assessing personality: effects of the depressive state on trait measurement. *American Journal of Psychiatry*, **140**, 695–699.

———, ———, LOVARI, P., *et al* (1989) Premorbid personality assessments of first onset of major depression. *Archives of General Psychiatry*, **46**, 345–350.

HOWLAND, R. H. (1991) Pharmacotherapy of dysthymia: a review. *Journal of Clinical Psychopharmacology*, **11**, 83–92.

KASAHARA, Y. (1991) The practical diagnosis of depression in Japan. In *The Diagnosis of Depression* (eds J. P. Feighner & W. F. Boyer), pp. 163–175. Chichester: Wiley.

KELLER, M. B., LAVORI, P. W., ENDICOTT, J., *et al* (1983) Double depression: two-year follow-up. *American Journal of Psychiatry*, **140**, 689–694.

———, ———, RICE, J., *et al* (1986) The persistent risk of chronicity in recurrent episodes of nonbipolar major depressive disorder: a prospective follow-up. *American Journal of Psychiatry*, **143**, 24–28.

KERNBERG, O. F. (1988) Clinical dimensions of masochism. *Journal of the American Psychoanalytic Association*, **36**, 1005–1029.

KLEIN, D. N. (1990) Depressive personality: reliability, validity, and relation to dysthymia. *Journal of Abnormal Psychology*, **99**, 412–421.

———, CLARK, D. C., DANSKY, L., *et al* (1988a) Dysthymia in the offspring of parents with primary unipolar affective disorder. *Journal of Abnormal Psychology*, **97**, 265–274.

———, TAYLOR, E. B., DICKSTEIN, S., *et al* (1988b) Primary early-onset dysthymia: comparison with primary nonbipolar nonchronic major depression on demographic, clinical, familial, personality, and socioenvironmental characteristics and short-term outcome. *Journal of Abnormal Psychology*, **97**, 387–398.

KLIBANSKY, R., PANOFSKY, E. & SAXL, F. (1979) *Saturn and Melancholy*. Liechtenstein: Nendeln, Kraus Reprint.

KOCSIS, J. H. & FRANCES, A. J. (1987) A critical discussion of DSM–III dysthymic disorder. *American Journal of Psychiatry*, **144**, 1534–1542.

Kovacs, M. & Beck, A. T. (1978) Maladaptive cognitive structures in depression. *American Journal of Psychiatry*, **135**, 525–533.

—— & Gastsonis, C. (1989) Stability and change in childhood – onset of depressive disorder: longitudinal course as a diagnostic validator. In *The Validity of Psychiatric Diagnosis*, (eds L. N. Robins & J. E. Barrett), pp. 57–73. New York: Raven Press.

Kraepelin, E. (1921) *Manic-depressive Insanity and Paranoia* (transl. R. M. Barclay, ed. G. M. Robertson). Edinburgh: E. S. Livingstone.

Kraines, S. H. (1967) Therapy of the chronic depressions. *Diseases of the Nervous System*, **28**, 577–584.

Kraus, A. (1978) Sozialverhalten und psychosenauslosung bei manisch–depressiven. *Zeitschrift fur Klinische Psychologie und Psychotherapie (Munchen)*, **26**, 149–160.

Kretschmer, E. (1936)*Physique and Character* (transl. E. Miller). London: Kegan, Paul, Trench, Trubner and Co.

Kukopoulos, A., Tundo, A., Floris, G. F., *et al* (1990) Changes in life habits that may influence the course of affective disorders. In *Psychiatry – A World Perspective* (eds C. N. Stefanis, A. D. Rabavilas & C. R. Soldatos), pp. 478–488. Amsterdam: Elsevier.

Lewinsohn, P. M., Hoberman, H. M. & Rosenbaum, M. (1988) A prospective study of risk factors for unipolar depression. *Journal of Abnormal Psychology*, **97**, 251–264.

——, Rohde, P., Seeley, J. R., *et al* (1991) Comorbidity of unipolar depression: I. Major depression with dysthymia. *Journal of Abnormal Psychology*, **100**, 205–213.

Liebowitz, M. R. & Klein, D. F. (1979) Hysteroid dysphoria. *Psychiatric Clinics of North America*, **2**, 555–575.

McCullough, J. P. (1991) Psychotherapy for dysthymia. A naturalistic study of ten patients. *Journal of Nervous and Mental Disease*, **179**, 734–740.

McGuffin, P. & Thapar, A. (1992) The genetics of personality disorder. *British Journal of Psychiatry*, **160**, 12–23.

Nystrom, S. & Lindegard, B. (1975) Predisposition for mental syndromes: a study comparing predisposition for depression, neurasthenia and anxiety state. *Acta Psychiatrica Scandinavica*, **51**, 69–76.

Parker, G., Blignault, I. & Manicavasagar, V. (1988) Neurotic depression: delineation of symptom profiles and their relation to outcome. *British Journal of Psychiatry*, **153**, 15–23.

Peron-Magnan, P. & Galinowski, A. (1991) La personnalité depressive. In *La Depression Etudes* (eds A. Feline, P. Hardy & M. de Bonis), pp. 93–115. Paris: Masson.

Perris, C., Eisemann, M., von Knorring, L., *et al* (1984) Personality traits in former depressed patients and in healthy subjects without past history of depression. *Psychopathology*, **17**, 178–186.

Perugi, G., Maremmani, I., McNair, D. M., *et al* (1988) Differential changes in areas of social adjustment from depressive episodes through recovery. *Journal of Affective Disorders*, **15**, 39–43.

——, Musetti, L., Simonini, E., *et al* (1990) Gender-mediated clinical features of depressive illness. The importance of temperamental differences. *British Journal of Psychiatry*, **157**, 835–841.

Phillips, K. A., Gunderson, J. G., Hirschfeld, R. M., *et al* (1990) A review of the depressive personality. *American Journal of Psychiatry*, **147**, 830–837.

Pilkonis, P. A. & Frank, E. (1988) Personality pathology in recurrent depression: nature, prevalence, and relationship to treatment response. *American Journal of Psychiatry*, **145**, 435–441.

Rihmer, Z. (1990) Dysthymia–a clinician's perspective. In *Dysthymic Disorder* (eds S. W. Burton & H. S. Akiskal), pp. 112–125. London: Gaskell.

Rosenthal, T. L., Akiskal, H. S., Scott-Strauss, A., *et al* (1981) Familial and developmental factors in characterological depressions. *Journal of Affective Disorders*, **3**, 183–192.

Roy-Byrne, P. P., Uhde, T. W. & Post, R. M. (1986) Effects of one night's sleep deprivation on mood and behaviour in panic disorder. Patients with panic disorder compared with depressed patients and normal controls. *Archives of General Psychiatry*, **43**, 895–899.

Rutter, M. (1987) Temperament, personality and personality disorder. *British Journal of Psychiatry*, **150**, 443–458.

Schneider, K. (1958) *Psychopathic Personalities* (transl. M. W. Hamilton). Springfield, Illinois: Charles C. Thomas.

SHEA, M. T., GLASS, D. R., PILKONIS, P. A., *et al* (1987) Frequency and implications of personality disorders in a sample of depressed outpatients. *Journal of Personality Disorders*, **1**, 27–42.

SIMONS, R. C. (1987) Psychoanalytic contributions to psychiatric nosology: forms of masochistic behavior. *Journal of the American Psychoanalytic Association*, **35**, 583–608.

SJOBRING, H. (1973) Personality structure and development (English translation of: Struktur och utveckling, en personlighetsteori. Lund: Gleerup 1958). *Acta Psychiatrica Scandinavica*, Suppl. 244.

STANDAGE, K. F. (1978) The diagnosis of personality disorders: a pilot study. *Canadian Psychiatric Association Journal*, **23**, 15–22.

TELLENBACH, H. (1980) *Melancholia* (transl. E. Eng). Pittsburgh: Duquesne University Press.

TYRER, P. (1988) *Personality Disorders: Diagnosis, Management and Course*. London: Butterworth & Co. Ltd.

———, SEIVEWRIGHT, N., FERGUSON, B., *et al* (1990) The Nottingham Study of Neurotic Disorder: relationship between personality status and symptoms. *Psychological Medicine*, **20**, 423–431.

VAN VALKENBURG, C., LILIENFELD, S. & AKISKAL, H. S. (1987) The impact of familial personality disorder and alcoholism on the clinical features of depression. *Psychiatrie et Psychobiologie*, **2**, 195–201.

VON ZERSSEN, D. & POSSL, J. (1990) The premorbid personality of patients with different subtypes of an affective illness. Statistical analysis of blind assignment of case history data to clinical diagnoses. *Journal of Affective Disorders*, **18**, 39–50.

WEISSMAN, M. M., LEAF, P. J., BRUCE, M. L., *et al* (1988) The epidemiology of dysthymia in five communities: rates, risks, comorbidity, and treatment. *American Journal of Psychiatry*, **145**, 815–819.

WIDIGER, T. A. (guest editor) (1987) The self-defeating personality disorder. *Journal of Personality Disorders* (*special feature*), **1**, 157–201.

WILLNER, P., WILKES, M. & ORWIN, A. (1990) Attributional style and perceived stress in endogenous and reactive depression. *Journal of Affective Disorders*, **18**, 281–287.

WINOKUR, G. (1987) Family (genetic) studies in neurotic depression. *Journal of Psychiatric Research*, **21**, 357–363.

8 Multiple personality

STEPHEN WILSON

We are inclined to take it for granted that each person has just one body which changes slowly with the passage of time. But the unity of mind or 'soul' has often seemed problematic – something not given, but rather achieved with difficulty. Thus Plato (*Republic*, 443) suggests that work is required in order to integrate the diverse parts of a man's inner self: ''Only when a man has linked these parts together in well-tempered harmony and has made himself one man instead of many, will he be ready to go about whatever he may have to do . . .'' (Kenny, 1973).

Inconsistencies in human experience and behaviour may therefore have seemed unremarkable until the notion of a unique unchanging identity, attributable to every man, gained general acceptance. That this should ever have happened requires some explanation. L. L. Whyte puts it nicely when he says:

''The intuitive sense of a persisting experiencing self constitutes a treacherous basis for an ordering of experience, because the direct awareness of the human individual does not justify the attribution to the self either of *permanence*, or of *unchanging identity*, or of *continuous awareness*. Indeed the facts of growth, aging, and death, and the transitory wandering character of awareness render this assumption of a permanent identical conscious subject most peculiar. Why did the human mind ever make such a strange, apparently perverse, 'inference'?'' (Whyte, 1978).

Whyte argues that self-awareness helps man to master his environment and satisfy his needs. In doing so it paradoxically reduces the disjunction between biological need and environmental provision, and thus destroys the basis for its own existence. 'Self-awareness is basically self-eliminating'. Seventeenth century rationalism failed to realise this and 'invented' a single, enduring, cognitive, rational self, which colonised man's identity and gave rise to a peculiarly modern malaise – the pain of unmitigated self-consciousness.

The notion of unconscious mental process, Whyte suggests, acted as a balm for this condition and provided a kind of counterbalance to Descartes' equation of mind with awareness. It was, he writes: "*conceivable* (in post-Cartesian Europe) around 1700, *topical* around 1800, and *fashionable* around 1870–1880."

Accordingly, throughout this period, interest in the discontinuities of human experience – altered states of consciousness, dreams, somnambulism, and automatism – the outer manifestations of a contradictory and hidden inner process, continued to grow.

Early case reports

Cases of abrupt changes in personality accompanied by disturbances in awareness have been reported for at least 200 years. One of the earliest examples dates from 1789. A young German woman, impressed by the arrival in Stuttgart of aristocratic refugees from the French Revolution, suddenly 'exchanged' her own personality for the manners and ways of a French-born lady, speaking French fluently and German as would a French woman. Eberhardt Gmelin, who published the case, was apparently able with a wave of his hand, to induce repeated changes between 'French' and 'German' states. In her French personality, the young woman had complete memory of all that she had said and done during her previous French states, but as a German she knew nothing of her French personality! (Ellenberger, 1970).

Another famous case, that of a young English woman called Mary Reynolds, was first published in 1816 by Dr John Kearsley Mitchell. She oscillated between two different personality states over a period of 15 or 16 years, finally settling in the second state until her death in 1854 at the age of 69. In her first state she was quiet, sober and thoughtful with a tendency to depression, while in her second state she was gay, cheerful, extravagant, fond of company and practical jokes, with a strong propensity for versification and rhyming.

Joseph Breuer's patient, Anna O (Breuer & Freud, 1893–95), sometimes credited with the birth of psychoanalysis (as well as a pseudocyesis that embarrassed her physician), also demonstrated a double personality. When Breuer took over her treatment in December 1880, she manifested two entirely distinct states of consciousness which alternated frequently and without warning. In one she recognised her surroundings, and was melancholy and anxious, but relatively normal. In the other she hallucinated and was 'naughty' – throwing cushions at people, tearing buttons from her bedclothes and producing numerous defects of speech and language. At one stage she apparently spoke only in English to the consternation of those around her! Later, after the death of her father in April 1881 a new feature of her 'condition seconde' developed – she appeared to be living in the winter of the preceding year. Breuer was easily able to induce a change of state by holding an orange before her eyes. She coined the terms 'talking cure' and 'chimney sweeping' to describe the hypnotic procedure whereby, through tracing the circumstances in which her symptoms originated, she was able to gain relief.

In 1886 a Dr Myers summarised the case of a male patient known as Louis V (*Science*, 1886) who was said to have six different states of consciousness, all of them more or less accompanied by distinct physical conditions, and different types of amnesia. The application of soft iron to his right thigh apparently restored most of his memory and temporarily dispelled all paralysis. Under other magnetic conditions, a sudden change of character occurred whereby, from being "arrogant, violent, and profane, with indistinct utterance and complete inability to write"; he became "quiet, modest, and respectful, speaking easily and clearly and able to write with a fair hand", although the greater part of his life remained a blank to him.

Ellenberger goes so far as to suggest that the entire 19th century was preoccupied with the problems that magnetism and hypnotism threw up regarding the constitution of the human mind. After the turn of the century most cases were reported as having more than two personalities (Prince, 1920). 'Dipsychism' – a dualistic concept – gave way to 'polypsychism' which saw the mind as a cluster of subpersonalities and finds its modern expression in psychoanalytic object-relations theory. Dr Henry Jekyll summarises the position well in Stevenson's famous novella:

"I thus drew steadily nearer to that truth by whose partial discovery I have been doomed to such a dreadful shipwreck: that man is not truly one, but truly two. I say two, because the state of my own knowledge does not pass beyond that point. Others will follow, others will outstrip me on the same lines; and I hazard the guess that man will be ultimately known for a mere polity of multifarious, incongruous and independent denizens."
(Stevenson, 1886)

Nosological status

The place of multiple personality phenomena in a classification of mental disorders is by no means settled. Several positions, not all mutually exclusive, need to be considered.

(a) *Multiple personality represents the normal but frequently unacknowledged condition of mankind. Hence it is a problem for grammar rather than medicine* (Tantam, 1990). This position fails to take account of the arresting fascination of case reports over two centuries. Mundane happenings do not normally stimulate such interest. The argument is easier to sustain in its weaker form – that multiple personality differs only in degree and not in kind from normal psychology. Freud adopted this view when he wrote the following lines, though he may have been oversanguine in thinking the concept of 'identification' was explanatory rather than merely descriptive:

> "perhaps the secret of the cases of what is described as 'multiple personality' is that the different identifications seize hold of consciousness in turn. Even when things do not go so far as this, there remains the question of conflicts between the various identifications into which the ego comes apart, conflicts which cannot after all be described as entirely pathological."
> (Freud, 1923)

(b) *Multiple personality is a factitious entity constructed by malingerers, or naively generated with iatrogenic help!* Illness confers alterations in social status, most notably release from normal social obligations, and possible legal defences against criminal charges (albeit with the simultaneous imposition of an alternative role). It may therefore be simulated for social gain. Professionals may be inclined to make diagnoses for the same reason, or because a given condition has become officially recognised or fashionable! Hypnotic suggestion might also encourage the manufacture of new identities (Chodoff, 1987). Such factors may explain the 'epidemic' of case reports emanating from North America over the last 20 years (Boor, 1982; Merskey, 1992). Sceptics, however, must explain those cases which seem to arise spontaneously, outside any legal context, and those (possibly as large a proportion as 90%) where dissimulation appears to have been attempted (Kluft, 1987a). There is a body of opinion which holds that it is impossible for a person to consistently fake multiplex cognitive, affective and behavioural patterns over an extended period of time (Watkins, 1984; Orne *et al*, 1984; Kluft, 1987b).

(c) *Multiple personality is a mental disorder* sui generis. This is the present orthodoxy expounded in DSM–III and DSM–III–R (American Psychiatric Association, 1980, 1987), where it is classified under the general rubric of dissociative disorders, and in ICD–10 (World Health Organization, 1992). In DSM–III–R, two or more distinct personalities (or personality states) are required to exist in the same person. A second criterion insists that the person's behaviour must be 'fully controlled' at different times by more than one of these personalities. The disorder is said to originate in childhood almost invariably, where there is frequently a history of physical and sexual abuse. More than 100 personalities may occur, with varying degrees of awareness and memory of each other. Transition between them is often sudden. The presence of amnesia between the 'primary personality' and others has been held to be important in eliminating false-positive diagnoses.

A 'personality' is defined as: "a relatively enduring pattern of perceiving, relating to, and thinking about the environment and one's self that is exhibited in a wide range of important social and personal contexts"; 'personality states' differ only in that they exhibit themselves in a narrower band of situations. Among the associated features, it is claimed that various personalities in the same person may have different physiological characteristics (e.g. skin-resistance, rate of vital functions, brain blood flow, electro-encephalogram (EEG), and visual acuity). They may also score differently on IQ tests, respond differently to pharmacological preparations and report themselves to be of different sex, age, or race, displaying supposedly characteristic behaviours.

Clearly, this definition introduces a controversial principle into the diagnostic process, in so far as it institutionalises the notion that human behaviour may be controlled not by individual persons but by a plurality of 'personalities' which inhabit persons. Thus the diagnosis of multiple personality disorder, according to DSM–III–R, automatically commits the diagnostician to an opinion which undermines the notion of individual autonomy. This, as we shall see, leads to extraordinary difficulties in assessing criminal responsibility, and is, to say the least, an unverifiable assumption. If the law is to avoid tautology, the existence of mental disorder giving rise to impaired responsibility must surely be established on other independent grounds.

(d) *Multiple personality is a symptom characteristic of a range of psychological disturbances.* These include hysteria, borderline personality disorder, affective and schizophrenic states and epileptic conditions. This is close to the position taken by DSM–II (American Psychiatric Association, 1968) and the conclusion felt to be most consistent with available evidence by Fahy (1988), after an extensive review of the literature. It is more satisfactory (although some might say shirks the issue) because it is fundamentally agnostic. Recognition and description of 'the symptom' does not entail commitment to a particular diagnosis, aetiological theory, treatment regime or untenable moral philosophy. Each case can be assessed on its merits, leaving the question of 'responsibility for the control of behaviour' out of the diagnostic criteria, for some transcendent legal or divine authority to decide!

Forensic implications

In modern times, one of the inherent assumptions in a society regulated by the Rule of Law, is the general recognition of the principle that responsibility is personal and individual (Lloyd, 1964). Individuals are accorded both rights and duties, and are only to be answerable for their own wrongdoing. The notion of individual moral responsibility may be an unjustifiable and unassessable metaphysical construct, yet the wellbeing of society seems to require it.

The putative existence of multiple identities in one body has far-fetched social consequences, and challenges assumptions which we normally take for granted. Is, for example, each identity to be awarded a separate vote? Does punishment of one identity offend against the principle that there should be no vicarious liability, if other 'innocent' identities must suffer along with the guilty one? Can a guilty identity escape justice by 'hiding' behind an innocent one? Can multiple identities give testimony to prove a felony?

The case of Kenneth Bianchi (The Los Angeles 'Hillside Strangler') is one in point. During the autumn and winter of 1977–78, the naked bodies of 10 women who had been raped and then strangled were found on various hillsides of Los Angeles County. In January 1979, two further victims were found in a vacant house in Bellingham, Washington, and physical evidence led to the arrest of Bianchi. After interrogation, the Los Angeles police did not consider Bianchi to be a likely suspect for the killings in their area.

Bianchi gave his defence attorney an alibi which was grossly at variance with the facts. When faced with this, he claimed to have invented the story in order to fill in gaps in his memory. His claim of amnesia led the defence to call in a forensic hypnotist, who elicited an alterpersonality, 'Steve', apparently unknown to Ken, claiming responsibility for the two local killings and 9 of the 10 Los Angeles deaths. John Watkins, the hypnotist, found Bianchi to be "a pleasant, mild young man who seemed to be earnestly seeking to understand what had happened and why he was in jail", and who at no time showed any concern for his legal fate (Watkins, 1984).

'Steve', however, when seen by another investigator out of trance, was described as "very crude and nasty, using the word "fuck" in every sentence, and claiming to have committed the crime to get Ken out of the way, so that he could control the body full-time" (Allison, 1984). In an attempt to discover whether Bianchi was malingering, it was suggested to him (in his normal state) that real cases of multiple personality invariably had at least three personalities. Under hypnosis a third personality, 'Billy', duly emerged, and this, together with other inconsistencies led prosecution witnesses to conclude that the correct diagnosis was Antisocial Personality Disorder with Sexual Sadism.

This split in expert opinion eventually resulted in a plea bargain, in which Bianchi pleaded guilty (avoiding the death penalty) and was sentenced to several terms of life imprisonment. Nevertheless, professional controversy regarding his diagnosis, and the means by which 'true' cases of multiple personality can be distinguished, continues unabated. It should be noted that at no stage in this case was the validity of multiple personality disorder *per se* called into question by the expert witnesses, although it has subsequently been suggested by one of them that determining the correct diagnosis in a death penalty case may be an impossible task (Allison, 1984).

Another case, under trial in Wisconsin at the time of writing, and reported in *The Times* (London), highlights the legal conundrums that the diagnosis engenders. Here the crime is said to have been made possible as a result of the victim's multiple personality!

> "Mark Peterson, a shop assistant, aged 29, is accused of raping Sarah by summoning 'Jennifer', a '20-year-old who likes to dance and have fun', and having sex with her in his car. During intercourse, a six-year-old personality known as Emily intruded. She told Sarah, who subsequently telephoned the police to report that she had been assaulted. On Wednesday the prosecutor and judge patiently questioned Sarah before 'summoning' and separately swearing in 'Jennifer' and 'Franny', a '30-year-old'." (*The Times*, 1990)

Clinical issues

From the psychodynamic point of view, multiple personality is regarded as a defence against anxiety, originally experienced in infancy. It has been suggested that the 'split' involved is in the ego, rather than between the ego and the id (Marmer, 1980). Object-relations language sees it both in the 'self' and its 'internal objects', or their 'representations'. The high prevalence of adverse childhood experiences reported in these patients is consistent with this, very general, hypothesis.

Another way of seeing this defence invokes the notion of 'self-hypnosis' (Bliss, 1980). Hypnosis is here regarded as a phylogenetically old CNS mechanism for protecting animals from danger. As a third alternative to fight and flight, self-hypnosis may produce physiological changes that allow the animal to remain immobile and 'freeze' for extended periods of time. In man this mechanism may lead to an altered state of consciousness whereby unpleasant experiences are forgotten or allocated out of awareness to alternative personalities. Most often discovered in childhood, it is suggested that in cases of multiple personality it thereafter develops into a primary method for coping with stress.

Information from split-brain observations also provides a biological model. It is clear that when the corpus callosum is severed the individual may engage in bewilderingly contradictory behaviour. In one case a husband embraced his wife with one hand and pushed her away with the other. A second person's right and left hand chose different clothes to wear (Sperry, 1965). These findings, together with the evidence of altered brain physiology in some cases, raise the possibility of an underlying biological basis for the dissociative states.

However we look at multiple personality, there can be no doubt that people do present to psychiatric services requiring help for this condition, and some workers feel it is insufficiently recognised (Ross, 1987). A wide range of therapeutic strategies has been tried, singly and in combination, including drugs, electroconvulsive therapy, hypnosis, and various forms of psychotherapy (Herzog, 1984; Ross & Gahan, 1984).

On the whole, these people are difficult to help and, in addition to personality change, frequently manifest depression, suicide attempts, substance abuse, amnesia, fugue, auditory hallucinations, and headaches (Cooms & Milstein, 1986). Hysterical conversion symptoms such as numbness, blindness, weakness, and convulsions are also often reported. Even experienced therapists who take on such patients find the work tedious and time consuming, and are prone to feel angry, exasperated, and emotionally exhausted by the task (Coons, 1986).

In in-patient settings physical restraint is required and sessions are frequently begun "in the seclusion room, knowing that angry, abusive alters are likely to be out of control when called out. Often orderlies are on standby outside the room" (Ross, 1987).

Apart from treating any underlying condition, therapeutic efforts are usually aimed at effecting 'integration' in the patient, for which Kluft (1982) has proposed six criteria:

(a) continuity of memory
(b) absence of dissociation
(c) subjective sense of unity
(d) absence of alter personalities under hypnosis
(e) modification of the transference consistent with fusion
(f) presence of previously segregated feelings, attitudes and memories in the fused personality.

This may come about swiftly (in eight out-patient sessions; Ross, 1987) or require prolonged psychotherapy lasting more than 10 years.

In the absence of controlled studies the efficacy of treatment is difficult to evaluate. What follow-up information there is does not give grounds for excessive optimism. Kluft's extensive outcome study over a period of ten years revealed only 15% of 161 treated patients to be integrated (Kluft, 1985), while Coons found three quarters of 20 patients to have remained unintegrated after a variable period of time (Coons, 1986). Antipsychotic medication appeared generally unhelpful in this group, but tricyclic antidepressants were judged effective in three of six patients. In a single case study, carbamazepine has also been reported to be useful in the control of dissociation and violent episodes (Fichter *et al*, 1990). Nevertheless it must be concluded that there is no unequivocal evidence to show that multiple personality is susceptible to anything other than spontaneous change.

References

ALLISON, R. B. (1984) Difficulties in diagnosing the multiple personality syndrome in a death penalty case. *International Journal of Clinical and Experimental Hypnosis*, **32**, 102–117.

AMERICAN PSYCHIATRIC ASSOCIATION (1968) *Diagnostic and Statistical Manual of Mental Disorders* (2nd edn) (DSM–II). Washington, DC: APA.

—— (1980) *Diagnostic and Statistical Manual of Mental Disorders* (3rd edn) (DSM–III). Washington, DC: APA.

—— (1987) *Diagnostic and Statistical Manual of Mental Disorders* (3rd edn, revised) (DSM–III–R). Washington, DC: APA.

BLISS, E. L. (1980) Multiple personalities: a report of 14 cases with implications for schizophrenia and hysteria. *Archives of General Psychiatry*, **37**, 1388–1397.

BOOR, M. (1982) The multiple personality epidemic. *Journal of Nervous and Mental Disease*, **170**, 302–304.

BREUER, J. & FREUD S. (1893–95) *Studies on Hysteria*, SE Vol. II (reprinted 1955). London: Hogarth.

CHODOFF, P. (1987) More on multiple personality disorder. *American Journal of Psychiatry*, **144**, 124.

COONS, P. M. (1986) Treatment progress in 20 patients with multiple personality disorder. *Journal of Nervous and Mental Disease*, **174**, 715–721.

—— & MILSTEIN, V. (1986) Psychosexual disturbances in multiple personality: characteristics, etiology, and treatment. *Journal of Clinical Psychiatry*, **47**, 106–110.

ELLENBERGER, H. F. (1970) *The Discovery of the Unconscious*, p. 127. London: Allen Lane.

FAHY, T. A. (1988) The diagnosis of multiple personality disorder: a critical review. *British Journal of Psychiatry*, **153**, 597–606.

FICHTER, C. G., KUHLMAN, D. T., GRUENFELD, M. J., et al (1990) Decreased episodic violence and increased control of dissociation in a carbamazepine-treated case of multiple personality. *Biological Psychiatry*, **27**, 1045–1052.

FREUD, S. (1923) *The Ego and the Id*, SE Vol. XIX (reprinted 1985). London: Hogarth.

HERZOG, A. (1984) On multiple personality: comments on diagnosis, etiology, and treatment. *International Journal of Clinical and Experimental Hypnosis*, **32**, 210–221.

KENNY, A. (1973) Mental health in Plato's Republic. In *The Anatomy of the Soul*, p. 8. Oxford: Blackwell.

KLUFT, R. P. (1982) Varieties of hypnotic intervention in the treatment of multiple personality. *American Journal of Clinical Hypnosis*, **24**, 230–240.

—— (1985) The treatment of multiple personality disorder: current concepts. *Directions in Psychiatry (New York)*, **5**, 1–9.

—— (1987a) The simulation and dissimulation of multiple personality disorder. *American Journal of Clinical Hypnosis*, **30**, 104–118.

—— (1987b) An update on multiple personality disorder. *Hospital and Community Psychiatry*, **38**, 363–373.

LLOYD, D. (1964) *The Idea of Law*, p. 163. London: Pelican.

MARMER, S. (1980) Psychoanalysis of multiple personality. *International Journal of Psycho-analysis*, **61**, 439.

MERSKEY, H. (1992) The manufacture of personalities: the production of multiple personality disorder. *British Journal of Psychiatry*, **160**, 327–340.

MITCHELL, J. K. (1816) A double consciousness or duality of person in the same individual. *Medical Repository*, **3**, 185–186.

ORNE, M. T., DINGES, D. F. & ORNE, E. C. (1984) The differential diagnosis of multiple personality disorder in the forensic context. *International Journal of Clinical and Experimental Hypnosis*, **32**, 118–167.

PRINCE, M. (1920) Miss Beauchamp: the psychogenesis of multiple personality. *Journal of Abnormal Psychology*, **16**, 67–137.

ROSS, A. & GAHAN, M. (1988) Techniques in the treatment of multiple personality disorder. *American Journal of Psychotherapy*, **XLII**, 40–52.

Ross, C. (1987) Inpatient treatment of multiple personality disorder. *Canadian Journal of Psychiatry*, **32**, 779–781.

Science (1886) Editorial. **7** (169), 397–399.

Sperry, R. (1965) Brain bisection and the mechanisms of consciousness. In *The Brain and Conscious Behaviour* (ed. J. C. Eccles). New York: Springer.

Stevenson, R. L. (1886) *The Strange Case of Dr Jekyll and Mr Hyde*, p. 82 (reprinted 1979). London: Penguin.

Tantam, D. (1990) Iatrogenic identities. *BJP Review of Books*, **1**, 19–21.

The Times (1990) 'Three faces' of Sarah give evidence. *Times*, Nov. 9.

Watkins, J. G. (1984) The Bianchi (L.A. Hillside Strangler) case: sociopath or multiple personality. *International Journal of Clinical and Experimental Hypnosis*, **32**, 86.

Whyte, L. L. (1978) *The Unconscious Before Freud*, p. 32. London: Julian Friedmann.

World Health Organization (1992) *The ICD–10 Classification of Mental and Behavioural Disorders*. Geneva: WHO.

9 Self-wounding and personality disorder

DIGBY TANTAM and JANE WHITTAKER

Favazza (1987), in an excellent review, gives numerous examples of the widespread human interest in hand-crafting the body which range from head-moulding in ancient Egypt, Central and North America and modern Europe, to Chinese foot-binding, which produced feet that were so small they could not bear their owner unsupported. Other types of anatomical rearrangement in the list include trepanation of the skull (world-wide, prehistoric), finger amputation (Pacific, Africa), and various types of genital rearrangement (Australia, Africa). In fact, he concludes that only the eyes and the anus have never been the target of socially sanctioned mutilation.

Such practices fill many Westerners with horror although, it must be said, Western practices of ear- and nose-piercing, circumcision, and skin-bronzing through radiation exposure are rarely abhorred with equal vigour. One reason for this may be the special status attached to the healthy (whole) body and the denigration of deformity in this culture. The pursuit of health and wholeness has become morally good, and deliberate self-injury is proportionally bad or 'sick'.

This is not so for other cultures, and has not always been so in the West. Mortification of the flesh has been an important theme in Christianity, resulting in epidemics of self-mutilation, notably the flagellants of the 14th century who, as disturbingly portrayed in Bergman's film *The Seventh Seal*, wandered in bands across Europe whipping themselves. Religiously motivated self-wounding by slashing, tearing, or ripping the skin and subcutaneous structures is also practised throughout the world. Menninger (1935) mentions Tongans, Chinese thigh-cutters, South American Indians, Bengalis, and a Russian sect of castrati, the skoptsi. Favazza (1987) adds dervishes in Morocco, Tamils in South India, North American Indians, Africans and native Australians. No doubt there are many others. Mutilation is a central theme in many religions. Christ was crucified, Odin gave an eye for knowledge, Attis/Osiris was castrated, and even Gautama Buddha is said in some traditions to have fed his own flesh to a hungry tiger (Evans-Wentz, 1968).

191

Favazza argues that self-mutilation in the context of a group and with a religious aim is psychologically distinct from the self-mutilation which leads to psychiatric referral, and quotes from Turner (1977): "deviant self-mutilators are not liminal objects . . . and the flow of their blood opens no significant channels between God and Man" (Favazza, 1987, p. 44). However, there may be an association between the familiarity of culturally sanctioned self-mutilation and attitudes to self-harm. Members of cultures in which the normative response to suffering is bathos are likely to have different motives for self-harm than the members of cultures where pathos is the rule. This leads to the speculation that the horror provoked by wounds, and the efforts to conceal them, may be in direct proportion to the frequency with which deviant self-wounding occurs.

Self-harm, self-injury, self-mutilation and self-wounding: some definitions

There is no generally agreed terminology but we will use the expression first put forward by Morgan (1979), 'deliberate self-harm' (or, simply, 'self-harm'), as the most general term for behaviour whose main purpose is bodily derangement. Deliberate self-harm ('parasuicide', 'attempted suicide', 'self-injury') may be brought about enterally or parenterally. The former we shall term self-poisoning ('overdosing'), the latter – the main topic of this review – self-injury ('slashing, 'cutting', 'wrist-cutting').

Simpson (1976) distinguishes 'wrist-slashers' from "the psychotic individual who mutilates himself" and "the person who makes one deep and dangerous cut in a highly lethal suicide attempt", and we follow his practice in differentiating between these different forms of self-injury, which we term 'self-wounding' (e.g. cutting, slashing), and 'self-mutilation' (e.g. castration, enucleation of the eye: see Table 9.1).

Dermatitis artefacta, malingering, and other types of socially motivated self-mutilation

Major anatomical change may occur as a secondary consequence of repeated self-injury, for example in people with learning disabilities who repeatedly bite or bang themselves. However, anatomical change is most commonly associated with those types of self-injury which are directed towards its production. Such self-mutilation may be pathological, performed in the context of a religious ritual, or be the means to a desired end ('motivated'), in which case the factitious nature of the injury is concealed. Motives include profit for the professional beggar, the avoidance of unpleasant duties or

TABLE 9.1
Some characteristics of different types of self-injury

Associated with:	Self-mutilation			Self-wounding		
	pathological	religious	motivated	reactive or habitual	depressive	motivated
unequivocal depression	–	–	–	–	+	–
borderline phenomena	–	–	–	+	–	+/–
psychosis	+	–	–	–	–	–
other habit disorders	–	–	–	+	–	+
Tendency to repeat many times	+	–	–	+	–	+
Much commoner in youth	–	–	–	+	–	–
Surgical correction often needed	+	+	+	–	+	–
Major anatomical change	+	–	+	–	–	–
May affect vital structures	+	–	–	–	+	–
Commonly life-threatening	–	–	–	–	–	–
Medical care rejected	–	–	–	+	–	–
Cause of injury concealed	–	–	+	–	–	+

consequences in the case of the malingerer, or the simulation of a pathological lesion in order, presumably, to obtain medical care.

Pathological lesions may be simulated in Munchausen's syndrome with or without actual self-mutilation, but in the related dermatitis artefacta, some degree of self-harm always occurs. Sneddon & Sneddon (1975) have described 45 patients, 38 of whom were women, who presented to hospital with self-inflicted skin lesions which included excoriations, burns, bruising, and ligature-induced lesions, but no cuts. Their ages ranged from 9 to 81 years, and they were suffering from a variety of psychiatric disorders which included dementia and learning disability. Of the 33 who could be traced 12 years later, 13 (39.4%) were still damaging their skins.

It is arguable whether such acts are *prima facie* evidence of personality disorder: we are inclined to think not, although they may be indicators of depression.

Pathological self-mutilation versus self-wounding

The amount of suffering that is experienced, although it may be considerable, does not appear to be relevant to final satisfaction, which may be genuine and lasting, with the result of self-mutilation. Those who wound themselves, on the other hand, often take steps to prolong or increase their suffering, but are indifferent to the final anatomical consequences.

The stated intention of self-mutilation is often to rid oneself of an offending organ or body part, typically one which the subject's culture attributes some moral and agentive qualities. Common targets are the eye (the evil eye, the roving eye), the genitalia (John Thomas), or the tongue (the filthy tongue, the tongue that runs away with you). Self-wounding may be directed to the genitalia but more often involves areas where wounds are likely to produce the greatest anxiety, for example the skin of the wrists, or the neck, which overlies vulnerable vital structures.

Self-mutilation is rare in our psychiatric experience, and certainly much rarer than other forms of self-injury. By contrast, treated rates of self-mutilation have been observed in Zambia to be higher than treated rates of self-wounding (Vanvaria & Haworth, personal communication), and this may be true of hospital practice in many developing countries.

Case descriptions of self-mutilation are, however, published more often than reports of self-wounding, perhaps because their more lurid nature appeals to journal editors. Many of them concern patients with psychosis, and it is commonly stated in literature reviews that there is a particular association between the two conditions. Thus Konicki & Schulz (1989, p. 556) state that "patients who injure themselves without clear suicidal intent can be divided into two classes: the psychotic patients and the patients with severe character pathology (personality disorders)''. They follow Pattinson & Kahan (1983) in using an age of first self-harm before 30 as a distinguishing criterion of the latter, 'early-onset' type. Walsh & Rosen (1988) distinguish between manipulative and self-punishing self-mutilators (which we subsume under our term 'self-wounding') and psychotic self-mutilators. Favazza (1989) considers that most of the latter, whom he terms 'major self-mutilators', are either psychotic, intoxicated with drugs, or suffering from an organic brain syndrome.

The 'self-wounding syndrome' and other types of self-wounding

As already noted, some people who are almost always severely depressed may wound themselves with the intention of killing themselves. Self-wounding may also occur as an incidental by-product of other behaviour, notably sexual practices: urethral and anal stimulation may lead to trauma, for example, and asphyxiation during masturbation may lead to haemorrhage or brain damage.

We distinguish these types from the reactive or habitual 'self-wounding syndrome' which is an end in itself (Table 9.1).

Epidemiology

Robinson & Duffy (1989) found that 656 of the 7887 patients admitted to the Edinburgh Regional Poisoning Treatment Centre between 1980 and 1986 had injured themselves. This is close to the 11.7% reported by Weissman (1975) and the 11.2% found by Clendenin & Murphy (1971). However, in a more comprehensive sub-study, a higher proportion of self-wounding was found in patients who discharged themselves or who were referred to other (mainly surgical) wards, and the ratio of self-wounding to self-poisoning was about one to two when these other patients were included. From this and from recently published rates of non-fatal self-harm in Edinburgh (Kreitman, 1990), it can be estimated that 1 in 600 adults deliberately wound themselves sufficiently to require hospital treatment. This is likely to be an underestimate since some deliberate self-harm will be concealed by relatives, friends or the person themselves, or will not be judged sufficiently severe to require hospital assessment.

A more thorough study in Ontario in the early 1970s surveyed incidents of 'self-injury' over 12 months in general practices, nursing homes, and gaols as well as hospitals (Johnson *et al*, 1975). The authors report an annual rate of 730 episodes of self-injury per 100 000 population, committed by 559 individuals per 100 000 population, but guessed that the 'true' rate was 1433 episodes per 100 000. Self-cutting accounted for 17.6% of the episodes.

In Favazza & Conterio's (1989) series of 240 women who regularly wounded themselves, the commonest method used was cutting (72%), followed by skin-burning (35%), hitting or punching parts of the body (30%), interfering with wound-healing (22%), scratching (22%), hair-pulling (10%), and breaking bones (8%). Damage was to the arms, especially the wrists (74%), the legs (44%), the abdomen (25%), the head (23%), the chest (18%), and the genitalia, including the vaginal wall (8%).

Damage is commonly produced by broken glass, needles, open scissors, razor blades, knives, hammers, cigarettes, irons, and hotplates, but almost any available household object can be adapted for the purpose. Other patients known to us have injected septic urine into the skin, tied tourniquets on the arms and legs, thrown themselves down or in front of vehicles, partly strangled themselves with coathangers, hanged themselves, and abused aperients sufficiently to produce incontinence. People, especially people with learning difficulties, may also bang their heads, swallow foreign objects, or bite themselves. No doubt this list could be expanded, seemingly the only limitation being the imagination of the patient.

According to Simpson (1976), "the typical wristcutter . . . is likely to be a young (usually 16–24 years of age) attractive woman", but this may reflect only the composition of those patients who are retained in treatment. Two surveys of patients entering treatment (Lester & Beck, 1980; Robinson & Duffy, 1989) show that self-mutilation is commoner in men than women, although they confirm the association with youth.

Self-wounding, once begun, tends to be repeated. In Favazza & Conterio's (1989) sample of women, which was partly recruited by advertisement and may therefore have been biased towards a more severe or chronic group, cutting often began in the early teens, and half the sample had wounded themselves on more than 50 occasions. Peak incidence, according to Favazza (1987), is in the early teens, and self-wounding typically continues for 5–10 years.

Association with other forms of self-harm

Self-wounding is associated with problem drinking (Fox & Weissman, 1975; Lester & Beck, 1980; Robinson & Duffy, 1989; Favazza & Conterio, 1989); drug misuse (Waldenberg, 1972; Simpson, 1976), particularly of oral drugs (Gossop *et al*, 1975); eating disorders (Simpson, 1976), especially bulimia nervosa (Lacey & Evans, 1986); offending (Waldenburg, 1972; Lacey & Evans, 1986), particularly violent offending (Bach-y-Rita, 1974); and self-poisoning, particularly repeated overdosing (Robinson & Duffy, 1989). Lacey & Evans (1986) have proposed that all of these activities are the expression of a unitary disorder which they call the "multi-impulsive personality". Others have proposed a 'deliberate self-harm syndrome' (Morgan, 1979; Kahan & Pattison, 1984) or a 'wrist-cutter syndrome' (Graff & Malin, 1967).

Self-wounding and personality disorder

Repeated self-wounding is one of the symptoms of borderline personality disorder in DSM–III–R (American Psychiatric Association, 1987) or of other 'flamboyant' personality disorders such as histrionic and narcissistic personality disorder (Konicki & Schulz, 1989) and there is an association between self-wounding and other symptoms of borderline personality disorder. There is also a close association with 'multiple personality disorder', a syndrome which lies on the borderline between hysteria and personality disorder. Putnam *et al* (1986), in one of the largest series of patients with multiple personality disorder to be published, found that 34% of patients had deliberately wounded themselves.

The validity of personality disorder diagnoses has been criticised (see Tantam, 1988; Lewis & Appleby, 1988, for a fuller discussion) and there is no personality disorder diagnosis which is unique to self-wounding. In one study (Gardner & Gardner, 1975) personality disorder was no more frequently diagnosed in psychiatric in-patients who had harmed themselves than in a control group of non-psychotic psychiatric in-patients.

The attribution of upsetting behaviour to abnormal personality tends to blunt the normal caring response of compassion and commonsense firmness, and may encourage an expectation of irresponsibility and the 'secondary deviance' of which labelling theorists have written (Lemert, 1967). Too often, further enquiry into the reasons for the behaviour, in particular into the situational determinants of self-wounding, stops once a diagnosis is made.

Disturbed behaviour is produced by disturbing situations or disturbed relationships as well as by disturbed personality, but the former is much harder to investigate and has, since the early days of psychoanalysis (Masson, 1985), been as systematically neglected by many psychotherapists as it has by neuropsychiatrists.

Hawton *et al*'s (1982) classification of self-poisoning among adolescents, which is applicable to other types of self-harm, has the advantage that it links impulsive behaviour and social relationships but without any comment on personality. They propose that self-poisoning may be (a) a response to conflict in one relationship, other relationships being generally satisfactory; (b) a response to an acute exacerbation of longer-standing and more pervasive problems in relationships; and (c) a less clearly motivated behaviour, part of a complex of impulsive behaviours, and associated with a lack of close or satisfying relationships.

Hawton considers that repeated self-harm is a symptom of another disorder, usually a personality disorder. We lean more to the arguments of other authors who argue for a diagnostic category of repeated, deliberate self-harm, *sui generis*, which could also include other impulsive and self-destructive behaviours, for instance those considered by Lacey & Evans (1986) to be part of the "multi-impulsive" personality.

Separation of a deliberate self-harm syndrome from the pervasive impairment of relationships and emotions characteristic of personality disorder would have the added advantage that it would make it possible to investigate how often repeated self-wounding leads to an impairment in relationships and emotions: whether, in other words, personality abnormality may be consequent on, rather than antecedent to, repeated self-harm.

Self-wounding and adversity

Emerson (1914), one of the first to describe a case of self-cutting, mentioned both abuse and disturbed relationships within the family. Zanarini *et al* (1989) found that patients with borderline personality disorder diagnoses were more likely than controls to have a history of neglect or abuse, Briere & Zaidi (1989) that a history of sexual abuse was linked to self-harm, substance abuse, sexual difficulties, multiple diagnoses and borderline personality disorder diagnoses, and Herman (1989) that 17 of 21 patients with borderline personality gave histories of trauma (71% physical, 68% sexual, 62% witnessing domestic violence).

Abuse for which the victim feels to blame, as is often the case with incest, may be particularly likely to lead to self-harm (Shapiro, 1987). Rape may have similar psychological effects, and may also lead to self-harm (Greenspan & Samuel, 1989).

Aetiology

Favazza (1989) considers 12 possible causes of self-wounding, and undoubtedly many more could be identified. We shall only consider the following: tension relief, alteration of consciousness, addictive self-stimulation, emotional privation, social learning, symbolic mediation of internal change, and the symbolic mediation of relationships.

Tension relief

Many patients report that cutting themselves reduces a dysphoria that is experienced as accumulating between episodes. Jones *et al* (1979) argue, on the basis of similarities between the circumstances of self-wounding in man and in animals, particularly primates, that there is a common physiological mechanism, which they call the relief of tension. Little direct human evidence exists for this, but there is mounting evidence that arousal leads to self-injury in man and animals. Caffeine (Peters, 1967), caffeine with low dose amphetamine (Mueller *et al*, 1982), pemoline (Genovese *et al*, 1969), or methylxanthine (Lloyd & Stone, 1981) all increase self-injury in rats. All these are dopamine precursors, whose administration has also been shown to increase self-injury in monkeys with brain lesions (Goldstein *et al*, 1986), and in four children with attention deficit disorder (Sokol *et al*, 1987).

It has been suggested that dopamine mediates goal-directed behaviour (van Praag *et al*, 1990), and arousal occurs when there is internal pressure towards purposive behaviour, but the opportunities for behaviour are not available, either because of internal constraints, such as the approach–avoidance conflict originally described by ethologists, or because of circumstances, for example the cage surrounding the laboratory animal. The association of brain injury and self-harm in some of the reports cited above could also be attributable to an interference with purposive activity.

People with learning disabilities are more likely to harm themselves than controls, particularly by hitting and biting (McKerracher *et al*, 1968). The frequency of self-injury increases with increasing learning disability (Ballinger, 1967) with a prevalence reaching 10% in some mental-handicap hospitals. Self-harm is also commoner in other institutions, being more frequent and of greater severity in prisoners (Claghorn & Beto, 1967), especially those meeting criteria for personality disorders and those kept in solitary confinement (Virkkunen, 1976).

The similarities of the self-injury in these human situations and that seen in animals is suggestive of dopamine-mediated 'tension relief' being a factor in both cases. Indeed Jones *et al*'s (1979) hypothesis was based on observations of laboratory animals (Jones & Barraclough, 1978) which, it is well-known, are more likely to show behavioural abnormalities than their free-ranging, feral conspecifics. As long ago as 1928, Tinkelpaugh reported self-harm in a captive male macaque who had been separated from his mate.

The injuries in the children with attention-deficit disorder cited above, the self-injury of patients with learning disability, especially those with Lesch-Nyhan (Nyhan, 1976) and De Lange syndrome (Singh & Pulman, 1979), and the dopamine-responsive isolation stereotypies that Ridley & Baker (1982) described in rhesus macaques are similar to each other, but different in kind from the type of self-wounding typified by wrist-cutting.

Dopamine- or amphetamine-related self-injury also differs from self-wounding in not being consummatory, but more like a displacement activity: a normal behaviour which would usually be suppressed by behaviour to meet environmental demands and which is therefore only apparent in circumstances when social or instrumental behavioural sequences have broken down. In this it has similarities with other frustration-induced behaviour, such as trichotillomania and lichen simplex, which incidentally produces self-injury and which is made worse by 'stress'.

The difference between self-injury due to behavioural restraint and other types of self-harm is exemplified by Yaroshevsky's (1975) observation that self-injury was common in Russian prisons among 'criminals', but not among 'politicals' who go on hunger strikes. Although he writes "Thus, both the hunger strikers and those who mutilate themselves in other ways remove themselves from the omnipotent control of their jailers, while simultaneously reproaching them morally", it seems clear that the 'politicals' are making a protest, a statement with a purpose, which the 'criminals' are failing to do.

We conclude that some forms of self-injury may be a direct consequence of the behavioural outflow of 'tension', itself the consequence of the inhibition of the normal behavioural expression of an agonistic or appetitive drive. However, this does not apply primarily to the self-wounding exemplified by wrist-cutting. We consider below the possibility that tension relief following self-wounding can be conditioned or otherwise learnt.

Alteration of consciousness

Grunebaum & Klerman (1967) were the first to emphasise the 'dissociation' which preceded self-harm. Depersonalisation is also often described as a prelude – Walsh & Rosen (1988) cite 5 other references – and self-wounding is sometimes described by patients as a means of restoring their sense of the reality of themselves or of their environment. Two-thirds of the respondents in Favazza & Conterio's (1989) sample reported feeling no pain while they wounded themselves, and this anaesthesia may persist for some hours (interestingly local anaesthesia is also associated with an increase in self-harm according to Dubovsky, 1978).

There is little other than anecdotal evidence for the often repeated suggestion that self-wounding is a measure adopted to terminate dissociation. It seems, in fact, rather more likely that dissociation enables self-wounding to occur (Pao, 1969). Biological explanations of dissociation have recently given way to social learning ones. Ross (1989), for example, considers that dissociation in multiple personality disorder develops from the need to escape from intolerable situations in childhood, such as incest. Because no physical escape is available, he suggests that the child experiences her/himself as an uninvolved observer, separate from her/his body.

We shall return to the social learning of self-wounding in a later section.

Addictive self-stimulation

Favazza (1987) has proposed that self-wounding is repeated because it is addictive. Further evidence for this is that it is associated with other types of behaviour with an addictive quality (eating disorder, impulsive disorder, self-harm, substance abuse, violence) and that, if it is prevented, it may be replaced by another of these addictive behaviours.

For the behaviour to be truly addictive, it must be shown to have an effect on one of the brain reward systems, and it is therefore of interest that there does seem to be a link between endogenous opiates and self-wounding.

Endorphins. Konicki & Charles (1989) have recently reviewed this subject. They note that either methadone or morphine administration produces stereotypies in rats, and that opiate antagonists have been shown to reduce self-injury by animals. Naloxone, but not haloperidol, has been shown to reduce self-mutilation in one patient with Tourette's syndrome (Gillman & Sandyk, 1985). Konicki & Charles review six other studies involving a total of 11 patients, all of them with learning disability, in whom either naloxone or naltrexone were given and self-injury monitored, with improvement reported in four (reviewed in Konicki & Schulz, 1989) and no change in two.

These findings suggest that an excess of endogenous opioid may increase self-injury. Coid *et al* (1983) found that 10 patients who repeatedly wounded themselves had higher plasma metenkephalin levels than 10 age- and sex-matched volunteers. However in the absence of surgical and psychiatric control groups, the alternative possibilities that metenkephalin is higher in psychiatric patients or that it is increased by injury cannot be excluded.

Konicki & Schulz (1989) consider two possible explanations of the putative causal association between raised endogenous opioids and self-injury. The first is that a constitutionally raised opioid level raises the pain threshold and so makes self-injury 'easier'. The second is that self-injury is maintained because it produces endogenous opioids which are associated with a 'high' which is behaviourally rewarding (Richardson & Zaleski, 1986).

Either of these abnormalities could result from an inborn biochemical diathesis or the effects of chronic stimulation, through repeated stress. We consider some possible characteristics of the latter below.

Emotional privation

Mason & Sponholz (1963) showed that partial isolation of rhesus macaques in early life predisposed to self-mutilation. Cross & Harlow (1965) raised macaques from birth onwards in individual wire cages from which they could see and hear conspecifics, but not touch them. They found that this resulted in the persistence of sucking and chewing behaviours long after normally reared age-mates were substituting other behaviours for them. Response to external threat was also impaired and after the age of three, partially isolated macaques were as likely to respond with self-directed aggression, particularly attacks on a bodily appendage or self-biting, as with outwardly directed attack. Self-directed aggression almost never occurred in socially reared monkeys.

Non-injurious self-stimulation, such as rocking, is commonly associated with more severe emotional isolation resulting, for example, from institutionalisation or autism. Self-injury, in monkeys at least, is associated with partial and inadequate nurturance, similar to what Rutter in his study of maternal deprivation (Rutter, 1981) terms 'strained relationship'.

In man, such relationships are associated with behavioural ambivalence in which both approach and avoidance elements occur; ambivalence in close relationships is, indeed, a characteristic feature of many people who harm themselves repeatedly who have a history of either having to lose the care of others or having to submit to them so that "whichever direction they move, they experience negative feedback" (Melges & Swartz, 1989).

Further evidence for intermittent emotional privation comes from retrospective studies. Caroll *et al* (1980) found that 14 self-wounding patients were significantly more likely to report separations before 12, family violence, and physical abuse than 14 psychiatric controls. Zanarini *et al* (1989) obtained accounts of their childhood from 50 patients with borderline personality disorder and compared these with the accounts of controls with dysthymia or antisocial personality disorder. Both abuse and neglect were significantly commoner in the borderline than in the other groups.

If the persistent oral stimulation and the autoaggression of emotionally deprived primates are a model of self-wounding then this would imply that the wound combines elements of pleasurable self-stimulation and of violence.

This suggestion is not new, having been made by Emerson (1914). He regarded self-cutting as a symbolic substitute for masturbation and also an act of self-punishment. This point of view has been further developed by Fenichel (1945) and Siomopoulos (1974). Siomopoulos, for example, attributes self-wounding to an excessive need for self-stimulation to compensate for a lack of maternal handling, which Rosenthal & Rosenthal (1984) consider may also lead to self-harm in young children.

The association of a vulnerability to addiction with a history of emotional privation suggests that these two explanations could be complementary. The opiate system is one possible common ground, but one of the many brain systems subserved by serotonergic neurons may be another. Winchel & Stanley (1991) summarise an impressive range of evidence for some association between lowered serotonin function and increased self-harm. One study (Valzelli & Bernasconi, 1979) that they cite, suggests a link between aggressiveness, vulnerability to isolation, and brain serotonin in mice. In this study, brain 5-HIAA and aggression were measured in mice of different strains. Mice strains which showed the greatest reduction in 5-HIAA turnover when kept in isolation also showed the greatest increase in aggression when kept isolated.

Social learning

Early studies, before self-wounding was widely publicised, found a high proportion of people who had worked in medical settings among patients who wounded themselves (McEvedy, 1963). Rosenthal *et al* (1972) found that 60% of patients diagnosed as having borderline personality disorder and who had wounded themselves, gave a history of surgery or hospital treatment before the age of five.

Walsh & Rosen (1985) studied 25 adolescents in a residential facility over a year and found that there were clusters of self-wounding suggesting that self-wounding was imitated. Further statistical analysis and a sociogram (Rosen & Walsh, 1989) led them to conclude that a few residents set the trend which was followed by those in their immediate circle.

Social learning may operate through conditioning processes, or through beliefs. Walsh & Rosen (1988, p. 156) ask themselves ''What is it about the thinking of self-mutilators that allows them to demean and deface themselves through self-inflicted wounds?'' and come to the conclusion that they have been taught to believe that:

''(a) self-mutilation is acceptable
(b) one's body and self are disgusting and deserving of punishment
(c) action is needed to reduce unpleasant feelings and bring relief
(d) overt action is necessary to communicate feelings to others.''

Learning through conditioning has received less attention than belief acquisition or imitation. This is surprising because operant conditioning, 'attention seeking', is so very often invoked in clinical settings. Evidence suggests that any attention provided is usually either punitive or critical, and unlikely therefore to be the reward that the conditioning explanation requires. However, it is possible that self-wounding in response to threat may successfully turn away the aggression or sexual desire of the threatening person and that, if this effect is repeated, this relief may become a classically conditioned response to self-wounding in the future. This is a possible explanation of the relief of tension that some cutters report.

Symbolic mediation of internal change

The importance of self-injury in religious observance underpins the symbolic significance of the wound. Psychoanalysts have interpreted this in various ways. Menninger (1935) proposed that self-wounding was a substitute for suicide, a 'partial suicide', which enables guilt to be expiated. Helen Deutsch (1944) considered it a symbol of the menses which the self-inflicted wound was an attempt to control. Others have also stressed the importance of the flowing blood, but as a symbol of comfort (Kafka, 1969).

As already noted, repeated self-wounding is commonly one aspect of the psychological and behavioural abnormalities which can be termed borderline personality disorder. Pines considers that ''What is common to all borderline personalities is that they remain . . . vulnerable to self-fragmentation and loss of a sense of identity in one or other degree'' (Pines, 1989, p. 63).

Kohut (1984) and other self-psychologists consider that this structural weakness arises from a failure of caregivers to ''affectively attune' to the infant, so that the normal development from a fused self and other representation, the 'self-object', does not occur. Kernberg (1984) proposes instead a chronic split between good and bad 'objects' resulting from a failure to fuse affection and hostility directed to the same person. These two models have different implications for treatment, but the psychological consequences are similar: over-identification ('fusion') with others, and marked inconsistency with sudden changes of attitude and emotional state ('splitting').

Both fusion and splitting weaken the behavioural continuities which others use to identify a person as 'that person'. They weaken, to use another psychoanalytically inspired metaphor, the 'ego-boundary', of which the skin is a particular symbol. It is not therefore surprising that self-wounding has often been considered to be a means of restoring the ego boundary (Kris, 1954; Kakfa, 1969) although it is not quite clear why this should be done by means of a wound, unless it is meant to symbolise the rents in the ego boundary.

A simpler explanation might be that self-wounding may be an expression of mastery or autonomy when other avenues are closed off. One of our patients, who was bullied both at school and at home, first cut herself when a girl at school threw a bottle at her. She picked up one of the fragments of shattered glass, and cut her wrist with it.

Even if adequately formed, it might be supposed that the 'ego boundary' could be broken down by subsequent damage, and the picture of a defensive wall being breached by attacks, or by Trojan horses, from outside fits well with the pervasive loss of mastery and shame that may follow sexual or physical abuse. Meares (1987) lays particular emphasis on the Trojan horse: an idea, memory, or experience which is a 'pathogenic secret', being too horrible or shameful to either utter or forget. We agree with Hill (Hill, 1991) that such secrets are common in the histories of patients who cut themselves. Examples of them from our own cases are, as well as sexual abuse, a father's promiscuity, a father's transvestism, and the patient's own incest with a sibling.

Symbolic mediation of relationship change

Like Kernberg (1987), we are uncomfortable with many of the metaphors applied to older-style psychodynamic explanations, preferring the, to us, clearer action language of Shafer (1983) and others. One of us (Tantam, 1986) has elsewhere proposed that non-verbal communication has both a meaning, and a burden. The meaning of a particular act of self-wounding can be looked for among some of the symbols considered in the previous section. The burden of self-wounding can be found in the changes in the quality of relationships with others that it effects.

Skin which is easily visible to others is deliberately damaged more often than skin which is rarely uncovered. Undoubtedly self-wounding is a powerful move in the game of personal relationships, one that often attracts the opprobrium of care-staff who term it 'manipulative'. The use of this term suggests, falsely, that people who wound themselves are better manipulators of others than most. Our experience is contrary to this: that people who wound themselves are less good at manipulating others, and consequently are more likely to resort to the last ditch strategy of self-wounding.

It has already been noted that close relationships with other people who veer from being profoundly rejecting to being seductively warm or overprotective may lead to self-injury. Self-wounding has the effect of both distancing others and protecting against rejection, and it may be developed as a means of controlling highly conflictual relationships and the ambivalent feelings that they arouse. Were it a successful method it would not lead to psychiatric intervention, but it is not. Indeed self-wounding recreates the same conflicts and inconsistencies in new relationships, including therapeutic relationships, that are present in formative, childhood relationships. This may be a significant factor in the maintenance of self-wounding.

The frequent use of dissociation by people who injure themselves may have the function of reducing cognitive dissonance between these inconsistencies in attitudes and behaviour. This may be reinforced by the greater social legitimacy of deviant or 'out of character' behaviour if it can be attributed to illness or altered psychological state in which the person was 'not themself'.

An aetiological reconstruction

We consider that many, if not all, of the aetiological factors considered here may be applicable to some patients or at some time in the development of the habit of repeated self-wounding. The following hypothetical case, based on clinical experience and the papers reviewed here, is designed to illustrate how the factors might combine.

Hypothetical case

A child finds herself impotent in the face of relationship conflicts which fill her with highly charged, but opposite feelings. She is likely to be socially isolated, and more self-preoccupied than most. She may have discovered that she feels transiently better when she is hurt, and she may have heard about girls who cut themselves. She tries it, and feels better: calmer, more alert, more cheerful, even more deserving.

It creates a stir which she quickly finds she can turn to her advantage. However, the adults with whom she lives are as self-preoccupied as she is, and resent her intrusion of her feelings into their awareness. Two parties form: those who think that she is being manipulative, and those that think she is desperately unhappy. The former want to punish her, the latter to take her over. She tries to mollify the disciplinarians by wounding herself as a form of punishment, but they interpret this as more manipulation. Her self-harm may also seem to be a good strategy to deal with the other party, by showing them how useless their help really is, but this party only interpret her actions as showing how much she needs them and claim that only they really understand her.

The only way out, for all concerned, is to attribute the problem neither to the family nor to the patient, but to a mystery illness or condition. There may be some relief and improvement in behaviour when this construction of events is completed, and legitimised by a doctor. However, the girl finds that all other relationships drop away leaving only those in which she is a patient. She feels trapped, inadequate, and more socially isolated. She also feels increasingly angry with doctors and medical treatment although fearful of giving them up. Activities, interests, and social contacts not involving self-harm dwindle. The only thing that reliably works to make her feel better is to wound herself, and as these thoughts occupy more and more of her waking day she begins to believe that they have an existence independent of her, and that she cannot defend herself against them. She begins to hear the thoughts in her head, as a voice, and may start to say that this is not her own. She starts to harm herself in other ways, for example, by starving herself, and identifies increasingly with other girls in a similar situation. To harm oneself very frequently or severely is regarded by this group as a sort of achievement and new methods of self-harm initiated by one member are quickly taken up by others.

Treatment

This has recently been reviewed by Feldman (1988), who stresses the lack of comparative studies and the reliance on single case reports.

Physical treatment

Neurosurgery. Vaernet & Madsen (1970) reported that amygdalectomy produced improvement in violent patients who mutilated themselves in response, probably, to psychotic experiences but it is not clear that these results would apply to the self-harming patients we are considering here. Burnham (1969) reported a single patient whose repeated self-cutting was treated by pre-frontal leucotomy. Her self-harm was diminished by the operation which, in the author's words, she 'provoked', but at considerable cost to her subsequent initiative and quality of life.

ECT has also been used but seems to have little to recommend it. Improvements tend, if they occur at all, to be short-lived (Feldman, 1988).

Drug treatment

Most types of psychotropic drug have been used at one time or another, including amphetamines (Favazza, 1987).

Antidepressants suggest themselves because of the obvious misery and low self-esteem of many people who repeatedly harm themselves. They may also complain of poor sleep, and have appetite and weight abnormalities which further suggest the presence of a depressive illness. The older antidepressants had the disadvantage of being highly dangerous in overdose, and this usually outweighed any possible advantage. Monoamine oxidase inhibitors have been found in one study (Cowdry & Gardner, 1988) to be associated with a non-significant reduction in self-wounding in patients diagnosed as having borderline personality disorder; the risk of abuse and of serious side-effects in patients who are not compliant with dietary advice is considerable.

Newer antidepressants are safer in overdose and those that act on serotonergic transmission may, it has been proposed, have a particular effect on impulsive behaviour and on obsessional symptoms which may sometimes be associated with self-damaging behaviour (Gardner & Gardner, 1975; Gupta *et al*, 1986).

One of the new 5-HT reuptake inhibitors has received adverse publicity about its relation to both suicidal and aggressive behaviour, but in a recent, open, study in 22 borderline and schizotypal patients its use in high dose was associated with a significant reduction in self-injury (Markovitz *et al*, 1991). Of the 22, 13 met DSM–III–R criteria for major depression, but the authors report that the presence or absence of depression was not related to outcome. This suggests a direct effect of serotonergic drugs on self-injury, and opens up a hopeful avenue of treatment possibilities. But, until further studies have been performed, it is still probably the best advice to avoid any antidepressant except when there is definite evidence of a recent onset of a depressive syndrome associated with a marked change of social and psychological function, or definite evidence of endogenous symptoms of depression.

Lithium has also been used in the treatment of self-harm, particularly when associated with learning disability. Again, reports are conflicting and often only anecdotal. It has been suggested that lithium's reputation rests on its value for those few patients whose self-harm is associated with undiagnosed recurrent depression. (Lithium also has the disadvantage of a low therapeutic index.) There are occasional reports of the value of anticonvulsants such as carbamazepine and sodium valproate in patients diagnosed as having borderline personality disorder (Gardner & Cowdry, 1986).

Neuroleptics, including depot neuroleptics, are regularly used in clinical practice and were found to reduce the frequency of self-injury in one placebo-controlled study (Montgomery & Montgomery, 1982). *Sedatives* such as the benzodiazepines, while they may alleviate anxiety, can also result in disinhibition or produce 'paradoxical responses' (Feldman, 1988), resulting in an exacerbation of self-harming behaviour. A detailed consideration of drug effects in the treatment of personality disorders is given by Stein (Chapter 11, this volume).

In conclusion, medication carefully chosen with clear therapeutic motives and for specific symptoms may well be of value in this group of patients but there is no evidence that drugs have any direct effect on the propensity to harm the self, and considerable evidence that they are often abused, sometimes with fatal consequences. The reader may well be advised to consider Lion & Conn's (1982) suggestion. ''It is obvious that there is no drug of choice for the self mutilating patient and the clinician might best focus on the avoidance of disinhibitory substances such as alcohol'' (p. 787) and, we might add, benzodiazepines.

Psychological treatment

Perhaps the largest body of literature available focuses on the analytic treatment of self-harm. It contains many practical hints about management which are applicable to long-term relationships between doctor and self-harming patient irrespective of the type of treatment that the doctor places faith in. Emerson (1914) writes of his patient that ''she was encouraged to believe in her own capacity . . . opportunity for sublimation was obtained for the patient and she was given a chance''. Crabtree (1967) noted that asking the patient about fantasies was counterproductive. Kafka (1969) stressed the importance of making explicit the feelings that the therapist arouses in the patient, and vice versa. Novotny (1972) stressed the need for flexibility within the therapeutic relationship and commented on the need for ''matter of fact'' handling of self-mutilatory behaviour.

Many of these practical manoeuvres can be seen as a means of maintaining the closest, least coercive and most enabling relationship with the patient which is possible in the circumstances: maintaining, that is, a 'holding' or 'containing' relationship as it is often termed after Winnicott and Balint.

Compulsory treatment

Containing the patient is not easy when she is threatening self-harm which is, or is thought to be, potentially fatal. Is some degree of coercion justified in these circumstances? Feldman (1988) points out that excessive restriction is likely to lead to an increase in self-harm, yet, paradoxically, removing those restrictions may also increase its frequency. Compulsory treatment is possible under the terms of the UK Mental Health Act, even in the absence of mental illness, if the patient's behaviour is such that a psychiatrist would diagnose a personality disorder and if deterioration in the patient's condition can thereby be prevented. There is little evidence, however, to enable a rational decision about the latter.

Every psychiatrist has stories of patients whose bloodcurdling threats were countered by professional refusal to 'take responsibility for your actions' with apparent success: at least, the patients survived. Some also know of patients who killed themselves in similar circumstances, although few of us recount these stories with as much readiness. It seems to us that detention is sometimes inescapable, that very occasionally it helps and that quite often it makes subsequent self-harm worse. Our clinical experience suggests that the decision should always be shared with as many of the staff team directly dealing with the patient as possible, that hospital staff are often more over-protective than social workers and other community carers, and that the period of compulsory treatment should be for the shortest possible period, which means not waiting until the situation has calmed down completely.

Hospital treatment

Many authors recommend the complete avoidance of hospital admission (e.g. Dawson, 1988) on the basis that the hospital environment removes responsibility from patients, reinforces the perception that the patient is ill, and exposes the patient to what is, very often, a divided staff. However, good results are also reported from in-patient treatment programmes in which these problems are anticipated and steps taken to remedy them. We consider that hospital admission is generally best avoided unless there is a specialist treatment unit with experienced staff, although it may sometimes be necessary to admit in a crisis. Hospital admission which has no purpose other than to protect the patient against herself should be minimised: a threat of suicide is not enough, in itself, to justify admission.

Specific therapeutic procedures

Hypnosis. Hypnosis has proved useful in the treatment of some unwanted habits, and there is at least one report of its use in deliberate self-wounding (Malan & Berardi, 1987) which indicates that it is well liked by patients who use it mainly as a means of reducing the tension that would otherwise lead to self-wounding.

Analytical psychotherapy. Analysts from Emerson (1914) onwards have stressed the value of translating the action of self-wounding into the feelings which it, supposedly, expresses, for example fears of abandonment and feelings of powerlessness (Kwawer, 1980), anger, hostility and dependence (Feldman, 1988), and sexual feelings (Favazza, 1987).

Nelson & Grunebaum (1971) followed up several recurrent cutters and over the course of the years asked them to identify the factors they felt most significant in their improvement. The factors they identified included the verbal capacity to express feelings, the presence of an accepting therapist with constructive action in crises and, in addition, the control of psychosis when this was present. However, they also note that insight into the genesis of the cutting behaviour did not afford relief.

If the retrospective judgements of these patients are correct and if they apply to other patients, the interpretation of feelings is effective if it assists the development of the relationship with the therapist, but not if it seeks to explain the historical development of self-harm. A concentration on interventions that increase the empathy and closeness between the therapist and the patient, rather than on plausible reconstructions of past determinants of present feelings, is therefore indicated. Intervention is most important when the patient is disappointed or angry with the therapist, since, unless these feelings are quickly identified, they may lead to the patient rejecting the therapist.

The analytical approach is not without side-effects. Silver (1985) lists these as "escalation of self-harm, substance abuse, suicide attempts, job losses and school failure" and later warns against "premature interpretation, a sudden threat of abandonment or a misperceived narcissistic attack". Given the frequency of these events in patients who harm themselves it is difficult to know whether there is a specific association between analytic practice and adverse events, but the point that he makes later in the same paper is well-taken: ". . . most of the theoretical underpinnings of psychodynamic therapy originally evolved from treating much less severely disturbed patients than those described. . . . As we move further away from the kinds of patients that the theories were initially based on, these models bear less directly on the clinical strategies or techniques used, while more flexible and novel treatment approaches must be encouraged".

These strictures are less applicable to those modern psychodynamic approaches which stress the actual, here-and-now relationship between patient and therapist, but even here Kernberg, one of the best-known practitioners of this approach, emphasises the skills that the therapist needs to sustain a working relationship with the patient rather than his or her interpretative abilities (Kernberg, 1987).

Structuring the therapeutic relationship by means of diagrams, letters, or contracts seems to work well for some therapists (Lansky, 1988; Ryle, 1990) perhaps because these methods ensure that the patient has some responsibility for, and control over, the treatment. Both Ryle and Lansky advocate explanation to patients and, where appropriate, relatives, Ryle in terms of ego-states, and Lansky in terms of regressive crises brought on by a failure of special treatment by others. Ryle advocates the use of a reformulation letter for this, coupled with diagrams of the relation of ego-states in relation to traps, snags, and predicaments. Lansky, who runs an in-patient programme, gives patients a recorded tape.

Prokaletic therapy. Kraupl Taylor's treatment method (Kraupl Taylor, 1969) combines behavioural, analytic and cognitive elements, although anticipating the formulation of the latter by Beck. It is unusual in having been specifically developed for deliberate self-harm. Taylor recognises the aversive nature of many interpretations, and advocates their deliberate use in this way. Thus the therapist may be invited to respond to self-wounding with solicitude, but instead expresses distaste at what he or she interprets to be a masturbation substitute. There has been no systematic evaluation.

Behavioural treatment. Behavioural treatment has been used widely in the treatment of self-harm by people with learning disabilities (Wolf *et al*, 1967; Lovaas & Simmons, 1969; Jones *et al*, 1974; Azrin *et al*, 1975). Corter *et al* (1971) compared the elimination of social response to self-harm, the reinforcement of non-injurious behaviour, and punishment by electrical shock on the frequency of face-banging and slapping, hair-pulling, and other self-harm by four people with profound learning disability. Punishment was clearly more effective than the other treatments but its effects were restricted to the setting in which it was delivered and its long-term consequences were not evaluated.

Behavioural techniques are also often used for people whose self-wounding is not associated with learning disability, but there has been no evaluation of their value in this rather different group.

Punishment may be an overt or a covert element in behavioural treatment but, irrespective of the ethical issues concerned, there is no evidence that it is of benefit. Punishment inevitably leads to a deterioration of the relationship between staff and patient and this may outweigh any transient value that it has in reducing the frequency of self-wounding. It would also be wrong to assume that punishment is always aversive. In the very disturbed families from which many people who repeatedly harm themselves come, punishment may have been a more desirable parental response than indifference or seduction.

Most clinicians will have anecdotes illustrating that the frequency of a particular patient's self-harm was altered by a change in contingencies, but the relationship between action and consequence is more complex than can be explained by conditioning or reinforcement. Carr (1977) has, however, made a case for the operant conditioning of self-wounding and both Linehan *et al* (1987) and Walsh & Rosen (1988) have put forward suggested treatment programmes based on cognitive and behavioural principles.

Although it seems reasonable, on the basis of what is currently known, to avoid 'rewarding' self-harm by extra attention or concern, there may be circumstances in which the patient's distress does need recognition and does need some special effort on the part of carers. Staff and patient need to be clear that the expression of distressed feelings will evoke appropriate concern, but that self-harm will be met with whatever medical treatment is needed to repair the damage but no particular emotional response. There is no place for punishment or criticism of self-harm, however much of a relief it may be for the staff to express these feelings. Aversion therapy is only effective if the operant response is, in fact, aversive: but there is every reason to believe that punishment may be rewarding for many people who repeatedly wound themselves.

Cognitive therapy. This relatively recent treatment approach aims to change the pathological thinking which is thought to lead to the repetition of self-wounding. Kendall & Braswell (1984), Walsh & Rosen (1988), and Salkovkis *et al* (1990) have given accounts of its application. Walsh & Rosen (1988) suggest the following steps: having patients monitor their thoughts, demonstrating the link between thought and self-wounding, challenging the patient to change by, for example, relabelling self-harm as disrespect to the body and therefore oneself, and focusing on the patient's positive qualities.

Walsh & Rosen (1988) argue that therapists need to restructure the client's tendency to act into an 'active thinking style', thereby helping the client to think differently about the way they communicate and about their relationships. This is particularly important as self-wounding may well have become the main form of communication of feelings and may have become an important part of the individual's relationships. Both Walsh & Rosen (1988) and Favazza (1987) comment that these individuals are very deficient in both social and relationship skills, and here the therapist can help in shaping and reinforcing social skills. Through the relationship with the therapist the patient may well learn to cope with the realities of life, developing some form of tolerance to interpersonal relationships. Walsh & Rosen (1988) argue for the value of desensitisation to relationship stresses as well as finding alternative routes to tension reduction.

Salkovkis *et al* (1990), in a controlled trial, found that self-wounding could be significantly reduced by cognitive therapy.

'*Detoxification*'. The addiction hypothesis of self-wounding discussed above implies that treatment must take account of the 'withdrawal symptoms' when it is given up. Favazza (1987) has outlined the steps in a detoxification-orientated treatment programme: voluntarily agreed observation of sufficient closeness to ensure that any self-harm can be prevented, if necessary by restraint; encouragement of the ventilation of the patient's feelings; "consistent and predictable reality experiences" provided by staff; and avoidance of the suppression of feelings by medication. Only patients with considerable motivation succeed with this approach.

Detoxification from opioids leads to dysphoria which can be abolished by reusing the drug (Crowley *et al*, 1985). Self-wounding seems to lead to a comparable dysphoria, described as an increasing sense of tension and restlessness. Hypnosis and drug treatments may reduce this dysphoria or 'stimulus hunger' (Lycacki *et al*, 1979) which had previously been 'treated' by self-wounding. The postulated action of 5-HT active antidepressants on impulsivity (Coccaro *et al*, 1989) suggests that they may act in the same way.

Social treatment

Perhaps because of the abhorrence of suffering in modern Western culture, self-wounding – and the patients who harm themselves – provoke strong emotional reactions from caregivers. Many authors (e.g. Grunebaum & Klerman, 1967; Podvoll, 1969; Nelson & Grunebaum, 1971) have commented on the fear, anger or anxiety that a person deliberately harming themselves produces in carers and in fellow patients in in-patient units. Perhaps the best statement of this is by Winnicott (1949): he uncompromisingly terms the carers' reaction to the rejection of care as 'hate'. Almost as potentially destructive to patients who harm themselves is the impulse to save them from themselves or from their families. Staff who idealise the patient and blame others for their plight are as likely to ignore the patient's own wishes and intentions as staff who blame the patient, and the conflict that readily develops between the two factions may dominate staff concerns to the exclusion of the patient's actual needs, and may even spread to involve other patients or family members (Kwawer, 1980; and see Main, 1957, for the classic account).

Podvoll (1969) comments that the identity of self-harming patients seems to become little more than their acts, and it is easy for their own aspirations or intentions to become drowned out by those of their carers. Carers may relieve their disappointment and frustration with the patient by stigmatising her as 'bad', 'attention-seeking' or 'manipulative', terms which have no explanatory value but do subtly devalue the patient's distress and can sometimes be used to justify either harsh or indifferent treatment. It is also arguable that apparently therapeutic manoeuvres such as ECT, high-dose medication, or the transfer of care may on occasions be a means of getting rid of a frustrating patient or even punishing her for her refractoriness.

Not that the patient herself does not sometimes redirect her own rage and hatred from past, often abusive, carers to the staff who seek to help her. Silver comments about patients who wound themselves that "despite deliberately seeking help from one therapist to another, before long they seem driven to sabotage, devalue, frustrate and destroy the therapeutic experience they so desperately seek" (Silver, 1985).

Not uncommonly, staff may transfer their frustration with the patient to anyone with whom the patient has a particular relationship. Often this is a relatively junior doctor, who may feel criticised for 'allowing the patient to get away with anything' or for failing to recognise a patient's 'obviously manipulative' motives (Grunebaum & Klerman, 1967).

Kafka (1969) considers that countertransference difficulties and staff divisions can be minimised by increased communication between staff members, including those who are acting as therapists for the patient, increased communication with the patient, and the use of group meetings. Written agreements between staff and patient may also be helpful, although they may also be abused by staff who consider them in some quasi-legal sense as binding contracts on the patient rather than, as should be the intention, binding on the staff. Communication may be especially difficult with night staff or emergency staff who may not know either the patient or the policy of the treating team. Careful summaries and agreements in the notes and the nursing cardex may assist in communication, but personal contact is often necessary. A member of the treating team may need to hold themselves available for telephone consultation about such patients if incorrect treatment is to be avoided.

Ross & MacKay (1979) described the reorganisation of an institution for disturbed adolescent women. They noted that intensive psychotherapy worsened self-harm. Improvement most often occurred when the 'negative' qualities of the residents were reframed into 'positive' qualities. Resident females were 'co-opted' as co-therapists and encouraged to take responsibility for themselves and others.

Limit-setting. Walsh & Rosen (1988) make a useful distinction between coercing others ('manipulative') and punishing oneself through self-wounding. Although these motives may often coexist in the same person, it is useful to consider to what extent self-wounding is intended to bring pressure to bear on others, whether they are emotionally vulnerable family members or the duty psychiatrist. Walsh & Rosen (1988) suggest that a lack of concealment of the wound, wounds which have a tendency to escalate in severity, a history of previously successful coercion by means of self-wounding, and a preoccupation with power may be indications of 'manipulation'. Threats of self-harm are commonly used to assist the coercion of others.

Coercive (we prefer this term to manipulative) self-wounding is like an attack in which the blow falls not on the victim but on the attacker. It is best approached as an assault, or the threat of an assault, and dealt with by negotiation. The principles of this are similar to those of negotiating under other types of threat, whether they be from terrorists or from hostile countries. A clear statement of the principles is contained in a now classic paper by Murphy & Guze (1960).

Group psychotherapy. Repeated self-harm is not a contraindication to group psychotherapy, but the self-harming patient may become marginalised within the group, and respond to this by an increased, and not decreased, investment in the expression of feelings through self-harm. Patient and group therefore need to be especially carefully matched.

Walsh & Rosen (1988) consider the value of using groups entirely composed of patients who wound themselves. These groups present special difficulties. Self-harm by one member may trigger off self-harm in others. Members may also harm themselves in the group, for example by burning themselves with cigarettes. A counterculture may develop in which self-harm confers rather than diminishes status. Despite these problems, they consider that homogeneous groups present some advantages. Within the group a person may learn to identify and practise more adaptive means of meeting their needs than self-harm. He or she may learn new skills, particularly communication skills, and may find greater self-understanding through sharing common experiences and common fears. Presumably because their groups are closed, they find that they pursue a predictable course and delineate the steps that they consider lead to a successful outcome:

(a) accurate labelling of self-harm as the intent to wound and not to kill

(b) drawing the group's attention to the use of self-harm to produce intimacy

(c) (i) predicting the repetition of the cycle of closeness–conflict–self-harm–closeness

    (ii) predicting the contagion of self-harm from one member to another

(d) redefining a nurturant response to self-harm as participation in a destructive process

(e) identifying and practising better means of getting looked after

(f) generalising interpersonal skills from the group to the rest of social life

(g) dealing with the loss of the therapist and of the group at termination.

These steps may also be applicable to individual psychotherapy.

Family therapy. The reaction of other household members, especially when they are family, to self-wounding is likely to have a marked influence on whether or not it is repeated. It is valuable to include any involved household members in the treatment process, partly to shift any preoccupation that they may have with suicide and partly to help them to identify and use non-reinforcing responses to self-harm.

As previously noted, many of the families in which self-wounding occurs are disturbed. Often these families have a secret, which may be intimated to a carer under strict instructions not to inquire further or to reveal it to other family members. The secret may be given as an explanation for self-wounding. Concealment of unpleasant facts or emotions, for example anger (Carroll *et al*, 1980), may be characteristic of all the family's interactions and may contrast strangely with the over-confidence with which one or both parents may say that they know exactly how other family members feel, without them having to say. The secret may be that one or both parents have a psychiatric disorder such as depression or a drink problem, that one family member is violent, or sexually abusive, or is having affairs outside the family. One of our patients concealed for a number of years that her father cross-dressed in women's clothing.

By the time these issues surface, the family may have broken down. We doubt that reconstituting the family to examine them is worthwhile, but when the self-wounding is still taking place in a family context it may be necessary to confront the family about the existence of a secret. This may result in the break-up of the family. It is essential that the step is only taken with the full and informed agreement of the patient, that the patient has failed to free her/himself of the secret unaided, and that greater harm will come to family members by colluding with the secrecy than by confronting it.

Outcome

Repetition of self-wounding

Hawton *et al* (1982) propose that repetition and successful suicide are both particularly likely when self-harm is part of a complex of impulsive behaviours. Myers (1988) found that scores on a scale developed by Buglass & Horton (1974), containing items relating to other forms of impulsive behaviour, could be used to predict the repetition of self-harm, but only in women and only with the low positive predictive value of 20–30%. Male repetition was best predicted by the answer to the question "What makes life worth living?".

Kreitman & Casey (1988) found that a forensic history, living alone, being battered, having a criminal conviction, being out of work, having a personality disorder, being a habitual user of drink or drugs, having had psychiatric treatment, and being separated from parents were all factors associated with repetition in a cohort of patients admitted to the Regional Poisoning Centre of the Edinburgh Royal Infirmary.

Van Egmond & Jonker (1988) found that 52% of a consecutive sample of patients admitted to hospital for treatment of a first episode of self-harm had been either sexually or physically abused, whereas 77% of those admitted for a repeat episode had been. Their sample was biased against patients well known to the hospital, who were then likely to be admitted, and patients who injured themselves, who were transferred to the surgical unit.

Suicide

Repeated self-wounding is often said to result in suicide only rarely. Simpson (1976) cited six references in support of his statement that "Although the wrist-cutter may be highly disturbed, such acts are usually of low lethality" and this distinction has been generally accepted. Walsh & Rosen (1988) cited 23 reports and a previous literature review all tending to this view, and expanded on Schneidman's distinction between suicide and parasuicide to produce 10 characteristics which differentiate them. Although they refer to three studies which found a minority of those who wounded themselves wished to die when doing so (Gardner & Gardner, 1975; Jones *et al*, 1979; Walsh, 1987), they conclude with Morgan (1979) that intent is too unreliably ascertained to be a useful measure of danger. Expressed intent may be a more reliable predictor, however (Pierce, 1977), and hopelessness certainly is (Beck *et al*, 1985).

However, although self-wounding may itself be "delicate self-cutting", as Pao (1969) described it, it may be associated in the same patient with more lethal self-harm, such as self-poisoning, hanging, or jumping from a height or in front of vehicles. Walsh (1987) studied 52 adolescents who had wounded themselves, and compared the 16 who had in the past jeopardised

TABLE 9.2
Five-year outcome of self-wounding

	Nelson & Grunebaum, 1971[1] (n = 19)	Reilly, 1983 (n = 16)
Suicide	3 (16%)	2 (13%)
Psychosis	2 (10.5%)	3 (18.8%)
'Improved'	10 (52.6%)	8 (50%)

1. Of six survivors described as psychotic at initial presentation, four improved: all three suicides came from the psychotic group.

their lives through self-harm with the remaining 36 who had not. The number of times that they harmed themselves, the staff's judgement about intent, the reasons given for self-wounding, the physical damage produced by the self-wounding, and the use of multiple methods all failed to distinguish the two groups. The 'in jeopardy' group had, however, experienced significantly more adverse events, especially sexual abuse as a child, but also including a recent, emotionally important loss or chronic peer conflict.

Follow-up studies

Nelson & Grunebaum (1971) followed up 23 wrist slashers, and succeeded in obtaining information on 19, five to six years after their initial contact. Their outcome was poor. Reilly (1983), in a study of patients with personality disorder admitted to a professorial unit over a two-year period, found 17 patients who had wounded themselves, of whom all but two had also poisoned themselves. He was able to obtain five-year follow-up information for 16. The outcome of these two studies is similar (Table 9.2): about 15% of patients killed themselves and about half improved after five years.

Discussion

Self-injury is not foreign to our experience. Not only is it surprisingly common in the general population, with about 1 in 600 people wounding themselves deliberately, but it also occupies an important place in our culture. We distinguish self-wounding from self-mutilation which has some aim in view. The latter includes psychotically driven bodily rearrangement, and failed suicide. We also distinguish self-wounding from non-consummatory self-injury, which is associated with learning disability and with social deprivation, and is shown by lower animals.

We agree with Favazza (1989) that self-wounding is intentional, and designed to relieve feelings which cannot be expressed in any other way. Often this is because the direct expression of feeling is either ignored or punished, or both. This situation often arises when families are concealing a secret, for example that of sexual abuse. Abused women may believe that their body is not their own, but the property of the abuser.

We also agree with Favazza that repetition becomes addictive. There may be two main reasons for this, which may often be combined: (a) coercive – self-wounding produces a desirable social response; and (b) relieving – self-wounding produces a desirable alteration of mood, perhaps by direct biochemical mechanisms, perhaps by conditioning, or perhaps symbolically. Addictive self-wounding may also lead to hospital addiction.

The response of carers may increase coercive self-harm by denying other means of self-assertion, depriving a person of self-determination, failing to set clear limits, and encouraging hospital addiction. Relief self-harm may be increased by hostility or criticism, by failing to provide for emotional needs, and by a lack of stability in close relationships, including therapeutic relationships.

Although self-wounding is rarely fatal, repeated self-wounding is associated with other self-harm which may be. Rarely this may be attributed to the supervention of a psychosis or a depressive illness, and careful screening for these is necessary. Social, especially family, circumstances also need careful investigation. Drug treatment may be valuable if a definite psychiatric illness is present, or as a temporary expedient during 'detoxification'. Hypnosis is also regarded as helpful for this. The mainstay of treatment is psychosocial. The first principle is to avoid further harm which is all too readily produced by the emotional reactions of carers, or by the encouragement of hospital addiction.

Self-wounding as a reaction to a highly stressful current situation may be fairly easy to manage. Once it becomes addictive and persists even when the situation has changed, treatment becomes much more difficult. The person who is addicted to self-wounding is likely to relate to others as if they are the neglectful, abusive parents or peers to whom they have been exposed in the past. It may be very difficult to maintain a compassionate and non-critical therapeutic relationship despite the provocations and frustrations. We think it helpful for the therapist to understand this type of self-wounding in the context of persistently disordered relationships, but do not consider that terming these a 'personality disorder' is particularly illuminating. Indeed it has a number of disadvantages.

The relationship difficulties crystallise in two practical problems: when to provide emergency succour, and when to take control. The former is often a special difficulty for a caregiver in the community, the latter for the hospital-based worker. When a client rings to say they want to take an overdose and implies that they certainly will unless you visit them, what do you do? When the in-patient or the patient in casualty insists on going home, darkly hinting that the remedy for all her troubles is there, in the shape of a full bottle of paracetamol, what do you do?

We cannot offer definitive guidance. We suggest that there are times when an emergency home visit, an extra consultation, or detaining a patient are indicated. If the decision is right, and there is an extraordinary need, the patient will recognise that it has been met and will feel empowered. If the decision is wrong, the patient will either feel rejected because their real need has been unrecognised or cheated because the caregiver has been unable to trust them to sort out the situation for themselves.

Clearly the decision is a difficult one, in which the patient may be asking for one thing and needing another. We therefore think that the decision should be made by an experienced staff member who knows the patient. Junior psychiatrists on call, community workers unfamiliar with the patient, and general practitioners should have telephone access to such a person out of hours. When the patient is completely unknown, we think that it is best to err on the side of safety until such time as a sufficient assessment has been made for an informed decision.

The principles which, we think, might usefully govern treatment are summarised below.

(a) Making and maintaining a relationship
    (i) understanding
    (ii) staying calm
    (iii) reframing self-wounding as an expression of feeling
    (iv) avoiding threats or promises
    (v) sticking to limits
    (vi) leaving the responsibility with the patient
    (vii) sticking with the patient.
(b) Breaking the habit
    (i) coping with withdrawal symptoms
    (ii) increasing determination to change.
(c) Maintaining change
    (i) rewards for new behaviour
    (ii) minimising medicalisation
    (iii) resolving emotional conflicts
    (iv) tackling coercion
    (v) training in intimacy.

References

AMERICAN PSYCHIATRIC ASSOCIATION (1987) *Diagnostic and Statistical Manual of Mental Disorders* (3rd edn, revised) (DSM–III–R). Washington, DC: APA.

AZRIN, N., GOTTLIEB, L., HUGHART, L., *et al* (1975) Eliminating self-injurious behavior by educative procedures. *Behavior Research and Therapy*, **13**, 101–111.

BACH-Y-RITA, G. (1974) Habitual violence and self-mutilation. *American Journal of Psychiatry*, **131**, 1018–1020.

BALLINGER, B. (1967) Minor self-injury. *British Journal of Psychiatry*, **118**, 535–538

BECK, A., STEAR, R., KARASS, M., *et al* (1985) Hopelessness and eventual suicide: a 10-year prospective study of patients hospitalised with suicidal ideation. *British Journal of Psychiatry*, **142**, 559–562.

BRIERE, J. & ZAIDI, L. Y. (1989) Sexual abuse histories and sequelae in female psychiatric emergency room patients. *American Journal of Psychiatry*, **146**, 1602–1606.

BUGLASS, D. & HORTON, J. (1974) A scale for predicting subsequent suicidal behaviour. *British Journal of Psychiatry*, **124**, 573–578.

BURNHAM, R. C. (1969) Symposium on impulsive self-mutilation. *British Journal of Medical Psychology*, **42**, 223–227.

CARR, E. G. (1977) The motivation of self-injurious behaviour. *Psychological Bulletin*, **84**, 800–816.

CARROLL, J., SCHAFFER, C., SPERSLEY, J., *et al* (1980) Family experiences of self-mutilating patients. *American Journal of Psychiatry*, **137**, 852–853.

CLAGHORN, J. & BETO, D. (1967) Self-mutilation in a prison mental hospital. *Journal of Social Therapy*, **13**, 133–141.

CLENDENIN, W. W. & MURPHY, G. E. (1971) 'Wrist cutting'. *Archives of General Psychiatry*, **25**, 465–469.

COCCARO, E. F., SIEVER, L. J., KLAR, H. M., *et al* (1989) Serotonergic studies in patients with affective and personality disorders. Correlates with suicidal and impulsive aggressive behaviour. *Archives of General Psychiatry*, **46**, 587–599.

COID, J., ALLOLIO, B. & REES, L. (1983) Raised plasma metenkephalin in patients who habitually mutilate themselves. *Lancet*, **ii**, 545–546.

CORTER, H., WOLFSON, A. & LOCKE, B. (1971) A comparison of procedures for eliminating self-injurious behaviour of retarded adolescents. *Journal of Applied Behaviour Analysis*, **4**, 201–213.

COWDRY, R. & GARDNER, D. (1988) Pharmacotherapy of borderline personality disorder. *Archives of General Psychiatry*, **45**, 111–119.

CRABTREE, L. M. (1967) A psychotherapeutic encounter with a self-mutilating patient. *Psychiatry*, **30**, 91–100.

CROSS, H. & HARLOW, H. (1965) Prolonged and progressive effects of partial isolation on the behaviour of macaque monkeys. *Journal of Experimental Research in Personality*, **1**, 39–49.

CROWLEY, T. J., WAGNER, J. E., ZERBE, G., *et al* (1985) Naltrexone-induced dysphoria in former opioid addicts. *American Journal of Psychiatry*, **142**, 1081–1084.

DAWSON, D. (1988) Treatment of the borderline patient, relationship management. *Canadian Journal of Psychiatry*, **33**, 370–374.

DEUTSCH, H. (1944) *Psychology of Women*, Vol. 1. Philadelphia: Grune and Stratton.

DUBOVSKY, S. (1978) Experimental self mutilation. *American Journal of Psychiatry*, **135**, 1240–1241.

EMERSON, L. E. (1914) A preliminary report of psychoanalytic study and treatment of a case of self-mutilation. *Psychoanalytic Review*, **1**, 42–52.

EVANS-WENTZ, R. (1968) *The Tibetan Book of the Great Liberation*. Oxford: Oxford University Press.

FAVAZZA, A. (1987) *Bodies Under Siege*. Baltimore: Johns Hopkins University Press.

—— (1989) Why patients mutilate themselves. *Hospital and Community Psychiatry*, **40**, 137–145.

—— & CONTERIO, K. (1989) Female habitual self-mutilators. *Acta Psychiatrica Scandinavica*, **79**, 283–289.

FELDMAN, M. D. (1988) The challenge of self mutilation, a review. *Comprehensive Psychiatry*, **29**, 252–269.

FENICHEL, O. (1945) *The Psychoanalytic Theory of Neurosis*. New York: W. W. Norton.

FOX, K. & WEISSMAN, M. (1975) Suicide attempts and drugs: contradiction between method and intent. *Social Psychiatry*, **10**, 31–38.

GARDNER, A. R. & GARDNER, A. J. (1975) Self-mutilation, obsessionality and narcissism. *British Journal of Psychiatry*, **127**, 127–132.

—— & COWDRY, R. (1986) Positive effects of carbamazepine on behavioral dyscontrol in borderline personality disorder. *American Journal of Psychiatry*, **143**, 519–522.

GENOVESE, E., NAPOLI, P. A. & BOLEGO-ZONTA, N. (1969) Self-aggressiveness: a new type of behavioural change induced by pemoline. *Life Sciences*, **8**, 513–514.

GILLMAN, M. A. & SANDYK, R., (1985) Opiate and dopaminergic functions and Lesch-Nyhan Syndrome. *American Journal of Psychiatry*, **142**, 1226.

GOLDSTEIN, M., KUSANO, N., MELLER, E., *et al* (1986) Dopamine agonist induced self-mutilative biting behavior in monkeys with unilateral ventromedial segmental lesions of the brain stem: possible pharmacological model for Lesch-Nyhan syndrome. *Brain Research*, **367**, 119–120.

GOSSOP, M., COBB, J. & CONNELL, P. (1975) Self-destructive behaviour in oral and intravenous drug-dependent groups. *British Journal of Psychiatry*, **126**, 266–269.

GRAFF, H. & MALLIN, R. (1967) The syndrome of the wrist cutter. *American Journal of Psychiatry*, **124**, 36–42.

GREENSPAN, G. S. & SAMUEL, S. E. (1989) Self cutting after rape. *American Journal of Psychiatry*, **146**, 789–790.

GRUNEBAUM, N. M. & KLERMAN, G. L. (1967) Wrist-slashing. *American Journal of Psychiatry*, **124**, 527–534.

GUPTA, M. A., GUPTA, A. K. & HABERMAN, H. F. (1986) Neurotic excoriations: a review and some new perspectives. *Comprehensive Psychiatry*, **27**, 381–386.

HAWTON, K., OSBORN, M., O'GRADY, J., *et al* (1982) Classification of adolescents who take overdoses. *British Journal of Psychiatry*, **140**, 124–131.

HERMAN, J. L. (1989) Childhood trauma in borderline personality disorder. *American Journal of Psychiatry*, **146**, 490–495.

HILL, J. (1991) Family therapy. In *Textbook of Psychotherapy in Practice* (ed. J. Holmes), pp. 117–138. Edinburgh: Churchill Livingstone.

JOHNSON, F., FRANKEL, B., FERRENCE, R., *et al* (1975) Self-injury in London, Canada: a prospective study. *Canadian Journal of Public Health*, **66**, 307–316.

JONES, I. & BARRACLOUGH, B. (1978) Auto-mutilation in animals and its relevance to self-injury in man. *Acta Psychiatrica Scandinavica*, **58**, 40–47.

——, CONGIU, L., STEVENSON, J., *et al* (1979) A biological approach to two forms of self-injury. *Journal of Nervous and Mental Disease*, **167**, 74–78.

JONES, F. H., SIMMONS, J. Q. & FRANKEL, F. (1974) An extinction procedure for eliminating self destructive behaviours in a 9-year-old autistic girl. *Journal of Autism and Childhood Schizophrenia*, **4**, 241–250.

KAFKA, J. (1969) The body as a transitional object: a psychoanalytic study of a self-mutilating patient. *British Journal of Medical Psychology*, **42**, 207–212.

KAHAN, J. & PATTISON, E. (1984) Proposal for a distinctive diagnosis: the deliberate self-harm syndrome. *Suicide and Life Threatening Behaviour*, **14**, 17–35.

KENDALL, P. C. & BRASWELL, L. (1984) *Cognitive–Behavioural Therapy for Impulsive Children*. New York: Academic Press.

KERNBERG, O. (1984) *Severe Personality Disorders: Psychotherapeutic Strategies*. New Haven: Yale University Press.

—— (1987) A psychodynamic approach. *Journal of Personality Disorders*, **1**, 344–346.

KONICKI, P. E. & SCHULZ, S. C. (1989) Rationale for clinical trials of opiate antagonists in treating patients with personality disorders and self-injurious behaviour. *Psychopharmacology Bulletin*, **25**, 556–563.

KRAUPL TAYLOR, F. (1969) Prokaletic measures derived from psychoanalytic techniques. *British Journal of Psychiatry*, **115**, 407–419.

KREITMAN, N. (1990) Research issues in the epidemiological and public health aspects of parasuicide and suicide. In *The Public Health Impact of Mental Disorder* (eds D. Goldberg & D. Tantam), pp. 73–82. Stuttgart: Hogrefe and Huber.

—— & CASEY, P. (1988) Repetition of parasuicide: an epidemiological and clinical study. *British Journal of Psychiatry*, **153**, 792–800.

KRIS, E. (1954) Problems of infantile neurosis. In *The Psychoanalytic Study of the Child*, Volume 9. New York: International Universities Press.

KWAWER, J. (1980) Some interpersonal aspects of self-mutilation in a borderline patient. *Journal of the American Academy of Psychoanalysis*, **8**, 203–216.

LACEY, J. H. & EVANS, C. D. H. (1986) The impulsivist: a multi-impulsive personality disorder. *British Journal of Addiction*, **81**, 641–649.

LANSKY, M. (1988) The subacute hospital treatment of the borderline patient – I: an educational component. *Hillside Journal of Clinical Psychiatry*, **10**, 24–37.

LEMERT, E. (1967) *Human Deviance, Social Problems and Social Control*. Englewood Cliffs, New Jersey: Prentice-Hall.

LESTER, D. & BECK, A. (1980) What the suicide's choice of method signifies. *Omega*, **81**, 271–277.

LEWIS, G. & APPLEBY, L. (1988) Personality disorder: the patients psychiatrists dislike. *British Journal of Psychiatry*, **153**, 44–49.

LINEHAN, M., CAMPER, P., CHILES, J., et al (1987) Interpersonal problem solving and parasuicide. *Cognitive Therapy and Research*, **11**, 1–12.

LION, J. R. & CONN, L. M. (1982) Self mutilation: pathology and treatment. *Psychiatric Annals*, **12**, 782–787.

LLOYD, H. G. E. & STONE, T. W. (1981) Chronic methylxanthine treatment in cats. *Pharmacology, Biochemistry and Behaviour*, **14**, 827–830.

LOVAAS, O. I. & SIMMONS, J. Q. (1969) Manipulation of self destruction in three retarded children. *Journal of Applied Behaviour Analysis*, **2**, 143–157.

LYCACKI, H., JOSEF, N. & MUNETZ, M. (1979) Stimulation and arousal in self-mutilators. *American Journal of Psychiatry*, **136**, 1223–1224.

MAIN, T. F. (1957) The ailment. *British Journal of Medical Psychology*, **30**, 129–145.

MALAN, D. & BERARDI, D. (1987) Hypnosis with self-cutters. *American Journal of Psychotherapy*, **41**, 531–541.

MARKOVITZ, P., CALABRESE, J., SCHULZ, S., et al (1991) Fluoxetine in the treatment of borderline and schizotypal personality disorders. *American Journal of Psychiatry*, **148**, 1064–1067.

MASON, W. A. & SPONHOLZ, F. (1963) Behaviour of rhesus monkeys raised in isolation. *Journal of Psychiatric Research*, **1**, 299–306.

MASSON, J. M. (1985) *The Assault on Truth: Freud's Suppression of the Seduction Theory*. Harmondsworth: Penguin.

McEVEDY, C. P. (1963) Self-inflicted injuries. Academic D.P.M. Dissertation. London: University of London.

McKERRACHER, D., LOUGHNANE, T. & WATSON, R. (1968) Self-mutilation in female psychopaths. *British Journal of Psychiatry*, **114**, 829–832.

MEARES, R. (1987) The secret and the self – on a new direction in psychotherapy. *Australia and New Zealand Journal of Psychiatry*, **21**, 545–559.

MELGES, F. & SWARTZ, M. S. (1989) Oscillations of attachment in borderline personality disorders. *American Journal of Psychiatry*, **146**, 1115–1120.

MENNINGER, K. A. (1935) A psychoanalytic study of the significance of self mutilations. *Psychoanalytic Quarterly*, **4**, 408–466.

MORGAN, H. G. (1979) *Death Wishes*. Chichester: John Wiley.

MONTGOMERY, S. & MONTGOMERY, D. (1982) Pharmacological prevention of suicidal behaviour. *Journal of Affective Disorders*, **4**, 291–298.

MUELLER, K., SABODA, S., PALMOUR, R., et al (1982) Self injurious behaviour produced in rats by daily caffeine and continuous amphetamine. *Pharmacology, Biochemistry and Behaviour*, **71**, 613–617.

MURPHY, G. & GUZE, S. (1960) Setting limits: the management of the manipulative patient. *American Journal of Psychotherapy*, **14**, 30–47.

MYERS, E. (1988) Predicting repetition of deliberate self-harm: a review of the literature in the light of a current study. *Acta Psychiatrica Scandinavica*, **77**, 314–319.

NELSON, S. & GRUNEBAUM, H. (1971) A follow-up study of wrist slashers. *American Journal of Psychiatry*, **127**, 1345–1349.

NOVOTNY, P. (1972) Self-cutting. *Bulletin of the Menninger Clinic*, **36**, 505–514.

NYHAN, W. (1976) Behavior in the Lesch-Nyhan syndrome. *Journal of Autism and Childhood Schizophrenia*, **6**, 235–252.

PAO, P. (1969) The syndrome of delicate self-cutting. *British Journal of Medical Psychology*, **42**, 195–206.

PATTINSON, E. M. & KAHAN, J. (1983) The deliberate self-harm syndrome. *American Journal of Psychiatry*, **140**, 867–872.

PETERS, J. M. (1967) Caffeine induced haemorrhagic automutilation. *Archives of Internal Pharmacodynamics*, **169**, 139–146.

PIERCE, D. (1977) Suicidal intent in self-injury. *British Journal of Psychiatry*, **130**, 377–385.

PINES, M. (1989) Borderline personality disorders and its [sic] treatment. *Current Opinion in Psychiatry*, **2**, 362–367.

PODVOLL, E. M. (1969) Self-mutilation within a hospital setting: a study of identity and social compliance. *British Journal of Medical Psychology*, **42**, 213–221.

REILLY, S. P. (1983) *A Study of Self-Mutilation and Prognosis in Personality Disorder*. MSc Thesis, University of Manchester.

RICHARDSON, J. & ZALESKI, W. (1986) Letter: endogenous opiates and self-mutilation. *American Journal of Psychiatry*, **143**, 938–939.

RIDLEY, R. & BAKER, H. (1982) Stereotyping in monkeys and humans. *Psychological Medicine*, **12**, 61–72.

ROBINSON, A. & DUFFY, J. (1989) A comparison of self-injury and self-poisoning from the Regional Poisoning Treatment Centre, Edinburgh. *Acta Psychiatrica Scandinavica*, **80**, 272–279.

ROSEN, F. M. & WALSH, B. W. (1989) Patterns of contagion in self mutilation epidemics. *American Journal of Psychiatry*, **146**, 656–658.

ROSENTHAL, R., RINZLER, C., WALSH, R., *et al* (1972) Wrist-cutting syndrome: the meaning of a gesture. *American Journal of Psychiatry*, **128**, 1363–1368.

—— & ROSENTHAL, S. (1984) Suicidal behaviour by pre-school children. *American Journal of Psychiatry*, **141**, 520–525.

ROSS, C. A. (1989) *Multiple Personality Disorder*. New York, Chichester, Brisbane, Toronto, Singapore: John Wiley & Sons.

ROSS, R. R. & MACKAY, H. B. (1979) *Self Mutilation*. Lexington: Lexington Books.

RUTTER, M. (1981) *Maternal Depression Reassessed* (2nd edn). Harmondsworth: Penguin.

RYLE, A. (1991) *Cognitive Analytic Therapy*. Chichester: John Wiley.

SALKOVKIS, P., ATHA, C. & STORER, D. (1990) Cognitive–behavioural problem solving in the treatment of patients who repeatedly attempt suicide. A controlled trial. *British Journal of Psychiatry*, **157**, 871–876.

SHAFER, R. (1983) *The Analytic Attitude*. New York: Basic Books.

SHAPIRO, S. (1987) Self-mutilation and self-blame in incest victims. *American Journal of Psychotherapy*, **41**, 46–54.

SILVER, D. (1985) Psychodynamics and psychotherapeutic management of self-destructive character-disordered patient. *Psychiatric Clinics of North America*, **8**, 357–375.

SIMPSON, M. A. (1976) Self-mutilation. *British Journal of Hospital Medicine*, **16**, 430–438.

SINGH, N. & PULMAN, R. (1979) Self-injury in the Cornelia de Lange syndrome. *Journal of Mental Deficiency Research*, **23**, 79–84.

SIOMOPOULOS, V. (1974) Repeated self cutting: an impulse neurosis. *American Journal of Psychotherapy*, **28**, 85–94.

SNEDDON, I. & SNEDDON, J. (1975) Self-inflicted injury. A follow-up of 40 patients. *British Medical Journal*, ii, 527–530.

SOKOL, M., CAMPBELL, M., GOLDSTEIN, M., *et al* (1987) Attention deficit disorder with hyperactivity and the dopamine hypothesis. *Journal of Child and Adolescent Psychiatry*, **26**, 428–433.

TANTAM, D. (1986) Towards a grammar of non-verbal communication. *Semiotica*, **58**, 41–57.

—— (1988) Personality disorders. In *Recent Advances in Clinical Psychiatry* (ed. K. Granville-Grossman). Edinburgh: Churchill Livingstone.

TINKELPAUGH, O. L. (1928) The self mutilation of a male macacus rhesus monkey. *Journal of Mammalogy*, **9**, 293–300.

VAERNET, K. & MADSEN, A. (1970) Stereotaxic amygdalotomy and basofrontal tractotomy in psychotics with aggressive behaviour. *Journal of Neurology, Neurosurgery and Psychiatry*, **33**, 856–863.

VALZELLI, L. & BERNASCONI, S. (1979) Aggressiveness by isolation and brain serotonin turnover changes in different strains of mice. *Neuropsychobiology*, **5**, 129–135.

VAN EGMOND, M. & JONKER, D. (1988) Sexual abuse and physical assault: risk factors for recurrent suicidal behaviour in women. *Tijdschraft die Psychiatrie*, **30**, 21–38.

VAN PRAAG, H. M., ASNIS, G. M., KAHN, R., *et al* (1990) Monoamines and abnormal behaviour. A multi-aminergic perspective. *British Journal of Psychiatry*, **157**, 723–734.

VIRKKUNEN, M. (1976) Self-mutilation in antisocial personality (disorder). *Acta Psychiatrica Scandanavica*, **54**, 347–352.

WALDENBERG, S. S. A. (1972) *Wrist-Cutting: a Psychiatric Enquiry*. M. Phil Dissertation, University of London.

WALSH, B. W. (1987) *Adolescent Self-Mutilation: an Empirical Study*. Unpublished doctoral dissertation. Boston College Graduate School of Social Work.

—— & ROSEN, P. M. (1985) Self-mutilation and contagion – an empirical test. *American Journal of Psychiatry*, **141**, 119–120.

—— & —— (1988) *Self-Mutilation: Theory, Research, and Treatment*. New York: Guilford Press.

WEISSMAN, M. M. (1975) Wrist-cutting. *Archives of General Psychiatry*, **32**, 1166–1171.

WINCHEL, R. & STANLEY, M. (1991) Self-injurious behaviour: a review of the behavior and biology of self-mutilation. *American Journal of Psychiatry*, **148**, 306–317.

WINNICOTT, D. (1949) Hate in the counter-transference. *International Journal of Psychoanalysis*, **30**, 69–74.

WOLF, M. M., RISLEY, T., JOHNSTON, M., *et al* (1967) Application of operant conditioning procedures to the behaviour problems of an autistic child: a follow-up and extension. *Behaviour Research and Therapy*, **5**, 103–111.

YAROSHEVSKY, F. (1975) Self-mutilation in Soviet prisons. *Canadian Psychiatric Association Journal*, **20**, 443–446.

ZANARINI, M. C., GUNDERSON, J. G., MARINO, M. F., *et al* (1989) Childhood experiences of borderline patients. *Comprehensive Psychiatry*, **30**, 18–25.

10 Psychotherapy in borderline and narcissistic personality disorder

ANNA HIGGITT and PETER FONAGY

The concept of personality disorder

Even a cursory examination of psychotherapeutic approaches to personality disorder reveals the diverse ways in which the term is used, broken down, or indeed systematically avoided, by authors of different theoretical orientations. Recent 'advances' in diagnostic strategies towards personality disorder, initiated largely by the cook-book approach to psychiatric diagnosis embodied in DSM–III–R (Widiger *et al*, 1988) and the evolution of the rating instruments which underpin the epidemiological validation of the DSM–III–R approach (Tyrer, 1989), might have had the potential to eradicate the confusion. Unfortunately, the present trend to refine the diagnosis of personality disorders and define relatively small, and descriptively apparently non-overlapping, subcategories may well encourage psychotherapists to persist with their tendency to use imprecise subtle definitions of patient groups on the basis of individual case material. No doubt, patients with personality disorders (like all individuals) profoundly differ from one another phenomenologically, dynamically, or behaviourally, but current knowledge does not permit us to link particular therapeutic strategies with specific personality disorders based on a descriptive diagnostic scheme such as ICD–10 (World Health Organization, 1986) or DSM–III–R. To the extent that evidence is available, it points away from over-reliance on descriptive diagnosis.

A recent report by Zanarini *et al* (1990*a*) concluded that many clinical features previously thought to be specific to particular personality disorders may be better viewed as general personality traits. A large-scale, careful investigation by Tyrer *et al* (1990) failed to identify any predictive value (in terms of response to a variety of treatments) associated with categories of personality disorder, implying that current classifications of personality disorder may be erring on the side of making over-refined descriptive distinctions with few, if any, practical benefits. In the USA, the National

Institute of Mental Health multicentre outcome study on the treatment of depression revealed that patients with personality disorders on the whole responded less well to all forms of treatment. Outcome, however, was not predicted by specific personality disorder clusters (Shea *et al*, 1990).

Rutter (1987), in a persuasive review, proposed abandoning the concept of trait-defined personality disorder and suggested lumping together a group of disorders whose abnormality derives from a pervasive difficulty in establishing and maintaining adequate social relationships. Such an approach may be particularly appropriate when considering the literature on psychotherapeutic treatment where respect for descriptive diagnostic distinctions is hardly widespread. The cluster termed 'dramatic' in DSM–III, consisting of the borderline, the antisocial, the histrionic and the narcissistic personality disorders corresponds broadly to Rutter's patient group. Much of the psychotherapeutic literature discussing the treatment of 'difficult patients' appears also primarily to concern this group. Often, the adjective or noun 'borderline', is used in designating such patients. We commence our review by briefly considering the borderline concept and go on to explore the psychotherapeutic literature pertinent to the group of patients fitting Rutter's definition. A full and definitive review of the borderline concept is provided by Tarnopolsky & Berelowitz (1987).

Concepts of 'borderline' psychopathology

The term borderline brings with it enormous ambiguity. Lang *et al* (1987) identify seven conceptually distinct ways in which the term is used in the psychotherapeutic literature which we draw upon here, in place of a single definition, which would be arbitrary and restricting.

(a) Kernberg (1967, 1975, 1976, 1984), supported by the majority of psychoanalytic authors, regards borderline as a *level of psychic functioning* referred to as borderline personality organisation. In this respect he continues Melanie Klein's and Herbert Rosenfeld's emphasis on personality organisation. The borderline personality organisation according to Kernberg rests on four critical features of the patient's personality structure:

   (i) non-specific manifestations of ego weakness which include poor capacities to tolerate anxiety, control impulses or to develop socially productive ways of channelling energy (sublimation)
  (ii) a propensity to shift towards irrational dream-like thinking patterns in the context of generally intact reality testing
 (iii) predominance of developmentally less mature psychological defences such as splitting, projection and projective identification (see below)
  (iv) identity diffusion and the related specific pathology of internal object relations, such that mental representations of important others are fragmented and strongly charged as either good or bad.

Thus Kernberg's concept of the borderline includes within it a range of personality disorders such as infantile personalities, narcissistic personalities, antisocial personalities, as-if personalities, and schizoid personalities. In fact, any patient manifesting significant disturbance of identity in Kernberg's system is either psychotic or, if in possession of intact reality testing, borderline.

This broad use of the term is viewed by many as unhelpful. By this definition, probably over 10% of the adult population in the 18–45-year age range could be characterised as borderline (Stone, 1987*a*). Furthermore, some preliminary empirical data from Perry & Cooper (1986) indicate that individuals with antisocial personality disorders do not use the defences of splitting and projective identification, and conversely some with DSM–III–R borderline diagnosis do not use omnipotence and primitive idealisation. Such evidence, if confirmed by further investigation, would suggest that narcissistic and borderline defences do not occur together and that personality disorders associated with these defences may need to be distinguished conceptually as well as descriptively. The literature on the high co-morbidity of personality disorders casts doubt over the findings (e.g. McGlashan, 1987; Fyer *et al*, 1988).

(b) Many regard the group of patients characterised by low achievement, impulsivity, manipulative suicide attempts, heightened affectivity, mild psychotic experiences, high socialisation and disturbed close relationships as a *distinct clinical syndrome* (e.g. Gunderson, 1984; Gunderson & Zanarini, 1987). This approach defines a much smaller and homogeneous group (2–4% of the clinical population; Baron *et al*, 1985). However, this use of the term is less congenial to authors who contribute to the psychotherapeutic field; the psychodynamic characteristics which this group may share (and which are necessary to guide therapeutic thinking) are neglected in favour of an emphasis upon the description of overt behaviour, being explicitly stated as part of the definition (see Freud, 1970; Shapiro, 1989). In a similar vein, Frosch (1988) proposed abolishing the term borderline in favour of a term more closely related to the psychodynamic features of the disorder, such as 'psychotic character'.

(c) As distinct from borderline as a syndrome, in current North American psychiatric nosology it is regarded as a *personality type* (an Axis II disorder). While Gunderson's work was an important motivator for the establishment of the DSM–III category of borderline personality disorder, the DSM–III–R definition is broader than this worker's conceptualisation had been. An Epidemiologic Catchment Area study of 1500 individuals identified 1.8% by DSM criteria as having a borderline personality disorder (Swartz *et al*, 1990). From a psychotherapeutic standpoint, its meaningfulness is reduced by the possibility of an individual being given a diagnosis of borderline personality disorder when not impulsive, with no history of unstable and intense interpersonal relationships and showing no inappropriate or intense anger. Furthermore, the link of the borderline concept with a personality type appears somewhat arbitrary because of unresolved issues concerning the trait characteristics that are more appropriately viewed as symptoms than a part of personality make-up (McReynolds, 1989).

In addition, the borderline concept has been (d) linked historically to an *attenuation of psychotic illness*, particularly schizophrenia; (e) used as an *indication of a failure of therapist empathy* (Kohut, 1984; Brandchaft & Stolorow, 1987); (f) hypothesised to be a *sub-affective disorder* (Akiskal *et al*, 1985) or an overlap of affective and personality disorder pathology (Frances & Widiger, 1987); and (g) employed as a *meaningless wastebasket* category (Abend *et al*, 1983).

Our view is that borderline is a 'heuristic device' (to compensate for the lack of a comprehensive psychological model), the days of which are probably numbered. As with many other terms within the psychoanalytic knowledge domain, it is currently valuable because of its ambiguity (what Sandler (1983) terms 'elasticity'), its capacity to take on many different meanings depending on the context. Perhaps all we can hope for at this time is 'a fruitful mis-understanding'. As the interface of psychotherapy and empirical science develops, terms such as borderline should be replaced by concepts which correspond more exactly to models of mental function (Fonagy, 1982). For the moment, however, it remains a useful term denoting the vast, and aetiologically probably extremely heterogeneous, otherwise unclassified group of patients who between them consume a disproportionate amount of therapeutic resources.

Elsewhere, we have drawn attention to three unequivocal features of this group (Fonagy & Higgitt, 1990). Firstly, there is marked heterogeneity of symptoms and diagnosable mental disorders which appear to co-occur with borderline personality organisation. Of 180 patients with borderline personality disorder, 91% had one additional diagnosis and 42% had two or more (Fyer *et al*, 1988). Affective features predominate among these (Perry, 1985; Weiler *et al*, 1988) but there is also a high incidence of eating disorders and substance abuse (Pope *et al*, 1987). Temporary (less than two days in duration) psychotic manifestations are also a common feature (Zanarini *et al*, 1990*b*), even compared to schizophrenic patients. It thus appears as if this type of character structure constituted a risk factor for other psychiatric disorders (see Tyrer *et al*, 1990, for a similar observation in a study of neurotic disorders).

Secondly, all major authorities point to the variability or lability in behaviour that is a constant feature of the disorder. Periods of improved adaptation are invariably followed by disintegration in a fashion approximating to the cyclical. This paradoxical combination of stable lability has led many workers to conceive of these patients' problems in terms of hypothetical 'pathological organisations' (Bion, 1962; Rey, 1979; Steiner, 1979, 1987). The American child analytic literature has, quite independently, captured the same feature in the concept of the stable instability in ego functioning (Ekstein & Wallerstein, 1954; Shapiro, 1983).

Finally, the most striking aspect of this group of patients is impairment of interpersonal relationships. Dramatic altercations, precipitated by what appear to be mild but emotional interactions, lead to fragmentation of the social world and a sense of disorganisation and chaos that cannot fail to strike anyone who comes into contact with this group of individuals, whether for therapeutic or social reasons. Their submissiveness can suddenly turn to disparagement or to rage, often related to what may seem to the clinician as totally unreasonable demands for understanding and gratification.

The core features of (a) numerous psychiatric diagnoses, (b) predictably varying intensity and (c) major interpersonal difficulties, identify for most experienced psychotherapists a highly specific group of patients. As long as epidemiological psychiatry cannot provide a realistic single description for this group the term 'borderline' will do. The term, however, is probably no more appropriate than one suggested by a colleague disenchanted with the prospect of mapping this aspect of psychiatric nosology onto psychotherapy practice: 'unwelcome referrals'.

Psychodynamic formulations of borderline and narcissistic personality disturbance

While the literature on psychodynamic formulations of borderline pathology is rich, diverse and well covered in reviews (see for example, Stone, 1986; Grotstein *et al*, 1987; Tarnopolsky & Berelowitz, 1987), descriptions of the psychoanalytic treatment of borderlines are sparse, frequently lacking in detail (particularly in the North American literature) and are poorly reviewed (see Aronson, 1989, for an exception). We suspect, along with, for example, Wallerstein (1988), that radically divergent theoretical constructions in the psychoanalytic field may mask a surprising homogeneity of clinical approaches. Limited space, the availability of appropriate reviews and their arguably limited relevance have led us to reduce the coverage of psychoanalytic formulations of borderline states in this paper to a minimum and we concentrate our coverage on treatment approaches. All theoretical contributions are helpful in providing the struggling clinician with at least the illusion of meaningful explanation for a set of disturbing types of behaviour on which neither the patient nor current psychiatric orthodoxy can cast a particularly helpful light.

Most modern psychoanalytic formulations of borderline personality disorder are primarily developmental in nature. Current psychoanalytic approaches to borderline states may be broadly classified into three groups. Kohut (1977, 1984) proposed a trauma-arrest model which has been expanded and elaborated in the context of borderline pathology by a number of North American authors including Buie & Adler (1982), Brandchaft & Stolorow (1987), Tolpin (1987) and Palombo (1987). In these models a profound fault in the child's early environment, for Kohutians the excessively unempathic responses of the selfobjects, frustrate normal developmental needs and fixate the child's self at a fragile, archaic level. (Kohut (1971) sees infants as perceiving the caretaking figure (the object) as part of themselves, hence the term selfobject. This person (in effect the mother), through her soothing and mirroring of her infant's needs, supplies them with the necessary functions of self-cohesion which infants cannot yet perform for themselves.) The borderline individual thus finds it necessary to make use of highly primitive selfobject relationships (grandiosity, rage, excitement or sedation through drugs or other addictions) to support self-cohesion as well as self-esteem. Kohut also evocatively describes the subjective experience of emptiness that is secondary to an inadequately developed self. The psychic pain associated with this state cannot be underestimated. A borderline patient described how she went to a casualty department to tell the psychiatrist about this empty state. When she felt unable to communicate it orally, she inscribed the phrase ''I am lost'' into her leg with a razor blade.

This theory is thus essentially a deficiency theory: deficiency of necessary facilitating experiences leading to a psychic deficit (viz. an inadequately developed sense of self). The characteristic manifestations of the borderline position may be understood as indications of the individual's tragic attempts to cope with the profound limitations of his/her intrapsychic world. (The term 'borderline position' is a useful metaphor originating in Kleinian writings (see especially Steiner) where it has specific theoretical significance. Here the term position refers simply to the adaptational task borderline patients face *vis-à-vis* their highly unsatisfactory mental functioning.) The clear therapeutic implication is that meaningful intervention must focus on the nature of the individual's deficit and aim at the provision of a therapeutic environment which may be expected to lead to personal growth to make good the early deprivation: in Kohutian terms the provision of a soothing and mirroring function that leads to the restoration of the self.

By contrast, Kernberg's highly influential psychostructural model (1975, 1984) emphasises the inevitability of psychic conflict and its by-products of anxiety, guilt and shame in the course of early human development. The root cause of borderline states in Kernberg's model is the intensity of destructive and aggressive impulses and the relative weakness of ego structures available to handle them. Kernberg sees the borderline individual as using developmentally early defences in an attempt to separate contradictory images of self and others in order to protect positive images from being overwhelmed by negative and hostile ones. The wish to protect the object from destruction with but the most rudimentary of psychic mechanisms at the infant's disposal leads to the defensive fragmenta-tion of self and object representations. Manifestations of the borderline condition therefore represent a continuation of a developmentally unresolved infantile conflict state. These conflicts may be reasonably expected to continue within the context of treatment and their interpretation is assumed to have therapeutic effects.

Kernberg's approach has much, but by no means everything, in common with British followers of Melanie Klein (Klein, 1950, 1957; Bion, 1957; Segal, 1964) who also stress the inevitability of pathological sequelae arising out of innate destructiveness. The crucial difference lies in more recent Kleinian thinking (see Spillius, 1988) concerning the defensive arrangements which many conditions linked to borderline pathology appear to have in common. The term organisation (e.g. narcissistic organisation (Sohn, 1985; Rosenfeld, 1987), defensive organisation (O'Shaughnessy, 1981), pathological organisation (Steiner, 1987)) refers to a relatively stable construction of impulses, anxieties and defences. This allows the individual to create a very precious internal state where he is protected from the chaos of earlier developmental stages but is nevertheless 'voluntarily' depriving himself of more advanced modes of psychic functioning which would lead to intolerable depressive anxiety. The psychic defences work together in an extremely rigid system making therapeutic progress difficult and rarely entirely successful. It is as if the psychic structure itself becomes the embodiment of the destructive impulses which called it into existence in the first place. Bion (1962) provides one explanation as to why this puzzling state of affairs should occur. His description is in terms of the ego's identification with an object which is felt to be full of envy and hate, resulting in an early disabling of certain psychic processes to do with understanding cognitive and affective aspects of interpersonal relationships. Thus, in this model a state of quasi-deficit is seen as arising as the pathological resolution of intrapsychic conflicts.

Numerous alternative formulations represent various degrees of compromise between the deficit and conflict views. One alternative formulation, which owes much to Kleinian writers, has been put forward from a contemporary Freudian perspective (Fonagy, 1989, 1991; Fonagy & Higgitt, 1990; Fonagy & Moran, 1991). These workers have proposed a model which also stresses the importance of a state of deficit, of a primarily cognitive nature, which arises as an adaptation to intrapsychic conflict. In contrast to Kleinian workers they see the root of borderline disturbance in the child's, generally accurate, perception of the caregiving figure as harbouring hostile and ultimately destructive thoughts about the child. To protect against the painful awareness of the violence, neglect, and vacuousness in the mind of the primary caregiver, the child defensively inhibits (or disavows) his capacity to think about the mental state of others. Their internal and external object relations are profoundly constrained by their failure to conceive of others as thinking, feeling, believing and desiring, that is, as being fully human. Later, especially when threatened by intense affect, such individuals will tend to think of themselves and others comfortably only as physical entities, without a meta-representation of their capacity to think and feel. Although there is no reason why this defensive inhibition could not take place at a relatively late developmental stage, within a developmental perspective, it is most likely to occur between the ages of two and four, when the child's ideas concerning the mental world are thought to be undergoing rapid development (Harris, 1989; Baron-Cohen, 1987, 1989; Baron-Cohen *et al*, 1985) and is thus most vulnerable to defensive inhibition (Fonagy & Moran, 1991).

The dynamic inhibition of the capacity to think about the mental states of others or even about one's own mental states leaves the individual profoundly vulnerable to psychic conflict. Pathological adaptation to conflict is therefore common, giving rise to a high frequency of psychiatric disorders associated with this condition. The slow rate of psychic change in these patients is seen as a consequence of the lack of availability of a psychological process, a 'theory of mind', a reflective or psychological self (Fonagy *et al*, 1991) that normally plays a central role in psychotherapeutic work. Notwithstanding its focus upon cognitive deficit, within this model the appropriate therapeutic intervention remains conflictual. It is through the consistent interpretation of the nature of threatening affects and ideas that the motivation for and the capacity to think about one's own and others' mental states is rediscovered.

Typical borderline mechanisms

Regardless of the model adopted by workers there is substantial 'common ground' between different psychoanalytic schools in their understanding of the unconscious mechanisms involved in creating the typical borderline clinical picture. The emphasis placed upon the mental mechanisms of splitting, projective identification and manic defence is a hallmark of most dynamic formulations.

Splitting is both a cause and a consequence of borderline individuals' difficulty in maintaining an ambivalent, balanced view of both self and object which, in Kleinian theory, would require the acknowledgement and mental confrontation of their experientially overwhelming destructive, annihilatory potential. Searles (1986) also stresses the importance of splitting in preventing the formation of a memory of an object which would then have to be mourned. Splitting, as seen by Kleinian theorists, may also be part of a reaction to claustrophobic anxieties associated with phantasy entrapment within the object consequent upon ego boundary difficulties.

The characteristic sadism and masochism of borderline patients are seen by these authors as reflecting split aspects of the self. With more than one object at their disposal, borderline individuals may succeed in externalising their incapacity to integrate good and bad objects by polarising people working with them and with constant attempts to attack the links between them (Main, 1957).

Equally important in psychoanalytic accounts of borderline behaviour both in and out of treatment, is the concept of *projective identification* originally described by Tausk (1919). For Melanie Klein (1957), projective identification is an unconscious infantile phantasy by which the infant is able to relocate its persecutory experiences by separating (splitting) them from its self-representation and making them part of its image of a particular object. Disowned unconscious feelings of rage or shame are firmly believed by the patient to exist within the therapist. Projective identification is qualitatively different from simple projection in that by acting in subtle but influential ways, the patient may achieve a confirming reaction of criticism or even persecution.

Projective identification has explanatory power far beyond that of a mechanism of defence. The phantasy of a magical control over an object may be achieved in this way. Furthermore, projective identification is not a truly internal process and involves the object who may experience it as manipulation, seduction or a myriad of other forms of psychic influence. Thus, projective identification has an important primitive communicative function.

Bion (1959) pointed to the necessity for projective identification in infancy, a time when the individual is ill-equipped to absorb impressions of the experiential world. By projecting these elements into another human mind (a container) that has the capacity of accepting, absorbing and transforming them into meanings, its survival is ensured. Thus for Bion, transference and countertransference are essentially about the transfer of intolerable mental pain, originally from infant to mother and in the treatment situation from patient to therapist.

Searles (1986), Giovacchini (1979, 1987) and many other North American analysts working with borderline patients make use of the construct of projective identification in this interpersonal sense. The concept is appealing because it conveys the undoubted ability of these patients to 'get under the skin' of all those with whom they develop close relations. Whether a psychologically implausible concept such as projective identification is essential to give an account of these phenomena or whether a more parsimonious explanation such as Sandler's (1976*a,b*) role responsiveness or King's (1978) reverse transference may be sufficient, is a controversial issue. Sandler (1976*a,b*, 1987) elaborates a model of the two-person interaction when the direct influence of one on the other is accounted for by the evocation of particular roles in the mind of the person who is being influenced. The behaviour or role adopted by the person doing the influencing is crucial in eliciting a complementary response from the participant. Sandler suggests that in this way infantile and childhood patterns of relationships may be actualised or enacted in the transference and in other relationships. King (1978) describes evocatively how patients at times take on the role of the other in re-enacting infantile relationships in the transference, thus forcing the therapist to take on the role of an unacceptable aspect of the patient's infantile self. These are alternative accounts for some of the communicational phenomena ascribed to projective identification by Kleinian writers.

Grandiosity, contempt and profound dependency of borderline patients are explained by Klein and Kernberg in terms of the notion of the manic defence (Klein, 1940). Their dependency causes them to feel intolerable vulnerability, the pain of which is warded off through unprovoked attacks on the good qualities of those whose dependability seems to mock their own feelings of helplessness and defectiveness. To deal with their envy they devalue their objects (their therapists, their spouses). Kohut's (1977) account of grandiosity and contempt invokes his model of self-development. As a result of developmental deprivations in empathy the borderline individual fails to step beyond the state of natural infantile grandiosity in the development of the self.

A further common feature of borderline patients on which psychoanalytic ideas cast a useful light is the self-destructiveness of such patients. Kernberg (1987) illustrates how self-mutilating behaviour and suicidal gestures tend to coincide with intense attacks of rage upon the object and they can serve to re-establish control over the environment by evoking guilt feelings or expressing unconscious guilt over the success of a deepening relationship. In some patients, self-destructiveness occurs because their self-image becomes 'infiltrated' with aggression so that they experience increased self-esteem and a confirmation of their grandiosity in self-mutilation or masochistic sexual perversions. The helpless caring professional can respond only with despair to such patients' obvious sense of triumph in their victory over pain and death. Their pleading efforts seem futile to the patient, who at an unconscious level experiences a sense of being in control over death. Self-mutilation, such as cutting, may also protect from the identity diffusion (derealisation) which is a constant threat to the fragmented internal world of the borderline.

All affects appear to occur in exaggerated form in these patients. Their anxiety appears qualitatively different from neurotic concern and seems much better described by terms such as Winnicott's (1960) 'unthinkable anxiety', Kohut's (1971) 'disintegration anxiety' or Bion's (1959) 'nameless dread'. There is rarely any doubt in the empathic clinician's mind that such fears concern the continuation of existence itself. In our experience it is the loss of a sense of a mental or psychological continuity, that is normally provided by adequately functioning mental processes, which is most profoundly feared.

Related to this intense anxiety is the proneness to profound depression associated with object loss. Masterson (1981) links borderline pathology closely to Margaret Mahler's (Mahler *et al*, 1975; Mahler & Kaplan, 1977) *rapprochement* sub-phase of the separation–individuation phase of development. He discusses abandonment depression as the consequence of the borderline individual's quest for separation from the withdrawing or aggressive maternal object who in turn, for pathological reasons of her own, wishes to keep the child in a symbiotic relationship with her. The withdrawing and rewarding object representations are kept rigidly separate to maintain the possibility of symbiotic union with the rewarding object and to ward off abandonment depression.

Between 15 and 22 months, when the toddler can physically separate from the mother, the infant's sense of individual identity takes a dramatic leap forward. The child, through identification with, and internalisation of, the mental representation of the mother, assumes the functions the mother had previously performed for him, thereby achieving firmer reality perception, impulse control, frustration tolerance and self–other boundaries. This process, in Masterson's view, is undermined by the failure of the borderline individual's mother (who would probably herself be described as borderline) to encourage and emotionally support the process of separation.

Borderline personality disorder is seen by Masterson as a developmental arrest in the *rapprochement* sub-phase. The borderline individual's dramatic response to actual separation is thus explained by his incomplete separation from his objects, with the psychological experience of separation becoming equivalent to a loss of a part of the self. Borderline patients' common vigorous pursuing of their therapists at home, in their holidays or in other professional activity can be understood in this way.

Modell (1963, 1968) was the first to describe the 'transitional relatedness' of borderline patients. This much overused concept of Donald Winnicott's (1953) refers to the use infants make of inanimate objects to soothe them in their mother's absence. Borderline individuals frequently make use of inanimate objects in their adult lives to serve this purpose. Even more striking is their use of other people as if they were inanimate to serve a self-regulating, soothing function, to be used, like a toddler uses a teddy bear, in primitive, demanding and tenacious ways. Searles and Giovacchini, in attempting to account for this, postulate that borderline patients may have been treated as transitional objects by their parents.

Treatment approaches

Psychoanalysis and intensive (expressive) psychoanalytic psychotherapy[1]

The distinction between psychoanalysis and psychoanalytic psychotherapy is an elusive one. In Britain, psychoanalysis is practised four or five times

---

1. Psychoanalytic clinicians undoubtedly pioneered numerous aspects of the psychotherapeutic treatment of borderline and narcissistic individuals. Many of their clinical findings have implications for diagnosis and management which go far beyond the practice of psychoanalysis or psychoanalytical psychotherapy. For convenience, clinical issues are included here.

a week, involves the use of the couch, and encourages the development of intense, sometimes regressive emotional experiences. Intensive psycho-analytic psychotherapy takes place two or three times a week and is more often conducted face to face. Most British psychoanalysts would agree that psychoanalysis is the treatment of choice for borderline individuals. British analysts, particularly Rosenfeld (1978, 1987), have been pioneers in treating borderline patients with psychoanalysis without compromising any of the parameters of classical psychoanalysis, for example the insistence upon interpreting the transference. They do, however, make recommendations about technique specific to this group of patients, for example, Rosenfeld's insistence on not interpreting oedipal transference phantasies with patients who are likely to concretise them.

In the United States, aside from certain special facilities, such as Chestnut Lodge and the Menninger Clinic, and particular individuals (Searles, 1986; Boyer, 1987; Giovacchini, 1987), the tradition until recently was opposed to interpretive psychotherapy for this group of patients. In part fuelled by the American discovery of British object relations theory (particulary the work of Kleinian authors and to some extent Fairbairn and Winnicott), this situation has now radically shifted. In particular, Kernberg's incorporation of Kleinian ideas into a theoretical framework relatively congenial to North American analysts led these clinicians to become increasingly enthusiastic about using interpretive techniques to achieve personality change in borderline patients through the resolution of intra-psychic structural conflicts and/or undoing deficits and unblocking arrested developmental processes.

In North America, some authors such as Masterson (1976), Kernberg (1984), and Buie & Adler (1982) advocate dynamically orientated face-to-face psychotherapy two to three times a week. These may be variously described as expressive, reconstructive, or uncovering approaches. Kernberg's approach has recently been clearly documented in a treatment manual (Kernberg *et al*, 1989). Other therapeutic approaches based on models of developmental arrest or deficit differ slightly (Bacal, 1981).

The shared aspects of these psychoanalytic and psychoanalytic–psychotherapeutic approaches are far more marked, although less frequently remarked upon, than are the differences between them. They are unlikely to formulate their goals for such patients in the context of specific formula-tions (e.g. as integrating split self and object images, promoting higher-level defensive functioning, working through abandonment depression to promote separation, etc.). Yet the manner in which these apparently diverse therapeutic goals are achieved may be at times hard to distinguish (Wallerstein, 1990).

The number of sessions per week may vary, but the overall duration is likely to be between two and seven years. The hallmarks of the treatment are the interpretation of the transference, particularly its pre-genital aspects; the interpretation of primitive defences as these enter the transference; careful attention to neutrality; and consistent limit-setting. All authors agree on the importance of a non-anxious, calm therapeutic attitude to this rather chaotic group of patients. The requirement of a certain degree of phlegmatism despite intense anxiety, acute crises and incessant provocation, perhaps more than any other, makes some therapists unsuited in character to work with borderline patients.

All intensive psychotherapeutic procedures are interpretive, focused on the transference, and permitting, if not promoting, regression. They emphasise the therapist's involvement in terms of increased activity compared with the prototypical silent analyst. Borderline patients respond poorly to the unstructured situation promoted by the therapist's silence. Nevertheless, the therapist has to maintain sufficient neutrality for the patient's reactions to the therapeutic situation to become meaningful and interpretable (Kernberg, 1975).

Transference reactions in the borderline patient are dramatic, rapid and unstable. Patients frequently express intense emotion, and the pretend tone and "I am behaving as if" character of neurotic transference is missing. Kohut (1971, 1977) distinguishes three common types of transference reaction with 'difficult' narcissistic patients based on his selfobject theory. In the 'merger transference' the therapist is seen as an extension of the patient's omnipotence and grandiosity and the patient demands total possession of the object. In the 'mirroring transference' the therapist is seen as someone whose sole function is to respond empathically to the patient's achievements. In the 'idealised transference' the patient looks to the therapist as a safe, containing, idealised other.

Rosenfeld (1978) describes even more primitive forms of transference where the patient's experience of the therapist is a delusional one. North American and British analysts, apparently independently, identified transference bordering on a confusional state where the patient enters into a state of massive projective identification, merger or symbiotic relatedness with the therapist. A number of workers emphasise that the therapist's ability to tolerate, and be able to verbalise, this experience is a critical component of the treatment.

Equally testing of the therapist's tolerance, but also generally recognised as essential, is the therapist's capacity to withstand the patient's angry and hostile transference. Winnicott (1949) describes the therapist's struggle with his/her own response of hatred and sadism to what are seen as unjustified verbal assaults. Under these circumstances it is easy, but highly counter-productive, to collude with the patient and minimise the destructive intent behind these attacks. Rather, the therapeutic aim should be to fully acknowledge them while understanding them in the context of the patient's current struggles. Thus the therapist must not retaliate against or abandon the patient with his/her rage, nor should the therapist relinquish therapeutic responsibility and feign indifference to slights and taunts.

In this, as in all other contexts, it is regarded as essential that clarifications and interpretations remain in the present, for some workers almost uniquely in the context of the therapeutic relationship. Explorations of the patient's past, and interpretations using childhood experience as an explanation of current behaviour, are unlikely to do more than divert attention from the pathological nature of the patient's current behaviour.

All those analysts who work with borderline individuals recognise that extra care needs to be taken about the constancy and reliability of the framework in which treatment takes place. Borderline patients make their attachments to physical objects as intensively as they do to people (Searles, 1986). The consistency and regularity confers what Tustin calls a 'rhythm of safety' (Grotstein *et al*, 1987) which is perhaps one of the most powerful arguments for intensive, five times weekly, treatment being offered to these patients. Disappointment and unmet expectation, which may be the norm in a psychiatric out-patient department, can assume catastrophic proportions in the mind of a borderline individual. The failure to deal with (i.e. acknowledge and work through the affective reaction to) irregularities when they have occurred either undermines the therapeutic relationship in the long run, or will lead to a drastic curtailment of the patient's voluntary participation in treatment.

Most workers recognise the difficulty in establishing such a stable environment in the face of what may appear as the patient's relentless attempts at undermining this by coming late, by insisting on leaving early, by remaining silent, by arriving under the influence of drugs or alcohol or injuring themselves just before or even during a session. (A patient treated by one of us was reported, while under the care of a previous therapist, to have put her head through a window in the middle of a session – without first opening it.)

Some workers (e.g. Selzer *et al*, 1987; Miller, 1990) recommend drawing up a contract between the therapist and the patient specifying what may constitute threats to the patient's treatment. Chessick (1979) explicitly demands the limitation of any behaviour that is 'future foreclosing' to the patient's life or treatment. He suggests that the therapist makes clear the range of responses to be utilised in case of the patient violating the contract, from simple confrontation and interpretation, to suspending a session, to enlisting the aid of others and even terminating treatment. This limit-setting function of the contract is seen as much to counteract the therapists' omnipotence and to get them to formally recognise their own limitations as to controlling the patient's behaviour. Such a contract may be invaluable at the initial stages of treatment; it is not expected, however, to deal with the constant threat of acting out, of turning unconscious fantasy into action. Ultimately it is only the accurate interpretation of the motives behind such actions that is thought in the long term to reduce their likely occurrence.

Also a part of this more active style is the therapist's commitment to repeatedly draw the patient's attention to the adverse consequences of self-destructive behaviours. Most such actions may be conceived of as primarily defensive in nature, protecting the patient from awareness of particular affects. Actions, self-destructive or otherwise, will be an important medium of the patient's communication with the therapist. The verbalisation of that communication, and drawing attention to the affect states from which it protects the patient, is essential to ensure that acting does not become a resistance to the awareness of the transference and thus to the progress of treatment.

There is also universal agreement that the therapist is in nearly as great a danger of acting out in the course of treatment as the patient. Borderline patients are extremely sensitive to dyadic relationships and can have an eerie empathic understanding of the vulnerability of others. They can confront the therapist with an almost infinite variety of situations for which no training can adequately prepare one. Being regarded by a patient variously as someone who has the capacity to make things better, but also as the person who is responsible for the patient's pain, someone who is irrelevant and then as the patient's last hope, yet also someone who is hopelessly inadequate and out of touch, it is inevitable that therapists develop intense reactions to their borderline patient.

Reason and understanding are the first casualty. Sooner or later all therapists are nudged into making mistakes. One may give in to the temptation to search for narcissistic gratification in the interaction, and to take on a heroic role, placing the patient at grave risk because all one is doing is enacting the patient's fantasies of omnipotence. Alternatively, the therapist may be overwhelmed by a sense of inadequacy and try to rescue the patient through sexual seduction or deal with the temptation to do so by being harsh, critical and rejecting, in either case probably running the risk not only of therapeutic disaster but also of litigation. More commonly, the therapist can become a vehicle for the patient's intolerable self-critical part and be nudged into the role of confronter and accuser.

Pines (1978) describes how the therapist finds himself being dragged, "unwillingly but inevitably as if by a great force, into the pattern imposed by the patient, so that we begin to feel provoked, hostile, persecuted and to behave exactly as the patients need us to, becoming rejecting and hostile" (p. 115). As Pines and others point out, the crucial aspect of this process is that interpretations or the other mature contributions of our intact mental function are neither real nor meaningful for these patients. Rather, the primitive impulses, hostilities, persecutions and mockeries that they engender feel to them as genuine and real, and validate the therapeutic process.

Racker's (1968) distinction between concordant countertransference, where the therapist identifies with the patient's feelings, and complementary countertransference, where the therapist experiences or acts out a role which complements a need in the patient, is relevant here. What may be a painful recognition for a therapist, inexperienced with border-line individuals, is that his role with the patient is not, from the patient's standpoint at least, as an interpreter or provider of a 'holding environment'. Rather, the therapist is a vehicle to be transformed magically and immediately by the patients' fantasies into a good or bad, protective or persecutory aspect of their internal world. If therapists are able to submit themselves to this process and tolerate the distortions to their conceptions of themselves induced by the patients' primitive projections, then they are in a position to make use of this valuable source of information about the patient's internal world (Sandler, 1976*b*). If their own identity is insufficiently well established, or they are temperamentally unsuited to the task for some other reason, they will endlessly find themselves in interminable arguments about the accuracy of the patients' judgement of them.

Thus the most important aspect of monitoring one's emotional reactions is to recognise, and avoid being sucked into, a destructive and hopeless sequence of interactions with the patient. This may be prevented by taking up opportunities for supervision or, for those with more experience, making extensive use of peer consultations (Adler, 1986). Searles (1986), perhaps the most skilled practitioner of a primarily countertransferential technique, warns that while the analyst may be a virtual sense organ for the patient's distress, he must at the same time recognise that he is also the cause of that distress, that there is a core of reality in even the most delusional of transference reactions. The importance of the awareness of one's own contribution to the transference–countertransference matrix is also highlighted by studies of infant development (Trevarthen, 1980; Stern, 1985; Murray, 1988) showing the constant reciprocity that maintains interaction and attunement in the mother–infant dyad. In the absence of developmentally later communication capacities, this complementarity becomes vital to the treatment of borderline patients.

Some controversial issues

There is considerable variation whether emphasis is placed upon the content of interpretations or on the general atmosphere of the treatment situation. It is not easy to see these two facets of treatment as independent of one another (an astute therapist creates a powerful holding environment by the use of his interpretations). Nevertheless, Kleinian analysts and others with classicial orientation (Segal, 1972; Masterson, 1976; Kernberg, 1984; Steiner, 1979; Boyer, 1987; Rosenfeld, 1987) advocate focus on the interpretation of defensive distortions of the transference and the self-destructive nature of the patient's stance.

Other analysts, particularly from the self-psychology tradition in North America, some members of the British Independent Group and other independent North American analysts (e.g. Volkan, 1987), regard experiential factors as being primary determinants, particularly in the early phase of the treatment. The 'holding environment', a term coined by Winnicott (1965) to designate an early stage of development when a mother is primarily concerned with her infant's welfare, is an often used and apparently highly apt metaphor for the therapeutic action. In this context, holding refers to the analyst's ability to create a safe milieu in which previously cut-off feelings can be explored.

Mellita Schmideberg (1947) described the great lengths she went to, in terms of non-interpretive contact (telephone calls, home visits, self-disclosures), in order to establish a therapeutic milieu. Others offer extra sessions, give vacation addresses and use transitional objects such as photographs and postcards. Gunderson (1984) stresses the importance of a holding environment in the early stages of treatment, when the patient's objectlessness provides only a doubtful base for interpretive interventions. Giovacchini (e.g. 1987), and those who use a self-psychology frame of reference (e.g. Brandchaft & Stolorow, 1987), tend to diminish the value of interpretation in favour of experiential learning. It is reasonably claimed that interpretations should not be expected to be heard until the patient has the necessary intrapsychic structures in place to understand them.

Bion's concept of the 'container' could well be regarded as the cognitive equivalent of holding. It is likely that affective and intellectual accommodation of the patient's mental state are both active therapeutic ingredients and are required from the therapists. Although individual therapeutic styles may place greater emphasis upon one or other of these approaches, it is likely that both exist in all successful therapeutic endeavours.

The psychoanalytic literature on borderlines also encompasses the controversy over the significance of early trauma. Masterson (1981) is convinced that the aetiology of the borderline includes early abuse and treats the transference manifestations of mistrust and rage as reactive to 'not-good-enough' mothering. Kernberg and Kleinian theorists tend to regard the transference manifestations of borderlines as distortions which need to be tackled whether or not early trauma or abuse was part of the picture. Brenman (1980), writing on the value of reconstruction, sees the analyst's role as furnishing the patient with experiences of an understanding current and real object who is able to bear within him what the patient feels to be unbearable and can thus replace faulty internal representations of inadequate parental introjects. Kernberg explicitly identifies how the more primitive distorted level of transference gradually gives way to a more realistic perception of childhood in the course of treatment.

Evidence (Herman *et al*, 1989; Ogata *et al*, 1990; Shearer *et al*, 1990; Swett *et al*, 1990; Westen *et al*, 1990) is accumulating to substantiate Masterson's radical stance on aetiology. Borderline patients are more likely to have experience of physical or sexual abuse than most other psychiatric samples.

Arguments and data concerning genetic predisposition blur the implications of the evidence confounding, as it does, physical and social inheritance. Stone (1986) favours an interactional model. He sees some individuals being pushed by genetic predisposition towards a borderline condition, no matter how protective their parenting might have been, while the social background of others appears to justify their borderline status without any help from genetics. From a therapeutic standpoint this would imply that Kernberg's approach may on balance be the safer one to adopt.

The most significant divergences in treatment recommendations arise out of the difference in relative emphasis placed upon deficit versus conflict. Analysts who prefer to regard the borderline individual as someone who lacks a holding, soothing and mirroring internalised caretaking figure tend not to interpret the patient's idealisations or derogations until a later phase of treatment. Giovacchini, for example, is of the view that early interpretation of the negative transference is likely to be heard as criticism. Searles, similarly, cautions against interpretation of the transference before the patient can identify clearly the experiences to which the therapist's comments refer. Kernberg, however, insists that unless the borderline patient's hostility is interpreted from the outset of the treatment, and thereby the therapist demonstrates his capacity to tolerate it, negative affects may be lost to the treatment and will be found to undermine the therapeutic endeavour.

A difference in emphasis exists concerning the aetiological significance of aggression and destructiveness. The interpretation of destructiveness and aggression is a hallmark of clinical work of Kleinian analysis, as well as Kernberg. Kohutian analysts see anger as arising from narcissistic injury. Anger is the patients' resistance to positive transference feelings and is interpreted as rooted in their fear of vulnerability within such trusting relationships. (Therapists' non-empathic responses are also seen as an integral cause of the patient's anger and destructiveness in treatment.)

The controversy crystallises around what some therapists see as the borderline individual's unrealistic positive transference, the wish to be with, and be loved by, the therapist in preference to almost anything else in their lives. Kohutian analysts (Kohut, 1971; Buie & Adler, 1982; Brandchaft & Stolorow, 1987) would see the emergence of these feelings as a positive move which, through clarifications and interpretations of the patient's disappointments, will gradually give way to a more realistic appraisal. Other analysts see such positive transference as defensive, immature and as serving to protect the borderline patient from their negative transference feelings. Thus Kleinian analysts, or those who follow Kernberg, are unlikely to talk of the patient's longings for holding or soothing, but see these wishes as perhaps part of an act of manic reparation serving to avoid guilt and depressive anxiety.

Related to the controversy over positive transference is the issue of 'corrective emotional experience' (Alexander, 1957). The question of whether the therapist's behaviour may be construed as in some way compensating for the sequence of past parental deficiency, is an emotional one for many analytical therapists as it appears to simplify what seems to them to be an enormously complex process. Self-psychologists, however, take the reasonable view that the capacity of holding oneself in adequate esteem cannot develop without a strong experience of having been valued. Acknowledging the patient's positive qualities therefore at a later stage of treatment becomes one of its important components.

At the other extreme, Kleinian analysts and Kernberg would regard such acts as counter-therapeutic and indicating the therapist's incapacity to deal with the patient's hostility. In their view, therapeutic advantage accrues from the therapist's capacity to withstand the patient's aggressive onslaughts which cumulatively reduce the patient's fears about his destructive impulses and lead to the reintegration into the self of its split-off aspects and object representations. Independently, Masterson and Gunderson both make specific recommendations about using supportive techniques at later phases of treatment. They recommend discussing with patients their new feelings, ideas and interests in an attempt to actively validate the patient's growing awareness of his/her emerging self and its continuing individuation.

Supportive psychotherapy

The psychoanalytic tradition which eschews the use of an interpretive approach with borderline patients (Knight, 1953; Zetzel, 1971; Grinker, 1975) is at least as distinguished as the one which espouses it. Supportive therapy has as its treatment aim the strengthening, through suggestion, education and a facilitating interpersonal relationship, of the patient's adaptive functioning. Understanding and interpretation of defences is seen as undermining the patient and is regarded as unhelpful or even dangerous. Transference regression and dependency are similarly discouraged as likely to lead to psychotic episodes, suicide or other forms of acting out. Nevertheless, the supplying of partial interpretations in an educational rather than a confrontational way may be recommended, for example, explaining to patients about their neediness, their sensitivity to rejection, their intense rage and guilt, their need to master feelings of helplessness and the relationship of these states to acts of self-destructiveness.

Psychotherapists favouring this approach talk of reinforcing the therapeutic situation by imposing strict limitations upon it. Thus therapy is conducted face to face, the patient is not encouraged to say whatever comes into his mind but rather direct his thinking towards clear and explicit goals. The therapist is directive, sometimes confrontational, but does not stop short of either suggestion or environmental intervention. Sessions are less frequent, perhaps once a week. Nevertheless, the treatment commitment is seen as long-term: several years, perhaps even indefinite (Federn, 1947; Zetzel,

J

1971). Schmideberg (1947) is particularly eloquent in showing how therapists are under obligation to adapt their style to the patient and be willing to be natural and self-revealing at the expense of therapeutic neutrality.

The therapist's reality and the partial gratifications this offers diminish negative transference. Positive transference may be used in the service of empowering the therapist's suggestion and advice as does the encouraging of the 'we are on the same side' attitude (Rockland, 1987). These workers consider that the warm, human, benevolent attitude, coupled with consistency and availability, may be of greater importance to the patient than the therapeutic communications themselves. They view the 'holding environment' as of paramount significance. As Fromm-Reichmann eloquently stated: "What these patients need is an experience, not an explanation". The importance of establishing a new and better relationship recommended by these authors is very close to what Alexander and French had in mind in their construct of the corrective emotional experience.

The potency of supportive techniques to bring about very substantial improvement is well documented by follow-up studies (see Wallerstein, 1986; Stone, 1987, 1989) and experimental studies of psychotherapy where 'placebo' control groups are used (Frank, 1988). The question of efficacy turns on what supportive therapy is thought to entail. The division between expressive techniques and supportive ones is of course in practice never as clear as it might seem in books and papers on technique. Many therapists committed to the interpretive approach use supportive techniques at the initial stages of their treatment (e.g. Masterson). Others may turn to such techniques at times of crisis or in the final stages of treatment.

Interpretive or expressive therapy cannot be the treatment of choice for all borderline patients since supportive therapy appears to have yielded such surprisingly favourable results. It should be remembered, however, that follow-up studies of insight-orientated techniques pertain to clinical interventions probably quite different in quality to what was described in the previous section. Psychoanalysis in its classical form, as practised in North America in the 1950s and 1960s, would be regarded as inappropriate by most psychoanalysts currently involved with borderline patients, technically and theoretically, whether Kohutian, Kleinian, or influenced by Kernberg or Masterson.

This is, however, not to say that the ideal technique is some combination of supportive and interpretive approaches. In reality, if supportive interventions are made in psychoanalytic psychotherapy without consideration and explicit working through of their transference implications, they are likely to be muddling for both the therapist and his/her already considerably confused patient. Similarly, an isolated transference interpretation, within a generally supportive framework, is unlikely to be helpful as the patient does not have the cognitive and emotional framework within which to make sense of such interventions. All authorities agree that this takes effort and time to establish reliably. Such mixing of techniques usually arises out of an inadequately formulated treatment plan leading to 'seat of the pants' intervention which gives maximum opportunity for countertherapeutic, countertransferential processes to hold sway and where the option of 'no therapy' as the treatment of choice should be given serious consideration. On present evidence, both expressive and supportive technique may be regarded as useful for some patients. There is no indication for the judicious combination of the two.

Group psychotherapy

Traditionally, borderline patients have not been considered suitable for group psychotherapy because their disruptive behaviours were regarded as interfering with the development of group cohesiveness. Their demands for exclusive attention, their paranoid tendencies, constant orientation towards bolstering their self-esteem as well as their general low level of personal accomplishment must be regarded as contraindications (Horwitz, 1987). These very characteristics, however, are also the ones most likely to be tackled rapidly in a group, with the group exerting gentle pressure on the patient to reduce such maladaptive behaviours. Psychotherapy groups can have a civilising and socialising influence upon the borderline patient, and as many, including Gunderson (1984) have found, the results of group treatments tend to be favourable.

Macaskill (1980, 1982) explored the therapeutic processes at work in group therapy. He asked patients to respond to Yalom's (1975) questionnaire on therapeutic factors and found, surprisingly, that self-understanding and altruism were the most valued aspects of the group process for borderline patients. Further detailed analysis of tapes of group sessions revealed that patients' insights and altruistic responses tended to follow therapists' empathic interventions in connection with narcissistic hurt experienced by a group member. The group may thus function to soothe and comfort patients by containing their anger and despair and yet remaining undamaged by them.

There are several advantages to the group approach clearly stated by Horwitz (1977, 1987). Horwitz recommends a special combination of individual and group treatments where both are administered by the same therapist. It is claimed to benefit the patient's reality orientation, to highlight maladaptive character traits at the same time as opening up a suitable context for dealing with them. Grobman (1980) describes the successful treatment of borderline patients in groups when they could not be effectively treated in individual therapy.

The adjunctive use of group therapy, where the group provides an interpersonal training ground alongside individual therapy, has been proposed equally by those who favour interpretive and supportive psychotherapy (Knight, 1953; Kernberg, 1975; Roth, 1980; Wong, 1980). Group therapists and analysts suggest that the process of individual therapy may frequently be accelerated if the patient concurrently participates in a therapy group where primitive fantasies are stimulated and where the structure of the group may provide feedback, support and encouragement leading to personal growth (Tuttman, 1990; Roth, 1990; Pines, 1990). Furthermore, the group may have the capacity to contain intense envy and narcissistic rage engendered by individual therapy and thus attenuate negative therapeutic reaction. Wong (1988) cautions against using different therapists for individual and group work as it can encourage splitting and cause countertransferential difficulties between the therapists.

Group therapists consider that most groups can rarely contain more than two borderline individuals (Horwitz, 1987; Pines, 1990). Chatham (1985) describes a group made up exclusively of borderline patients and stresses the importance of directiveness, modelling and nurturance strategies in group leaders. Kutter (1982) gives an example where a psychoanalytic group made up entirely of borderlines failed to avoid mutual destructiveness and emotional chaos. The entry of patients into the group may also need to be facilitated (Stone & Gustafson, 1982). Macaskill's work also showed that the individualised aspect of group function, rather than group processes *per se*, were perceived by borderline group members as of benefit.

There is no compelling evidence available at the moment to recommend group therapy over individual therapy other than those deriving from economic and practical considerations. There is some indication that patients with narcissistic disorders do not respond well to group treatment which confronts them with the pathological aspects of their narcissism; indeed the patient as a result may well be scapegoated (Horner, 1975).

Family therapy

Families of borderline patients have been implicated in an aetiological context in at least two ways. Firstly, pedigree studies (Stone, 1977; Siever & Gunderson, 1979; Loranger *et al*, 1982) suggest that borderline personality disorders are familial disorders, although this has not been borne out by twin studies (Torgerson, 1984). Secondly, descriptive studies of families of borderline individuals frequently point to serious psychiatric disturbance, neglect, rejection and abuse as typical of family structure (Akiskal, 1981; Andrulonis *et al*, 1981; Soloff & Millward, 1983; Herman *et al*, 1989; Shearer *et al*, 1990). Feldman & Guttman (1984), in an empirical study, identified a group of parents who seemed characterised by extreme literal-mindedness and lack of empathy and a second where the parents' borderline features made the child an easy target for the parents' projection and distortions of reality.

Family therapy is frequently offered to adolescent borderline patients and is regarded by many as the treatment of choice in that context (Solomon,

1987; Brown, 1987). There is little in the literature concerning family interventions specifically with borderline individuals (but see Mandelbaum, 1977; Jones, 1987; Brown, 1987). Yet both systemic and dynamic family approaches evolved from the treatment of patient groups in which borderline personality organisation is common. (See for example Minuchin's work with anorexic patients.)

The involvement of the family has the effect of taking the onus off the patients while at the same time giving the therapist a clearer view of the interactions which may be creating the disturbance in both the patient and the family. The full gamut of pathological interactions may be readily observed in most borderline families including alliances and manipulations, scapegoating, double-binding, splitting, and the 'parentifying' of children by the parents (Schane & Kovel, 1988). Lansky (1987) describes the subtle and not so subtle use of shame and blaming in borderline families. Lansky (1989) gives an account of emergency family sessions to deal with the sequelae of acute suicide cases. Kennedy (1989) describes the treatment of borderline families in an in-patient psychoanalytically orientated setting (see also Haugsgjerd, 1987).

The potency of family-based interventions is evident to all those who have witnessed a well conducted family session. The efficacy of this form of treatment in terms of empirical studies, however, is no better or worse established than any of the other treatment modalities.

In-patient treatment and the therapeutic community

The use of hospital admission in the treatment of borderline patients remains controversial. Controversy surrounds the danger of regression following admission and whether the goal of in-patient treatment should be stabilisation and the preparation for further treatment or the internalisation of a new structure. Some analytically orientated North American psychiatrists feel strongly about the importance and value of relatively long-term hospital care in the treatment of borderline patients (Kernberg, 1976; Adler, 1977; Hartocollis, 1980; Brown, 1981; Silver, 1983; Fenton & McGlashen, 1990). In an early paper Kernberg (1976) outlines the indications for long-term hospital admission as low motivation, severe ego weakness and poor object relations. Interestingly, evidence, to the extent that it exists, suggests that it is the relatively healthier borderline patients that draw more benefit from long-term admission (Masterson & Costello, 1980; Greben, 1983). None of the outcome investigations offer strong support for long-term hospital admission.

For borderline patients to benefit from long-term hospital stays, they should probably be admitted to a unit specialising in the care of such patients (see for example Jackson & Pines, 1986). The therapeutic community approach to long-term hospital admission is a multi-component treatment programme, where individual therapy, ward groups, active patient participation in the maintenance of the community, and the constant monitoring of group processes are all used to confront and counteract manifestations of the borderline personality organisation. A useful description of current North American approach is given by Fenton & McGlashen (1990).

Main's (1957) classic paper on the patients who could be "recognised essentially by the object relations formed" described eloquently the regressions which ensued and the countertransference difficulties for the treatment team created by these patients. More recently, Gabbard (1989) described splitting and its management in the hospital setting. He concludes that as a process it must be monitored but not necessarily eradicated as it provides a useful safety valve.

A number of workers have independently commented on the therapeutic benefits of brief periods of custodial care for severely disturbed individuals (e.g. Singer, 1987). Friedman (1975) advocates a hospital milieu encouraging positive rapport, limit setting, special attention to the therapeutic alliance and the use of countertransference as an indication of the failure of limit-setting. Miller (1990) considers that drawing up a contract between the patient and the admitting doctor is essential to the success of in-patient treatment. Nurnberg & Suh (1980) have specifically stressed the importance of specifying discharge dates soon after initial admission in the context of a focused approach which avoids the historical perspective. Wishnie (1975) sees a two-week hospital admission as ideal. Rosenbluth (1987), in reviewing this literature, concludes that long-term hospital admission should be avoided and that the goals of admission should be limited to diagnosis and stabilisation. He stresses the importance of a clear definition of goals for the patient upon discharge as well as the team's readmission criteria.

The alternative approach to hospital treatment of brief admission at times of crisis has been termed 'adaptational' by Gordon & Beresin (1983). Detailed descriptions of such programmes are also available in the literature (e.g. Sansone & Madakasira, 1990). In some ways the controversy over in-patient treatment maps on to the distinction between supportive interventions as opposed to interpretive psychotherapy in that those in favour of short-term hospital admission tend also to take an anti-regression stance.

The current trend is away from long-term admissions, favouring brief admissions and crisis management (see Miller, 1989, for a review). In the absence of controlled studies with very substantial follow-up periods (perhaps as long as 10 years), it would seem that this change in pattern of care is driven primarily by economic rather than clinical or scientific consideration. There is a great deal of clinical evidence (and some empirical, Vaglum *et al*, 1990) to support the value of therapeutic communities such as the Henderson or the Cassel Hospitals or Dr Jackson's ward at the Maudsley Hospital.

Such centres may function as sanctuaries from an intolerable environment. They can be robust containers for aggressive and self-destructive acts. They can act as training grounds for human relationships, teaching the values of trust, openness and tolerance. Usually, it is combination of all these plus individual and/or group psychotherapy which constitutes the background to substantial clinical improvements following in-patient care.

Cognitive–behavioural approaches

Singular cognitive–behavioural approaches to the management of borderline behaviour are difficult to identify as such strategies tend to be evaluated in a problem-orientated way, and as the nature of the problem behaviours of borderline individuals are so diverse it is highly likely that many behavioural treatment studies of substance abuse, violent or challenging behaviour, eating disorders or depression in fact concern borderline individuals. Cognitive–behavioural psychotherapists are also likely to eschew the use of such a vague and imprecise term as borderline.

Linehan (1987) describes a special treatment package for young, parasuicidal borderline women which combines a structured weekly individual approach with twice-weekly group treatment lasting one year. The bulk of the treatment is aimed at both teaching the patient new coping strategies and helping her to find meaning in the reality of her current life. There is also a substantial supportive component, as well as a contractual agreement specifying the patient's responsibilities. The therapist acts as a selective reinforcer of the patient's behaviours, taking an irreverent attitude towards dysfunctional problem-solving attempts while validating the patient's emotional responses by accurate emotional empathy and accurate reflection of expectations, beliefs and assumptions. The use of behavioural skill-acquisition techniques and problem-solving cognitive-therapy approaches differentiate this package from more traditional forms of supportive psychotherapy. Westen (1991) provides a review of the use of cognitive–behavioural interventions in psychoanalytic psychotherapy, targeting self-regulation and social-cognitive processes, and offering coping strategies to these patients.

The variable success of behavioural approaches (e.g. Turner, 1989) is consistent with that of more traditional psychotherapeutic endeavours. The NIMH multicentre trial of treatment for affective disorders suggests that patients with major depression and borderline personality disorder benefit somewhat more from 16 weeks of cognitive–behavioural therapy than from interpersonal therapy (Shea *et al*, 1990). The differences between the groups were not large, and 16 weeks may not be the ideal duration for measuring the effect of psychotherapy on this severely handicapped group. The current state of understanding is some way from allowing us to identify those patients or those problems best helped by a behavioural approach.

Combinations of drug and psychotherapy

The efficacy of pharmacological treatments in borderlines is now well established and is reviewed elsewhere (Zanarini *et al*, 1988). The rationale and strategies for combining pharmacological treatments with psychotherapy is also beyond the scope of our review, although interested readers should turn to Perry (1990) for a clinical perspective and Elkin *et al* (1988*a,b*) for the conceptual and research problems that combined treatment raises. The nature of the borderline character, however, raises some special psychological problems with regard to the combination of these two forms of therapies.

There is a high rate of affective disorder in those with borderline personality disorder. Some workers have suggested that the relatively high suicide rates (up to 10%) reported in borderline personality disorder (Gunderson, 1984; Akiskal *et al*, 1985; Stone *et al*, 1987) may merely reflect the associated depressive disorders. These are indications that antidepressant medication should prove helpful. The potential for the abuse of prescribed medication, however, is also great.

The aetiology of borderline states is unclear. As with most other psychiatric disorders, a combination of social risk factors (severe abuse in early life), and biological vulnerability (genetic loading for manic–depressive psychosis) is indicated (Stone, 1990). The precise balance of the two probably holds the key to many outstanding controversies concerning diagnostic heterogeneity. It is unlikely, however, that either the presence of known family history or adverse psychosocial circumstances provides unambiguous grounds for recommending either drug treatment or psychotherapy as uniquely suitable.

The majority of borderline individuals have specific problems with dependency on drugs and on individuals and have a potential for abusing both. The act of prescription is thus intricate with borderline patients and invariably has meaning beyond that of a medical treatment whether in the context of psychotherapy or outside it. The borderline patient may be as likely to relate to medication as a transitional object as to a therapist (Adelman, 1985). The patient may use medication to soothe him in the therapist's absence or may attach power to it quite beyond the drug's pharmacological potential and develop a remarkable level of psychological dependence so that he cannot envisage his life without it.

The borderline patient's tendency towards splitting, idealising and denigrating extends to the opposition between pharmacological and psychological treatments. They are likely to speak disparagingly or in glowing terms about both depending on their perception of the views of those they are talking to, and on their current mood. Both psychopharmacologists and psychotherapists, with inadequate experience with this group of patients, may well find themselves either disheartened or part of a collusive attempt to destroy the image and self-respect of a fellow-professional.

Waldinger & Frank (1989) surveyed 40 North American clinicians with experience of psychotherapy with borderline patients in private practice. Of these clinicians, 90% were in the habit of prescribing medication to these patients, often in response to their own or the patient's pessimism about the progress of therapy. Problems of patients abusing their prescribed medication at some time were reported by 87% of therapists. These problems were reported to occur in conjunction with the patient's experience of loss, the patient's expression of strong positive or negative feelings, or the therapist's attempt at setting limits. It is advised that psychotherapists should not be shy of tackling issues raised by medication in the context of therapy.

The long-term follow-up of psychotherapy

There is little by way of specific empirical evidence to guide a clinician to favour a particular therapeutic approach. Kernberg's (1972) report on the findings of the Menninger Clinic Psychotherapy Outcome Study contrasting supportive with interpretive techniques was extremely influential. It revealed that borderlines did best with an expressive analytically orientated technique that utilised meticulous attention to transference issues in conjunction with limit setting. The schizophrenic group with whom the borderline patients were contrasted did poorly with this type of treatment and did better in supportive therapy, a conclusion now confirmed by several follow-up investigations (see Mueser & Berenbaum, 1990).

It is difficult to underestimate the impact of these findings which, in conjunction with the long-term follow-up of borderline patients treated in several psychoanalytic settings (see McGlashen, 1986, Chestnut Lodge; Stone *et al*, 1987; Stone, 1990, Psychiatric Institute), appeared to confirm the value of an interpretive psychotherapeutic approach. These follow-up studies identified a number of borderline patients who benefited dramatically from therapy and an equal number for whom therapy failed miserably. Some of the latter group appeared later to have been 'rescued' through a change in life circumstance, usually an important relationship.

All studies with borderlines emphasise the importance of extremely long follow-ups as the benefits of therapy may not be apparent upon discharge. Of course, longer-term follow-ups are very hard to interpret because of intervening variables, and none of these studies can be considered much more than studies of prognosis. A five-year follow-up study of treatment offered at the Cassel Hospital (Richmond, UK) found that those patients who on admission showed borderline pathology tended to be those who showed a poor response to the in-patient psychotherapeutic programme offered and did no better at the Cassel than at a standard psychiatric institution (Rosser *et al*, 1987). Stone's (1990) 16-year follow-up takes a longer-term perspective and finds that patients use long-term hospital admission (8–18 months) as a springboard to self-sufficiency and a move towards autonomy and independence.

Wallerstein's (1986) follow-up of the Menninger sample complicates the issue further as it shows that the treatment outcomes of interpretively and supportively treated patients tend to converge rather than diverge over the course of the follow-up. Wallerstein's monograph, which is a monumental contribution to the literature on borderline patients, concludes with far less unequivocal support for the long-term superiority of insight-orientated treatments. The contrasting conclusions of Kernberg's (1972) and Wallerstein's (1986) follow-up should be considered in the context of what is now known to be the natural course of the disorder. Stone's (1990) 20-year follow-up of 502 patients strongly indicates that the long-term prognosis is good, and approximately 66% of patients end up functioning normally or only with minimal symptoms. It is as if maturation and decreased energy levels and impulsivity with ageing brought about a developmental cure (Frances, 1990). Wallerstein's later follow-up, showing the surprising efficacy of supportive interventions, had a greater chance to capitalise on the tendency for spontaneous remission. Kernberg's earlier findings perhaps underscore the capacity of expressive techniques to 'accelerate' the process of natural cure.

Empirical data are urgently required to identify which subgroup of borderline patients is most likely to respond to psychotherapy. We may hope that Kernberg's (1992) planned outcome trial will yield more definite conclusions. Outcome research with this group of patients, however, will always be problematic (Elkin *et al*, 1988*a,b*). Systematic studies show that early drop-out rates, even in the most expert settings, are unusually high (around 35% in the first six months of treatment, e.g. Gunderson *et al*, 1989; Tucker *et al*, 1987). They are also, as Stone (1986) points out, the patients least likely to allow themselves to be randomised, and those who do are hardly likely to constitute a representative sample.

These problems suggest that a multi-centre quasi-experimental comparison of ordinary treatment strategies performed on a large scale may in the long run be more informative than single randomised control trials. In the meantime, perhaps all we can do here is draw together the results of follow-up and outcome studies to date (Akiskal, 1981; Wallerstein, 1986; McGlashan, 1986, 1987; Paris *et al*, 1987; Stone, 1987*b*, 1990; McGlashan & Heinssen, 1988) and received clinical wisdom (e.g. Meissner, 1987) to make practical recommendations concerning psychotherapy for borderline patients.

> (a) Some borderline patients are treatable in psychotherapy but these probably fall into a higher-order, less ill group.
> (b) The aim of psychotherapy may as often be the reduction of suicide risk as the alleviation of symptoms (particularly for patients aged under 30 years).

(c) Patients with chronic depression, high motivation, high psychological-mindedness, low impulsivity and relatively more secure living environment may be the most appropriate subgroup for expressive therapy.

(d) Patients with impulse control disorders (substance abuse, eating disorders, etc.) appear to benefit from help from a limit-setting group or a therapist who is supportive of their attempts to struggle with uncontrollable impulses.

(e) If interpretive–expressive therapy is used, focus should be placed upon the unconscious aspects of current human relationships, particularly the relationship between patient and therapist.

(f) Therapist commitment and enthusiasm appears to be of special significance and subjective aspects of patient–therapist 'fit' (complementarity) may be particularly important for this group of patients.

(g) Patients whose problems include substance abuse require their dependency problems to be specifically addressed before commencing psychotherapy.

Unfortunately, suitability (or otherwise) for treatment will most commonly become self-evident only after several months of heartache, of struggling with negative therapeutic reaction, of massive distress during breaks, of insistent demands for special treatment, of severe resistances including the constant devaluation of the therapist and periodic narcissistic rage, of serious self-destructive behaviours, non-adherence to medical recommendations, of suicidal gestures, and sometimes physical violence. All psychotherapists of the borderline patient are likely to encounter such phenomena. Sadly, none appears to guarantee either therapeutic success or failure.

Acknowledgements

The authors wish to express their gratitude to Professor Peter Tyrer, Dr George Moran and two anonymous referees for helpful comments on earlier drafts of this manuscript. We also wish to thank Julia Curl for help in preparing the manuscript.

References

ABEND, S. M., PORDER, M. S. & WILLICK, M. S. (1983) *Borderline Patients: Psychoanalytic Perspectives*. Monograph 7 of the Kris Study Group. New York: International Universities Press.

ADELMAN, A. (1985) Pills as transitional objects: a dynamic understanding of the use of medication in psychotherapy. *Psychiatry*, **48**, 246–253.

ADLER, G. (1977) Hospital management of borderline patients and its relation to psychotherapy. In *Borderline Personality Disorders* (ed. P. Hartocollis), pp. 307–323. New York: International Universities Press.

—— (1986) *Borderline Psychopathology and its Treatment*. New York: Jason Aronson.

AKISKAL, H. S. (1981) Subaffective disorders: dysthymic, cyclothymic, and bipolar II disorders in the "borderline" realm. *Psychiatric Clinics of North America*, **4**, 25–36.
——, CHEN, S. E., DAVIS, G. C., *et al* (1985) Borderline: an adjective in search of a noun. *Journal of Clinical Psychiatry*, **46**, 41–48.
ALEXANDER, F. (1957) *Psychoanalysis and Psychotherapy*. London: George Allen.
ANDROLUNIS, P. A., GLUECK, B. C., STROEBEL, C. F., *et al* (1981) Organic brain dysfunction and borderline personality disorder. *Psychiatric Clinics of North America*, **4**, 61–66.
ARONSON, T. A. (1989) A critical review of psychotherapeutic treatments of the borderline personality: historical trends and future directions. *Journal of Nervous and Mental Disease*, **177**, 511–527.
BACAL, H. (1981) Notes on some therapeutic challenges in the analysis of severely regressed patients. *Psychoanalytical Inquiry*, **1**, 29–56.
BARON, J., GRUEN, R., ASNIS, L., *et al* (1985) Familial transmission of schizotypal and borderline personality disorders. *American Journal of Psychiatry*, **142**, 927–934.
BARON-COHEN, S. (1987) Autism and symbolic play. *British Journal of Developmental Psychology*, **5**, 139–148.
—— (1989) The autistic child's theory of mind: a case of specific developmental delay. *Journal of Child Psychology and Psychiatry*, **30**, 285–298.
——, LESLIE, A. M. & FRITH, U. (1985) Does the autistic child have a "theory of mind"? *Cognition*, **21**, 37–46.
BION, W. R. (1957) Differentiation of the psychotic from the non-psychotic personalities. *International Journal of Psychoanalysis*, **38**, 266–275.
—— (1959) Attacks on linking. *International Journal of Psychoanalysis*, **40**, 308–315.
—— (1962) *Learning from Experience*. London: Heinemann.
BOYER, L. B. (1987) Regression and countertransference in the treatment of a borderline patient. In *The Borderline Patient: Emerging Concepts in Diagnosis, Psychodynamics and Treatment* (eds J. S. Grotstein, M. F. Solomon & J. A. Lang). Hillsdale, NJ: The Analytic Press.
BRANDCHAFT, B. & STOLOROW, R. D. (1987) The borderline concept: An intersubjective view. In *The Borderline Patient: Emerging Concepts in Diagnosis, Psychodynamics and Treatment, Vol. 2* (eds J. S. Grotstein, M. F. Solomon & J. A. Lang), pp. 103–126. Hillsdale, NJ: The Analytic Press.
BRENMAN, E. (1980) The value of reconstruction in adult psychoanalysis. *International Journal of Psychoanalysis*, **61**, 53–60.
BROWN, L. J. (1981) A short-term hospital program preparing borderline and schizophrenic patients for intensive psychotherapy. *Psychiatry*, **44**, 327–336.
BROWN, S. L. (1987) Family therapy and the borderline patient. In *The Borderline Patient: Emerging Concepts in Diagnosis, Psychodynamics and Treatment, Vol. 2* (eds J. S. Grotstein, M. F. Solomon & J. A. Lang), pp. 201–210. Hillsdale, NJ: The Analytic Press.
BUIE, D. H. & ADLER, G. (1982) Definitive treatment of the borderline personality. *International Journal of Psychoanalytic Psychotherapy*, **9**, 51–87.
CHATHAM, P. (1985) *Treatment of the Borderline Personality*. New York: Aronson.
CHESSICK, R. D. (1979) A practical approach to the psychotherapy of the borderline patient. *American Journal of Psychiatry*, **33**, 531–546.
EKSTEIN, R. & WALLERSTEIN, R. (1954) Observations of the psychology of borderline and psychotic children. *Psychoanalytic Study of the Child*, **9**, 344–369.
ELKIN, I., PILKONIS, P. A., DOCHERTY, J. P., *et al* (1988*a*) Conceptual and methodological issues in comparative studies of psychotherapy and pharmacotherapy, I: Active ingredients and mechanisms of change. *American Journal of Psychiatry*, **145**, 909–917.
——, ——, ——, *et al* (1988*b*) Conceptual and methodological issues in comparative studies of psychotherapy and pharmacotherapy, II: Nature and timing of treatment effects. *American Journal of Psychiatry*, **145**, 1070–1076.
FEDERN, P. (1947) Principles of psychotherapy in latent schizophrenia. *American Journal of Psychotherapy*, **1**, 129–144.
FELDMAN, R. D. & GUTTMAN, H. A. (1984) Families of borderline patients: literal-minded parents, borderline parents and parental protectiveness. *American Journal of Psychiatry*, **141**, 1392–1396.

FENTON, W. S. & MCGLASHEN, T. H. (1990) Longterm residential care: treatment of choice for refractory character disorders. *Psychiatric Annals*, **20**, 44–49.

FONAGY, P. (1982) Psychoanalysis and empirical science. *International Review of Psychoanalysis*, **9**, 125–145.

—— (1989) On tolerating mental states. *Bulletin of the Anna Freud Centre*, **12**, 91–115.

—— (1991) Thinking about thinking: some clinical and theoretical considerations concerning the treatment of a borderline patient. *International Journal of Psychoanalysis*, **72**, 639–656.

—— & HIGGITT, A. (1990) A developmental perspective on borderline personality disorder. *Revue Internationale de Psychopathologie*, **1**, 125–159.

—— & MORAN, G. M. (1991) Understanding psychic change in child psychoanalysis. *International Journal of Psychoanalysis*, **72**, 15–22.

——, STEELE, M., STEELE, H., *et al* (1991) The capacity for understanding mental states: the reflective self in parent and child and its significance for security of attachment. *Infant Mental Health Journal*, **13**, 200–216.

FRANCES, A. J. (1990) Foreword. In *The Fate of Borderline Patients* (ed. M. H. Stone). New York: Guilford Press.

—— & WIDIGER, T. (1986) The classification of personality disorders: an overview of problems and solutions. In *American Psychiatric Association Annual Review, Vol. 5* (eds A. J. Frances & R. E. Hales). Washington DC: American Psychiatric Press.

FRANK, J. D. (1988) Specific and non-specific factors in psychotherapy. *Current Opinion in Psychiatry*, **1**, 289–292.

FREUD, A. (1970) *The Writings of Anna Freud: Vol. 8. Psychoanalytic Psychology of Normal Development 1970–1980*. London: Hogarth Press and the Institute of Psychoanalysis.

FRIEDMAN, H. J. (1975) Psychotherapy of borderline patients: the influence of theory on technique. *American Journal of Psychiatry*, **132**, 1048–1052.

FROSCH, J. (1988) Psychotic character versus borderline. *International Journal of Psychoanalysis*, **69**, 445–456.

FYER, M. R., FRANCES, A. J., SULLIVAN, T., *et al* (1988) Comorbidity of borderline personality disorder. *Archives of General Psychiatry*, **45**, 348–352.

GABBARD, G. O. (1989) Splitting in hospital treatment. *American Journal of Psychiatry*, **146**, 444–451.

GIOVACCHINI, P. L. (1979) *Treatment of Primitive Mental States*. New York: Aronson.

—— (1987) The 'unreasonable' patient and the psychotic transference. In *The Borderline Patient: Emerging Concepts in Diagnosis, Psychodynamics and Treatment, Vol. 1* (eds J. S. Grotstein, M. F. Solomon & J. A. Lang), pp. 59–68. Hillsdale, NJ: The Analytic Press.

GORDON, C. & BERESIN, E. (1983) Conflicting treatment models for the inpatient management of borderline patients. *American Journal of Psychiatry*, **140**, 979–983.

GREBEN, S. E. (1983) The multi-dimensional inpatient treatment of severe character disorders. *Canadian Journal of Psychiatry*, **28**, 97–101.

GRINKER, R. R. (1975) Neurosis, psychosis and the borderline states. In *Comprehensive Textbook of Psychiatry* (eds A. M. Freedman, H. I. Kaplan & B. J. Saddock), pp. 845–850. Baltimore: Williams and Wilkins.

GROBMAN, J. (1980) The borderline patient in group psychotherapy: a case report. *International Journal of Group Psychotherapy*, **30**, 299–318.

GROTSTEIN, J. S., LANG, J. A. & SOLOMON, M. F. (1987) Convergence and controversy: II. Treatment of the borderline. In *The Borderline Patient: Emerging Concepts in Diagnosis, Psychodynamics and Treatment, Vol. 1* (eds J. S. Grotstein, M. F. Solomon & J. A. Lang), pp. 261–310. Hillsdale, NJ: The Analytic Press.

GUNDERSON, J. G. (1984) *Borderline Personality Disorder*. Washington DC: American Psychiatric Press.

—— & ZANARINI, M. C. (1987) Current overview of borderline diagnosis. *Journal of Clinical Psychiatry*, **48** (suppl.), 5–11.

——, FRANK, A. F., RONNINGSTAM, E. F., *et al* (1989) Early discontinuance of borderline patients from psychotherapy. *Journal of Nervous and Mental Disease*, **177**, 38–42.

HARRIS, P. L. (1989) *Children and Emotion: The Development of Psychological Understanding*. Oxford: Basil Blackwell.

HARTOCOLLIS, P. (1980) Long-term hospital treatment for adult patients with borderline and narcissistic personality disorders. *Bulletin of the Menninger Clinic*, **44**, 212–226.

HAUGSGJERD, S. (1987) Toward a theory for milieu treatment of hospitalized borderline patients. In *The Borderline Patient: Emerging Concepts in Diagnosis, Psychodynamics and Treatment, Vol. 2* (eds J. S. Grotstein, M. F. Solomon & J. A. Lang), pp. 211–226. Hillsdale NJ: Analytic Press.

HERMAN, J. L., PERRY, C. & VAN DER KOLK, B. A. (1989) Childhood trauma in borderline personality disorder. *American Journal of Psychiatry*, **146**, 490–495.

HORNER, A. J. (1975) A characterological contraindication for group psychotherapy. *Journal of American Academy of Psychoanalysis*, **3**, 301–305.

HORWITZ, L. (1977) A group-centred approach to group psychotherapy. *International Journal of Group Psychotherapy*, **27**, 423–439.

—— (1987) Indications for group psychotherapy with borderline and narcissistic patients. *Bulletin of the Menninger Clinic*, **51**, 248–260.

JACKSON, M. & PINES, M. (1986) In-patient treatment of borderline personality. *Neurologia et Psychiatrica*, **9**, 54–87.

JONES, S. A. (1987) Family therapy with borderline and narcissistic patients. *Bulletin of the Menninger Clinic*, **51**, 285–295.

KENNEDY, R. (1989) *The Family as In-patient*. London: Free Association Books.

KERNBERG, O. (1967) Borderline personality organisation. *Journal of the American Psychoanalytic Association*, **15**, 641–685.

—— (1972) Final report of the Menninger Foundation's psychotherapy research project: summary and conclusions. *Bulletin of the Menninger Clinic*, **36**, 181–195.

—— (1975) *Borderline Conditions and Pathological Narcissism*. New York: Jason Aronson.

—— (1976) Technical considerations in the treatment of borderline personality organisation. *Journal of the American Psychoanalytic Association*, **24**, 795–829.

—— (1984) *Severe Personality Disorders: Psychotherapeutic Strategies*. New Haven, CT: Yale University Press.

—— (1987) Borderline personality disorder: a psychodynamic approach. *Journal of Personality Disorders*, **1**, 344–346.

—— (1992) Measurements of change in the psychodynamic psychotherapy of the borderline patient. In *New Approaches to Psychoanalytic Research* (eds P. Fonagy & O. Kernberg). London: IPA (in press).

——, SELZER, M., KOENIGSBERG, H. W., *et al* (1989) *Psychodynamic Psychotherapy of Borderline Patients*. New York: Basic Books.

KIBEL, H. D. (1988) Combined individual and group treatment with borderline and narcissistic patients. *Borderline and Narcissistic Patients in Therapy* (ed. N. Slavinska-Holy), pp. 17–45. Madison, Connecticut: International Universities Press, Inc.

KING, P. (1978) Affective response of the analyst to the patient's communications. *International Journal of Psychoanalysis*, **59**, 329–334.

KLEIN, M. (1940) Mourning and its relation to manic–depressive states. In *The Writings of Melanie Klein*. London: Hogarth Press.

—— (1950) *Contributions to Psycho-Analysis, 1921–1945*. London: Hogarth Press.

—— (1957) Envy and gratitude. In *The Writings of Melanie Klein, Vol. 3*, pp. 176–235. London: Hogarth Press.

KNIGHT, R. (1953) Borderline states. *Bulletin of the Menninger Clinic*, **17**, 1–12.

KOHUT, H. (1971) *The Analysis of the Self*. New York: International Universities Press.

—— (1977) *The Restoration of the Self*. New York: International Universities Press.

—— (1984) *How Does Analysis Cure?* Chicago: University of Chicago Press.

KUTTER, P. (1982) *Basic Aspects of Psychoanalytic Group Therapy*. London: Routledge & Kegan Paul.

LANG, J. A., GROTSTEIN, J. S. & SOLOMON, M. F. (1987) Convergence and controversy: 1. Theory of the borderline. In *The Borderline Patient: Emerging Concepts in Diagnosis, Psychodynamics and Treatment, Vol. 1* (eds J. S. Grotstein, M. F. Solomon & J. A. Lang), pp. 385–422. Hillsdale, NJ: The Analytic Press.

LANSKY, M. R. (1987) Shame in the family relationships of borderline patients. In *The Borderline Patient: Emerging Concepts in Diagnosis, Psychodynamics and Treatment, Vol. 2* (eds J. S. Grotstein, M. F. Solomon & J. A. Lang), pp. 187–200. Hillsdale, NJ: The Analytic Press.

—— (1989) The subacute hospital treatment of the borderline patient: Management of suicidal crisis by family intervention. *Hillside Journal of Clinical Psychiatry*, **11**, 81–97.

LINEHAN, M. M. (1987) Dialectical behavioral therapy: a cognitive behavioral approach to parasuicide. *Journal of Personality Disorders*, **1**, 328–333.

LORANGER, A., OLDHAM, J. & TULLIS, E. (1982) Familial transmission of DSM–III borderline personality disorder. *Archives of General Psychiatry*, **39**, 795–799.

MACASKILL, N. D. (1980) The narcissistic core as a focus in the group therapy of the borderline patient. *British Journal of Medical Psychology*, **53**, 137–143.

—— (1982) Therapeutic factors in group therapy with borderline patients. *International Journal of Group Psychotherapy*, **32**, 61–74.

McGLASHAN, T. H. (1986) The Chestnut Lodge follow-up study: III. Long-term outcome of borderline personalities. *Archives of General Psychiatry*, **43**, 20–30.

—— (1987) Borderline personality disorder and unipolar affective disorder: longterm effects of co-morbidity. *Journal of Nervous and Mental Disease*, **175**, 467–473.

—— & HEINSSEN, R. K. (1988) Hospital discharge status and longterm outcome for patients with schizophrenia, schizoaffective disorder, borderline personality disorder and unipolar affective disorder. *Archives of General Psychiatry*, **45**, 363–368.

McREYNOLDS, P. (1989) Diagnosis and clinical assessment: current status and major issues. *Annual Review of Psychology*, **40**, 83–108.

MAHLER, M. S., PINE, F. & BERGMAN, A. (1975) *The Psychological Birth of the Human Infant*. New York: Basic Books.

—— & KAPLAN, L. (1977) Developmental aspects in the assessment of narcissistic and so-called borderline personalities. In *Borderline Personality Disorders* (ed. P. Hartocollis), pp. 71–85. New York: International Universities Press.

MAIN, T. (1957) The ailment. *British Journal of Medical Psychology*, **30**, 129–145.

MANDELBAUM, A. (1977) The family treatment of the borderline patient. In *Borderline Personality Disorders* (ed. P. Hartocollis), pp. 423–438. New York: International Universities Press.

MASTERSON, J. (1976) *Psychotherapy of the Borderline Adult*. New York: Brunner/Mazel.

—— (1981) *The Narcissistic and Borderline Disorders*. New York: Brunner/Mazel.

—— & COSTELLO, J. L. (1980) *From Borderline Adolescent to Functioning Adult, the Test of Time*. New York: Brunner/Mazel.

MEISSNER, W. W. (1987) A contribution to the issues of borderline diagnosis. In *The Borderline Patient: Emerging Concepts in Diagnosis, Psychodynamics and Treatment, Vol. 1* (eds J. S. Grotstein, M. F. Solomon & J. A. Lang), pp. 73–82. Hillsdale, NJ: The Analytic Press.

MILLER, L. J. (1989) Inpatient management of borderline personality disorder: a review and update. *Journal of Personality Disorders*, **3**, 122–134.

—— (1990) The formal treatment contract in the inpatient management of borderline personality disorder. *Hospital and Community Psychiatry*, **41**, 985–987.

MODELL, A. (1963) Primitive object relationships and the predisposition to schizophrenia. *International Journal of Psychoanalysis*, **44**, 282–291.

—— (1968) *Object Love and Reality*. New York: International Universities Press.

MUESER, K. T. & BERENBAUM, H. (1990) Psychodynamic treatment of schizophrenia: Is there a future? *Psychological Medicine*, **20**, 253–262.

MURRAY, L. (1988) Effects of post-natal depression on infant development: Direct studies of early mother–infant interactions. In *Motherhood and Mental Illness* (eds R. Kumar & I. F. Brockington). London: Wright.

NURNBERG, H. G. & SUH, R. (1980) Limits: Short-term treatment of hospitalized borderline patients. *Comprehensive Psychiatry*, **21**, 70–80.

O'SHAUGHNESSY, E. (1981) A clinical study of a defensive organization. *International Journal of Psychoanalysis*, **62**, 359–369.

OGATA, S. N., SILK, K. R., GOODRICH, S., *et al* (1990) Childhood sexual and physical abuse in adult patients with borderline personality disorder. *American Journal of Psychiatry*, **147**, 1008–1013.

PALOMBO, J. (1987) Selfobject transference in the treatment of borderline neurocognitively impaired children. In *The Borderline Patient: Emerging Concepts in Diagnosis, Psychodynamics and Treatment, Vol. 1* (eds J. S. Grotstein, M. F. Solomon & J. A. Lang), pp. 317–346. Hillsdale, NJ: The Analytic Press.

PARIS, J., BROWN, R. & NOWLIS, D. (1987) Longterm follow-up of borderline patients in a general hospital. *Comprehensive Psychiatry*, **28**, 530–535.

PERRY, J. C. (1985) Depression in borderline personality disorder: lifetime prevalence at interview and longitudinal course of symptoms. *American Journal of Psychiatry*, **142**, 15–21.

—— & COOPER, S. H. (1986) A preliminary report on defenses and conflicts associated with borderline personality disorder. *Journal of the American Psychoanalytic Association*, **34**, 863–893.

PERRY, S. (1990) Combining antidepressants and psychotherapy: rationale and strategies. *Journal of Clinical Psychiatry*, **51**, (suppl.), 16–20.

PINES, M. (1978) Group analytic psychotherapy of the borderline patient. *Group Analysis*, **11**, 115–126.

—— (1990) Group analytic psychotherapy and the borderline patient. In *The Difficult Patient In Group: Group Psychotherapy with Borderline and Narcissistic Disorders* (eds B. E. Roth, W. N. Stone & H. D. Kibel), pp. 31–44. Madison, Connecticut: International Universities Press, Inc.

POPE, H. G., FRANKENBURG, F. R., HUDSON, J. I., et al (1987) Is bulimia associated with borderline personality disorder? A controlled study. *Journal of Clinical Psychiatry*, **48**, 181–184.

RACKER, H. (1968) *Transference and Countertransference*. London: Hogarth Press.

REY, J. H. (1979) Schizoid phenomena in the borderline. In *Advances in the Psychotherapy of the Borderline Patient* (eds J. le Boit & A. Lapponi), pp. 449–484. New York: Jason Aronson.

ROCKLAND, L. H. (1987) A supportive approach: psychodynamically oriented supportive therapy – treatment of borderline patients who self-mutilate. *Journal of Personality Disorders*, **1**, 350–353.

ROSENBLUTH, M. (1987) The inpatient treatment of the borderline personality disorder: a critical review and discussion of aftercare implications. *Canadian Journal of Psychiatry*, **32**, 228–237.

ROSENFELD, H. (1978) Notes on the psychopathology and psychoanalytic treatment of some borderline patients. *International Journal of Psychoanalysis*, **59**, 215–221.

—— (1987) *Impasse and Interpretation*. London: Tavistock Publications.

ROSSER, R. M., BIRCH, S., BOND, H., et al (1987) Five year follow-up of patients treated with inpatient psychotherapy at the Cassel Hospital for Nervous Diseases. *Journal of the Royal Society of Medicine*, **80**, 549–555.

ROTH, B. E. (1980) Understanding the development of a homogenous identity impaired group through countertransference phenomena. *International Journal of Group Psychotherapy*, **30**, 404–412.

—— (1990) The group that would not relate to itself. In *The Difficult Patient In Group: Group Psychotherapy with Borderline and Narcissistic Disorders* (eds B. E. Roth, W. N. Stone & H. D. Kibel), pp. 127–155. Madison, Connecticut: International Universities Press, Inc.

RUTTER, M. (1987) Temperament, personality and personality disorder. *British Journal of Psychiatry*, **150**, 443–458.

SANDLER, J. (1976a) Countertransference and role-responsiveness. *International Review of Psychoanalysis*, **3**, 43–47.

—— (1976b) Actualisation and object relationships. *Journal of the Philadelphia Association of Psychoanalysis*, **3**, 59–70.

—— (1983) Reflections on some relations between psychoanalytic concepts and psychoanalytic practice. *International Journal of Psychoanalysis*, **64**, 35–45.

—— (1987) *Projection, Identification, Projective Identification*. London: Karnac Books.

SANSONE, R. A. & MADOKASIRA, S. (1990) Borderline personality disorder: guidelines for evaluation and brief inpatient management. *Psychiatric Hospital*, **21**, 65–69.

SCHANE, M. & KOVEL, V. (1988) Family therapy in severe personality disorders. *International Journal of Family Psychiatry*, **9**, 241–258.

SCHMIDEBERG, M. (1947) The treatment of psychopathic and borderline patients. *American Journal of Psychotherapy*, **1**, 45–71.

SEARLES, H. F. (1986) *My Work with Borderline Patients*. Northvale, NJ: Jacob Aronson.

SEGAL, H. (1964) *Introduction to the Work of Melanie Klein*. New York: Basic Books.

—— (1972) A delusional system as a defence against the emergence of a catastrophic situation. *International Journal of Psychoanalysis*, **53**, 393–402.

SELZER, M. A., KOENIGSBERG, H. W. & KERNBERG, O. F. (1987) The initial contract in the treatment of borderline patients. *American Journal of Psychiatry*, **144**, 927–930.

SHAPIRO, T. (1983) The borderline syndrome in children: a critique. In *The Borderline Child* (ed. K. Robson), pp. 11–30. New York: McGraw Hill.

—— (1989) Psychoanalytic classification and empiricism with borderline personality disorder as a model. *Journal of Consulting and Clinical Psychology*, **57**, 187–194.

SHEA, M. T., PILKONIS, P. A., BECKHAM, E., *et al* (1990) Personality disorders and treatment outcome in the NIMH treatment of depression collaborative research program. *American Journal of Psychiatry*, **147**, 711–718.

SHEARER, S. L., PETERS, C. P., QUAYTMAN, M. S., *et al* (1990) Frequency and correlates of childhood sexual and physical abuse histories in adult female borderline patients. *American Journal of Psychiatry*, **147**, 214–216.

SIEVER, L. J. & GUNDERSON, J. G. (1979) Genetic determinants of borderline conditions. *Schizophrenia Bulletin*, **5**, 59–86.

SILVER, D. (1983) Psychotherapy of the characterologically difficult patient. *Canadian Journal of Psychiatry*, **28**, 513–521.

SINGER, M. (1987) Inpatient hospitalization for borderline patients: process and dynamics of change in long- and short-term Treatment. In *The Borderline Patient: Emerging Concepts in Diagnosis, Psychodynamics and Treatment, Vol. 2* (eds J. S. Grotstein, M. F. Solomon & J. A. Lang), pp. 227–242. Hillsdale, NJ: The Analytic Press.

SOHN, L. (1985) Narcissistic organisation, projective identification and the formation of the identificate. *International Journal of Psychoanalysis*, **66**, 201–213.

SOLOFF, P. H. & MILLWARD, J. W. (1983) Psychiatric disorders in the families of borderline patients. *Archives of General Psychiatry*, **40**, 37–44.

SOLOMON, M. F. (1987) Therapeutic treatment of borderline patients by non-analytic practioners. In *The Borderline Patient: Emerging Concepts in Diagnosis, Psychodynamics and Treatment, Vol. 2* (eds J. S. Grotstein, M. F. Solomon & J. A. Lang), pp. 243–260. Hillsdale, NJ: The Analytic Press.

SPILLIUS, E. B. (1988) General introduction. In *Melanie Klein Today: Developments in Theory and Practice. Vol. 1: Mainly Theory* (ed. E. B. Spillius). London: Routledge.

STEINER, J. (1979) The border between the paranoid–schizoid and the depressive positions in the borderline patient. *British Journal of Medical Psychology*, **52**, 385–391.

—— (1987) The interplay between pathological organisations and the paranoid–schizoid and depressive positions. *International Journal of Psychoanalysis*, **68**, 69–80.

STERN, D. (1985) *The Interpersonal World of the Child*. New York: Basic Books.

STONE, M. H. (1977) The borderline syndrome: evolution of the term, genetic aspects and prognosis. *American Journal of Psychotherapy*, **31**, 345–365.

—— (ed.) (1986) *Essential Papers on Borderline Disorders: One Hundred Years at the Border*. New York: New York University Press.

—— (1987a) Systems for defining a borderline case. In *The Borderline Patient: Emerging Concepts in Diagnosis, Psychodynamics and Treatment* (eds J. S. Grotstein, M. F. Solomon & J. A. Lang), pp. 13–35. Hillsdale, NJ: The Analytic Press.

—— (1987b) Psychotherapy of borderline patients in light of longterm follow-up. *Bulletin of the Menninger Clinic*, **51**, 231–247.

—— (1989) Long-term follow-up of narcissistic borderline patients. *Psychiatric Clinics of North America*, **12**, 621–641.

——, HURT, S. W. & STONE, D. K. (1987) The PI 500: Long-term follow-up of borderline inpatients meeting DSM–III criteria: I. Global outcome. *Journal of Personality Disorders*, **1**, 291–298.

—— (1990) *The Fate of Borderline Patients: Successful Outcome and Psychiatric Practice*. New York: The Guilford Press.

STONE, W. N. & GUSTAFSON, J. P. (1982) Technique in group psychotherapy of narcissistic and borderline patients. *International Journal of Group Psychotherapy*, **32**, 29–47.

SWARTZ, M., BLAZER, D., GEORGE, L., *et al* (1990) Estimating the prevalence of borderline personality disorder in the community. *Journal of Personality Disorders*, **4**, 257–272.

SWETT, C., SURREY, J. & COHEN, C. (1990) Sexual and physical abuse histories and psychiatric symptoms among male psychiatric outpatients. *American Journal of Psychiatry*, **147**, 632–636.

TARNOPOLSKY, A. & BERELOWITZ, M. (1987) Borderline personality: a review of recent research. *British Journal of Psychiatry*, **151**, 724–734.

TAUSK, V. (1919) On the origin of the 'influencing machine' in schizophrenia. Reprinted (1933) in *Psychoanalytic Quarterly*, **2**, 519–556.

TOLPIN, M. (1987) Injured self-cohesion: Developmental, clinical and theoretical perspectives. In *The Borderline Patient: Emerging Concepts in Diagnosis, Psychodynamics and Treatment, Vol. 1* (eds J. S. Grotstein, M. F. Solomon & J. A. Lang), pp. 233–249. Hillsdale, NJ: The Analytic Press.

TORGERSEN, S. (1984) Genetic and nosological aspects of schizotypal and borderline personality disorders. *Archives of General Psychiatry*, **41**, 546–554.

TREVARTHEN, C. (1980) The foundations of intersubjectivity: development of interpersonal and cooperative understanding in infants. In *The Social Foundations of Language and Thought* (ed. D. R. Olson). Toronto: Norton.

TUCKER, L., BAUER, S. F., WAGNER, S., et al (1987) Long-term hospital treatment of borderline patients: a descriptive outcome study. *American Journal of Psychiatry*, **144**, 1443–1448.

TURNER, R. M. (1989) Case study evaluations of a bio-cognitive–behavioral approach to the treatment of borderline personality disorder. *Behavior Therapy*, **20**, 477–489.

TUTTMAN, S. (1990) Principles of psychoanalytic group therapy applied to the treatment of borderline and narcissistic disorders. In *The Difficult Patient In Group: Group Psychotherapy with Borderline and Narcissistic Disorders* (eds B. E. Roth, W. N. Stone & H. D. Kibel), pp. 7–29. Madison, Connecticut: International Universities Press, Inc.

TYRER, P. (1989) Clinical importance of personality disorder. *Current Opinion in Psychiatry*, **2**, 240–243.

———, SEIVEWRIGHT, N., FERGUSON, B., et al (1990) The Nottingham study of neurotic disorder: relationship between personality status and symptoms. *Psychological Medicine*, **20**, 423–431.

VAGLUM, P., FRIIS, S., IMON, T., et al (1990) Treatment response of severe and nonsevere personality disorders in a therapeutic community day unit. *Journal of Personality Disorders*, **4**, 161–172.

VOLKAN, V. D. (1987) Six constellations of psychoanalytic psychotherapy of borderline patients. In *The Borderline Patient: Emerging Concepts in Diagnosis, Psychodynamics and Treatment, Vol. 2* (eds J. S. Grotstein, M. F. Solomon & J. A. Lang), pp. 5–24. Hillsdale, NJ: The Analytic Press.

WALDINGER, R. J. (1987) Intensive psychodynamic therapy with borderline patients: an overview. *American Journal of Psychiatry*, **144**, 267–274.

——— & FRANK, A. F. (1989) Clinicians' experiences in combining medication and psycho-therapy in the treatment of borderline patients. *Hospital and Community Psychiatry*, **40**, 712–718.

WALLERSTEIN, R. (1986) *Forty-two Lives in Treatment.* New York: Guilford Press.

——— (1988) One psychoanalysis or many? *International Journal of Psychoanalysis*, **69**, 5–21.

——— (1990) Psychoanalysis: the common ground. *International Journal of Psychoanalysis*, **71**, 3–20.

WEILER, M. A., VAL, E. R., GAVIRIA, M., et al (1988) Panic in borderline personality disorder. *Psychiatric Journal of the University of Ottowa*, **13**, 140–143.

WESTEN, D. (1991) Cognitive–behavioural interventions in the psychoanalytic psychotherapy of borderline personality disorders. *Clinical Psychology Review*, **11**, 211–230.

———, LUNDOLPH, P., MISLE, B., et al (1990) Physical and sexual abuse in adolescent girls with borderline personality disorder. *American Journal of Orthopsychiatry*, **60**, 55–66.

WIDIGER, T. A., FRANCES, A., SPITZER, R. L., et al (1988) The DSM-III personality disorders: an overview. *American Journal of Psychiatry*, **145**, 786–795.

WINNICOTT, D. W. (1949) Hate in the countertransference. *International Journal of Psychoanalysis*, **30**, 69–75.

——— (1953) Transitional objects and transitional phenomena. *International Journal of Psychoanalysis*, **34**, 89–97.

——— (1960) The theory of the parent–infant relationship. In *The Maturational Process and the Facilitating Environment*, pp. 37–55. New York: International Universities Press.

—— (1965) *The Maturational Process and the Facilitating Environment*. London: Hogarth Press.

WISHNIE, H. A. (1975) Inpatient therapy with borderline patients. In *Borderline States in Psychiatry* (ed. J. E. Mack). New York: Grune and Stratton.

WONG, N. (1980) Combined group and individual treatment of borderline and narcissistic patients: heterogenous vs. homogenous groups. *International Journal of Group Psychotherapy*, **30**, 389–404.

—— (1988) Combined individual and group treatment with borderline and narcissistic patients. In *Borderline and Narcissistic Patients in Therapy* (ed. N. Slavinska-Holy). Madison: Connecticut: IUP.

WORLD HEALTH ORGANIZATION (1986) *Draft of Chapter V*. Geneva: WHO.

YALOM, I. D. (1975) *The Theory and Practice of Group Psychotherapy* (2nd edn). New York: Basic Books.

ZANARINI, M. C., FRANKENBERG, F. R. & GUNDERSON, J. G. (1988) Pharmacotherapy of borderline patients. *Comprehensive Psychiatry*, **29**, 372–378.

——, GUNDERSON, J. G., FRANKENBURG, F. R., *et al* (1990*a*) Discriminating borderline personality disorder from other Axis II disorders. *American Journal of Psychiatry*, **147**, 161–167.

——, —— & —— (1990*b*) Cognitive features of borderline personality disorder. *American Journal of Psychiatry*, **147**, 57–63.

ZETZEL, E. R. (1971) A developmental approach to the borderline patient. *American Journal of Psychiatry*, **127**, 867–871.

11 Drug treatment of the personality disorders

GEORGE STEIN

"If anything is impressive in the literature on the treatment of the borderline syndrome it is that nothing seems to work very well or for very long." (Dryud, 1972)

The treatment of the personality disorders is a topic surrounded with much pessimism, and most clinicians firmly believe that these disorders are essentially untreatable and that subjects with a personality disorder have little capacity for change. Despite this, ever since the first description of the borderline syndrome by Stern (1938), a few psychotherapists have taken a keen interest in these patients, and over the last two decades there has been an increasing number of articles describing the techniques and difficulties of psychotherapy with the borderline. This implies that there are at least *some* psychotherapists who believe that *some* change may be possible for at least *some* patients, albeit with difficulty. Stone (1985) considers these patients to be "just barely treatable".

There has also been a steady trickle of drug studies, focusing mainly on the use of neuroleptics. The whole area of drug treatment has recently sprung to life with the publication of three large, well designed drug trials with properly defined groups of borderline and schizotypal subjects (Goldberg *et al*, 1986; Soloff *et al*, 1986*a*; Cowdrey & Gardner, 1988), and the topic was even given an editorial in the *Lancet* (1986).

The principal stimulus for these trials and the most striking advance in personality disorder research in recent years has been in the area of classification and diagnosis. Clear operational criteria are now available in DSM–III–R (American Psychiatric Association, 1987) for each category of personality disorder, and this has enabled drug trials to be conducted in well defined patient groups, although only borderline personality disorder (BPD) and schizotypal personality disorder (SPD) (Table 11.1) have been the focus of any systematic psychopharmacological research. Even though the term 'borderline personality disorder' is more commonly used in the

Table 11.1

DSM–III–R criteria for borderline and schizotypal personality disorders (the two categories where drug treatments have been applied)

Borderline personality disorder (BPD)	Schizotypal personality disorder (SPD)
(1) Unstable or intense interpersonal relationships	(1) Ideas of reference
(2) Impulsiveness which may be self-damaging	(2) Excessive social anxiety
(3) Affective instability	(3) Odd beliefs and magical thinking
(4) Inappropriate or intense anger, temper	(4) Unusual perceptual experience, e.g. illusions
(5) Recurrent suicidal threats or self-mutilation	(5) Odd or eccentric behaviour or appearance
(6) Identity disturbance	(6) No close friends (or only one) apart from first-degree relatives
(7) Chronic feelings of emptiness or boredom	(7) Odd speech which may be impoverished, vague or abstract
(8) Frantic efforts to avoid real or imagined abandonment	(8) Inappropriate or constricted affect
	(9) Suspiciousness or paranoid ideation

For both disorders the onset should be in early adulthood and at least *five* items are required to make the diagnosis.

American literature than the English, the condition is equally frequent in the UK. Kroll *et al* (1982), using Gunderson's diagnostic interview for borderlines (Gunderson *et al*, 1981), showed that 14.5% of the patients on an admission ward in Fulbourne Hospital in Cambridge had BPD, although only 8.5% fulfilled DSM–III criteria for BPD. English clinicians preferred to use the labels of 'hysterical', 'explosive' or 'immature' personality disorders for the same subject.

Personality disorders are common. Of all psychiatric admissions in the UK, 7.5% had a personality disorder (Department of Health and Social Security, 1985), and a figure of 7.5% for BPD has been given for the USA (Soloff, 1981). The personality disorders also have a considerable morbidity and mortality. Thus the standardised mortality ratio for the 20–39-year age group is raised sixfold, a rise similar to that reported for schizophrenia and affective disorder (Zilber *et al*, 1989).

From a purely pragmatic point of view, psychotropic drugs are often prescribed to BPD in-patients, yet this is done without any empirical guidance or definite indications. Androlunis *et al* (1982) concluded from a survey of fellow clinicians that 84% of women and 87% of men with BPD received medication while in hospital, yet the clinicians in the survey admitted they had no clear reasons for selecting the particular drugs they prescribed. Soloff (1981), in a retrospective study, reported that 53% of an in-patient sample with BPD received medication and of these, 62% showed "clear and unequivocal progress" compared with only 18.7% of those who received no medication.

Although it is clear that large numbers of individuals with personality disorders are being medicated during their stay in hospital, there are no guidelines in the literature on drug use, nor is the topic considered in any of the major textbooks on psychiatry (Hill *et al*, 1986; Kendell & Zealley, 1988; Gelder *et al*, 1989; Kaplan & Sadock, 1989). As Chessick (1969) aptly put it, "these individuals seem to lie on the periphery of psychiatry, on the periphery of society and the periphery of penology".

This review focuses on the recent major drug trials. These studies are of three types: firstly there are a few studies where the effect of a drug on a specific personality disorder is examined; secondly, there are those studies which focus on a specific syndrome or behaviour pattern in subjects with a personality disorder; and thirdly there are a few studies of the effect of drugs on DSM–III–R axis I disorders such as depression in BPD subjects. In addition, some of the older literature appertaining to drug effects among subjects with personality disorders is considered. To merit inclusion in this review, a study should describe the effects of a pharmacological agent on a patient, or a group of patients, with a primary diagnosis of personality disorder. Some drug studies in other disorders where the prevalence of the personality disorders is known to be high have also been included. These are disruptive delinquents, aggressive prisoners, clinic alcoholics, recurrent parasuicides, aggressive and self-mutilating mentally handicapped subjects, and adults with attentional deficit disorders. The emphasis throughout this review is on the effects of drugs, beneficial or otherwise, on the personality disorder, rather than their known effects or side-effects on normal volunteers, or on patients with DSM–III–R axis I disorders.

Low-dose neuroleptic therapy – early uncontrolled studies

The introduction of chlorpromazine for the treatment of schizophrenia by Delay *et al* (1954) dramatically advanced the science of therapeutics in psychiatry. The discovery of the very much lesser but also beneficial effect that small doses of neuroleptics sometimes have on subjects with personality disorders has been a much slower, more haphazard, and less publicised affair. The earliest observations were made by a few American psychoanalysts who had a long-standing interest in borderline personality disorder.

Winkleman (1955) was the first to report the relief chlorpromazine gave to neurotic symptoms, particularly agitation, anxiety, phobias, and obsessions, as well as confirming its effects in acute schizophrenia. Winkleman (1975) described his experience with neuroleptics as adjuvant treatment to 30 of his own patients who were attending for psychoanalysis:

> "during drug months using a phenothiazine, a diminished intensity of what are classically called id drives and derivatives was observed, which allows psychotherapy to proceed more effectively. Anxiety was reduced and primary process material seemed less threatening and was also more amenable to interpretation. There was improved reality testing, better interpersonal

relationships and less fantasy, symbolisation and displacement. In proper dosage and at the proper time these neuroleptic effects benefited the psychotherapeutic process''.

Other analysts such as Schmideberg (1959) and Kernberg (1968) also suggest the use of tranquillising medication when a borderline patient's anxiety begins to interfere with analysis. Mandell (1976) also mentions the use of a small dose of a neuroleptic in a borderline subject to help ''tighten up his associations''. Needless to say, not all analysts with an interest in BPD were so favourably disposed to neuroleptics. Dryud (1972) wrote, ''phenothiazines, which should theoretically help with the postulated lack of central inhibition, have in my experience yielded no improved affect; possibly they lengthen the periods of unpleasant affects and in a larger dose result in depressed behaviour''.

A second and quite independent impetus to the exploration of the role of neuroleptics in the personality disorders came from Belgium, where the pharmaceutical company Janssen had recently synthesised pimozide, a potent dopamine receptor antagonist, and they sought to explore its role in all categories of psychiatric illness. Reyntjens *et al* (1972) supported by Janssen gave 2–8 mg pimozide (mean dose 3 mg) to 120 patients with DSM–II personality disorders (American Psychiatric Association, 1968) and found an excellent global outcome in 69% of subjects. His study was subsequently replicated by Collard (1976) using a lower dose of pimozide (1–2 mg daily). He studied his patients for up to nine months, and showed that beneficial effects often took up to three months to appear, but between three and nine months there was little further improvement.

The next significant contribution was made in the UK by Perinpanayagam & Haig (1977) working with a much more severely disturbed in-patient group. They described ten seriously disturbed adolescent girls who were in a secure unit, and wrote:

> ''they were disturbed, violent and aggressive girls, two of whom had schizophrenia, who were not influenced by tender loving care and they were started on depot tranquillisers. The girls on this regime benefited, in that their disturbed behaviour subsided. They became approachable in the psychotherapeutic framework and were more co-operative and psychologically more stable''.

In the USA, Brinkley *et al* (1979) first coined the term 'low dosage of neuroleptic therapy' and reported five therapy-resistant patients with a diagnosis of BPD. Two patients responded to perphenazine (2–6 mg daily), two responded to thiothixene (in dosages up to 10 mg daily), and one responded to thioridazine (25 mg at night). These doses are considerably lower than those required for the treatment of schizophrenia and are also lower than the dosages reported when neuroleptics are used to treat

TABLE 11.2
Studies using neuroleptics in the personality disorders

Author	Diagnostic group	n	Design	Drug	Result
Hedberg *et al* (1971)	Pseudo neurotic schizophrenia	28	Compared with schizophrenics	Tranylcypromine 20–30 mg, trifluoperazine 8 mg, and both drugs combined	50% responded to tranylcypromine alone, 22% to trifluoperazine alone, 28% to the combination
Reyntjens *et al* (1972)	DSM–III personality disorders (mixture of schizoid, paranoid and other groups)	120	Multicentre open study	Pimozide 1–3 mg mean dosage 3 mg	Marked improvement in many affective and psychotic symptoms and social functioning
Perinpanayagam & Haig (1977)	Disturbed adolescent girls in a secure unit	10	Open case reports	Fluphenazine 12.5–25 mg i.m., flupenthixol 25–40 mg monthly	All benefited, disturbed behaviour subsided and they became approachable in a psychotherapeutic framework
Collard (1976)	DSM–III personality disorders. Some with secondary neuroses and mixed personality disorders	60	Multicentre open study, for six months	Pimozide 1–3 mg, mean dosage 2 mg	Significant improvements in anxiety, affective and psychotic symptoms. Improvements during the first two months but little further change between months 3 and 6
Brinkley *et al* (1979)	Borderline personality disorder resembling Gunderson and Singer criteria	5	Open case reports	Perphenazine 16 mg, thiothixene 10 mg, thioridazine 25 mg	Marked reduction in severe chronic anxiety and maladaptive behaviour, and improvement in interpersonal relationships
Leone (1982)	Borderline subjects from private practice (Gunderson and Kolb criteria)	80	Double-blind comparison between drugs 6 weeks	Loxapine mean 14.5 mg, chlorpromazine mean 110 mg	Loxapine superior to chlorpromazine for depression, anger and anxiety. Both drugs improved from baseline score. High frequency of extrapyramidal side effects for both drugs

Study	Sample	N	Design	Drug/dose	Results
Montgomery & Montgomery (1982)	Recurrent suicide attempters: DSM–III histrionic 12: BPD 30	42	Double-blind placebo controlled. 6 months	Flupenthixol 20 mg i.m. every 4 weeks	Significant reduction in frequency of suicide attempts apparent after six months
Serban & Siegel (1984)	Consecutive admissions Personality disorder with mild psychotic episode 14 SPD, 16 BPD, 16 both SPD and BPD	52	Double-blind comparison between drugs	Thiothixene 4 mg, haloperidol 1.6 mg	Reduction from baseline scores for both drugs but thiothixene superior to haloperidol. Overall 56% markedly improved, 28% moderately, 12% no change, 2% worse. Cognitive symptoms, ideas of reference and derealisation, anxiety, and low self image did best
Soloff et al (1986a)	Referrals from other physicians with a diagnosis of personality disorder 3 SPD, 29 BPD, 32 both SPD and BPD	64	Double-blind placebo controlled	Amitriptyline 100–175 mg, mean 147 mg, haloperidol 4–16 mg, mean 7.2 mg	Haloperidol superior to both placebo and amitriptyline. Haloperidol improved depression, anxiety, paranoia and psychoticism. Amitriptyline showed some improvement on HRSD scores, but made some patients worse
Goldberg et al (1986)	Recruited by advertisements and scored for DSM–III personality disorder. 17 BPD, 13 SPD, 20 both SPD and BPD	50	Double-blind placebo controlled	Thiothixene 5–40 mg	Significant drug placebo differences for illusions, ideas of reference, psychoticism, and obsessive–compulsive symptoms, but not depression
Cowdry & Gardner (1988)	Referred by a private psychotherapist. 16 BPD all with behavioural dyscontrol	16	Double-blind placebo controlled longitudinal crossover study six weeks	Trifluoperazine 7.8 mg (7 took drug for three weeks)	Trifluoperazine poorly tolerated but significant improvement in behavioural dyscontrol, anxiety and depression

depression (Robertson & Trimble, 1982). Brinkley *et al* (1979) commented that dosage titration was "a critical aspect of the use of neuroleptics in this population because the margin between the symptom free state and the onset of sedative side effects is fine".

Two American retrospective case-note studies (Soloff, 1981; Cole *et al*, 1984) provided further uncontrolled evidence that neuroleptics may benefit borderline subjects. In Soloff's (1981) study, 5 out of 11 (45%) cases of BPD had a good outcome, while Cole *et al* (1984) noted that 10 out of 17 (58%) BPD subjects did well on neuroleptics, although those with a co-existing schizophrenia-like illness or depression seemed to benefit most. In an open trial, Leone (1982) compared loxapine (a tricyclic antipsychotic drug) with chlorpromazine; loxapine reduced anger hostility somewhat more than chlorpromazine in the early phase of the trial, but by six weeks the drugs appeared to be equally effective. Side-effects, particularly drowsiness and various dyskinesias, resulted in poor compliance for both drugs and a high drop-out rate.

Most of the drug studies described above were drawn from private analytical practice, and therefore represent a very biased sample. Furthermore, the absence of placebo controls in these studies makes it difficult to estimate the magnitude (if any) of the reported drug effect.

One prominent symptom of BPD is a tendency to repeated overdoses. Of those attempting suicide, 48–65% have personality disorders (Philips, 1970; Ovenstone *et al*, 1973). Casey (1989) also reports a frequency of 65%, although Jacobson & Tribe (1972) report a rather lower prevalence. Prospective studies have demonstrated that social-work intervention (Oast & Zitrin, 1975) and intensive out-patient supervision (Chowdrey *et al*, 1973) do not reduce the frequency of subsequent suicidal behaviour. Montgomery & Montgomery (1982) compared the effects of 20 mg intramuscular flupenthixol monthly with placebo and 30 mg mianserin. They selected subjects who had twice attempted suicide, but had no concurrent axis I disorder. Most subjects had BPD (by DSM–III criteria (American Psychiatric Association, 1980)) but a few had histrionic or dependent personality disorders. For the first three months of the trial there were no differences between drug and placebo groups, but by six months the flupenthixol-treated group attempted suicide significantly fewer times than the placebo group. The parallel group treated with mianserin derived no benefit.

Serban & Siegel (1984) conducted a large prospective study on 52 consecutive patients with either DSM–III BPD or SPD or both, who presented to the Bellevue Walk in Clinic in New York. Thiothixene (mean dose 9.8 mg) and haloperidol (mean dose 3.0 mg) were compared in a parallel design, but the study lacked a placebo control group. Overall 56% of the patients showed marked improvement; 28% did moderately well; 12% showed no change; and one subject (2%) was worse. Symptoms improving most were cognitive disturbance, derealisation, ideas of reference, anxiety, and depression. One finding of particular interest was that 'low self-image' – a psychological symptom traditionally held to respond only to psychotherapy – improved dramatically with both these neuroleptics. Thiothixene but not haloperidol resulted in an overall improvement on the Borderline Syndrome Index (Conte *et al*, 1980), suggesting that core borderline features may also change in response to drug therapy.

Although the majority of reports on the use of neuroleptics in BPD are favourable, Steiner *et al* (1979) describe an adverse reaction which they call 'behavioural toxicity'. They reported nine subjects with DSM–II borderline schizophrenia (DSM–II 295.5), although the limited case material provided in the text suggests that six had schizoid rather than schizotypal personality disorder, and three had pure BPD, but none were initially psychotic. In an attempt to treat their 'pre-schizophrenia' they were given 150–500 mg chlorpormazine or 7–12 mg haloperidol daily, and this resulted in the precipitation of psychotic symptoms and 'behavioural toxicity', characterised by psychomotor agitation, conceptual disorganisation, paranoid delusions, depersonalisation, and derealisation. There were no associated Parkinsonian or other extrapyramidal symptoms. The mechanism of this unusual reaction is uncertain and the authors postulated either a psychodynamic mechanism, or that the drugs precipitated an atropine-like psychosis.

Placebo-controlled trials of neuroleptics

In the first of these trials, Goldberg *et al* (1986) compared thiothixene with placebo in 50 patients. Subjects were recruited through an advertisement in a local newspaper outlining the main features of DSM–III BPD. Respondents were subsequently screened using the Structured Interview for Borderlines (Baron, 1981) and were only included if they fulfilled DSM–III criteria for BPD or SPD and had experienced the behaviour in question for at least three months. Patients who also had schizophrenia, mania, melancholia, or severe physical illness were excluded. Twenty-nine were women, 17 had BPD, 13 SPD and 20 had both SPD and BPD. Patients took a variable dosage of thiothixene in 2 mg and 5 mg tablets and were asked to titrate their own dosage up to a maximum of 40 mg daily. At the end of the trial the average dose of thiothixene taken was 8.67 mg while the average placebo dose was 26.36 mg. This difference, both large and significant, suggests that the drug was either more effective or produced more side-effects than placebo (or both). Large drug–placebo differences were demonstrated for delusions, ideas of reference, psychotic anger and hostility, phobic anxiety, and obsessive–compulsive symptoms. Rather smaller drug–placebo differences were present for somatisation, depersonalisation, derealisation, suspiciousness, and paranoia. There were negligible effects for hallucinations and depressive hostility and sensitivity to interpersonal rejection. 'Anger hostility' and sensitivity to interpersonal rejection showed a large placebo response, and because of this Goldberg *et al* (1986) suggested that the patients presenting with these symptoms might benefit more from psychotherapy than from drugs. Measurement of the 'personality cluster items', that is, borderline criteria and schizotypal criteria, showed large significant improvements over time for both placebo and the active drug, but there were no significant drug–placebo differences, and it is possible that the improvement in these measures was the result of psychotherapy after the drug trial.

In the second trial, Soloff *et al* (1986*a*) compared haloperidol (mean dosage 7.24 mg) with placebo and amitriptyline (mean dosage 147 mg). Because their subjects were an in-patient group they may have been rather more disturbed, yet at the same time more representative of hospital clinical populations and therefore more relevant to clinical practice than the community-based subjects studied by Goldberg *et al* (1986). All subjects were screened using the Diagnostic Interview for Borderlines: 43% had BPD, 6% SPD, and 51% both BPD and SPD. Haloperidol was superior to amitriptyline and there were large drug–placebo differences for haloperidol for a broad spectrum of neurotic and psychotic symptoms as well as measures of behavioural dyscontrol. Depression improved only according to the self-rated Beck Depression Inventory, not according to the observer-rated Hamilton Rating Scale for Depression. Haloperidol also led to a significant improvement in the Schizotypal Symptom Inventory, a scale purported to measure core features for schizotypal personality disorder.

The third placebo-controlled study is that of Cowdrey & Gardner (1988), and although only 16 subjects with pure BPD were examined, the study itself had an elegant design. Taking advantage of the chronicity of personality disorders, these authors repeatedly challenged their patients with four different drugs as well as placebo for consecutive six-week periods in a longitudinal crossover trial. The drugs tested were trifluoperazine (mean daily dose 7.8 mg), carbamazepine (820 mg daily), tranylcypromine (40 mg daily), alprazolam (4.7 mg daily), and placebo. Only 10 patients started the trifluoperazine trial and three dropped out in the first three weeks (two because of orthostatic hypotension and one because of extrapyramidal disorder), and a further two dropped out between three and six weeks, indicating that only 50% of the subjects were able to tolerate trifluoperazine. For those who completed the trial there was significantly less tendency to suicide attempts and behavioural dyscontrol, although the improvement was less than with carbamazepine in the same patients. There were also modest improvements in depression, anxiety, and sensitivity to rejection. The results of the trial were complex, with each drug showing beneficial effects on different aspects of BPD. Only tranylcypromine was superior to placebo over a broad range of measures of self- and observer-rated mood changes and behavioural dyscontrol. Carbamazepine was superior to placebo for behavioural dyscontrol but not for measures of dysphoria. Alprazolam was significantly worse than placebo for behaviourial dyscontrol, although for 2 of the 16 subjects, alprazolam emerged as the best drug.

The studies by Goldberg *et al* (1986) and Soloff *et al* (1986*a*) are methodologically sound, incorporating sizeable numbers of subjects as well as placebo controls, and both show a broad spectrum of efficacy for neuroleptics over a wide range of both neurotic and psychotic symptoms in subjects with well defined BPD and SPD. They therefore confirm the earlier reports of the American psychoanalysts and the open studies reported from the UK, US, and Belgium. The more definite indication for neuroleptic use appears to be brief psychotic episodes and episodes of severe behavioural dyscontrol. Neuroleptics taken over a longer period may benefit a few subjects who previously derived some benefit during an acute episode of dyscontrol or psychosis. In general, the high-potency preparations, such as pimizode, thiothixene or trifluoperazine, in low dosage have been preferred because they lack sedative side-effects which are apparently much abhorred by these patients. However, some patients prefer small doses of the low-potency preparations such as thioridazine and chlorpromazine because these drugs are less prone to cause extrapyramidal reactions, while their sedative effects are often valued.

Tricyclic antidepressants in borderline subjects

The poor response to tricyclics among subjects with personality disorders was observed in one of the first open trials of imipramine. Klein & Fink (1962) identified 13 subjects with "histrionic labile affects and a manipulative character" who responded poorly. Kiloh *et al* (1962), in a discriminant-function analysis, also found that self-pity, irritability and hysterical features were associated with a poor response to imipramine. Paykel (1972) treated 85 women with depression and classified them according to the typology of Overall *et al* (1966) into psychotic depressives, anxious depressives, hostile depressives, and young depressives with personality disorders. Psychotic depressives did best, while 'anxious depressives' were least responsive. Deykin & Dimascio (1972) found the only items to show any predictive association with a positive tricyclic response were a stable occupational record and a previous history of a substance abuse. Shawcross & Tyrer (1985) examined 17 out-patients who failed to respond to either a tricyclic or a monoamine oxidase inhibitor (MAOI), and of these, 12 (70%) had a recognisable personality disorder.

The first prospective study of the tricyclics in subjects with personality disorders was conducted by Akiskal *et al* (1980). They recruited 65 patients with 'characterological depression' who had: (a) a history of mild depressive

TABLE 11.3
Antidepressant studies in the personality disorders

	Subjects	n	Design	Drug	Result
Klein & Fink (1962)	All subjects received the drug	215	Open study	Imipramine	40 non-responders included a group of 13 subjects "with histrionic labile affect, manipulative character"
Paykel (1972)	Depressed females, 21 were young depressives with personality disorders	85	Open study	Amitriptyline 100–200 mg, daily	Personality disorder depressives did better than "anxious depressives" but worse than "psychotic depressives"
Akiskal et al (1980)	Characterological depression. More than 5 years duration	50	Open study, 40 unipolar controls	Amitriptyline or clomipramine 150–200 mg, daily	31% responded. Predictors were hypersomnia, or superimposed major depression
Soloff et al (1986a)	In-patients with DSM–III BPD, SPD, and BPD and SPD combined	60	Double-blind placebo controlled	Amitriptyline 147 mg, haloperidol 4.8 mg	Haloperidol superior to amitriptyline for depression. Some patients got better, others were much worse with paradoxical reactions
Hedberg et al (1971)	Pseudoneurotic schizophrenia	32	Open drug comparison	Tranylcypromine 30 mg, trifluoperazine 8–16 mg	50% responded to tranylcypromine, 22% to trifluoperazine, 28% to the combination
Liebowitz & Klein (1981)	Hysteroid dysphoria but most subjects also fulfilled DSM–III BPD criteria	16	Open study followed by placebo controlled withdrawal	Phenelzene 15–75 mg	11 out of 16 (68%) improved during open phase of the trial. Most relapsed during the drug withdrawal study
Cowdry & Gardner (1988)	DSM–III BPD with behavioural dyscontrol	12	Longitudinal placebo-controlled crossover	Tranylcypromine mean dose 40 mg/day	Produced the greatest improvement in mood, in comparison with trifluoperazine, apraxolam carbemazepine, and placebo

symptons for five or more years, (b) onset before the age of 25 years, (c) depressive symptoms for most of the year, (d) a condition that did not represent the residuum of a well defined depressive episode requiring hospital admission. Treatment was initially with a tricyclic antidepressant with mainly noradrenergic properties (desimipramine or nortriptyline) in full dosage, and if this failed a serotonergic drug such as amitriptyline or clomipramine was prescribed also in full therapeutic dosage (150–200 mg daily). Out of the 65 subjects, 20 (31%) responded well to tricyclic therapy. Responsiveness was associated with: a history of major depression; hypersomnia; a mild hypomanic episode in response to tricyclics; and female sex. Non-responders were more often male and had an unstable personality and a history of abusing hypnotics, alcohol or psychostimulants; they also had a poorer social outcome.

In antidepressant studies where the primary aim is the treatment of depression rather than the personality disorder, tricyclics are less successful among those with co-existing personality disorders than among subjects who are free of personality disorders. Black *et al* (1988), in a retrospective case-note study, compared 75 subjects with major depression and co-existing personality disorder with 152 with pure major depression. Of those with pure depression, 64% responded well to adequate tricyclic treatment, compared with only 27% of those with personality disorder. This study has relevance for hospital-based practitioners because it was based on a large in-patient sample, and the difference between the two groups was both large and significant. Using a similar retrospective design, Pfohl *et al* (1984) also showed that the response to antidepressants (not specified as tricyclics) was worse among patients with personality disorder (16%) compared with patients with pure depression (50%). However, as the main outcome measure was made after only two weeks' treatment, these figures are unreliable and probably too pessimistic.

Surprisingly there is only one prospective, well controlled, double-blind trial in the literature which compares amitriptyline with placebo and haloperidol among subjects with properly diagnosed DSM–III BPD or SPD, some of whom also had major depression according to Research Diagnostic Criteria (Soloff *et al*, 1986*a*). As a group, the depressed subjects treated with amitriptyline did only marginally better on the Hamilton and the Beck scales than subjects receiving placebo, whereas patients on haloperidol did markedly better on these scales. However, more detailed scrutiny of individual cases showed that some patients treated with amitriptyline responded well, while others became much worse.

In another paper, possibly on the same subjects, Soloff *et al* (1986*b*) reported that the 13 amitriptyline responders improved on ratings of depressed mood and in many areas of impulsive behaviour, including temper tantrums, assaultive threats, and manipulative behaviour. But the 13 amitriptyline non-responders deteriorated progressively and by six weeks were far worse than the placebo group on measures of global functioning, paranoid ideation, and impulsive behaviour. Non-responders were also more demanding, expressed more suicidal threats, and made more physical assaults. Responders and non-responders had similar plasma tricyclic levels, and it is of note that the non-responders were not over-medicated, under-medicated, nor hypomanic. Because of this, Soloff *et al* (1986*b*) cautioned, "clinicians should be aware of the potential of paradoxical effects of tricyclics in borderline patients".

Similar paradoxical effects and rage reactions had also been observed many years previously among a group of emotionally unstable adolescents (Klein & Fink, 1962), and Rampling (1978) reported four depressed subjects who experienced severe aggressive outbursts within a few hours of taking a tricyclic. This generally poor response of BPD depression to tricyclic antidepressants may explain why they often prove to be disappointing among depressive in-patients, since more than half of the in-patients with unipolar depression also have personality disorders (Baxter *et al*, 1984).

Monoamine oxidase inhibitors

All three studies in the literature on the effects of MAOIs on the personality disorders report beneficial effects (Hedberg *et al*, 1971; Liebowitz & Klein, 1981; Cowdry & Gardner, 1988). Hedberg *et al* (1971) examined 96 patients with a diagnosis of schizophrenia, but among the subjects there were 32 patients with pseudoneurotic schizophrenia, the probable forerunner of BPD. Half the patients with pseudoneurotic schizophrenia responded to tranyl-cypromine alone, 28% to trifluoperazine alone, and 22% to the combination. Prompted by this observation, Liebowitz & Klein (1981) gave phenelzine (mean dose 75 mg) to 16 women, aged between 18 and 45, who were bright and articulate and were all suffering from 'hysteroid dysphoria'. Fourteen of these 16 subjects also fulfilled DSM–III criteria for BPD. They also received twice-weekly dynamically orientated psychotherapy by experienced psychiatric social workers throughout the trial. Eleven of the 16 (68%) responded well to this combination of MAOIs and psychotherapy, but five failed to respond. Of these, two suffered from alcoholic relapses, one had to be admitted for worsening depression, and two dropped out because of side-effects, including delusional parasitosis. By the end of the open phase of the trial, the number of patients who continued to fulfil DSM–III criteria for BPD had fallen from 11 to 6. At the end of three months the 11 improved patients entered a double-blind placebo-controlled withdrawal study, and 8 (73%) relapsed, with an increasing frequency of physically self-damaging acts, feelings of emptiness and boredom, and the break up of relationships which had been going well during the open phase of the trial.

A third longitudinal crossover, placebo-controlled trial of MAOIs was conducted by Cowdry & Gardner (1988) in 12 patients with DSM–III BPD. In this trial, patients with comorbid schizophrenia or manic or major depression were excluded, but those with lesser degrees of affective disturbance were included. Nine patients completed a trial on tranylcypromine and there was marked improvement for anxiety, depression, and sensitivity to rejection. Behavioural dyscontrol also improved but this was less impressive than for carbamazepine among the same patients. In studies where MAOIs have been used to treat depressive disorders, rather than the personality disorder itself, MAOIs emerge as less effective antidepressants among subjects with combined depression and personality disorder, than when used to treat depression uncomplicated by personality disorder. Shawcross & Tyrer (1985) in a study of depressed neurotic out-patients found 68% of the non-responders had a personality disorder (mainly anancastic and passive dependent) compared with only 18% of the phenelzine responders. There are divergent views as to whether the beneficial effects of MAOIs on the personality disorders are due to their antidepressant effects, as in cases of atypical depression (Cowdry & Gardner, 1988), or whether it is their psychostimulant properties that are of critical importance (Wender *et al*, 1981).

Electroconvulsive therapy

While the immediate response to electroconvulsive therapy (ECT) may be good, there is a high relapse rate among BPD subjects with depression. Zimmerman *et al* (1986) treated 25 patients who had major depression with ECT. Ten subjects also suffered from a variety of personality disorders, while the remaining 15 had major depression only. The short-term response to ECT was good in both groups, but by six-month follow-up, five out of the ten subjects with personality disorder had been readmitted compared with only one out of the 15 with pure depression. Kramer (1982) also reported five BPD subjects with depression: two showed little or no response to ECT, two had an equivocal response with rapid relapse, and only one had a good response, but this was also soon followed by relapse. In a retrospective study where the primary aim of the ECT was to treat depression, Black *et al* (1988) found that 11 out of 14 (79%) patients with pure major depression responded well to ECT, but the response rate for depression in the personality disorder group was similar at 75%. Using a similar design, Pfohl *et al* (1984) found that 65% of their patients with pure depression responded well to ECT compared with only 40% of those with depression and personality disorders. Possibly as a consequence of the poor response to ECT, this type of depression is less commonly treated with ECT; thus Black *et al* (1988) found that only 45% of patients with a combined diagnosis of major depression

K

and personality disorder received ECT compared with 65% of those who had major depression alone. Figures in the study by Pfohl *et al* are lower but show a similar trend – 27% for pure major depression, and only 13% for depression combined with personality disorder.

However, ECT may be useful in certain instances. Firstly, anyone, regardless of their previous personality, may suffer a series of catastrophes and as a consequence develop a severe depressive illness which may respond to ECT. Secondly, Perry (1985) found that some BPD subjects experienced 'double depression' – discrete episodes of major depression superimposed on chronic dysphoria. During these phases, there is an abrupt and apparently inexplicable regression, and patients enter a phase of severe and frequent behaviour dyscontrol with daily or almost daily suicidal attempts and self-mutilation. ECT is often beneficial in breaking the cycle and stopping repetitive self-damaging acts. Even though the effect of ECT may be short lived, it can be life saving, while the extra time given may provide a breathing space, enabling the development of alternative treatment strategies.

Lithium

Cade's original discovery that lithium might be a cure for mania stemmed from his observation that lithium had a tranquillising effect on guinea pigs (Cade, 1949). A calming effect on the aggressive behaviour of other animal species such as Siamese fighting fish, and the territorial behaviour of hamsters, was also later demonstrated by Weischer (1969).

Only in the USA has it been possible to study the effect of lithium on the more seriously violent individuals found in prison populations (Sheard, 1971; Tupin *et al*, 1973; Sheard *et al*, 1976). Tupin *et al* (1973) studied 27 male convicts, approximately half of whom had personality disorders of a mainly explosive type, the remainder having schizophrenia; they all had a pattern of recurring, easily triggered violence. A high dose of lithium (1800 mg) was used, although the mean plasma level was only 0.82 mEq/l. Tupin *et al* (1973) commented that this group may handle lithium differently to the usual manic–depressive population, or alternatively be less cooperative about taking medication. Fifteen (56%) of their subjects showed a marked decrease in the number of prison infractions, 3 (11%) showed an increase, and 4 (14%) showed no change. Two patients became increasingly psychotic on lithium, presumably as a consequence of the high dosage and lithium toxicity. Many subjects reported an increased capacity to reflect, a frame of mind Monroe (1970) calls 'reflective delay', or as one convict aptly put it, "now I can think whether to hit him or not".

Sheard's first study was an open trial of lithium in 12 aggressive violent delinquents (mean age 19) from the Cheshire Correctional Institution in Connecticut. Serious aggressive episodes showed a much larger reduction with lithium than minor antisocial acts. However, a normal or high serum lithium level was a critical factor, the reduction in aggressive episodes only occurring if the level was above 0.6 mmol/l. Improvement for the whole group was largely accounted for by three (25%) subjects who appeared to be particularly responsive to lithium (Sheard, 1971).

In a second and much larger study, Sheard *et al* (1976) studied 66 subjects mainly with severe personality disorders who had been convicted of a serious aggressive crime, such as manslaughter, rape or assault, who continued to have chronic assaultive behaviour in prison. Improvement was measured objectively by counting the total number of major and minor infractions of the institution's rules. Major infractions were assaults or serious threatening behaviour, and these were punished with time "in the hole" (the seclusion unit). Minor infractions were offences such as possession of contraband, or being out of place at the wrong time, and these were usually punished by a loss of recreational privileges. For the first month all subjects were drug free; then half the subjects took lithium while half took placebo for the next three months, and this was followed by a further drug-free period. The infraction rate was similar for the two groups during the first drug-free month. However, during lithium therapy the frequency of major infractions steadily declined to zero by three months, whereas subjects taking placebo continued to have a high rate (a significant difference). However, minor infractions showed little or no change in the treatment group, indicating that lithium did not cause a global inhibition of behaviour. On stopping the lithium there was an immediate rebound increase in the number of major infractions in the treatment group.

Lithium may also be useful in some mentally retarded subjects prone to aggressive episodes and self-mutilation. The cause of this behaviour is unknown but is presumably an admixture of brain damage and character pathology rather than affective disorder. Wickham & Reed (1987), pooling the results of three controlled trials (Worral *et al*, 1975; Tyrer *et al*, 1984; Craft *et al*, 1987), found an overall response rate of around 70–75% compared with a placebo response rate of 30% (Craft *et al*, 1987). Side-effects such as polydipsia and polyuria (Dostal & Zvolsky, 1970) and episodes of lithium toxicity (Worrall *et al*, 1975), probably secondary to unrecognised episodes of intercurrent illness such as diarrhoea, may limit the use of lithium in this population, while Craft *et al* (1987) also observed one or two subjects who became more aggressive while on lithium.

The only placebo-controlled study of lithium in the personality disorders was among a group of female adolescents with brief spontaneous mood swings of elation, depression, anger, and overtalkativeness who suffered from "the emotionally unstable character disorder" (Rifkin *et al*, 1972). In their six-week double-blind crossover trial, patients were randomly allocated to placebo or lithium. Of the 21 patients studied, 14 were judged to be better on lithium, four on placebo, and three showed no improvement. The only

TABLE 11.4

Clinical studies of lithium in aggression and impulsiveness in subjects without major affective disorder or mental handicap[1]

	Subjects	n	Design	Drug	Results
Rifkin *et al* (1972)	Adolescent girls with emotionally unstable character disorder	21	Double-blind placebo controlled crossover trial	Lithium level 0.6–1.5 meq/l	14 better on lithium, 4 better on placebo. Significant reduction in within-day mood lability
Sheard (1971)	Aggressive convicts	12	Placebo-control crossover 6 weeks	Lithium level 0.6–1.5 meq/l	Significant reduction in number of serious aggressive episodes
Sheard (1975)	Aggressive delinquent convicts	12	Control was a period on low dose lithium (level below 0.6 meq/l)	Lithium serum level 0.6–1.5 meq/l	Reduction in aggressive episodes only present at serum lithium levels above 0.6 meq/l
Sheard *et al* (1976)	Habitually aggressive convicts, mainly with non-psychotic personality disorders	66	Double-blind placebo controlled trial	Lithium levels 0.6–1.0 meq/l	Almost complete cessation of all severe violent episodes while on lithium, with rebound recurrence after lithium was stopped
Tupin *et al* (1973)	Aggressive convicts 12 schizophrenia, 12 with sociopathy, 3 other violent subjects	27	Open study 3–18 months	Lithium mean level 0.82 meq/l	Reduction in violence in 68% no change in 18%, worse in 14%

1. Lithium studies of aggression in the mentally handicapped are extensively reviewed elsewhere (Wickham & Reed, 1987).

statistically significant change due to lithium was a decrease on 'within-day mood fluctuations'.

Lithium may also be helpful for a few alcoholics. Among attenders at an out-patient clinic with alcoholism there may be a high prevalence of personality disorders. Tyrer *et al* (1988) gave a figure of 69%, while Valgum & Valgum (1989) estimated that 30% of female alcoholics admitted to hospital had both BPD and SPD, which was ten times the rate in non-alcoholic female admissions. Dryud (1972) has suggested that alcohol and drug addictions may represent a form of self-medication to escape from the intolerable moods associated with BPD. Both Klein *et al* (1974) and Merry *et al* (1976) found lithium gave some benefit to clinic alcoholics, particularly where there was co-existing depression. Fawcett *et al* (1987) reported that 67% of detoxified alcoholics who took lithium remained abstinent for 12 months, compared with only 42% of controls, but these effects were independent of any previous depression.

Finally, Stone (1990) reported that around 8% of his large sample with DSM–III BPD developed affective disorder. A few suffered from bipolar II disorder, and some of these showed a gratifying response to lithium. There are thus reports that lithium can help small numbers of subjects with diverse personality disorders, such as emotionally unstable adolescents, some violent criminals, aggressive mentally retarded subjects, a few alcoholics, and a few borderline subjects who show bipolar features. In the absence of any useful clinical predictors, picking out the small minority of responders is almost impossible. Affective features and a family history of classic affective disorder may be useful indicators, while Goetzl (1977) and Eichelmann (1988) on the basis of single case histories suggest that a family history of alcoholism may also be relevant. In some cases a two-month therapeutic trial of lithium may be the only way of selecting lithium-responsive subjects from the large majority of non-responders.

Benzodiazepines

Benzodiazepines are contraindicated in personality disorder because of their propensity to disinhibit and to induce rage reactions and states of drug dependency. The early reports of chlordiazepoxide-induced rage reactions showed that these episodes were almost exclusively confined to subjects with 'pseudoneurotic schizophrenia' (Tobin *et al*, 1960). Many of the earlier, more favourable reports included mixtures of patients, some of whom had personality disorders, schizophrenia and epilepsy, and any beneficial effects on personality disorders were mixed with the known beneficial anti-epileptic effects of benzodiazepines.

Kalina (1964) studied 52 mainly male prison inmates with diagnoses of schizophrenia, schizoid personality disorders and epilepsy who were "constant sources of friction and unrest with mainly hostile aggressive manifestation". Diazepam (20–30 mg daily) given for 6–12 months led to a complete resolution of symptoms of violence, destructiveness and belligerence in 33 (63%) of the subjects, while a further 3 (6%) were improved and 16 (31%) were unchanged. As might be expected, the diazepam helped the epilepsy and seven out of eight epileptics became seizure free. Diazepam reduced the symptom of interictal belligerence among a group of epileptic in-patients (Goddard & Lokare, 1970) while intramuscular diazepam (5–10 mg) reduced both fit frequency and aggressive outbursts. The drug had a "favourable effect improving some undesirable aspects of personality function".

Lion (1979) found that both oxazepam (120 mg daily) and chlordiazepoxide (100 mg daily) were superior to placebo in controlling episodes of aggression and temper among subjects with explosive personality disorders (none of whom had epilepsy) and that oxazepam was superior to chlordiazepoxide. Intramuscular lorazepam is also useful for the treatment of violent episodes among in-patients who have either psychotic or non-psychotic aggression (Bick & Hannah, 1986).

A more novel use of rapidly absorbed short-acting benzodiazepines is reported by Griffiths (1985). He described two patients with Monroe's episodic behavioural disorders (see below) who were able to abort their rage attacks by taking triazolam (0.5 mg) at the onset of their prodromal symptoms. In his first case a patient presented with a ten-year history of uncontrolled paroxysms of rage. Although these rage attacks were usually triggered by external events, the patient experienced a prodromal period of gradually escalating hallucinations, irritability, racing thoughts, loud speech, hyperactivity, and insomnia. Once the rage began, however, he experienced himself as a passive observer watching the destruction of a wall or the door of his car. Both triazolam (0.5 mg) and clorazepate (15 mg), administered during the prodromal phase, were able to abort these rages in 80% of instances, but a daily dosage of clorazepate proved ineffective. Because the triazolam was rapidly absorbed, peak levels were present only one hour after ingestion. In our own unit a man with BPD, alcoholism, depression and self-mutilation discovered himself that he could abort some episodes of self-mutilation by taking lorazepam (1 mg) sublingually as soon as he felt an episode of self-mutilation was imminent, as this markedly reduced his anxiety within 15 minutes. Eichelmann (1988) also reports a case of a 57-year-old man, prone to severe destructive rages, and fulfilling DSM–III criteria for intermittent explosive disorder who experienced a complete resolution of his rages by taking oxazepam.

Faltus (1984) reported three cases of BPD with histories of alcohol and substance abuse, multiple admission to hospital, and failure to respond to a variety of other drugs including tricyclics, neuroleptics and lithium who responded well to a small dose of alprazolam. Although the Cowdry &

Gardner (1988) trial in BPD subjects was mainly unfavourable to benzodiazepines, alprazolam emerged as the best drug for 2 out of their 16 (12%) well defined BPD subjects; it was superior to placebo, tranylcypromine, carbamazepine, and trifluoperazine. However 7 out of 12 (58%) of their patients taking alprazolam had serious episodes of dyscontrol, compared with only 2 out of the 13 (14%) taking placebo. Aggressive episodes on alprazolam were both more frequent and more severe. Thus one woman who had previously only shouted at her child threw a chair at him, while another who had never previously mutilated herself slashed her neck (Gardner & Cowdry, 1985).

The prescription of benzodiazepines should therefore be confined to those with intermittent explosive disorder or the interictal personality disorder of temporal lobe epilepsy, although rapidly acting benzodiazepines may sometimes help abort episodes of dyscontrol. Occasional patients with BPD, particularly those with a history of drug and alcohol abuse who fail to respond to other regimes, may also respond. The main caveat to their use is their propensity to cause rage reactions, and some authorities such as Tyrer (1988) feel they are almost absolutely contraindicated because of this. Deitch & Jennings (1988) however have recently questioned this view and they quote a large controlled series where the prevalence of such rage reactions is found to be around 1% among subjects taking benzodiazepines and among placebo control groups.

Impulsiveness, episodic phenomena, and the anti-epileptics

The most seriously disruptive symptom of personality disorder is episodes of impulsive aggression. These take the form of rage reactions, assaults on others, self-mutilation, commonly wrist or body slashing, self-inflicted burns, and impulsive overdoses. Cowdry & Gardner (1988) consider that the behavioural dyscontrol manifested by BPD subjects may represent one of the types of episodic disorder, as described by Monroe (1970, 1982). The episodic disorders according to Monroe are common, with the core feature being "an abrupt onset of intense mixed dysphoric effects". This abruptly appearing recurrent maladaptive behaviour interrupts the lifestyle or 'life flow' of the individual. The content of this dysphoria varies according to the underlying illness: thus if dysphoria takes the form of panic attacks, the underlying illness is an anxiety neurosis; if it takes the form of a brief psychotic episode the underlying disorder is a functional psychosis; and if it is an attack of violence the underlying disorder may be psychopathy. The behaviour is not only out of character for the individual but also out of context when it occurs, and patients sometimes report a compulsion in such behaviour. Between these episodes there is a symptom-free interval when neither the patient nor relatives are able to offer any rational explanation

TABLE 11.5

Use of anti-epileptics in the management of impulsivity, aggression and behavioural dyscontrol

	Year	Subjects	n	Design	Trial drug	Result
Monroe	1970	Uncontrolled psychotic patients with episodic aggression in a high security ward	55	Open study	Combined phenothiazenes, mysoline and chlordiazepoxide	42% no acting out, 30% minimal episodes, 28% unchanged
Resnick	1967	Impulsive irritable prisoners, irritable delinquents	11	Placebo crossover 'medical guess' 1 week trial	Diphenylhydantoin 150–200 mg, daily	Medical guess correct in 10/11
Lefkowitz	1969	Disruptive, hyperactive delinquents	6 / 50	Placebo-controlled cohort study 10 weeks	Diphenylhydantoin 100 mg, b.d.	Marked improvement noted. Placebo superior to diphenylhydantoin
Rosenblatt et al	1976	Irritable child abusing parents with poor self-control	13	Placebo-controlled crossover 6 weeks	Diphenylhydantoin 200 mg, b.d.	Improvement in depression and anxiety but no effect on aggressiveness, hostility, or impulsiveness
Neppe	1983	Non-epileptic subjects with an EEG abnormality in the temporal lobe. Some chronic schizophrenic, miscellaneous diagnoses	15	Placebo crossover, 15 weeks	Carbemazepine 200 mg, t.d.s.	50% reduction in the severity of aggression. 30% reduction in frequency 'reflective delay' apparent
Luchens	1984	7 chronically violent patients (7 schizophrenic, 1 personality disorder)		Placebo-controlled crossover 6 weeks	Carbemazepine 200 mg, t.d.s.	67% reduction in frequency and severity of violent episodes. Abnormal EEG not predictive of outcome
Mattes	1984	Heterogeneous aggressive non-psychotic psychiatric patients.	34	Open, uncontrolled study 2–3 months	Carbemazepine 200 mg, t.d.s.	86% reduction in the frequency and severity of aggressive outbursts. Response independent of organicity
Gardner & Cowdry	1985	DSM–III borderline personality disorder, with behavioural dyscontrol	11	Placebo-controlled crossover trial	Carbemazepine	Serious episode in 63% of placebo patients but only 9% of treated patients

for the behaviour but sometimes refer to these episodes as 'spells', 'attacks' or 'seizures', and so liken them to true epilepsy.

Even though Monroe (1970, 1982) does not believe that the episodic disorders are truly epileptic, there are often prodromal symptoms, particularly mounting anxiety, motor agitation, and sometimes even auras reminiscent of classic temporal lobe epilepsy such as light headedness, visual distortions, olfactory and other sensory phenomena. These prodromal symptoms are followed abruptly by a florid disturbance that is sometimes accompanied by mild confusion and disorientation. After the episode there is commonly much relief of tension and some satisfaction as well as tranquillity and partial amnesia for the episode itself. As with epilepsy, patients with episodic disorders can often predict the impending acute phase and may make frantic attempts to abort attacks. Common precipitating factors for these episodes of behavioural dyscontrol are small amounts of alcohol or drugs which would have little effect on most individuals, irregular eating and sleeping habits, psychological stress, physical exhaustion, and excessive sensory stimulation.

Despite some resemblance between the symptoms of BPD and those of temporal lobe epilepsy, the changes on electroencephalography (EEG) in temporal lobe epilepsy are uncommon in BPD. Cowdry *et al* (1985) examined the EEG changes in 39 subjects with BPD and found only one subject with atypical temporal lobe spike and wave activity, and a further three with some focal abnormalities in the temporal lobe, although there was an increased rate of non-focal posterior spike and wave activity in comparison with a control group of unipolar depressives. Androlunis *et al* (1982) found no difference in the prevalence of abnormal EEGs between their BPD and schizophrenic subjects, nor was there an increased rate of EEG abnormalities among their 'organic borderline' subgroup. However, abnormal slow-wave activity followed by bursts of fast-wave activity was reported in 38% of BPD subjects in another study (Cowdry *et al*, 1985). Similar diffuse non-focal slow-wave activity has also been reported among subjects incarcerated for recurrent violence and among some recurrently suicidal individuals, and this pattern has been referred to as an immature EEG (see Cowdry *et al*, 1985).

Resnick (1967) was the first to report some benefit for diphenylhydantoin among a group of disruptive prisoners and some improvement in academic and social performance among a few impulsive hyperactive delinquents. Sadly, this early optimistic report was not replicated by Lefkowicz (1969), who conducted a more rigorous placebo-controlled trial in 50 "disruptive delinquents". In his study, staff ratings for disruptive behaviour fell by 40% for those taking placebo, but only by 26% for those taking diphenylhydantoin. There was even a suggestion that diphenylhydantoin made some individuals rather worse when compared with placebo, particularly on measures of distress, unhappiness, negativism, and aggressiveness. This very large placebo effect is consistent with Beecher's (1955) original figure of a 35% response rate to placebo in 15 studies on diverse medical conditions. The high placebo response rate suggests that drug trials on the personality disorders which lack a placebo control group may be meaningless.

A similar, equally negative finding for diphenylhydantoin was reported from the placebo crossover trial of Rosenblatt *et al* (1976) among a group of child-abusing parents. Diphenylhydantoin had beneficial effects only on anxiety, depression and somatic symptoms, but there was no improvement for the core symptoms of aggressiveness, impulsivity, or hostility.

The first description of the successful use of carbamazepine in episodic behavioural dyscontrol is probably the remarkable case described by Tunks & Dermer (1977). Their patient had congenital rubella and severe aggressive behaviour at the age of 10, resulting in admission at 13. She remained in hospital for the next ten years. A severe aggressive episode occurred every four days and 12–24 hours before the episode she would develop a glazed fixed expression in her eyes. Head-banging, scratching, and biting then followed. She failed to respond to phenothiazines, benzodiazepines, antidepressants, primidone, and oral contraceptives, but 800 mg carbamazepine daily (blood level 14 mg/l) led to a complete resolution of the disorder. Reducing the dosage led to a recurrence of episodes, and Tunks & Dermer concluded that a higher plasma level of carbamazepine was required for the control of episodic dyscontrol than for the control of epilepsy.

The realisation that carbamazepine may be an important psychotropic drug, as well as a useful anti-epileptic agent, started with the demonstration by Okuma *et al* (1981) of its anti-manic effects. Other workers soon found that the addition of carbamazepine to lithium could prevent relapse among lithium-resistant manic–depressives (Ballenger & Post, 1980). Furthermore, the addition of carbamazepine to chlorpromazine led to a dramatic reduction in the frequency of violent episodes among schizophrenics in a high-security hospital (Hakola & Laulumaa, 1982) and when combined with haloperidol, resulted in better control for schizophrenic excitement (Klein *et al*, 1983).

The first placebo-controlled trial of the effect of carbamazepine on behavioural dyscontrol was by Neppe (1983) among a group of treatment-resistant, long-stay, mainly schizophrenic, in-patients. Out of 15 patients, nine improved on carbamazepine but only one improved on placebo. Carbamazepine reduced the severity of overt aggression by half, and the frequency of aggressive outbursts was decreased by two-thirds. Luchens (1984) carried out a similar six-week placebo-controlled crossover trial among seven violent patients (six with schizophrenia, one with personality disorder) and found the frequency of aggressive acts was decreased by 67% during the carbamazepine trial. He replicated these findings in a second series, of eight patients, five of whom had a normal EEG while three had an abnormal EEG. There was no significant EEG effect on the frequency of either verbal or physical aggression. The presence of an abnormal EEG was however associated with carbamazepine therapy leading to a greater reduction in the use of medication 'as required' (p.r.n.). Mattes (1984) also reports a beneficial effect for carbamazepine on aggression which was independent of EEG status and neuropsychological measures of organicity. He treated 34 subjects with heterogeneous psychiatric diagnoses, many of whom had personality disorders and all of whom suffered from aggressive outbursts, with carbamazepine (200 mg three times daily) for two to three months. On a rating scale of 0–4 (4 = severe physical assaults) the patients' average score of 2.56 at base line fell to only 0.35 at discharge.

The most relevant study on the effect of carbamazepine on behavioural dyscontrol among the personality disorders is that of Gardner & Cowdry (1986). They conducted a six-week double-blind crossover trial of carbamazepine (200 mg three times daily) in 14 women with pure BPD, and a history of severe behavioural dyscontrol. Eleven of the placebo trials had to be discontinued because of clinical deterioration, compared with only one out of 14 carbamazepine trials. Seven (63%) patients while on placebo had episodes of severe major dyscontrol compared with only one (9%) on carbamazepine. Aggressive episodes during the carbamazepine trials were relatively minor, usually verbal outbursts only. Promising as this result appeared, it was not without its price: one subject developed psychotic depression and four others developed allergic skin reactions, leading to discontinuation of the drug in two cases. In both these cases substitution with diphenylhydantoin failed to show the same beneficial effect. Both Neppe (1983) and Gardner & Cowdry (1986) commented that carbamazepine appeared to induce a state of 'reflective delay', permitting patients to contemplate their actions, rather than acting immediately on their impulses.

Adult attention deficit disorder and the psychostimulants

Follow-up studies of hyperactive children during adolescence have shown these individuals are often impulsive, disorganised, or may have a poor self-image, and up to a quarter may be delinquent (Weiss *et al*, 1979). Men with minimal brain dysfunction are more sociopathic and assaultive, while women tend to depression, promiscuity, and suicidal gestures, and the most frequent adult diagnoses are immature and impulsive personality disorders rather than the functional psychoses. Family and cross-fostering studies have indicated a possible genetic link between attention deficit disorder and childhood and adult personality disorders, particularly alcoholism, sociopathy, and hysteria (Morrison & Stewart, 1971; Cantwell, 1972).

Hill (1944) was the first to use amphetamines in the personality disorders, in eight patients with a history of hyperactivity in childhood, enuresis, deep sleep, and abnormal EEGs. "The personalities which responded are those showing an aggressive bad temper and a generally hostile tendency. . . .

TABLE 11.6

Use of stimulants for the management of impulsivity, aggression and behavioural dyscontrol in adults

Study	Subjects	n	Design	Drug	Results
Hill (1944)	Aggressive psychopaths with previous childhood hyperactivity, enuresis, deep sleep	8	Open study	Amphetamine	Calming of dyscontrol, decrease in alcohol abuse, improved sleep and intellectual performance, weight maintained after initial loss
Wood *et al* (1976)	Adults with residual type attention deficit disorder	11	Placebo-controlled crossover	Methylphenidate 20–60 mg	57% had a good response
		15	Open trial	Pemoline, imipramine amitriptyline	37% improved on pemoline but only 8% on amitriptyline
Wender *et al* (1981)	Adults with residual type attention deficit	48	Double-blind placebo controlled	Pemoline 37.5–150 mg	Significant drug placebo differences for motor hyperactivity stress intolerance. Pemoline showed a bigger effect for those with severe hyperactivity during childhood.
Mattes (1984)	Adults with symptoms of attentional deficit disorder	61	Double-blind placebo-controlled trial	Methylphenidate mean 48.2 mg, daily	25% of subjects in both groups responded. Previous history of drug abuse but not previous childhood hyperactivity predictive of a positive response to methylphenidate
Shekim *et al* (1989)	Adults with residual type attention deficit disorder	18	Open trial	Nomifensene	80% showed an excellent response

The most satisfactory patients are those predominantly aggressive characters who are capable of making interpersonal relationships but continually wrecking such relationships'' (Hill, 1944). These drugs, with their propensity to addiction and to trigger paranoid psychoses (Connell, 1958), rapidly fell into disrepute and their use nowadays is confined to the rare disorder of narcolepsy and as aids to slimming.

Attempts to revive the use of psychostimulants in the treatment of adults with unstable temperaments and personality disorders were investigated by Wood *et al* (1976). In their first study, methylphenidate (up to 60 mg daily) was compared with placebo in subjects with adult impulsive disorders and a history of childhood hyperactivity. There were significant drug–placebo differences for tension, concentration and temper but not for depression. In the second study, Wender *et al* (1981) also showed that pemoline (37.5–150 mg) was superior to placebo for concentration, temper, impulsivity and stress intolerance, but these effects were confined to subjects with a history of severe childhood hyperactivity. Mattes *et al* (1984) failed to discern much benefit for methylphenidate among these adults, but Shekim *et al* (1989) found that nomifensine was sometimes of great benefit. Even though nomifensine has now been withdrawn, because of fatal liver complications, it is of interest that it inhibits the reuptake of noradrenalin and dopamine, an action it shares with amphetamine.

Just occasionally a severely violent patient may show a dramatic sedative response to d-amphetamine. Richmond *et al* (1978) described a 30-year-old man with severe recurrent bouts of aggression, including hurling a carton of condemned dynamite across a motorway, and at other times karate-chopping his wife in the neck. The patient had a history of childhood hyperactivity; his father and two brothers were ''always on a short fuse'', while his own daughter was maintained on d-amphetamine. His marriage was described as good in terms of their ''dynamite sexual relationship''. Computerised tomography and sleep EEGs with sphenoidal leads were all normal. All his symptoms resolved with 20 mg d-amphetamine twice daily. The patient commented ''this stuff makes me orderly. I can take things one at a time or if something is bothering me I can lay it aside and put it on the shelf. The only problem is the stuff makes me put on weight''.

The amphetamine-responsive patients described almost 50 years ago by Hill (1944) seem to differ little clinically from the MAOI-responsive borderlines described by Cowdry & Gardner (1988), except that Hill's patients were male and were labelled as psychopaths. Childhood hyperactivity was a common predictor for treatment responsiveness for both groups. There may be some overlap between subjects responsive to amphetamine and MAOIs. Thus Klein *et al* (1980) were able to switch some long-standing amphetamine users to MAOIs. Amphetamine responsiveness can be predicted formally by amphetamine testing, or more informally from the history of drug abuse. Mattes (1984) reported that such a history was the only useful predictor for a successful response to methylphenidate in adults, while Deykin & DiMascio (1972), but not Akiskal *et al* (1980), found it also predicted a responsiveness to tricyclics. Amphetamine testing predicts a successful response to pimozide in schizophrenia (Van Kammen *et al*, 1982) and, in depression, responsiveness to both imipramine (Fawcett & Siomopouloo, 1971; Van Kammen & Murphy, 1979) and to lithium (Van Kammen & Murphy, 1979). Amphetamine testing consists of measuring the effect of 30 mg d-amphetamine daily on mood-sensitive scales. In Fawcett's study three consecutive days on amphetamine were compared with three days on placebo, but in Van Kammen's study two days on d-amphetamine separated by at least two days on placebo were compared with the mean mood changes over four days of taking placebo. A significant alleviation of mood due to amphetamine was taken as a positive response. An assessment of the predictive power of amphetamine testing in BPD subjects might enable MAOI, amphetamine, or possible drug-responsive subjects to be more accurately identified at an earlier stage than is presently feasible.

Drugs and psychotherapy combined

Paykel (1989) graphically describes the debate that rages between the advocates of drugs and those who believe in psychotherapy in the treatment of depression. Historically, drugs and psychotherapy have often been diametrically opposed, with the proponents of each treatment arguing that the other was at best limited, and at worst harmful. Each camp was opposed to combined therapy, drug therapists arguing that psychotherapy aroused feelings that made patients worse, while psychotherapists suggested that drugs would fixate patients on somatic issues.

In the area of the personality disorders this debate has been far less acrimonious and combined therapies have been used for a long time. Possibly the high spontaneous remission rates in uncomplicated depression afford therapists the luxury of the belief that their particular therapy has been curative. However, among the personality disorders spontaneous remission in the short term is unusual and the response to both drugs and psychotherapy is meagre. Because of this therapists who favour one treatment approach are more willing to adopt the techniques of the opposite camp when indicated. Kernberg (1986), a leading authority on the pyschotherapeutic treatment of BPD, when considering the issue of suicide, writes "in all cases the treatment of the psychotic syndrome takes precedence over the treatment of underlying personality disorder, at least brief hospitalisation, possibly electroconvulsive treatment, may be required". By contrast Cowdry & Gardner (1988), both psychopharmacologists, permitted patients to take part in their drug trial only on the precondition that they continued to attend their psychotherapist.

A survey of American psychotherapists with an interest in psychotherapy for BPD showed that successful therapy was often two or three times weekly extending over four years (Waldinger & Gunderson, 1984). In addition, Gunderson (1984) writes that psychotherapists should have special attributes to treat BPD subjects, which include "a comfort with aggression, sensitivity to separation experiences, a sense of adventurousness and clarity of conceptual organisation". Perhaps these qualities or at least a generally tolerant attitude are also required even for those psychiatrists who adopt a mainly pharmacological approach. Possibly they should also be prepared to continue to see their patients for perhaps some three to six years, albeit at a rather lesser intensity than their more psychotherapeutically minded colleagues.

Although the majority of psychotherapists dislike the use of drugs, most will employ physical treatments for the more definite indications of suicide, severe behavioural dyscontrol, violent mood swings, and brief psychoses. Rather more controversial is their longer-term use as an adjuvant to psychotherapy. There are, however, two valid reasons why drug therapy can be viewed favourably in such circumstances. First, psychotherapy with BPD is associated with a drop-out rate of around 60% over six months (Gunderson *et al*, 1989) and some of this early drop-out may be prevented by concomitant drug therapy. Soloff (1987) puts the case even more strongly, and suggests that since drug trials have shown a consistent beneficial effect of small doses of neuroleptics, such treatments should be offered much earlier than after years of failure in psychotherapy. A second reason for favouring adjuvant drug therapy is the sheer expense of prolonged analytical psychotherapy which, as Gelenberg (1987) points out, puts it beyond the reach of all but the most wealthy. Supportive psychotherapy, once weekly, combined with a drug to help alleviate dysphoria, is more affordable and therefore may be made more widely available.

Prescribing for borderline subjects

All authors who write on the subject (Sweeney, 1987; Cowdry, 1987; Soloff, 1987) acknowledge there may be special psychological difficulties in prescribing drugs for BPD subjects which are quite distinct from the well known pharmacological side-effects of the drugs. Thus medication is sometimes used as another medium for acting out in therapy, while histrionic patients may grossly exaggerate side-effects and this may lead to the premature cessation of pharmacotherapy. Sweeney (1987) describes how some patients have a strong anti-medication bias before any treatment. The prescription of medication is experienced unconsciously as the doctor's attempt to take control. To surmount this, both Sweeney (1987) and Gunderson (1987) advocate that prescribing should only be done in the context of a good therapeutic alliance, where both the doctor and patient act jointly as colleagues in a trial of the drug, with the patient assuming some control over dosage and the time of day to take the drug. This manoeuvre may help dispel fantasies of medical omnipotence and so diminish anti-authoritarian feelings and the tendency to act out.

Gunderson (1986) also highlights the clinging dependency of many BPD subjects who have underlying fears of abandonment. They may either fail to recognise or deliberately deny that a particular treatment has been helpful because to make such an admission could result in the termination of therapy. Also the addition of any new treatment, whether a different therapist, a new group, or a new drug, may be experienced by a borderline with marked rejection sensitivity as an intense negative event and result in a relapse. Drug treatment, like psychotherapy, for the borderline is difficult to conduct and often has a poor outcome and should not be embarked on lightly, as many patients may do well without drugs while others may be worsened by medication. Response rates to the drugs are far worse than in the functional psychoses, yet some patients may derive a modest benefit, although for a few subjects the relief may be striking. However, there should be no unrealistic expectation that drugs can alter any ingrained character traits or in some way compensate for childhood abuse or deprivation, which is common among BPD subjects (Stone, 1990).

Caution is required when prescribing for BPD subjects with suicidal tendencies. The lethality of the drug in overdose should be an important consideration in drug selection. Often it is better to avoid prescribing drugs at all, but if a drug has to be used then a benzodiazepine or neuroleptic is relatively safe in overdose. Winkleman (1975) recommends chlorpromazine for those "who are prone to take handfuls of tablets at random". Montgomery & Montgomery (1982) have demonstrated that flupenthixol injections can reduce the frequency of such overdoses. Tricyclics and MAOIs are moderately lethal drugs in overdose and so they should be used sparingly among these subjects. Lithium is highly lethal in overdose and among those who take repeated overdoses, it may be contraindicated, except possibly as a trial during an admission.

Conclusions and future research

Only a decade ago Soloff (1981) commented that even though drugs were commonly prescribed for BPD there were no published guidelines for their use. Our knowledge and skill in prescribing has improved since then, not because any marvellous new drugs have been discovered, but more as a result of better diagnostic methods and a few well designated placebo-controlled trials. There is now reasonable evidence that many cases of BPD may respond to small doses of neuroleptics. Thiothixene, haloperidol and trifluoperazine have been shown to be superior to placebo, while perphenazine and thioridazine emerge favourably in open studies. These drugs seem to help a wide spectrum of symptoms including hostility, anger, suspiciousness, anxiety, depressed mood, delusions, behavioural dyscontrol, suicidal tendencies and sensitivity to rejection in cases of BPD. A rather more controversial area relates to their prolonged use as an adjunct to psychotherapy. Three studies suggest that MAOIs may also benefit a broad spectrum of symptoms in BPD subjects, but dietary restrictions and their risks with alcohol and in overdose may restrict their use. What limited information there is on pure SPD also suggests that neuroleptics may help in some cases (Goldberg *et al*, 1986) and a trial of low doses of neuroleptics may be indicated (Cowdry, 1987).

Psychotic episodes in BPD respond well to brief admissions, often without the use of drugs, but when drugs are prescribed, neuroleptics are indicated. The doses required for the psychotic episodes of BPD are usually considerably lower than those used in the treatment of schizophrenia and there is a suggestion that higher doses may actually make some patients worse. When a psychotic episode has responded well to a particular drug the individual patient may also benefit from taking a smaller dose of the same drug for longer.

Behavioural dyscontrol is undoubtedly the most serious management problem posed by subjects with BPD and in these cases pharmacotherapy should be combined with some form of psychotherapy and, if necessary, institutional care. In some cases, a strong manipulative element is present, and the wish to control staff or relatives is obvious; in these instances psychotherapy may play a more pivotal role. However, most subjects with BPD who mutilate themselves do so on their own, and repeatedly, as a means of relieving intolerable states of inner tension.

Drug trials have shown that the neuroleptics and to a lesser extent benzodiazepines can help some patients, and these drugs should certainly be given a trial first, before moving on to the more potent, but medically more dangerous drugs, carbamazepine and lithium. Carbamazepine may be specifically useful in the dyscontrol of BPD (Cowdry & Gardner, 1988) even in the absence of EEG or psychometric evidence of organicity (Mattes, 1984). There are as yet no trials of lithium in the behavioural dyscontrol of BPD but empirically a few cases may respond. Useful pointers to lithium responsiveness include mood disturbance, aggressive behaviour in the context of anger, a family history of classic affective disorder, and a personal or family history of alcoholism. Patients with serious episodes of aggressive behaviour extending over years should be given the benefit of a three-month trial of lithium (Sheard *et al*, 1976).

Depression and other mood disorders are common in the personality disorders. Thus classic DSM–III–R axis I syndromes, such as major depression, may sometimes respond to a tricyclic, although the response of major depression to tricyclics, MAOIs and ECT in BPD subjects is often equivocal and certainly much worse than in major depression uncomplicated by BPD. Panic disorder is also common and because panic attacks can sometimes act as a trigger for episodes of behavioural dyscontrol it is worth trying to treat. The mood disorders most characteristically associated with BPD are feelings of emptiness, boredom and frustration. This type of dysphoria usually responds poorly to drugs, but if drug therapy is attempted neuroleptics and MAOIs may be of more use than the tricyclics.

Attempts to subdivide the borderline syndrome into different subsyndromes, each responding to a particular drug, have not proved to be of much clinical value. A subgroup with spontaneously occurring mood swings, termed 'subaffectives' by Akiskal *et al* (1989) or 'emotional unstable character disorders'' by Rifkin *et al* (1972), may respond to lithium. In contrast, another subgroup where mood changes only occur in response to external stress, the 'hysteroid dysphorics', may do well with MAOIs (Liebowitz & Klein, 1981). Androlunis *et al* (1982) subdivided the borderline syndrome into organic and functional subtypes. They found that 38% of their sample had a significant organic contribution such as a previous head injury, epilepsy, encephalitis or a history of childhood attentional deficit disorder. Organic borderlines were more often male, had a younger age of onset and presentation, and more often had a family history of alcohol or drug abuse. The non-organic borderline was more commonly female, tended to break-down in the later school years, with depression, or brief psychotic episodes, and more often had a family history of affective disorder. Androlunis *et al* (1982) recommend that organic borderlines should be treated in a structured environment with psychostimulants and anti-epileptics, whereas non-organic borderlines allegedly do better with psychotherapy, antidepressants, neuro-leptics, or lithium. Ellison & Adler (1984) provide a neat but also unvalidated formulation that divides borderline personality disorder into four subgroups: schizophrenic, affective, organic, and a true personality disorder group. Remedies appropriate to the axis I disorders should be applied, while the personality disorder subtype, that is those patients who lack any co-morbid axis I disorder, should be treated by psychotherapy alone.

Most of the subdivisions described above have little proven clinical usefulness, but the drug trial of Cowdry & Gardner (1988) in BPD, covering trifluoperazine, MAOIs, carbamazepine and alprazolam, led to two important clinical observations, the one helpful, the second less so. The good news was that most of the subjects with BPD responded to one or other of the trial drugs. The bad news was that there were no useful clinical predictors in the patient's history as to which drug might be helpful, with the possible exception of a history of childhood hyperactivity and MAOI responsiveness. A pragmatic approach may therefore be the best, with patients being offered two or three drugs in a sequential trial in the hope that one drug will be found that is both beneficial and well tolerated.

When conducting such a therapeutic trial the clinician should always watch for drug-induced clinical deterioration as well as the more common medical side-effects. The following types of drug-induced deterioration are described: increased behavioural dyscontrol, or paradoxical rage reactions, with benzodiazepines (Gardner & Cowdry, 1985) and also with tricyclic antidepressants (Soloff *et al*, 1986*b*); severe depression with both propanolol and carbamazepine (Gardner & Cowdry, 1986); increased psychoses and 'behavioural toxicity' with neuroleptics (Steiner *et al*, 1979); and increased aggression with lithium (Tupin *et al*, 1973; Craft *et al*, 1987).

Methods of drug trials

Drug trials on subjects with personality disorders are difficult to conduct and this probably explains the dearth of published trials. The treatment of even a single borderline individual with psychotherapy, with or without drugs, is a major undertaking that makes considerable demands on a doctor's skill and reserves of emotional energy (Dawson, 1988), and so taking on a whole group of subjects for treatment must represent a daunting prospect. Main (1957) in his classical paper "The ailment" has graphically described how some female patients with severe personality disorders have the potential to make their therapists not only feel quite uncomfortable, but almost ill, as well. Disruptiveness, the occasional anti-authoritarian stance, and a propensity to abuse medication by taking repeated overdoses, or becoming addicted, are all clinical aspects of BPD which may jeopardise the completion of any drug trial. Quite apart from these practical difficulties in the management of BPD subjects during a drug trial, there are theoretical problems concerning the design of trials, their duration, diagnostic difficulties, subject recruitment, and the selection of suitable instruments for measuring change. Finally, ethical issues such as the use of placebos and the role of psychotherapy should also be addressed. Presently there is no accepted treatment of choice for BPD which can act as a standard for comparison, nor any agreed trial protocol or any generally accepted instrument to measure change. Despite these difficulties, much useful information can be gleaned by scrutinising the methods of the existing studies and this may assist in the design of future trials.

Making the diagnosis

Until comparatively recently, the diagnosis of a personality disorder was rather vague and most investigators just made up their own criteria for inclusion in their study and then recruited subjects from hospitals, prisons, or the out-patient population. Pseudoneurotic schizophrenia, an early forerunner of BPD, was so named because it was thought to be a variant of schizophrenia (Hoch & Polatin, 1949). This diagnosis was used in one of the first trials of MAOIs by Hedberg *et al* (1971). The ''emotionally unstable character disorder'' as described by Rifkin *et al* (1972) and hysteroid dysphoria as described by Liebowitz & Klein (1981) were both thought to have their basis in affective disorder.

Much of the confusion surrounding the diagnosis of these three different, yet probably closely related syndromes was clarified by Gunderson *et al* (1981), who not only laid down explicit operational criteria for 'borderline personality disorder' but also devised a special interview 'The Diagnostic Interview for Borderlines'. This instrument has now assumed a central place in all the more recent BPD studies, perhaps analogous to the PSE in studies on schizophrenia, or the SADS in affective disorder research. Gunderson's criteria also formed the basis for the DSM–III–R criteria of borderline personality disorder which are shown in Table 11.1. The only other group of personality disorders to figure prominently in drug trials are the schizotypal illnesses.

Even though it is most unlikely that DSM–III–R categories of BPD and SPD are the result of a single biochemical lesion, responsive to a single drug, they represent a coherent patient group. In future, drug trials are likely to be confined to these DSM–III–R categories rather than some of the earlier more esoteric formulations such as 'pseudoneurotic schizophrenia', 'hysteroid dysphoria', 'characterological depression' or 'emotionally unstable character disorder'.

Recruiting subjects for the drug trials

A wide variety of settings has been used to recruit patients for drug trials. These range from high security prisons (Sheard *et al*, 1976) to seeking out members of the general public via newspaper advertisements (Goldberg *et al*, 1986), or private practice, or particular patient groups where the prevalence of personality disorders is known to be high, such as clinic alcoholics (Fawcett *et al*, 1987), irritable or disruptive delinquents (Lefkowitz, 1969), or the parasuicide population (Montgomery & Montgomery, 1982). Very few, if any, of the reported trials have adhered to the accepted convention of subject recruitment, that is, a 'consecutive series of patients meeting diagnostic criteria'. Because of this, the published trials are not as truly representative of the whole population of personality disorders as they might be and, as a consequence, the value of their findings for daily clinical work is somewhat diminished. Many of the published trials have also stipulated in their inclusion criteria that a certain symptom or syndrome previously known to be responsive to the trial drug should also be present. While biases of this type, particularly if made explicit, do not detract from the scientific validity of the trial, they leave important clinical questions unanswered. In particular, it is impossible to know whether any beneficial effects of the drug are simply the result of its already known ability to alleviate one particular symptom or whether the drug has had a more global influence on the patient's personality disorder. Thus, the discovery that neuroleptics are helpful in those personality disorders which are associated with a transient psychosis (Serban & Siegel, 1984; Goldberg *et al*, 1986) can hardly be described as new because their efficacy in psychotic symptoms in other disorders such as schizophrenia or depression is well known. However, the observation that small doses of neuroleptics may also sometimes lead to improvements in interpersonal relationships and social functioning in the absence of a psychosis represents a rather more interesting and novel observation (Collard, 1976; Brinkley *et al*, 1979).

Despite the obvious difficulties in recruiting suitable subjects for trials there appears to be only one attempt at a multicentre trial. Collard (1976) together with 36 colleagues who each recruited a few cases, was able to report on the effect of pimozide in 60 subjects with DSM–II personality disorders (American Psychiatric Association, 1968). Studies on the more severe cases, for example, those with a forensic history, may in the future become rather more difficult to conduct because of severe legal and administrative restraints and therefore the fascinating study of lithium on violent offenders is unlikely ever to be replicated (Sheard *et al*, 1976). However, the milder community cases, who probably do not even require drugs, studied by Goldberg *et al* (1986), although easier to recruit, are less representative of the more morbid populations found in hospitals and prisons. To the hospital-based clinician, the population that really matters, and should therefore be the focus of further drug studies, are those subjects with BPD or SPD who are admitted to hospital, because it is those patients who will probably be medicated in any case (Soloff, 1981; Cole *et al*, 1984). Despite these criticisms, the very real difficulties in recruiting suitable subjects and running drug trials should be acknowledged and perhaps we should be grateful for the pioneering drug trials that have hitherto been conducted.

Design of the studies

Many of the earlier reports (for example, Reyntjen *et al*, 1972; Collard, 1976; Perinpanayagam & Haig, 1977; Brinkley *et al*, 1979) examined cases in an open fashion relying solely on a clinician's impression of improvement often even without using a rating scale. More recently, some studies have compared baseline scores with post-treatment scores, without placebo controls. This method is unsatisfactory because placebo effects may be large and spontaneous remissions can sometimes occur. Only three studies considered in this review (Lefkowitz, 1969; Goldberg *et al*, 1986; Fawcett *et al*, 1987) give any information on the magnitude of the placebo effect in the personality disorders, but these studies suggest it is large. In Lefkowitz's (1969) study on disruptive institutionalised delinquents, placebo resulted in a 40% reduction in global measures of disruptiveness. Fawcett's study on the effect of lithium in alcoholics showed that 42% of subjects who took placebo were cured compared with only 7% who stopped taking placebo, indicating a placebo effect of around 35%. Within the placebo effect there are probably a host of other therapeutic effects, such as improvement due to psychotherapy, beneficial social influences, and the subjects' motivation, any one of which may be more important than a specific drug effect. Thus only a trial which incorporates placebo controls and strict randomisation has any hope of balancing out these non-specific effects between the treatment and control group and can therefore detect a true pharmacological effect, which may quite possibly be smaller than the placebo effect.

The use of placebos in two recent trials has also facilitated the detection of adverse drug reactions, particularly the increased frequency and severity of episodes of behavioural dyscontrol. This was strikingly demonstrated for aprazolam by Cowdry & Gardner (1988) and for amitriptyline by Soloff *et al* (1986*b*). These adverse reactions would almost certainly have been missed in a trial design based solely on measures of change from a single baseline score. Three different placebo-controlled designs have been adopted. First, the classical parallel group design, as described by Goldberg *et al* (1986) and Soloff *et al* (1986*a*). This design is probably optimal, because it controls for other beneficial treatment effects such as psychotherapy, and provides an estimate of the size of drug–placebo differences, as well as the magnitude of the placebo effect. The main drawback to this design is that large numbers of cooperative subjects are required, for example Soloff *et al* (1986*a*) had to recruit 60 subjects for their trial of haloperidol, amitriptyline, and placebo, with only 20 subjects in each group. The second design is the longitudinal crossover study as described by Cowdry & Gardner (1988) and Rosenblatt *et al* (1974) in their study of child-abusing parents. Smaller numbers can be used, and the design is helpful for comparing drugs as well as detecting adverse drug effects. However, ordering effects may be important, and because there is a general tendency for patients to improve during a drug trial merely with the passage of time, the reliability of a crossover trial lasting for several months is questionable. The third type of placebo-controlled trial is the drug-withdrawal study as described by Liebowitz & Klein (1981). This is the least satisfactory, because illnesses caused by drug withdrawal are often quite severe in their own right, and may bear little relationship to the original disorder. Thus even normal individuals when given powerful psychotropic drugs may develop severe drug-withdrawal illnesses.

Another area of uncertainty in trial design is the optimum duration of the study. Beneficial effects for pimozide were observed up to the third month but not beyond (Collard, 1976) while gradual improvement for lithium occurred for up to two to three months in trials of lithium in aggression (Sheard *et al*, 1976; Wickham & Reed, 1987). Conventional antidepressant trials usually end after six weeks, but because drug effects in the personality disorders are probably rather weaker, a 12-week trial period may be more useful, if smaller beneficial drug effects are not to be missed.

A further important issue in the design of drug trials relates to the role of psychotherapy. Psychotherapy is commonly used in the treatment of personality disorders (for review see Kernberg, 1986) although its efficacy is uncertain. Should the patients who take part in a drug trial also be given psychotherapy during the trial or should it be withheld? Collard (1976) argued that it would be unethical to withhold psychotherapy because many subjects are deeply distressed and require support. His solution was to use 'the minimum amount of psychotherapy compatible with ethics', although not surprisingly no description of this amount of psychotherapy is given in his paper. Liebowitz & Klein (1981) adopted a much more generous approach and ensured that all their patients had twice-weekly dynamic psychotherapy throughout the trial. Cowdry & Gardner (1988) had an even more elegant solution to the problem of ensuring that all the trial patients received the same type and quantity of psychotherapy. Patients were only eligible for inclusion in the drug trial if they had been referred by one psychotherapist, and had given a firm commitment to remain in psychotherapy with the same psychotherapist for the duration of the study. Although such a solution is ideal it can only be applied in a single centre study comprising relatively few patients.

The measurement of change

Because of their pleomorphic psychopathology several different groups of symptoms have to be followed throughout the trial. Firstly, there should be a wide-ranging scale which covers a broad spectrum of symptoms such as the Hopkins Symptom Checklist (Derogatis *et al*, 1973) or other similar scales which cover a wide range of symptoms, such as the in-patient multidimensional psychiatric scale (Lorr & Klett, 1966). Secondly, special attention should be given to the measurement of depression and behavioural dyscontrol as these are the two most common presenting and distressing symptoms in BPD, and finally there should be some measure of the core personality disorder features throughout the trial. The measurement of depression in personality disorders is more complicated than measuring depression in a depressive illness because the picture is usually one of complaints of boredom, misery and emptiness rather than more classical melancholic features. For this reason, the Hamilton Rating Scale for Depression (Hamilton, 1967) may be rather less useful than self-rating scales such as the Beck Depression Inventory (Beck *et al*, 1961). Self-rated depression and anxiety should be assessed because unless a drug provides some subjective relief it is unlikely to be taken for a prolonged period. Thus, carbamazepine produced a substantial reduction in behavioural dyscontrol but only a very modest improvement on subjective depression on the Beck

Depression Inventory and was not much favoured by the patients (Cowdry & Gardner, 1988). On the other hand, tranylcypromine had rather less effect on behavioural dyscontrol but may be more likely to be taken for a longer period because it gave more relief from anxiety and depression (Cowdry & Gardner, 1988).

Behavioural dyscontrol and impulsiveness need to be quantified, and two separate approaches have been adopted. First, the simpler and probably superior method consists of simply counting the total number of severe episodes occurring over a fixed period of time. Montgomery & Montgomery (1982) counted the total number of suicide attempts made over six months in a trial of flupenthixol. Sheard *et al* (1976) counted the total number of serious episodes of violence among prisoners on lithium, while Cowdry & Gardner (1988) counted the frequency, and also rated the severity, of individual episodes of behavioural dyscontrol. The second approach, which may be less satisfactory, is to rely on self-rating scales such as the Buss Durkee Scale (Buss & Durkee, 1957) specifically designed for the assessment of impulsivity. Scores on these self-rated scales also tend to pick up anxiety, depression and other dysphoric affects and also fail to capture the episodic nature of the dyscontrol found among BPD subjects. The Overt Aggression Scale (Yudovsky *et al*, 1986) and the Ward Scale for impulsive action (Soloff *et al*, 1986a) may be used for measuring behavioural dyscontrol.

The final area requiring assessment is the severity of the personality disorder itself. Relevant scales include the Diagnostic Interview for Borderlines (Gunderson *et al*, 1981), the interview for borderlines (Baron, 1981), or the Borderline index (Conte *et al*, 1980) or the schizotypal symptom inventory (Meehl, 1964) as well as the DSM–III criteria for BPD. These scales measure core features of personality disorder which can sometimes change during a drug trial. Thus Liebowitz & Klein (1981) found at the start of their trial 12 out of 16 subjects fulfilled DSM–III criteria for BPD, but after three months treatment with a combination of MAOIs and psychotherapy, only six subjects still fulfilled the criteria. In the study of Goldberg *et al* (1986) scores on the schizotypal symptom inventory had a large fall during the trial, with both placebo and thiothixene, but there was no difference between the two groups.

Drug compliance is an additional interesting measure of drug efficacy in the personality disorders and Cowdry & Gardner (1988) found a trend for greater compliance with the more effective drugs. Thus only 37% of their subjects completed a placebo trial as compared with 75% who completed a trial of MAOIs. However, using compliance as a measure of efficacy may be confounded by the addictive nature of certain drugs such as the benzodiazepines and possibly even the MAOIs.

Drug trials on the personality disorders may be difficult to conduct, time consuming, and expensive, but funding bodies should view them favourably because of their clinical importance. Once acceptable protocols for these trials have been devised, newer drugs and other non-pharmacological remedies can be subjected to proper scientific scrutiny and so hasten the search for a cure for these debilitating disorders.

Acknowledgements

The author wishes to thank Professor Peter Tyrer, Professor Patricia Casey, and Susan Ritter for their helpful comments on an earlier draft of this paper, and Mrs Penny Nicholson for patiently retyping the manuscript.

References

AKISKAL, H. S., ROSENTHAL, T. L., HAYKAL, R. F., *et al* (1980) Clinical and sleep EEG findings separating "subaffective dysthymias" from "character spectrum disorders". *Archives of General Psychiatry*, **37**, 777–793.

AMERICAN PSYCHIATRIC ASSOCIATION (1968) *Diagnostic and Statistical Manual of Mental Disorders* (2nd edn) (DSM–II). Washington, DC: APA.

—— (1980) *Diagnostic and Statistical Manual of Mental Disorders* (3rd edn) (DSM–III). Washington, DC: APA.

—— (1987) *Diagnostic and Statistical Manual of Mental Disorders* (3rd edn, revised) (DSM–III–R). Washington, DC: APA.

ANDROLUNIS, P. A., GLUECH, B. C., STROEBEL, C. F., *et al* (1982) Borderline personality disorder subcategories. *Journal of Nervous and Mental Disease*, **170**, 670–679.

BALLENGER, J. C. & POST, R. M. (1980) Carbamazepine in manic depressive illness: a new treatment. *American Journal of Psychiatry*, **137**, 782–790.

BARON, M. (1981) *Schedule for Interviewing Borderlines*. New York: New York State Psychiatric Institute.

BAXTER, L., EDELL, W., GERNER, R., *et al* (1984) Dexamethazone suppression test and axis I diagnosis of inpatients with DSM–III borderline disorder. *Journal of Clinical Psychiatry*, **45**, 150–153.

BECK, A. T., WARD, C. H., MENDELSON, M., *et al* (1961) An inventory for measuring depression. *Archives of General Psychiatry*, **4**, 561–571.

BEECHER, H. K. (1955) The powerful placebo. *Journal of the American Medical Association*, **159**, 1602–1606.

BICK, P. A. & HANNAH, A. L. (1986) Intramuscular lorazepam to restrain violent patients. *Lancet*, i, 206.

BLACK, D. W., BELL, S., HULBERT, J., *et al* (1988) The importance of Axis II in patients with major depression. *Journal of Affective Disorders*, **14**, 115–122.

BRINKLEY, J. R., BEITMAN, B. D. & FRIEDEL, R. O. (1979) Low dose neuroleptic regimes in the treatment of borderline patients. *Archives of General Psychiatry*, **36**, 319–326.

BUSS, A. H. & DURKEE, A. (1957) An inventory for assessing different kinds of hostility. *Journal of Consulting Psychology*, **21**, 343–349.

CADE, H. F. H. (1949) Lithium salts in the treatment of psychotic excitement. *Medical Journal of Australia*, **36**, 249–352.

CANTWELL, D. P. (1972) Psychiatric illness in the families of hyperactive children. *Archives of General Psychiatry*, **27**, 414–417.

CASEY, P. R. (1989) Personality disorder and suicidal intent. *Acta Psychiatrica Scandinavica*, **79**, 290–295.

CHESSICK, R. D. (1969) The borderline patient. In *American Handbook of Psychiatry* (ed. S. Arieti). New York: Basic Books.

CHOWDREY, N., HICKS, R. C. & KREITMAN, N. (1973) Evaluation of an aftercare service for parasuicidal patients. *Social Psychiatry*, **8**, 67–81.

COLE, J. O., SALOMON, M., GUNDERSON, J. G., *et al* (1984) Drug therapy in borderline patients. *Comprehensive Psychiatry*, **25**, 249–262.

COLLARD, J. (1976) Pimozide in the treatment of some "social maladjustments" in "personality disorders". *Acta Belgica Psychiatrica*, **79**, 686–703.

CONNELL, P. H. (1958) *Amphetamine Psychosis.* Maudsley Monograph, No. 5. London: Chapman and Hall.

CONTE, H. R., PLUTCHIK, R., KARASU, T. B., *et al* (1980) A self-report borderline scale: discriminative validity and preliminary norms. *Journal of Nervous and Mental Disease*, **168**, 428–435.

COWDRY, R. (1987) Round table discussion. Treatment of outpatients with borderline personality disorder. *Journal of Clinical Psychiatry*, **48** (suppl. 8), 36–37.

——, PICKAR, D. & DAVIES, R. (1985) Symptoms and EEG findings in the borderline syndrome. *International Journal of Psychiatry and Medicine*, **15**, 201–211.

—— & GARDNER, D. L. (1988) Pharmacotherapy of borderline personality disorder. *Archives of General Psychiatry*, **45**, 111–119.

CRAFT, M., ISMAIL, I. A., KRISHNAMURTHI, D., *et al* (1987) Lithium in the treatment of aggression in mentally handicapped patients: a double blind trial. *British Journal of Psychiatry*, **150**, 685–689.

DAWSON, D. F. (1988) Treatment of the borderline patient relationship management. *Canadian Journal of Psychiatry*, **33**, 370–374.

DEITCH, J. T. & JENNINGS, R. K. (1988) Aggressive dyscontrol in patients treated with benzodiazepines. *Journal of Clinical Psychiatry*, **49**, 184–188.

DELAY, J., DENIKER, P. & HARL, J. M. (1954) Traitement des etats d'excitation et d'agitation par une methode medicamenteuse derivee de l'hibernotherapie. *Annals Medicale et Psychologique*, **110**, 267–273.

DEPARTMENT OF HEALTH AND SOCIAL SECURITY (1985) *Mental Illness Hospitals and Units in England. Results from the Mental Health Enquiry.* Statistical Bulletin. Government Statistical Service. London: HMSO.

DEROGATIS, L. R., LIPMAN, R. S., RICKELS, K., *et al* (1973) The Hopkins Symptom Checklist (HSCL): a self-report symptom inventory. *Behavioural Science*, **19**, 1–15.

DEYKIN, E. Y. & DIMASCIO, A. (1972) The relationship of patient background characteristics to efficacy of pharmacotherapy in depression. *Journal of Nervous and Mental Disease*, **155**, 209–215.

DOSTAL, T. & ZVOLSKY, P. (1970) Anti-aggressive effects of lithium salts in severely retarded adolescents. *International Pharmacopsychiatry*, **5**, 203–207.

DRYUD, J. E. (1972) The treatment of the borderline syndrome. In *Modern Psychiatry and Clinical Research* (eds E. Offer & D. X. Freedman), pp. 159–193. New York: Basic Books.

EICHELMANN, B. (1988) Towards a rational pharmacotherapy for aggressive and violent behaviour. *Hospital & Community Psychiatry*, **39**, 31–39.

ELLISON, J. M. & ADLER, D. A. (1984) Psychopharmacologic approaches to borderline syndromes. *Comprehensive Psychiatry*, **25**, 255–262.

FALTUS, F. J. (1984) The use of alprazolam in the treatment of three patients with borderline personality disorder. *American Journal of Psychiatry*, **141**, 802–803.

FAWCETT, J. & SIOMOPOULOO, J. (1971) Dextroamphetamine response as a possible predictor of improvement with tricyclic therapy in depression. *Archives of General Psychiatry*, **25**, 244–247.

——, CLARK, D. C., AAGESEN, C. A., *et al* (1987) A double blind placebo controlled trial of lithium carbonate therapy for alcoholism. *Archives of General Psychiatry*, **44**, 248–256.

GARDNER, D. L. & COWDRY, R. W. (1985) Alprazolam-induced dyscontrol in borderline personality disorder. *American Journal of Psychiatry*, **142**, 98–100.

—— & —— (1986) Positive effects of carbamazepine on behavioural dyscontrol in borderline personality disorder. *American Journal of Psychiatry*, **143**, 519–522.

GELDER, M., GATH, D. & MAYOU, R. (1989) *Oxford Textbook of Psychiatry* (2nd edn). Oxford: Oxford University Press.

GELENBERG, A. J. (1987) Round table discussion. Psychopharmacology of borderline personality disorder: a review. *Journal of Clinical Psychiatry*, **48** (suppl. 8), 23–25.

GODDARD, P. & LOKARE, V. G. (1970) Diazepam in the management of epilepsy. *British Journal of Psychiatry*, **117**, 213–214.

GOETZL, V. (1977) Lithium carbonate in the management of hyperactive aggressive behaviour of the mentally retarded. *Comprehensive Psychiatry*, **18**, 599–606.

GOLDBERG, S. C., SCHULZ, S. C., SCHULZ, P. M., *et al* (1986) Borderline and schizotypal personality disorders treated with low-dose thiothixene vs placebo. *Archives of General Psychiatry*, **43**, 680–686.

GRIFFITHS, J. L. (1985) Treatment of episodic behavioural disorders with rapidly acting benzodiazepines. *Journal of Nervous and Mental Disease*, **173**, 312–315.

GUNDERSON, J. G. (1984) *Borderline Personality Disorder.* Washington, DC: American Psychiatric Press.

—— (1986) Pharmacotherapy for patients with borderline personality disorder. *Archives of General Psychiatry*, **48**, 698–700.

—— (1987) Round table discussion. Treatment of outpatients with borderline personality disorder. *Journal of Clinical Psychiatry*, **48** (suppl. 8), 36–37.

——, KOLB, J. E. & AUSTIN, V. (1981) The diagnostic interview for borderline patients. *American Journal of Psychiatry*, **138**, 896–903.

——, FRANK, A. F., RONNINGSTAM, E. F., *et al* (1989) Early discontinuance of borderline patients from psychotherapy. *Journal of Nervous and Mental Disease*, **171**, 38–42.

HAKOLA, H. P. A. & LAULUMAA, V. A. O. (1982) Carbamazepine in the treatment of violent schizophrenics. *Lancet*, **i**, 1358.

HAMILTON, M. (1967) Development of a rating scale for primary depressive illness. *British Journal of Social and Clinical Psychology*, **6**, 278–296.

HEDBERG, D. L., HAUCH, J. H. & GLEUCH, B. C. (1971) Tranylcypromine–trifluoperazine combination in the treatment of schizophrenia. *American Journal of Psychiatry*, **127**, 1141–1146.

HILL, D. (1944) Amphetamine in psychopathic states. *British Journal of Addiction*, **44**, 50–54.

HILL, P., MURRAY, R. M. & THORLEY, A. (1986) *Essentials of Post Graduate Psychiatry.* London: Grune and Stratton.

HOCH, P. & POLATIN, P. (1949) Pseudoneurotic forms of schizophrenia. *Psychiatric Quarterly*, 1949.

JACOBSON, S. & TRIBE, P. (1972) Deliberate self injury (attempted suicide) in patients admitted to hospital in mid Sussex. *British Journal of Psychiatry*, **121**, 379–386.

KALINA, R. K. (1964) Diazepam: its role in a prison setting. *Diseases of the Nervous System*, **25**, 101–107.

KAPLAN, H. I. & SADOCK, B. I. (1989) *Comprehensive Textbook of Psychiatry* (5th edn). Baltimore: Williams & Wilkins.

KENDELL, R. E. & ZEALLEY, A. K. (1988) *Companion to Psychiatric Studies* (4th edn). Edinburgh: Churchill Livingstone.

KERNBERG, O. (1968) The treatment of patients with borderline personality organisation. *International Journal of Psychoanalysis*, **49**, 600–619.

—— (1986) The suicidal patient. In *Severe Personality Disorders: Psychotherapeutic Strategies*, pp. 254–263. New Haven: Yale University Press.

KILOH, L. G., BALL, J. R. B. & GARSIDE, R. F. (1962) Prognostic factors in treatment of depressive states with imipramine. *British Medical Journal*, **i**, 1225–1227.

KLEIN, D. F. & FINK, M. (1962) Psychiatric reaction patterns to imipramine. *American Journal of Psychiatry*, **119**, 432–438.

——, GITTLEMAN, R., QUITKIN, F., *et al* (1980) *Diagnosis and Drug Treatment of Psychiatric Disorders.* Baltimore: Williams and Wilkins.

KLEIN, E., BENTAL, E., LERER, B., *et al* (1983) Carbamazepine and haloperidol vs. placebo haloperidol in excited psychoses. *Archives of General Psychiatry*, **41**, 165–170.

KLEIN, N. S., WREN, R. C., COOPER, T. B., *et al* (1974) Evaluation of lithium therapy in chronic and periodic alcoholism. *American Journal of Medical Science*, **268**, 15–20.

KRAMER, B. A. (1982) Poor response to ECT in patients with a combined diagnosis of major depression and personality disorder. *Lancet*, **i**, 1048.

KROLL, J., CARLEY, K., SINES, L., *et al* (1982) Are there borderlines in Britain? A cross-validation of US findings. *Archives of General Psychiatry*, **39**, 60–63.

LANCET (1986) Management of borderline personality disorders. *Lancet, ii*, 846–847.

LEFKOWITZ, M. (1969) Effects of diphenylhydantoin in disruptive behaviour: study of male delinquents. *Archives of General Psychiatry*, **20**, 643–651.

LEONE, N. F. (1982) Response of borderline patients to loxapine and chlorpromazine. *Journal of Clinical Psychiatry*, **43**, 148–150.

LIEBOWITZ, M. R. & KLEIN, D. G. (1981) Inter-relationship of hysteroid dysphoria and borderline personality disorder. *Psychiatric Clinics of North America*, **4**, 67–87.

LION, J. R. (1979) Benzodiazepine in the treatment of aggressive patients. *Journal of Clinical Psychiatry*, **40**, 70–71.

LORR, M. & KLETT, J. (1966) *Inpatient Multidimensional Psychiatric Scale Manual*. Palo Alto, California: Consulting Psychologists Press.

LUCHENS, D. J. (1984) Carbamazepine in violent non-epileptic schizophrenics. *Psychopharmacological Bulletin*, **20**, 569–571.

MAIN, T. F. (1957) The ailment. *British Journal of Medical Psychology*, **30**, 127–145.

MANDELL, A. J. (1976) Dr. Hunter S. Thompson and the new psychiatry. *Psychiatry Digest*, **37**, 12–17.

MATTES, J. A. (1984) Carbamazepine for uncontrolled rage outburst. *Lancet, ii*, 1164–1165.

MEEHL, P. E. (1964) *Manual for Use with Checklist of Schizotypal Signs*. Minneapolis: University of Minnesota.

MERRY, J., REYNOLDS, C. M., BAILY, J., *et al* (1976) Prophylactic treatment of alcoholism by lithium carbonate. *Lancet, ii*, 481–482.

MONROE, R. R. (1970) *Episodic Disorders*. Cambridge: Harvard University Press.

—— (1982) DSM–III style diagnoses for the episodic disorders. *Journal of Nervous and Mental Disease*, **170**, 664–669.

MONTGOMERY, S. A. & MONTGOMERY, D. (1982) Pharmacological prevention of suicidal behaviour. *Journal of Affective Disorders*, **4**, 291–298.

MORRISON, J. R. & STEWART, M. A. (1971) A family study of the hyperactive child syndrome. *Biological Psychiatry*, **3**, 189–195.

NEPPE, V. W. (1983) Carbamazepine as an adjunctive treatment in non-epileptic chronic inpatients with EEG temporal lobe abnormalities. *Journal of Clinical Psychiatry*, **44**, 326–331.

OAST, S. P. & ZITRIN, A. (1975) A public health approach to suicide prevention. *American Journal of Public Health*, **65**, 144–147.

OKUMA, T., INANAGA, K., OTSUKI, S., *et al* (1981) A preliminary double-blind study of the efficacy of carbamazepine in the prophylaxis of manic depressive illness. *Psychopharmacology (Berlin)*, **73**, 95–96.

OVENSTONE, I. K. (1973) Spectrum of suicidal behaviours in Edinburgh. *British Journal of Prevention and Social Medicine*, **27**, 27–35.

OVERALL, J. E., HOLLISTER, L. E., JOHNSON, M., *et al* (1966) Nosology of depression and differential response to drugs. *Journal of the American Medical Association*, **195**, 946–948.

PAYKEL, E. S. (1972) Depressive typologies and response to amitriptyline. *British Journal of Psychiatry*, **120**, 147–156.

—— (1989) Treatment of depression, the relevance of research for clinical practice. *British Journal of Psychiatry*, **155**, 754–763.

PERINPANAYAGAM, M. S. & HAIG, R. A. (1977) Use of depot tranquillisers in disturbed adolescent girls. *British Medical Journal, i*, 835–836.

PERRY, C. J. (1985) Depression in borderline personality disorder. Lifetime prevalence at interview and longitudinal course of symptoms. *American Journal of Psychiatry*, **142**, 15–21.

PFOHL, B., STAUGH, D. & ZIMMERMAN, M. (1984) The implication of DSM–III personality disorders for patients with major depression. *Journal of Affective Disorders*, **7**, 309–318.

PHILIPS, A. E. (1970) Traits, attitudes and symptoms in a group of attempted suicides. *British Journal of Psychiatry*, **116**, 475–482.

RAMPLING, D. (1978) Aggression – a paradoxical response to tricyclic antidepressants. *American Journal of Psychiatry*, **135**, 117–118.

RESNICK, O. (1967) The psychoactive properties of diphenylhydantoin experiences with prisoners and juvenile delinquents. *International Journal of Neuropsychiatry*, **3** (suppl. 2), 30–36.

REYNTJENS, A. M. (1972) A series of multicentre trials with pimozide in psychiatric practice. *Acta Psychiatrica Belgica*, **72**, 653–661.

RICHMOND, J. S., YOUNG, J. R. & GROVES, J. E. (1978) Violent dyscontrol responsive to D-amphetamine. *American Journal of Psychiatry*, **135**, 365–366.

RIFKIN, A., QUITKIN, F., CARRILLO, C., *et al* (1972) Lithium carbonate in emotionally unstable character disorders. *Archives of General Psychiatry*, **27**, 519–523.

ROBERTSON, M. M. & TRIMBLE, M. R. (1982) Major tranquillisers used as antidepressants, a review. *Journal of Affective Disorders*, **4**, 173–193.

ROSENBLATT, S., SCHAIFFER, D. & ROSENTHAL, J. S. (1976) Effects of diphenylhydantoin on child-abusing parents: a preliminary report. *Current Therapeutic Research*, **19**, 332–336.

SCHMIDEBERG, M. (1959) The borderline patient. In *American Handbook of Psychiatry* (ed. S. Arieti), vol. 1, pp. 398–416. New York: Basic Books.

SERBAN, G. & SIEGEL, S. (1984) Response of borderline and schizotypal patients to small doses of thiothixene and haloperidol. *American Journal of Psychiatry*, **141**, 1455–1458.

SHAWCROSS, C. R. & TYRER, P. (1985) The influence of personality on response to monoamine oxidase inhibitors and tricyclic antidepressants. *Journal of Psychiatric Research*, **19**, 557–562.

SHEARD, M. H. (1971) Effect of lithium on human aggression. *Nature*, **230**, 113–114.

—— (1975) Lithium in the treatment of aggression. *Journal of Nervous and Mental Disease*, **160**, 108–118.

——, MARINI, J. L., BRIDGES, C. I., *et al* (1976) The effect of lithium on unipolar aggressive behaviour in man. *American Journal of Psychiatry*, **133**, 1409–1413.

SHEKIM, W. O., MASTERSON, A., CANTWELL, O. P., *et al* (1989) Nomifensine maleate in adult attention deficit disorder. *Journal of Nervous and Mental Disease*, **177**, 296–299.

SOLOFF, P. H. (1981) Pharmacotherapy of borderline disorders. *Comprehensive Psychiatry*, **22**, 535–543.

—— (1987) Round table discussion. Treatment of outpatients with borderline personality disorder. *Journal of Clinical Psychiatry*, **48** (suppl. 8), 36–37.

——, GEORGE, A., NATHAN, R. S., *et al* (1986a) Progress in pharmacotherapy of borderline disorders: a double-blind study of amitriptyline, haloperidol and placebo. *Archives of General Psychiatry*, **43**, 691–697.

——, ANSELM, G., NATHAN, S., *et al* (1986b) Paradoxical effects of amitriptyline on borderline patients. *American Journal of Psychiatry*, **143**, 1603–1605.

STEINER, M., ELIZUR, A. & DAVIDSON, S. (1979) Behavioural toxicity: neuroleptic induced paradoxical behavioural toxicity in young borderline schizophrenics. *Confinia Psychiatrica*, **2**, 226–233.

STERN, A. (1938) Psychoanalytic investigation of and therapy in the borderline group of neuroses. *Psychiatric Quarterly*, **7**, 467–489.

STONE, M. H. (1985) Analytically orientated psychotherapy in schizotypal and borderline patients: at the border of treatability. *Yale Journal of Biology and Medicine*, **58**, 275–288.

—— (1990) *The Fate of Borderline Patients*. New York: Guilford Press.

SWEENEY, D. R. (1987) Treatment of outpatients with borderline personality. *Journal of Clinical Psychiatry*, **48** (suppl. 8), 32–35.

TOBIN, J. M., BIRD, I. F. & BOYLE, D. F. (1960) Preliminary evaluation of librium in the treatment of anxiety reactions. *Diseases of the Nervous System*, **21** (March suppl.), 11–19.

TUNKS, E. R. & DERMER, S. W. (1977) Carbamazepine in the dyscontrol syndrome associated with limbic dysfunction. *Journal of Nervous and Mental Disease*, **164**, 56–63.

TUPIN, J. P., SMITH, D. B., CLANON, T. L., *et al* (1973) The long-term use of lithium in aggressive prisoners. *Comprehensive Psychiatry*, **14**, 311–317.

TYRER, P. (1988) The management of personality disorder. In *Personality Disorders* (ed. P. Tyrer), pp. 112–118. London: Wright.

——, CASEY, P. & FERGUSON, B. (1988) Personality disorder and mental illness. In *Personality Disorders* (ed. P. Tyrer), pp. 93–104. London: Wright.

TYRER, S. P., WALSH, A., EDWARDS, D. E., *et al* (1984) Factors associated with a good response to lithium in aggressive mentally handicapped subjects. *Progress in Neuropsychopharmacology & Biological Psychiatry*, **8**, 751–755.

VALGUM, S. & VALGUM, P. (1989) Co-morbidity for borderline and schizotypal personality disorders. A study of alcoholic women. Progress in neuro-psychopharmacology and biological psychiatry. *Journal of Nervous and Mental Disease*, **177**, 279–284.

VAN KAMMEN, D. P. & MURPHY, D. L. (1979) Prediction of antidepressant response to lithium carbonate by a one day administration of d-amphetamine in unipolar depressed women. *Neuropsychobiology*, **5**, 266–273.

—— , DOCHERTY, J. P., MARDER, S. R., *et al* (1982) Antipsychotic effects of pimozide in schizophrenia. Treatment response prediction with acute dextro-amphetamine response. *Archives of General Psychiatry*, **39**, 261–266.

WALDINGER, R. J. & GUNDERSON, J. G. (1984) Completed psychotherapies with borderline patients. *American Journal of Psychotherapy*, **38**, 190–202.

WEISCHER, M. L. (1969) Uber die antiagressive wirkung von Lithium. *Psychopharmacologia*, **15**, 245–254.

WEISS, G., HECHTMAN, L., PERIMAN, T., *et al* (1979) Hyperactives as young adults: a controlled prospective ten-year follow-up of 75 children. *Archives of General Psychiatry*, **36**, 675–681.

WENDER, P. H., REIMHERR, F. W. & WOOD, D. R. (1981) Attention deficit disorder (minimal brain dysfunction) in adults. *Archives of General Psychiatry*, **38**, 449–456.

WICKHAM, E. A. & REED, J. V. (1987) Lithium in the control of aggression and self-mutilating behaviour. *International Clinical Psychopharmacology*, **2**, 181–190.

WINKLEMAN, N. W. (1955) Chlorpromazine in the treatment of neuropsychiatric disorders. *Journal of The American Medical Association*, **155**, 18–21.

—— (1975) The use of neuroleptic drugs in the treatment of non-psychotic patients. In *Rational Psychopharmacotherapy and the Right to Treatment* (ed. F. Ayd), p. 161. Baltimore: Ayd Medical Communications.

WOOD, R. D., REIMHERR, F. W., WENDER, P. H., *et al* (1976) Diagnosis and treatment of minimal brain dysfunction in adults. *Archives of General Psychiatry*, **33**, 1453–1460.

WORRALL, E. P., MOODY, J. P. & NAYLOR, G. J. (1975) Lithium in non-manic–depressives: anti-aggressive effect and red blood cell lithium values. *British Journal of Psychiatry*, **126**, 464–468.

YUDOFSKY, S. C., SILVER, J. M., JACKSON, W., *et al* (1986) The Overt Aggression Scale for the objective rating of verbal and physical aggression. *American Journal of Psychiatry*, **143**, 35–39.

ZILBER, N., SCHUFMAN, N. & LERNER, Y. (1989) Mortality among psychiatric patients, the groups at risk. *Acta Psychiatrica Scandinavica*, **79**, 248–256.

ZIMMERMAN, M., CORYELL, W., PFOHL, B., *et al* (1986) ECT response in depressed patients with and without a DSM-III personality disorder. *American Journal of Psychiatry*, **143**, 1030–1032.

12 Antisocial (psychopathic) personality disorders and dangerousness: two potentially dangerous concepts

HERSCHEL PRINS

"Psychopathic personalities as such cannot be regarded as medical problems, although they are very prone to develop abnormal reactions which would bring them into the medical domain." (Curran & Guttman, 1949)

"In its present stage of development the concept of psychopathy is fuzzy at the edges and in need of refinement." (Roth, 1990)

"Dangerousness is a dangerous concept." (Shaw, 1973)

Some preliminary comments on terminology

This chapter focuses deliberately on a somewhat narrow but clinically important area of concern. This is currently under great debate and also is highlighted in Dr Coid's chapter in this book. The now more accepted restricted clinical term antisocial personality disorder as used in DSM–III–R (American Psychiatric Association, 1987) is bracketed with the word 'psychopathic' merely to enable the term to also be discussed in its non-clinical sense, as for example in the 1983 Mental Health Act for England and Wales. This enables the topics of aggression and possible dangerousness to be discussed. For the sake of brevity, the use of the term dangerousness in this chapter will be confined to dangerousness towards others, although it is of course acknowledged that many personality-disordered individuals act in ways that are dangerous, both indirectly and directly, to themselves. Since, for a variety of ill-understood reasons, women are less often diagnosed as psychopathic, most of the discussion in this chapter is focused on men.

Context

The relationship between mental disorder and criminality is, at best, equivocal. In the first instance, much will depend upon how one defines crime; since definitions of crime change at different points in historical time, criminal behaviour will not be a static phenomenon. For example, the crimes of attempted suicide and homosexuality between consenting adult males in private disappeared in the 1960s by sweeps of the legislative pen. Much also depends on how one defines and classifies mental disorder. If one follows the redoubtable Professor Szasz (1987) one will incline to the view that much of it does not exist, but if one adopts the rather less rhetorical views of Professors Roth & Kroll (1986) one may consider that Szasz's 'myths' are more substantial than they at first appear. To add to the problem, there appear to be variations in the volume and presentation of mental disorders at different periods in history. This is exemplified by apparent variations in the prevalence of schizophrenia in earlier times (Hare, 1983; Scull, 1984). It seems likely that some physically defined disorders were more common in earlier times and this might, at least in part, be due to inadequate diet and related issues (Prins, 1990*a*).

Mental abnormality and crime

Penal and criminal populations

Studies of the prevalence of mental disorders in penal and criminal populations deal, inevitably, with highly selected groups of people. This fact has important implications; incarceration itself may well exacerbate an underlying psychiatric condition, or its effects may be severe enough to precipitate mental disorder in a vulnerable individual (Schorer, 1965; Guze, 1976; Gunn *et al*, 1978; Coid, 1984, 1988*a,b*; and also Coid in this volume, Chapter 6). Feldman (1977), and more recently Robertson (1988), have pointed out that the mentally abnormal may be more easily caught in criminal activities, the police may charge some of them more readily, and pleas of guilty by them may be more frequent.

More than 20 years ago, Scott (1969) suggested that even allowing for the high degree of selectivity in penal and remand populations, the proportion of clearly identifiable psychiatric diagnoses was only somewhere in the region of 15%. However, Scott was conservative in his attribution of diagnoses and, in a later study, Gunn *et al* (1978) put the figure much higher; they estimated that about one-third of a sample of 629 prisoners they studied could have been regarded as requiring psychiatric attention at the time of interview. The numbers of persons in custody suffering from a degree of mental disorder severe enough to satisfy the fairly stringent criteria of the 1983 Mental Health Act are quite small; until very recently they have shown a decline; from about 800 in 1977 to about 350 in 1986 and 235 in 1988 (NACRO, 1987 and House of Commons written reply 22.12.88). At the time of writing there has been a slight up-swing, to about 330 in 1988–1989. This up-swing has been confirmed in a more recent study by Gunn *et al* (1991), who found an increase in psychiatric morbidity among sentenced prisoners; Grounds (unpublished) has found comparable morbidity in the remand population.

This increase has also been accompanied by a disturbing increase in the numbers of suicides in prison (*Independent*, 10 July 1990; Griffiths, 1990*a*).

Moreover, it is important to note that in addition to prisoners who can be formally classified as mentally disordered within the relevant legislation, there is an unknown number of mentally abnormal persons who are not so classifiable. These range from certain notorious individuals to a large number of socially inadequate people who constitute the 'stage army' described so graphically by Rollin (1969) – in and out of institutions of various kinds between ever-decreasing periods at large in the community. Over a decade ago I examined some 20 studies carried out on penal and court clinic populations during a 50-year period. The detailed results are described elsewhere (Prins, 1980*a,b*; Howells, 1982), but in summary the percentage of offenders found to be suffering from functional psychoses ranged from 0.5%–26%, from mental subnormality 2.4%–28%, from psychopathy 5.6%–70%, and from alcoholism/excessive drinking 11%–80%. This tremendous variation is, as Howells concluded, to be expected in view of the range of populations surveyed, extending from homicides to approved schoolboys. However, he suggested that "in spite of these disparities, these studies do suggest a high level of mental disturbance in criminal groups" (Howells, 1982, p. 165). More recent confirmation of this may be found in a study of sentenced male prisoners serving over six months in a large London prison. The researcher (an experienced prison medical officer) found that those prisoners with extensive criminal histories showed a higher incidence of mental illness than the less criminally involved (Griffiths, 1990*b*).

In a recent work, Bavidge suggests of philosophers who wish to discuss "issues of responsibility and the law . . . [that they take] on the thankless task of stalking the boundaries between law, psychiatry and philosophy, which like most border territories are matters of wars and disputes, of danger and confusion" (Bavidge, 1989, p. 11). He might equally well have been writing about anyone wishing to explore the problem of psychopathic personality disorder. Such a disorder must, of course, be located along the spectrum of personality disorders in general. The history of the concept is a long and somewhat tortuous one and is discussed by Berrios (Chapter 2) and Coid (Chapter 6) in this book as well as elsewhere (Prins, 1980*a,b*, 1986).

Despite "little agreement on the nature of the conditions encompassed by the term psychopathic disorder . . . it is a concept that remains at the core of clinical practice in forensic psychiatry" (Coid, 1989, p. 750). Over the years, contributions to the debate about psychopathic disorder have come from both within and outside the profession of psychiatry; few disciplines have been held to lack relevance to such discussion. Acute observations have come from both social scientists and lawyers who have raised important philosophical and epistemological issues. Many psychiatrists must have felt beleaguered by those who have suggested that the disorder they had been trying to treat for many years was in fact a 'non-condition' in the medical sense. Many years ago, Barbara Wootton pointed to the nature of the circular arguments that bedevil our true understanding of the condition: "the . . . circular process by which mental abnormality is inferred from anti-social behaviour while anti-social behaviour is explained by mental abnormality" (Wootton, 1959, p. 250). Some of these criticisms and reservations about treatability and arguments as to which institutions should treat such individuals are probably justified, and have been well illustrated by Grounds (1987). Despite these continuing concerns, psychiatrists and their close colleagues are asked to assess, and sometimes treat, such people. For these reasons it is probably not unreasonable to suggest that the personality disorders in general and psychopathic disorders in particular are the 'Achilles' heel' of psychiatry (Prins, 1988a). Tyrer has rather wittily suggested that "the diagnosis of personality disorder is similar to an income tax form, it is unpleasant and unwanted, but cannot be avoided in psychiatric practice" (Tyrer, 1989, p. 240).

Others have gone further in their criticisms, suggesting that the concept is no less than a moral judgement pretending to be a diagnosis (e.g. Blackburn, 1988; Lewis & Appleby, 1988). Coid (Chapter 6, this volume) and Roth (1990) have re-stated some of the key features of the psychopath; egoism, immaturity in its various manifestations, aggressiveness, low frustration tolerance, and the inability to learn from experience so that social demands and expectations are never met. To these essential characteristics we should probably wish to add the following; curious superego lacunae rather than total lack of conscience, a greater than average need for excitement and arousal, and a capacity for the creation of chaos among family, friends and those involved in trying to manage them. This latter characteristic strikes me as being one of the most accurate indicators of the true, as distinct from the pejoratively labelled, psychopath (Prins, 1986). It is this element of the chaotic that carries with it the impression of quite remorseless, causeless behaviour, coupled with a gratuitousness and complete lack of justification. It has an almost eldritch quality in the weirdness of its impact and does not appear to be seen in any other kind of mentally aberrant state. It is therefore not to be wondered at that some people, in sheer explanatory desperation describe such behaviour as 'evil' – as did the bewildered governor of Strangeways prison at the height of the riots in the early summer of 1990 (*Independent*, 9 May 1990). The nature of behaviour that some would describe as psychopathic and others as 'evil' and an attempt at differentiation is made by Peck (1989). The other important characteristic is the veneer of charm and sophistication that only serves to mask the underlying themes of chaos and potential for mayhem. This veneer – the 'mask of sanity' – is graphically described by Cleckley in his classical accounts of different types of psychopaths (Cleckley, 1976). Such a veneer is well depicted by the aged Duchess of York in the description of her son Richard III; "Thy age confirmed, proud, subtle, sly and bloody, More mild but yet more harmful – kind in hatred" (Richard III Act IV Scene iv; Shakespeare).

The veneer of sincerity and truth has been described in more recent times as the psychopath's capacity to "know the words and not the music" (Johns & Quay, 1962). The search for proven aetiology continues and the research literature grows with its accounts of social analysis and laboratory-based experiments involving levels of anxiety arousal, cortical immaturity, brain biochemistry and the importance of neurological damage in the form of major and minor cerebral insults (Weller, 1986). The scope for future research is enormous and the current state of the art is usefully summed up by Coid when he says "current research trends suggest that it may be best to broadly conceptualise it [psychopathic disorder] as a development disorder, or series of disorders. The sheer range of psychopathology makes it more appropriate therefore to think of the psychopathic *disorders* [italics added] rather than a single entity" (Coid, 1989, p. 755). The results of a recent postal survey of forensic practitioners (forensic psychiatrists, clinical forensic psychologists and probation officers) suggest a fairly high level of agreement that the concept still has use in day-to-day practice and communication (Tennent *et al*, 1990). Finally, for those wishing for an insightful, descriptive account of psychopathy in the young a recent work by Masters will repay careful scrutiny (Masters, 1990).

Dangerous psychopaths

Dangerousness as a concept

Dangerousness means different things to different people. Indeed, if asked to rank a group of people in order of dangerousness we should probably find ourselves in great difficulty, thus emphasising what a dangerous concept it is. Of the following, who, for example, is the most dangerous? The bank robber, the bigoted patriot or blinkered politician, the over-zealous chief of police, the persistent paedophile, the person who peddles heroin for profit to children, the person who drives, knowing him/herself to be unfit through drink or other drugs, the swimmer who uses the public baths knowingly suffering from a highly contagious and dangerous disease, or the consortium which disposes of toxic waste without proper safeguards? All of the foregoing present potential hazards of some kind; it is this capacity to create a potential hazard to the safety of others that is at the heart of our concern. This safety of others implies a relationship. Dangerousness does not exist in isolation; the relationship between proximate persons and events is best demonstrated in Scott's deceptively simple equation:

"Offender + victim + circumstances = offence" (Scott, 1977, p. 130).

For present purposes we can best define dangerousness (paraphrasing Scott, 1977) as a tendency to inflict serious physical injury or psychological harm on others.

Can dangerousness be predicted?

If, by prediction, we mean the capacity to be right every time, the short answer is no. If we have more modest goals and ask, are there measures, based upon past experience, that will reduce the possibility of dangerous conduct, then the answer is yes. Pollock & Webster (1990) put the issues very clearly:

"From a scientific perspective . . . [the] question is impossible to answer since it is based on an unscientific assumption about dangerousness, namely that it is a stable and consistent quality existing within the individual. Translating the question into more appropriate terms would require the following question . . . 'what are the psychological, social and biological factors bearing on the defendant's violent behaviour and what are the implications for future violence and the potential for change?' " (p. 493).

In fact, psychiatrists appear to be no worse at predicting dangerousness than other professionals, and in relation to potentially dangerous *mentally ill* offenders are better at it than others (Greenland, 1980, 1985). All professionals might perform better if attempts at prediction were less global and confined to specific types of offender-patients (Hamilton & Freeman, 1982; Prins, 1990*b*). It is probably wisest to assert that our endeavours in this field are currently more at the 'art' than 'science' stage. Great caution should be exercised before labelling anyone as dangerous. For this reason, a greater degree of tolerance of ambiguity and uncertainty has to be shown in this area of psychiatric practice than many others. Our work is made additionally difficult because some of it has to be carried out under legal and administrative constraints (Prins, 1990*c*).

Are all psychopaths dangerous?

Not all psychopaths present universally potentially dangerous characteristics. However, if we adopt the 1983 Mental Health Act terminology it is legitimate to make an assumption of potential dangerousness since people so labelled must, *ipso facto*, have shown a long-standing course of antisocial conduct coupled with aggressiveness. In addition, there will be limited expectations of treatability since the Act emphasises alleviation of the condition and prevention of its deterioration and not cure as part of the grounds for compulsory hospital admission. Within the context of this contribution, the individuals I have in mind are those who have shown persistent, aggressive, antisocial behaviour (which at some point has brought them into conflict with the law) and who demonstrate most of the key characteristics of psychopathic disorder already mentioned. The essential features can be reinforced at this point in the Report of the Butler Committee (Home Office & Department of Health & Social Security, 1975):

"Since its introduction more than 90 years ago the term 'psychopathic disorder' has been subject to a variety of different practical usages; it has been taken to cover a narrow or broad group of mental disorders, and to indicate differences either of causation or of clinical manifestation from other mental disorders. In consequence there is now a multiplicity of opinions as to the aetiology, symptoms and treatment of 'psychopathy' which is only to be understood by reference to the particular sense in which the term is [employed] by the psychiatrist in question" (para 5.2).

More recently the psychopath has been described in the following terms by a clinician:

"a social isolate on the fringes of organised society, uncertain of how he stands in relation to others, and of what is expected of him, and of what he should expect of them. It often seems that his behaviour is designed to cause the maximal emotional response in others which somehow might overflow on to him and give him some brief existence in a world of real interaction." (Whiteley, 1982, p. 9)

Whiteley's description of a need for 'maximal emotional response' stresses the importance of the creation of chaos already mentioned. In addition, it is necessary to re-state a characteristic also referred to earlier, namely the need for a high state of excitement and arousal. This need is well illustrated in the personality of Colin Pitchfork, described in Wambaugh's (1989) book. Pitchfork was convicted of the rape and murder of two teenage girls in Leicestershire during the period 1983–1986. In interviews with the police, it is said that he told them he obtained a 'high' during episodes of indecent exposure to women and from the knowledge that his victims or likely victims were virginal. He also described an additional aspect of excitement, namely that derived from obtaining sex outside marriage and his attempts to conceal this from his wife. He, too, demonstrated the veneer of charm already described and was able by this means to induce his wife to forgive his persistent unfaithfulness on more than one occasion. Many, but by no means all, such individuals would satisfy the criteria for hospital admission under restriction orders (Sections 37/41 Mental Health Act, 1983) and would most likely receive initial placement in a Special Hospital because of the immediate and grave threat they presented to the public. Others would receive life or long determinate prison sentences. Indeed, if experience is anything to go by, serendipity often seems to enter into the disposal of such cases.

Management

Preparation for management – first stage

Before beginning to intervene with the serious and potentially dangerous psychopath, it is necessary to examine one's own attitudes and to try to come to terms with them. There is little doubt that some seriously psychopathic individuals engender feelings of revulsion, distaste and even horror because of their behaviour and the crimes they have committed. The need for self-inspection is well demonstrated by Treves-Brown: "so long as a doctor believes that psychopaths are mostly 'bad' his successful treatment rate will be dismal. Since it takes two to form a relationship, an outside observer could be forgiven for suspecting that a doctor who describes a patient as unable to form a relationship is simply justifying his own hostility to this patient" (Treves-Brown, 1977, p. 62).

There is little doubt that therapists, of whatever persuasion, will bring what I have described elsewhere as a degree of 'ambivalent investment' to the task (Prins, 1988*b*). Three elements in this investment may be discerned. Firstly, the difficulty in having to come to terms with the feelings of revulsion and horror already mentioned. Secondly, the need to deal with the very considerable burden of responsibility presented by the conflicting needs of the offender and the public. Thirdly, the therapist's high psycho-therapeutic investment in seeing that things are going well because of his/her personal and professional motivation to assist people with a variety of difficulties, both medical and social. Having had to work very hard to overcome the aforementioned hurdles, there is likely to be an overall investment in seeing that things are going well. For this reason, therapists may be ambivalently receptive to the disclosure of 'bad news' and because of this ignore half-spoken or hinted at messages that all is not well, from both offender/patient and or family. This is likely to result in missed opportunities for the release and catharsis of frightening thoughts and fantasies. In the case of the seriously psychopathic, it may hinder attempts to confront undesirable and antisocial behaviour. The stage of personal preparation by the therapist is therefore very important and is one that must be continually renewed if we are to remain 'tuned in' and able to exercise professional vigilance. Walker (1991) has recently emphasised this need for vigilance on the part of the supervisor of such patients/clients. He prefers the term 'monitor' as describing more unambiguously the true nature of the relationship.

Preparation for management – second stage

The second stage of preparation is concerned with becoming sufficiently aware of the detailed facts of the case to facilitate effective intervention. As Scott suggested in his seminal paper on this topic:

> "It is patience, thoroughness and persistence in this process (of data collection), rather than any diagnostic or interviewing brilliance that produces results. In this sense, the telephone, the written request for past records and the checking of information against other informants, are the important diagnostic devices. Having collected the facts under the headings (1) the offence; (2) past behaviour; (3) personal data; (4) social circumstances, it is useful to scan them from a number of different directions with a view to answering certain key questions relating to dangerousness." (Scott, 1977, p. 129)

As Scott suggests, there are some very simple (but easily overlooked) techniques which facilitate the assessment of the dangerous psychopathic offender-patient. Full details of the index offence or offences and what a variety of professional observers thought at the time about the individual's motivation and attitudes are essential. Equally important are details of previous convictions, if any. For example, most indecent exposers do not go on to commit more serious sex offences (although they frequently continue to expose themselves). Those who expose themselves and accompany their exposure by threats, gestures and open masturbation may go on to commit more serious sexual offences (Bluglass, 1980). In similar fashion, the offence of rape which is always a very grave assault on a woman's rights, may offer prognostic distinctions, as for example when it occurs under so-called 'normal' conditions, and when it occurs against a background of highly sadistic and deviant sexual activity as indulged in by some sexual psychopaths. Persistent and coercive paedophiles often try to present themselves in the best possible light, blaming their victims for their crimes. Only close persistent questioning and confrontation of such sexually psychopathic offenders will reveal a different picture – namely slow, determined seduction on the part of the offender (Wiest, 1981). In working with the seriously psychopathic offender, it is useful to approach them in a general spirit of scepticism, disbelief and taking nothing at face value. The male burglar who steals only the shoes belonging to the female occupant of the house or slashes the bedclothes with a knife needs to be distinguished clearly from the burglar who behaves in a more conventional fashion (Morneau & Rockwell, 1980). Sometimes, our perceptions are sharpened if we obtain the photographs of the victim(s) and/or scene of crime reports. These serve to remind us of the gravity of what has taken place and they also may help us to continually confront those who are seriously psychopathic with the true nature of their behaviour. This is important since they frequently attempt to deny or minimise its seriousness.

A degree of scepticism is also useful when judging apparent institutional success. Intellectual achievement (such as that obtained on an Open University course) is very laudable and a matter for congratulation on the part of all concerned. However, it should not blind us to the need for a degree of equal achievement in the development of personal awareness and social maturation. It is not difficult for the seriously psychopathic to hide behind an intellectual facade; in fact they do so frequently. In similar fashion, the man with a life-long history of achieving his goals by violent means may win praise for his involvement in body-building classes in prison. A more realistic appraisal might be to consider that he was preparing himself for further mayhem on discharge!

Those supervising the dangerously psychopathic may need to be more intrusively involved in their social environments than in most other therapeutic encounters. Had those responsible for the supervision of Graham Young gained access to his living accommodation they would have found revealing pictorial evidence of his continuing preoccupation with poisons and death (Holden, 1974; Prins, 1986). Much more recently, had those involved in the supervision of Daniel Mudd, on conditional discharge from special hospital, adopted a more questioning stance concerning his interest, behaviour and activities, it is possible that a murder might have been avoided (Wiltshire County Council, 1988). In Young's case, he appeared to be engaging in a rich ongoing psychopathic fantasy life which was accompanied by murderous activity. Such fantasies, which may sometimes be made more readily accessible to therapists than is realised, may well be evidence of a form of 'wishful rehearsal' for actual behaviour (McCulloch *et al*, 1983). This kind of material, provided it is viewed alongside other evidence, may be of very great value, both diagnostically and prognostically. The benefits of first-hand knowledge of the social environment and the detailed factual accounts of grave crimes are graphically described by non-clinical writers. The crime novelist P. D. James notes in compelling fashion that "people's living space, and the personal possessions with which they surround themselves . . . [are] . . . inevitably fascinating . . . an affirmation of identity, intriguing both in themselves and as a betrayal of character, interests, obsessions" (James, 1987, p. 241).

Ongoing management

Those with a capacity for evasion, self-deception and the projection of blame (such as is shown by the seriously psychopathic) need to be firmly confronted with their tendencies from the outset. When such persons are subject to statutory supervision by psychiatrists (as for example through the medium of conditional discharge, life-licence, or, more rarely, parole from a determinate prison sentence) the implications of such supervision and its requirements need to be spelled out from the outset; such implications and requirements may have to be repeated on more than one occasion. The special nature of this relationship cannot be fudged. If such fudging occurs, it is likely to make the need for reality confrontation that much more difficult when it arises, as for example when procedures for recall on the grounds of adverse behaviour have to be invoked. If fudging has been avoided, there is far less chance of the offender-patient being able to say in reality, "I didn't realise you would have to take such action".

Management is likely to be enhanced if such matters are grasped firmly from the outset. It will also be enhanced if the therapist has certain areas of questioning firmly in mind. Such questions may be difficult to ask for the reasons given earlier, but failure to do so may fail to protect both offender-patient (from the trauma of his own vulnerability) and the public from the commission of further harm. The following are a series of suggested areas of questioning to be borne in mind. They are, of course, relevant to all stages of work with psychopathic offender-patients and not just ongoing management. They are also relevant to patients who are not psychopathic offenders and the distinctions made are, to some extent, arbitrary. I would stress, however, that they are of special relevance to the potentially dangerous psychopathic individual.

(a) How much 'unfinished business' (Cox, 1979, p. 310) does this person still have to complete? For example, the morbidly jealous personality (who may or may not be diagnosable as being formally mentally ill) may well begin to establish a relationship with someone who clearly and ominously resembles their first victim. Close, ongoing scrutiny of changes in social relationships is essential in such cases.

(b) Have we observed sufficiently well that current employments are all too similar to past employments and, as such, are they likely to increase vulnerability? With hindsight, one may ask how wise it was to allow Graham Young to obtain employment with a firm of optical equipment manufacturers given his past obsession with poisons? One is mindful of King John when he says: "How oft the sight of means to do ill deeds makes deeds ill done." (*King John*, Act III, Scene iii, Shakespeare). Employments may also provide prognostic hints. Brittain (1970), in his classic paper on sadistic murderers, suggests how such killers have frequently worked in abattoirs and in the butchery trade. It is therefore of interest to note that Dennis Nilsen, the serial killer of numerous young men, had served in the Army Catering Corps and possibly learned some of the skills he needed to dissect his victims while so serving.

(c) To what extent have past precipitants and stresses been removed? Has the history been 'scanned' sufficiently in Scott's terms (above) to determine whether foreseeable vulnerability has been avoided, or at least recognised as far as possible?

(d) What is this offender-patient's current capacity for coping with provocation? It is as well to remember Scott's advice that aggression may be displaced "from a highly provoking source to one that may be scarcely provoking at all", as for example in the case of the legendary Medea, who killed her baby, wishing to get back at her husband, saying "that will stab thy heart" (Scott, 1977, p. 130). We all know that the most worrying cases are those where very serious assaults have been inflicted upon the innocent stranger in the street for no immediately discernible reason. For example, the psychopathic young adult male who has never been able to deal with hatred for his father may, given just the necessary amount of provocation, take his vengeance upon the first male stranger he meets who just happens to look like his hated father. In such cases detailed records of previous provoking incidents, and the response of the offender-patient, are essential.

(e) How does this offender-patient continue to view himself? Does the need for a 'macho' self-image, based upon unresolved conflicts around relationships with women, make him likely to continue to take his revenge on them by way of psychopathic sexual assaults involving extreme violence and sexual degradation?

(f) To what extent can we assess changes for the better of the individual's capacity to feel empathy towards others? The acknowledgement of this capacity in the potentially dangerous psychopath is vital to ongoing management. Do such individuals still treat those around them as 'objects' rather than persons upon whom to indulge their deviant desires? (See for example, Masters, 1985; Holmes & de Burger, 1988). The true psychopath tends to see all around him as malevolently disposed. For this reason, their behaviour is less likely to be indulged in as a reaction to a specific and clearly defined 'last straw' sequence of events than would be the case with some other offender-patients.

(g) To what extent does the behaviour seem person-specific or as a means of getting back at society in general, as in the case of some arsonists who, like the Monster in Mary Shelley's *Frankenstein* are "malicious because . . . [they are] . . . miserable"? (Prins, 1987). To what extent are thoughts of killing or injury still present? Is there a pleasurable feel to their talk of violent acts or thoughts? Is there still an interest in such matters as violent pornography, Nazi atrocities, the occult, torture, etc.?

(h) If the psychopathic disorder (particularly if of the highly aggressive type) appears to be associated with demonstrable neurological damage, does the condition appear to be responsive to medication? If so, does the individual seem willing to continue to take such medication or are they likely to take it only spasmodically or, perhaps worse, take it in conjunction with non-prescribed drugs and/or alcohol? What social and community resources are available for endeavouring to ensure compliance with such treatment?

(i) How much cognisance has been taken of what the offender-patient actually did at the time of the crime? Was the offence so horrendous to them that they blotted it out of consciousness? It would be a mistake to conclude that even the seriously psychopathic do not sometimes use such defences. Are we in possession of sufficient facts concerning these matters? Did they wander off in a fugue-like state or, upon realising what they had done, summon help immediately (a not very likely response in the severely psychopathic)? Or did they, having cut the body up in little pieces, or mutilated it in some other way, go off happily to supper and a night's dream-free sleep? Have we assessed adequately the role played by alcohol and other drugs? In his postscript to Master's book about Nilsen, Anthony Storr suggests that the importance of alcohol upon Nilsen's behaviour may have been underestimated (Masters, 1985, pp. 317–325). Prisons and, to a lesser extent, hospitals are not the best places for monitoring offenders' and offender-patients' likely future capacities for handling such substances. Graded and highly controlled exposure to these and other temptations (such as, for example, small children) are what is required.

(j) To what extent has the individual begun to come to terms with what they did – at least in part? We may be disquieted if the individual continues to talk about the offence or offences in an apparently guilt-free or callous manner. Disquiet may be felt when protestations of guilt or remorse are not forthcoming. Wiest (1981) suggests that offenders and offender-patients may go through five stages in working through guilt and remorse: confession, acceptance of punishment, denial, grieving, and remorse. Distortion and denial can, of course, occur at all stages and for this reason each stage merits most careful attention. Some offenders and offender-patients may have committed their crimes so long ago that a degree of loss or distortion of memory may have occurred for events long past. We should consider also the possibility that some offender-patients may not *in fact* be guilty. Individuals suffering from severe mental illness or mental impairment may have been found to be under disability (unfit to plead) and the facts of their cases never reviewed subsequently by the courts in the past. Recent legislation now remedies this (Criminal Procedure (Insanity and Unfitness to Plead) Act 1991).

Conclusions

Work with the psychopathically dangerous individual requires a high degree of surveillance and this may be a difficult notion for some psychiatric professionals to espouse. It also requires a capacity to acknowledge accountability to the public, to central government (notably the Home Office) and a very active degree of cooperation with other professionals. It also requires a capacity to ask 'unaskable' questions and to be in a state that Cox describes as "balanced hovering attentiveness" because important "developments will often most frequently occur when the worker is least prepared" (Cox, 1990, pp. x, xi). It is useful also to remember that work with such difficult people is affected by public attitudes. The degree to which members of the public are sympathetic to the psychopathic must affect the way in which professionals feel able to carry out their tasks. On the rare occasions when things go badly wrong and further mayhem is repeated, psychiatrists and their colleagues feel very alienated and alone in their tasks. Such tasks are not made easier by the fulminations of the less responsible elements in the media who merely seek to sensationalise. In addition, political attitudes that are based firmly on 'keeping the lid' on socially problematic behaviour and that give a very low priority to madness and badness are also likely to make the work of professionals significantly more difficult. It becomes all too easy to blame the professionals for public and political failure, and for politicians and the public to sit back and find refuge in distancing themselves from the army of refractory and potentially dangerous 'outsiders'. We should, therefore, as dispassionately as possible, but with compassion, "consider the subject's life longitudinally, his existential manner of being in the world, what roles he has sought or was pushed into, and by whom" (Scott, 1977, p. 139). In doing this we should adopt in our counselling and therapeutic interventions the qualities of quiet *insistence*, *persistence* and *consistency* since these seem to be the most effective in work with the dangerously psychopathic (see Prins, 1980*a*, 1986). If we do this, we shall go some way in avoiding the dangers of being too facile in our understanding of the concepts of psychopathy and dangerousness.

References

AMERICAN PSYCHIATRIC ASSOCIATION (1987) *Diagnostic and Statistical Manual of Mental Disorders* (3rd edn, revised) (DSM–III–R). Washington, DC: APA.

BAVIDGE, M. (1989) *Mad or Bad?* Bristol: Classical Press.

BLACKBURN, R. (1988) On moral judgements and personality disorder: the myth of psychopathic personality revisited. *British Journal of Psychiatry*, **153**, 505–512.

BLUGLASS, R. (1980) Indecent exposure in the West Midlands. In *Sex Offenders in the Criminal Justice System* (ed. D. J. West), pp. 171–180. Cambridge: Cambridge Institute of Criminology.

BRITTAIN, R. P. (1970) The sadistic murderer. *Medicine, Science and the Law*, **10**, 198–208.

CLECKLEY, H. (1976) *The Mask of Sanity* (5th edn). St. Louis: C. V. Mosby.

COID, J. W. (1984) How many psychiatric patients in prison? *British Journal of Psychiatry*, **145**, 78–86.

——— (1988*a*) Mentally abnormal prisoners on remand – (i) Accepted or rejected by the NHS. *British Medical Journal*, **296**, 1779–1882.

——— (1988*b*) Mentally abnormal prisoners on remand – (II) Comparison of services provided by Oxford and Wessex regions. *British Medical Journal*, **296**, 1783–1784.

—— (1989) Psychopathic disorders. *Current Opinion in Psychiatry*, **2**, 750–756.

COX, M. (1979) Dynamic psychotherapy with sex offenders. In *Sexual Deviation* (2nd edn) (ed. I. Rosen), pp. 306–350. Oxford: Oxford University Press.

—— (1990) Foreword to *Bizarre Behaviour: Boundaries of Psychiatry* (H. Prins). London: Tavistock/Routledge.

CURRAN, D. & GUTTMAN, E. (1949) *Psychological Medicine* (3rd edn). Edinburgh: Livingstone.

FELDMAN, M. (1977) *Criminal Behaviour: A Psychological Analysis*. London: Wiley.

GREENLAND, C. (1980) Psychiatry and the prediction of dangerousness. *Journal of Psychiatric Treatment and Evaluation*, **2**, 97–103.

—— (1985) Dangerousness, mental disorder and politics. In *Dangerousness: Probability and Prediction, Psychiatry and Public Policy* (eds C. D. Webster, M. H. Ben Aron & S. J. Hucker). Cambridge: Cambridge University Press.

GRIFFITHS, A. W. (1990*a*) Correlates of suicide history in male prisoners. *Medicine, Science and the Law*, **30**, 217–218.

—— (1990*b*) High and low offenders compared. *Medicine, Science and the Law*, **30**, 214–216.

GROUNDS, A. T. (1987) Detention of 'psychopathic disorder patients' in special hospitals: critical issues. *British Journal of Psychiatry*, **151**, 474–478.

GUNN, J. (1977) Criminal behaviour and mental disorder. *British Journal of Psychiatry*, **130**, 317–329.

——, ROBERTSON, G., DELL, S., *et al* (1978) *Psychiatric Aspects of Imprisonment*. London: Academic Press.

——, MADEN, T. & SWINTON, M. (1991) *Mentally Disordered Prisoners*. London: Home Office.

GUZE, S. (1976) *Criminality and Psychiatric Disorders*. Oxford: Oxford University Press.

HAMILTON, J. R. & FREEMAN, H. (eds.) (1982) *Dangerousness: Psychiatric Assessment and Management*. London: Gaskell Books.

HARE, E. (1983) Was insanity on the increase? *British Journal of Psychiatry*, **142**, 439–455.

HOLDEN, A. (1974) *The St. Albans Poisoner: The Life and Crimes of Graham Young*. London: Hodder and Stoughton.

HOLMES, R. M. & DE BURGER, J. (1988) *Serial Murder*. London: Sage Publications.

HOME OFFICE AND DEPARTMENT OF HEALTH AND SOCIAL SECURITY (1975) *Report of the Committee on Mentally Abnormal Offenders*. (Butler report), cmnd 6244. London: HMSO.

HOWELLS, K. (1982) Mental disorder and violent behaviour. In *Developments in the Study of Criminal Behaviour, Vol. 2*. Violence (ed. M. Feldman). Chichester: Wiley.

INDEPENDENT, THE (1990*a*) 10 July, p. 5.

—— (1990*b*) Facing the moral dilemma of how to judge evil. 9 May, p. 3.

JAMES, P. D. (1987) *A Taste for Death*. London: Sphere Books.

JOHNS, J. H. & QUAY, H. C. (1962) The effect of social reward on verbal conditioning in psychopathic and neurotic military offenders. *Journal of Consulting Psychology*, **26**, 217–220.

LEWIS, G. & APPLEBY L. (1988) Personality disorder: the patients psychiatrists dislike. *British Journal of Psychiatry*, **153**, 44–49.

MacCULLOCH, M. J., SNOWDEN, P. R., WOOD, P. J. W., *et al* (1983) Sadistic phantasy; sadistic behaviour and offending. *British Journal of Psychiatry*, **143**, 20–29.

MASTERS, B. (1985) *Killing for Company: The Case of Dennis Nilsen*. London: Cape.

—— (1990) *Gary*. London: Jonathan Cape.

MORNEAU, R. M. & ROCKWELL, B. S. (1980) *Sex, Motivation and the Criminal Offender*. Springfield, Illinois: Charles C. Thomas.

NACRO (1987) NACRO Briefing. *Mentally Disordered Offenders*. London: Clapham.

PECK, M. S. (1989) *People of the Lie: The Hope for Healing Human Evil*. London: Rider.

POLLOCK, N. & WEBSTER, C. (1990) The clinical assessment of dangerousness. In *Principles and Practice of Forensic Psychiatry* (eds R. Bluglass & P. Bowden), pp. 489–497. Edinburgh: Churchill Livingstone.

PRINS, H. (1980*a*) *Offenders, Deviants or Patients? An Introduction to the Study of Socio-Forensic Problems*. London: Tavistock.

—— (1980*b*) Mad or bad? Thoughts on the equivocal relationship between mental disorder and criminality. *International Journal of Law and Psychiatry*, **3**, 421–433.

—— (1986) *Dangerous Behaviour, The Law and Mental Disorder*. London: Tavistock.

—— (1987) Up in smoke; the psychology of arson. *Medico-Legal Journal*, **55**, 69–84.

—— (1988a) The status of personality disorder. *Current Opinion in Psychiatry*, **1**, 184–187.

—— (1988b) Dangerous clients: further observations on the limitation of mayhem. *British Journal of Social Work*, **18**, 593–609.

—— (1990a) Mental abnormality and criminality: an uncertain relationship. *Medicine, Science and the Law*, **30**, 247–258.

—— (1990b) Dangerousness – a review. In *Principles and Practice of Forensic Psychiatry* (eds R. Bluglass & P. Bowden), pp. 499–505. Edinburgh: Churchill Livingstone.

—— (1990c) Supervision of dangerous offender-patients. *British Journal of Psychiatry*, **156**, 157–162.

ROBERTSON, G. (1988) Arrest patterns among mentally disordered offenders. *British Journal of Psychiatry*, **153**, 313–316.

ROLLIN, H. (1969) *The Mentally Abnormal Offender and the Law*. Oxford: Pergamon.

ROTH, M. (1990) Psychopathic (sociopathic) personality. In *Principles and Practice of Forensic Psychiatry* (eds R. Bluglass & P. Bowden), pp. 437–449. Edinburgh: Churchill Livingstone.

—— & KROLL, J. (1986) *The Reality of Mental Illness*. Cambridge: Cambridge University Press.

SCHORER, C. E. (1965) The Ganser syndrome. *British Journal of Criminology*, **5**, 120–131.

SCOTT, P. D. (1969) Crime and delinquency. *British Medical Journal*, i, 424–426.

—— (1977) Assessing dangerousness in criminals. *British Journal of Psychiatry*, **131**, 127–142.

SCULL, A. (1984) Was insanity on the increase? A response to Edward Hare. *British Journal of Psychiatry*, **144**, 432–436.

SHAW, S. H. (1973) The dangerousness of dangerousness. *Medicine, Science and the Law*, **13**, 269–271.

SZASZ, T. (1987) *Insanity: The Idea and Its Consequences*. New York: Wiley.

TENNENT, G., TENNENT, D., PRINS, H., *et al* (1990) Psychopathic personality – a useful clinical concept? *Medicine, Science and the Law*, **30**, 39–44.

TREVES-BROWN, C. (1977) Who is the psychopath? *Medicine, Science and the Law*, **17**, 56–63.

TYRER, P. (1989) Clinical importance of personality disorder. *Current Opinion in Psychiatry*, **2**, 240–243.

WALKER, N. (1991) Dangerous mistakes. *British Journal of Psychiatry*, **158**, 752–757.

WAMBAUGH, J. (1989) *The Blooding*. London: Bantam Books.

WELLER, M. P. I. (1986) Medical concepts in psychopathy and violence. *Medicine, Science and the Law*, **26**, 131–143.

WIEST, J. (1981) Treatment of violent offenders. *Clinical Social Work Journal*, **9**, 271–281.

WHITELEY, S. (1982) Assessing dangerousness in psychopaths. *Dangerousness: Psychiatric Assessment and Management* (eds J. R. Hamilton & H. Freeman), pp. 55–60. London: Gaskell.

WILTSHIRE COUNTY COUNCIL (1988) *Report of a Departmental Enquiry into the Discharge of Responsibilities of the Wiltshire Social Services in relation to Daniel Mudd from his release from Broadmoor in May, 1983 until his arrest in December, 1986 for the murder of Ruth Perrett*. Trowbridge: County Hall.

WOOTTON, B. (1959) *Social Science and Social Pathology*. London: Allen and Unwin.

13 Long-term outcome in personality disorders

MICHAEL H. STONE

"Man is like a novel: one doesn't know until the very last page how the thing will end." (Yevgeny Zamyatin, *We* (1924))

Long-term follow-up has been considered the psychiatrist's 'microscope' (S. Heller, personal communication). As with real microscopy, we must familiarise ourselves with a number of special factors, in order to make sense out of what we are viewing. In the domain of chronic conditions such as personality disorders, short-term follow-up is of little value in providing clues as to the most likely life trajectory. But long-term studies, besides being arduous, are fraught with problems affecting validity. Diagnostic criteria change from one generation to another. Patterns of illness also shift, such that long-term results, even if accurately assessed, may begin to lose relevance *vis-à-vis* the conditions confronting clinicians when the seal is broken on the results of conditions treated 25 years earlier which are no longer familiar. The longer the interval, the greater the multiplication of intervening variables. Data about outcome are more secure, but inferences about the efficacy of the initial treatment become riskier. Retrospective study design is burdened not only by the evanescence of memory but also by the spottiness of the old records with respect to variables whose importance was not suspected a quarter of a century ago. Prospective design reduces the memory problem, but forces the investigators to rely only on the variables they know at the outset are important; they cannot enquire systematically about factors whose significance will have hit home only in the distant future.

In the realm of personality disorders, there is a unique problem affecting the clinician observer – patients exhibiting severe and socially offensive traits are often at pains to hide these traits from the diagnostician or, at follow-up, from the interviewer. The existence and long-term fate of antisocial tendencies, in particular, present great difficulties to the investigator.

Personality disorders also show, to an even greater extent than the psychoses, the property of existing within a bell-curve of variation. The readily-diagnosed conditions represent 'outliers'. Next to them are 'borderline cases' (schizotypal and schizoid personalities are thus 'borderline' with respect to schizophrenia; cyclothymia, with respect to manic–depression). The fatter mid-portions of the curve contain those persons who would not be identified within psychiatry as 'cases'.

The personality disorders defined in DSM–III (American Psychiatric Association, 1980) or in ICD–9 (World Health Organization, 1978) may thus be seen as extreme examples of tendencies observable in the general population. Several of the standard personality disorders bear a close relationship to the symptom disorders enumerated in DSM–III's Axis-I. If agoraphobia is brought under control, for example, there is usually a residue of 'avoidant personality'. The lines between 'depressive personality' (Phillips *et al*, 1990) and 'major depressive disorder' are often indistinct. Many patients with obsessive–compulsive *disorder* do not have an underlying obsessive–compulsive *personality*, but in those that do the two conditions seem like different degrees of the same tendency.

Another problem arises with regard to personality disorders, stemming from the narrowness of the personality domain in DSM/ICD compared with the larger realm of maladaptive personalities recognisable within society as a whole. Many persons exhibit one or a few irritating traits (stinginess, intrusiveness, abrasiveness) with adverse social effects. Yet these traits need not 'add up' to an officially defined personality disorder. For the purposes of this review, we have little choice but to concentrate upon disorders within the standard nomenclature. The outcome studies published so far chiefly rely upon this common language.

Also complicating the analysis of outcome (besides the frequent admixture, in clinical practice, of *personality* disorders with well-defined *symptom* disorders) is the even more frequent admixture with 'other' personality disorders as currently defined. The latter situation is often called, in the United States, 'co-morbidity'. This is an unfortunate term, since it suggests the accidental coexistence of two or more unrelated conditions (like measles and tuberculosis), and blurs our recognition of how arbitrary our personality labels really are.

Since antisocial or psychopathic persons are, for example, by definition, self-seeking and contemptuous of others, they are therefore also 'narcissistic'. As Oldham has documented (1988), 'borderline' patients almost invariably have enough other traits to warrant a 'co-morbid' personality diagnosis. As a result, BPD needs, even more than the other categorically-defined personality disorders, to be understood also in dimensional terms (Stone, 1980). The importance of the dimensional approach to personality and its aberrations has been stressed by Eysenck (1947), Mezzich (1988), Tyrer & Alexander (1988), Liveseley (1986, 1987) and Liveseley *et al* (1987). I have recently offered a compendium of over 500 maladaptive traits (Stone, 1990a), analysable into some 66 'dimensions'. All the just-cited dimensional systems cover not only the entirety of the personality-disorder sections of DSM-III and ICD-9, but much that is left unnoticed by the latter category-based systems.

Personality traits, strictly defined, should reflect enduring and habitual qualities of interaction with others, that are for the most part egosyntonic and non-disruptive to the self. Symptoms and symptomatic acts (e.g. wrist-cutting, illusions, shoplifting) cannot be considered personality traits, whereas tactfulness, generosity, even temperedness (and their opposites, rudeness, stinginess, cantankerousness) clearly are. The current definitions of border-line, antisocial and schizotypal depend heavily upon symptomatic acts and general dispositions of mind (identity disturbance). One might actually divide the Axis-II section of DSM into a larger group of 'true' personality disorders, defined entirely by traits, and a smaller group of mixed disorders whose definitions include symptoms as well as traits. 'Paranoid' is a true personality disorder, whose ingredients (mistrustfulness, suspiciousness, grudge-holding, guardedness, hypervigilance, over-reactiveness, and jealousy) are all traits. Three of the DSM disorders – antisocial, borderline, and schizotypal – are mixed, as are two additional disorders of the ICD: affective and explosive.

As noted, the domain of traits is more extensive than the domain of personality disorders. The diagnosis of a 'disorder' is reserved for more serious conditions that would awaken the interest of a therapist or a forensic specialist. Some traits (frivolousness, silliness), even in their extreme form, remain, psychiatrically speaking, beyond the fringe. Still other traits, although clearly pathological, inhabit a disputed territory where there is not sufficient agreement among clinicians, or sufficient interest, to situate them within or outside the domain of obvious disorders. Traits such as lascivious, vampish, dandified, bigoted, and witchy are reminiscent of certain disorders (histrionic, narcissistic, passive–aggressive) but are not among their itemised descriptors. Cultural factors also enter the equation, so much so as to render the establishment of universal standards for the diagnosis of personality disorders an unrealisable goal.

A few examples will illustrate:

When in South America some years ago, I chanced to learn of an elderly judge who shot and killed his wife at a dinner party because, or so he believed, she looked at another man. This did not excite the attention of the legal community in that country, although it did receive mention in one of the inner pages of the local newspaper. Still less did his actions earn him the diagnosis, in that country, of either 'paranoid' or 'aggressive'.

Many people whose acts produce only a shrug of the shoulders in New York would be experienced, in Tokyo, as rude enough to warrant a diagnosis of 'aggressive' personality disorder. Those whom even New Yorkers would dub 'aggressive' would stretch Japanese vocabulary beyond its limits.

The foregoing remarks should help one understand that the literature on outcome in personality disorders is confined to a small region within the

M

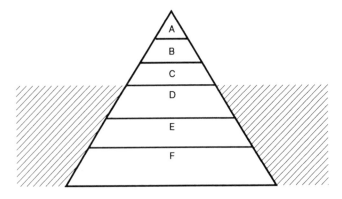

Fig. 13.1. Compartments within the domain of personality (A Personality disorder (PD) correctly identified via DSM/ICD criteria; cases followed-up long-term via reliable methods; B Persons seeking therapy; diagnosed correctly as examples of PD via standardised criteria; C Persons seeking treatment for personality problems not meeting standardised criteria for a 'personality disorder'; D Persons with severe personality problems warranting a PD diagnosis, but not seeking help or becoming identified as 'cases'; E Persons with several bothersome traits, short of meeting PD criteria; F Remainder of the general population)

totality of abnormal or 'disordered' personality. Even that region will have indistinct boundaries because inter-rater reliability for personality disorders is less than that for conditions marked by severe symptoms. In Fig. 13.1, the relative size (Region A: the tip of the iceberg) and unrepresentativeness of the disorders captured in this literature are shown in relation to the domain of *all* personality problems (Regions A through E of the 'iceberg'). Compartments A, B and C represent the portion of the 'iceberg' exposed to the mental health professions. The larger compartments, D and E, of personality pathology remain below the surface, apart from notorious figures in forensic, political and other realms whose abnormal personalities suddenly come into public view.

Outcome studies and their results

The outcome studies thus far reported have concentrated, understandably enough, on personality disorders associated with good reliability and with greatest interest to clinical and forensic specialists. These happen to be the 'mixed' (symptom and trait) disorders: borderline, antisocial, and schizotypal. Partly, this relates to the ease with which symptoms (e.g. self-damaging acts) can be reliably rated, in comparison with traits (e.g. vanity, indecisiveness). In a search of the literature spanning 1980–1989 there emerged some 61 outcome studies in this area, mostly devoted to borderline (24), antisocial (13), or schizotypal (9) personalities. Among the remainder, only narcissistic, obsessive–compulsive, and schizoid received attention, apart from a few articles on 'mixed' disorders. Because of the greater ease in conducting follow-up studies with in-patients rather than with ambulatory patients, almost all the data available concern patients who were originally in residential treatment centres.

Borderline personality disorders

The first follow-up studies of borderline patients, stemming from the 1970s, were of brief duration (three to five years) and used a variety of diagnostic criteria – mostly broad and unsystematic. Their results are reviewed elsewhere (Stone, 1989*a*). The life course appeared unfavourable, scarcely distinguishable from that of schizophrenics, except for the better socialisation noted among the borderline patients.

During the 1980s a number of studies based on larger numbers and longer intervals were reported, beginning with that of Plakun *et al* (1985) at Austin Riggs. This and the subsequently reported studies of McGlashan (1986*a*), Stone *et al* (1987), Paris *et al* (1987), and Kroll *et al* (1985) were more homogeneous with respect to diagnosis, all utilising DSM–III or the closely related Gunderson (Gunderson *et al*, 1981) criteria. The DSM criteria utilised in these studies were those of the 1980 edition. At least five of the following eight 'items' were necessary to confirm the diagnosis: unstable interpersonal relationships, impulsiveness, affective instability, inappropriate anger, self-damaging acts, identity disturbance, chronic boredom, and problems tolerating being alone. Curiously, none of these is a true personality trait. 'Impulsiveness' might have been included except the DSM definition stresses such examples as shoplifting or binge eating, which are symptomatic acts, not traits. Unstable relationships, impulsiveness, and anger are considered the key items.

Of these studies, ours (Stone *et al*, 1987; Stone, 1990*b*) had been based on the largest number (550: of which the BPD patients comprised the largest subgroup: 206), with the highest trace-rate (currently: 95%). In this study, referred to as the PI–500 (for New York State *P*sychiatric *I*nstitute), all but a dozen of the original patients were known to me personally. This acquaintance facilitated the tracing-process and enhanced cooperation with questions about current status. The patients were predominantly middle to upper-middle class, socio-economically: 87% came from families in Hollingshead & Redlich's (1958) socio-economic status (SES) I, II or III. Half the patients came from New York City; the remainder, from the rest of New York State. Their religious affiliations were largely Jewish (52%) or Protestant (22%). Almost all were single (91%); their average age when admitted to hospital, 22 years. Average length of stay was 12½ months. A quarter of the patients had never been admitted before. Most had completed at least some college; average IQ was 118. Although the levels of parental abusiveness, physical or sexual, had not been negligible, their homes, and the patients themselves, had been less violence-prone than is the case with many samples of BPD patients in the recent literature (Stone *et al*, 1988).

In the combined studies, all socio-economic groups are represented: the patients traced by McGlashan and by Plakun were predominantly SES I, II and III; those of Paris and of Kroll, of SES III, IV and V. All these studies (including the PI–500) are in agreement that when borderline patients have been traced at intervals of 10–30 years, outcome is generally favourable. Two-thirds of the patients in each study were clinically well at follow-up. Many had residual mild symptoms. About 20% were asymptomatic, working well and had established a gratifying long-term sexual partnership. This was more apt to be true of women than of men.

In our study, the marriage rate was half the national average for persons from their respective culture and era. The percentage of the former BPD women who now had children was about a quarter of the general population average. Only about one patient in four, as the group entered the fourth or fifth decade of life, still retained enough clinical features of BPD to justify its diagnosis by DSM–III criteria. The majority would currently be diagnosed as manifesting one of the milder personality disorders (e.g. histrionic, avoidant, obsessive–compulsive).

McGlashan has reported (1986*a*) that some BPD patients, as they enter their 40s, become symptomatic (usually depressed) again, owing to the loss of a sustaining relationship. Death of a spouse was the precipitant in some cases, but more often separation or divorce, prompted by the irascibility of the borderline spouse.

Subsequent readmission during the follow-up years was, in our series, only a third as likely for a BPD, as for a schizophrenic patient (28% v. 77%). Similarly, BPD patients were much more likely to have worked during half or more of the follow-up period than were the schizophrenics (66% v. 18%), and to have worked at higher levels of complexity (executive/professional). Among the borderline patients at follow-up, we found ten who had become psychologists, six lawyers, five doctors, three clergymen, ten teachers, two manufacturers, and one television executive. The 99 schizophrenic patients (all but two of whom have been traced), apart from one lawyer and one accountant, were either still unemployed or else working at jobs of less complexity than was characteristic of their families of origin.

One of the factors implicated in delayed recovery or in poor outcome is substance abuse – a common accompaniment of BPD especially in patients under 30 years of age. As they approached 30, many of the patients lost their enthusiasm for marijuana, amphetamines, etc. or, if alcohol had been their main addiction, had conquered their habit with the help of Alcoholics Anonymous (AA).

In our series (Stone, 1990*b*, p. 162) 37 of the BPD patients had, concomitantly, serious problems with alcohol. Of these, 10 were able to maintain a lasting relationship with AA and all are now well. But the suicide rate – 7 of 37 (19%) – was over twice the level in the BPD group as a whole. Among the AA-refusers, the rate jumps to 7 of 27 (26%). More striking still: of the 13 BPD females co-morbid for both alcoholism and major affective disorder (MAD), there were five suicides (38%). This combination – BPD × MAD × Alc – constituted one of the most fatal subgroups within the entire PI–500, matched only by the suicide rate among BPD patients exhibiting all eight DSM–III items. In this group of 15, there were 6 suicides (40%) (p. 208). Our findings are in line with those of Zilber *et al* (1989), who noted that in psychiatric patients of all diagnostic groups, the suicide risk was substantially greater than in the general population and that the standard mortality rate (SMR) in those with a personality disorder who also abused alcohol or drugs was three times that of those who did not abuse substances (21% v. 7%).

The one-third of the BPD patients who did not do well belonged to two broad categories: suicides and the chronically impaired. In the patients of our series, traced after an average of 16½ years, the suicide rate was 8½% (17 of 196: Stone *et al*, 1987), a rate similar to that noted by Paris *et al* (1988) – of 8%. In McGlashan's (1987) series, only the BPD patients with concomitant unipolar depression showed suicide rates in this range. In the large remainder the rate was 3%. The lower suicide rate in McGlashan's series is partly a reflection of the older average age (26) of the patients when first admitted at Chestnut Lodge, compared with that of the PI–500 series (Stone, 1990*b*); the Chestnut Lodge patients had, in effect, passed through more of what is now the main age of risk (20–29) in the USA for suicide (Solomon & Murphy, 1984).

In addition to the 17 suicides within the traced BPD patients of the PI–500, we could identify five patients who had made suicide attempts of such lethality that their survival seemed miraculous. Two had hanged themselves in the shower-room of the hospital ward and were cut down by the nursing staff seconds before the effects would have been irreversible. One hurled himself under an oncoming subway train, only to have the entire train pass over him without inflicting injury. Another, trying to die by oven-gas, was saved when the ensuing explosion blew him out of a room that was otherwise engulfed in flames. The last, having taken an overdose of heroin, was rescued in a hospital emergency-room with only a minute to go before brain-death. Each of these patients responded in a manner reminiscent of Gloucester, who, when fooled by his son into thinking he had jumped off a cliff, promised, on discovering himself still alive: "Henceforth I'll bear affliction till it do cry out itself 'enough, enough,' and die" (*King Lear* IV, vi: Shakespeare). For each of these suicide-*manqués* the near-fatal attempt was the last: each has gone on to clinical recovery. The man who nearly died from heroin, for example, is now on the lecture-circuit for Narcotics Anonymous, speaking to groups of young people about the dangers of drug abuse.

The opposite situation also occurs: a depressed person, not intending to die, makes a suicide gesture that turns out to be fatal. Two patients in the PI–500 took overdoses of a sleeping compound, expecting to be rescued by the return of a roommate who never showed up. The death of Marilyn Monroe (Summers, 1985) was probably an example of this phenomenon. In a depressed state on the night she died, she may have inadvertently taken an overdose of hypnotics, without having consciously willed her death. The details of her biography suggest she showed the combination of BPD, MAD and substance abuse – a combination associated with a high risk of suicide or fatal acts of carelessness.

Factors contributing importantly to suicide in BPD patients include continuing alcohol abuse, chaotic impulsivity and a history of parental brutality or sexual molestation (Stone, 1990*b*). The alcoholic BPD patients who refused AA tended to show more impatience, denial of illness, uncooperativeness, and disdain of authority. These 'hidden' personality factors interacted synergistically with the traits of BPD to drive the life-trajectory downwards towards either chronic impairment or early death. In the PI–500 the violence commonly associated with alcohol abuse was directed mostly against the self, although one of the alcoholic BPD females who eventually committed suicide had been arrested for molesting children and a second had burnt down her apartment; one of the BPD male suicides had been jailed for arson, and another had been violent toward his parents. The only alcoholic BPD patient with a history of violence who did not commit suicide was a woman arrested for abusing her own child. In general, the connection between alcohol abuse and violence is strong, as underlined in the study of Norton & Morgan (1989): high percentages of persons exposed to alcohol have been involved in violence (3% to 92%, depending on the series).

Table 13.1 shows the frequency of affective disorder, alcohol abuse and other variables, in relation to the 19 borderline patients of the PI–500 series who

TABLE 13.1
The PI–500 series[1]: 19 suicides in borderline patients

Diagnosis	History of affective disorder[3]	History of alcohol abuse	History of incest[4]	At least one psychiatrically ill relative[5]
BPD (*n* = 17)	13	7	5	8
BP organisation[2] (*n* = 2)	2	1	0	0

1. Stone (1990*b*)
2. Kernberg (1967)
3. Atypical depression (2), unipolar recurrent depression (5), bipolar illness during follow-up interval (1), bipolar II illness during follow-up interval (1) and solitary episodes of major affective disorder (MAD) (4).
4. As defined by Russell (1986).
5. Both parents alcoholic (2), both parents depressed, alcoholic and committed suicide (1), one parent depressed and committed suicide (1), one parent with MAD (4).

committed suicide. Fifteen of these suicides occurred within five years of leaving the hospital.

The chronically-impaired group consisted in addition of chronically hostile persons who undermine otherwise sustaining relationships (and often signed out of hospital against medical advice: McGlashan & Heinssen, 1988), of those whose self-esteem had been shattered by severe sexual or physical abuse, of persons, many of whom were chaotically impulsive, who never developed hobbies or work skills, and of 'co-morbidly' affectively ill (BPD × MAD) patients whose condition evolved during the follow-up years into unipolar or bipolar manic–depressive illness. The latter accounted for 8% of the BPD patients in the PI–500 series. Among the men, although not among the women, in this series, BPD × MAD was associated with a doubling of the suicide risk as compared with BPD alone (18% v. 8%). Many of the BPD × MAD males showed the personality characteristics mentioned by Benjaminsen *et al* (1990) that are considered a predisposition to suicidal behaviour: moodiness, pessimism, introversion, and dependency.

Evolution into schizophrenia was rare in the American series (Akiskal, 1981; Fenton & McGlashan, 1989; Stone, 1990*b*), but reached 20% in Scandinavia (Dahl, 1986), where admixture with schizotypal traits is more common in samples of BPD patients than is the case in the USA.

The presence of strong antisocial traits also predicted chronic impairment in BPD (Woolcott, 1985; Gabbard & Coyne, 1987; Stone, 1989*a*). Males are more likely to show this combined picture than are females. In the PI–500 series, the suicide rate among those with BPD × ASP (antisocial personality) was nearly three times that of the BPD group as a whole: 3 of 13 (23%).

Chronic impairment was also noted when schizotypal traits were prominent in a BPD patient (McGlashan, 1986*a*), presumably because the key schizotypal traits (odd communication, suspiciousness, social isolation: McGlashan, 1987) interfere grossly with the creation of sustaining, intimate and other relationships.

Because outcomes at long-term follow-up of BPD spanned the entire range from suicide to recovery with success in all areas of life, it becomes important to ascertain what factors might contribute to the extremes of this wide range. In the PI–500 series BPD patients whose outcomes were distinctly better than the average tended to show one or more of the following attributes: (a) high intelligence, (b) unusual talent in music, art, writing, etc., (c) unusual attractiveness, (d) concomitant obsessive–compulsive traits, or (e) in the case of alcoholics, adherence to AA. Woolcott (1985) also includes the quality of likeability. The value of the obsessive–compulsive traits probably lay in the self-discipline, work-orientatedness and ability to structure leisure time constructively that are typical ingredients of this personality type. In contrast, BPD patients who are particularly sensation-seeking and dependent on other people become disorganised and anxious when alone; unless treatment succeeds in fostering self-discipline, their extramural life

TABLE 13.2

Borderline patients of the PI–500. Impact of certain variables upon outcome

Factor	No. traced	No.	%	
		Follow-up GAS[1] scores >60		
Borderline × alcoholism × AA	10	10	100.0	
Borderline × artistic talent	9	8	88.9	More than 1 ½
BPD × obsessive–compulsive personality	17	15	88.2	GAS deciles above average
Borderline × attractiveness (1 s.d. above group mean)	25	22	88.0	
Borderline × IQ (2 s.d. above group mean)	18	15	83.3	
BPD female; no MAD	37	28	75.7	
Dysthymic borderlines	34	25	73.5	
Borderline × male homosexuality	13	9	69.2	
BPD × anorexia nervosa/bulimia nervosa	22	15	68.2	
BPD × MAD female	100	66	66.0	
All BPD	185	118	63.8	
Borderline females who eloped	33	21	63.6	
BPD × MAD male	27	17	63.0	
Borderline female × incest	35	22	62.9	
BPD–MDP	26	15	57.7	
BPD × alcoholism	35	19	54.3	
BPD female × incest	28	15	53.6	
Borderline × male/female homosexuality/bisexuality	23	12	52.2	
Borderline × parental brutality	30	15	50.0	
BPD female × incest with father/stepfather	22	10	45.5	
Borderline × STP	14	6	42.8	
BPD × parental brutality	22	9	40.9	
BPD with all eight DSM items	15	6	40.0	More than 1 ½
Borderline × firesetting	8	3	37.5	GAS deciles
BPD male; no MAD	24	9	37.5	below average
Borderline males who eloped	9	2	22.2	
BPD × ever raped	7	1	14.3	
BPD × ever jailed	8	1	12.5	
(schizophrenia)	95	8	8.4	
BPD × ASP	13	1	7.4	

1. GAS = Global Assessment Score (Endicott *et al*, 1976) – an anchored rating scale ('0' to '100') of overall function. Scores of 1–30 indicate clinical incapacitation; 31–50, marginal function; 51–60, 'fair' (persistence of moderate symptoms and social handicaps); 61–70, 'good' (mild symptoms, generally functioning pretty well); >70 clinically recovered. Group scores *exceeding* 1 ½ GAS deciles (i.e. 15 points) represent statistically significant deviations from the average of the whole population.

is a succession of calamities. Outcomes distinctly worse than the average were noted in BPD patients with (a) a history of parental brutality, (b) a history of father–daughter incest (Stone *et al*, 1988), (c) concomitant schizotypal features or (d) concomitant antisocial features. The observation of Links *et al* (1990) that marked impulsivity and poor premorbid functioning correlated with (continuing) poor function at two-year follow-up remains valid, in the light of long-term studies, at 10 and 20 years after initial treatment.

The associations between outcome in borderline patients and negative factors, as well as some additional factors are shown in Table 13.2, derived from the PI–500 series. Most of the associations concern a given variable in relation to BPD as the standard condition, but in some instances a broader definition of 'borderline' is used. The latter definition is that of Kernberg (1967), which includes BPD plus a number of other non-psychotic clinical states of intermediate severity (e.g. anorexia/bulimia; agoraphobia). In the PI–500 series there were an additional 93 patients who were borderline only by Kernberg, and not by DSM–III, criteria.

The impact of many variables is difficult to assess owing to their sheer number and also to sample differences. The coexistence of major affective illness led, for example, to a worsening of outcome in Plakun *et al*'s (1985) series, whereas Stone (1990*b*) noted that, in males with BPD, affective illness was associated with a generally better outcome (although a higher suicide rate) – because in the remainder of the male patients there was an over-representation of antisocial comorbidity. The counterintuitive finding of Modestin & Villiger (1989) that outcome at 4½ years was similar in BPD and in other personality disorder may also be a reflection of sample peculiarities.

In the PI–500 series, parental brutality emerged, in analysis of variance, as the most important negative factor; that is, as the factor with the greatest power to divert the life trajectory downwards towards a 'worse than average' outcome. This makes sense clinically. Being reared in an atmosphere of withering rejection and cruelty is likely to have more damaging effects upon the humanisation of children – upon their ability to trust, love and feel compassionate towards others – than most other traumata. Even father–daughter incest is not as uniformly shattering as parental brutality, since in some cases the daughter is the victim 'merely' of betrayal and perverted love, whereas in the worst cases, parental love was absent and in its place only sadistic exploitation. Of the latter, Case 1 below is an example.

The consistently poor outcomes noted in borderline patients who had ever been jailed (even for one day, after being caught 'joyriding' in a stolen car) were related in some cases to a life-long pattern of impulsivity and flaunting the law; in other cases, to antecedent parental cruelty, which had led to demoralisation and counter-aggressivity, culminating in a persistent pattern of antisociality.

More so than most other personality-disordered patients, those with BPD are exquisitely sensitive to initial conditions (Stone, 1988). Minor events lead to major upsets; major events that most people take in their stride lead to catastrophe. In the pathway analysis of the man who almost died of the heroin overdose, we saw that he was developing normally until his mother died of cancer when he was 11 years old. His father remarried. The step-mother was abusive and rejecting. The patient ran away from home, lived with a delinquent gang, became addicted to heroin, stole, was jailed, remanded to our unit, eloped, resumed his heroin habit, overdosed, and almost died. The near-death set in motion a favourable trend (perhaps galvanising long-buried positive qualities into re-emergence), just as the stepmother's behaviour had sparked the destructive trend. If the mother had not died, his life-course might never have passed through such a turbulent phase.

The following clinical vignettes, taken from the PI–500, illustrate the range of outcome we noted in the BPD patients, and also the way in which the outcome in some patients overturned the initial expectations of the hospital staff.

Case 1

Miss T was admitted to our unit when 20 years old because of suicide gestures, marijuana abuse, promiscuous relationships with both men and women, depression, and episodic rage outbursts. Her heiress mother had married a dissolute, narcissistic man who verbally humiliated their three sons (two of whom committed suicide) and who had incestuous relations with the patient when she was twelve. She became anorexic and was admitted to hospital elsewhere for two years. Attractive, and talented in ballet, she seemed headed for a successful career in dancing. In addition she was well-liked, projected a certain 'charisma', and was thought to have an excellent prognosis. She remained four months on our unit, then eloped. For a time she found employment in a prestigious dance company, but was eventually fired because of lateness to her own performances. A series of chaotic love affairs culminated in a suicide gesture (setting fire to her apartment), for which she was readmitted. A year later she married a man she had known for only a few weeks. Embarrassed about her past, and despondent about the future, she committed suicide a month later. Diagnostically, she had displayed all eight DSM 'items' for BPD.

Case 2

Miss N, a woman of 18, was admitted to our unit because of multiple drug abuse and a serious suicide attempt following a failed love affair. In addition she was unable to maintain her studies at college and was asked to leave after one semester. Her father, an affluent lawyer, had sexual relations with her for several years during her early adolescence. At 15 she briefly ran away from home. On the unit she was noted to be attractive, moody and impulsive. Five months later, she was discovered having brought alcohol onto the unit and was administratively discharged, presumably to reside with her parents. She disappeared, however, and for 10 years was a 'missing person'. The story as it emerged when she was traced 18 years after discharge was that she lived by her wits in Central America for those 10 years, had become alcoholic, and had been supported by a series of men. The last of these, a recovered alcoholic, persuaded her to enrol in AA. Her recovery began with that step. She became abstinent, returned to college, and became an alcoholic-rehabilitation counsellor. Later she married and had a child.

Antisocial personality

The current DSM criteria for antisocial personality (ASP) emphasise acts (e.g. stealing, aggressive behaviour) rather than traits. The corresponding ICD category (301.7) lays more stress upon traits such as, irresponsibility, callousness, and affective coldness. This difference in approach may account for the poor correlation between DSM–III–R (American Psychiatric Association, 1987) ASP and ICD–10's dissocial personality (Blashfield, 1990; World Health Organization, 1992). Blackburn (1988) has expressed serious misgivings about the moral judgements implicit in our traditional concepts of the 'psychopath' – the term once popular in referring to persons manifesting ASP. Blackburn's *caveat* aside, the definition of a 'psychopath' advanced by Cleckley (1972) was built primarily around traits: unreliability, emotional unresponsiveness, impoverished affect, egocentricity, insincerity, and remorselessness. This constellation of traits seems like a truer measure of whatever 'antisocial personality' or 'psychopathy' might signify, because the definition of a personality disorder should rest upon traits, not upon symptomatic acts. Unfortunately for the discussion of outcome, however, antisocial acts are much easier to record in the anamnesis and to agree upon between raters, whereas to register such traits as *insincerity*, *mendacity* and *irresponsibility* requires long (and usually painful) personal experience with whomever the diagnostician is evaluating. The outcome studies that exist have relied almost exclusively upon the recent DSM criteria and are thus largely uninformative concerning the fate of persons exhibiting the Cleckleyan traits.

Briefly, the presence of ASP generally betokens a pessimistic prognosis and an unfavourable life trajectory as tracked in the various outcome studies. This is no more than one would expect. Occasionally, there are reports of improvement or recovery – and it is in these instances we would most want to know whether these persons originally manifested the callousness, glibness, etc. of which Cleckley spoke. Or were they persons of a more sympathetic character who got caught up transitorily in antisocial acts?

As for DSM–III ASP, Gabbard & Coyne (1987) noted that of 33 patients at Menninger's so diagnosed in their survey, 19 were 'completely unresponsive to treatment' (p. 1183); 21 left the hospital prematurely and only five met initial treatment goals. Predictors of a negative response included a history of a felony arrest or of repeated lying and 'conning'. An early onset of dissocial behaviour during childhood was a worse prognostic sign than later onset (Offord & Reitsma-Street, 1983). Patients with opioid dependency did worse if they also met ASP criteria than if free of such signs (Woody *et al*, 1985); the case was similar with alcoholic patients (Rounsaville *et al*, 1987). Incarcerated rapists who did not meet ASP criteria showed less recidivism four years after release than did their ASP counterparts (Rice *et al*, 1990). In the Chestnut Lodge study, McGlashan noted that patients with BPD, BPD + ASP traits, and BPD + Narcissistic PD traits showed similar life trajectories. But in the ASP group, there were not sufficient antisocial traits to make an independent ASP diagnosis; the traits that were present were milder and well short of felonious acts, ruthless exploitativeness, etc. McGlashan's findings are in accord with the outcome patterns noted in the PI–500 study; namely, that a history of antisocial acts before a psychiatric hospital admission was not always an indicator of a bad prognosis nor of 'psychopathic' personality (in Cleckley's terms). Many of the ASP patients in the PI–500 were adolescent males remanded to the unit because of violent acts or serious non-violent crimes, alongside depression or other symptoms suggestive of psychiatric disturbance. These patients, almost all of whom were male, did uniformly poorly. But several of the males and most of the adolescent females whose antisocial acts had been less serious (truancy, shoplifting, running away from home) eventually made good adjustments. Almost invariably, these patients came from abysmal environments. They had been young persons of fundamentally decent character, forced by parental rejection or cruelty to take to the streets and survive by their wits. Some had become rebellious and, while on the treatment unit, were arrogant and indifferent. They left the unit (usually against advice) as treatment failures, yet were amenable to rescue by some other agency: most often, an 'Anonymous' group or a non-standard church. Some simply outgrew their wildness as they reached 30 years of age, settling down into respectable jobs and conventional lives. One such patient, 20 years later, became the mayor of a town in the Mid-West US; another, a manufacturer; a third, a counsellor in AA.

The tendency towards spontaneous remission, such that few persons diagnosed ASP in adolescence would still be so diagnosed in their 30s, has also been noted in the large series of Robins *et al* (1991). In their epidemiological study, only 47% of persons diagnosed ASP had arrest records, and only 37% of a group of arrestees met DSM–III criteria for ASP.

One reason for the equivocal findings in outcome studies of ASP is the conflation, within this diagnostic heading, of both transitory delinquents and continuous antisocials. As Dilalla & Gottesman (1990) point out, there are many delinquent young persons who do not go on to commit criminal acts during adulthood. In contrast the 'continuous antisocials', who probably have a "higher loading of either genetic or environmental influences or both" (p. 346), show criminal activity at a younger age, and persist in this pattern. ASP patients in the follow-up studies conducted by McGlashan and by our group were predominantly of the transitory delinquent type, hence the tendency towards 'mellowing' as they entered their late 20s or 30s.

Schizotypal personality disorder

Patients with schizotypal personality (STP) are rarely admitted to hospital in the United States and have thus received less comment in American follow-up studies than have borderline or antisocial patients. In Scandinavia, where this personality type is more common, a different designation is sometimes used. Many of the adolescent in-patients who formed the basis of Aarkrog's monograph on 50 consecutively admitted 'borderlines' (1981) would be schizotypal by DSM–III/DSM–III–R criteria. She has recently begun a long-term follow-up of these patients.

Among the American studies, that of McGlashan (1986*b*) compared 10 patients with STP with 18 in whom the traits of STP and BPD were combined. Outcomes were less favourable in the 'pure' STP group than in those with BPD as well. The latter did not fare quite as well as those with BPD who were not 'co-morbid' for STP, whereas the pure STP patients had outcomes only slightly better than those with frank schizophrenia. STP patients showed considerable residual impairment socially and usually worked at occupations considered below their 'potential' as this had been estimated during their youth. Few achieved closeness with a sexual partner and most lived as marginal 'loners'. Less tempestuous than affectively ill patients, the schizotypal patients seemed to have a suicide rate lower than that of patients with BPD or either schizophrenia or manic–depression (Stone, 1990*b*), although their small number makes comparison with the more populous diagnostic groups hazardous.

Minichiello *et al* (1987) reported underachievement in patients with obsessive–compulsive disorder (OCD) if STP was also present: behaviour therapy and pharmacotherapy led to improvement in 16 of 19 patients with OCD alone – but in only 1 of 10 with OCD × STP in the original article; 1 in 14 (Jenike, 1986), in a later paper.

Evidence for viewing STP as a condition within the spectrum of schizophrenia has been presented from many sources. A schizophrenic *dénouement* is common in patients first diagnosed STP, who showed magical thinking, suspiciousness, and social isolation (Fenton & McGlashan, 1989). In the PI–500 only one of 196 traced BPD patients went on to develop schizophrenia, and only one other a schizoaffective psychosis (Stone, 1990*b*).

Of the 12 patients with STP × BPD in the PI–500, the ten thus far traced include three recovered persons who are self-supporting and raising families, a murderer currently imprisoned, a suicide, and two chronically incapacitated persons receiving public assistance. Three others are working, but severely constricted socially (one took holy orders and lives in a monastery). Those with the worst outcomes usually showed strong paranoid features as well.

Narcissistic personality disorder

In-patients with narcissistic personality disorder (NPD) represent a highly skewed sample, since most persons with NPD come to the attention neither of psychiatric nor forensic authorities. Psychoanalysts, such as Kohut (1971) and his colleagues, who specialise in the treatment of narcissistic patients have used different and less well-defined diagnostic criteria, making comparisons with DSM-defined patients difficult. Follow-up studies of psychoanalysts working with narcissistic patients have not been carried out.

In his comparison of 17 in-patients with NPD and 33 with BPD Plakun (1989) found that the NPD group showed a higher rate of admission at long-term follow-up than did the BPD patients, and also a poorer overall level of function and sexual satisfaction. McGlashan & Heinssen (1989), and Stone (1989*b*) in their series found no appreciable differences in long-term outcome in BPD patients with or without concomitant NPD, unless ASP was added to the BPD × NPD combination (Stone, 1989*b*). Of the 13 patients meeting all three criteria, 12 were male; 2 of the 11 traced had committed suicide, one has been jailed for the past 22 years for multiple murder, six others are living marginal existences, and only two are now well (Stone, 1990*b*). As with BPD patients, those with NPD as well spanned the whole range of outcomes, from suicide to total recovery. One might suspect that, in this generation, young males with prominent narcissistic features (especially, overweening ambition and preoccupation with wealth and power) would be particularly prone to suicide. In the currently available studies, the sample sizes were too small to permit testing of this hypothesis. BPD males with depressive illness in the PI–500 did have a suicide rate of 18% – three times that of the males without depressive illness, and 2½ times that of BPD females (with or without concomitant depressive disorder). Narcissistic features appear to have played a role in the excess mortality: many of these males were acutely distressed over their inability, because of the underlying depressive illness, to 'live up to their potentials', become self-supporting, etc. – narcissistic injuries to which males in our society are especially sensitive.

Other personality disorders

The literature is sparse on outcome in personality disorders other than those just mentioned. The very nature of paranoid personality militates against the cooperation of patients with this disorder in long-term follow-up work. Patients in whom paranoid elements predominate lack the 'feedback' mechanism upon which successful therapy of personality disorders depends. This mechanism consists of a collective of positive traits: introspection, humility, candour, and a willingness to acknowledge imperfections. Paranoid persons, in contrast, tend to externalise and to relate with evasiveness rather than candour. Schizoid persons seldom seek help from the psychiatric profession; those that do seldom remain long in treatment (Stone, 1989*c*). The ten-year follow-up by Wolff & Chick (1981) of 22 boys, aged 5–14, with schizoid personality did not address the issue of change in function, mentioning merely that 18 still met the criteria for this disorder 10 years after initial evaluation.

The four disorders of DSM-Cluster 'C' – obsessive–compulsive (anankastic), passive–dependent, avoidant and passive–aggressive – seldom lead into residential treatment or to incarceration. Because of the ambulatory status of most such patients, they are only glimpsed peripherally by investigators pursuing long-term follow-up work. These disorders are often found in conjunction with the symptom-neuroses. Tyrer *et al* (1983) demonstrated the kind of dynamic equilibrium that exists between anxiety disorders and passive–dependent personality, and obsessional neurosis and anankastic personality. Anxious, including agoraphobic (Stone, 1991), persons when not under stress may emerge as passive–dependent or as avoidant; forced into uncomfortable social and other situations, the anxiety symptoms resurface. Patients in whom avoidant personality had been preceded by severe agoraphobia represent, as their long-term life path suggests, the severe end of the avoidant spectrum. Only two of the ten agoraphobic in-patients in the PI–500 have recovered; two are still housebound, and the remainder lead markedly constricted lives (Stone, 1991). Patients with milder forms of phobia/avoidant personality often respond favourably to the behavioural methods pioneered by Marks (1987), such that they become less phobic and less socially withdrawn.

There are only anecdotal reports about the long-term fate of patients with passive–aggressive personality. Such patients often develop their personality style in response to parental intrusiveness and pressure to conform – the response being one of covert hostility, defiance, sabotage and general non-compliance. In the course of therapy these attitudes quickly become apparent, manifesting themselves typically as a need to prove the therapist incompetent. Given time enough, and a commitment to the process of change, the passive–aggressive patients might eventually overcome these maladaptive patterns. But many quit treatment (a passive–aggressive act in itself) before any positive changes can occur. Hence passive–aggressive personality has the reputation of being particularly resistant to treatment (Liebowitz *et al*, 1986).

Ironically, follow-up data are least available on the personality disorders that are the most common. For the most part, histrionic, obsessive–compulsive, masochistic ('self-defeating') and depressive patients are ambulatory. These are the patients who have formed the bulk of the caseloads for three generations of psychoanalysts and, more recently, for therapists of psychoanalytic, behavioural, cognitive, and other orientations. Most of the literature on the short- and long-term fate of these patients is anecdotal (Pfeffer, 1961; Schlesinger & Robbins, 1974). The focus is seldom on personality or 'character' disorders *per se*, but rather on transference responses and related variables (Kantrowitz *et al*, 1990), from which inferences about personality types and their differential outcomes cannot be drawn.

The few follow-up studies that exist of patients treated with psychoanalysis either lack systematic diagnoses of personality (or 'character') or else do not present outcome data with precision. The review by Knapp *et al* (1960) of 100 cases mentioned that of 27 patients considered least suitable initially, 9 had obsessive characteristics and 13 had hysterical characteristics. All but one of the obsessives improved, whereas the hystericals showed wider variation in outcome – some doing very well, others poorly. In the 5–10 year follow-up of 183 analysis patients studied by Sashin *et al* (1975), no significant differences were observed among the various diagnostic groups (predominantly: hysterical, obsessive–compulsive and depressive), but 'outcome' was reported as a measure not of current function, but of whether treatment had ended (as in six out of seven cases it did) by mutual consent. The report of Weber and his colleagues at Columbia Psychoanalytic Center, although more extensive in scope than the preceding, did not analyse their results in relation to personality/character diagnosis at the outset and did not use the more common outcome scales (Weber *et al*, 1985a,b; Bachrach *et al*, 1985).

With regard to treatability, there is considerable indirect evidence for positive response to therapy, within the realm of mild character and personality disorders. In Mavissakalian *et al*'s (1990) study, for example, patients with obsessive–compulsive disorder who responded favourably to treatment became measurably less histrionic, avoidant, dependent and compulsive, according to standardised rating scales. Still, suicide risk is greater in those with any 'personality disorder' by a factor of three; and in those showing 'neuroticism', by a factor of two, when compared with the general population (Allebeck *et al*, 1988). Similarly, patients with depression alone fare better than those with concomitant personality disorders (Andreoli *et al*, 1989; Duggan *et al*, 1990). The most persuasive evidence comes from the elegant study of Smith *et al* (1980). They concluded, from statistical analysis of 475 studies, that ''psychotherapy is beneficial, consistently so and in many different ways'' (p. 183). Although their focus was on the different types of psychotherapy, the articles they reviewed included many devoted to patients with hysterical, obsessive–compulsive, passive–aggressive, 'as-if' and other personality disorders. It is an inference, admittedly, but not a rash inference, to claim that patients with these personality disorders are often capable of sustained improvement. This was the general conclusion of the psychoanalytic studies of Weber and Sashin cited above. Smith and her colleagues noted, however, that the various and competing forms of therapy they reviewed appeared equally effective (p. 185). Efficacy seemed to depend at least as much on certain key patient variables as on the length and variety of therapy. The key variables are, in effect, the *positive* personality traits of motivation, the strength to face weakness, the confidence to trust another person, and the flexibility to weigh and select among contingencies. These qualities, when present, can offset many of the maladaptive traits that make up the item-lists of the standard personality disorders. Paranoid, antisocial, schizoid, and sadistic, along with some borderline, narcissistic and passive–aggressive persons are deficient in one or several of these key traits. One could argue that, *de fortiori*, persons exhibiting the other disorders ought to show long-term outcomes at least as favourable as those of, say, the borderline and narcissistic patients mentioned above – if not more favourable. Indeed, one of the chief stumbling blocks to the follow-up study of the milder personality disorders is the patients' relatively good occupations and interpersonal function at the outset. What researchers are left to evaluate, years later, are subtle measures of satisfaction with life, quality of friendships, and the like, rather than such easily measured variables as whether one has a job or is on public assistance, etc.

General issues

Existing follow-up studies have been devoted almost entirely to the severe end of the personality-disorder spectrum. In this region of the spectrum, admixture of traits with symptoms (including, in the case of ASP, unlawful acts) is routinely found. The interaction between traits and symptoms is such that the prognosis of a symptom disorder (such as an affective disorder) is worse in the presence of a personality disorder, and *vice versa*. Paradoxically, alleviation of certain symptoms (e.g. by use of antidepressants in a unipolar patient) often reduces the intensity of accompanying traits (such as low self-esteem, pessimism). Similarly, successful therapeutic work with certain traits may bring about reduction of symptoms. Depressive patients who learn to become less self-critical may, for example, become less anxious henceforth in social situations.

Outcome in all personality disorders depends in part upon the balance between maladaptive and adaptive traits, but the effects of this balance can be seen more clearly when the clinical picture is not clouded by the presence of disabling symptoms. Candour and introspectiveness were mentioned earlier as examples of positive traits. Related to introspectiveness is the willingness to accept responsibility for contributing – perhaps greatly – to the creation of one's interpersonal difficulties. The opposite trait is externalisation, where all blame is localised in persons other than oneself – a trait especially prominent in paranoid patients, but common as well in the anti-social/psychopathic, narcissistic, borderline, passive–aggressive, and sadistic disorders. While psychotherapy can succeed in reversing the tendency to externalise in patients with the mild forms of these disorders, the task becomes insuperable in the face of massive externalisation. Premature rupture of the treatment contract is the customary 'outcome' in the latter case. There is a parallel between the concepts of externalisation versus introspectiveness and the no longer so popular psychoanalytic terms, 'alloplastic' versus 'autoplastic'. Those who would mould the external world so as to suit their wishes (the 'alloplastic' strategy) tend to blame, as well as to manipulate and coerce, others. Personality disorders characterised chiefly by alloplastic manoeuvres are many times more resistant to treatment than are those whose approach (blaming oneself, changing oneself) is autoplastic. The 'classical' psychoneuroses that served as the inspiration for the development of psychoanalysis involve chiefly autoplastic patterns. The hysterical, obsessional, phobic, depressive, masochistic, and dependent neurotics of Freud's day suffered mainly from inhibitions that interfered with normal sexual life. Psychoanalytic therapy helped lift these inhibitions. To the extent that similar patients nowadays can be diagnosed with a personality disorder, the disorder will usually be within DSM's anxious cluster, with the exception of histrionic PD. Psychoanalytic and related methods are less well suited to the treatment of alloplastic disorders, including those personality disorders where externalisation is an identifying feature. Persons whom others consider offensive or obnoxious, whether diagnosable in standard terms or not, make heavy use of alloplastic defences, although certain clingingly dependent patients manage to be simultaneously offensive yet autoplastic and self-reproachful.

Most of the standard personality disorders may be understood as midway points along spectra at whose extremes one finds either mild traits or, at the opposite end, severe symptom disorders. This situation is illustrated in Table 13.3. In this table, the personality disorders are presented dimensionally, in keeping with Millon's remark (1988) that personality is our first line of (interpersonal) defence – a line which, when breached, leads to less adaptive 'breakdown' symptoms. Some personality disorders are not easily visualised as belonging only to one spectrum. Anger and moodiness are both central to our current concept of BPD, for which reason this personality disorder is placed between those two spectra. Cyclothymic personality, as Kraepelin (1921) mentioned, is a blend of depressive and hypomanic attributes.

This dimensional view of personality disorders highlights the severity factor alluded to earlier: outcome depends on severity (i.e. how pervasive and how ingrained are the maladaptive traits) in such a way that persons with mild paranoid traits may fare better in treatment, and in life, than will persons with extremely dependent traits, despite the aura of ominousness that ordinarily surrounds the paranoid label.

As one moves towards milder expressions of personality aberrations, one departs from the medical model of illness, and departs also from DSM and ICD. Many persons, for example, have integrated and reasonably tolerable personalities except for one or two offensive or obnoxious traits. Included here would be persons who are markedly jealous, smug, stingy, abrasive, garrulous, aimless, bigoted, boring, risqué, cynical, or vacuous (to mention but a few). Such persons do not fit comfortably into our standard nomenclature. Their traits, nevertheless, may render them just as handicapped, or more so, than some persons with diagnosable

TABLE 13.3

Spectrum aspects of personality disorders

Traits – increasing severity	Personality disorder	Severe symptom disorder
Shy	**Schizoid/Schizotypal**	Schizophrenic
Aloof		
Sceptical	**Paranoid**	Delusional
Mistrustful		
Restrained	**Obsessive–compulsive**	Obsessive–compulsive
Orderly	(anankastic)	
Overmeticulous		
Lacking self-confidence	**Passive dependent**	Phobic
	Avoidant	
	Passive–aggressive	
Cranky	**Sadistic**	Violent
Irritable		Explosive
Angry		
Verbally abusive	**Borderline**	
Abrasive		
Over-reactive	'Impulse-ridden	
Impulsive	character'	
Unreasonable, very		
impulsive		
Mercurial		
Stormy		
Moody	**Depressive**	Unipolar depression
Pessimistic		
	Cyclothymic	Bipolar mania
	Hypomanic	
Outgoing	**Histrionic**	'Hysterical psychosis'
Extroverted		
Dramatic	Infantile (BPD ×	
Flirtatious	Histrionic PD)	
Irresponsible	**Antisocial**	Career criminal with
Glib		ASP
Amoral		
Sociopathic;	Psychopath	
dissocial		
Self-centred	**Narcissistic**	
Ambitious		
Vain		
Condescending		

personality disorders – whose overall personalities are more pleasing. It is for this reason that Woolcott (1985) stressed the prognostic importance of likeability. Opposite to likeability is of course unlikeability, which immediately invokes the thorny issues of moral judgment, raised by Blackburn (1988), and of countertransference feelings in therapists, confronted by psychopathic or obnoxious persons (Winnicott, 1949). Among the latter are persons who display anger more often and more intensely than other persons in similar life situations. Highly irascible persons offend co-workers and superiors, destroy intimate relationships, alienate their children and undermine any attempts at treatment. The impact of 'inordinate anger' (BPD diagnostic 'item') upon outcome is great enough to cause a downward shift in the life trajectory of BPD patients who are relatively asymptomatic – in comparison with BPD patients co-morbid for eating disorders and depression, but whose anger level is not high.

Personality disorders (including the single-trait disturbances sketched above) derive, in part, from patterns of thought and behaviour that appear to be 'hard-wired' into the central nervous system (in pathways that probably involve the basal ganglia 'habit memory' system; Mishkin *et al*, 1984) during the first five or six years of life. Heredofamilial factors play a role in many of the standard disorders (schizoid PD, schizotypal PD and some instances of paranoid PD as 'spectrum' cases of the schizophrenic genotype; depressive and hypomanic personalities as attenuated forms of manic–depression; Pössl & von Zerssen, 1990). Deeply etched as these disorders are in the neurophysiological framework of our minds, it is small wonder that personality disorders are hard to modify and slow to change. The follow-up studies outlined in this paper, even though centred on the more severe disorders, suggest nonetheless that beneficial changes can often occur, and that current treatment approaches can often be instrumental in effecting these positive changes. All methods of treatment aim at the same goal: the gradual conquest by new, more adaptive habits of thought and behaviour – over the pre-existing, maladaptive habits; in effect, the conquest of reason over habit.

References

AARKROG, T. (1981) The borderline concept in childhood, adolescence and adulthood. *Acta Psychiatrica Scandinavica*, **64** (suppl. 243).

AKISKAL, H. S. (1981) Subaffective disorders: dysthymic, cyclothymic and bipolar-II disorders in the 'borderline' realm. *Psychiatric Clinics of North America*, **4**, 25–46.

ALLEBECK, P., ALLGULANDER, G. & FISHER, L. D. (1988) Predictors of completed suicide in a cohort of 50,465 young men: role of personality and deviant behaviour. *British Medical Journal*, **297**, 176–178.

AMERICAN PSYCHIATRIC ASSOCIATION (1980) *Diagnostic and Statistical Manual of Mental Disorders* (3rd edn) (DSM-III). Washington, DC: APA.

——— (1987) *Diagnostic and Statistical Manual of Mental Disorders* (3rd edn, revised) (DSM-III-R). Washington, DC: APA.

ANDREOLI, A., GRESSOT, G., AAPRO, N., *et al* (1989) Personality disorders as a predictor of outcome. *Journal of Personality Disorders*, **3**, 307–320.

BACHRACH, H. M., WEBER, J. J. & SOLOMON, M. (1985) Factors associated with the outcome of psychoanalysis (clinical and methodological considerations): report of the Columbia Psychoanalytic Center Research Project: IV. *International Review of Psychoanalysis*, **12**, 379–389.

BENJAMINSEN, S., KRARUP, G. & LAURITSEN, R. (1990) Personality, parental rearing behavior and parental loss in attempted suicide. *Acta Psychiatrica Scandinavica*, **82**, 389–397.

BLACKBURN, R. (1988) On moral judgments and personality disorders: The myth of psychopathic personality revisited. *British Journal of Psychiatry*, **153**, 505–512.

BLASHFIELD, R. K. (1990) An American view of the ICD-10 personality disorders. *Acta Psychiatrica Scandinavica*, **82**, 250–256.

CLECKLEY, H. (1972) *The Mask of Sanity* (5th edn). St. Louis: C. V. Mosby.

DAHL, A. A. (1986) Prognosis of borderline disorders. *Psychopathology*, **19**, 68–79.

DILALLA, L. F. & GOTTESMAN, I. I. (1990) Heterogeneity of causes of delinquency and criminality: lifespan perspectives. *Development & Psychopathology*, **1**, 339–349.

DUGGAN, C. F., LEE, A. S. & MURRAY, R. M. (1990) Does personality predict long-term outcome in depression? *British Journal of Psychiatry*, **157**, 19–24.

ENDICOTT, J., SPITZER, R. L., FLEISS, J. L., *et al* (1976) The global assessment scale. *Archives of General Psychiatry*, **33**, 766–771.

EYSENCK, H. J. (1947) *The Dimensions of Personality*. London: Kegan Paul, Trench and Trubner.

FENTON, W. S. & MCGLASHAN, T. H. (1989) Risk of schizophrenia in character disordered patients. *American Journal of Psychiatry*, **146**, 1280–1284.

GABBARD, G. O. & COYNE, L. (1987) Predictors of response of antisocial patients to hospital treatment. *Hospital and Community Psychiatry*, **38**, 1181–1185.

GUNDERSON, J. G., KOLB, J. & AUSTIN, V. (1981) The diagnostic interview for borderline patients. *American Journal of Psychiatry*, **138**, 896–903.

HOLLINGSHEAD, A. B. & REDLICH, F. C. (1958) *Social Class and Mental Illness*. New York: J. Wiley.

JENIKE, M. A., MINICHIELLO, W. E., SCHWARTZ, C. E., *et al* (1986) Concomitant obsessive-compulsive disorder and schizotypal disorder. *American Journal of Psychiatry*, **143**, 530–532.

KANTROWITZ, J. L., KATZ, A. L. & PAOLITTO, F. (1990) Follow-up of psychoanalysis five to ten years after termination: II. Development of the self-analytic function. *Journal of the American Psychoanalytic Association*, **38**, 637–654.

KERNBERG, O. F. (1967) Borderline personality organization. *Journal of the American Psychoanalytic Association*, **15**, 641–685.

KNAPP, P., LEVIN, S., MCCARTER, R. H., *et al* (1960) Suitability for psychoanalysis: A review of one hundred supervised cases. *Psychoanalytic Quarterly*, **29**, 459–477.

KOHUT, H. (1971) *Analysis of the Self*. NY: International Universities Press.

KRAEPELIN, E. (1921) *Manic Depressive Insanity and Paranoia*. Edinburgh: E. & S. Livingstone.

KROLL, J. L., CAREY, K. S. & SINES, L. K. (1985) Twenty year follow-up of borderline personality disorder: A pilot study. In *IV World Congress of Biological Psychiatry* (vol. VII) (ed. C. Shagass), pp. 577–579. New York: Elsevier.

LIEBOWITZ, M. R., STONE, M. H. & TURKAT, I. D. (1986) Treatment of personality disorders. *Annual Review of Psychiatry*, Vol. V, pp. 356–393. Washington, DC: American Psychiatric Press.

LINKS, P., MITTON, J. E. & STEINER, M. (1990) Predicting outcome for borderline personality disorder. *Comprehensive Psychiatry*, **31**, 490–498.

LIVESELEY, W. J. (1986) Trait and behavioral prototypes of personality disorders. *American Journal of Psychiatry*, **143**, 728–732.

—— (1987) A systematic approach to the delineation of personality disorders. *American Journal of Psychiatry*, **144**, 772–777.

——, REIFFER, L. I. & WEST, M. (1987) Prototypicality ratings of DSM-III criteria for personality disorders. *Journal of Nervous and Mental Disease*, **175**, 395–401.

MARKS, I. M. (1987) *Fears, Phobias & Rituals*. London: Oxford University Press.

MAVISSAKALIAN, M., HAMANN, M. S. & JONES, B. (1990) DSM-III personality disorders in obsessive–compulsive disorder: changes with treatment. *Comprehensive Psychiatry*, **31**, 432–437.

MCGLASHAN, T. H. (1986a) The Chestnut Lodge follow-up study: III. Long-term outcome of borderline personalities. *Archives of General Psychiatry*, **43**, 20–30.

—— (1986b) Chestnut Lodge follow-up study: VI. Long-term follow-up perspectives. *Archives of General Psychiatry*, **43**, 329–334.

—— (1987) Borderline personality disorder and unipolar affective disorder: long term effects of comorbidity. *Journal of Nervous and Mental Disease*, **175**, 467–473.

—— & HEINSSEN, R. K. (1988) Hospital discharge status and long term outcome for patients with schizophrenia, schizoaffective disorder, borderline personality disorder and unipolar affective disorder. *Archives of General Psychiatry*, **45**, 363–368.

—— & —— (1989) Narcissistic, antisocial and non-comorbid subgroups of borderline disorder: are they distinct entities by long-term clinical profile? *Psychiatric Clinics of North America*, **12**, 653–670.

MEZZICH, J. (1988) ICD-9 personality types as dimensions. Presented at the *First International Congress of Personality Disorders*, Copenhagen, 18 August.

MILLON, T. (1988) Overview of personality disorders. Keynote address: *First International Congress of Personality Disorders*, Copenhagen, 19 August.

MINICHIELLO, W. E., BAER, L. & JENIKE, M. A. (1987) Schizotypal personality disorder: a poor prognostic indicator for behavior therapy in the treatment of obsessive–compulsive disorder. *Journal of Anxiety Disorders*, **1**, 273–276.

MISHKIN, M., MALAMUT, B. & BACHEVALIER, J. (1984) Memories and habits: The neural system. In *Neurobiology of Learning and Memory* (eds G. Lynch, J. McGaugh & N. M. Weinberger), pp. 65–77. New York: Guilford Press.

MODESTIN, J. & VILLIGER, C. (1989) Follow-up study on borderline versus non-borderline personality disorders. *Comprehensive Psychiatry*, **30**, 236–244.

NORTON, R. N. & MORGAN, M. Y. (1989) The role of alcohol in mortality and morbidity from interpersonal violence. *Alcohol*, **24**, 565–576.

OFFORD, D. R. & REITSMA-STREET, M. (1983) Problems of studying antisocial behavior. *Psychiatric Development*, **1**, 207–224.

OLDHAM, J. M. (1988) Patterns of personality disorder comorbidity in patients with borderline personality. Presented at the *1st New York State Office of Mental Health Research Conf*. Albany, 2 Dec.

—— & MORRIS, L. B. (1990) *The Personality Self-Portrait*. New York: Bantam Books.

PARIS, J., BROWN, R. & NOWLIS, D. (1978) Long-term follow-up of borderline patients in a general hospital. *Comprehensive Psychiatry*, **28**, 530–535.

——, NOWLIS, D. & BROWN, R. (1988) Developmental factors in the outcome of borderline personality disorder. *Comprehensive Psychiatry*, **29**, 147–150.

PFEFFER, A. Z. (1961) Single case report: follow-up study of a satisfactory analysis. *Journal of the American Psychoanalytic Association*, **9**, 698–718.

PHILLIPS, K. A., GUNDERSON, J. G., HIRSCHFELD, R. M. A., *et al* (1990) A review of the depressive personality. *American Journal of Psychiatry*, **147**, 830–837.

PLAKUN, E. M. (1989) Narcissistic personality disorder: a validity study and comparison to borderline personality disorder. *Psychiatric Clinics of North America*, **12**, 603–620.

——, BURKHARDT, P. E. & MULLER, J. P. (1985) Fourteen year follow-up of borderline and schizotypal personality disorders. *Comprehensive Psychiatry*, **26**, 448–455.

PÖSSL, J. & VONZERSSEN, D. (1990) A case history analysis of the 'manic type' and the 'melancholic type' of premorbid personality in affectively ill patients. *European Archives of Psychiatry and Neurological Sciences*, **239**, 347–355.

RICE, M. E., HARRIS, G. T. & QUINSEY, V. L. (1990) A follow-up of rapists assessed in a maximum-security psychiatric facility. *Journal of Interpersonal Violence*, **5**, 435–448.

ROBINS, L. N., TIPP, J. & PRZYBECK, T. (1991) Antisocial personality. In *Psychiatric Disorders in America* (eds L. N. Robins & D. A. Regier), pp. 258–290. N.Y.: Macmillan.

ROUNSAVILLE, B. J., DOLINSKY, Z. S., BABOR, T. F., *et al* (1987) Psychopathology as a predictor of treatment outcome in alcoholics. *Archives of General Psychiatry*, **44**, 505–513.

RUSSELL, D. (1986) *The Secret Trauma*. New York: Basic Books.

SASHIN, J. I., ELDRED, S. H. & VANAMERONGEN, S. J. (1975) A search for predictive factors in institute-supervised cases: a retrospective study of 183 cases from 1959–1966 at the Boston Psychoanalytic Society & Institute. *International Journal of Psychoanalysis*, **56**, 343–359.

SCHLESINGER, N. & ROBBINS, F. (1974) Assessment and follow-up in psychoanalysis. *Journal of the American Psychoanalytic Association*, **22**, 542–567.
SMITH, M. L., GLASS, G. V. & MILLER, T. I. (1980) *The Benefits of Psychotherapy*. Baltimore: The Johns Hopkins University Press.
SOLOMON, M. I. & MURPHY, G. E. (1984) Cohort studies of suicide. In *Suicide in the Young* (eds H. S. Sudak, A. B. Ford & N. B. Rushforth), pp. 1–14. Boston: John Wright.
STONE, M. H. (1980) *The Borderline Syndromes*. New York: McGraw Hill.
—— (1988) Toward a psychobiological theory of borderline personality disorder. *Dissociation*, **1**, 2–15.
—— (1989a) The course of borderline personality disorder. *Annual Review of Psychiatry*, Vol. VIII, pp. 103–122. Washington, DC: American Psychiatric Association Press.
—— (1989b) Long-term follow-up of narcissistic/borderline patients. *Psychiatric Clinics of North America*, **12**, 621–641.
—— (1989c) Schizoid personality disorder. In *Treatments of Psychiatric Disorders*, vol. III (ed. T. B. Karasu), pp. 2712–2718. Washington, DC: American Psychiatric Association Press.
—— (1990a) Toward a comprehensive typology of personality. *Journal of Personality Disorders*, **4**, 416–421.
—— (1990b) *The Fate of Borderline Patients*. New York: Guilford Press.
—— (1991) Psychotherapy for the treatment of anxiety disorders. In *Handbook of Anxiety*. Vol. IV (eds R. Noyes, Jr, M. Roth & G. D. Burrows), pp. 389–404. Amsterdam: Elsevier.
——, HURT, S. W. & STONE, D. K. (1987) The PI–500: Long term follow-up of borderline in-patients meeting DSM III criteria. I. Global outcome. *Journal of Personality Disorders*, **1**, 291–298.
——, UNWIN, A., BEACHAM, B., *et al* (1988) Incest in female borderlines: its frequency and impact. *International Journal of Family Psychiatry*, **9**, 277–293.
SUMMERS, A. (1985) *Goddess: The Secret Lives of Marilyn Monroe*. New York: Macmillan.
TYRER, P. & ALEXANDER, J. (1988) Personality assessment schedule. In *Personality Disorders: Diagnosis, Management and Course* (ed. P. Tyrer), pp. 43–62. London: Wright.
——, CASEY, P. & GALL, J. (1983) Relationship between neurosis and personality disorder. *British Journal of Psychiatry*, **142**, 404–408.
WEBER, J. J., BACHRACH, H. M. & SOLOMON, M. (1985a) Factors associated with the outcome of psychoanalysis: Report of the Columbia Psychoanalytic Center Research Project: II, III. *International Review of Psychoanalysis*, **12**, 127–141, 251–262.
——, SOLOMON, M. & BACHRACH, H. M. (1985b) Characteristics of psychoanalytic clinic patients: report of the Columbia Psychoanalytic Center Research Project: I. *International Review of Psychoanalysis*, **12**, 13–26.
WINNICOTT, D. W. (1949) Hate in the counter-transference. *International Journal of Psychoanalysis*, **30**, 69–74.
WOLFF, S. & CHICK, J. (1981) Schizoid personality in childhood: a controlled follow-up study. *Annual Progress in Child Psychiatry and Child Development*, 550–580.
WOODY, G. E., MCLELLAN, A. T., LUBORSKY, L., *et al* (1985) Sociopathy and psychotherapy outcome. *Archives of General Psychiatry*, **42**, 1081–1086.
WOOLCOTT, P. Jr (1985) Prognostic indicators in the psychotherapy of borderline patients. *American Journal of Psychotherapy*, **39**, 17–29.
WORLD HEALTH ORGANIZATION (1992) *The ICD–10 Classification of Mental and Behavioural Disorders*. Geneva: WHO.
ZILBER, N., SCHUFMAN, N. & LERNER, Y. (1989) Mortality among psychiatric patients – the groups at risk. *Acta Psychiatrica Scandinavica*, **79**, 248–256.

Index

Compiled by STANLEY THORLEY